The Sources of Science, No. 88

THE SOURCES OF SCIENCE

Editor-in-Chief: HARRY WOOLF

WILLIS K. SHEPARD PROFESSOR OF THE HISTORY OF SCIENCE
THE JOHNS HOPKINS UNIVERSITY

A Selection of Titles in this Series:

AGASSIZ. *Bibliographia Zoologiae et Geologiae.* 4 vols. (No. 20).

BIRCH. *History of the Royal Society of London.* 4 vols. With a new Introduction by A. Rupert Hall and a Bibliographical Note by Marie Boas Hall. (No. 44).

Catalogus Bibliothecae Historico-Naturalis Josephi Banks. 5 vols. Compiled by Jonas Dryander. (No. 22).

CHARLETON. *Physiologia Epicuro-Gassendo-Charltoniana.* With Indexes and a new Introduction by Robert Hugh Kargon. (No. 31).

CORNUT. *Canadensium Plantarum.* With a new Introduction by Jerry Stannard. (No. 37).

DARMSTAEDTER. *Naturforscher und Erfinder.* (No. 26).

DARWIN. *The Life and Letters of Charles Darwin.* 3 vols. (No. 102).

Essayes of Natural Experiments made in the Academie del Cimento. Translated by Richard Waller. With a new Introduction by A. Rupert Hall. (No. 1).

GREW. *The Anatomy of Plants.* With a new Introduction by Conway Zirkle. (No. 11).

HALLIWELL. *A Collection of Letters Illustrative of the Progress of Science in England from the Reign of Queen Elizabeth to that of Charles II.* With a new Introduction by Carl B. Boyer. (No. 12).

HERSCHEL. *A Preliminary Discourse on the Study of Natural Philosophy.* With a new Introduction by Michael Partridge. (No. 17).

The Interpretation of Animal Form. Essays by Jeffries Wyman, Carl Gegenbaur, E. Ray Lankester, Henri Lacaze Duthiers, Wilhelm His and H. Newell Martin. With Translations and an Introduction by William Coleman. (No. 15).

MAUPERTUIS. *The Earthly Venus*. Translated by Simone Brangier Boas and with an Introduction by George Boas. (No. 29).

POWER. *Experimental Philosophy*. With an Introduction by Marie Boas Hall. (No. 21).

ROHAULT. *A System of Natural Philosophy*. 2 vols. With a new Introduction by L. L. Laudan. (No. 50).

SCHLEIDEN. *Principles of Scientific Botany*. Translated by Edwin Lankester. With a new Introduction by Jacob Lorch. (No. 40).

TAYLOR. *Scientific Memoirs*. Selected from the Transactions of Foreign Academies of Science and Learned Societies, and from Foreign Journals. 7 vols. With a new Preface by Harry Woolf. (No. 7).

WARD. *The Lives of the Professors of Gresham College*. (No. 71).

WILSON. *The Cell in Development and Inheritance*. With a new Introduction by Hermann J. Muller. (No. 30).

WOOD. *Athenae Oxonienses*. 4 vols. Edited by Philip Bliss. (No. 55).

Zeitschrift für wissenschaftliche Botanik. Vol. 1. Edited by M. J. Schleiden and Carl Nägeli. (No. 27).

The History of New-Hampshire

THE
HISTORY
OF
NEW-HAMPSHIRE

BY

JEREMY BELKNAP

With a New Introduction by
JOHN KIRTLAND WRIGHT

I

The Sources of Science, No. 88

New York and London

1970

This 2-volume edition reproduces the Dover (N.H.) editions
of 1831 and 1812 as follows:

Volume I: A reprint of Volume 1, 1831
(This is a revision of Volumes 1–2
of the 1812 edition)

Volume II: A reprint of Volume 3, 1812

A second volume of the 1831 edition was never published.
It would have been a revision of Volume 3 of the 1812 edition.

Library of Congress Catalog Card Number: 70-122255

Printed in the U.S.A.

INTRODUCTION

If by "source of science" we mean a flowing spring or fountainhead of scientific inspiration and influence, Jeremy Belknap's *History of New-Hampshire* would not so qualify. Its author was a clergyman, a patriot, and a historian, but not a scientist, and his book is certainly not in the class of the *Principia Mathematica* or the *Kosmos* (though it did have a stimulating effect on other writers of state histories.[1] If, however, by "source" we mean a pool that reveals and reflects the nature of its contemporaneous science and by "science" we mean something nearer to the *scientia* of earlier times than to the "hard" sciences of today, the *History* is surely a "source of science." It testifies to scientific habit of mind on the part of its author and it mirrors qualities that existed in this country during the last quarter of the eighteenth century in the studies of history, physical geography, botany, zoology, and mineralogy, in the use of statistics, and in the pursuit of technology.

In this Introduction we shall begin with a few remarks about Belknap and a few generalities about his *History*. Then we shall consider the *History* itself, first as a historical work and then in greater detail as a contribution to geography. This disproportionate emphasis may be justified on the ground that most readers of this book will probably be more interested in the geographical than in the historical parts.

BIOGRAPHY[2]

Born in Boston in 1744, Jeremy Belknap as a boy developed a love of history and of writing. He was graduated from Harvard with the Class of 1762 at the age of eighteen; but he was not an infant prodigy. College boys were younger in those days than

[1] Merle Curti, *The Growth of American Thought* (New York: Harper, 1951), p. 152. Brooke Hindle, *The Pursuit of Science in Revolutionary America, 1735–1789* (Chapel Hill, N. C.: University of North Carolina Press, 1956), p. 318.

[2] For sketches of Belknap's life as a whole (there is no "full-length biography) see *Life of Jeremy Belknap, D. D. . . . Collected and Arranged by his Grand-daughter* [Jane Belknap Marcou] (New York: Harper, 1847), henceforth cited as "Marcou"; Charles Deane, "Prefatory Note" in Vol. 1 of *Belknap Papers*, pp. v–xii (see next paragraph of this note); J. S.

they now are.[3] After a few years of teaching school (while also studying for the ministry) Belknap served from 1766 to 1786 at the Congregational Church in Dover, New Hempshire.[4] This was a dramatic time: the surge of the frontier northward in New England after the conquest of Quebec[5] and the winning of national independent affected Belknap's career and the nature of his *History*. Approximately two-thirds of the latter is a narrative of the development of New Hampshire from the early explorations along the coast to the ratification of the Constitution of the United States in 1790, and the remainder a geographical description of the State as it was in the 1780's. The historical part gained flavor and fervor from Belknap's personal involvement in the winning of political liberty[6] by his country; and the geograph-

---

[3] In a total of 208 students entering Harvard with the classes of 1748–1755 37 were 18 or over, 83 were between 15 and 18, and 83 were 15 or under (figures kindly furnished me by Mr. Hamilton Vaughan Bail of Hartland, Vermont, who compiled them from data in C. K. Shipton, *Biographical Sketches of Those Who Attended Harvard College* (constituting *Sibley's Harvard Graduates*, Vols. 12 and 13, Boston: Massachusetts Historical Society, 1962, 1963) pertaining to the last classes covered in that work. Comparable ratios no doubt held for Belknap's class.

[4] See G. B. Spalding, *The Dover Pulpit During the Revolutionary War: A Discourse Commemorative of the Distinguished Service Rendered by Rev. Jeremy Belknap, D. D., to the Cause of American Independence* . . . (Dover, New Hampshire, 1867; 31 pp.)

[5] This "surge" is revealed on a map on which "isochronic lines" show the limits of settlement in New England at successive 20-year intervals, 1640–1820, accompanying S. D. Dodge, "The Frontier of New England in the Seventeenth and Eighteenth Centuries and its Significance in American History," *Papers of the Michigan Academy of Science, Arts, and Letters*, 28 (1942), 435–439.

[6] On Belknap as a patriot see Bassett, *Middle Group*, pp. 29–30, and C. W. Cole, "Jeremy Belknap: Pioneer Nationalist," *New England Quarterly*, 10 (1937), 743–751. Cole draws attention to Belknap's advocacy of the advancement of science in the interests of national development. See BP 1, p. 655.

Bassett, *The Middle Group of American Historians* (New York: Macmillan, 1917), pp. 24–37; S. A. Eliot, "Jeremy Belknap" . . ., *Proceedings of the Massachusetts Historical Society*, 66 (1936–1941), 96–106; L. S. Mayo, biography of Belknap in *Dictionary of American Biography*, Vol. 2, 1929, p. 147.

The most comprehensive single source of information concerning Belknap's life is the "Belknap Papers," published in 3 volumes of the *Collections of the Massachusetts Historical Society* [Vols. 42, 43, 54] (Ser. 5, Vols. 2 and 3, 1877; Ser. 6, Vol. 4, 1891; cited hereafter as BP 1, 2, and 3, respectively); BP 1 and BP 2 consist of correspondence with Ebenezer Hazard, BP 3 of correspondence with others than Hazard and largely of letters *to* Belknap.

ical part was affected by his proximity to the "pioneer fringe."

Difficulties concerning his salary led to Belknap's resignation from the Dover pulpit in 1786,[7] and a year later he accepted a call to the Congregational Church on Long Lane[8] (later the Federal Street Congregational Church) in Boston, where he remained until his death in 1796. During these last years he finished the *History*, wrote for publication several works on historical, geographical, religious, and other themes,[9] and, as an early member of the then-recently-founded American Academy of Arts and Sciences and as one of the founders of the Massachusetts Historical Society, he was active as an organizing statesman of institutionalized scholarship. In the Preface to the first volume of the *History* he deplored the destruction of Thomas Prince's collection of historical manuscript's by the British troops in Boston in 1775: "Had we suffered it by the hands of *Saracens*, the grief had been less poignant" (I:viii).[10] The launching of the Massachusetts Historical Society, felt by one historian to be Belknap's "best service,"[11] was motivated by a "born" archivist's desire to see historical documents preserved and by a "born" historian's desire to see them published.

Although he was probably a "born" historian, I am inclined to think, that Belknap "acquired geography" and "had mathematics thrust upon him." His geographical interests were largely a by-product of his interest in history and in people, rather than a primary passion, and this taste was itself partly historical, as shown in various works in which geographical attributes of historical events are treated, and partly regional, as shown by travel and by the gathering of geographical data at first hand. That Belknap liked to travel is obvious from the realistic manner

7 Marcou, *Life*, pp. 119–121; Bassett, *Middle Group*, pp. 25–27.

8 BP 1, p. 457.

9 See Charles Evans, *American Bibliography, 1639–1800* (14 vols., Chicago and Worcester, 1903–1959), Index under Belknap; Jacob Blanck, *Bibliography of American Literature* . . . (New Haven: *Yale University* Press, 4 Vols., 1955–1963), Vol. 1, pp. 185–191. For location of manuscripts, see *American Literary Manuscripts: A Checklist of Holdings* . . . *in the United States* (Austin, Texas: University of Texas Press, 1960; indicates that the largest collection of Belknap manuscripts is in the Massachusetts Historical Society, the second largest in the New Hampshire Historical Society).

10 References in this form are to the pages in the Dover edition of 1831.

11 Bassett, *Middle Group*, p. 37; see also Oscar Zeichner, editor, "Jeremy Belknap and the William Samuel Johnson Correspondence," *New England Quarterly*, 14 (1941), 362–374.

in which he narrated his journeys and described scenes. That he was not a "passionate" traveler could be deduced from the limited extent of his travels—or, perhaps, it might be fairer to say that his *Wanderlust* was not strong enough to overcome his sense of duty to his Church and to his large family.[12] In the Preface to the geographical volume of the *History* he mentions "several journeys to the northern and western parts" of New Hampshire (II[III]:iii).[13] Detailed accounts of two of these are available in print today.[14] The first, in July 1774, took him from Dover via Plymouth and Orford to Hanover (where he attended the Dartmouth Commencement exercises) and thence homeward down the Connecticut valley and by way of Keene.[15] Ten years later, in company with the Reverend Menasseh Cutler and others, he penetrated the mysterious fastnesses of the White Mountains on what was, for those times, a veritable scientific exploring expedition (II[III], 37–39).[16] Several of the party, but not Belknap, reached the top of the highest peak, which some years later

[12] "He had six children and no other dependence for their support than his own efforts" (Bassett, *Middle Group*, p. 27).

[13] References in this form are to the pages in Volume III of the Dover edition of 1812, reprinted herewith as Volume II of the present edition.

[14] In letters to Hazard, Belknap mentions having visited Gay Head at the western end of Martha's Vineyard Island "when very young" and as having been impressed by the "beautiful appearance which it exhibits at a distance from the reflection of the sun-beams on its various coloured cliffs" (BP 1, p. 253), and also having "been about thirty miles into the country" from Dover in September 1782 (BP 1, pp. 154–156). On the latter occasion he "ascended with difficulty a very high mountain called *The Moose*" but got no pleasure out of the view because of the woods on the summit. The ascent and descent took four hours. There is a Moose Mountain near Sanbornville, New Hampshire, some 25 miles north of Dover.

[15] See Jeremy Belknap, *Journey to Dartmouth in 1774*, edited by E. C. Lathem (Hanover, New Hampshire: Dartmouth Publications, 1950).

[16] For a transcript of Belknap's diary concerning this trip (July 20–31, 1784) see BP 1, pp. 386–401 (also Jeremy Belknap, *Journal of a Tour to the White Mountains in July, 1784 . . . printed from the original manuscript, with a prefatory note by the editor* C[harles] D[eane] (Boston: Massachusetts Historical Society, 1876). For letters to Hazard concerning this journey ("substantially the same as the journal") see BP 2, pp. 168–189 (includes reproduction of a rough sketch map by Belknap of the country between Mt. Washington [not so named, however] and Conway, 1784; 2 miles to an inch. On this map Belknap had drawn two profiles showing "the appearance of the White Mountains" from the east and northwest. Are these the first pictorial representations of the Presidential Range?). See also Jeremy Belknap, "A Description of the White Mountains," *Transactions of the American Philosophical Society* 2, (1786), 42–49.

was named "Mount Washington."[17] In September and October 1785 he journeyed to Philadelphia,[10] where he visited his friend Ebenezer Hazard, then Postmaster of the United States, who had helped him arrange for the publication of the first volume of the *History*.[19] His last long journey, carried out in 1796 in company with the Reverend Jedidiah Morse, author of the *American Geography* (1789), was for a missionary visit to the Oneida Indians in northwestern New York State.[20]

Religion and politics were probably Dr. Belknap's foremost public concerns, and history, geography (broadly construed), and graceful literary expression his foremost concerns as a scholar and writer. Not only his historical and biographical writing but also his sermons shed light on his political interests, since several of the sermons were political in tone. His personal theology was based on a more literal interpretation of the Bible than is usual today in this country except in "fundamentalist" denominations.[21] He believed, however, that each person should interpret the Bible for himself: "I have long since utterly discarded all confessions or standards of human authority," he wrote Hazard in 1784.[22] He advocated religious toleration and the separation of Church and State: Chapter 3 of Volume I of the *History*, which deals with this subject, was praised by de Tocqueville, as was the whole *History*.[23] Perhaps Belknap was unconsciously characterizing himself in the concluding para-

---

[17] Lawrence Martin, "Who Named Mount Washington?" *Geographical Review* 28 (1938), 303–305. Colonel Martin thought the name may have been given to the summit either by Belknap, Cutler, or someone else between 1786 and 1792.

[18] See Marcou, *Life*, pp. 107–119.

[19] On how Belknap enlisted and obtained Hazard's help in getting Volume I of the History published, see L. S. Mayo, "Jeremy Belknap and Ebenezer Hazard, 1782–1784," *New England Quarterly* 2 (1929), 183–198.

[20] Belknap's narrative is in *Proceedings of the Massachusetts Historical Society*, 19 (1881–1882) 393–423; also in Jeremy Belknap, *Report on the Oneida, Stockbridge, and Brotherton Indians* (New York: Museum of the American Indian, Heye Foundation, 1955). See also Marcou, *Life*, pp. 233–236.

[21] See BP 1, pp. 14–15, 67, 138–141, 190–193, 363–368; BP 3: 18–23, 379–380.

[22] BP 1, p. 325. See also BP 3, pp 253–257, and below, note 47.

[23] Alexis de Tocqueville, *Democracy in America* . . . Vol. 2 (New York: Knopf, 1945), Appendix F, pp. 348–349; see also Marcou, *Life*, p. 129; Bassett, *Middle Group*, p. 31.

graph of the text of the *History* where he pictures the "happy society" as a New England town in which there would be, among others, "a clergyman of any denomination, which should be agreeable to the majority, a man of good understanding, of a candid disposition and exemplary morals; not a metaphysical, nor a polemic, but a serious and practical preacher" (II[III]: 251). Though he devoted a good many pages in the *History* to ecclesiastical issues and interdenominational controversies, he refrained—in that work, at any rate—from theological interpretation of either the course of human events or the nature of geographic reality, as Cotton Mather and other earlier New England divines had done (see page xxvi). Nor have I read anything to suggest that he had any definite "philosophy" of either history or geography. Arguments of the kind that are not infrequent in academic circles today concerning how the historian should write history and the geographer should write geography would probably have struck Dr. Belknap as too "metaphysical and polemic" for his taste. But then, like Herodotus and Gibbon, like Ptolemy and Humboldt, he was a mere amateur. History and geography had not yet been taken over by professionals with all their associated metaphysics and polemics.

From the literary point of view Dr. Belknap's last dozen years were the most vigorous, in terms of publication. In this period he completed the *History of New-Hampshire. The Foresters: An American Tale, being a sequel to the History of John Bull, the Clothier*, which first appeared in serial form in 1787 and was later published as a book, was a politico-historical spoof.[24] The *American Biography*, which was announced in the Preface to the original third volume of the *History of New-Hampshire* (II[III]: vii), was published in two volumes (1794, 1798), of which the second was in the press when its author died. There were also several lesser works, one of which, in particular, along with parts of the *American Biography*, is exceptional among early American historical writings in that it treats broadly of the history of geographical ideas and exploration. On October 23, 1792, Belknap delivered in Boston *A Discourse Intended to Commemorate the Discovery of America by Christopher Columbus*, on the

---

[24] *The Foresters* (Boston, 1792) had originally appeared in the *Columbian Magazine* in 1787; it was republished at Exeter, New Hampshire, 1831. For a specimen passage see Bassett, pp. 32–34; Marcou, pp. 207–211.

three-hundredth anniversary of that event.[25] Justin Winsor a
century later praised this as "the earliest considerable recounting of the story of Columbus in America."[26] Actually the short
sketch of Columbus' career and theories in this work seems less
significant than does the setting in which they are placed.
Belknap, who had a sense of humor, felt that Columbus' exploit
was "a splendid instance of the accomplishment of that remarkable prediction of the prophet Daniel, Ch. xii, ver. 4: 'Many
shall run to and fro and knowledge shall be increased.'" The
main essay, in which he sought to place Columbus' achievement
in relation to "its causes," "its execution," and "its consequences," is accompanied by four "Dissertations": (1) on the
circumnavigation of Africa by the Ancients; (2) on Behaim's
pretensions to a pre-Columbia discovery of America; (3) on
whether or not the honeybee is native to America; and (4) on
the color of the native American and the recent population of
this continent;[27] and in the first volume of the *American Biography* further attention is given to most of these matters. The
main text of the *American Biography* presents sketches of the
lives, (among others) of some fifteen early explorers of the
North American coastlines from "Biron" (Bjarni) and Madoc
to Mason and Gorges of New Hampshire fame.

---

[25] A comparable celebration was held in London on October 12, 1792,
at which the Rev. Elhanan Winchester (1751–1797), an American Uni-
versalist clergyman then living there (1787–1794; see *Dictionary of American Biography*, Vol. 20, 1936, pp. 377–378) delivered an *Oration on the
Discovery of America* (London, 2nd ed., 1792). Was the discovery celebrated in 1692? in 1592? This suggests the possibility of a study of the
impact of anniversaries upon the writing of history. A paper by Belknap
entitled "Has the Discovery of America Been Helpful or Hurtful to
Mankind?" [*Boston Magazine*, 1 (1784), p. 281; available in micro-
film] is mentioned by Michael Kraus in a discussion of the impact of the
early exploration of America upon historiography in *The Atlantic Civilization: Eighteenth-Century Origins* (Ithaca, New York: Cornell University
Press, 1949), p. 5.

[26] Justin Winsor, *Christopher Columbus* (Boston, 1892), pp. 55–56.

[27] "My second dissertation is intended as an answer to a Memoir of
M. Otto, in the second volume of Philosophical Transactions. . . . the 3d
and 4th dissertations are the same, for substance, which were printed in
Carey's Museum, though with some additions. The 1st is entirely new, and
is intended to establish the ancient circumnavigation of the African Continent" (Letter from Belknap to Hazard, Nov. 6, 1792, in BP 2, p. 315).
By "Philosophical Transaction" Belknap meant, no doubt, the *Transactions
of the American Philosophical Society*; he had been a corresponding
member of the Philosophical Society since 1784 (BP 1, p. 300). On the
honeybee paper see BP 2, pp. 321, 328.

Before we turn to a closer view of the *History of New-Hampshire*, be it noted that some forty years after Dr. Belknap's death, when a new county was set apart on the shores of Lake Winnipesaukee, it was named after him. Several New England counties have been named for generals and statesmen (Franklin, Washington, Sullivan, Lincoln, Knox, Hancock, Waldo, etc.) but no other has been so honored with the name of a historian-geographer.

THE HISTORY OF NEW-HAMPSHIRE

Bibliographical History[28]

The first edition of the *History of New-Hampshire* appeared in three volumes: Vol. I, Philadelphia, 1784; Vols. II and III, Boston, 1791, 1792. This was reprinted in Boston, in three volumes, 1792–1793. A second edition with minor changes, also in three volumes, was published in Dover, New Hampshire, in 1812 and an unauthorized version was published in Boston in 1813.[29] In these editions the text of Volumes I and II includes the historical narrative from the early seventeenth century to 1790. In Volume I there is also an appendix in which 48 letters and other documents dating from 1629 to 1703 are printed from manuscripts; the appendix in Volume II comprises five tables and a letter from George Washington. The text of Volume III (Vol. II of this reprint) presents the geographical description of the state. This volume also contains an appendix comprising 33 items, of which all but the last three date from 1708 to 1790, are in continuation of the items in the appendix to Volume I, and are pertinent to the text of the original Volume II.

In 1831 at Dover, New Hampshire, Volumes I and II, the historical volumes proper of the earlier editions, were republished together as "Volume I" of a new edition, with continuous pagination. This incorporated corrections and annotations by

---

[28] Mr. R. Kolvoord, proprietor of the Old Settler Bookshop, Walpole, New Hampshire, informs me that used-book dealers regard the various editions of the *History* as "scarce" rather than "rare," in the technical terminology of the book trade; also that the demand for the Dover 1831 edition tends to exceed that for the earlier editions.

[29] "Nothing more than the Dover, 1812, edition reissued with cancel title pages" and a different map (Blanck, *Bibliography*, Vol. 1, p. 191; Wright Howes, *U. S.-iana (1700–1950): A Descriptive Check-list of 11,450 Printed Sources Relating to those Parts of Continental North America now Comprising the United States* [Boston: Bowker, 1954], p. 42; Howes annotation that "all" the *History* was reprinted in 1831 is incorrect).

Dr. Belknap and the editor, Dr. John Farmer, as explained in the latter's Preface (I:iv–v). "Volume II," however, never appeared. It would have been a revision of the original Volume III, the geographical part of the earlier editions. This failure to publish Volume II distressed Belknap's granddaughter. In her biography of him, after calling attention to a favorable comment on the geographical volume in a London magazine, she added that the "omission of the third volume has mutilated the work and done great injustice to its author."[30] There was reason for this complaint. The "geography" formed a logical conclusion for all that had gone before and the omission of the appendix notes pertinent to the original Volume II was a positive "mutilation." On the other hand, Farmer's edition was an improvement over the previous versions of Volumes I and II in that mistakes were corrected in the text and additional information was furnished in the notes. Volume I of the present reprint, accordingly, is from Volume I of the Dover edition of 1831 and Volume II is from Volume III of the Dover edition of 1812.

The "Historical" Part of the *History*

Professor Bassett commended Belknap for his "fine sense of proportion."[31] A historian shows a good sense of proportion by not allowing personal bias to warp his value judgments so that he either expresses himself intemperately or lets whims determine the manner in which he apportions space to different topics. That Belknap's overtly expressed value judgments of men, motives, situations, and ideas are on the whole temperately stated is a proposition that cannot be demonstrated mathematically. Yet I believe most present-day readers would agree to it. His apportionment of space to different subjects likewise seems as well balanced as could be expected and is a proposition concerning which a few figures may be given.

---

30 Marcou, *Life*, p. 134; Mrs. Marcou pointed out that in the *London Monthly*, October 1793, the hope was expressed that Belknap would write a general account of the United States. On December 8, 1787, Belknap wrote Hazard "I have been thinking of an American Gazetteer, and have made some preparations for it" (BP 1, p. 497), but when Hazard informed him soon after that Jedidiah Morse was intending to publish "both a Geography and Gazetteer" (BP 2, p. 1), Belknap abandoned the project [BP 2, p. 13; see also R. H. Brown, "The American Geographies of Jedidiah Morse," *Annals of the Association of American Geographers* 31 (1941), 145–217; 152–154].

31 Bassett, *Middle Group*, p. 24.

An author is privileged to write about anything he pleases. In the case of fiction the title need not fit the subject, but in serious works of history or geography there should be some relation between title (or at least subtitle) and contents. If, for example, three-quarters of the *History of New-Hampshire* had been devoted to proof of some pet theory of its author he would have been open to legitimate criticism. Actually, about seven-tenths of the entire text (as distinguished from appendixes) is historical (Vol. I) and the remainder geographical (Vol. II[III]), a suitable ratio in a work entitled *"History of . . . ."*

Volume I covers a span of about 175 years, from 1615 to 1790, in such a way that (in the 1831 edition) the average number of pages per annum is 2.32. Unlike some averages this is not *totally* meaningless. It conveys a modicum of meaning when compared with similar averages for different parts of the volume. When I was a boy I kept a "Line-a-Day" diary in which I wrote four or five lines each day regardless of what happened. Unlike my diary, Belknap's *History* exhibits considerable deviations from the mean, and one could work out the standard deviation if one wished (I don't). Especially eventful years such as 1745 and 1775 receive a dozen or more pages, counterbalanced by briefer treatment of less interesting years; and naturally Belknap, unlike the annalist or diarist, did not treat each year as a watertight compartment. The story flows along smoothly, with occasional digressions in which generalities are considered. It is an agreeable stream, and the reader senses a rational correlation between the amount of attention devoted to different historical events and their relative "importance."[32] As time advanced and New Hampshire's population grew larger and its spirit of independence more and more intense, the course of events increased in complexity and in its direct bearing upon the state of society that existed in Belknap's own time, as described in Volume II[III]. Hence, as might be expected, with the quickening of the reader's interest there is a progressive deceleration of the chronological pace, or, what amounts to the same thing, a progressive gain in the quantity of information and comment provided per annum: for the first hundred years the mean is 1.8 pages per annum, for the last 75 years 2.9, and for the exciting and troublous final

---

[32] One might assess the relative historical "importance" of events in terms of (1) the number of persons affected, (2) the quality and potency of the effects, and (3) the duration of the effects. But how?

15 years 3.2 Though he tells graphically of campaigns, battles, and other wartime happenings, Belknap was not obsessed with military affairs. For some 47 "war years" the mean is only 2.5 pages per annum, or slightly in excess of the over-all mean. It would be possible, of course, to work out such statistics in much greater detail for other subjects covered in the *History*, but it would not add much to what you can see for yourself by perusing the tables of contents, and, as regards Belknap's "fine sense of proportion," would be like gilding the lily with statistical gilt.

Though "fine," Jeremy Belknap's sense of historical proportion was not perfect. No historian's is. One feels in Volume I a disproportionate amount of quoting and paraphrasing of legal and governmental documents. Many more crucial human conflicts have been waged and resolved in law courts, legislative assemblies, and council chambers than on battlefields, and hence have been recorded in the language of lawyers. This makes for hard reading, and, like the tangled growths in the upper Nile, renders occasional reaches of Belknap's stream less agreeable to navigate than others. The careful documentation is admirable, but a more adroit if not necessarily more scholarly historian could have stripped off some of the verbiage.

Dr. Samuel Atkins Eliot a quarter century ago commended Belknap for finding his material "as much in the private as in the public life of the community" and for the attention he gave to social conditions; but this applies predominantly to Volume II [III].[33] In Volume I the stress is almost wholly on public affairs, (wars, politics, ecclesiastical controversies, the progress of settlement, etc.), and there is relatively little about the "life of the people" as it was prior to Belknap's own time. Hence, as viewed in the light of later standards, the book shows a lack of balance as a general history. But it must be remembered that what a historian or geographer writes about, though initially foreshadowed by his predilections and desires, is closely circumscribed by the scholarly mores of his time and field of interest and no less by the availability of sources of information. Belknap would have been a historian of exceptional originality had he felt a strong impulse to round out his book with a fuller treatment of what we should now call economic, social, and cultural history

---

[33] Eliot, "Jeremy Belknap", pp. 103–104.

and the history of ideas.[34] But even if he had wanted to do this and had been fully conscious of the fascination and values of such kinds of historical study, he would have been more or less stymied. Nowadays the would-be student by going to certain libraries and historical societies can readily find the printed texts of manuscripts and guides to the location of unpublished manuscripts that were entirely out of Jeremy Belknap's reach or ken.

Geography in Belknap's *History*

A brief dialogue follows. The speakers are a bright young American academic geographer of today and the shade of Jeremy Belknap.

BYAG: "Mr. Belknap, I'd appreciate it, sir, if you would explain where you would draw the line between history and geography. For example, where would you draw it in your *History of New-Hampshire?*

SJB: "I wouldn't try to draw any such line."

BYAG: "Oh, come sir; surely you think it is important to recognize the difference."

SJB: "Of course there is a difference, but that doesn't mean that history can be sharply differentiated from geography. History aims to narrate and interpret the course of human events, geography to describe and interpret the earth or parts thereof,[35] but in a particular study they may become so mixed or compounded that it serves no useful purpose to separate them; in fact, it is positively misleading to draw sharp boundary lines between most broad fields of human understanding."

BYAG: "But should not history and geography be segregated and sharply distinguished so that the professors won't poach on each others' preserves?"

SJB: "I fail to comprehend what you are talking about and I

---

[34] As did, for example, the Rev. Samuel Miller in his learned and far from "brief" *A Brief Retrospect of the Eighteenth Century: Part First, in Two Volumes, Containing a Sketch of the Revolutions and Improvements in Science, Arts, and Literature During That Period* (New York, 1803; the second part, which was never published, would have dealt with theology, morals, and politics. The chapter on the United States was reprinted with an introduction by L. H. Butterfield, *William and Mary Quarterly (3rd ser.)* 10 (1953), 579–627. Like Merle Curti's *The Growth of American Thought* (see above, note 1), Miller's *Retrospect* places Belknap's *History*, both as history and as geography, against a broader background of intellectual movement.

[35] This, I believe, is what Belknap might well have said; I have no knowledge of his ever having defined either "history" or "geography."

disrelish polemical argument about such matters. Things must
have changed since my time."

That things have changed must be borne in mind in making
value judgments concerning the geographical parts of Belknap's
History. Let us consider these under two headings: (1) geographical history and (2) contemporaneous geography.

Geographical History. American geographers tend to distinguish
the "history of geography" from "historical geography" and
sometimes they differentiate "geographical history" from both.[36]
To avoid a bog of semantics we shall lump together as "geographical history" all those parts of Belknap's *History* that deal
historically with any geographical aspect of the course of human
events, as contrasted with those parts (in Volume II[III]) that
deal geographically with contemporaneous *conditions* in New
Hampshire.

One large aspect of the course of human events has been the
growth of geographical knowledge ("history of geography").
Although, as we have seen, Belknap was a pioneer in the study of
this subject in this country, he does not seems to have thought
either of it or of its cognate study, "historical geography," as a
distinctive field worthy of a distinctive name. By piecing together scattered passages in the *History,* however, one could
compile a summary account of the advancement of geographical
knowledge of New Hampshire from the time of the early voyages
along the coast to Cutler's and Belknap's visit to the White Mountains. The account would tell something of the reconnoitering
trips to the mountains in the mid-1600's, of the inhibiting effect
on exploration of the Indian menace, which kept most of the interior a *terra incognita* for about a century, and of the gaining of
geographical intelligence by frontier scouts and small military
operations during the Indian Wars and through the harrowing
tales recounted by women and others freed from captivity. Some
of the account would deal with the acquisition of geographical
information through surveys. In Volume I there is considerable
detail regarding the surveys by which the straight-line southern

---

36 The term "geographical history" was used in 1600 by John Pory and
has been used off and on since then (letter from Professor Gary S. Dunbar
to J. K. Wright, 1963); on a possible distinction between the meanings of
"historical geography," "geographical history," and "history of geography," see J. K. Wright and Elizabeth T. Platt, *Aids to Geographical Re-
search* . . . (New York: Columbia University Press and American
Geographical Society, 1947), pp. 100–101.

and eastern boundaries of New Hampshire were established, and
certain of the original documents will be found in the Appendix
to Volume II[III]. Belknap writes vividly of the difficulties of
surveying in the woods, whether for locating roads or running
town lines; he explains how errors had been made through ignorance of the behavior of the compass, and he tells something
of the special problems encountered in marking out a curious
semicircular line across southern and eastern New Hampshire.
This line, which was claimed in the mid-eighteenth century by
the heirs of John Mason as the northern and western limit of
their land holding according to a "patent under the common seal
of the council of Plymouth" (1629) in the reign of Charles I, is
still discernible on maps showing New Hempshire's present-day
town and county boundaries.[37]

Surveyors apply and use geographical knowledge, and hence
the history of surveying links together the histories of technology
and of geography. But surveyors also serve as agents of governments or landholders or entrepreneurs in helping establish the
geometric areal frameworks requisite for the orderly channeling
of human affairs; and, indeed, mankind could dispense with
their services only a shade less catamitously than with the services of doctors. "Historical geography" is largely concerned with
changes in the earth's surface as wrought by engineers and with
social, political, and economic conflicts regarding the extent of
governmental jurisdictions over territory and regarding the
ownership and use of land, water, and natural resources—in all
of which the surveyor's work is initial and fundamental. In the
life of a region that in being frequently opened up to settlement,
engineering operations and conflicts over land bulk large, and
there is much in Belknap's *History* that bears on these matters.
The most serious territorial conflicts were those with Massachusetts over the southern tiers of New Hampshire townships
(settled by the running of the state line in 1741), with New York
over the "New Hampshire Grants" (settled nominally in 1763),
and with the Vermont that grew out of the Grants; and within
New Hampshire over the complexities of the claims of the Ma-

---

[37] See G. B. Upham, "New Hampshire Town Boundaries Determined by
Mason's Curve," *Granite Monthly*, 52 (1920), 19–27; W. H. Fry, *New
Hampshire as a Royal Province* (New York: Columbia University Press,
1928).

sonian proprietors and counterclaims of the people and government. A large fraction of the legal verbiage to which attention has been called relates to these intricate proceedings.

Other matters that lie within the general scope of "geographical history" are the spread of settlement and population on the one hand, and wars, on the other. The former brought about long-enduring patterns of population distribution, still readily recognizable in New Hampshire's "human geography." Most of the battles, sieges, military campaigns, etc., although having marked geographic attributes and relationships at the time when they occurred, were of only a few hours or days or weeks or months duration and, except for two or three decisive events (e.g., Louisbourg, Bennington), without lasting geographic aftereffects.

Contemporaneous Geography. Some of Volume II[III] might not pass muster as "geography" under academic definitions of that subject that are in vogue today. Our concern here, however, is what this volume *is* rather than with whether it should be called "geography" or not. As may be seen from the Table of Contents the first half of the text, more or less, bears upon the natural environment and the Indians (evidently conceived as an ingredient of the environment), and the latter parts with the population and its economic, political, and cultural life. As might be expected of a regional geography for the general reader, the book is essentially factual rather than theoretical. Perhaps its chief virtue is that nearly all the facts were fresh at the time when Belknap gathered them and were not culled from older publications. He obtained his information either directly from personal observation and experience or from other contemporary sources of first-hand information. By contrast, most of the *ideas* to which the book gives expression were derivative, for Belknap was not a particularly original thinker. Whence came these derivative ideas?

To answer this question adequately would call for a far greater fund of knowledge than I possess but some hints may be given.

Every book—even a telephone book—expresses ideas implicitly—ideas that govern the manner in which facts are chosen and treated. In Volume II[III] the selection of subjects, their classification, the order in which they are taken up, and the terminology conform with standard practice in English and

American geographical writings of the period[38]—the books of Guthrie, Morse, Jefferson, Williams, and others. The English style is also, in a sense, derivative in being simple, straightforward, and "classic," without displays of stylistic originality or idiosyncracy. The following passage is typical:

The mountains of New Hampshire "appear of different colours . . . according to the distance of the observer . . . If he is very nigh, they appear of the grey colour of the rock, and the farther he recedes, their appearance is a paler blue, till it becomes nearly the colour of the sky. The woody parts of the mountains when viewed at a small distance, are green, at a greater distance, blue. From some favorable situations, all these varieties may be seen at once[39] mountains of different shades, textures and elevations, are presented to the eye of the curious observer.[40]

This shows keen powers of observation, but the results are expressed as many another of Belknap's literate contemporary compatriots would have expressed them. The style of the following passage, concerning the higher part of the White Mountains, is even more obviously derivative: "A poetic fancy may find full gratification amidst these wild and rugged scenes . . . Almost every thing in nature, which can be supposed capable of inspiring ideas of the sublime and beautiful, is here realized. Aged mountains, stupendous elevations, rolling clouds, impending rocks, verdant woods, chrystal streams, the gentle rill, and the roaring

---

[38] In a letter informing Belknap of Belknap's election to the American Philosophical Society (Jan. 24, 1784) Hazard wrote: "Can't you sketch out a short Natural History of N. Hampshire?" Replying (Feb. 27), Belknap pointed out that he had "made some beginning, which I intend as a part of my second volume, together with some other observations in the form of our geographical grammars." See BP 1, pp. 301, 306. "Geographical grammar" was part of the title of eighteenth-century British textbooks by Patrick Gordon, William Guthrie, Thomas Salmon, and others. Michael Joy, an American residing at the time in London, wrote Belknap (Aug. 7, 1789): ". . . the present rage, next to politics, is for natural history. The more of this, therefore, you introduce, the more you will attract the present class of reader. Topographical descriptions, remarks on the climates, soils, minerals, marine productions, indigenous vegetables, & animals, are sought for & read with eagerness. . . . A full account of the aborigenes of N. Hampshire would be a most desireable & interesting, as well as a natural, appendix to the History" (BP 3, p 446).

[39] This and subsequent references in this form are to pages in Volume II[III] (see above, note 13).

[40] Belknap had described the colors of the mountains as seen from a distance in almost identical terms in a letter to Hazard written soon after his return from the trip (Aug. 19, 1784; see BP 2, pp. 188–189).

torrent, all conspire to amaze, to soothe and to enrapture" (p. 39).[41] This makes us wonder what Belknap had been reading. It is gothic and romantic.[42] In the same chapter we find: "When amazement is excited by the grandeur and sublimity of the scenes presented to view, it is necessary to curb the imagination, and exercise judgment with mathematical precision; or the temptation to romance will be invincible" (p. 32). For the most part Belknap successfully resisted this temptation.

In a number of places he gave *explicit* expression to ideas derived from others either by attacking or adopting them. These passages protrude amidst the more factual elements like rocky outcrops in a New Hampshire pasture.

Of the geographical volume the French traveler Volney wrote: "If we overlook some effusions of prejudice, natural to the author's character as an American and clergyman, and which show themselves in declamation against the philosophers and travellers of Europe, his work is one of the most instructive and philosophical with which America is capable of enriching our language"[43] [Volney had in mind its translation into French].

Being an American, I find little that seems objectionable in the "declamations" to which Volney took exception, nor are there many of them. In Chapter 5 Belknap criticizes European theories concerning the sinuosity and descent of rivers and throws in this *obiter dictum:* "It is amusing to observe how the European writers, in their accounts of America, entertain themselves and their readers, with a detail of circumstances, which have no foundation but in their own fancies" (p. 50). If not the quintessence of tact, this was more or less true. In Chapter 14 Belknap rallies to the defense of the climate of America (or at least of New Hampshire) against Robertson, Raynal, and other "European philosophers" who had condemned it as unhealthful.

---

41 In a footnote in his diary concerning the tour of the White Mountains Belknap had written of this scenery in almost the same words (BP 1, p. 395, see also BP 2, p. 183).

42 See the chapter on "The Aesthetics of the Infinite" in Marjorie Nicolson, *Mountain Gloom and Mountain Glory* (Ithaca, New York: Cornell University Press, 1959. New York: Norton paperback, 1963).

43 C. F. Volney, *A View of the Soil and Climate of the United States of America. . . .* Translated with Occasional Remarks, by C. B. Brown (Philadelphia and Baltimore, 1804), pp. 320–321.

This was a bitter issue at the time,[44] and in rebuttal Belknap marshaled a variety of statistical data of variable worth concerning the healthiness and longevity of his fellow New Hampshiremen. His motives here were quite as much patriotic as they were scientific.

As one reads along in the chapters on natural history one's attention is arrested by the following comments: "The beaver is not only an amphibious animal, but is said to form a connecting link between quadrupeds and fishes" (p. 113): "The only *mamillary biped* which we have is the Bat (*vespertilio murinus*) which forms the connecting link between the beasts and the birds" (p. 121) ;[45] and similarly Dr. Cutler is quoted as saying that the fibers in peat "seem to form the link between the vegetable and fossil kingdom" p. 84n). The classification of animals as "quadrupeds" and "bipeds," the distinction between the animal, the vegetable, and the "fossil" kingdoms, and the concept of the beaver, the bat, and peat as "connecting links" are tiny outcrops of immense substrata of now obsolete biological lore. The doctrine that certain creatures are "connecting links" ties in with the magnificent theory of the Great Chain of Being, so brilliantly interpreted by the late Professor Lovejoy.[46]

As compared with some of the geographical writings of other American clergymen of the period before 1800, Belknap's geographical volume shows little evidence of the influence of theology. The book, in fact, seems almost totally devoid of what I have ventured elsewhere to call "geopiety" (the expression of "piety aroused by awareness of terrestrial diversity"), the most

---

[44] See E. T. Martin, *Thomas Jefferson: Scientist* (New York: Schuman, 1952), pp. 148–159; Gilbert Chinard, "Eighteenth Century Theories on America as a Human Habitat" (*Proceedings of the American Philosophical Society*, 91 (1947): 27–57); C. J. Glacken, *Traces on the Rhodian Shore: Nature and Culture in Western Thought from Ancient Times to the End of the Eighteenth Century* (Berkeley and Los Angeles: University of California Press, 1967), pp. 681–685.

[45] Hazard wrote Belknap (May 30, 1792): "What will those critics say to the assertion in your 3d volume, that 'bats are the only *mamillary bipeds* in New Hampshire'? Let them say what they will, I think you will get honour, if not profit, by your History. The last volume will be the most interesting to persons who are not inhabitants of the State" (BP 2, p. 296).

[46] A. O. Lovejoy, *The Great Chain of Being* (Cambridge, Mass.: Harvard University Press, 1936. New York: Harper Torchbooks, 1960), Chapter 8. See also D. J. Boorstin, *The Lost World of Thomas Jefferson* (New York: Holt, 1948. Beacon paperback, 1960), Chapter 1.

"geopious" pages not being Belknap's but in General Benjamin Lincoln's letter on the migration of fishes (pp. 334–343).[47]

Chapter 8 opens thus: "Few persons in this country, have studied natural history as a science. . . . With much diffidence I enter on this part of my work, sensible that my knowledge of the subject is imperfect, yet, desirous of contributing something, to promote a branch of science, now in its infancy." Chapter 10, on the native animals, begins with a similar disavowal of competence, and in Chapter 11, on "Caverns, Stones, Fossils, and Minerals" we read: "This chapter must be extremely imperfect as many parts of the country are yet unexplored; and of those which are known, the knowledge is mostly confiend to the surface and its vegetation" (p. 138). Also, "Mineralogy is a branch of science which is but little cultivated. Men of genius and science have not leisure to pursue objects from which present advantages cannot be drawn" (p. 143). Belknap's clear-eyed recognition of the shortcomings of contemporaneous natural history and candid disavowal of any particular ability of his own in this domain reveals a scientific spirit if not a high order of scientific knowledge or technical proficiency.[48] Had he not been so honest, perhaps certain writers in the mid-nineteenth century might not have taken his words at their face value and condemned the

---

[47] See J. K. Wright, *Human Nature in Geography* . . . (Cambridge, Mass.: Harvard University Press, 1966), p. 251. See also letter from Lincoln to Belknap (Jan. 21, 1792) in BP 3, pp. 512–517. For light on how Belknap's thought concerning the date of the peopling of America (as expressed in letters written in 1781 and 1782, was colored by theological presuppositions see BP 1, pp. 127, 135–142; BP 3, pp. 219-222. In a letter to Hazard (Oct. 22, 1789) however, Belknap wrote: "I wish you was [sic] here to laugh with me at Dr. [Cotton] Mather's 'Wonders of the Invisible World' which I have taken out of the College Library" (BP 2, pp. 198–199); he referred to Mather's observations on the Devil's ability to raise storms (see Wright, *Human Nature*, p. 271). John Thayer, a Roman Catholic convert and fellow Bostonian, wrote a long undated letter to Belknap accusing him of anti-Catholic prejudice in dealing with certain matters geographical and historical (BP 3, pp. 539–546); since it contains references to "Volume 2" of Belknap's *History* and to his *Discourse on the Discovery of America*, this letter must date from the end of 1792 or later.

[48] On March 13, 1780, Belknap wrote Hazard "I wish I had some good system of Natural History" (BP 1, p. 40), to which Hazard replied (April 1): "I have not read anything upon *natural history*, nor can I tell you who is the best author upon that subject. . . ." (BP 1, p. 45). In July 1782 Hazard referred Belknap to Oliver Goldsmith's "History of the Earth and Animated Nature" in "eight or nine volumes 8vo" and suggested that he also read "Sir Robert Boyle's works" (BP 1, p. 137). Belknap refer to Goldsmith's book in the *History* (II[III]: 50 n., 115, 123).

parts of his *History* relating to natural science as "worth little."[49]
In my opinion they are worth a great deal. They furnish entertaining information about the useful and the noxious properties
of the better-known plants, animals, birds, insects, fish, caverns,
stones, fossils, and minerals of New Hampshire and about the
actual uses to which many of these were being put. Along with
the parts of the book on forest industries, "husbandry," the
fisheries, manufactures, and surveying, they are sources from
which reliable data may be obtained concerning the state of
technology in New Hempshire, and by extension over large parts
of the United States, in Revolutionary times. Their value, however, is as compendia of isolated data, classified and described
but otherwise ungeneralized. In the matter of generalization and
integration—of "binding" together facts in coherent units that
make sense in terms of cause and effect or otherwise—Belknap's
chapters on natural history are almost as deficient as the medie-
val herbals, bestiaries, and lapidaries; they are what these would
be if expurgated of the marvelous, the monstrous, and the
fabulous.

Add 2 to 3 and call it 5 and you have made a quantitative
nongeographical generalization. Add an apple to a pear and call
them fruit and your generalization is both nonquantitative and
nongeographical. Where Belknap wrote: "The Snow Bird is
smaller than the sparrow, and appears in little flocks, in the
winter, enlivening the gloom of that dreary season" (p. 127)[50]
his generalization was nonquantitative and, except insofar as
broadly pertinent to New Hampshire, nongeographical. Here is
another generalization of the same sort: "Their [the Indians']
method of girdling trees to kill them . . . is not only a lazy fashion
but quite inexcusable where axes may be had" (p. 70). Here
too, the generalization is nongeographical, except as pertinent to
the Indians of New Hampshire and those who followed their
"bad" example. Where Belknap wrote "The greater part of New-
Hampshire is by nature shut off from any commercial inter-

[49] See articles on Belknap in William Allen, *The American Biographical
Dictionary* (Boston, 1958, 3rd ed.) and in Appleton's *Cyclopaedia of
American Biography*, Vol. 1, 1887.

[50] Belknap lists some 130 different kinds of birds, giving both English
and Latin names, but he comments on only eight or ten. No representative
of the numerous tribe of warblers seems to be mentioned. The "Yellow
Bird," which he designates as *Fringilla tristis* (hence a member of the
finch-sparrow family) was probably the Goldfinch rather than the Yellow
Warbler.

course with the only port in the State" (p. 153), the generalization is still nonquantitative but more truly geographical, since it relates to geographic diversity within the area of New Hampshire. The following comment, an extremely simple generalization, is *both* quantitative and genuinely geographical: the sea breezes "do not reach more than twenty or thirty miles into the country, and the lighter ones not so far" (p. 18).

One cannot talk sensibly without generalizing (classifying, integrating, explaining, interpreting, describing), but there are different levels of quantitative and nonquantitative sophistication at which this may be done, and the levels have risen since Dr. Belknap's time. For one thing, vastly more geographical data have become available to generalize about; for another, there have been mighty strides in the techniques of generalization (culminating in the generalizers that may end all generalization —computers and such); and, finally, demands have arisen for generalized, classified, and integrated information that would have astounded Dr. Belknap's ghost. A few more examples should suffice to illustrate the scope and quality of his geographical generalizations, and first of some nonquantitative ones:

"Mountainous countries are observed to be most subject to earthquakes; and the nearer any lands are to mountains, it may be expected that these commotions will be more frequent. . . . In 1727 and 1755 . . . shocks were more frequent in New-Hampshire than in Boston" (pp. 27–28).[51]

"That the coldness of our northwest wind is owing to the great lakes, is a vulgar error, often retailed by geographical writers, and adopted by unthinking people. All the great lakes lie westward of the N.W. point, and some of them southward of W. It is more natural to suppose that the immense wilderness, but especially the mountains, when covered with snow, give a keenness to the air. . . ." (p. 15).[52]

"In the new and uncultivated parts [of New Hampshire], the soil is distinguished by the various kinds of woods which grow upon it, thus: White oak land is hard and stony. . . .," etc. (p. 95). "After going through the catalogue of forest trees, it may

---

[51] See also BP 1, pp. 299, 328, 424.

[52] This description appears also in almost identical words in Belknap's diary of his tour of the White Mountains (BP 1, p. 393). The northwest wind seems almost invariably mentioned and described by seventeenth- and eighteenth-century writers on the geography of eastern North America.

be proper to observe, that all woods, which grow on high land, are more firm and solid, and better for timber or fewel, than those which grow in swamps" (p. 88). Each of these ecological observations is followed by examples.

"Before the Revolution, the people of the different parts of New-Hampshire, had but little connexion with each other. They might be divided into three classes. Those of the older towns, and the emigrants from them. Those on the southern border, most of whom were emigrants from Massachusetts; and those on Connecticut River, who came chiefly from Connecticut" (p. 191).[53] After this come specific comments on the economic and political effects of this cleavage, which was partly areal and partly social; its influence was implicit upon many of the events discussed in detail in Volume I.

Now for a few examples of quantitative geographical generalization:

On May 19, 1780, darkness due to forest-fire smokes extended more than 200 miles from north to south and from "beyond Albany" to at least "fifteen leagues eastward of Cape Anne" (pp. 22–23).[54] The native black rat retires back into the country as the gray rat, introduced from shipwrecks, advances. Since 1764 the latter has advanced about thirty miles, and farther, along the great roads (p. 119). The lumber trade "is drawn from the distance of thirty or forty miles, to the heads of the tide in the branches of the river [Pascataqua]" (p. 150).

Such generalizations are not on a high plane of geographico-statistical sophistication, and neither are any of the other geographical statistics that may be found scattered through the text of Volume II [III]. These relate to the situation, dimensions, and area of the State; to the heights of two or three mountains; to divers productions and commodities and their prices; to taxes; and to deaths, births, and diseases in a few towns where the clergy had kept records. The only quantitative data that could possibly have been plotted on a base map showing town boundaries so as to yield a dot or choropleth map of the kinds so

[53] This passage is paraphrased and commented on in S. E. Morison and H. S. Commager, *The Growth of the American Republic* (New York, etc.; Oxford University Press, 1934) pp. 61–62.

[54] For more extended and vivid comments on this "dark day," see Belknap's correspondence with Hazard (BP 1, pp. 52–55, 58). Belknap's friend, John Eliot, also had much to say about it in letters to Belknap (June 3, Sept. 11, 1780) (BP 3, pp. 191–194, 197).

frequent in present-day geographical writings, are those for population and tax rates in the tables in Volume II[III] on pages 226–243, and for taxation in relation to representation in the assembly (1773) in Vol. I(II), p. 374, but such maps were unheard of in the eighteenth century. Belknap's normal method of using statistical data was simple: he gave the figures in text or table and let the reader draw his own conclusions. When, on one occasion, he tried a mathematical calculation in an attempted forecast of the growth of population, he made an elementary mistake in arithmetic reasoning, as Dr. James Freeman explained in a letter that Belknap printed in the Appendix (II[III]: 344–353).

As compared with what is easily accessible today, Belknap's fund of information concerning New Hampshire was meager and he was quite unaware of techniques of generalization that are common knowledge of every first-year graduate student in our burgeoning university departments of geography. But he did the best he could with what he had, and it was no fault of his that we look in vain for graphs and dot maps and mathematical correlation in his book or that in some places the facts seem to float about like croutons in a watery soup.

The facts themselves are not only delightful but for the most part genuine and not fancies, and where they seem the most fanciful they are questioned (except now and then, as with reference to the man who is said to have walked from Portsmouth to Boston and back in two days at the age of 80 and then continued to have lived to the age of 115). Of the entire work the parts I enjoy the most are the early chapters of Volume II[III]. These tell of familiar things: winds and storms,[55] the "face of

---

[55] Writing to Hazard (Dec. 1, 1783), Belknap inquired whether Hazard kept "a journal of the weather." He explained that he wanted data concerning the beginning and ending of storms, and to this end he gave some information about storms in November 1783 and on Jan. 2, 1784 (BP, pp. 280, 291). Possibly Hazard failed to receive Belknap's letters, for soon after (Jan. 24, 1784) he asked whether Belknap made meteorological observations (BP 1, p. 301). Was Belknap's thought in this connection influenced by Lewis Evans' (or possibly Benjamin Franklin's) speculations concerning the movement of storms? (see inscription on Evans' map of 1749, and letters of Franklin to Jared Eliot, 1747, 1749–1750, as published, respectively, in L. H. Gipson, *Lewis Evans* [Philadelphia: Historical Society of Philadelphia, 1939], pp. 11, 223, and in *The Works of Benjamin Franklin* . . . with notes by Jared Sparks (Boston, 1836–1840), Vol. 6, pp. 79, 105, 219; see also W. M. Davis, "Was Lewis Evans or Benjamin Franklin the First to Recognize that Our Northeast Storms Come from the Southwest?" *Proceedings, American Philosophical Society*, 45 (1906) 129–130, 183.

the country," the White Mountains, the forest. At about the age of five, from a pasture high on a hillside in Hancock, I first saw a wide New Hampshire horizon and was told the magical names of distant blue summits: Monadnock, the Uncanoonucs, Joe English Hill, Crotched Mountain, Kearsarge. Since then there have been few years when I have not felt New Hampshire's summer heats or heard its thunder or camped in its forests or smelled its forest fires or climbed its mountains and sketched their outlines as seen from afar, and for the last eleven years I have lived happily in one of its smaller villages. Jeremy Belknap also knew of these things and knew how to describe them.

John Kirtland Wright

Pendleton's Lithog.y Boston

JEREMY BELKNAP, D.D.

Born June 4.th 1744 }
Died June 20.th 1798. } Aged 54.

THE

HISTORY

OF

NEW-HAMPSHIRE.

BY JEREMY BELKNAP, D. D.,

MEMBER OF THE AMERICAN PHILOSOPHICAL SOCIETY, OF THE AMERICAN ACAD-
EMY OF ARTS AND SCIENCES, AND CORRESPONDING SECRETARY OF
THE MASSACHUSETTS HISTORICAL SOCIETY.

FROM

A COPY OF THE ORIGINAL EDITION,

HAVING THE AUTHOR'S LAST CORRECTIONS.

TO WHICH ARE ADDED

NOTES,

CONTAINING VARIOUS CORRECTIONS AND ILLUSTRATIONS OF THE TEXT,
AND ADDITIONAL FACTS AND NOTICES OF PERSONS AND
EVENTS THEREIN MENTIONED.

BY JOHN FARMER,

CORRESPONDING SECRETARY OF THE N. H. HISTORICAL SOCIETY.

VOL. I.

DOVER:

S. C. STEVENS AND ELA & WADLEIGH.

1831.

EDITOR'S PREFACE.

THE first volume of the History of New-Hampshire was published at Philadelphia, in 1784, with the following title-page : " THE HISTORY OF NEW-HAMPSHIRE. VOLUME I. COMPREHENDING THE EVENTS OF ONE COMPLETE CENTURY FROM THE DISCOVERY OF THE RIVER PASCATAQUA. BY JEREMY BELKNAP, A. M. Member of the American Philosophical Society held at Philadelphia for promoting useful knowledge.

> Tempus edax rerum, tuque invidiosa vetustas,
> Omnia destruitis : vitiataque dentibus ævi
> Paulatim lenta consumitis omnia morte.
> Hæc perstant.   OVID.

Philadelphia : Printed for the author by ROBERT AITKEN, in Market Street, near the Coffee House. M. DCC. LXXXIV."

The author was then the minister of Dover, and it being difficult for him, at such a distance from the press, to superintend the publication of the work, it was entrusted to his friend, EBENEZER HAZARD, Esquire, a gentleman well acquainted with the history and antiquities of our country, who faithfully executed the trust committed to him.

The second volume of the work was published at Boston in the year 1791, after the author had removed from New-Hampshire, and had been installed over the Congregational church in Federal Street. The title of this volume is as follows : " THE HISTO-RY OF NEW-HAMPSHIRE. VOLUME II. COMPREHENDING THE EVENTS OF SEVENTY FIVE YEARS, FROM MDCCXV. to MDCCXC. Illustrated by a Map. By JEREMY BELKNAP, A. M. Member of the Philosophical Society in Philadelphia, and

of the Academy of Arts and Sciences in Massachusetts. Printed
at Boston for the Author, by ISAIAH THOMAS & EBENEZER T. AN-
DREWS, Faust's Statue, No. 45, Newbury Street. MDCCXCI."
It is believed that there was a reprint of the first volume soon after the publication of the second.

The work having been nearly all sold, a new edition was called
for by the public in 1810, and Mr. Samuel Bragg, of Dover, commenced the printing of it from a copy, into which had been transcribed the marginal notes and corrections made by the author at
different times in a printed copy which he kept for this purpose.
The printing had not proceeded far before the office of Mr. Bragg,
with his printing materials and the corrected copy of the first volume, which contained nearly all the corrections and additions
made to the historical part of the work, was consumed by fire. A
new edition however appeared in 1812, printed at Dover by JOHN
MANN and JAMES K. REMICH, for O. CROSBY & J. VARNEY, but
without the advantages of the corrected copy of the first volume,
which had been used by Mr. Bragg, and which it was supposed
could never be replaced. Some of the copies, and it is believed
a considerable part of the impression, have a false title page, purporting that the work was published at Boston by Bradford & Read,
and that it contains " large additions and improvements from the
author's last manuscript," but it is not apprehended that either
the original publishers or printers had any agency in such a gross
imposition on the public.

After the copy for the present edition had been prepared for the
press, I received from JOHN BELKNAP, Esquire, of Boston, son of
the venerated author, a letter respecting the work, of which the
following is an extract. " When I sold to Mr. BRAGG and Mr.
VARNEY the *corrected copy*, with the right to print an edition,
with the corrections, two other copies had all the corrections transcribed into them, and remain in the family. My object in writing, is to offer you an opportunity to avail yourself of these corrections, in case you proceed in the publication, which may be
done, by exchanging one of these corrected copies, for a copy of
your new edition " I lost no time in accepting the kind offer of
Mr. BELKNAP, and soon received the copy which had been corrected
by the author, together with the original appendix which had been
prepared by him, and in his hand writing. The corrections and
additions of the historical part have been introduced into this vol-

ume ; and the appendix of original papers and public documents
has been printed from the manuscript copy of the author.

In the Notes which I have added to the work, endeavors have
been made to correct the errors occasioned by the author's reliance on the authenticity of the Wheelwright deed of 1629 ; to
supply some facts which had been omitted for want of information,
and to give short biographical notices of some of the most prominent characters mentioned in the course of the history. The notes
which I have added are included within brackets.

At the head of the left hand page, is the running title of the
former editions ; at the head of the right hand page, stands the
name of the governor or chief magistrate for the time being. The
authorities, which were placed on the side margin of the former
editions, are here placed next after the text, at the bottom of the
page. The references to them in the text may be sometimes misplaced, as none had before been used, but they are believed to be
generally correct. In spelling the names of persons, autographs
have been followed, whenever they could be obtained. This has
occasioned a difference in the orthography of the names of Andros,
Chamberlain, Cutt, Endecott, Godfrey, Holyoke, Leveridge,
Moodey, Wheelwright and Wiggin, which were before printed, An-
drosse, Chamberlayne, Cutts, Endicot, Godfrie, Holiock, Leverich,
Moody, Whelewright and Wiggen. The name of Pickering was
often, at an early period, written by those bearing it, Pickerin.
The name of Hinckes which occurs a number of times in the
text should probably be Hinks. The spelling of the names of
places has been altered in a number of instances ; and the orthography of common words and the punctuation have undergone
some changes. The latter might have been still further improved.
In all these alterations, great care has been taken to preserve the
text unimpaired, and no changes affecting that have been allowed.

A copious General Index, embracing every important subject
and every name in the text, notes, and tables to the 418th page,
has been prepared with considerable labor, but is necessarily omitted. It may, however, appear with the second volume.

Concord, 2 February, 1831.

CORRECTIONS.

Page 4, *wherefore*, in the 6th line, should be *whereof*.
    74, *Pequawet*, in the 18th line, should be *Pequawket*.
   100, in the 2d and 3d lines of second note, 9 December, 1687, may be
       substituted for *about the year* 1689.
   110, after *to*, in the 20th line, *be* should be inserted.
   116, insert the name of John Cummings as one of the founders of the
       church in Dunstable.
   133, *is*, in the 11th line, should be *his*.
   144, the figures 13 against Groton, and under *Wounded*, should be placed
       under *Capt'd*.
   164, *council*, in the 14th line, should be *counsel*.
   166, *Gen-men*, in the 8th and 9th lines, should be *Gentlemen*.
   285, *St. Frances*, in the 19th line, should be *St. Francis*.
   292, *Shattack's* in the 9th line, should be *Shattuck's*.
   336, *Charlestown*, in the 9th line, should be *Charleston*.
   355, *neat*, in the 40th line, should be *net*.
   390, *which*, in the last line of the text, should be *with*.
   410, the year 1681, preceding Job Clements, should be placed before
       Robert Mason, and the year 1717, after Job Clements, Dover, should
       be 1683.
   411, the year 1745, in the first note, should be 1715.
   412, *Gamling*, in the 7th line, should be *Gambling*.
   413, the year 1778, in the 2d line, should be 1776.
   416, the year 1669, in the 11th line, should be 1699.
   " the list of Treasurers requires the following corrections :
          1809, Thomas W Thompson, Concord, 1810.
          1810, Nathaniel Gilman,   Exeter,   1814.
          1814, William Austin Kent, Concord,   1816.
   418, the list of Representatives in Congress requires the following ad-
       dition : 1825, Nehemiah Eastman, 2 years.
   " the year 1830, in the last line, should be 1823.
   422, the *Nos.* 55 and 59, in the 20th line, should be 58, 59 and 62.
   464, after *they*, in the 41st line, the word *freely* should be inserted, and
       conferred, in the same line, should be *confessed*.
   " *continuance*, in the 45th line, should be *contrivance*.
   " *admit*, in the last line, should be *attaint*.
   480, *sew*, in the 34th line, should be *serve*.

It may be gratifying to some readers to know something further respecting the three men, who commenced the first settlement of New-Hampshire.—The following note is therefore added.

EDWARD HILTON lived at Dover between fifteen and twenty years, and then removed to Squamscot patent, or Exeter, and died about the year 1671, leaving sons, Edward, William, Samuel, and Charles, who administered on his estate, which was appraised at £2204. WILLIAM HILTON removed from Dover, and his name is found at several places, particularly at Newbury, where five of his children were born. He was a representative at the General Court at Boston, at the March and May sessions in 1644. He finally removed to Charlestown, where he died 7 September, 1675. Of DAVID THOMPSON I had concluded that nothing farther could be known than what is given in the text and notes, page 5, when unexpectedly the Rev. Joseph B. Felt, of Hamilton, Massachusetts, sent me from the Mass. Colony Records some extracts, which enable me to state, that Thompson took possession of the island known by his name, situated within the present limits of the town of Dorchester, in the year 1626 ; that he died in 1628, or soon after that time, leaving an infant son, John, who, in 1648, claimed the island which belonged to his father, as he had done before, and which was granted to him by the General Court of Massachusetts. Descendants of the Hiltons are numerous in the state of New-Hampshire, and in Maine. Of a name so common as that of Thompson, it would be difficult to identify any of the posterity of the first settler of Little-Harbor.

PREFACE

TO THE FIRST VOLUME.

WHEN a new publication appears, some prefatory account of the reasons which led to it, and the manner in which it has been conducted, is generally expected.

The compiler of this history was early impelled by his natural curiosity to inquire into the original settlement, progress, and improvement of the country which gave him birth. When he took up his residence in New-Hampshire, his inquiries were more particularly directed to that part of it. Having met with some valuable manuscripts which were but little known, he began to extract and methodise the principal things in them ; and this employment was (to speak in the style of a celebrated modern author) his " hobby horse."

The work, crude as it was, being communicated to some gentlemen, to whose judgment he paid much deference, he was persuaded and encouraged to go on with his collection, until the thing became generally known, and a publication could not decently be refused.

He owns himself particularly obliged to the public officers both in this and the neighboring state of Massachusetts, under the former as well as the present constitutions, for their obliging attention in favoring him with the use of the public records or extracts from them. He is under equal obligation to a number of private gentlemen, who have either admitted him to their own collections of original papers or procured such for him. In the course of his inquiry. he has frequently had reason to lament the loss of many valuable materials by fire and other accidents : But what has pained him more severely, is the inattention of some persons, in whose hands original papers have been deposited, and who have suffered them to be wasted and destroyed as things of no value. The very great utility of a public repository for such paper- under proper regulations, has appeared to him in the strongest light, and he is persuaded that it is an object worthy the attention of an enlightened legislature.

The late accurate and indefatigable Mr. PRINCE, of Boston, (under whose ministry the author was educated, and whose memory he shall always revere) began such a collection in his youth and continued it for above fifty years. By his will, he left it to the care of the Old South Church, of which he was pastor, and it was deposited with a library of ancient books in an apartment of their meeting-house. To this collection, the public are obliged for some material hints in the present work, the author having had frequent access to that library before the commencement of the late war. But the use which the British troops in 1775 made of that elegant building, having proved fatal to this noble collection of manuscripts ; the friends of science and of America must deplore the irretrievable loss. Had we suffered it by the hands of *Saracens,* the grief had been less poignant !

Historians have mentioned the affairs of New-Hampshire only in a loose and general manner. Neal and Douglass, though frequently erroneous, have given some hints, which, by the help of original records and other manuscripts, have, in this work, been carefully and largely pursued. Hutchinson has said many things, which the others have omitted. His knowledge of the antiquities of the country was extensive and accurate, and the public are much obliged by the publication of his history ; but he knew more than he thought proper to relate. The few publications concerning New-Hampshire, are fugitive pieces dictated by party or interest. No regular historical deduction has ever appeared. The late Mr. FITCH, of Portsmouth, made a beginning of this sort, about the year 1728. From his papers, some things have been collected, which have not been met with elsewhere. The authorities from which information is derived, are carefully noted in the margin. Where no written testimonies could be obtained, recourse has been had to the most authentic tradition, selected and compared with a scrupulous attention, and with proper allowance for the imperfection of human memory. After all, the critical reader will doubtless find some chasms, which, in such a work, it would be improper to fill by the help of imagination and conjecture.

The author makes no merit of his regard to truth. To have disguised or misrepresented facts, would have been abusing the reader. No person can take more pleasure in detecting mistakes, than the author in correcting them, if he should have opportunity. In tracing the progress of controversy, it is impossible not to take a side, though we are ever so remote from any personal interest in it. Censure or applause, will naturally follow the opinion we adopt. If the reader should happen to entertain different feelings from the writer, he has an equal right to indulge them ; but not at the expense of candor.

The Masonian controversy lay so directly in the way, that it could not be avoided. The rancor shewn on both sides in the early stages of it, has now subsided. The present settlement is so materially connected with the general peace and welfare of the people, that no wise man or friend to the country, can, at this day wish to overthrow it.

Mr. HUBBARD, Dr. MATHER and Mr. PENHALLOW, have published narratives of the several Indian wars. These have been compared with the public records, with ancient manuscripts, with CHARLEVOIX's history of New-France, and with the verbal traditions of the immediate sufferers or their descendants. The particular incidents of these wars, may be tedious to strangers, but will be read with avidity by the posterity of those, whose misfortunes and bravery were so conspicuous. As the character of a people must be collected from such a minute series, it would have been improper to have been less particular.

The writer has had it in view not barely to relate facts, but to delineate the characters, the passions, the interests and tempers of the persons who are the subjects of his narration, and to describe the most striking features of the times in which they lived. How far he has succeeded, or wherein he is defective, must be left to the judgment of *every candid reader,* to which this work is most respectfully submitted.

Dover, June 1, 1784.

PREFACE

TO THE SECOND VOLUME.

———

WHEN the first volume was printed, I had not seen the ' Political Annals' of the American Colonies, published in 1780, by George Chalmers, Esq. This gentleman, being in England, was favored with some advantages, of which I was destitute ; having access to the books and papers of the Lords of Trade and Plantations, from the first establishment of that Board. He seems to possess the diligence and patience which are necessary in a historian ; but either through inadvertence or want of candor, has made some misrepresentations respecting New-Hampshire, on which I shall take the liberty to remark.*

In page 491, speaking of the first Council, of which President CUTT was at the head, he says, ' they refused to take the accustomed oaths, as the English law required, because liberty of conscience was allowed them.' In the first volume of my history, page 91, I have said, ' they published the commission and took the oaths ;' for which I cited the Council records ; and on recurring to them, I find the following entry, in the hand writing of Elias Stileman, Secretary.

' January 21, 1679—80.

' His Majesty's Commissioners, nomynated in said commission, tooke their respective oathes, as menconed in said commission.'

That the oaths were really taken, is a fact beyond all dispute ; but if there is any ground for what Mr. Chalmers is pleased to call a refusal, it must have been respecting the *form* of swearing ; which was usually done here by lifting the hand, and not by laying it on the bible, as was the form in England. Was it a forced construction of the clause respecting liberty of conscience, to suppose, that this indulgence was granted to them ? What other use could they have made of this liberty, than to act according to the dictates of their consciences ? Is it then consistent with candor, to publish an assertion, so worded as to admit the idea, that these gentlemen *refused* to obey an

* [It appears from the History of the Rise and Progress of the United States of North America, till the British Revolution in 1688, by James Graham, Esq., that Mr. Chalmers commenced his acquaintance with colonial history in this country. Prior to the American revolution, he emigrated to the American colonies, and settled as a lawyer at Baltimore, but adhering to the royal cause, he returned to England, and was rewarded by an appointment from the Board of Trade. The North American Review, No. LXX. (January, 1831,) p. 179, has pronounced a severe, but probably just sentence on the character of the work above mentioned.]

2

essential part of the duty prescribed by the commission, which they undertook to execute ? Or is it consistent with the character which he gives of
the President, Cutt, p. 492, that ' he was allowed to have been an honest
' man and a loyal subject ?' The commission required them to take the oaths
of allegiance and supremacy, and an oath of office, which last is recited in
the commission; but not a word is said of the mode and form, in which the
oaths should be taken ; neither was it said that they should be taken ' as the
' English law required.' They were therefore left at their liberty, to take
them in any form which was agreeable to their conscience, or their former
usage.

In the same page (491) he says ; ' An Assembly was soon called, which, by
' means of the usual intrigues, was composed of persons, extremely favorable
' to the projects of those who now engrossed power.' And in a note (page
507) ' the Council transmitted to the towns, a list of those who should be al-
' lowed to vote.'

With what propriety can it be said that these gentlemen *engrossed* power,
when they were commissioned by the king; and it is acknowledged, that not
only their appointment, but their entering on office, was contrary to their
inclinations ?

That the persons chosen into the Assembly should be ' favorable' to the
sentiments of the Council, or of ' the wise men of Boston,' was not the result
of any intrigues ; but because the majority of the people were of the same
mind. As to sending ' a list of those who should be allowed to vote ;' the
true state of the matter was this. The commission provided for the calling of
an Assembly, within three months after the Council should be sworn, by summons under seal, ' using and observing therein such rules and methods, as to
' the persons who are to choose the deputies, and the time and place of meet-
' ing, as they (the Council) shall judge most convenient.' The mode which
they judged most convenient was, to order the select men of the four towns,
to take a list of the names and estates of their respective inhabitants, according to their usual manner of making taxes, and send it to the Council. The
Council then issued an order, appointing *the persons therein named*, to meet in
their respective towns, and elect by a major vote, three persons from each, to
represent them in a general Assembly, on the 16th of March ; and in the
order, there is this proviso, ' Provided that wee do not intend that what is
' now done be presidential for the future, and that it shall extend noe farther,
' than to the calling this first assembly.'

Now as the rules and methods of calling an assembly, and the persons who
were to choose deputies, were left to the discretion of the Council ; what
more proper method could they have taken, than to call for a list of the inhabitants and their estates, and by that means to determine, who were qualified in point of property and habitancy to be electors ? And as the numbers
were few, and the persons well known, was it not as proper to name them at
once, in the writs, as to establish qualifications, and appoint other persons to
judge of those qualifications ; especially when there was no law in force by
which they could be judged? It is observable that each voter was ordered to take
the oath of allegiance, if he had not taken it before ; and in the list of names
in the book, a mark is set against several persons, who did not take the oath ;
and another against those who did not appear at the election. Has this the
appearance of *intrigue ?*

In page 492, he says, ' they were extremely slow in conforming to present
' requisitions, and passed no laws during the first session.' Having again
consulted the records, I find in the Journal of the Council this entry, ' At a
' general Assembly held in Portsmouth, the 16th of March, 1679—80. Pres-
' ent, &c. Sundry laws and ordinances made *at this session* are in another
' booke, for that purpose.'

In that other book, a body of laws is recorded, in the same hand writing,
viz. of Stileman the Secretary, which bears the following title ; ' The general
' laws and liberties of the Province of New-Hampshire, made by the general
' Assembly in Portsmouth, the 16th day of March, 1679—80, and approved by
' the President and Council.'

It appears from the books, that this Assembly held four sessions within the
year, viz. on the 16th of March, the 7th of June, the 12th of October, and the
7th of December. As there is not a particular date to each law, but the whole

code bears the date of the first session in March ; it may fairly be inferred, that the business was begun in the first session, and continued through the other three ; and when completed, was immediately sent to England ; for Mr. Chalmers himself tells us, that ' the laws which they transmitted, in conform-' ity to their Constitution, had not the good fortune to please, and were disap-' proved of, by the Lords of the Committee of Plantations, *in December*, 1681.'

From this statement it may be concluded, that they were not slower in ' es-' saying their legislative talents,' than the necessity of proceeding with due deliberation required ; and that there was no just cause for the reproach which he has cast upon them.

In page 494, he gives this account of the character of the people of New-Hampshire. ' When CRANFIELD arrived, he found the Province containing ' four thousand inhabitants, extremely poor from the devastation of the Indian ' war. But when he spoke contemptuously of the country which he had been ' sent to rule, he seems not to have reflected, that all colonies had once known ' the like paucity of numbers, the same weakness, and the same poverty ; ' animated only by a *dissimilar spirit* from that of New-Hampshire, which ' now disdained that *independence on her neighbors*, that other provinces had ' contended for with enthusiasm. And other plantations, actuated by very ' different maxims, had not complained, even in their weakest days, of their ' inability to defend their frontiers, against the attacks of a foe, that has never ' proved dangerous, except to the *effeminate*, the factious, or the *cowardly*. ' When New-Plymouth consisted only of two hundred persons, of all ages ' and sexes. it repulsed its enemies and secured its borders, with a gallantry ' worthy of its parent country ; because it stood alone, in the desert, without ' hope of aid.'

That the people of New-Hampshire ever deserved the character of *effem-inate* or *cowardly*, can by no means be admitted. Innumerable facts evince the contrary beyond a doubt. Had this author ever resided among them, espe-cially in time of war, he would have thought quite otherwise of them. That the native savages have ' never proved a *dangerous* foe, to any but the effem-' inate, the factious and the cowardly,' is an assertion totally unfounded.— Their manner of attacking was always by surprise, and the bravest and best men may sometimes be deficient in vigilance, where no suspicion of danger exists.

If the people of New-Hampshire ' disdained independence,' let it be con-sidered, that they had been, for about 40 years. connected with Massachusetts, to their mutual satisfaction ; and the proposed ' independence' which he means was but another name for subjection to a landlord. When independence, in its genuine meaning, became necessary, in 1776, they freely joined with their brethren in asserting it, and in bravely defending it.

Without any disparagement to the first settlers of Plymouth, who, from the year 1643, were protected by a confederacy of the four New-England colo-nies, it may with truth be said, that the people of New-Hampshire were nev-er behind them, in vigorous exertions for their own defence, when they were conducted by officers in whom they could place confidence ; but in Cranfield's time, there was no war with the Indians ; though he attempted to frighten them into an apprehension of danger, from the Indians, to serve his own pur-poses.

The account which Mr. Chalmers gives of Cranfield's administration differs not very materially from mine, except in one instance.

He represents ' the ministers as very attentive to him, because they deem-' ed him gained over to the Independents.' I have met with no evidence of this ; the deception, if any, must have been very short lived.

Mr. Chalmers says nothing of the prosecution of Moodey, and of Cran-field's endeavors to ruin him, for his non-conformity to the Church of Eng-land ; but tells us that he ' deemed it unsafe, to remain any longer among the ' ministers, who ruled an enthusiastic people, with the same sway as did the ' popish clergy during the darkest ages ;' and that in his letters to England, he ' gave warning that while the clergy were allowed to preach, no true alle-' giance would be found in those parts.' This may be considered as a corrob-orating evidence of his bigotry and intolerance. Truth obliges me to add, that his opponents were not deficient in those unhappy qualities, which were too much in fashion among all parties in that age.

Mr. Chalmers concludes his account of New-Hampshire in these words :—
' Being excluded from the charter granted to Massachusetts, it has continued
' to the present time, a different, though *inconsiderable* settlement; ||irregular
' and factious in its economy, affording no precedents that may be of exem-
' plary use to other colonies.'||* What justice there is in this remark, the
reader will be able to determine, from the following portion of its history,
which, after much unavoidable delay, is now submitted to his perusal.

Boston, August 1, 1791.

* [The words between parallels appear to be *quoted* by Chalmers. After
" irregular," the words, " as we are assured," occur in Chalmers, but are
omitted by Dr. Belknap.]

CONTENTS.

APPENDIX.

LIST OF PAPERS IN THE APPENDIX.

NOTE. Those papers to which a star is prefixed were not published in the former editions.

HISTORY

OF

NEW-HAMPSHIRE.

CHAPTER I.

Discovery of the country. Establishment of the Council of Plymouth. Their grants to Mason and others. Beginning of the settlements at Portsmouth and Dover. Wheelwright's Indian purchase. Neal's adventures. Discouragements. Dissolution of the Council. Mason's death. Causes of the failure of his enterprise.

IT is happy for America that its discovery and settlement by the Europeans happened at a time, when they were emerging from a long period of ignorance and darkness. The discovery of the magnetic needle, the invention of printing, the revival of literature and the reformation of religion, had caused a vast alteration in their views, and taught them the true use of their rational and active powers. To this concurrence of favorable causes, we are indebted for the precision with which we are able to fix the beginning of this great American empire ; an advantage of which the historians of other countries almost universally are destitute ; their first eras being either disguised by fiction and romance, or involved in impenetrable obscurity.

Mankind do not easily relinquish ancient and established prejudices or adopt new systems of conduct, without some powerful attractive. The prospect of immense wealth, from the mines of Mexico and Peru, fired the Spaniards to a rapid conquest of those regions and the destruction of their numerous inhabitants ; but the northern continent, presenting no such glittering charms, was neglected by the European princes for more than a century after its discovery.[1] No effectual care was taken to secure to themselves the possession of so extensive a territory, or the advantage of a friendly traffic with its natives, or of the fishery on its coasts ; till private adventurers at a vast expense, with infinite hazard and persevering zeal, established settlements for themselves, and thereby enlarged the dominions of their sovereigns.

(1) Prince's Annals.

3

Of the voyagers who visited the northern coast of America, for the sake of its furs and fish, one of the most remarkable was Captain John Smith, who ranged the shore from Penobscot to Cape Cod, and, in this route, discovered the river Pascataqua ; which he found to be a safe harbor, with a rocky shore. He returned to England in one of his ships, and there published a description of the country, with a map of the sea-coast, which he presented to Prince Charles, who gave it the name of NEW-ENGLAND.[1]   The other ship, he left behind under the care of Thomas Hunt, who decoyed about twenty of the natives on board and sold them for slaves at Malaga. This perfidious action excited a violent jealousy in the natives, and bitterly enraged them against succeeding adventurers. Two of those savages having found their way back as far as Newfoundland, then under the government of Captain John Mason, were restored to their native country by his friendly interposition, and reported the strong disapprobation, which the English in general entertained of the mischievous plot, by which they had been carried off. By this means, together with the prudent endeavors of Captain Thomas Dermer,* and afterward of the Plymouth settlers, tranquillity was re-established between the Indians and the adventurers, which was tolerably preserved for many years.[2]   However fond we may have been of accusing the Indians of treachery and infidelity, it must be confessed that the example was first set them by the Europeans. Had we always treated them with that justice and humanity which our religion inculcates, and our true interest at all times required, we might have lived in as much harmony with them, as with any other people on the globe.

The importance of the country now began to appear greater than before, and some measures were taken to promote its settlement. A patent had been granted by King James in 1606, limiting the dominion of Virginia, from the thirty-fourth, to the forty-fourth degree of northern latitude ; which extent of territory had been divided into two parts, called North and South Virginia. The latter was assigned to certain noblemen, knights and gentlemen of London ; the former to others in Bristol, Exeter and Plymouth.[3]   Those who were interested in the northern colony, finding that the patent did not secure them from the intrusions of others, petitioned for an enlargement and confirmation of their privileges. After some time, the king, by his sole authority, con-

(1) Smith's Voyage.   (2) Hubbard's printed Narrative of the troubles with the [Eastern] Indians, p. 6, 7.   (3) Gorges' Narrative.

* [This industrious and prudent gentleman having spent almost two years in searching the coast between New-England and Virginia, the fruit of whose labors and hazards many others afterwards reaped, was at the last, on his return to Virginia, set upon by some malicious savages in some parts beyond Cape Cod, from whom he received fourteen or fifteen wounds, upon which occasion, retiring to Virginia, he there ended his days, about the year 1621.—Hubbard, Hist. New-England, 40.]

stituted a council, consisting of forty noblemen, knights and gentlemen,* by the name of "The council established at Plymouth, "in the county of Devon, for the planting, ruling and governing "of New-England, in America."[1]   They were a corporation with perpetual succession, by election of the majority ; and their territories extended from the fortieth to the forty-eighth degree of northern latitude.   This patent, or charter, is the foundation of all the grants that were made of the country of New-England. But either from the jarring interests of the members, or their indistinct knowledge of the country, or their inattention to business, or some other cause which does not fully appear, their affairs were transacted in a confused manner from the beginning ; and the grants which they made were so inaccurately described, and interfered so much with each other, as to occasion difficulties and controversies, some of which are not yet ended.

Two of the most active members of this council were Sir Ferdinando Gorges and Captain John Mason.   Gorges had been an officer in the navy of Queen Elizabeth, intimately connected with Sir Walter Raleigh, of whose adventurous spirit he had a large share.[2]   After the peace which King James made in 1604, he was appointed governor of the fort and island of Plymouth in Devonshire.   Whilst he resided there, Captain Weymouth, who had been employed by Lord Arundel in search of a northwest passage, but had fallen short of his course and put in at Pemaquid, brought from thence into the harbor of Plymouth, five natives of America, three of whom were eagerly seized by Gorges, and retained in his service for three years.   Finding them of a tractable and communicative disposition, and having won their affections by gentle treatment, he learned from them many particulars concerning their

(1) Ms. copy in Superior Court files. [Hubbard, Hist. New-England, 80, 217.   Hazard, Coll. i. 103—118.   Trumbull, Hist. Connecticut, Appx.]— (2) Hume.

* [Lodowick] Duke of Lenox,
[George] Marquis of Buckingham,
[James] Marquis of Hamilton,
[William] Earl of Pembroke,
[Thomas] Earl of Arundel,
[William] Earl of Bath,
[Henry] Earl of Southampton,
[William] Earl of Salisbury,
[Robert] Earl of Warwick,
[John] Viscount Haddington,
[Edward] Lord Zouche,
[Edmund] Lord Sheffield,
[Edward] Lord Gorges,
Sir Edward Seymour,
Sir Robert Mansell,
Sir Edward Zouche,
Sir Dudley Digges,
Sir Thomas Roe,
Sir Ferdinando Gorges,
Sir Francis Popham,

Sir John Brookes,
Sir Thomas Gates,
Sir Richard Hawkins,
Sir Richard Edgecombe,
Sir Allen Apsley,
Sir Warwick Heale,
Sir Richard Catchmay,
Sir John Bourchier,
Sir Nathaniel Rich,
Sir Edward Giles,
Sir Giles Mompesson,
Sir Thomas Wroth, Knights,
Matthew Sutcliffe, [dean of Exeter]
Robert Heath, [recorder of London]
Henry Bourchier,
John Drake,
Rawley Gilbert,
George Chudley,
Thomas Haymon,
John Argall, Esquires.

[There is a copy of this Patent entire in Hazard's Collections, i. 103—118.]

country, its rivers, harbors, islands, fisheries and other productions ; and the numbers, force, disposition and government of the
natives ; and from this information, he conceived sanguine hopes
of indulging his genius, and making his fortune, by a thorough
discovery of the country.[1]   For this purpose, he, in conjunction with others, ventured several ships, wherefore some met with
peculiar misfortunes ; and others brought home accounts, which,
though discouraging to some of his associates, made him determine upon farther attempts,wherein his resolution and perseverance
were more conspicuous than any solid gain.   These transactions
were previous to the establishment of the council ; in soliciting
which, Gorges was so extremely active, that he was appointed
their president, and had a principal share in all their transactions.
Mason was a merchant of London, but became a sea-officer, and,
after the peace, governor of Newfoundland, where he acquired a
knowledge of America, which led him, on his return to England,
into a close attachment to those who were engaged in its discovery ; and upon some vacancy in the council, he was elected a mem-
1621. ber and became their secretary ; being also governor of
       Portsmouth in Hampshire.   He procured a grant from the
council, of all the land from the river of Naumkeag, now Salem,
round Cape Anne, to the river Merrimack ; and up each of those
rivers to the farthest head thereof ; then to cross over from the head
of the one to the head of the other ; with all the islands lying within three miles of the coast.   This district was called MARIANA.
The next year, another grant was made to Gorges and Mason
jointly, of all the lands between the rivers Merrimack and Saga-
dehock, extending back to the great lakes and river of Canada,
and this was called LACONIA.

Under the authority of this grant, Gorges and Mason, in conjunction with several merchants of London, Bristol, Exeter, Plymouth, Shrewsbury and Dorchester, who styled themselves " the
company of Laconia," attempted the establishment of a colony
1623. and fishery at the river Pascataqua ; and in the spring of the
       following year, sent over David Thompson, a Scotchman,
Edward and William Hilton, fishmongers of London,with a number
of other people, in two divisions, furnished with all necessaries to
carry on their design.   One of these companies landed on the
southern shore of the river, at its mouth, and called the place
Little-Harbor.   Here, they erected salt-works, and built an house
which was afterwards called Mason-Hall ;* but the Hiltons set

(1) Gorges' Narrative.

* [The site of this house was on a peninsula, or point of land, now called
Odiorne's point, which is formed by Little-Harbor on the northeast, and a creek
on the south, with a large tract of salt marsh on the west.   This place was selected with great judgment.   The peninsula contains about five hundred acres
of land, on which is a commanding eminence ; where are evident remains of
an ancient fort, and situated so as to be a complete defence against the incursions of a savage enemy.   The house was erected a few rods to the northward

up their stages eight miles further up the river, toward the north-west, on a neck of land which the Indians called Winnichahannat, but they named Northam, and afterward Dover.[1] Thompson not being pleased with his situation, removed the next spring to an island in the bay of Massachusetts;* this the General Court afterward confirmed to him, and it still bears his name.[2]

These settlements went on but slowly for several years, but the natives being peaceable and several other small beginnings being made along the coast as far as Plymouth, a neighborly intercourse was kept up among them, each following their respective employ-ments of fishing, trading and planting, till the disorderly behaviour of one Morton, at Mount Wollaston in the bay of Massachu- 1628. setts, caused an alarm among the scattered settlements as far as Pascataqua.   This man had, in defiance of the king's procla-mation, made a practice of selling arms and ammunition to the In-dians, whom he employed in hunting and fowling for him; so that the English, seeing the Indians armed in the woods, began to be in terror.   They also apprehended danger of another kind; for Morton's plantation was a receptacle for discontented servants, whose desertion weakened the settlements, and who, being there without law, were more formidable than the savages themselves. [3] The principal persons of Pascataqua therefore readily united with their neighbors, in making application to the colony of Plymouth, which was of more force than all the rest, to put a stop to this growing mischief; which they happily effected by seizing Mor-ton and sending him prisoner to England.†

(1) Hubbard, MS. [p. 214 of the printed copy.]   (2) Prince's Annals.— (3) Prince's Annals.

of the fort. The present possessors of the land point out the spot where it stood. They think they have discovered the foundation of the chimney and the cellar walls. These were standing when Mr. Hubbard wrote in 1680.— Three or four thousand acres of land were annexed to this building, with an intention of forming a manor there, according to the English custom. Ad-ams, Annals of Portsmouth, 10, 11.]

* [It appears from Bradford, in Prince, i. 161, that Thompson was living at Pascataquack in 1626, and probably about that time, and not as in the text, in 1624, removed to the Massachusetts Bay, and took possession of "a very fruit-ful island and a very desirable neck of land, which is afterwards confirmed to him by the General Court of the Massachusetts Colony."]

† [The apportionment of the charges of this united effort of the earliest plantations to check the progress of Morton, as given by Governor Bradford in 1 Coll. Mass. Hist. Soc. iii. 63, may serve to show their relative importance at this time.

" Plimouth,	£2 10	Natascot,	£1 10
Naumkeak,	1 10	Thomson,	0 15
Pascataquack,	2 10	Blackston,	0 12
Jeffrey and Burslem,	2 00	Edward Hilton,	1 00
		Total,	£12 7 "

This assessment alone enables us to correct the error in Dr. Holmes, (An-nals of America, i. 209) who says, under the year 1631, " Portsmouth began to be settled this year."

The settlement of this place commenced in the spring of 1623 by David Thompson, and appears from several authorities, not to have been broken up,

|| 1629.   Some of the scattered planters in the bay of Massa-
chusetts, being desirous of making a settlement in the neighborhood of Pascataqua, and following the example of those at Plymouth, who had purchased their lands of the Indians, which they
conscientiously thought necessary to give them a just title, procured a general meeting of Indians, at Squamscot falls, where
they obtained a deed from Passaconaway, sagamore of Penacook,
Runnaawitt of Pawtucket, Wahangnonawit of Squamscot, and
Rowls of Newichwannock : wherein they expressed their 'desire
' to have the English come and settle among them as among their
' countrymen in Massachusetts, whereby they hope to be strength-
' ened against their enemies the Tarrateens; and accordingly
' *with the universal consent of their subjects,* for what they deem-
' ed a valuable consideration in coats, shirts and kettles, sell to
' John Wheelwright of the Massachusetts bay, late of England,
' minister of the gospel, Augustine Story (or Storer) Thomas
' Wight, William Wentworth, and Thomas Leavit, "all that part
" of the main land bounded by the river Pascataqua and the
" river Merrimack, to begin at Newichwannock falls in Pascata-
" qua river aforesaid, and down said river to the sea ; and along
" the sea-shore to Merrimack river ; and up said river to the falls
" at Pawtucket ; and from thence upon a northwest line, twenty
" English miles into the woods ; and from thence upon a straight
" line northeast, till it meet with the main rivers that run down
" to Pawtucket falls, and Newichwannock falls aforesaid ;* the
" said rivers to be the bounds from the thwart or head line to the
" aforesaid falls, and from thence the main channel of each river
" to the sea to be the side bounds ; together with all the islands
" within the said bounds ; as also the isles of shoals so called."
The conditions of this grant were, ' that Wheelwright should
' within ten years, begin a plantation at Squamscot falls ; that
' other inhabitants should have the same privileges with him ;
' that no plantation should exceed ten miles square ; that no lands

although Thompson himself removed within a few years to the Massachusetts
colony.   From Governor Bradford, in Prince, i. 161, it is evident that he was
at Pascataquack in 1626 ; and from the preceding apportionment, it appears
that this place was of sufficient consequence in 1628, to pay a sum equal to
that of Plymouth.   Again, from Prince, i. 196, it seems that the inhabitants on
Pascataqua river in 1629, entered into a combination for the erecting a government among themselves, and from Adams, Annals of Portsmouth, 18,
there were in 1631, at least, 50 men employed by Mason, as stewards and servants, besides ten Danes, who were occupied in sawing lumber and making
potash.   Some persons may have doubts whether Thompson's settlement and
Pascataquack were the same, which will be removed by recurring to Edward
Winslow's *Good Newes from New-England,* which informs us that David Tom-
son, a Scotchman, began in the spring of 1623 "a plantation twenty-five
leagues north-east from us [Plymouth] near Smith's Isles, at a place called
Pascataquack."]

* The NW. line here described, will end within the township of Amherst ;
and the NE. line from thence will cross the river Merrimack about Amuskeag
falls, and passing through Chester, Nottingham, Barrington, and Rochester,
will strike Newichwannock river about ten miles above the Salmon falls.

'should be granted but in townships; and that these should be
'subject to the government of the Massachusetts colony, until
'they should have a settled government among themselves ; that
'for each township there should be paid an annual acknowledg-
'ment of "one coat of trucking cloth," to Passaconaway the chief
'sagamore, or his successors, and two bushels of Indian corn to
'Wheelwright and his heirs. The Indians reserved to them-
'selves free liberty of fishing, fowling, hunting and planting with-
'in these limits.'[1] The principal persons of Pascataqua and
the province of Maine were witnesses to the subscribing of this
instrument, and giving possession of the lands.||*

(1) MS. copy in Superior Court files.

* [The portion of the text above and on the preceding page, included within
parallels,and those portions thus distinguished which follow, must be rejected,as
they are founded upon documents which are proved to be spurious. It is much to
be regretted that any part of our history has thus become vitiated, but no blame
can be imputed to the careful and laborious author for relying on authorities
which were supposed to be genuine when he wrote,and which were so considered
until within a few years. The Wheelwright deed of 1629 was supposed to be an
authentic document until June, 1820, when the Hon. James Savage, of Boston,
in preparing Notes for the new edition of Governor Winthrop's Journal, or
History of New-England, published in 1825 and 1826, had his suspicion excited in regard to the authenticity of this instrument. A critical and laborious
scrutiny into all the circumstances of the case resulted in the conviction that
it was a forgery. His ingenious and elaborate argument, by which the forgery of the deed is indisputably proved, and which is too long to be introduced
here, may be found in the Appendix to the first volume of his edition of Winthrop, 405—424.

If any person should remain skeptical on the subject after reading that argument, let him read the testimony of Rev. Mr. Wheelwright and Edward
Colcord, two of the original grantees, in an actual purchase of lands of the Indians, nine years posterior to the pretended one. This testimony, which relates to the purchase made in 1638, mentioned by Governor Winthrop, (Hist.
N. E. i. 290) and of which the original deeds are in possession of the editor,
and have been published in the Coll. of the N. H. Hist. Soc. i. 147—149, was
found among the records of the ancient county of Norfolk, kept at Salem.

Testimony of Rev. John Wheelwright.
"I John Wheelwright, pastor of the church of Salisbury, doe testify that
when I, with others, first came to sit downe at Exeter, we purchased of the
Indians, to whom (so far as we could learne) the right did belong, a certain
Tract of land about thirty miles square, to run from Merrimack river, East-
ward, and so up into the Country, of wch. lands we had a graunt in writing
signed by the[m.]   JOHN WHEELWRIGHT."
"April 15, 1668."

Edward Colcord's Testimony.
"Mr. Edward Colcord testifieth to all above written, and further saith that
one northerly bound mentioned in our agreemt. with Wehahnonowet, the
chiefe Sagamore was, the westerly part of Oyster River, called by the Indians
Shankhassick,wch. is about foure miles northerly beyound Lampereele River."

"We the abovesaid witnesses doe further testefy yt. they of the town of
Exeter, did dispose and possesse divers parcels of land about Lamprel River
by virtuee of sd. Indian Right before such time as it was actually taken in by
the Jurisdiction of the Massachusetts, without interruption of Dover or any
other."

To the above is also added the Testimony of Rev. Samuel Dudley.
"Mr. Samuel Dudly doth testifie that he did see the agreemt. in writing
betweene the towne of Exeter and the Sagamores for that land wch. is above
mentioned, and the said Sagamore's hands to the same."

"Sworn before the Court ye. 14th : 2 mo : 1668."
                                THOMAS BRADBURY, *Rec.*

By this deed, the English inhabitants with these limits obtained a right to the soil from the original proprietors, more valuable in a moral view, than the grants of any European prince could convey. If we smile at the arrogance of a Roman Pontiff in assuming to divide the whole new world between the Spaniards and Portuguese, with what consistency can we admit the right of a king of England, to parcel out America to his subjects, when he had neither purchased nor conquered it, nor could pretend any other title, than that some of his subjects were the first Europeans who discovered it, whilst it was in possession of its native lords? The only validity which such grants could have in the eye of reason was, that the grantees had from their prince a permission to negotiate with the possessors for the purchase of the soil, and thereupon a power of jurisdiction subordinate to his crown.

The same year, Captain Mason procured a new patent, under the common seal of the council of Plymouth, for the land " from " the middle of Pascataqua river, and up the same to the farthest " head thereof, and from thence northwestward, until sixty miles " from the mouth of the harbor were finished ; also, through Mer- " rimack river, to the farthest head thereof, and so forward up into " the land westward, until sixty miles were finished; and from " thence to cross over land to the end of the sixty miles account- " ed from Pascataqua river ; together with all islands within five " leagues of the coast."[1]   This tract of land was called NEW-HAMPSHIRE : it comprehended the whole of Wheelwright's purchase ; and unless Mason's intention was to frustrate his title, it is difficult to assign a reason for the procurement of this patent, as the same land, with much more, had been granted to Gorges and Mason jointly, seven years before. If there was an agreement between them to divide the province of Laconia, and take out new patents from the council, in preference to the making a deed of partition ; it is not easy to conceive why the western boundary should be contracted to sixty miles from the sea, when the lakes and river Canada were supposed to be but ninety or an hundred miles from Pascataqua.[2]   If this grant was intended as an equivalent for the patent of Marianna, which the council had the preceding year included in their deed to the Massachusetts company, it is impossible to account for the extension of New-Hampshire to the river Merrimack, when the grant of Massachusetts reached to " three miles north of that river and of every part " of it."*

1630.
Mar. 12.

(1) MS. in files of Superior Court.   (2) Gorges' History of America, p. 48.

The boundaries described in the true deed, dated " the third day of Aprill, 1638," are " within three miles on the Northerne side of ye river Meremake extending thirty miles along by the river from the sea side and from the sayd river side to Pisscataqua Patents thirty miles up into the countrey North West, and soe from the ffals of Piscataqua to Oyster river thirty miles square eury way."]

*Mr. Hubbard in his MS. history says, " it hath been affirmed by Mr. Josse-

The west country adventurers were not less attentive to their interest; for in the following spring, they obtained a patent from the council, whereby " all that part of the river Pascataqua called "or known by the name of Hilton's Point, with the south side of "the said river, up to the falls of Squamscot, and three miles into "the main land for breadth," was granted to Edward Hilton. This patent, sealed with the common seal of the council, and subscribed by the Earl of Warwick, sets forth, that Hilton and his associates had, at *their own* proper cost and charges, transported servants, built houses and planted corn at Hilton's Point, now Dover, and intended the further increase and advancement of the plantation.[1] William Blackstone, William Jeffries and Thomas Lewis, or either of them, were impowered to give possession of the premises; which was done by Lewis and the livery and seizin endorsed. 1631. Within these limits are contained the towns of Dover, Durham, and Stratham, with part of Newington and Greenland. It was commonly called Squamscot patent, but sometimes Bloody-point patent, from a quarrel between the agents of the two companies about a point of land in the river which was convenient for both; and, there being no government then established, the controversy would have ended in blood, if the contending parties had not been persuaded to refer the decision of it to their employers. [2]

The London adventurers also thought it prudent to have some security for the interest which they had advanced, and accordingly obtained a grant from the council, of " that part of the patent "of Laconia, on which the buildings and salt-works were erected, "situate on both sides the harbor and river of Pascataqua to the "extent of five miles westward by the sea-coast, then to cross "over towards the other plantation in the hands of Edward Hil-"ton."[3] The grantees named in this patent* were, Sir Ferdi-

(1) MS. copy in Proprietary Office. (2) Hubbard's MS. [p. 217 of the printed copy.] (3) Hutch. vol. 1, p. 316.

lyn, who first came over into New-England on Capt. Mason's account, that there was an agreement made between Mr. Matthew Cradock (the first Governor of the Massachusetts company) and Captain John Mason, that the bounds of the Massachusetts should reach to *three miles northward of the Merrimack*, and the remainder of the land betwixt that line and Pascataqua river, should be left for Captain Mason's patent."

The commissioners sent by Charles II, in 1664, report that " Mr. Mason had a patent for some land about Cape Anne before the Massachusetts had their first patent; whereupon Captain Mason and Mr. Cradock agreed that the Massachusetts should have that land, which was granted to Capt. Mason about Cape Anne, and Capt. Mason should have *that land which was beyond Merrimack and granted to the Massachusetts*. This agreement was sent to Mr. Henry Jocelyn to get recorded at Boston, but before he could have leisure to go there, he heard that Capt. Mason was dead, and therefore went not. Of this, he made affidavit, before the Commissioners." Hutch. Collection Papers, p. 423.

* Mr. Hubbard says, that this patent was in the hands of some gentlemen at Portsmouth when he wrote. I have seen no copy of it but what is preserved in his MS. history. There is among the ancient files in the Recorder's office, an invoice of goods sent over in 1631, subscribed by all the above names, except the last, in whose stead is subscribed William Gyles.

nando Gorges, Captain John Mason, John Cotton, Henry Gardner, George Griffith, Edwin Gay, Thomas Warnerton, Thomas
Eyre and Eliezer Eyre, who, it is said, had already expended
three thousand pounds in the undertaking. They were to pay
forty-eight pounds per annum by way of acknowledgment to the
president and council, if demanded.[1] Captain Camocke, a relation of the Earl of Warwick,* with Henry Jocelyn, who were
then intending a voyage hither, were appointed to put the grantees in possession. Within this patent are comprehended the
towns of Portsmouth, Newcastle and Rye, with part of Newington and Greenland.

The whole interest being thus divided into two parts, Captain
Thomas Wiggin was appointed agent for the upper, and Captain
Walter Neal for the lower plantation;[2] with him were associated Ambrose Gibbons, George Vaughan, Thomas Warnerton,
Humphrey Chadbourne† and one Godfrey,‡ as superintendants
of the several businesses of trade, fishery, salt-making, building
and husbandry. Neal resided at Little-Harbor with Godfrey,
who had the care of the fishery. Chadbourne built a house at
Strawberry-bank, which was called *the great house,* in which Warnerton resided. Gibbons had the care of a saw-mill, and lived in
a palisaded house at Newichwannock,‖ where he carried on trade
with the Indians. He afterward removed to Sanders'-point, where
the adventurers gave him a settlement for his faithful services.
He was succeeded at Newichwannock by Chadbourne, whose
posterity are persons of principal figure and interest there at this
day. The proprietors were also careful to provide for the defence of their plantations, and sent over several cannon which
they directed their agents to mount in the most convenient place
for a fort. They accordingly placed them on the northeast point
of the Great-Island at the mouth of the harbor, and laid out the
ground " about a bow-shot from the water-side to a high rock, on
" which it was intended in time to build the principal fort."[3]

(1) Hubbard's MS. (p. 216 of the printed copy.) (2) MS. letters. (3) MS.
in the Recorder's files.

* [He was nephew to the Earl of Warwick. He lived sometime at Pascataqua, but died at Scarborough, Me. in 1663. Prince, Annals, ii. 70. 2 Coll.
Mass. Hist. Soc. v. 216, 224.]

† [Humphrey Chadbourne came to this country as early as 1631, on the invitation of Sir Ferdinando Gorges and Capt. John Mason, and under them
erected the large house as stated in the text. In 1643, he purchased a tract of
land of an Indian called Knowles, being a neck between the Bason and Ne-
wichawannock river at Quampeagan, (Sullivan.) He afterwards lived in Kittery, and represented that town in the General Court at Boston in 1657 and
1659.]

‡ [Edward Godfrey, on whom, Mr. Savage, in Winthrop's Hist. N. E. i. 90,
91, bestows a very valuable note, was one of the first aldermen of Agamenticus,
(York) and governor of the province of Maine, 1651. See Belknap's Biog. 1.
386. Adams's Annals of Portsmouth, 18.]

‖ [The pronunciation of this name two centuries ago appears to have been
Ne-ge-won-nuck. Capt. Danforth, an eminent surveyor, wrote it *Negewonnick*
in 1679.]

A great part of Captain Neal's errand was to penetrate the interior part of the province of Laconia, concerning which the adventurers had formed very sanguine expectations.[1] It was described as containing divers lakes, and extending back to a great lake and river in the country of the Iroquois. This river was said to be fair and large, containing many fruitful islands ; the air pure and salubrious ; the country pleasant, having some high hills ; full of goodly forests, fair valleys and fertile plains ; abounding in corn, vines, chestnuts, walnuts, and many other sorts of fruit ; the rivers well stored with fish, and environed with goodly meadows full of timber-trees. In the great lake, were said to be four islands, full of pleasant woods and meadows, having great store of stags, fallow-deer, elks, roe-bucks, beavers and other game, and these islands were supposed to be commodiously situated for habitation and traffic, in the midst of a fine lake, abounding with the most delicate fish. No one who is acquainted with the interior part of the country in its wilderness state, can forbear smiling at this romantic description, penned in the true style of adventurers : yet such an impression had the charms of Laconia made on the minds of our first settlers, that Neal set out on foot, in 1632. company with Jocelyn and Darby Field, to discover these beautiful lakes, and settle a trade with the Indians by pinnaces, imagining the distance to be short of an hundred miles. In the course of their travels, they visited the white mountains,* which they described in the same romantic style, to be a ridge, extending an hundred leagues, on which snow lieth all the year, and inaccessible but by the gullies which the dissolved snow hath made : on one of these mountains they reported to have found a plain of a day's journey over, whereon nothing grows but moss ; and at the further end of this plain, a rude heap of massy stones, piled up on one another a mile high ; on which one might ascend from stone to stone, like a pair of winding stairs, to the top, where was another level of about an acre, with a pond of clear water. [2] This summit was said to be far above the clouds, and from hence they beheld a vapor like a vast pillar, drawn up by the sunbeams, out of a great lake into the air, where it was formed into a cloud. The country beyond these mountains northward, was said to be " daunting terrible," full of rocky hills, as thick as mole-hills in a meadow, and clothed with infinite thick woods. They had great expectation of finding precious stones on these mountains ; and something resembling crystal being picked up, was sufficient to give them the name of the CRYSTAL-HILLS.[3] From hence they continued their route in search of the lake ; till finding their

(1) Gorges' History of America, p. 47.   (2) Jocelyn's rarities of New-England.   (3) Hubbard's Ms. Hist. [p. 381, printed copy.]

* [The visit to the White Mountains by Darby Field should be referred to the year 1642, under which, see the account of it as given by Winthrop, Hist. N. E. ii. 67, 68.]

provision almost spent, and the forests of Laconia yielding no supply, they were obliged to return when they supposed themselves
so far advanced, that "the discovery wanted but one day's jour-
"ney of being finished."*1

This expedition, being ended, was succeeded by one of another kind. The coast was alarmed by the report of a pirate, one
Dixy Bull; who, with fifteen others, being employed in the Indian trade at the eastward, had taken several boats and rifled the
fort at Pemaquid. Neal, in conjunction with the others, equipped four pinnaces and shallops, manned with forty men, being all
the force that both plantations could spare, who, being joined by
twenty more in a bark from Boston, proceeded to Pemaquid; but
contrary winds and bad weather obliged them to return without
meeting the pirates, who made their way farther to the eastward,
and at length got to England, where Bull met with his deserts.
1633. The company on their return hanged, at Richmond's island, an Indian who had been concerned in the murder of
an Englishman.2

|| The next year, Neal and Wiggin joined in surveying their
respective patents, and laying out the towns of Portsmouth and
Northam, and another which was called Hampton, though no settlement had been made there. They also agreed with Wheelwright that the plantation which he had undertaken to make at
Squamscot falls, should be called Exeter; and determined the
bounds between his land and theirs. This survey was made by
order of the company of Laconia, who gave names to the four
towns, and the transaction was duly reported to them :3 soon af-
ter which Neal returned to England.||†

(1) Gorges' History of America, p. 48.   (2) Prince's Annals, vol. 2. p. 73,83.
(3) MS. in Recorder's office.

* Mr. Hubbard, and after him, Governor Hutchinson, place this discovery
of the White Hills in 1642. But as Neal had positive orders to discover the
lakes, and tarried but three years in the country, employing great part of his
time in seaching the woods, it is probable that Mr. Hubbard mistook one figure in his date.

[On this note, Mr. Savage, in Winthrop, ii. 67, makes the following remarks:
"Here, as he has often done elsewhere, Hubbard might indeed have mistaken
a figure, but he faithfully copied Winthrop, whose work was unknown to Dr.
Belknap, when his history of N. H. was published. A greater mistake is
however chargeable on Belknap, in making Josselyn the companion of Neal,
who was gone home four years before Josselyn came over. Nor did Josselyn
make the journey according to his own account, before his second voyage to
New-England in 1663. That Neal ever went to the White mountains, is not
rendered probable by any authorities cited by Belknap ; and as the circumstance would have been for him a great matter of boasting, we may be confident of the first journey of Field." Mr. Savage mistakes, in saying that the
work of Winthrop was unknown to Dr. Belknap when his history of N. H.
was published. The work was both known and used by Dr. Belknap when
he compiled his history, and he has copied from it, as may be seen under the
years 1635 and 1640.]

† [The authority for this paragraph is the "Letter from Neal and Wiggin, relating to the division of Lands at Pascataqua, 1633," which is No. VI, in the
Appendix to the i. vol. of the former editions of this work, and which without

From a number of letters that passed between the adventurers and Gibbons, their factor, and which are yet preserved, it appears that their views were chiefly turned toward the discovery of the lakes and of mines; the cultivation of grapes, and the advantages of trade and fishery; and that little regard was had to agriculture, the surest foundation of all other improvements in such a country as this. They often complain of their expenses, as indeed they might with reason; for they had not only to pay wages to their colonists, but to supply them with provisions, clothing, utensils, medicines, articles of trade, implements for building, husbandry and fishing, and to stock their plantations with cattle, swine, and goats. Bread was either brought from England in meal, or from Virginia in grain, and then sent to the wind-mill at Boston, there being none erected here.[1] Very little improvement was made on the lands; the lakes were not explored; the vines were planted but came to nothing; no mines were found but those of iron, and these were not wrought; three or four houses only were built within the first seven years; the peltry trade with the Indians was of some value, and the fishery served for the support of the inhabitants; but yielded no great profit to the adventurers, who received but inadequate returns in lumber and furs. They saw their interest sinking apace, and grew dispirited; and the major part of them either relinquished the design, or sold their shares to

(1) Prince's Annals, vol. 2, p. 30, 70.

doubt is spurious, and was fabricated for the purpose of supporting the Indian deed of 1629. That this letter is a forgery, and of the most palpable kind, will appear from the following considerations :

I. That there was no such purchase of " the Indyans at Squamscutt falls," by Mr. Wheelwright, so early as 1633, as is alleged in the letter, nor an implied promise that he would name the plantation *Exeter*, five years before the settlement of that place was made.

II. That Thomas Wiggin, one of the signers of the letter, who is pretended to write at " North-ham on Pascataway river in New-England, 13 August, 1633," was about embarking at that time, at London, in the ship James, for New-England, with power from Lords Say and Brook. He arrived at Salem, 10 October, 1633, in eight weeks passage. Winthrop, Hist. N. E. i. 115.

III. Walter Neal, the other signer, was in Boston, or on his passage to England with Capt. Graves, when this letter was dated. He wrote to Gov. Winthrop on that very day, (13 August) " to excuse his not coming to see" him, as " he had been in the bay above ten days and came not all that time to see the governor." (Winthrop, Hist. N. E. i. 106, 107.) Ambrose Gibbons in a letter, which is numbered V. in the Appx., and dated in July, 1633, says, " the governor" (Neal) " departed from the plantation the fifteenth of July in the morning."

IV. The name of Northam was not given to Dover until the arrival there of Thomas Larkham in 1640, when it was *changed* from the name of DOVER, which it had received the year before, (Winthrop, i. 326) to NORTHAM, probably to gratify Larkham, who had been a preacher at a place of that name, near Barnstable, in England.

V. The settlement at Pascataqua, or Portsmouth, was called Strawberry-Bank until 1653, when the inhabitants petitioned the General Court of Massachusetts for an enlargement of territory, and humbly desiring " that the name of the plantation, being Strawberry Banke (accidentally soe called by reason of a banke where Strawberries *was* found in this place)" might be called PORTSMOUTH, " beinge a name most sutable for the place, it beinge the River's *mouth*, and a good *harbour* as any in this land." MS. Petition.]

Mason and Gorges, who were more sanguine than the rest, and became (either by purchase or tacit consent of the others) the principal, if not sole proprietors. These gentlemen renewed their exertions with greater vigor, sent over a fresh supply of servants, and materials 1634. for carrying on the settlement, and appointed Francis Williams their governor. He was a gentleman of good sense and discretion; and so very acceptable to the people, that when they combined in a body politic, they continued him at their head.

The charter by which the council at Plymouth was established, 1635. had been from the beginning disrelished by the Virginia company; who spared no pains to get it revoked.[1] Their applications to the king proved fruitless; but when the parliament began to inquire into the grievances of the nation, this patent was complained of as a monopoly. Sir Ferdinando Gorges, being summoned, appeared before them, and both in person and by his council defended it in a masterly manner, but in vain; for when the national grievances were presented to the throne, the patent of New-England was the first.[2] The council also was in disrepute with the high-church party, for having encouraged the settlement of the Plymouth and Massachusetts colonists, who fled from their persecutions. These prejudices against them, operating as discouragements to their undertaking, induced the council to resign their charter to the king; having previously taken care to secure some portion of the expiring interest to such of themselves as were disposed to accept it. The scheme they had in view was to divide their territory into twelve provinces, under as many proprietary governors, subject to one general governor; and they went so far as to nominate Gorges, then threescore years of age, for the person, and build a ship of war, which was to bring him over and remain in the service of the country. But the ship fell and broke in the launching; and their project not being sufficiently attended to by those in power, they were obliged to be content with such grants as they could make of those districts, into which they had divided the country.[3] That which was made to Mason comprehended both his former patents, extending from Naumkeag to Pascataqua, and sixty miles northwestward within the land, together with the south half of the Isles of Shoals, and ten thousand acres at Sagadahock; saving to those already settled within these limits, the property of their lawful grants on paying "some small acknowledgment" to the proprietor.[4] This grant was dated the twenty-second of April.* [5] In June following,

(1) Hubbard's MS. Hist. (2) Gorges' Narrative, p. 22 and 44. (3) Hubbard's MS. Hist. (4) Files of the Superior Court. (5) Hubbard's MS. Hist.

* Whether Captain Mason had his title confirmed by the king after the surrender of the charter is a point that has been questioned. I shall here collect what evidence I have met with on both sides.

In a pamphlet published in 1728, containing a detail of the grants and transactions of Capt. Mason, it is said "King Charles I. by charter dated "Aug. 19, 1635, gives, grants and confirms unto Capt. John Mason, then

the council surrendered their charter to the king; and in September, Gorges sold to Mason a tract of land on the northeast side of the river Pascataqua, extending three miles in breadth, and following the course of the river from its mouth to its farthest head, including the saw-mill which had been built at the falls of Newichwannock.[1]

But death which puts an end to the fairest prospects, cut off all the hopes which Mason had entertained of aggrandizing his fortune, by the settlement of New-Hampshire. By his last will, which he signed a few days before his death, he disposed of his American estate in the following manner, viz. 'To the corpora-'tion of Lynn Regis in Norfolk, the place of his nativity, he gave 'two thousand acres of land in New-Hampshire, subject to the 'yearly rent of one penny per acre to his heirs, and two fifths of 'all mines royal; on condition that five families should within five 'years be settled thereupon. To his brother in law John Wallas-'ton, three thousand acres, subject to the yearly rent of one shil-'ling. To his grandchild Anne Tufton, ten thousand acres at 'Sagadahock. To Robert Tufton, his grandson, he gave his 'manor of Mason-hall, on condition that he should take the sur-'name of Mason. He also gave to his brother Wallaston in trust, 'one thousand acres for the maintenance of "an honest, godly "and religious preacher of God's word;" and one thousand more 'for the support of a grammar-school; each of these estates to 'be conveyed to feoffees in trust, and their successors, paying an-

(1) Printed state of Allen's title.

" called treasurer and paymaster of his army, his heirs and assigns, all the " aforesaid tract of land, granted to him by the council of Plymouth, by the " name of the province of New-Hampshire; *with power of government*, and as " ample jurisdiction and prerogatives as used by the bishop of Durham; cre-" ating him and his aforesaids *absolute lords and proprietors* of the province of " New-Hampshire, with power of conferring honors, &c. On this authori-ty (I suppose) Douglass has asserted the same thing.(1) On which Hutchin-son remarks "This is not probable. His heirs were certainly unacquainted " with it, or they would have made mention of it before the king in council " in 1691."(2) The report of the Lords Chief Justices in 1677, wherein the several grants are recited, makes no mention of this: But on the contrary it is said, "As to Mr. Mason's *right of government* within the soil he claimed, " their lordships, and indeed his own council, agreed *he had none;* the great " council of Plymouth, under whom he claimed, having no power to transfer " government to any." The Lords of Trade in a report to the king in 1753, say, "It is alleged that this last grant to Mason was ratified and confirmed " by the crown, by charter dated Aug. 19, 1635, with full power of civil juris-" diction and government, but *no such charter as this appears upon record*."

None of Mason's heirs ever attempted to assume government by virtue of such a charter, as the heirs of Gorges did in the province of Maine. Robert Mason was appointed counsellor by mandamus, and Samuel Allen, who purchased the title, was governor by commission from the crown.

There is an original letter in the Recorder's files, written by George Vaughan to Ambrose Gibbons, both factors for the company of Laconia, April 10, 1636, long before any controversy arose on this point, which may give more light to it than any thing that has yet been published. [This letter is in the Appendix of first edition.]

(1) Doug. Summary, i. 413   (2) Hist. Mass. i. 317.

'nually one penny per acre to his heirs. The residue of his es-
'tate in New-Hampshire he gave to his grandson John Tufton, he
'taking the surname of Mason, and to his lawful issue; or in want
'thereof to Robert Tufton and his lawful issue; or in want there-
'of to Doctor Robert Mason, chancellor of the diocese of Win-
'chester, and his lawful issue; or, in want of such issue, to his
'own other right heirs forever; provided that it should not go out
'of the name of Mason. The residuary legatee was required to
'pay five hundred pounds out of this estate to his sister Mary and
'all the grandchildren were to relinquish their right to one thou-
'sand pounds due from this estate to their father Joseph Tufton.'
The estate in America was valued in the inventory at ten thousand pounds sterling.

The Massachusetts planters viewed Mason as their enemy, [1]
because he, with Gorges, had privately encouraged some persons
whom they had censured and sent home, to petition against them
as disaffected to the government; and had endeavored to get their
charter set aside, to make way for the scheme of a general governor.*

But though Mason and Gorges had not the same religious views
with the Massachusetts planters, yet their memory deserves respect. They were both heartily engaged in the settlement of the
country; they sunk their estates in the undertaking, and reaped
no profit to themselves; yet their enterprising spirit excited emulation in others, who had the advantage of improving their plans
and avoiding their mistakes. Gorges accounted for the ill success of his adventures in the following manner.[2] 1. He began
when there was no hope of any thing for the present but loss;
as he had first to seek a place; which, being found, was a wilderness; and so gloomy was the prospect, that he could scarce
procure any to go, much less to reside in it; and those whom he
at length sent, could not subsist but on the provisions with which
he supplied them. 2. He sought not barely his own profit, but
the thorough discovery of the country; wherein he went so far

(1) MS. in Superior Court files.   (2) Gorges' Narrative, p. 49.

* Mr. Hubbard relates the following anecdote, without mentioning the name
of the person.* "One of the gentlemen who was known to be one of the
"greatest adversaries to the affairs of the Massachusetts, fell sick and died.
"In his sickness, he sent for the minister, and bewailed his enmity against
"them: and promised if he recovered, he would be as good a friend to New-
"England, as he had been an enemy; but his fatal hour being come, his pur-
"poses of that nature were cut off. The passage aforegoing was certified by
"letters from Lord Say and others to the governor of New-England about the
"year 1635."
    Governor Winthrop has the following remark in his Journal. "1636. The
"last winter Captain Mason died. He was the chief mover, in all attempts
"against us; and was to have sent the general governor; and for this end was
"providing ships. But the Lord, in mercy, taking him away, all the business
"fell on sleep." [Winthrop, Hist. N. E. i. 187.]
    * [Dr. Belknap has added in the corrected copy this note: "It appears
from Winthrop's Journal that this was Morton. p. 208."]

(with the help of his associates) as to open the way for others to
make their gain. 3. He never went in person to oversee the
people whom he employed. 4. There was no settled government to punish offenders, or mispenders of their masters' goods.
Two other things contributed to the disappointment in as great, if
not a greater degree, than what he has assigned. The one was
that instead of applying themselves chiefly to husbandry, the original source of wealth and independence in such a country as this;
he and his associates, being merchants, were rather intent on trade
and fishery as their primary objects. These cannot be profitable
in a new country, until the foundation is laid in the cultivation of
the lands. If the lumber trade and fishery cannot now be carried
on to advantage, without the constant aid of husbandry in their
neighborhood, how could a colony of traders and fishermen make
profitable returns to their employers, when the husbandry necessary for their support was at the distance of Virginia or England?
The other mistake which these adventurers fell into was the idea
of lordship, and the granting of lands not as freeholds, but by leases
subject to quit-rents. To settle a colony of tenants in a climate
so far northward, where the charges of subsistence and improvement were much greater than the value of the lands, after the improvements were made; especially in the neighborhood of so respectable and growing a colony as that of Massachusetts, was indeed a chimerical project; and had not the wiser people among
them sought a union with Massachusetts, in all probability the
settlements must have been deserted.

CHAPTER II.

Troubles at Dover.   Settlements of Exeter and Hampton.   Ruin of Mason's
interest.   Story of Underhill.   Combinations at Portsmouth and Dover.—
Union of New-Hampshire with Massachusetts.

WHILST the lower plantation on the river Pascataqua lay under
discouragement by the death of its principal patron, the upper
settlement, though carried on with more success, had peculiar
difficulties to struggle with. Two thirds of this patent belonged
to some merchants of Bristol, the other third to some of Shrewsbury; and there was an agreement that the division should be
made by indifferent men. Captain Wiggin who was sent over to
superintend their affairs, after about one year's residence in the
country made a voyage to England, to procure more ample
means for carrying on the plantation. In the mean time, those
of Bristol had sold their interest to the lords Say and Brook,
George Willys and William Whiting, who continued Wiggin in

the agency, and procured a considerable number of families in
the west of England, some of whom were of good estates, and
1633.   "of some account for religion," to come over and increase
        the colony.[1] It appears from ancient records that Wiggin
had a power of granting lands to the settlers;[2] but, as trade was
their principal object, they took up small lots, intending to build
a compact town on Dover Neck, which lies between two branches of the river, and is a fine, dry, and healthy situation; so high
as to command all the neighboring shores, and afford a very extensive and delightful prospect. On the most inviting part of this
eminence they built a meeting-house, which was afterward surrounded with an entrenchment and flankarts, the remains of which
are still visible. Wiggin also brought over William Leveridge, a
worthy and able puritan minister; but his allowance from the adventurers proving too small for his support in a new country, where
all the necessaries of life were scarce and dear, he was obliged to
remove to the southward; and settled at Sandwich in the colony
of Plymouth.* This proved an unhappy event to the people,
who, being left destitute of regular instruction, were exposed to
the intrusions of artful impostors.

1634.   The first of these was one Burdet.† He had been a
        minister at Yarmouth in England; but either really or
pretendedly taking offence at the extravagancies of the bishops
and spiritual courts, came over to New-England, and joined with
the church in Salem, who employed him for a year or two as a
preacher, being a good scholar and plausible in his behaviour;[3]
But, disgusted with the strictness of their discipline, he removed
1636.   to Dover; and continued for sometime in good esteem
        with the people as a preacher; till by artful insinuations
he raised such a jealousy in their minds against Wiggin their gov-

(1) Hubbard's MS. Hist.   (2) Dover Records.   (3) Hubbard's MS. Hist.

* [Rev. William Leveridge arrived at Salem in the ship James, on the 10
October, 1633, in company with Captain Thomas Wiggin of Pascataqua. He
remained at Dover less than two years, and went from thence to Boston, where
he was admitted a member of the First church, 9 August, 1635. He was at
Sandwich in 1640, and, it is believed as late as 1652. In 1657, he was employed as a missionary by the commissioners of the United Colonies. He accompanied the people who made the first settlements at Huntington and Oyster-
Bay, on Long-Island, who seem, says Mr. Wood, " to have composed one company, or to have arrived at nearly the same time. He settled in Huntington,
and is mentioned as the minister of that place in the earliest records of the
town. He remained there until 1670, when he removed to Newtown, on the
same island. Hubbard characterises him as " an able and worthy minister."
Mr. Wood says, that in one of the books among the town records of Newtown,
there is a commentary on a large part of the old testament, presumed to have
been made by him. Some of his posterity still reside at Newtown, and are
among the most respectable people of that place. Johnson, Hist. N. E. 226.
Winthrop, Hist. N. E. i. 115, 331. Hubbard, Hist. N. E. 221, 603. Wood,
Hist. Sketch of the Towns on Long-Island, 3d edit. 43—45. Records of First
Church Boston.]

† [His name was George. He was admitted freeman, 2 September, 1635.—
The authorities for what is said of him are, Hubbard, Hist. N. E. 221, 263, 353
—356, 361, and Winthrop, Hist. N. E. i. 276, 281, 291, 298, 326. ii. 10.]

ernor, that they deprived him of his office, and elected Burdet in
his place.

During his residence here, he carried on a correspondence with
Archbishop Laud to the disadvantage of the Massachusetts   1637.
colony, representing them as hypocritical and disaffected,
and that under pretence of greater purity and discipline in matters of
religion, they were aiming at independent sovereignty ; it being accounted perjury and treason by their general court, to speak of appeals to the king.   The prelate thanked him for his zeal in   1638.
the king's service, and assured him that care should be taken
to redress those disorders when leisure from their other concerns
would permit.   This letter of the archbishop was intercepted, and
shewn to the governor of Massachusetts.   Burdet's villainy was
considered as the more atrocious, because he had been admitted
a freeman of their corporation, and had taken the oath of fidelity.
A copy of his own letter was afterward found in his closet.

About this time, the Antinomian controversy at Boston having
occasioned the banishment of the principal persons of that sect,
several of them retired to this settlement, being without the jurisdiction of Massachusetts.   When this was known, Governor Winthrop wrote to Wiggin, Burdet and others of this plantation, ' that
' as there had hitherto been a good correspondence between them
' it would be much resented if they should receive the exiles ; and
' intimating the intention of the general court to survey the utmost
' limits of their patent, and make use of them.'[1]   To this Burdet
returned a scornful answer, refusing to give the governor his title.
The governor thought of citing him to court to answer for his contempt ; but was dissuaded from it by Dudley, the deputy-govern-
or, who judged it imprudent to exasperate him, lest he should
avenge himself by farther accusing them to their enemies in England.   The governor contented himself with sending to Hilton an
account of Burdet's behaviour, inclosing a copy of his letter, and
cautioning the people not to put themselves too far under his power.   His true character did not long remain secret ; for being detected in some lewd actions he made a precipitate removal to
Agamenticus, now York, in the province of Maine, where he also
assumed to rule, and continued a course of injustice and adultery
till the arrival of Thomas Gorges, their governor, in 1640, who
laid a fine on him, and seized his cattle for the payment of it.*
He appealed to the king, but his appeal not being admitted, he
departed for England full of enmity against these plantations.
When he arrived, he found all in confusion ; and falling in with
the royalists was taken and imprisoned by the parliamentary party,
which is the last account we have of him.[2]

One of the exiles on account of the Antinomian controversy,

(1) [Winthrop, Hist. N. E. i. 276.]   (2) [Hubbard, Hist. N. E. 361.]

* The records of the court mention him as " a man of ill name and fame, in-
famous for incontinency." Lib. A. Sept. 8th, 1640.

was John Wheelwright, brother to the famous Anne Hutchinson. He had been a preacher at Braintree, which was then part of Boston, and was a gentleman of learning, piety and zeal. ‖ Having engaged to make a settlement within ten years, on the lands he had purchased of the Indians at Squamscot falls,‖ he with a number of his adherents began a plantation there, ‖which according to the agreement made with Mason's agents, they called Exeter.‖ Having obtained a dismission from the church in Boston,* they formed themselves into a church; and judging themselves without the jurisdiction of Massachusetts, they combined into a separate body politic,† and chose rulers and assistants, who were sworn to the due discharge of their office, and the people were as solemnly sworn to obey them. Their rulers were Isaac Grosse, Nicholas Needham, and Thomas Wilson; each of whom continued in office the space of a year, having two assistants. [1] The laws were made in a popular assembly and formally consented to by the rulers. Treason, and rebellion against the king, (who is styled "the Lord's anointed") or the country, were made capital crimes; and sedition was punishable by a fine of ten pounds, or otherwise, at the discretion of the court. This combination subsisted three years.

About the same time, a plantation was formed at Winnicumet,‡ which was called Hampton. The principal inducement to the making this settlement was the very extensive salt-marsh, which was extremely valuable, as the uplands were not cultivated so as to produce a sufficiency of hay for the support of cattle. With a

(1) Exeter Records.

* The names of those who were thus dismissed were—

John Wheelwright,	Philemon Purmot,	George Baytes,
Richard Morrys,	Isaac Grosse,	Thomas Wardell,
Richard Bulgar,	Christopher Marshall,	William Wardell.

Boston Church Records.

† [The persons who entered into an agreement at this time ' to erect and set up among themselves, such government as should be to their best discerning, agreeable to the will of God,' were the following :

George Barlow,	Edmund Littlefield,	Thomas Pettit,
Richard Bulgar,	Philemon Purmont,	Samuel Walker,
William Cole,	Henry Roby,	James Wall,
John Cram,	Francis Matthews,	George Walton,
Thomas Crawley,	Richard Morris,	Thomas Wardhall,
Henry Elkins,	Nicholas Needham,	William Wardhall,
Godfrey Dearborn,	George Rawbone,	William Wentworth,
Darby Field,	Robert Read,	John Wheelwright,
Ralph Hall,	Edward Rishworth,	William Winborne,
Christopher Helme	Robert Seward,	Thomas Wilson,
Christopher Lawson,	Robert Smith,	Thomas Wright.
Thomas Leavitt,	Augustine Storre,	

Descendants of several of the persons here named are still found in Exeter and its neighborhood. The name of Storre has been variously written, as *Star, Starr, Stor* and *Story*, but I am assured by John Kelly, Esq., of Northwood, that his signature to the agreement alluded to, is *Storre*. The name of Wardhall is found written *Wardell* and *Wardwell*. Rawbone may be a mistake for Rathbone.]

‡ [This name is called Winicowett by Winthrop.]

view to secure these meadows, the general court of Massachusetts had, in 1636, empowered Mr. Dummer* of Newbury, with John Spencer,† to build an house there at the expense of the colony, [1] which was to be refunded by those who should settle there.   Accordingly, an house was built, and commonly called the Bound-house; though it was intended as a mark of possession rather than of limits.   The architect was Nicholas Easton, who soon after removed to Rhode-Island, and built the first English house in Newport.[2] ‡

This entrance being made, a petition was presented to the court by a number of persons, chiefly from Norfolk in England, praying for liberty to settle there, which was granted them.[3]   They began the settlement by laying out a township in one hundred and forty-seven shares;[4] and having formed a church, chose Stephen Batchelor for their minister, with whom Timothy Dalton was soon after associated.   The number of the first inhabitants was fifty-six.||

(1) Massa. Records.   (2) Callender's Century Sermon, p. 73.   (3) MS. of Mr. Gookin.   (4) Massa. Records, Sept. 8, 1638.

* [Richard Dummer was one of the principal men of the Massachusetts colony.   He was born at Bishop-Stoke, England, and came to N. E. in 1632, resided first at Roxbury, from whence he soon removed to Newbury, where he died 14 December, 1679, aged 88.   He was elected an assistant in 1635 and 1636, and representative in 1640, and from 1645 to 1647.]

† [John Spencer resided in Ipswich and Newbury.   He was representative one year in 1635.   He returned to England in 1638, and died in 1648.]

‡ [Nicholas Easton, one of the first settlers of Ipswich, for which place he was elected a deputy to the General Court of Massachusetts in March, 1635, but did not hold his seat, after a short residence at Newbury, removed to Rhode-Island, where he was elected governor in 1672 and 1673.   He died in 1685, aged 83.]

|| Some of their names are mentioned in the Court Records, viz.

Stephen Batchelor,	Thomas Molton,
Christopher Hussey,	William Estow,
Mary Hussey, widow,	William Palmer,
Thomas Cromwell,	William Sargeant,
Samuel Skullard,	Richard Swayne,
John Osgood,	William Sanders,
Samuel Greenfield,	Robert Tucke,
John Molton,	John Cross.

[Among the files of the ancient county of Norfolk, kept in the office of the clerk of the court of common pleas, in Salem, is " A Note of the Families in Hampton, the first summer Mr. Batchelor came to Hampton," which will be here added.   The names of baptism are generally omitted, but I have endeavored to supply them, including them in parentheses.   Those with a || prefixed are styled *Goodman;* the year added to each shows the time of admission as freemen.

		Married Men.	
" John Browne	1638 ?		
Mr. (Christopher) Hussey	1634	||(Philemon) Dalton	1636
||(Edmund) Johnson		||(John) Huggins	
||(Robert) Tucke	1639	||(Jeoffry) Mingay	1640
Thomas Jones	1638	Thomas Moulton	1638
||(Robert) Saunderson	1639	John Moulton	1638
||(James) Davis	1640	William Palmer	1638
||(Richard) Swaine	1640	||(Thomas) Marston	1641
||(Samuel) Greenfield	1635	||(William) Estowe	1638
Abraham Perkins	1640	Lieut. (William) Hayward	1640

The authority of Massachusetts having established this settlement, they, from the beginning, considered it as belonging to their colony.[1]   Though the agent of Mason's estate made some objection to their proceeding, yet no legal method being taken to controvert this extension of their claim, the way was prepared for one still greater, which many circumstances concurred to establish.

After the death of Captain Mason, his widow and executrix sent over Francis Norton as her "general attorney;" to whom she committed the whole management of the estate.[2]   But the expense so far exceeded the income, and the servants grew so impatient for their arrears, that she was obliged to relinquish the care of the plantation, and tell the servants that they must shift for themselves; upon which, they shared the goods and cattle.   Norton drove above an hundred oxen to Boston, and there sold them for twenty-five pounds sterling per head, which it is said was the current price of the best cattle in New-England at that time.*   These were of a large breed, imported from Denmark, from whence Mason had also procured a number of men skilled in sawing plank and making potashes.   Having shared the stock and other materials, some of the people quitted the plantation ;

(1) MS. Deposition in Superior Court files.   (2) Anne Mason's Letters, and MS. Depositions in Superior Court files.

Isaac Perkins	1642	Robert Cassell	
Francis Peabody	1642	‖(John) Cross	1639
Young Men that had Lots.		William Sargeant	
William Wakefield	1638	Arthur Clark	1640
William Fifield		*The second Summer.*	
Moses Cox		‖(Robert) Page	1642
Thomas King		‖(William) Marston	
Anthony Taylor		‖(Joseph) Austin	
Thomas Ward	1637	‖(Joseph) Smith	
Giles Fuller		‖(John) Philbrick	
‖(William) Saunders		‖(William) English	1642
Daniel Hendrick		‖(Walter) Roper	1642
John Wedgewood		‖(Henry) Ambrose	1641
Thomas Chase		Widdow Parker	
‖(William) Fuller	1641		

The names of Stephen Batchelor, Timothy Dalton, Mary Hussey, widow, Thomas Cromwell, Samuel Skullard and John Osgood, which are in Dr. Belknap's list, do not appear in the preceding.   Cromwell and Skullard resided in Newbury, and Osgood settled at Andover, where he died in October, 1651, aged 56.   Most of the first settlers of Hampton had previously lived in other towns in the Massachusetts colony, after their emigration from England. In 1643, I find the following additional names at Hampton, viz. James Davis, jr., Francis Swaine, William Marston, jr., Thomas Linnet, William Sanborn, John Sanborn, Stephen Sanborn, William Huntington, Aquila Chase, ancestor of the Chase families in New-Hampshire, Richard Knight and Edward Tucke.]

* [Norton did not return to New-Hampshire, but took up his residence at Charlestown, and being, as Johnson says in Hist. N. E., 192, "a man of a bold and cheerful spirit, well disciplined, and an able man,". was admitted freeman of the colony in 1642; chosen a member of the Ancient and Honorable Artillery Company in 1643, and captain of the Charlestown train band. He was elected a deputy to the General Court eleven years, viz. in 1647, 1650, 1652—1661, excepting 1656 and 1657.   He died 27 July, 1667.]

others of them tarried, keeping possession of the buildings and improvements, which they claimed as their own; the houses at Newichwannock were burned; and thus Mason's estate was ruined. These events happened between 1638 and 1644.

Among the Antinomians who were banished from Boston, and took refuge in these plantations, was Captain John Underhill, in whose story will appear some very strong characteristics of the spirit of these times.[1] He had been a soldier in the Netherlands, and was brought over to New-England by Governor Winthrop, to train the people in military discipline. He served the country in the Pequod war, and was in such reputation in the town of Boston, that they had chosen him one of their deputies.[2] Deeply tinctured with Antinomian principles, and possessed of an high degree of enthusiasm, he made a capital figure in the controversy; being one of the subscribers to a petition in which the court was censured, with an indecent severity, for their proceedings against Wheelwright. For this offence, he was disfranchised. He then made a voyage to England; and upon his return petition- Nov. 15, ed the court for three hundred acres of land which had 1637. been promised him for his former services, intending to remove after Wheelwright. In his petition, he acknowledged his offence in condemning the court, and declared "that the Lord had brought " him to a sense of his sin in that respect, so that he had been in " great trouble on account thereof." On this occasion, the court thought proper to question him concerning an offensive expression, which he had uttered on board the ship in which he came from England, "that the government at Boston were as zealous as the " scribes and Pharisees, and as Paul before his conversion." He denied the charge, and it was proved to his face by a woman who was passenger with him, and whom he had endeavored to seduce to his opinions. He was also questioned for what he had said to her concerning the manner of his receiving assurance, which was " that having long lain under a spirit of bondage, he could get no " assurance; till at length as he was taking a pipe of tobacco, " the spirit set home upon him an absolute promise of free grace, " with such assurance and joy that he had never since doubted of " his good estate, neither should he, whatever sins he might fall " into." This he would neither own nor deny; but objected to the sufficiency of a single testimony. The court committed him for abusing them with a pretended retraction, and the next day passed the sentence of banishment upon him. Being allowed the liberty of attending public worship, his enthusiastic zeal broke out in a speech in which he endeavored to prove "that as the Lord " was pleased to convert Saul while he was persecuting, so he " might manifest himself to him while making a moderate use of " the good creature tobacco; professing withal that he knew not " wherein he had deserved the censure of the court." The el-

(1) Hubbard's MS. Hist.   (2) Prince's Annals, MS.

ders reproved him for this inconsiderate speech; and Mr. Cotton
told him, "that though God often laid a man under a spirit of
" bondage while walking in sin, as was the case with Paul, yet
" he never sent a spirit of comfort but in an ordinance, as he did
" to Paul by the ministry of Ananias; and therefore exhorted him
" to examine carefully the revelation and joy to which he preten-
" ded." The same week he was privately dealt with on suspicion
of adultery, which he disregarded; and therefore on the next
sabbath was questioned for it before the church; but the evidence
not being sufficient to convict him, the church could only admon-
ish him.

These proceedings, civil and ecclesiastical, being finished, he
removed out of their jurisdiction; and after a while came to Dover, where he procured the place of governor in the room of Burdet. Governor Winthrop hearing of this, wrote to Hilton and
others of this plantation, informing them of his character. Underhill intercepted the letter, and returned a bitter answer to Mr.
Cotton; and wrote another letter full of reproaches against the
governor to a gentleman of his family, whilst he addressed the
governor himself in a fawning, obsequious strain, begging an ob-
literation of former miscarriages, and a bearing with human infirmities. These letters were all sent back to Hilton; but too
late to prevent his advancement.

Being settled in his government, he procured a church to be
gathered at Dover, who chose Hanserd Knollys for their minister.
He had come over from England the year before; but being an
Anabaptist of the Antinomian cast, was not well received in Massachusetts, and came here while Burdet was in office, who forbade
his preaching; but Underhill, agreeing better with him, prevailed
to have him chosen their minister. To ingratiate himself with
his new patron, Knollys wrote in his favor to the church in Boston;
styling him "the right worshipful, their honored governor." Notwithstanding which, they cited him again to appear before them;
the court granting him safe conduct. At the same time, complaint was made to the chief inhabitants on the river, of the breach
of friendship in advancing Underhill after his rejection; and a
copy of Knollys's letter was returned, wherein he had written that
" Underhill was an instrument of God for their ruin," and it was
inquired whether that letter was written by the desire or consent
of the people.[1] The principal persons of Portsmouth and Dover
disclaimed his miscarriages, and expressed their readiness to call
him to account when a proper information should be presented;
but begged that no force might be sent against him. By his instigation, Knollys had also written to his friends in England, a
calumnious letter against the Massachusetts planters, representing
them as more arbitrary than the high-commission court, and that
there was no real religion in the country. A copy of this letter

(1) [Winthrop, i. Hist. N. E. 281, 292.]

being sent from England to Governor Winthrop, Knollys was so ashamed at the discovery, that obtaining a license, he went to Boston ; and at the public lecture before the governor, magistrates, ministers and the congregation, made confession of his fault, and wrote a retraction to his friends in England, which he left with the governor to be sent to them.[1]

Underhill was so affected with his friend's humiliation, and the disaffection of the people of Pascataqua to him, that he resolved to retrieve his character in the same way. Having obtained safe conduct, he went to Boston, and in the same public manner acknowledged his adultery, his disrespect to the government and the justice of their proceedings against him. But his confession was mixed with so many excuses and extenuations that it gave no satisfaction ; and the evidence of his scandalous deportment being now undeniable, the church passed the sentence of excommunication, to which he seemed to submit, and appeared much dejected whilst he remained there.

Upon his return, to please some disaffected persons at the mouth of the river, he sent thirteen armed men to Exeter to rescue out of the officer's hand one Fish, who had been taken into custody for speaking against the king. The people of Dover forbade his coming into their court till they had considered his crimes and he promised to resign his place if they should disapprove of his conduct ; but hearing that they were determined to remove him, he rushed into court in a passion, took his seat, ordered one of the magistrates to prison, for saying that he would not sit with an adulterer, and refused to receive his dismission, when they voted it. But they proceeded to choose another governor, Roberts, and sent back the prisoner to Exeter.

A new scene of difficulty now arose. Thomas Larkham, a native of Lyme, in Dorsetshire, and formerly a minister at Northam near Barnstable, who had come over to New-England, and not favoring the doctrine, nor willing to submit to the discipline of the churches in Massachusetts, came to Dover ; and being a preacher of good talents, eclipsed Knollys, and raised a party who determined to remove him. He therefore gave way to popular prejudice, and suffered Larkham to take his place ; who soon discovered his licentious principles by receiving into the church persons of immoral characters, and assuming, like Burdet, the civil as well as ecclesiastical authority. The better sort of the people were displeased and restored Knollys to his office, who excommunicated Larkham. This bred a riot, in which Larkham laid hands on Knollys, taking away his hat on pretence that he had not paid for it ; but he was civil enough afterward to return it. Some of the magistrates joined with Larkham, and forming a court, summoned Underhill, who was of Knollys's party, to appear before them, and answer to a new crime which they had to allege

1640.

(1) [Winthrop, Hist. N. E. i. 306, 326.]

against him. Underhill collected his adherents : Knollys was
armed with a pistol, and another had a bible mounted on an hal-
bert for an ensign.   In this ridiculous parade, they marched against
Larkham and his party, who prudently declined a combat, and
sent down the river to Williams, the governor, at Portsmouth, for
assistance. He came up in a boat with an armed party, beset
Knollys's house, where Underhill was, guarded it night and day
till a court was summoned, and then, Williams sitting as judge,
Underhill and his company were found guilty of a riot, and after
being fined, were banished the plantation. The new crime which
Larkham's party alleged against Underhill was, that he had been
secretly endeavoring to persuade the inhabitants to offer themselves to the government of Massachusetts, whose favor he was
desirous to purchase, by these means, as he knew that their view
was to extend their jurisdiction as far as they imagined their limits
reached, whenever they should find a favorable opportunity.[1] The
same policy led him with his party to send a petition to Boston,
praying for the interposition of the government in their case.   In
consequence of which, the governor and assistants commissioned
Simon Bradstreet, Esq., with the famous Hugh Peters, then minister of Salem, and Timothy Dalton, of Hampton, to inquire into
the matter, and effect a reconciliation, or certify the state of things
to them.   These gentlemen travelled on foot to Dover, and finding both sides in fault, brought the matter to this issue, that the
one party revoked the excommunication, and the other the fines
and banishment.

In the heat of these disputes, a discovery was made of Knollys's
failure in point of chastity. He acknowledged his crime before
the church ; but they dismissed him and he returned to England,
where he suffered by the severity of the long parliament in 1644 ;
and being forbidden to preach in the churches, opened a separate
meeting in Great St. Helen's, from which he was soon dislodged,
and his followers dispersed.[2] He also suffered in the cause of
non-conformity in the reign of King Charles the second, and at
length (as it is said) died " a good man in a good old age," September 19, 1691, Æt. ninety-three.[3]

Underhill having finished his career in these parts, obtained
leave to return to Boston, and finding honesty to be the best policy, did in a large assembly, at the public lecture, and during the
sitting of the court, make a full confession of his adultery and hypocrisy, his pride and contempt of authority, justifying the church
and court in all that they had done against him, declaring that his
pretended assurance had failed him, and that the terror of his
mind had at some times been so great, that he had drawn his
sword to put an end to his life. The church being now satisfied,
restored him to their communion.[4] The court, after waiting six

(1) [Winthrop, Hist. N. E. ii. 27, 28.]   (2) Neal's Hist. Puritans. 4to. vol.
ii. p. 118.   (3) Neal's Hist. N. E. vol. i. p. 216.   Mather's Magnal. lib. 8. p.
7.   (4) Prince's Annals.

months for evidence of his good behaviour, took off his sentence of banishment, and released him from the punishment of his adultery : the law which made it capital having been enacted after the crime was committed, could not touch his life. Some offers being made him by the Dutch at Hudson's river, whose language was familiar to him, the church of Boston hired a vessel to transport him and his family thither, furnishing them with all necessaries for the voyage.[1] The Dutch governor gave him the command of a company of an hundred and twenty men, and he was very serviceable in the wars which that colony had with the Indians, having, it is said, killed one hundred and fifty on Long-Island, and three hundred on the Main. He continued in their service till his death.*

We find in this relation a striking instance of that species of false religion, which, having its seat in the imagination, instead of making the heart better and reforming the life, inflames the passions, stupifies reason, and produces the wildest effects in the behaviour. The excesses of enthusiasm have often been observed to lead to sensual gratifications; the same natural fervor being sufficient to produce both. It cannot be strange that they who decry morality, should indulge such gross and scandalous enormities as are sufficient to invalidate all those evidences of their religious character on which they lay so much stress. But it is not so surprising that men should be thus misled, as that such frantic zealots should ever be reduced to an acknowledgment of their offences; which, in this instance, may be ascribed to the strict discipline then practised in the churches of New-England.

(1) Hubbard's MS. Hist. [p. 365 printed copy.]

* [Mr. Wood says he settled at Stamford in Connecticut, and was a delegate from that town to the court of New-Haven in 1643, and was appointed an assistant justice there. In the war between the Dutch and Indians from 1643 to 1646, he had a principal command. After this war, which was terminated by a great battle at Strickland's plain, and in which the Dutch with difficulty obtained the victory, he settled at Flushing, on Long-Island. He had some agency in detecting and exposing the intrigues of the Dutch treasurer in 1653. In 1665, he was a delegate from the town of Oyster-Bay to the Assembly, holden at Hempstead by Governor Nicolls, and was appointed by him, under-sheriff of the north riding of Yorkshire or Queen's county. In 1667, the Matinecoc Indians gave him 150 acres of land, which has remained in the family ever since, and is now in possession of one of his descendants that bears his name. It is supposed that Captain Underhill died at Oyster-Bay in the year 1672. See Wood's Sketch of the First Settlement of the several Towns on Long-Island, 3d edit. 1828, 76. The author of this work in a letter to me, dated at Huntington, L. I., 5 November, 1827, says, "the descendants of Captain Underhill are numerous and very respectable. His eldest son John was a magistrate and a man of influence and very serviceable. The most of his posterity have changed the warlike habiliments of their ancestor for the Quaker habit. One of his female descendants, who resides within six miles of Huntington, is clerk of a meeting in that neighborhood, an office of considerable importance among the Friends. She is regarded as a woman of superior talents and acquirements." The name of Underhill still exists in New-Hampshire. Whether those bearing it are descendants of Capt. John Underhill, I have not ascertained. There was a Giles Underhill in New-Hampshire in 1668, who is mentioned in the N. H. Republican of 29 January, 1823, printed at Dover.]

The people of Dover and Portsmouth during all this time had no power of government delegated from the crown; but finding the necessity of some more determinate form than they had yet enjoyed, combined themselves each into a body politic after the example of their neighbors at Exeter. The inhabitants of Dover, by a written instrument, signed by 41 persons, agreed to submit to the laws of England, and such others as should be enacted by a majority of their number, until the royal pleasure should be known.[1] The date of the combination at Portsmouth is uncertain, their first book of records having been destroyed in 1652, after copying out what they then thought proper to preserve.[2] Williams, who had been sent over by the adventurers, was by annual suffrage continued governor of the place, and with him were associated Ambrose Gibbons and Thomas Warnerton* in quality of assistants. During this combination, a grant of fifty acres of land for a glebe was made by the governor and inhabitants† to Thomas Walford‡ and Henry Sher-

Oct. 22.

May 25.

(1) Hubbard, MS. Hist.   (2) Portsmouth Records.

---

* Warnerton had been a soldier. Upon the division of Mason's stock and goods he carried his share to Penobscot, or some part of Nova-Scotia, where he was killed in a fray with the French inhabitants. 1644. (Hubbard.)—[Winthrop, Hist. N. E. ii. 178, gives the circumstances of his death, and Mr. Savage has added a valuable note pp. 177, 178, which serves more fully to develope the character of Warnerton, or Wannerton as spelled by Winthrop.]

† This grant is subscribed by

Francis Williams, Governor,	John Landen, 1
Ambrose Gibbons, Assistant,	Henry Taler,
William Jones,	John Jones,
Renald Fernald,	William Berry,
John Crowther,	John Pickerin,
Anthony Bracket,	John Billing,
Michael Chatterton,	John Wotten,
John Wall,	Nicholas Row,
Robert Pudington,	Matthew Coe,
Henry Sherburne,	William Palmer.

Portsmouth Records.

(1) [Adams, Annals of Portsmouth, 395, has this name Lander. The name of Wotten above, he reads Wolten.]

‡ [Thomas Walford was among the earliest emigrants to the Massachusetts colony. He was found at Charlestown in 1628, by those who went from Salem, in the summer of that year, to settle that place. He occupied an " English thatched house pallisadoed," and was employed as a smith by trade. He removed to Pascataqua within a few years, where he appears to have acquired a considerable estate for those days, as his property at the time of his death, in 1657, was inventoried at £1433 3 8. He possessed some influence, and served in several offices of responsibility. Jane Walford, supposed to be his wife, fell under the censure of dealing in witchcraft, and a prosecution [probably the first, and perhaps the only one of the kind in New-Hampshire,] was instituted against her, in 1657, which Mr. Adams supposes was dropped, as twelve years afterwards, she brought against her prosecutor an action of slander, and obtained a verdict of five pounds, and costs of court. Mr. Walford probably left descendants as the name continued many years in the eastern parts of the state. From this early artisan of New-England, a mechanic's News Room, lately established at Charlestown, Massachusetts, has received the name of " Walford hall." See Hubbard, Hist. N. E. 220.—Hutch. Hist. Mass. i. 17.—2 Coll. Mass. Hist. Soc. ii. 163.—Coll. of N. H. Hist. Soc. i. 255 –257.—Savage, Notes in Winthrop, i. 44, 53.—Adams, Annals of Portsmouth, 26, 38, 39, 40, 395.]

burne,* church-wardens, and their successors forever, as feoffees
in trust ;[1] by virtue of which grant the same land is still held, and
being let on long leases, a considerable part of the town of Portsmouth is built upon it.   At this time, they had a parsonage house
and chapel, and had chosen Richard Gibson for their parson, the
patronage being vested in the parishoners.   Gibson was sent from
England as minister to a fishing plantation belonging to one Tre-
lawney.   He was "wholly addicted to the hierarchy and disci-
" pline of England, and exercised his ministerial function" according to the ritual.[2]   He was summoned before the court at
Boston for " scandalizing the government there, and denying
" their title ;" but upon his submission, they discharged him
without fine or punishment, being a stranger and about to depart
the country.   After his departure, the people of Portsmonth had
James Parker† for their minister,[3] who was a scholar, and had
been a deputy in the Massachusetts court.   After him, they had

(1) Portsmouth Records.   (2) Gov.Winthrop's Journal, MS. [Vol. ii. p. 66,
Mr. Savage's edition.]   (3) Portsmouth Records.

* [Henry Sherburne, it appears from a deposition found among the old
colony files of Massachusetts, was born about the year 1612.   He therefore,
if the same who is mentioned in the text, must have come to New-England
before he was 20 years of age. He was the deputy of Portsmouth to the General Court of Massachusetts in 1660, and was living in 1665, and probably at
a later period.   The Sherburne family in New-Hampshire has been a distinguished one from the earliest settlement of the state.   Capt. Samuel Sherburne, of Portsmouth, a worthy officer who was killed by the Indians at Mac-
quoit, is named in this history, sub anno 1691.   Samuel Sherburne, who
graduated at Harvard College in 1719, was a merchant of Portsmouth.   Henry Sherburne was appointed a mandamus counsellor in 1728, and died 29 December, 1757, aged 83.   Henry Sherburne, born in 1710, graduated at Harvard
College in 1728 ; was engaged in mercantile business ; was elected representative of Portsmouth twenty-one years in succession, from January, 1745 ; was
speaker of the House of Representatives from 1755 to 1766, when he was appointed counsellor by mandamus.   In 1765, he received the appointment of
Justice of the Superior Court of Common Pleas for the province.   He died 30
March, 1767, in the 58th year of his age. (Adams, in Annals of Portsmouth,
220, 221, gives an account of his character.)   Joseph Sherburne was appointed
a counsellor of the province in 1733, sworn into office, 1 January, 1734, and
died 3 December, 1744, aged 64.   John Sherburne, the fourth counsellor of
the name, received his appointment the year before the revolution commenced, and served only one year.   He died 10 March, 1797, in his 77th year.
John Samuel Sherburne, Judge of the U. S. District Court for the New-
Hampshire District, is of this family.]

† Governor Winthrop gives this account of him and his ministry. (1642.
10 mo :) " Those of the lower part of Pascataquack invited Mr. James Par-
" ker of Weymouth, a godly man [and a scholar] to be their minister. He,
" by advising with divers of the magistrates and elders, accepted the call, and
" went and taught among them, this winter, and it pleased God to give great
" success to his labors, so as above forty of them, whereof the most had been
" very profane, and some of them professed enemies to the way of our church-
" es, wrote to the magistrates and elders, acknowledging the sinful course
" they had lived in, and bewailing the same, and blessing God for calling them
" out of it, and earnestly desiring that Mr. Parker might be settled amongst
" them.   Most of them fell back again in time, embracing this present
" world." 1 He afterward removed to Barbadoes and there settled. (vide
Hutchinson's Collection of papers, p. 155 and 222.)   Hutchinson supposes
him to have been minister of Newbury, mistaking him for Thomas Parker.
        (1) MS. Journal. [Vol. ii. p. 93 of Mr. Savage's edition.]

one Browne; and Samuel Dudley,* a son of Deputy Governor Dudley; but these were only temporary preachers, and they did not obtain the regular settlement of a minister for many years.

Four distinct governments (including one at Kittery on the north side of the river) were now formed on the several branches of Pascataqua. These combinations being only voluntary agreements, liable to be broken or subdivided on the first popular discontent, there could be no safety in the continuance of them. The distractions in England at this time had cut off all hope of the royal attention, and the people of the several settlements were too much divided in their opinions to form any general plan of government which could afford a prospect of permanent utility. The more considerate persons among them, therefore thought it best to treat with Massachusetts about taking them under their protection. That government was glad of an opportunity to realize the construction which they had put upon the clause of their charter wherein their northern limits are defined. For a line drawn from east to west, at the distance of "three miles to the "northward of Merrimack river and of any and every part there-"of," will take in the whole province of New-Hampshire, and the greater part of the province of Maine, so that both Mason's and Gorges's patents must have been vacated.[1] They had already intimated their intention to run this east and west line, and presuming on the justice of their claim, they readily entered into a negotiation with the principal settlers of Pascataqua respecting their incorporation with them. The affair was more than a year 1641. in agitation, and was at length concluded by an instrument Apr. 14. subscribed in the presence of the general court, by George Willys, Robert Saltonstall, William Whiting, Edward Holyoke, and Thomas Makepeace, in behalf of themselves and the other partners of the two patents; by which instruments, they resigned the jurisdiction of the whole to Massachusetts, on condition that the inhabitants should enjoy the same liberties with their own people, and have a court of justice erected among them. The property of the whole patent of Portsmouth, and of one third part of Oct. 8. that of Dover, and of all the improved lands therein, was reserved to the lords and gentlemen proprietors, and their heirs forever.

The court on their part consented that the inhabitants of these towns should enjoy the same privileges with the rest of the colony, and have the same administration of justice as in the courts of Salem and Ipswich; that they should be exempted from all public charges, except what should arise among themselves, or for their own peculiar benefit; that they should enjoy their former liberties of fishing, planting and selling timber; that they should send

(1) Massa. Records.

* Dudley settled at Exeter in 1650, and died there in 1683, aged 77. "He was a person of good capacity and learning." Fitch's MS.

two deputies to the general court; and that the same persons who
were authorized by their combinations to govern them, should
continue in office till the commissioners named in this order should
arrive at Pascataqua. These commissioners were invested with
the power of the quarter courts of Salem and Ipswich, and, at
their arrival, they constituted Francis Williams, Thomas Warnerton and Ambrose Gibbons of Portsmouth, Edward Hilton, Thomas Wiggin and William Waldron of Dover, magistrates, who were
confirmed by the general court.*

By a subsequent order, a very extraordinary concession was
made to these towns, which shows the fondness that
government had of retaining them under their jurisdiction. 1642.
A test had been established by law, but it was dispensed Sept. 8.
with in their favor; their freemen were allowed to vote in town
affairs, and their deputies to sit in the general court though they
were not church-members.[1]

The people of Dover being left destitute of a minister by the
sudden departure of Larkham, who took this method to avoid the
shame which would have attended the discovery of a crime similar to that for which Knollys had been dismissed, wrote to Massachusetts for help. The court took care to send them Daniel
Maud, who had been a minister in England.† He was an honest man, and of a quiet and peaceable disposition, qualities much
wanting in all his predecessors.[2] Larkham returned to England,
where he continued to exercise his ministry till ejected by the act
of uniformity in 1662, from Tavistock in Devon. He is said to
have been "well known there for a man of great piety and sin-
"cerity," and died in 1669, Æ. 69.[3] ‡

(1) Hubbard's MS. [Winthrop, Hist. N. E. ii. 92. Savage, Winthrop, ii.
92.] (2) Math. Mag. (3) Calamy's account of ejected ministers, p. 24.]

* [Hubbard says, " on Sept. 24, 1641, the inhabitants on the south side of
Pascataqua, both at Dover and Strawberry-Bank (since Portsmouth) were declared to belong to the Massachusetts jurisdiction, and in pursuance thereof,
a committee was chosen to order matters accordingly." Hist. N. E. 372.]

† [Daniel Maud came to New-England as early as 1635, in which year, on
the 25 October, he was admitted freeman by the Massachusetts colony. He
was employed while at Boston as a schoolmaster. He was the minister of
Dover about thirteen years, and died in 1655.]

‡ [1642. The visit of Darby Field to the White Mountains should be placed
under this year. The season of the year, when this visit was made is determined by the following note, among the chronological items in the Rev. Samuel Danforth's almanac for 1647. " 1642. (4) [i. e. June] The first discovery
of the great mountaine (called the Christall Hills) to the NW. by Darby Field."
The expedition was deemed so important and atttended with so much labor
and fatigue, that it may be proper to give Gov. Winthrop's account of it
entire.
" One Darby Field, an Irishman, living about Pascataquack, being accompanied with two Indians, went to the top of the White hill. He made his
journey in 18 days. His relation at his return was, that it was about one hundred miles from Saco ; that after 40 miles travel, he did, for the most part ascend, and within 12 miles of the top, was neither tree nor grass, but low sav-
ins, which they went upon the top of sometimes, but a continual ascent upon
rocks, on a ridge between two valleys filled with snow, out of which came

The inhabitants of Exeter had hitherto continued their combination; but finding themselves comprehended within the claim of
Massachusetts, and being weary of their inefficacious mode of
Sept. 8. government they petitioned the court, and were readily
admitted under their jurisdiction. William Wenborne,
Robert Smith, and Thomas Wardhall were appointed their magistrates; and they were annexed to the county of Essex.[1] Upon
this, Wheelwright who was still under sentence of banishment,
with those of his church who were resolved to adhere to him, removed into the province of Maine, and settled at Wells, where his
posterity yet remain. He was soon after restored, upon a slight
acknowledgment, to the freedom of the colony, and removed to
Hampton, of which church he was minister for many years; until he went to England where he was in favor with Cromwell.
But, after the restoration, he returned and settled at Salisbury,
where he died in 1680.[2] *

(1) Mass. Records.   (2) Hubbard's MS. [pp. 351, 365–368 of the printed
copy.]

two branches of Saco river, which met at the foot of the hill, where was an Indian town of some 200 people. Some of them accompanied him within 8
miles of the top, but durst go no further, telling him that no Indian ever dared to go higher, and that he would die if he went. So they staid there till his
return, and his two Indians took courage by his example and went with him.
They went divers times through the thick clouds for a good space, and within
4 miles of the top they had no clouds, but very cold. By the way, among
the rocks, there were two ponds, one a blackish water, the other reddish.—
The top of all was plain about 60 feet square. On the north side there was
such a precipice, as they could scarce discern to the bottom. They had neither cloud nor wind on the top, and moderate heat. All the country about
him seemed a level, excepting here and there a hill rising above the rest, but
far beneath them. He saw to the north a great water which he judged to be
about 100 miles broad, but could see no land beyond it. The sea by Saco
seemed as if it had been within 20 miles. He saw also a sea to the eastward,
which he judged to be the gulph of Canada: he saw some great waters in
parts to the westward, which he judged to be the great lake which Canada
river comes out of. He found there much muscovy glass. They could rive
out pieces of 40 feet long, and 7 or 8 broad." Winthrop, Hist. N. E. ii. 67, 68.
Field again visited the mountains about a month afterwards, in company with
five or six persons. At this time, they brought away some stones which they
supposed were diamonds, but which proved to be crystal. It is to be regretted that the other " relation, *more true and exact*," to which Gov. Winthrop
refers as subsequent, is not to be found in his History. There have been many accounts of the White Mountains published in the periodicals of the day,
the most satisfactory of which may be found in the N. E. Journal of Medicine
and Surgery, for January, 1816, vol. v. 321—338, and in Farmer and Moore's
Collections for April, 1823, vol. ii. 97—107.]

* [Rev. John Wheelwright died 15 November, 1679, at an advanced age,
and probably between 80 and 90 years, as he is said to have been at the University with Oliver Cromwell, who, when Wheelwright, while in England,
waited upon him after he became Protector, declared to the gentlemen then
about him, " that he could remember the time when he had been more afraid
of meeting Wheelwright at foot-ball, than of meeting any army since in the
field, for he was infallibly sure of being *tript up* by him " (Mather, in Appx.
to iii. vol. Belknap, 225.) Mr. Wheelwright came from Lincolnshire to New-
England in 1636. Soon after his arrival, he preached a sermon at Boston,
which, being considered by the magistrates as " tending to sedition," occasioned his banishment from the colony in November, 1637. Mr. Savage
who has seen the sermon, says, in Winthrop, i. 215, " that it was not such as

After his departure from Exeter, an attempt was made by the remaining inhabitants to form themselves into a church, and call the aged Stephen Batchelor to the ministry, who had been dismissed from Hampton for his irregular conduct. But the general court here interposed and sent them a solemn prohibition, importing " that their divisions were such that " they could not comfortably, and with approbation, proceed in so " weighty and sacred affairs," and therefore directing them " to " defer gathering a church, or any other such proceeding, till they " or the court at Ipswich, upon further satisfaction of their recon- " ciliation and fitness, should give allowance therefor."1 *

1644.

May 29.

(1) Massa. Records.

as can justify the court in their sentence for *sedition* and *contempt*, nor pre-vent the present age from regarding that proceeding as an example and a warning of the usual tyranny of ecclesiastical factions." There is a copy of the sermon in MS. in the library of the Massachusetts Historical Society.— The following exhortation from it is copied by Mr. Savage. " Thirdly, let us have a care, that we do show ourselves holy in all manner of good conver-sation, both in private and public ; and, in all our carriages and conversations, let us have a care to endeavor to be holy as the Lord is ; let us not give occa-sion to those that are coming on, or manifestly opposite to the ways of grace, to suspect the way of grace ; let us carry ourselves, that they may be ashamed to blame us ; let us deal uprightly with those with whom we have occasion to deal, and have a care to guide our families and to perform duties that belong to us ; and let us have a care that we give not occasion to say, we are liber-tines or antinomians."

Mr. Wheelwright, on his banishment, came to New-Hampshire and settled Exeter as has been stated in the text, having obtained from several Indian Sagamores, by purchase, a tract of territory thirty miles square—" lying with-in three miles on the northern side of Merrimack river, extending thirty miles along by the river from the sea side, and from the said river to Pascataqua pa-tent, thirty miles up into the country north west, and so from the falls of Pascataqua to Oyster River, thirty miles square every way." From Exeter he went to Wells, in Maine, where he remained, some time, but being releas-ed from his sentence of banishment, he went to Hampton in 1647, where he ap-pears to have remained until 1654, and perhaps later. He was in England in 1658, but returned to this country after the restoration, and succeeded Rev. William Worcester at Salisbury. His will, made 25 of May, 1679, names his son Samuel, who lived at Wells, his son-in-law Edward Rishworth, his grand-children Edward Lyde, Mary White, Mary Maverick, William, Thomas and Jacob Bradbury, to whom he gave his estate in Lincolnshire, in England, and his lands and tenements and personal property in New-England. Two of his daughters were living when Mather wrote the letter in Appx. to iii. vol-ume of Belknap, already cited.]

* [After this, the town of Exeter did not settle a minister until 1650. The town records show the contract to have been made with Rev. Samuel Dudley on the 13 of May, that year. He then, in consideration of the stipulated sal-ary, &c. " agreed to come and inhabit at Exeter, to be a minister of God's word to the people there, until such time as God should be pleased to make way for the gathering of a church, and then he is to be ordained Pastor and Teacher according to the ordinance of God—and was not to leave till death or some more than ordinary call of God otherways." MS. Note communica-ted by Hon. Jeremiah Smith, LL. D.

Rev. Samuel Dudley was born in 1606, and probably came to New-Eng-land with his father in 1630. He resided a short time at Cambridge, then at Boston, and removed to Salisbury as early as 1641, and represented that town in the General Court, at the March and May sessions in 1644. His first wife, who was Mary, daughter of Gov. Winthrop, died at Salisbury, 12 April, 1643. He afterwards married a second and third wife, by all of whom he had as many as fifteen children. His eldest son, Thomas, graduated at Harvard

7

Such a stretch of power, which would now be looked upon as
an infringement of christian liberty, was agreeable to the principles of the first fathers of New-England, who thought that civil
government was established for the defence and security of the
church against error both doctrinal and moral.   In this sentiment
they were not singular, it being universally adopted by the reformers, in that and the preceding age, as one of the fundamental
principles of their separation from the Romish church, and necessary to curtail the claims of her Pontiff, who assumed a supremacy over " the kings of the earth."*

CHAPTER III.

Observations on the principles and conduct of the first planters of New-England.   Causes of their removal.   Their fortitude.   Religious sentiments.—
Care of their posterity.   Justice.   Laws.   Theocratic prejudices.   Intolerance and persecutions.

A UNION having been formed between the settlements on Pascataqua and the colony of Massachusetts, their history for the
succeeding forty years is in a great measure the same.   It is not
my intention to write the transactions of the whole colony during
that period ; but, as many of the people in New-Hampshire had
the same principles, views and interests with the other people of
New-England, I shall make some observations thereon, and in-
tersperse such historical facts as may illustrate the subject.

In the preceding century the holy scriptures, which had long
lain hid in the rubbish of monastic libraries, were brought to public
view by the happy invention of printing ; aud as darkness vanish-
es before the rising sun, so the light of divine truth began to dis-
sipate those errors and superstitions in which Europe had long

College in 1651, and died 7 November, 1655, aged 21. Several of his sons
were active useful men, and their descendants have been numerous in this
state.]

* [Under this year, 1644, Governor Winthrop (Hist. N. E. ii. 177) speaks
of " the contentions in Hampton as grown to a great height." "The whole
town was divided into two factions, one with Mr. Batchellor their late pastor,
and the other with Mr. Dalton their teacher, both men very passionate, and
wanting discretion and moderation. Their differences were not in matters of
opinion but of practice. Mr. Dalton's party being the most of the church,
and so freemen, had great advantage of the other, though a considerable party, and some of them of the church also, whereby they carried all affairs both
in church and town according to their own minds, and not with that respect
to their brethren and neighbors which had been fit. Divers meetings had
been both of magistrates and elders, and parties had been reconciled, but
brake out presently again, each side being apt to take fire upon any provocation. Whereupon Mr. Batchellor was advised to remove, and was called to
Exeter." It was then that the General Court of Massachusetts interposed as
related in the text.]

been involved. At the same time, a remarkable concurrence of circumstances gave peculiar advantage to the bold attempt of Luther, to rouse Germany from her inglorious subjection to the Roman Pontiff, and effectuate a reformation, which soon spread into the neighboring countries. But so intimately were the political interests of kingdoms and states blended with religious prejudices, that the work, though happily begun, was greatly blemished and impeded.

Henry the VIIIth of England took advantage of this amazing revolution in the minds of men, to throw off the papal yoke, and assert his native claim to independence. But so dazzling was the idea of power, and the example of the first christian princes, who had exercised a superintendency in spirituals, as well as temporals, that he transferred to himself that spiritual power which had been usurped and exercised by the bishops of Rome, and set up himself as supreme head on earth of the church of England; commanding both clergy and laity in his dominions to swear allegiance to him in this newly assumed character.

This claim was kept up by his son and successor Edward the Sixth, in whose reign the reformation gained much ground; and a service-book was published by royal authority as the standard of worship and discipline for his subjects. This excellent prince was taken out of the world in his youth; and his sister Mary, who then came to the throne, restored the supremacy of the pope, and raised such fiery persecution against the reformers, that many of them fled into Germany and the Netherlands; where they departed from that uniformity which had been established in England, and became divided in their sentiments and practice respecting ecclesiastical affairs: the native effect of that just liberty of conscience which they enjoyed abroad, pursuing their own inquiries according to their respective measures of light; uninfluenced by secular power, or the hope of acquiring dignities in a national establishment.

The accession of Elizabeth inspired them with new hopes; and they returned home, resolving to attempt the reformation of the church of England, agreeably to the respective opinions which they had embraced in their exile. But they soon found that the queen, who had been educated in the same manner with her brother Edward, was fond of the establishment made in his reign, and was strongly prejudiced in favor of pomp and ceremony in religious worship. She asserted her supremacy in the most absolute terms, and erected an high-commission court with jurisdiction in ecclesiastical affairs. Uniformity being rigorously enjoined, and no abatement or allowance made for tender consciences, (though it was conceded that the ceremonies were indifferent) a separation from the establishment took place. Those who were desirous of a farther reformation from the Romish superstitions, and of a more pure and perfect form of religion were denominated *Puritans;* whose principles, as distinguished from those of the other reformers who were in favor with the queen, are thus represented.[1]

" The queen and court-reformers held, 1. That every prince had the sole authority to correct all abuses of doctrine and worship within his own territories. 2. That the church of Rome was a true church, though corrupt in some points of doctrine and government; that all her ministrations were valid, and that the pope was a true Bishop of Rome though not of the universal church. 3. That the scriptures were a perfect rule of faith, but not a standard of discipline; and that it was left to the discretion of the christian magistrate, to accommodate the government of the church to the policy of the state. 4. That the practice of the primitive church for the first four or five centuries was a proper standard of church government and discipline; and in some respects better than that of the Apostles, which was only accommodated to the infant state of the church, while it was under persecution; whereas the other was suited to the grandeur of a national establishment. 5. That things indifferent in their own nature, as rites, ceremonies, and habits, might be settled, determined and made necessary by the command of the civil magistrate, and that in such cases, it was the duty of the subject to observe them."

" On the other hand, the Puritans, 1. Disowned all foreign jurisdiction over the church, but could not admit of that extensive power which the crown claimed by the supremacy. However, they took the oath, with the queen's explication, as only restoring her majesty to the ancient and natural rights of sovereign princes over their subjects. 2. They held the pope to be antichrist, the church of Rome a false church, and all her ministrations superstitious and idolatrous. 3. That the scriptures were a standard of discipline as well as doctrine, and if there was need of a discretionary power, it was vested not in the magistrate, but in the officers of the church. 4. That the form of government ordained by the Apostles was aristocratical, and designed as a pattern to the church in after ages, not to be departed from in its main principles. 5. That those things which Christ had left indifferent ought not to be made necessary; and that such rites and ceremonies as had been abused to idolatry and superstition, and had a manifest tendency to lead men back thereto, were no longer indifferent but unlawful."

" Both parties agreed too well in asserting the necessity of uniformity in public worship, and of using the sword of the magistrate for the support and defence of their respective principles; which they made an ill use of in their turns, whenever they could grasp it in their hands. The standard of uniformity according to the bishops, was the queen's supremacy and the laws of the land;

(1) Neal's Hist. Puritans, vol. i. p. 95, 98, 4to.

according to the Puritans, the decrees of national and provincial synods, allowed and enforced by the civil magistrate. Neither party were for admitting that liberty of conscience and freedom of profession which is every man's right, as far as is consistent with the peace of civil government. Upon this fatal rock of *uniformity*, was the peace of the church of England split."

It is melancholy to observe what mischiefs were caused by the want of a just distinction between civil and ecclesiastical power, and by that absurd zeal for uniformity, which kept the nation in a long ferment, and at length burst out into a blaze, the fury of which was never thoroughly quelled till the happy genius of the revolution gave birth to a free and equitable *toleration*, whereby every man was restored to the natural right of judging and acting for himself in matters of religion. All the celebrated wisdom of Elizabeth's government could not devise an expedient so successful. Though her reign was long and prosperous, yet it was much stained with oppression and cruelty toward many of her best subjects; who, wearied with ineffectual applications, waited the accession of James, from whom they expected more favor, because he had been educated in the presbyterian church of Scotland, and professed an high veneration for that establishment. But they soon found that he had changed his religious principles with his climate, and that nothing was to be expected from a prince of so base a character, but insult and contempt.

In the beginning of his reign, a great number of the Puritans removed into Holland, where they formed churches upon their own principles. But not relishing the manners of the Dutch, after twelve years, they projected a removal to America, and laid the foundation of the colony of Plymouth. The spirit of uniformity still prevailing in England, and being carried to the greatest extent in the reign of Charles the First, by that furious bigot Archbishop Laud; many of the less scrupulous, but conscientious members of the church of England, who had hitherto remained in her communion, seeing no prospect of rest or liberty in their native country, followed their brethren to America, and established the colony of Massachusetts, from which proceeded that of Connecticut.

By such men, influenced by such motives, were the principal settlements in New-England effected. The fortitude and perseverance which they exhibited therein will always render their memory dear to their posterity. To prepare for their enterprise, they had to sell their estates, some of which were large and valuable, and turn them into materials for a new plantation, with the nature of which they had no acquaintance, and of which they could derive no knowledge from the experience of others. After traversing a wide ocean, they found themselves in a country full of woods, to subdue which required immense labor and patience; at a vast distance from any civilized people; in the neighborhood of none but ignorant and barbarous savages; and in a climate,

where a winter much more severe than they had been accustomed to, reigns for a third part of the year. Their stock of provisions falling short, they had the dreadful apprehension of perishing
by famine, one half of their number dying before the first year
was completed ; the ocean on one side separated them from their
friends, and the wilderness on the other, presented nothing but
scenes of horror, which it was impossible for them to conceive of
before they endured them.

But under all these difficulties, they maintained a steady and
pious resolution; depending on the providence of the supreme
ruler, and never repenting the business on which they had come
into this wilderness. As purity in divine administrations was the
professed object of their undertaking, so they immediately set
themselves to form churches, on what they judged the gospel plan.
To be out of the reach of prelatic tyranny, and at full liberty to
pursue their own inquiries, and worship God according to their
consciences, (which had been denied them in their own country)
was esteemed the greatest of blessings, and sweetened every bitter cup which they were obliged to drink. They always professed that their principal design was to erect churches on the primitive model, and that the consideration of temporal interest and
conveniency had but the second place in their views.*

In the doctrinal points of religion, they were of the same mind
with their brethren of the church of England, as expressed in
their articles. The Massachusetts planters left behind them,
when they sailed, a respectful declaration importing that they did
not consider the church of England as anti-christian, but only
withdrew from the imposition of unscriptural terms of communion.[1] Some of the Plymouth planters had embraced the narrow
principles of the Brownists, the first who separated from the
church of England ; but by the improvements which they made
in religious knowledge under the instruction of the renowned John
Robinson, their pastor in Holland, they were in a great measure
cured of that sour leaven. The Congregational system of church
government was the result of the studies of that truly pious, learned, humble and benevolent divine, who seems to have had more
of the genuine spirit of the reformation, and of freedom from bigotry, than any others in his day. His farewell charge to those of
his flock who were embarking in Holland for America, deserves
to be had in perpetual remembrance.[2] " Brethren, (said he)
" we are now quickly to part from one another, and whether I

_____

(1) Hutch. Hist. vol. i. p. 487.   (2) Neal's Hist. N. E. vol. i. p. 84.

* " It concerneth New-England always to remember, that they are orig-
" inally a plantation religious, not a plantation of trade. The profession of
" the purity of doctrine, worship and discipline is written upon her forehead.
" Let merchants, and such as are increasing cent. per cent. remember this,
" that worldly gain was not the end and design of the people of New-Eng-
" land but religion. And if any man among us make religion as twelve, and
" the world as thirteen, such an one hath not the spirit of a true New-Eng-
" land man." Higginson's Election Sermon, 1663.

" may ever live to see your face on earth any more, the God of
" heaven only knows ; but whether the Lord hath appointed that
" or no, I charge you before God and his blessed angels that you
" follow me no further than you have seen me follow the Lord
" Jesus Christ. If God reveal any thing to you by any other
" instrument of his, be as ready to receive it, as ever you were
" to receive any truth by my ministry ; for I am verily persuaded,
" I am very confident, the Lord has more truth yet to break forth
" out of his holy word. For my part, I cannot sufficiently be-
" wail the condition of the reformed churches, who are come to
" a period in religion, and will go at present no farther than the
" instruments of their reformation. The Lutherans cannot be
" drawn to go beyond what Luther saw ; whatever part of his
" will our good God has revealed to Calvin, they will rather die
" than embrace it. And the Calvinists you see stick fast where
" they were left by that great man of God, who yet saw not all
" things. This is a misery much to be lamented ; for though
" they were burning and shining lights in their times, yet they
" penetrated not into the whole counsel of God ; but where they
" now living, would be as willing to embrace farther light, as that
" which they at first received. I beseech you to remember it as
" an article of your church covenant, *that you be ready to re-*
" *ceive whatever truth shall be made known to you from the writ-*
" *ten word of God.* Remember that, and every other article of
" your sacred covenant. But I must herewithal exhort you to
" take heed what you receive as truth. Examine, consider and
" compare it with other scriptures of truth, before you receive it ;
" for it is not possible the christian world should come so lately
" out of such thick antichristian darkness, and that perfection of
" knowledge should break forth at once." It is much to be regretted
that this excellent man did not live to come to New-England, and to
diffuse more generally such truly catholic and apostolic principles.

Many of the first planters of New-England were persons of
good education, and some of them eminent for their abilities and
learning. Such men could not but see the necessity of securing
to their posterity the advantages which they had so dearly purchased. One of their first concerns was to have their children
considered, from their earliest years, as subjects of ecclesiastical
discipline. This became a matter of controversy, and was largely
discussed in sermons and pamphlets, and at length determined
by the authority of a synod. A regular course of academical
learning was a point of equal importance, and admitted of no dispute. They saw that the reputation and happiness of the whole
country depended greatly upon it. They therefore took early
care for the establishment of schools, and within ten years from
their first settlement, founded a college at Cambridge,* which,

* " When New-England was poor, and we were but few in number, there
" was a spirit to encourage learning, and the college was full of students."—
Result of a Synod in 1679.

from small beginnings, by the munificence of its patrons, has made a distinguished figure in the republic of letters. Many eminent men have there been formed for the service of the church and state ; and without this advantage, the country could not have arrived, in so short a time, at its present respectable state ; nor have been furnished with men capable of filling the various stations of usefulness, and of defending our civil and religious liberties.

Though the first planters derived from the royal grants and charters a political right as subjects of the crown of England, to this territory ; yet they did not think themselves justly entitled to the property of it, till they had fairly purchased it of its native lords, and made them full satisfaction.* Nor did they content themselves with merely living peaceably among them, but exerted themselves vigorously in endeavoring their conversion to christianity, which was one of the obligations of their patent, and one of the professed designs of their settlement in this country. This painful work was remarkably succeeded, and the names of ELIOT and MAYHEW will always be remembered as unwearied instruments in promoting it. Great care was taken by the government to prevent fraud and injustice toward the Indians in trade, or violence to their persons. The nearest of the natives were so sensible of the justice of their English neighbors, that they lived in a state of peace with them, with but little interruption, for above fifty years.

Slavery was thought so inconsistent with the natural rights of mankind, and detrimental to society, that an express law was made prohibiting the buying or selling of slaves, except those taken in lawful war, or reduced to servitude for their crimes by a judicial sentence ; and these were to have the same privileges as were allowed by the laws of Moses. There was a remarkable instance of justice in the execution of this law in 1645, when a negro who had been fraudulently brought from the coast of Africa, and sold in the country, was, by the special interposition of the general court, taken from his master in order to be sent home to his native land.† How long after this the importation of blacks

---

* The Abbe Raynal in his elegant History of the East and West Indies, speaks of the purchase made of the Indians by William Penn in 1681, as " an example of moderation and justice in America, which was never thought " of before, by the Europeans." It can be no derogation from the honor due to the wise founder of Pennslyvania that the example of this moderation and justice was first set by the planters of New-England, whose deeds of convey-ance from the Indians were earlier than his by half a century.

In some parts of the country the lands purchased of the Indians are subject to quit-rent, which is annually paid to their posterity. They have lands re-served to their use, which are not allowed to be purchased of them without the consent of the legislature.

† " 14. 3d mo. 1645. The court thought proper to write to Mr. Williams " of Pascataqua, (understanding that the negroes which Capt. Smyth brought " were fraudently and injuriously taken and brought from Guinea, by Capt. " Smyth's confession and the rest of the company) that he forthwith send the

continued to be disallowed, is uncertain; but if the same resolute justice had always been observed, it would have been much for the credit and interest of the country; and our own struggles for liberty would not have carried so flagrant an appearance of inconsistency.

Severe laws conformable to the principles of the laws of Moses were enacted against all kinds of immorality. Blasphemy, idolatry, adultery, unnatural lusts, rape, murder, man-stealing, false witness, rebellion against parents, and conspiracy against the commonwealth, were made capital crimes; and because some doubted whether the magistrate could punish breaches of the four first commands of the decalogue, this right was asserted in the highest tone, and the denial of it ranked among the most pestilent heresies, and punished with banishment. By the severity and impartiality with which those laws were executed, intemperance and profaneness were so effectually discountenanced that Hugh Peters, who had resided in the country twenty years,* declared before the parliament, that he had not seen a drunken man, nor heard a profane oath during that period. The report of this extraordinary strictness, while it invited many of the best men in England to come over, kept them clear of those wretches who fly from one country to another to escape the punishment of their crimes.

The professed design of the plantation being the advancement of religion, and men of the strictest morals being appointed to the chief places of government, their zeal for purity of every kind carried them into some refinements in their laws which are not generally supposed to come within the sphere of magistracy, and in larger communities could scarcely be attended to in a judicial way. The drinking of healths, and the use of tobacco were forbidden, the former being considered as an heathenish and idolatrous practice, grounded on the ancient libations; the other as a species of intoxication and waste of time. Laws were instituted to regulate the intercourse between the sexes, and the advances toward matrimony: they had a ceremony of betrothing, which preceded that of marriage. Pride and levity of behaviour came under the cognizance of the magistrate. Not only the richness but the mode of dress, and cut of the hair were subject to state-regulations. Women were forbidden to expose their arms or bosoms to view; it was ordered that their sleeves should reach down to their wrist, and their gowns be closed round the

---

" negro which he had of Capt. Smyth hither, that he may be sent home,
" which this court doth resolve to send back without delay. And if you have
" any thing to allege, why you should not return him to be disposed of by
" the court, it will be expected you should forthwith make it appear either by
" yourself or your agent." Massachusetts Records.

* [The length of time above stated which the Rev. Hugh Peters passed in this country may have been a typographical error. He was here not quite six years, having arrived on the 6 October, 1635, and sailed for England, 3 August, 1641.]

neck.   Men were obliged to cut short their hair, that they might
not resemble women.   No person not worth two hundred pounds
was allowed to wear gold or silver lace, or silk hoods and scarfs.
Offences against these laws were presentable by the grand jury ;
and those who dressed above their rank were to be assessed accordingly.   Sumptuary laws might be of use in the beginning of
a new plantation ; but these pious rulers had more in view than
the political good.   They were not only concerned for the external appearance of sobriety and good order, but thought themselves
obliged, as far as they were able, to promote real religion and
enforce the observance of the divine precepts.

As they were fond of imagining a near resemblance between
the circumstances of their settlement in this country and the redemption of Israel from Egypt or Babylon ; it is not strange that
they should look upon their " commonwealth as an institution of
" God for the preservation of their churches, and the civil rulers
" as both members and fathers of them."[1]   The famous John
Cotton, the first minister of Boston, was the chief promoter of
this sentiment.   When he arrived in 1633, he found the people
divided in their opinions.   Some had been admitted to the privileges of freemen at the first general court, who were not in communion with the churches.   After this, an order was passed, that
none but members of the churches should be admitted freemen ;
whereby all other persons were excluded from every office or
privilege civil or military.   This great man by his eloquence
confirmed those who had embraced this opinion, and earnestly
pleaded "that the government might be considered as a theocracy,
" wherein the Lord was judge, lawgiver and king ; that the laws
" which he gave Israel might be adopted, so far as they were of
" moral and perpetual equity ; that the people might be consid-
" ered as God's people in covenant with him ; that none but per-
" sons of approved piety and eminent gifts should be chosen
" rulers ; that the ministers should be consulted in all matters of
" religion ; and that the magistrate should have a superintending
" and coercive power over the churches."[2] *   At the desire of

(1) Increase Mather's Life, p. 57.   (2) Mather's Magnalia, lib. 8, p. 20.

* [There is a very scarce work which was published in 1663, at Cambridge,
by Samuel Green and Marmaduke Johnson, entitled " A Discourse about
Civil Government in a new Plantation whose Designe is Religion, Written
many years since. By that Reverend and Worthy Minister of the Gospel,
John Cotton, B. D. and now published by some Undertakers of a new Plantation, for General Direction and Information."   The object of it seems to be,
" to prove the expediency and necessity of entrusting free Burgesses which
are members of churches gathered amongst them according to Christ with the
power of choosing among themselves, magistrates, and men to whom the
managing of all public civil affairs of importance is to be committed—and to
vindicate the same from an imputation of an under-power upon the churches
of Christ which hath been cast upon it through a mistake of the true state of
the question."   The work seems to be addressed to a brother in the ministry,
who had affirmed, that " the limiting of the right and power of choosing civil
officers unto free burgesses that are members of churches, brought that tyran-

the court, he compiled a system of laws founded chiefly on the laws of Moses, which was considered by the legislative body as the general standard; though they never formally adopted it, and in some instances varied from it.[1]

These principles were fundamentally the same with those, on which were grounded all the persecutions which they had endured in England, and naturally led to the same extremes of conduct which they had so bitterly complained of in those civil and ecclesiastical rulers, from whose tyranny they had fled into this wilderness. They had already proceeded a step farther than the hierarchy had ever attempted. *No test-law had as yet taken place in England ;* but they had at one blow cut of all but those of their own communion, from the privileges of civil offices, however otherwise qualified. They thought that as they had suffered so much in laying the foundation of a new state, which was supposed to be " a model of the glorious kingdom of Christ on earth,"* they had an exclusive right to all the honors and privileges of it ; and having the power in their hands, they effectually established their pretensions, and made all dissenters and disturbers feel the weight of their indignation.

In consequence of the union thus formed between the church and state on the plan of the Jewish theocracy, the ministers were called to sit in council, and give their advice in matters of religion and cases of conscience which came before the court, and without them they never proceeded to any act of an ecclesiastical nature. As none were allowed to vote in the election of rulers

(1) Hutch. Coll. Papers, p. 161.

ny into the Romish Church, which all the churches of Christ complain of." In reply to this, the author says, " it would well have become you to have better digested your own thoughts, before such words had passed through your lips ; for you will never be able to produce any good author that will confirm what you say. The truth is quite contrary ; for that I may instance in Rome itself : Had Churches been rightly managed when the most considerable part of that city embraced the Christian faith, in the ceasing of the *Ten Persecutions,* that only such as had been fit for that estate, had been admitted in church-fellowship, and they alone had had power, out of themselves to have chosen magistrates, such magistrates would not have been chosen, as would have given their power to the Pope ; nor would those churches have suffered their pastors to become worldly princes and rulers, as the Pope and his Cardinals are ; nor would they have given up the power of the Church from the Church into the officers hands, but would have called upon them to *fulfil their ministry which they had received of the Lord ;* and if need were, would by the power of Christ have compelled them so to do : and then where had the Pope's supremacy been, which is made up of the spoils of the ecclesiastical and civil state ? but had by the course which now we plead for, been prevented."]

* " I look upon this as a little model of the glorious kingdom of Christ on " earth. Christ reigns among us in the commonwealth as well as in the " Church, and hath his glorious interest involved in the good of both societies " respectively. He that shall be treacherous and false to the civil government, " is guilty of high treason against the Lord Jesus Christ, and will be proceed-
' ed against as a rebel and traitor to the King of kings, when he shall hold his " great assizes at the end of the world." President Oakes's Election Sermon, 1673.

but freemen, and freemen must be church members; and as none
could be admitted into the church but by the elders, who first
examined, and then propounded them to the brethren for their
vote, the clergy acquired hereby a vast ascendency over both
rulers and people, and had in effect the keys of the state as well
as the church in their hands. The magistrates, on the other
hand, regulated the gathering of churches, interposed in the settlement and dismission of ministers, arbitrated in ecclesiastical
controversies and controled synodical assemblies. This coercive
power in the magistrate was deemed absolutely necessary to preserve " the order of the gospel."

The principle on which this power is grounded is expressed in
the Cambridge Platform in terms as soft as possible.[1] "The
" power and authority of magistrates is not for the restraining of
" churches, or any other *good* works, but for the helping in, and
" furthering thereof, and therefore the consent and countenance
" of magistrates *when it may be had*, is not to be slighted or
" lightly esteemed; but, on the contrary, it is a part of the honor
" due to christian magistrates to desire and crave their consent
" and approbation therein : which being obtained, the churches
" may then proceed in their way with *much more* encouragement
" and comfort." This article (like divers others in that work) is
curiously and artfully drawn up, so that there is an appearance of
liberty and tenderness, but none in reality : for although the magistrate was not to restrain any good works, yet *he* was to be the
judge of the good or evil of the works to be restrained; and what
security could churches have that they should not be restrained in
the performance of what *they* judged to be good works ? They
might indeed think themselves safe, whilst their rulers were so
zealous for the purity of the churches of which themselves were
members, and whilst their ministers were consulted in all ecclesiastical affairs; but if the civil powers had acted without such
consultation, or if the ministers had been induced to yield to the
opinion of the magistrates, when contrary to the interest of the
churches, what then would have become of religious liberty ?

The idea of liberty in matters of religion was in that day strangely understood, and mysteriously expressed. The venerable Higginson, of Salem, in his sermon on the day of the election, 1663,
speaks thus : " The gospel of Christ hath a right paramount to
" all rights in the world; it hath a divine and supreme right to be
" received in every nation, and the knee of magistracy is to bow
" at the name of Jesus. This right carries liberty along with it,
" for all such as profess the gospel, to walk according to the faith
" and order of the gospel. That which is contrary to the gospel
" hath no right, and therefore should have no liberty." Here
the question arises, who is to be the judge of what is agreeable
or contrary to the gospel? If the magistrate, then there is only

(1) Chap. 17. Sec. 3.

a liberty to believe and practice what the magistrate thinks right. A similar sentiment occurs in the sermon of the learned President Oakes on the same occasion, in 1673 : "The outcry of some " is for liberty of conscience. This is the great Diana of the " libertines of this age. But remember that as long as you have " liberty to walk in the faith and order of the gospel, and may " lead quiet and peaceable lives in all godliness and honesty, you " have as much liberty of conscience as Paul desired under any " government." Here the question recurs, would Paul have sub- mitted to walk according to the opinion which the magistrate might entertain of the faith and order of the gospel ? But this was all the freedom allowed by the spirit of these times. Liberty of conscience and toleration were offensive terms, and they who used them were supposed to be the enemies of religion and gov- ernment. " I look upon toleration (says the same author) as the " first born of all abominations; if it should be born and brought " forth among us, you may call it Gad, and give the same reason " that Leah did for the name of her son, *Behold a troop cometh,* " a troop of all manner of abominations." In another of these election sermons,[1] (which may generally be accounted the echo of the public voice, or the political pulse by which the popular opinion may be felt) it is shrewdly intimated that toleration had its origin from the devil, and the speech of the demoniac who cried out, " what have we to do with thee, let us alone, thou " Jesus of Nazareth," is styled " Satan's plea for toleration." The following admonition to posterity, written by the Deputy- Governor Dudley, is another specimen.

" Let men of God in courts and churches watch
" O'er such as do a toleration hatch ;
" Lest that ill egg bring forth a cockatrice,
" To poison all with heresy and vice.
" If men be left and otherwise combine,
" My epitaph's, *I dy'd no libertine.*"[2]*

The champion of these sentiments was Cotton, who though eminently meek, placid and charitable, yet was strongly tinctured with the prevailing opinion, that the magistrate had a coercive power against heretics. The banishment of Roger Williams, minister of Salem, occasioned a vehement controversy on this point. Williams having written in favor of liberty of conscience, and styled the opposite principle " the bloody tenet;" was an- swered by Cotton, who published a treatise, in 1647, with this strange title, " The bloody tenet washed, and made white in the " blood of the Lamb." In this work, he labors to prove the law- fulness of the magistrate's using the civil sword to extirpate her- etics, from the commands given to the Jews to put to death blas-

(1) Shepard's Election Sermon, 1672.　(2) Morton's Memorial, p. 179. [257 of Judge Davis's edition.]

* [These verses, says Morton, were found in his pocket after his death.]

phemers and idolaters.　To the objection, that persecution serves
to make men hypocrites, he says, " better tolerate hypocrites, and
" tares than briars and thorns.　In such cases, the civil sword
" doth not so much attend the conversion of seducers, as the pre-
" venting the seduction of honest minds by their means."　He
allows indeed, that " the magistrate ought not to draw the sword
" against seducers till he have used all good means for their con-
" viction : but if after their continuance in obstinate rebellion
" against the light, he shall still walk toward them in soft and gentle
" commiseration, his softness and gentleness is excessive large to
" foxes and wolves ; but his bowels are miserably straitened and
" hardened against the poor sheep and lambs of Christ.　Nor is it
" frustrating the end of Christ's coming, which was to save souls,
" but a direct advancing it, *to destroy*, if need be, *the bodies* of
" those wolves, who seek to destroy the souls of those for whom
" Christ died."　In pursuing his argument, he refines so far as to
deny that any man is to be persecuted on account of conscience
" till being convinced in his conscience of his wickedness, he do
" stand out therein, not only against the truth, but against the light
" of his own conscience, that so it may appear he is not persecuted
" for cause of conscience, but punished for sinning against his
" own conscience."　To which he adds, " sometimes it may be
" an aggravation of sin both in judgment and practice that a man
" committeth it in conscience."　After having said, that " it was
toleration which made the world anti-christian," he concludes his
book with this singular ejaculation, " the Lord keep us from being
" bewitched with the whore's cup, lest while we seem to reject
" her with open face of profession, we bring her in by a back
" door of toleration ; and so come to drink deeply of the cup of
" the Lord's wrath, and be filled with her plagues."

But the strangest language that ever was used on this, or perhaps on any other subject, is to be found in a book printed in 1645
by the humorous Ward of Ipswich, entitled, " The Simple Cob-
ler of Aggawam."　" My heart (says he) hath naturally detested
" four things ; the standing of the Apocrypha in the bible : for-
" eigners dwelling in my country, to crowd out native subjects in-
" to the corners of the earth : alchymized coins : toleration of
" divers religions or of one religion in segregant shapes.　He that
" willingly assents to the last, if he examines his heart by day-
" light, his conscience will tell him, he is either an atheist, or an
" heretic, or an hypocrite, or at best a captive to some lust.　Poly-
" piety is the greatest impiety in the world.　To authorize an un-
" truth by toleration of the state, is to build a sconce against the
" walls of heaven, to batter God out of his chair.　Persecution of
" true religion and toleration of false are the Jannes and Jambres
" to the kingdom of Christ, whereof the last is by far the worst.
" He that is willing to tolerate any unsound opinion, that his
" own may be tolerated though never so sound, will for a need,

" hang God's bible at the devil's girdle.   It is said that men ought
" to have liberty of conscience and that it is persecution to debar
" them of it : I can rather stand amazed than to reply to this ; it
" is an astonishment that the brains of men should be parboiled in
" such impious ignorance."

From these specimens, (of which the reader will think he has
had enough) it is easy to see how deeply the principle of intoler-
ancy was rooted in the minds of our forefathers.   Had it stood
only in their books as a subject of speculation, it might have been
excused, considering the prejudices of the times ; but it was drawn
out into fatal practice, and caused severe persecutions which cannot be justified consistently with christianity or true policy.—
Whatever may be said in favor of their proceedings against the
Antinomians, whose principles had such an effect on the minds of
the people as materially affected the foundations of government,
in the infancy of the plantation ; yet the Anabaptists and Quakers
were so inconsiderable for numbers, and the colony was then so
well established that no danger could have been rationally apprehended to the commonwealth from them.   Rhode-Island was settled by some of the Antinomian exiles on a plan of entire religious
liberty ; men of every denomination being equally protected and
countenanced, and enjoying the honors and offices of government. [1]
The Anabaptists, fined and banished, flocked to that new settlement, and many of the Quakers also took refuge there ; so that
Rhode-Island was in those days looked upon as the drain or sink
of New-England ; and it has been said that " if any man had lost
" his religion, he might find it there, among such a general mus-
" ter of opinionists."   Notwithstanding this invective, it is much
to the honor of that government that there never was an instance
of persecution for conscience sake countenanced by them.—
Rhode-Island and Pennsylvania afford a strong proof that toleration conduces greatly to the settlement and increase of an infant
plantation.

The Quakers at first were banished ; but this proving insufficient, a succession of sanguinary laws were enacted against them,
of which imprisonment, whipping, cutting off the ears, boring the
tongue with an hot iron, and banishment on pain of death, were
the terrible sanctions.   In consequence of these laws, four persons
were put to death at Boston, bearing their punishment with patience and fortitude ; solemnly protesting that their return from
banishment was by divine direction, to warn the magistrates of
their errors, and intreat them to repeal their cruel laws ; denounc-
ing the judgments of God upon them ; and foretelling that if they
should put them to death, others would rise up in their room to fill
their hands with work.* [2]   After the execution of the fourth per-

(1) Callender's Century Sermon, 1738.   (2) Sewel's History of the Quakers.

* The following passages extracted from William Leddra's letter to his

son, an order from King Charles the second, procured by their friends in England, put a stop to capital executions.*

Impartiality will not suffer a veil to be drawn over these disgraceful transactions. The utmost that has been pleaded in favor of them, cannot excuse them in the eye of reason and justice. The Quakers, it is said, were heretics; their principles appeared to be subversive of the gospel, and derogatory from the honor of the Redeemer. Argument and scripture were in this case the proper weapons to combat them with; and if these had failed of success they must have been left to the judgment of an omniscient and merciful God. They were complained of as disturbers of

friends, written the day before his execution, March 15, 1660, shew an elegance of sentiment and expression, not common in their writings.

" Most dear and inwardly beloved,
" The sweet influence of the morning star, like a flood, distilling into my
" innocent habitation hath so filled me with the joy of the Lord in the beauty
" of holiness, that my spirit is as if it did not inhabit a tabernacle of clay, but
" is wholly swallowed up in the bosom of eternity from whence it had its being."
" Alas, alas! what can the wrath and spirit of man that lusteth to envy, ag-
" gravated by the heat and strength of the king of the locusts which came out
" of the pit, do unto one that is hid in the secret places of the Almighty ? or
" to them that are gathered under the healing wings of the Prince of Peace ?
" O my beloved, I have waited as the dove at the window of the ark, and have
" stood still in that watch, which the master did at his coming reward with the
" fulness of his love; wherein my heart did rejoice that I might speak a few
" words to you, sealed with the spirit of promise. As the flowing of the
" ocean doth fill every creek and branch thereof, and then retires again toward
" its own being and fulness and leaves a savour behind it; so doth the life
" and virtue of God flow into every one of your hearts, whom he hath made
" partakers of his divine nature ; aed when it withdraws but a little, it leaves
" a sweet savour behind it, that many can say they are made clean through
" the word that he has spoken to them. Therefore, my dear hearts, let the
" enjoyment of the life alone be your hope, your joy and your consolation.
" Stand in the watch within, in the fear of the Lord which is the entrance of
" wisdom. Confess him before men, yea before his greatest enemies. Fear
" not what they can do to you : Greater is he that is in you than he that is
" in the world, for he will clothe you with humility and in the power of his
" meekness you shall reign over all the rage of your enemies." Sewel's Hist.
Quakers, p. 274.

* [The Mandamus of King Charles is dated at Whitehall, the 9th day of September, 1661, and is directed " To our trusty and well-beloved John Endecott, esquire, and to all and every other the governor or governors of our plantations of New-England, and of all the colonies thereunto belonging, that now are or hereafter shall be, and to all and every the ministers and officers of our plantations and colonies whatsoever within the continent of New-England." There is a copy of it in Hazard's Collections, ii. 595, in Sewel's History of the Quakers, i. 475, and in the Journal of George Fox, pp. 326, 327. Fox gives the following account of its being presented to the governor. It was brought over in 1661, by Samuel Shattock, who had been banished by the government of Massachusetts for being a Quaker. He and Ralph Goldsmith, the commander of the ship in which they came, " went through the town [of Boston] to the governor's, John Endecott's door, and knocked. He sent out a man to know their business. They sent him word their business was from the king of England, and they would deliver their message to none but the governor himself. Thereupon they were admitted in, and the governor came to them ; and having received the deputation and the Mandamus, he put off his hat and looked upon them. Then going out, he bid the friends follow. He went to the deputy governor, and after a short consultation, came out to the friends, and said, ' We shall obey his majesty's commands.' " George Fox, Journal, folio. p. 326.]

the peace, revilers of magistracy, " malignant and assiduous pro-
" moters of doctrines, directly *tending* to subvert both church and
" state ;" and our fathers thought it hard, when they had fled from
opposition and persecution in one shape to be again troubled with
it in another.[1] But it would have been more to their honor to
have suffered their magistracy and church order to be insulted,
than to have stained their hands with the blood of men who deserved pity rather than punishment. The Quakers indeed had no
right to disturb them ; and some of their conduct was to an high
degree indecent and provoking ; but they were under the influence of a spirit which is not easily quelled by opposition. Had
not the government appeared to be jealous of their principles, and
prohibited the reading of their books before any of them appeared
in person, there could not have been so plausible a pretext for
their reviling government. It was said, that the laws by which
they were condemned, were grounded on the laws in England
against Jesuits. But the case was by no means parallel, (as
the Quakers pleaded) their principles and practices not being
equally detrimental to society.[2] It was moreover urged in excuse
of the severities exercised against the Quakers, that the magistrates thought themselves "bound in conscience to keep the passage with the point of the sword : this (it was said) could do no
harm to him that would be warned by it : their rushing on it was
their own act, and they brought the blood on their own heads.
Had they promised to depart the jurisdiction and not return without leave, the country would have been glad to have rid themselves of the trouble of executing the laws upon them. It was
their presumptuous returning after banishment, that caused them
to be put to death."[3] This was the plea which the court used in
their address to the king ; and in another vindication published
by their order, the unhappy sufferers are styled " felones de se,"
or self-murderers.[4] But this will not justify the putting them to
death, unless the original crimes for which they were banished
had deserved it.[5] The preamble to the act, by which they were
condemned, charges them with "altering the received laudable
custom of giving respect to equals and reverance to superiors ;
that their actions *tend* to undermine the civil government and
destroy the order of the churches, by denying all established
forms of worship, by withdrawing from orderly church fellowship,
allowed and approved by all orthodox professors of the truth,
and instead thereof, and in opposition thereto, frequently meeting themselves, insinuating themselves into the minds of the simple, whereby divers of our inhabitants have been infected."
Did these offences deserve death ? Had any government a right
to terrify with capital laws persons guilty of no other crimes than

(1) Hutch. Coll. Papers, p. 327.   (2) Sewel's History Quakers.   (3) Mass.
Records.   (4) Sewel, b. 6, p. 272.   (5) Ibid. p. 199.

these, especially, when they professed that they were obliged to go the greatest lengths in maintaining those tenets which they judged sacred, and following the dictates of that spirit which they thought divine ? Was not the mere "holding the point of the sword" to them, really inviting them to "rush on it," and seal their testimony with their blood ? and was not this the most likely way to strengthen and increase their party ? Such punishment for offences which proceeded from a misguided zeal, increased and inflamed by opposition, will never reflect any honor on the policy or moderation of the government; and can be accounted for only by the strong predilection for coercive power in religion, retained by most or all of the reformed churches ; a prejudice which time and experience were necessary to remove.*

* From the following authorities, it will appear that the government of New-England, however severe and unjustifiable in their proceedings against the Quakers, went no farther than the most eminent reformers; particularly the Bohemians, the Lutherans, the celebrated Calvin and the martyr Cranmer.

In the war which the Emperor Sigismond excited against the Bohemian reformers, who had the famous Zisca for their general ; "The acts of barbarity which were committed on both sides were shocking and terrible beyond expression. For notwithstanding the irreconcileable opposition between the religious sentiments of the contending parties, they both agreed in this one horrible point, that it was innocent and lawful to persecute and extirpate with fire and sword, the enemies of the true religion, and such they reciprocally appeared to be in each others eyes." Mosheim's Eccl. Hist. vol. 3. p. 261.

" It were indeed ardently to be wished, that the *Lutherans* had treated with more mildness and charity those who differed from them in religious opinions. But they had unhappily imbibed a spirit of persecution in their early education. This was too much the spirit of the times, and it was even a leading maxim with our ancestors (this author was a Lutheran) that it was both lawful and expedient to use severity and force against those whom they looked upon as heretics. *This maxim was derived from* ROME; and even those who separated from that church did not find it easy to throw off all of a sudden that despotic and uncharitable spirit, that had so long been the main spring of its government and the general characteristic of its members. Nay in their narrow view of things, their very piety seemed to suppress the generous movements of fraternal love and forbearance, and the more they felt themselves animated with a zeal for the divine glory, the more difficult did they find it to renounce that ancient and favorite maxim, that whoever is found to be an enemy to God, ought also to be declared an enemy to his country." Mosheim, vol. 4, page 437.

" Michael Servetus, a Spanish physician, published seven books in which he attacked the sentiments adopted by far the greatest part of the christian church, in relation to the divine nature and a trinity of persons in the Godhead. Few innovaters have set out with a better prospect of success : But all his views were totally disappointed by the vigilance and severity of Calvin, who, when Servetus was passing through Switzerland, caused him to be apprehended at Geneva in the year 1553, and had an accusation of blasphemy brought against him before the council. Servetus adhering resolutely to the opinions he had embraced, was declared an obstinate heretic and condemned to the flames." Mosheim, vol. 4. page 171.

Dr. Macclaine in his note on this passage, says, " It was a remaining portion of *the spirit of popery* in the breast of Calvin that kindled his unchristian zeal against the wretched Servetus, whose death will be an indelible reproach upon the character of that great and eminent reformer."

In the reign of Edward the Sixth of England, anno, 1549, " A woman " called Joan Bocher, or Joan of Kent, was accused of heretical pravity. Her " doctrine was, "that Christ was not truly incarnate of the virgin, whose " flesh being the outward man was sinfully begotten and born in sin ; and

The mistakes on which their conduct was grounded cannot be detected in a more masterly manner, than by transcribing the sentiments of Doctor Increase Mather, who lived in those times, and was a strong advocate for the coercive power of the magistrate in matters of religion; but afterward changed his opinion on this point. " He became sensible that the example of the Israel-" itish reformers inflicting penalties on false worshippers would not " legitimate the like proceedings among christian gentiles : for the " holy land of old was, by a deed of gift from the glorious God, " miraculously and indisputably granted to the Israelitish nation, " and the condition on which they had it was their observance of " the Mosaic institutions. To violate them was high treason " against the king of the theocracy, an iniquity to be punished by " the judge. At the same time, sojourners in the land were not " compelled to the keeping those rites and laws which Moses had " given to the people. Nay, the Israelites themselves fell, many " of them, into the worst of heresies, yet whilst they kept the " laws and rites of Moses, the magistrate would not meddle with " them. The heresy of the Sadducees in particular struck at the " foundation of all religion ; yet we do not find that our Saviour " ever blamed the Pharisees for not persecuting them. The " christian religion brings us not into a temporal Canaan, it knows " no weapons but what are purely spiritual. He saw that until " persecution be utterly banished out of the world, and Cain's

" consequently he could take none of it; but the word by the consent of the " inward man of the virgin was made flesh." A scholastic nicety, not capable of doing much mischief! but there was a necessity for delivering the woman to the flames for maintaining it. The young king though in such tender years, had more sense than all his counsellors and preceptors ; and he long refused to sign the warrant for her execution. CRANMER, with his superior learning, was employed to persuade him to compliance, and he said, that the prince, being God's deputy, ought to repress impieties against God, in like manner as the king's deputies were bound to punish offenders against the king's person. He also argued from the practice of the Jewish church in stoning blasphemers. Edward overcome by importunity more than reason at last submitted, and told Cranmer with tears in his eyes, that if any wrong was done, the guilt should lie entirely on his head. The primate was struck with surprise ; but after making a new effort to reclaim the woman and finding her obstinate, he at last committed her to the flames. Nor did he ever renounce his burning principles so long as he continued in power." Hume's Hist. Eng. 4to. vol. 3. p. 320. Neal's Hist. Puritans, 4to. vol. 1. p. 41.

It ought also to be remembered, that at the same time that the Quakers suffered in New-England, penal laws against them were made and rigorously executed in England ; and though none of them suffered capital executions, yet they were thrown into prison and treated with other marks of cruelty, which in some instances proved the means of their death. And though the lenity of King Charles the IId. in putting a stop to capital executions here has been much celebrated, yet in his letter to the Massachusetts government the next year, wherein he requires liberty for the church of England among them, he adds, " Wee cannot be understood hereby to direct, or wish that " any indulgence should be graunted to Quakers, whose principles, being in-" consistent with any kind of government. Wee have found it necessary " with the advise of our parliament here to make a sharp law against them, " and are well content you doe, the like there." Records of Deeds, Province Maine, lib. i. fol. 129.

" club taken out of Abel's hand, 'tis impossible to rescue the
" world from endless confusions. He that has the power of the
" sword will always be in the right and always assume the power
" of persecuting. In his latter times, therefore, he looked upon
" it as one of the most hopeful among the signs of the times, that
" people began to be ashamed of a practice which had been a
" mother of abominations, and he came entirely into that golden
" maxim, *Errantis poena doceri*."

Divers others of the principal actors and abettors of this tragedy
lived to see the folly and incompetency of such sanguinary laws,
to which the sufferings of their brethren, the nonconformists in
England, did not a little contribute. Under the arbitrary government of King James, the Second, when he, for a shew of liberty
and as a leading step to the introduction of popery, issued a proclamation of indulgence to tender consciences, the principal men
of the country sent him an address of thanks, for *granting* to
them what they had formerly *denied* to others. It is but justice
to add, that all those disgraceful laws were renounced and repealed, and the people of New-England are now as candidly disposed
toward the Quakers as any other denominations of christians. To
keep alive a spirit of resentment and reproach to the country, on
account of those ancient transactions which are now universally
condemned, would discover a temper not very consistent with
that meekness and forgiveness which ought to be cultivated by all
who profess to be influenced by the gospel.

But though our ancestors are justly censurable for those instances of misconduct, yet they are not to be condemned as unworthy the christian name, since some of the first disciples of our
Lord, in a zealous imitation of the prophet Elias, would have
called for fire from Heaven to consume a village of the Samaritans
who refused to receive him. Their zeal was of the same kind ;
and the answer which the benevolent author of our religion gave
to his disciples on that occasion, might with equal propriety be
addressed to them, and to all persecuting christians, " Ye know
" not what spirit ye are of, for the Son of man is not come to
" destroy men's lives but to save them."

CHAPTER IV.

Mode of Government under Massachusetts. Mason's efforts to recover the property of his ancestor. Transactions of the King's Commissioners. Opposition to them. Political principles. Internal transactions. Mason discouraged.

DURING the union of these plantations with Massachusetts, they were governed by the general laws of the colony, and the terms of the union were strictly observed.* Exeter and Hamp-

* [One of the most important events of this period was the confederacy of the colonies of Massachusetts, (which included New-Hampshire) New-Plymouth, Connecticut and New-Haven, which continued nearly forty years. This union was proposed by the colonies of Connecticut and New-Haven, as early as 1638, but was not finally completed until 1643. "Besides its agency in guiding the events of the time, it was the prototype of the confederacy of the states during the revolution, which was in fact the germ and vivifying principle of our existence as a nation." The features of this confederacy are thus described by Mr. Pitkin, in his Civil and Political History of the United States. "By the articles of confederation, as they were called, these colonies entered into a firm and perpetual league of *friendship and amity*, for offence and defence, mutual advice and succor, upon all just occasions, both for preserving and propagating the truth and liberties of the Gospel, and for their own mutual safety and welfare. Each colony was to retain its own peculiar jurisdiction and government, and no other plantation or colony was to be received as a confederate, nor any two of the confederates to be united into one jurisdiction, without the consent of the rest. The affairs of the united colonies were to be managed by a legislature to consist of two persons, styled commissioners, chosen from each colony. These commissioners had power to hear, examine, weigh, and determine all affairs of war or peace, leagues, aids, charges, and number of men for war,—division of spoils, and whatsoever is gotten by conquest—receiving of more confederates for plantations, into combination with any of the confederates; and all things of a like nature, which are the proper *concomitants* and *consequences* of such a confederation for amity, offence, and defence; not intermeddling with the government of any of the jurisdictions, which, by the third article, is preserved entirely to themselves. The commissioners were to meet annually, in each colony, in succession, and when met, to choose a president, and the determination of any six to be binding on all.

"The expenses of all just wars to be borne by each colony, in proportion to its number of male inhabitants of whatever quality or condition, between the ages of sixteen and sixty.

"In case any colony should be suddenly invaded, on motion and request of three magistrates of such colony, the other confederates were immediately to send aid to the colony invaded in men, Massachusetts one hundred, and the other colonies forty-five each, or for a less number, in the same proportion.

"The commissioners, however, were very properly directed, afterwards, to take into consideration the cause of such war or invasion, and if it should appear that the fault was in the colony invaded, such colony was not only to make satisfaction to the invaders, but to bear all the expenses of the war.

The commissioners were also authorised "to frame and establish agreements and orders in general cases of a civil nature, wherein all the plantations were interested, for preserving peace among themselves, and preventing as much as may be all occasions of war, or difference with others, as about the free and speedy passage of justice, in every jurisdiction, to all the confederates equally as to their own, receiving those that remove from one plantation to another, without due certificates.

"It was also very wisely provided in the articles that runaway servants,

ton were at first annexed to the jurisdiction of the courts at Ips-
1643.   wich, till the establishment of a new county which was
called Norfolk, and comprehended Salisbury, Haverhill,
Hampton, Exeter, Portsmouth, and Dover. These towns were
then of such extent as to contain all the lands between the rivers
Merrimack and Pascataqua, The shire town was Salisbury;
but Dover and Portsmouth had always a distinct jurisdiction,
though they were considered as part of this new county; a court
being held in one or the other, sometimes once and sometimes
twice in the year, consisting of one or more of the magistrates or
assistants, and one or more commissioners, chosen by the General
Court out of the principal gentlemen of each town. This was
called the court of associates; and their power extended to
causes of twenty pounds value. From them, there was an appeal to the board of Assistants, which being found inconvenient,
it was, in 1670, ordered to be made to the county court of Norfolk.[1] Causes under twenty shillings in value were settled in
each town, by an Inferior Court, consisting of three persons.
After some time, they had liberty to choose their Associates,
1647.   which was done by the votes of both towns, opened at a
joint meeting of their selectmen, though sometimes they
requested the court to appoint them as before.[2] That mutual
confidence between rulers and people, which springs from the
genius of a republican government, is observable in all their
transactions.*

(1) Mass. General Court Records.   (2) Dover and Portsmouth Records.

and fugitives from justice, should be returned to the colonies where they belonged, or from which they had fled.
  "If any of the confederates should violate any of the articles, or, in any
way injure any one of the other colonies, "such breach of agreement, or injury, was to be considered and ordered" by the commissioners of the other colonies. This confederacy, which was declared to be perpetual, continued
without any essential alteration, until the New-England colonies were deprived of their charter by the arbitrary proceedings of James II. In the year
1648, some of the inhabitants of Rhode-Island requested to be admitted into
the confederacy, but they were informed that the island was within the patent granted to New-Plymouth, and therefore their request was denied."—
Pitkin, Hist. U. S., 50, 51.]

  * In 1652, the number of people in Dover was increased so that they were
allowed by law to send two deputies to the General Court. Hampton continued sending but one till 1669, and Portsmouth till 1672. The names of
the representatives which I have been able to recover, are as follows: [As
the years for which the representatives were chosen, and the names of a
number of them are omitted by Dr. Belknap, his list is left out, and the following, which is nearly complete, substituted.

	Dover.	Portsmouth.	Hampton.
1642	———————	———————	
1643	Edward Starbuck		William Hayward
1644	William Hilton	Stephen Winthrop	William Hayward
1645	William Heath		William Hayward
1646	William Waldron	———————	William Hayward
	Edward Starbuck		William English

This extension of the colony's jurisdiction over New-Hampshire, could not fail of being noticed by the heirs of Mason : but the distractions caused by the civil wars in England were invincible bars to any legal inquiry. The first heir named in Mason's will dying in infancy, the estate descended after the death of the executrix to Robert Tufton, who was not of age till 1650. In two years after this, Joseph Mason came over as agent to the executrix, to look after the interest of her deceased husband. He found the lands at Newichwannock occupied by Richard

	Dover.	Portsmouth.	Hampton.
1647	————————	————————	William English
1648	————————	————————	William Estowe
1649	————————	————————	William Estowe
1650	John Baker	————————	Jeoffry Mingay
1651	————————	————————	Roger Shaw
1652	Valentine Hill		Roger Shaw
1653	Valentine Hill	Bryan Pendleton	Roger Shaw
1654	Richard Waldron Valentine Hill	Bryan Pendleton	Anthony Stanyan
1655	Valentine Hill		Henry Dow
1656	Richard Waldron	————————	Henry Dow
1657	Richard Waldron	————————	Roger Page
1658	Richard Waldron	Bryan Pendleton	Christopher Hussey
1659	Richard Waldron	————————	Christopher Hussey
1660	Richard Waldron	Henry Sherburne Bryan Pendleton (2)	Christopher Hussey
1661	Richard Waldron	Bryan Pendleton	William Fuller
1662	Richard Waldron	————————	Samuel Dalton
1663	Richard Waldron	Bryan Pendleton	William Gerrish
1664	————————	————————	William Gerrish Samuel Dalton (2)
1665	Richard Waldron	Richard Cutt	Samuel Dalton
1666	Richard Waldron	Nathaniel Fryer	Samuel Dalton
1667	Richard Waldron	Elias Stileman	William Fuller
1668	Richard Waldron	Elias Stileman	Robert Page
1669	Richard Waldron	Richard Cutt	Samuel Dalton Joshua Gilman
1670	Richard Waldron Richard Cooke	Richard Cutt	Samuel Dalton
1671	Richard Waldron Richard Cooke	Elias Stileman	Samuel Dalton
1672	Richard Waldron Peter Coffin	Richard Cutt Richard Martyn	Joseph Hussey
1673	Richard Waldron Peter Coffin	Elias Stileman	Samuel Dalton
1674	Richard Waldron Anthony Miller	Richard Cutt	Samuel Dalton
1675	Richard Waldron Anthony Miller	Richard Cutt	Samuel Dalton
1676	Anthony Miller	Richard Cutt	Samuel Dalton
1677	Richard Waldron	Elias Stileman	Thomas Marston
1678	————————	————————	Samuel Dalton
1679	Richard Waldron Peter Coffin	Richard Martyn	Samuel Dalton

Richard Waldron was speaker of the house of deputies or representatives in the years 1666, 1667, 1668, 1673, 1674, 1675 and 1679. A dash under the town against the year shows that no representative was chosen that year.— Where (2) is annexed, it shows that the person was elected for the 2d session of the court. It does not appear that Exeter sent any deputies to court during this union.]

Leader,* against whom he brought actions in the county court of
Norfolk; but a dispute arising whether the lands in question
were within the jurisdiction of Massachusetts, and the court of
Norfolk judging the action not to be within their cognizance, recourse was had to the general court ; who, on this occasion, ordered an accurate survey of the northern bounds of their patent
to be made ; a thing which they had long meditated.[1] A com-
mittee† of the general court, attended by Jonathan Ince, and John
Sherman surveyors, and several Indian guides, went up the river
Merrimack to find the most northerly part thereof, which the Indians told them was at Aquedochtan, the outlet of the lake Winnipiseogee.‡   The latitude of this place was observed to be 43

(1) Massa. Records.

* [One of this name was agent for the Iron Works at Lynn about this time
Lewis, Hist. Lynn, 96.]

† [The committee of the general court were Capt. Edward Johnson, author
of the History of New-England, and Capt. Simon Willard, afterwards an assistant and commander of a portion of the Massachusetts forces in the Indian
war of 1675. The expedition took up nineteen days in the months of July
and August, and the whole expense was not less than £84. The report of
the surveyors, written by a neat chirographist, has been obtained from the
Massachusetts colony files, and a copy of it is here added :
   " The Answer of John Sherman, serjt. at Watertown, and Jonathan Ince,
student at Harvard College, in Cambridge, to Captain Simon Willard and
Captain Edward Johnson, Commissioners of the General Court, held at Boston, May 27, 1652, concerning the Latitude of the Northermost pt. of Merrimack River—
   " Whereas wee John Sherman and Jonathan Ince were procured by the
aforesaid Commissioners to take the latitude of the place abovenamed, Our
Answer is, that at Aquedahcan, the name of the head of Merrimack, where it
issues out of the Lake called Winnapusseakit, upon the first of August, one
thousand, six hundred and fifty two, wee observed and by observation found
that the Latitude of the place was fourty three degrees, fourty minutes and
twelve seconds, besides those minutes which are to be allowed for the three
miles more North wch. run into the Lake. In witnesse whereof, wee have
subscribed our names this nineteenth of October, one thousand, six hundred,
fifty two.   JOHN SHERMAN,
                                                  JONATHAN INCE.
        Jur. coram me,   JOH. ENDECOTT, Gubr.]

‡ [The variations in the orthography of this word, which was probably pro-
nounced *Win-ne-pis-se-ock-ee*, are somewhat remarkable. The following have
occurred in the course of my investigations.
   Winnepisseockegee. Captain Alden's Treaty with Indians, 1690. 3 Coll.
   Winnopisseag. Mather, Magnalia, ii. 513.   [Mass. Hist. Soc. i. 112.
   Wenapesioche. Douglass, Summary, i. 420.
   Winnepasiake. Ibid. i. 423.
   Winnapissiaukee. Hutchinson, Hist. Mass. i. 358.
   Winnepissiaukee. Ibid. ii. 346.
   Winnepissocay. Penhallow, in Coll. N. H. Hist. Soc. i. 112.
   Winnepesiaukee. Trumbull, Hist, Connecticut, ii. 78.
   Winnapuseakit. Sherman and Ince's Report, above.
   Winnipesocket. Bartlett, Narrative of Captivity, 5.
   Winnipishoky. Petition in Moore's Annals of Concord.
   Winnipisioke. MS. Charter of Kingswood.
   Wennepisseoka. MS. Letter of Lieut. Gov. Wentworth.
   Winipisseoca. MS. Records of General Assembly of N. H.
   Winipisinket. Douglass, Summary, i. 456.
   Winipisiakit. Ibid. i. 390.
   Winipisiackit. Ibid. ii, 346.
   Winnipessioke. N. H. Gazette, 18 March, 1789.]

degrees, 40 minutes and 12 seconds, to which three miles being added, made the line of the patent, according to their construction, fall within the lake, in the latitude of 43 degrees, 43 minutes and 12 seconds. Two experienced ship-masters, Jonas Clarke and Samuel Andrews, were then dispatched to 1653. the eastern shore, who found the same degrees, minutes, and seconds, on the northern point of an island in Casco Bay, called the Upper Clapboard Island. An east and west line, drawn through these points from the Atlantic to the South sea, was therefore supposed to be the northern boundary of the Massachusetts patent, within which the whole claim of Mason, and the greater part of that of Gorges were comprehended. When this grand point was determined, the court were of opinion, that " some " lands at Newichwannock, with the river, were by agreement of " Sir Ferdinando Gorges and others, apportioned to Captain Ma- " son, and that he also had right by purchase of the Indians, as " also by possession and improvement ;" and they ordered " a " quantity of land proportionable to his disbursements, with the " privilege of the river, to be laid out to his heirs." The agent made no attempt to recover any other part of the estate ; but having tarried long enough in the country to observe the temper of the government, and the management used in the determination of his suit, he returned ; and the estate was given up for lost unless the government of England should interpose.*

* [The 9 June, 1654, there was a storme of thunder and haile, such as hath not been heard of in N. E. since the first planting thereof, which haile fell in the bounds of Hampton betwixt the towne and the mills at ye falles—the which haile was so violent as that where the strength of the storm went, it shaved the leaves, twigs and fruit from the trees, and beat down the corne, both rye and Indian, and pease and other things, so battering and burying the same as that men had beaten it down with thrashing instruments ; the haile being to admiration for the multitude thereof, so as that in some places it remained after the storm was over, 12 inches in thickness above the ground, and was not all dissolved 2 days after the storme in many places, as we are informed by many eye witnesses and many of which haile were said to be 3 or 4 inches in length. Hampton Town Records, copied by Mr. Joshua Coffin, S. H. S. Mass.

1656. The delusion respecting witchcraft, which extended itself generally throughout New-England, appeared in a few instances in New-Hampshire. Mr. Adams, in his Annals of Portsmouth, gives the following account of one case which occurred in that town, this year.

" Goodwife Walford was brought before the court of assistants for this offence, upon the complaint of Susannah Trimmings. A recital of the testimony will shew how far a disordered imagination contributed to make a person believe she was bewitched ; and what degree of credulity was necessary, to fix the offence upon the person accused. Mrs. Trimmings testified, " As I was going home on Sunday night, the 30th of March, I heard a rustling in the woods, which I supposed to be occasioned by swine, and presently there appeared a woman, whom I apprehended to be old Goodwife Walford. She asked me to lend her a pound of cotton ; I told her I had but two pounds in the house, and I would not spare any to my mother. She said I had better have done it, for I was going a great journey, but should never come there. She then left me, and I was struck as with a clap of fire on the back ; and she vanished toward the water side, in my apprehension, in the shape of a cat. She had on her head a white linen hood, tied under her chin, and her waist-

10

During the commonwealth, and the protectorate of Cromwell, there could be no hope of relief, as the family had always been attached to the royal cause, and the colony stood high in the favor of the parliament and of Cromwell. But the restoration of 1660. King Charles the second encouraged Tufton, who now took the surname of Mason, to look up to the throne for favor and assistance. For though the plan of colonization adopted by his grandfather was in itself chimerical, and proved fruitless, yet he had expended a large estate in the prosecution of it, which must have been wholly lost to his heirs, unless they could recover the possession of his American territories. Full of this idea, Mason petitioned the king ; setting forth ' the encroachment of the ' Massachusetts colony upon his lands, their making grants and ' giving titles to the inhabitants, and thereby disposessing him and keeping him out of his right.' The king referred the petition to to his attorney-general Sir Geoffrey Palmer, who reported that

coat and petticoat were red, with an old green apron, and a black hat upon her head." Oliver Trimmings, her husband, said, " my wife came home in a sad condition. She passed by me with her child in her arms, laid the child on the bed, sat down on the chest, and leaned upon her elbow. Three times I asked her how she did. She could not speak. I took her in my arms, and held her up, and repeated the question. She forced breath, and something stopped in her throat, as if it would have stopped her breath. I unlaced her clothes, and soon she spake, and said, Lord have mercy upon me, this wicked woman will kill me. I asked her what woman. She said Goodwife Walford. I tried to persuade her, it was only her weakness. She told me no, and related as above, that her back was as a flame of fire, and her lower parts, were, as it were, numb and without feeling. I pinched her, and she felt not. She continued that night, and the day and night following, very ill, and is still bad of her limbs, and complains still daily of it."

Nicholas Rowe testified, " that Jane Walford, shortly after she was accused, came to the deponent in bed, in the evening, and put her hand upon his breast, so that he could not speak, and was in great pain till the next day. By the light of the fire in the next room, it appeared to be Goody Walford, but she did not speak. She repeated her visit about a week after, and did as before ; but said nothing."

Eliza Barton deposed, " that she saw Susannah Trimmings at the time she was ill, and her face was colored and spotted with several colors. She told the deponent the story, who replied that it was nothing but her fantasy ; her eyes looked as if they had been scalded."

John Puddington deposed, that " three years since, Goodwife Walford come to his mother's. She said that her own husband called her an old witch ; and when she came to her cattle, her husband would bid her begone, for she did overlook the cattle, which is as much as to say in our country, bewitching."

Agnes Puddington deposes, that " on the 11th of April, the wife of W. Evans came to her house, and lay there all night ; and a little after sunset the deponent saw a yellowish cat ; and Mrs. E. said she was followed by a cat, wherever she went. John came and saw a cat in the garden—took down his gun to shoot her ; the cat got up on a tree, and the gun would not take fire, and afterward the cock would not stand. She afterwards saw three cats,— the yellow one vanished away on the plain ground ; she could not tell which way they went."

On the 20 October, 1657, " a boat going out of Hampton River, was cast away, and the persons drowned, who were eight in number, who all perished in the Sea." Records of Norfolk County. The records give the names of seven who were lost, viz. Em. Hilliar, John Philbrick, Anne Philbrick, his wife, Sarah Philbrick, their daughter, Alice Cox, wife of Moses Cox, John Cox, his son, and Robert Read.]

" Robert Mason, grandson and heir to Captain John Mason, had " a good and legal title to the province of New-Hamp- Nov. 8. " shire."[1] Nothing farther was done at this time, nor was the matter mentioned in the letter which the king soon after sent to the colony, though some offensive things in their conduct were therein reprehended, and divers alterations enjoined. [2] 1662. But the directions contained in this letter not being strictly attended to, and complaints being made to the king, of disputes which had arisen in divers parts of New-England concerning the limits of jurisdiction, and addresses having been presented by several persons, praying for the royal interposition ; a commission was issued under the great seal to Colonel Richard Nicholls, Sir Robert Carr, knight, George Cartwright* and Samuel 1664. Maverick, esquires, impowering them " to visit the several Apr. 25. " colonies of New-England ; to examine and determine all com- " plaints and appeals in matters civil, military and criminal ; to " provide for the peace and security of the country, according to " their good and sound discretion, and to such instructions as they " should receive from the king, and to certify him of their pro- " ceedings."[3] †

This commission was highly disrelished by the colony, as inconsistent with the rights and privileges which they enjoyed by their charter, and which the king had sacredly promised to confirm. It is therefore no wonder that the commissioners were treated with much coolness at their arrival ; but they severely repaid it in their report to the king.[4]

(1) MS. in Sup. Court files.   (2) Hutch. Coll. of papers, p. 377.   (3) Hutch. Hist. Mass. vol. i. p. 535.   (4) Hutch. Coll. papers, 417.

* [This name is Carteret in the former editions, but it should doubtless be Cartwright as will appear from 2 Coll. Mass. Hist. Soc. viii. 58-90.]

† [Rev. Timothy Dalton, minister of Hampton, died 28 December, 1661, being somewhat advanced in years.   Mr. Savage, in Winthrop, ii. 28, has given him descendants, but none are named in a copy of his last will and testament which I have seen.   He gave a portion of his property to Samuel, the son of Philemon Dalton, who was probably brother to the minister, and from a sermon of Rev. Jonathan French of North-Hampton, 1820, it appears that the ministerial fund in that town and Hampton arose from a liberal donation he made to the last named town.   Mrs. Ruth Dalton, his widow, died at Hampton, 12 May, 1666.   Johnson (Hist. N. E. 135) has bestowed some verses upon him, which will conclude this brief note on one of the earliest and most worthy of the ecclesiastical fathers of New-Hampshire.

" DOULTON doth teach perspicuously and sound,
" With wholesome truths of Christ thy flock doth feed,
" Thy honour with thy labour doth abound,
" Age crounes thy head in righteousnesse, proceed
" To batter doune, root up, and quite destroy
" All Heresies and Errors, that draw back
" Unto perdition, and Christ's folk annoy ;
" To warre for him, thou weapons dost not lack :
" Long dayes to see, that long'd-for day to come,
" Of *Babel's* fall, and *Israel's* quiet peace :
" Thou yet maist live of dayes so great a sum
" To see this work, let not thy warfare cease."]

In their progress through the country, they came to Pascataqua, and inquired into the bounds of Mason's patent. They heard
June. the allegation of Wheelwright, who when banished by the colony, was permitted to reside immediately beyond what was called the bound-house, three large miles to the northward of the river Merrimack. They took the affidavit of Henry Jocelyn concerning the agreement between Governor Cradock and Captain Mason, that the river should be the boundary of their respective patents. They made no determination of this controversy in their report to the king ; but having called together the inhabi-
Oct. 10. tants of Portsmouth, Sir Robert Carr, in the name of the rest, told them that " they would release them from the " government of Massachusetts, whose jurisdiction should come " no farther than the bound-house."[1] They then proceeded to appoint justices of the peace and other officers, with power to act according to the laws of England, and such laws of their own as were not repugnant thereto, until the king's pleasure should be farther known.

There had always been a party here who were disaffected to the government of Massachusetts.[2] One of the most active among them was Abraham Corbett, of Portsmouth, who, since the arrival of the commissioners at Boston, and probably by authority derived from them, had taken upon him to issue warrants in the king's name on several occasions, which was construed a high misdemeanor, as he had never been commissioned by the authority of the colony.[3] Being called to account by the general court, he was admonished, fined five pounds, and committed till the sentence was performed. Irritated by this severity, he was the fitter instrument for the purpose of the commissioners, who employed him to frame a petition to the king in the name of the four towns, complaining of the usurpation of Massachusetts over them, and praying to be released from their tyranny. Corbett, in a secret manner, procured several persons both in Portsmouth and Dover to subscribe this petition, but the most of those to whom he offered it refused.

The sensible part of the inhabitants now saw with much concern, that they were in danger of being reduced to the same unhappy state, which they had been in before their union with the colony. Awed by the supercilious behaviour of the commissioners, they knew not at first how to act ; for to oppose the king's authority was construed treason, and it was said that Sir Robert Carr had threatened a poor old man with death for no other crime than forbidding his grandchild to open a door to them. But when the rumor was spread that a petition was drawn, and that Corbett was procuring subscribers, the people, no longer able to bear the abuse, earnestly applied to the general court, praying " that in

(1) Mass. Records.   (2) Hutch. Coll. papers, 488.   (3) Mass. Records.

" some orderly way they might have an opportunity to clear them-
" selves of so great and unjust aspersions, as were by this petition,
" drawn in their name, cast upon the government under which
" they were settled; and also to manifest their sense of such per-
" fidious actions, lest by their silence it should be concluded they
" were of the same mind with those who framed the petition."
In consequence of this petition, the court commissioned Thomas
Danforth, Eleazar Lusher, and Major General Leverett to inquire
into the matter, and settle the peace in these places according to
their best discretion.

These gentlemen came to Portsmouth, and having assembled
the inhabitants, and published their commission, they told them
that they were informed of a petition subscribed in behalf
of that and the neighboring towns, complaining of the   Oct. 9.
government; and desired them if they had any just grievances to
let them be known, and report should be immediately made to the
general court. The next day, they assembled the people of Dover and made the same challenge. Both towns respectively protested against the petition, and professed full satisfaction with the
government, which they signified in addresses to the court. Dudley, the minister of Exeter, certified under his hand to the committee, that the people of that town had no concern directly nor
indirectly with the obnoxious petition.* They received also full
satisfaction with regard to Hampton; a certificate of which might
have been obtained, if they had thought it necessary.

They then proceeded to summon Corbett before them for seditious behaviour; but he eluded the search that was made for him,
and they were obliged to leave a warrant with an officer to cite
him to the court at Boston. The commissioners had now gone
over into the province of Maine, from whence Sir Robert Carr in
their name sent a severe reprimand to this committee, forbidding
them to proceed against such persons as had subscribed the petition, and inclosing a copy of a letter which the said commissioners
had written to the governor and council on the same subject.

The committee returned and reported their proceedings to the
court, and about the same time, the commissioners came from their
eastern tour to Boston; where the court desired a conference
with them, but received such an answer from Sir Robert Carr as
determined them not to repeat their request. A warrant was then
issued by the secretary, in the name of the whole court, to apprehend Corbett and bring him before the governor and magistrates,

---

* [The certificate of Mr. Dudley, in the files of the Massachusetts colony
records, is as follows : " This may certify whom it may concern, that concerning the Question that is in hand, whether the town of Exeter hath subscribed to that petition sent to his Majesty for the taking of Portsmouth, Dover, Hampton and Exeter under his immediate government, I do affirm to my
best apprehension and that by more than probable conjecture, that the town
of Exeter hath no hand in that petition directly or indirectly. Witness my
hand, 10. 8. 65.   SAMUEL DUDLEY."]

" to answer for his tumultuous and seditious practices against the
       " government." The next spring, he was seized and
1666. brought before them ; and after a full hearing was adjudg-
May 23. ed guilty of sedition, and exciting others to discontent
with the government and laws, and of keeping a disorderly house
of entertainment, for which crimes he was sentenced to give a bond
of one hundred pounds, with security for his peaceable behaviour
and obedience to the laws ; he was prohibited retailing liquors ;
disabled from bearing any office in the town or commonwealth,
during the pleasure of the court ; and obliged to pay a fine of
twenty pounds, and five pounds for the costs of his prosecution.

This severity in vindication of their charter-rights, they thought
fit to temper with something that had the appearance of submission to the royal commands. The king's pleasure had been signified to the commissioners, that the harbors should be fortified.
This instruction came to hand while they were at Pascataqua, and
they immediately issued warrants to the four towns, requiring
them to meet at a time and place appointed to receive his majesty's orders.[1] One of these warrants was sent by express to Boston, from whence two officers were dispatched by the governor
and council to forbid the towns on their peril to meet, or obey the
commands of the commissioners. But by their own authority,
they ordered a committee to look out the most convenient place
for a fortification, upon whose report " the neck of land on the
" eastward of the Great Island, where a small fort had been al-
" ready built, was sequestered for the purpose, taking in the Great
" Rock, and from thence all the easterly part of the said island." [2]
The court of associates being impowered to hear and determine
the claims of those who pretended any title to this land ; a claim
was entered by George Walton,* but rejected ; and the appropriation confirmed. The customs and imposts on goods imported
into the harbor were applied to the maintenance of the fort, and
the trained bands of Great-Island and Kittery-Point were discharged from all other duty to attend the service of it, under
Richard Cutt, esquire, who was appointed captain.

The people of Massachusetts have, both in former and latter
times, been charged with disloyalty to the king in their conduct
towards these commissioners, and their disregard of authority derived from the same source with their charter. To account for
their conduct on this occasion, we must consider the ideas they
had of their political connexion with the parent state. They had

(1) Hutch. Coll. papers, 419.   (2) Mass. Records.

* [George Walton appears to have been of Exeter in 1639, having previously resided at Pascataqua. He finally settled on Great Island, where he
died in 1686, aged about 71 years. See Mather, ii. Magnalia, 393. Adams,
Annals of Portsmouth, 44, 398. Coll. N. H. Hist. Soc. i. 322. It is probable
that he was the father of Col. Shadrach Walton, who is several times mentioned in this history.]

been forced from it by persecution : they came at their own charges into a wilderness, claimed indeed by the crown of England ; but really in possession of its native lords ; from whom they had purchased the soil and sovereignty, which gave them a title, considered in a moral view, superior to the grant of any European prince. For convenience only, they had solicited and accepted a patent from the crown, which in their opinion constituted the only bond of union between them and their prince, by which the nature and extent of their allegiance to him was to be determined. This patent they regarded as a solemn compact, by which the king had granted them undisturbed possession of the soil, and power of government within certain limits ; on condition that they should settle the country, christianize the natives, yield a fifth of all gold and silver mines to the crown, and make no laws repugnant to those of England. They had, on their part, sacredly performed these conditions ; and therefore concluded that the grant of title, property and dominion which the crown had made to them was irrevocable. And although they acknowledged themselves subjects of the reigning prince, and owned a dependence on the royal authority ; yet they understood it to be only through the medium of their charter.

The appointment of commissioners who were to act within the same limits, independently of this authority, and to receive appeals from it ; whose rule of conduct was not established law, but their own " good and sound discretion," was regarded as a dangerous stretch of royal power, militating with and superseding their charter. If the royal authority was destined to flow through the patent, it could not regularly be turned into another channel : if they were to be governed by laws made and executed by officers of their own choosing, they could not at the same time be governed by the " discretion" of men in whose appointment they had no voice, and over whom they had no control. Two ruling powers in the same state was a solecism which they could not digest. The patent was neither forfeited nor revoked ; but the king had solemnly promised to confirm it, and it subsisted in full force. The commission therefore was deemed an usurpation and infringement of those chartered rights, which had been solemnly pledged on the one part, dearly purchased and justly paid for on the other. They regarded " a royal donation under the great seal (to use their own words) as the greatest security that could be had in human affairs ;"[1] and they had confidence in the justice of the supreme ruler, that if they held what they in their consciences thought to be their rights, and performed the engagements by which they had acquired them, they should enjoy the protection of his providence,* though they should be obliged to abandon the

(1) Hutch. Hist. Mass. vol. i. p. 543.

* " Keep to your patent. Your patent was a royal grant indeed ; and it is " instrumentally your defence and security. Recede from that, one way or

country, which they had planted with so much labor and expense, and seek a new settlement in some other part of the globe.

These were the principles which they had imbibed, which they openly avowed and on which they acted. Policy might have dictated to them the same flexibility of conduct, and softness of expression, by which the other colonies on this occasion gained the royal favor.   But they had so long held the sole and uninterrupted sovereignty, in which they had been indulged by the late popular government in England ; and were so fully convinced it was their right ; that they chose rather to risk the loss of all, than to make any concessions; thereby exposing themselves farther to the malice of their enemies and the vengeance of power.

The commissioners, having finished their business, were recalled by the order of the king, who was much displeased with the ill treatment they had received from the Massachusetts government, which was the more heinous, as the colonies of Plymouth, Rhode-Island and Connecticut had treated the commission with acknowledged respect.   By a letter to the colony, he commanded

Apr. 10. them to send over four or five agents, promising " to hear " in person, all the allegations, suggestions, and pretences to right " or favor, that could be made on behalf the colony," intimating that he was far from desiring to invade their charter ; and commanding that all things should remain as the commissioners had settled them until his farther order ; and that those persons who had been imprisoned for petitioning or applying to them should be released.[1] The court, however, continued to exercise jurisdiction, appoint officers, and execute the laws in these towns as they had done for twenty-five years, to the general satisfaction of the people who were united with them in principles and affection.

This affection was demonstrated by their ready concurrence with the proposal for a general collection, for the purpose of

1669. erecting a new brick building* at Harvard college, the old wooden one being small and decayed.   The town of Portsmouth, which was now become the richest, made a subscription of sixty pounds per annum for seven years; and after five years, passed a town vote to carry this engagement into effect.— Dover gave thirty-two, and Exeter ten pounds for the same laudable purpose.[2]

The people of Portsmouth, having for some time employed

1671. Joshua Moodey as a preacher among them, and erected a new meeting house, proceeded to settle him in regular

(1) Hutch. p. 547.   (2) Harvard College Records.

" the other, and you will expose yourself to the wrath of God and the rage of
" man.   Fix upon the patent, and stand for the liberties and immunities con-
" ferred upon you therein ; and you have GOD and the king with you, both
" a good cause and a good interest : and may with good conscience set your
" foot against any foot of pride and violence that shall come against you."—
President Oakes's Election Sermon, 1673.

* This building was erected in 1672, and consumed by fire in 1764.

order.   A church consisting of nine brethren* was first gathered; then the general court having been duly informed of it, and
having signified their approbation, according to the established
practice, Moodey was ordained in the presence of Governor Leverett and several of the magistrates.[1] †

The whole attention of the government in England being at
this time taken up with things that more immediately concerned themselves, nothing of moment relating to Ma-   1674.
son's interest was transacted.   He became discouraged, and
joined with the heirs of Gorges in proposing an alienation of their
respective rights in the provinces of New-Hampshire and Maine
to the crown, to make a government for the duke of Monmouth.
The duke himself was greatly pleased with the scheme, as he
had been told that an annual revenue of five thousand pounds or
more might be collected from these provinces.   But by the more
faithful representations of some persons who were well acquainted
with the country, he was induced to lay aside the project.   Many
complaints were made against the government of Massachusetts;
and it was thought to be highly expedient that more severe measures should be used with them; but the Dutch wars, and other
foreign transactions, prevented any determination concerning
them, till the country was involved in all the horrors of a general
war with the natives.[2]

CHAPTER V.

Remarks on the temper and manners of the Indians.   The first general war
with them called Philip's war.

At the time of the first discovery of the river Pascataqua by
Captain Smith, it was found that the native inhabitants of these
parts differed not in language, manners, nor government, from
their eastern or western neighbors.   Though they were divided
into several tribes, each of which had a distinct sachem, yet they
all owned subjection to a sovereign prince, called Bashaba, whose
residence was at Penobscot.   It was soon after found that the

(1) Portsmouth Church Records.   [Adams, Annals of Portsmouth, 51—55,
where is a particular account of the measures preparatory to the ordination of
Mr. Moodey.]   (2) Hutch. Collection of papers, 451, 472.

* Joshua Moodey, John Cutt, Richard Cutt, Richard Martyn, Elias Stileman, Samuel Haynes, James Pendleton, John Fletcher, John Tucker.

† [1671. April 1.   A great storme of driving snow came out of the N. W.
and drove up in drifts about 6 feet deep, as appeared by those that measured
the banks of snow.   For the space of 14 days after, it was a sad time of rain,
not one whole fair day, and much damage done to mills and other things by
the flood which followed.   Town Records of Hampton.]

11

Tarrateens, who lived farther eastward, had invaded his country, surprised and slain him, and all the people in his neighborhood, and carried off his women, leaving no traces of his authority. [1] Upon which the subordinate sachems, having no head to unite them, and each one striving for the pre-eminence, made war among themselves ; by which means many of their people, and much of their provision were destroyed. When Sir Richard Hawkins visited the coast in 1615, this war was at its height; and to this succeeded a pestilence, which carried them off in such numbers that the living were not able to bury the dead ; but their bones remained at the places of their habitations for several years. [2] During this pestilence, Richard Vines and several others, whom Sir Ferdinando Gorges had hired, at a great expense, to tarry in the country through the winter, lived among them and lodged in their cabins, without receiving the least injury in their health, " not so much as feeling their heads to ache the whole time." [3] By such singular means did divine providence prepare the way for the peaceable entrance of the Europeans into this land.

When the first settlements were made, the remains of two tribes had their habitations on the several branches of the river Pascataqua ; one of their sachems lived at the falls of Squamscot, and the other at those of Newichwannock; their head quarters being generally seated in places convenient for fishing. Both these, together with several inland tribes, who resided at Pawtucket and Winnipiseogee, acknowledged subjection to Passaconaway the great sagamore of Pannukog, or (as it is commonly pronounced) Penacook. He excelled the other sachems in sagacity, duplicity and moderation ; but his principal qualification was his skill in some of the secret operations of nature, which gave him the reputation of a sorcerer, and extended his fame and influence among all the neighboring tribes. They believed that it was in his power to make water burn, and trees dance, and to metamorphose himself into flame ; that in winter he could raise a green leaf from the ashes of a dry one, and a living serpent from the skin of one that was dead."[4]

An English gentleman, who had been much conversant among the Indians, was invited in 1660, to a great dance and feast ; on which occasion, the elderly men, in songs or speeches recite their histories, and deliver their sentiments, and advice, to the younger. At this solemnity, Passaconaway, being grown old, made his farewell speech to his children and people ; in which, as a dying man, he warned them to take heed how they quarrelled with their English neighbors ; for though they might do them some damage, yet it would prove the means of their own destruction. He told them that he had been a bitter enemy to the English, and by the

(1) Smith's Voyage. (2) Gorges's Narrative, p. 17, 54.   Prince's Annals. (3) Gorges, page 12. (4) Hutch. Hist. Mass. vol. i. p. 474.

arts of sorcery had tried his utmost to hinder their settlement and increase; but could by no means succeed. This caution perhaps often repeated, had such an effect, that upon the breaking out of the Indian war fifteen years afterwards, Wonolanset, his son and successor, withdrew himself and his people into some remote place, that they might not be drawn into the quarrel.[1]

Whilst the British nations had been distracted with internal convulsions, and had endured the horrors of a civil war, produced by the same causes which forced the planters of New-England to quit the land of their nativity; this wilderness had been to them a quiet habitation. They had struggled with many hardships; but providence had smiled upon their undertaking; their settlements were extended and their churches multiplied. There had been no remarkable quarrel with the savages, except the short war with the Pequods, who dwelt in the south-east part of Connecticut. They being totally subdued in 1637, the dread and terror of the English kept the other nations quiet for near forty years. During which time, the New-England colonies being confederated for their mutual defence, and for maintaining the public peace, took great pains to propagate the gospel among the natives, and bring them to a civilized way of living, which, with respect to some, proved effectual; others refused to receive the missionaries, and remained obstinately prejudiced against the English. Yet the object of their hatred was at the same time the object of their fear; which led them to forbear acts of hostility, and to preserve an outward shew of friendship, to their mutual interest.

Our historians have generally represented the Indians in a most odious light, especially when recounting the effects of their ferocity. Dogs, caitiffs, miscreants and hell-hounds, are the politest names which have been given them by some writers, who seem to be in a passion at the mentioning their cruelties, and at other times speak of them with contempt.[2] Whatever indulgence may be allowed to those who wrote in times when the mind was vexed with their recent depredations and inhumanities, it ill becomes us to cherish an inveterate hatred of the unhappy natives. Religion teaches us a better temper, and providence has now put an end to the controversy, by their almost total extirpation. We should therefore proceed with calmness in recollecting their past injuries, and forming our judgment of their character.

It must be acknowledged that human depravity appeared in these unhappy creatures in a most shocking view. The principles of education and the refinements of civilized life either lay a check upon our vicious propensities, or disguise our crimes; but among them human wickedness was seen in its naked deformity.

(1) Hubbard's printed Narrative, page 9, 31. (2) Hubbard's Narrative and Mather's Magnalia.

Yet, bad as they were, it will be difficult to find them guilty of any crime which cannot be paralleled among civilized nations.

They are always described as remarkably *cruel*; and it cannot be denied that this disposition indulged to the greatest excess, strongly marks their character. We are struck with horror, when we hear of their binding the victim to the stake, biting off his nails, tearing out his hair by the roots, pulling out his tongue, boring out his eyes, sticking his skin full of lighted pitch-wood, half roasting him at the fire, and then making him run for their diversion, till he faints and dies under the blows which they give him on every part of his body. But is it not as dreadful to read of an unhappy wretch, sewed up in a sack full of serpents and thrown into the sea, or broiled in a red hot iron chair; or mangled by lions and tigers, after having spent his strength to combat them for the diversion of the spectators in an amphitheatre? and yet these were punishments among the Romans in the politest ages of the empire. What greater cruelty is there in the American tortures, than in confining a man in a trough, and daubing him with honey that he may be stung to death by wasps and other venomous insects; or fleaing him alive and stretching out his skin before his eyes, which modes of punishment were not inconsistent with the softness and elegance of the ancient court of Persia? or, to come down to modern times; what greater misery can there be in the Indian executions, than in racking a prisoner on a wheel, and breaking his bones one by one with an iron bar; or placing his legs in a boot and driving in wedges one after another; which tortures are still, or have till lately been used in some European kingdoms? I forbear to name the torments of the inquisition, because they seem to be beyond the stretch of *human* invention. If civilized nations, and those who profess the most merciful religion that ever blessed the world, have practised these cruelties, what could be expected of men who were strangers to every degree of refinement either civil or mental?

The Indians have been represented as *revengeful*. When any person was killed, the nearest relative thought himself bound to be the avenger of blood, and never left seeking, till he found an opportunity to execute his purpose. Whether in a state, where government is confessedly so feeble as among them, such a conduct is not justifiable, and even countenanced by the Jewish law may deserve our consideration.[1]

The *treachery* with which these people are justly charged, is exactly the same disposition which operates in the breach of solemn treaties made between nations which call themselves christians. Can it be more criminal in an Indian, than in an European, not to think himself bound by promises and oaths extorted from him when under duress?

(1) Numbers, ch. 35, v. 19.   Deuteronomy, ch. 19, v. 12.

Their *jealousy and hatred* of their English neighbors may easily be accounted for, if we allow them to have the same feelings with ourselves. How natural is it for us to form a disagreeable idea of a whole nation, from the bad conduct of some individuals with whom we are acquainted ? and though others of them may be of a different character, yet will not that prudence which is esteemed a virtue, lead us to suspect the fairest appearances, as used to cover the most fraudulent designs, especially if pains are taken by the most politic among us, to forment such jealousies to subserve their own ambitious purposes ?

Though the greater part of the English settlers came hither with religious views, and fairly purchased their lands of the Indians, yet it cannot be denied that some, especially in the eastern parts of New-England, had lucrative views only ; and from the beginning used fraudulent methods in trade with them. Such things were indeed disallowed by the government, and would always have been punished if the Indians had made complaint : but they knew only the law of retaliation, and when an injury was received, it was never forgotten till revenged. Encroachments made on their lands, and fraud committed in trade, afforded sufficient grounds for a quarrel, though at ever so great a length of time ; and kept alive a perpetual jealousy of the like treatment again.*

Such was the temper of the Indians of New-England when the first general war began. It was thought by the English in that day, that Philip, sachem of the Wompanoags, a   1675. crafty and aspiring man, partly by intrigue, and partly by example, excited them to such a general combination. He was the son of Massassoit, the nearest sachem to the colony of Plymouth, with whom he had concluded a peace, which he maintained more through fear than good will, as long as he lived. His son and immediate successor Alexander, preserved the same external show of friendship ; but died with choler on being detected in a plot against them. Philip, it is said, dissembled his hostile purposes ; he was ready, on every suspicion of his infidelity, to renew his submission, and testify it even by the delivery of his arms, till he had secretly infused a cruel jealousy into many of the neighboring Indians ; which excited them to attempt the recovering their country, by extirpating the new possessors. The plot, it is said, was discovered before it was ripe for execution : and as he could no longer promise himself security under the mask of friendship, he was constrained to shew himself in his true charac-

* Mons. du Pratz gives nearly the same account of the Indians on the Mississippi. " There needs nothing but prudence and good sense to pursuade " these people to what is reasonable, and to preserve their friendship without " interruption. We may safely affirm, that the differences we have had with " them have been more owing to the French than to them. When they are " treated insolently, or oppressively, they have no less sensibility of injuries " than others." History of Louisiana, lib. 4, cap. 3.

ter, and accordingly began hostilities upon the plantation of Swanzey, in the colony of Plymouth, in the month of June, 1675.

Notwithstanding this general opinion, it may admit of some doubt, whether a single sachem, whose authority was limited, could have such an extensive influence over tribes so remote and unconnected with him as the eastern Indians; much more improbable is it, that those in Virginia should have joined in the confederacy, as it hath been intimated. The Indians never travelled to any greater distance than their hunting required; and so ignorant were they of the geography of their country, that they imagined New-England to be an island,[1] and could tell the name of an inlet or strait by which they supposed it was separated from the main land. But what renders it more improbable that Philip was so active an instrument in exciting this war, is the constant tradition among the posterity of those people who lived near him, and were familiarly conversant with him, and with those of his Indians who survived the war : which is, that he was forced on by the fury of his young men, sorely against his own judgment and that of his chief counsellors; and that as he foresaw that the English would, in time, establish themselves and extirpate the Indians, so he thought that the making war upon them would only hasten the destruction of his own people. It was always a very common, and sometimes a just excuse with the Indians, when charged with breach of faith, that the old men were not able to restrain the younger from signalizing their valor, and gratifying their revenge, though they disapproved their rashness. This want of restraint was owing to the weakness of their government; their sachems having but the shadow of magistratical authority.

The inhabitants of Bristol shew a particular spot where Philip received the news of the first Englishmen that were killed, with so much sorrow as to cause him to weep; a few days before which he had rescued one who had been taken by his Indians, and privately sent him home.[2] Whatever credit may be given to this account, so different from the current opinion, it must be owned, that in such a season of general confusion as the first war occasioned, fear and jealousy might create many suspicions, which would soon be formed into reports of a general confederacy, through Philip's contrivance; and it is to be noted that the principal histories of this war, (Increase Mather's and Hubbard's) were printed in 1676 and 1677, when the strangest reports were easily credited, and the people were ready to believe every thing that was bad of so formidable a neighbor as Philip. But as the fact cannot now be precisely ascertained, I shall detain the reader no longer from the real causes of the war in these eastern parts.

There dwelt near the river Saco, a sachem named Squando,

(1) Hubbard's Narrative, page 12. Neal's Hist. N. E. vol. i. p. 21.   (2) Callender's Century Sermon, p. 78.

a noted enthusiast, a leader in the devotions of their religion, and one who pretended to a familiar intercourse with the invisible world. These qualifications rendered him a person of the highest dignity, importance and influence among all the eastern Indians. His squaw passing along the river in a canoe, with her infant child, was met by some rude sailors, who having heard that the Indian children could swim as naturally as the young of the brutal kind, in a thoughtless and unguarded humor overset the canoe. The child sunk, and the mother instantly diving fetched it up alive, but the child dying soon after, its death was imputed to the treatment it had received from the seamen ; and Squando was so provoked that he conceived a bitter antipathy to the English, and employed his great art and influence to excite the Indians against them.[1] Some other injuries were alleged as the ground of the quarrel ; and, considering the interested views and irregular lives of many of the eastern settlers, their distance from the seat of government, and the want of due subordination among them, it is not improbable that a great part of the blame of the eastern war belonged to them.

The first alarm of the war in Plymouth colony spread great consternation among the distant Indians, and held them awhile in suspense what part to act ; for there had been a long external friendship subsisting between them and the English, and they were afraid of provoking so powerful neighbors. But the seeds of jealousy and hatred had been so effectually sown, that the crafty and revengeful, and those who were ambitious of doing some exploits, soon found means to urge them on to an open rupture ; so that within twenty days after Philip had begun the war at the southward, the flame broke out in the most northeasterly part of the country, at the distance of two hundred miles.[2]

The English inhabitants about the river Kennebeck, hearing of the insurrection in Plymouth colony, determined to make trial of the fidelity of their Indian neighbors, by requesting them to deliver their arms. They made a show of compliance ; but in doing it, committed an act of violence on a Frenchman, who lived in an English family ; which being judged an offence, both by the English and the elder Indians, the offender was seized ; but upon a promise, with security, for his future good behaviour, his life was spared, and some of them consented to remain as hostages ; who soon made their escape, and joined with their fellows in robbing the house of Purchas, an ancient planter at Pegypscot.

The quarrel being thus begun, and their natural hatred of the English, and jealousy of their designs, having risen to a great height under the malignant influence of Squando and other leading men ; and being encouraged by the example of the western Indians,

(1) Hubbard, [Wars with the Eastern Indians, p. 61.]   Magnalia, lib. 7, p. 55.   (2) Hubbard, [Indian Wars] page 13.

who were daily making depredations on the colonies of Plymouth, and Massachusetts; they took every opportunity to rob and murder the people in the scattered settlements of the province of Maine; and having dispersed themselves into many small parties, that they might be the more extensively mischievous, in the month of September, they approached the plantations at Pascataqua, and made their first onset at Oyster river, then a part of the town of Dover, but now Durham. Here, they burned two houses belonging to two persons named Chesley; killed two men in a canoe, and carried away two captives; both of whom soon after made their escape. About the same time, a party of four laid in ambush near the road between Exeter and Hampton, where they killed one,* and took another,† who made his escape. Within a few days an assault was made on the house of one Tozer at Newichwannock, wherein were fifteen women and children, all of whom, except two, were saved by the intrepidity of a girl of eighteen. She first seeing the Indians as they advanced to the house, shut the door and stood against it, till the others escaped to the next house, which was better secured. The Indians chopped the door to pieces with their hatchets, and then entering, they knocked her down, and leaving her for dead, went in pursuit of the others, of whom two children, who could not get over the fence, fell into their hands. The adventurous heroine recovered, and was perfectly healed of her wound.[1]

The two following days, they made several appearances on both sides of the river, using much insolence, and burning two houses and three barns, with a large quantity of grain. Some shot were exchanged without effect, and a pursuit was made after them into the woods by eight men, but night obliged them to return without success. Five or six houses were burned at Oyster river, and two more men killed.‡ These daily insults could not be borne without indignation and reprisal. About twenty young men, chiefly of Dover, obtained leave of Major Waldron, then commander of the militia, to try their skill and courage with the Indians in their own way.[2] Having scattered themselves in the woods, a small party of them discovered five Indians in a field near a deserted house, some of whom were gathering corn, and others kindling a fire to roast it. The men were at such a distance from their fellows that they could make no signal to them without danger of a discovery; two of them, therefore, crept along

(1) Hubbard, [Wars with Eastern Indians] p. 19.   (2) [Hubbard, Eastern Wars, 20.]   (3) Hubbard, [Eastern Wars] page 21.

* [Goodman Robinson, of Exeter, who, with his son, was going to Hampton. He was shot through his back, the bullet having pierced through his body. The son escaped by running into a swamp, and reached Hampton about midnight. Hubbard, Wars with Eastern Indians, 19, 20.]

† [Charles Ranlet, who escaped by the help of an Indian. Ibid. 20.]

‡ [William Roberts and his son-in-law. Ibid. 21]

silently, near to the house, from whence they suddenly rushed upon those two Indians, who were busy at the fire, and knocked them down with the butts of their guns; the other three took the alarm and escaped.

All the plantations at Pascataqua, with the whole eastern country, were now filled with fear and confusion. Business was suspended, and every man was obliged to provide for his own and his family's safety. The only way was to desert their habitations, and retire together within the larger and more convenient houses, which they fortified with a timber wall and flankarts, placing a sentry-box on the roof. Thus the labor of the field was exchanged for the duty of the garrison, and they, who had long lived in peace and security, were upon their guard night and day, subject to continual alarms, and the most fearful apprehensions.[1]

The seventh of October was observed as a day of fasting and prayer; and on the sixteenth, the enemy made an assault upon the inhabitants at Salmon-falls, in Berwick. Lieutenant Roger Plaisted, being a man of true courage and of public spirit, immediately sent out a party of seven from his garrison to make discovery. They fell into an ambush; three were killed, and the rest retreated. The Lieutenant then despatched an express to Major Waldron and Lieutenant Coffin at Cochecho, begging most importunately for help, which they were in no capacity to afford, consistently with their own safety. The next day, Plaisted ventured out with twenty men, and a cart to fetch the dead bodies of their friends, and unhappily fell into another ambush. The cattle affrighted ran back, and Plaisted being deserted by his men, and disdaining either to yield or fly, was killed on the spot, with his eldest son and one more; his other son died of his wound in a few weeks.* Had the heroism of this worthy family been imitated by the rest of the party, and a reinforcement arrived in season, the enemy might have received such a severe check as would have prevented them from appearing in small parties. The gallant behaviour of Plaisted, though fatal to himself and his sons, had this good effect, that the enemy retreated to the woods; and the next day, Captain Frost came up with a party from Sturgeon creek, and peaceably buried the dead. But before the month had expired a mill was burned there, and an assault made on Frost's garrison, who though he had only three boys with him, kept up a constant fire, and called aloud as if he were commanding a body of men, to march here and fire there: the stratagem succeeded, and the house was saved. The enemy then proceed-

(1) Ibid. 22.

* [Soon after this, they assaulted a house at Oyster River, which was garrisoned. Meeting with a good old man without the garrison, whose name was Beard, they killed him upon the place, and in a barbarous manner cut off his head and set it on a pole in derision. Hubbard, Eastern Wars, 22.]

ed down the river, killing and plundering as they found people off
their guard, till they came opposite to Portsmouth; from whence
some cannon being fired they dispersed, and were pursued by
the help of a light snow which fell in the night, and were overtaken by the side of a swamp, into which they threw themselves,
leaving their packs and plunder to the pursuers. They soon after did more mischief at Dover, Lamprey river* and Exeter;
and with these small, but irritating assaults and skirmishes, the autumn was spent until the end of November; when the number of
people killed and taken from Kennebeck to Pascataqua amounted to upwards of fifty.[1]

The Massachusetts government being fully employed in defending the southern and western parts, could not seasonably send
succors to the eastward. Major General Denison, who commanded the militia of the colony, had ordered the majors who commanded the regiments on this side of the country, to draw out a
sufficient number of men to reduce the enemy, by attacking them
at their retreat to their head-quarters at Ossipee and Pequawet.†
But the winter setting in early and fiercely, and the men being
unprovided with rackets to travel on the snow, which by the tenth
of December was four feet deep in the woods, it was impossible
to execute the design. This peculiar severity of the season however proved favorable. The Indians were pinched with famine,
and having lost by their own confession about ninety of their
number, partly by the war, and partly for want of food, they
were reduced to the necessity of suing for peace. With this
view, they came to Major Waldron, expressing great sorrow for
what had been done, and promising to be quiet and submissive.
By his mediation, a peace was concluded with the whole body of
eastern Indians, which continued till the next August; and might
have continued longer, if the inhabitants of the eastern parts had
not been too intent on private gain, and of a disposition too un-
governable to be a barrier against an enemy so irritable and vindictive. The restoration of the captives made the peace more
pleasant. A return from the dead could not be more welcome
than a deliverance from Indian captivity.

The war at the southward, though renewed in the spring, drew
toward a close. Philip's affairs were desperate; many
1676. of his allies and dependents forsook him; and in the month
of August, he was slain by a party under Captain Church. [2]

(1) Hubbard, [Eastern Wars] p. 23, 24, 25.   (2) Church's Memoirs, p. 44.

* [One was killed near this place; and between Exeter and Hampton, they
killed one or two men in the woods as they were travelling homewards.—
Hubbard's Eastern Wars, 25.]
† [This name was spelled *Pigwacket* in the former editions, but the true
orthography, which conveys the aboriginal pronunciation, is said to be as given
above in the text. It is variously written by the early historians. Winthrop
has it *Pegwaggett;* Hubbard, *Pigwauchet;* and Sullivan, *Peckwalket* and
Pickwocket.]

Those western Indians who had been engaged in the war, now fearing a total extirpation, endeavored to conceal themselves among their brethren of Penacook who had not joined in the war, and with those of Ossipee and Pequawket, who had made peace. But they could not so disguise themselves or their behaviour as to escape the discernment of those who had been conversant with Indians. Several of them were taken at different times and delivered up to public execution. Three of them, Simon, Andrew and Peter, who had been concerned in killing Thomas Kimball of Bradford, and captivating his family, did, within six weeks, voluntarily restore the woman and five children. It being doubted whether this act of submission was a sufficient atonement for the murder, they were committed to Dover prison till their case could be considered. Fearing that this confinement was a prelude to farther punishment, they broke out of prison, and going to the eastward, joined with the Indians of Kennebeck and Ameriscoggin in those depredations which they renewed on the inhabitants of those parts, in August, and were afterward active in distressing the people of Pascataqua.

This renewal of hostilities occasioned the sending of two companies to the eastward under Captain Joseph Syll, and Captain William Hathorne. In the course of their march, they came to Cochecho, on the sixth of September, where four hundred mixed Indians were met at the house of Major Waldron, with whom they had made the peace, and whom they considered as their friend and father. The two captains would have fallen upon them at once, having it in their orders to seize all Indians, who had been concerned in the war. The major dissuaded them from that purpose, and contrived the following stratagem. He proposed to the Indians, to have a training the next day, and a sham fight after the English mode ; and summoning his own men, with those under Capt. Frost of Kittery, they, in conjunction with the two companies, formed one party, and the Indians another. Having diverted them a while in this manner, and caused the Indians to fire the first volley ; by a peculiar dexterity, the whole body of them (except two or three) were surrounded, before they could form a suspicion of what was intended. They were immediately seized and disarmed, without the loss of a man on either side. A separation was then made : Wonolanset, with the Penacook Indians, and others who had joined in making peace the winter before, were peaceably dismissed ; but the strange Indians, (as they were called) who had fled from the southward and taken refuge among them, were made prisoners, to the number of two hundred ; and being sent to Boston, seven or eight of them, who were known to have killed any Englishmen, were condemned and hanged ; the rest were sold into slavery in foreign parts.

This action was highly applauded by the general voice of the colony ; as it gave them opportunity to deal with their enemies in a judicial way, as rebels, and, as they imagined, to extirpate those troublesome neighbors. The remaining Indians, however, looked upon the conduct of Major Waldron as a breach of faith ; inasmuch as they had taken those fugitive Indians under their protection, and had made peace with him, which had been strictly observed with regard to him and his neighbors, though it had been broken elsewhere. The Indians had no idea of the same government being extended very far, and thought they might make peace in one place, and war in another, without any imputation of infidelity ; but a breach of hospitality and friendship, as they deemed this to be, merited, according to their principles, a severe revenge, and was never to be forgotten or forgiven. The major's situation on this occasion was indeed extremely critical ; and he could not have acted either way without blame. It is said that his own judgment was against any forcible measure, as he knew that many of those Indians were true friends to the colony ; and that, in case of failure, he should expose the country to their resentment ; but had he not assisted the forces in the execution of their commission, (which was to seize all Indians who had been concerned with Philip in the war) he must have fallen under censure, and been deemed accessary, by his neglect, to the mischiefs which might afterward have been perpetrated by them. In this dilemma, he finally determined to comply with the orders and expectations of government ; imagining that he should be able to satisfy those of the Indians whom he intended to dismiss, and that the others would be removed out of the way of doing any further mischief ; but he had no suspicion that he was laying a snare for his own life. It was unhappy for him, that he was obliged in deference to the laws of his country, and the orders of government, to give offence to a people who, having no public judicatories and penal laws among themselves, were unable to distinguish between a legal punishment and private malice.*

Two days after this surprisal, the forces proceeded on their route to the eastward, being joined with some of Waldron's and Frost's men ; and taking with them Blind Will, a sagamore of the Indians who lived about Cochecho, and eight of his people for pilots. The eastern settlements were all either destroyed or deserted, and no enemy was to be seen ; so that the expedition proved fruitless, and the companies returned to Pascataqua.

It was then thought advisable, that they should march up to-

---

* The above account of the seizure of the Indians is given from the most authentic and credible tradition that could be obtained within the last sixteen years, from the posterity of those persons who were concerned in the affair. It is but just mentioned by Hubbard and Mather, and not in connexion with its consequences. Neal, for want of better information, has given a wrong turn to the relation, and so has Wynne who copies from him. Hutchinson has not mentioned it at all.

ward the Ossipee ponds ; where the Indians had a strong fort of timber fourteen feet high, with flankarts ; which they had a few years before hired some English carpenters to build for them, as a defence against the Mohawks, of whom they were always afraid. It was thought that if the Indians could be surprised on their first return to their head-quarters, at the beginning of winter, some considerable advantage might be gained against them ; or if they had not arrived there, that the provisions, which they had laid in for their winter subsistence, might be destroyed.   Accordingly, the companies being well provided for a march at that season, set off on the first of November ; and after travelling four days through a rugged, mountainous wilderness, and crossing several rivers, they arrived at the spot ; but found the fort and adjacent places entirely deserted, and saw not an Indian in all the way.   Thinking it needless for the whole body to go further, the weather being severe, and the snow deep, a select party was detached eighteen or twenty miles above ; who discovered nothing but frozen ponds, and snowy mountains ; and supposing the Indians had taken up their winter quarters nearer the sea, they returned to Newich-wannock, within nine days from their first departure.

They had been prompted to undertake this expedition by the false accounts brought by Mogg, an Indian of Penobscot, who had come in to Pascataqua, with a proposal of peace ; and had reported that an hundred Indians were assembled at Ossipee. This Indian brought with him two men of Portsmouth, Fryer* and Kendal, who had been taken on board a vessel at the eastward ; he was deputed by the Penobscot tribe to consent to articles of pacification ; and being sent to Boston, a treaty was drawn and subscribed by the governor and magistrates on the one part, and by Mogg on the other ; in which it was stipulated, that if the Indians of the other tribes did not agree to this transaction, and cease hostilities, they should be deemed and treated as enemies by both parties.   This treaty was signed on the sixth of November ; Mogg pledging his life for the fulfilment of it.   Accordingly, vessels being sent to Penobscot, the peace was ratified by Madokawando the sachem, and two captives were restored.   But Mogg, being incautiously permitted to go to a neighboring tribe, on pretence of pursuading them to deliver their captives, though he promised to return in three days, was seen no more.   It was at first thought that he had been sacrificed by his countrymen, as he pretended to fear when he left the vessels ; but a captive who escaped in January, gave a different account of   1677. him ; that he boasted of having deceived the English, and laughed

---

* [James Fryer was the eldest son of Nathaniel Fryer, who was afterwards one of the council.   He had received a wound in his knee from the Indians at Richmond's island, which proved mortal a few days after his return to his father's house, at Great Island.   Kendal, whose name according to Hubbard should be Gendal, was taken prisoner at the same time with Fryer.   Hubbard, Indian Wars from Pascataqua to Pemaquid, 46, 47.]

at their kind entertainment of him. There was also a design talked of among them to break the peace in the spring, and join with the other Indians at the eastward in ruining the fishery.— About the same time, it was discovered that some of the Narraganset Indians were scattered in the eastern parts ; three of them having been decoyed by some of the Cochecho Indians into their wigwams, and scalped, were known by the cut of their hair.— This raised a fear in the minds of the people, that more of them might have found their way to the eastward, and would prosecute their revenge against them.

From these circumstances, it was suspected, that the truce would be but of short continuance. The treachery of Mogg, who was surety for the performance of the treaty, was deemed a full justification of the renewal of hostilities; and the state of things was, by some gentlemen of Pascataqua, represented to be so dangerous, that the government determined upon a winter expedition. Two hundred men, including sixty Natick Indians, were enlisted and equipped, and sailed from Boston the first week in February, under the command of Major Waldron ; a day of prayer having been previously appointed for the success of the enterprise.

At Casco, the major had a fruitless conference, and a slight skirmish with a few Indians, of whom some were killed and wounded. At Kennebeck, he built a fort, and left a garrison of forty men, under the command of Captain Sylvanus Davis.* At Pemaquid, he had a conference with a company of Indians, who promised to deliver their captives on the payment of a ransom : Part of it being paid, three captives were delivered, and it was agreed that the conference should be renewed in the afternoon, and all arms be laid aside. Some suspicion of their infidelity had arisen, and when the major went ashore in the afternoon with five men, and the remainder of the ransom, he discovered the point of a lance hid under a board, which he drew out and advanced with it toward them ; charging them with treachery in concealing their arms so near. They attempted to take it from him by force ; but he threatened them with instant death, and waved his cap for a signal to the vessels. While the rest were coming on shore, the major with his five men secured the goods. Some of the Indians snatching up a bundle of guns which they had hid, ran away. Captain Frost, who was one of the five, seized an Indian, who was well known to be a rogue, and with

* [Sylvanus Davis resided some time at Sheepscot in Maine. He was an officer in the war of 1675, and received a wound from the Indians, as related by Hubbard in his Account of the Wars with the Eastern Indians in 1675, p. 41. Hutchinson (ii. 21) says that he was " the commander of the fort at Casco, where he was taken prisoner and carried to Canada." He was nominated by Rev. Increase Mather as one of the counsellors in the charter of William and Mary, granted in 1691, and his name was inserted as one of the twenty-eight appointed. There is an account written by him, of the management of the war against the English in the Eastern parts of New-England by the Indians, in 3 Coll. Mass. Hist. Soc. i. 101—112.]

Lieutenant Nutter, carried him on board. The major searching about, found three guns, with which he armed his remaining three men ; and the rest being come on shore by this time, they pursued the Indians, killed several of them before they could recover their canoes, and after they had pushed off, sunk one with five men, who were drowned ; and took four prisoners, with about a thousand pounds of dried beef, and some other plunder. The whole number of the Indians was twenty-five.

Whether the casual discovery of their arms, which they had agreed to lay aside, was sufficient to justify this severity, may be doubted ; since, if their intentions had really been hostile, they had a fine opportunity of ambushing or seizing the major and his five attendants, who came ashore unarmed ; and it is not likely that they would have waited for the rest to come ashore before they opened the plot. Possibly, this sudden suspicion might be groundless, and might inflame the prejudice against the major, which had already been excited by the seizure of their friends at Cochecho some time before.

On the return of the forces, they found some wheat, guns, anchors and boards at Kennebeck, which they took with them.—They killed two Indians on Arrowsick Island, who, with one of the prisoners taken at Pemaquid, and shot on board, made the number of Indians killed in this expedition thirteen. They returned to Boston on the 11th of March, without the loss of a man, bringing with them the bones of Captain Lake,[*] which they found entire in the place where he was killed.[†]

There being no prospect of peace at the eastward, it became necessary to maintain great circumspection and resolution, and to make use of every possible advantage against the enemy. A long and inveterate animosity had subsisted between the Mohawks and the eastern Indians, the original of which is not mentioned, and perhaps was not known by any of our historians ; nor can the oldest men among the Mohawks at this day give any account of it. These Indians were in a state of friendship with their English neighbors ; and being a fierce and formidable race of men, their

* [Capt. Thomas Lake was a merchant of good character, and was the joint owner with Major Clarke of Boston of Arrowsick island, in Maine, where he had a house and occasionally resided. It was while residing here, that he was killed by the Indians on the 14 of August, 1676. Hubbard, Eastern Wars, 41, 42. Hutch. Hist. Mass. i. 209. Records of the 2d church in Boston.—Hubbard, page 72, states that " the body of Capt. Lake, was preserved entire and whole and free from putrefaction by the coldness of the long winter." By what means the body could be so long preserved from decomposition, Captain Lake having been killed in the preceding August, it may be difficult to explain, but we must seek for an additional cause to the one assigned by Hubbard.]

† Here ends Hubbard's printed Narrative. The account of the remainder of this war is taken from his MS. history, from sundry original letters, and copies of letters, and from a MS. journal found in Prince's collection, and supposed to have been written by Capt. Lawrence Hammond of Charlestown.

name carried terror where ever it was known.   It was now thought, that if they could be induced to prosecute their ancient quarrel with the eastern Indians, the latter might be awed into peace, or incapacitated for any farther mischief. The propriety of this measure became a subject of debate ; some questioning the lawfulness of making use of their help, " as they were heathen ;" but it was urged in reply, that Abraham had entered into a confederacy with the Amorites, among whom he dwelled, and made use of their assistance in recovering his kinsman Lot from the hands of their common enemy.[1] With this argument, the objectors were satisfied ; and two messengers, Major Pynchon of Springfield, and Richards of Hartford were dispatched to the country of the Mohawks ; who treated them with great civility, expressed the most bitter hatred against the eastern enemy, and promised to pursue the quarrel to the utmost of their power.[2]

Accordingly, some parties of them came down the country about the middle of March, and the first alarm was given at Amuskeag falls ; where the son of Wonolanset being hunting, discovered fifteen Indians on the other side, who called to him in a language which he did not understand ; upon which he fled, whilst they fired near thirty guns at him without effect. Presently after this, they were discovered in the woods near Cochecho. Major Waldron sent out eight of his Indians, whereof Blind Will was one, for farther information.[3] They were all suprised together by a company of the Mohawks ; two or three escaped, the others were either killed or taken : Will was dragged away by his hair ; and being wounded, perished in the woods, on a neck of land, formed by the confluence of Cochecho and Ising-glass rivers, which still bears the name of Blind Will's Neck. This fellow was judged to be a secret enemy to the English, though he pretended much friendship and respect ; so that it was impossible to have punished him, without provoking the other neighboring Indians, with whom he lived in amity, and of whose fidelity there was no suspicion.[4] It was at first thought a fortunate circumstance that he was killed in this manner ; but the consequence proved it to be otherwise ; for two of those who were taken with him escaping, reported that the Mohawks threatened destruction to all the Indians in these parts without distinction.[5] So that those who lived in subjection to the English grew jealous of their sincerity, and imagined, not without very plausible ground, that the Mohawks had been persuaded or hired to engage in the war, on purpose to destroy them ; since they never actually exercised their fury upon those Indians who were in hostility with the English, but only upon those who were in friendship with them ; and this only in such a degree as to irritate, rather than to weaken

(1) Genesis, chap. 14.   (2) Hubbard's MS. Hist. [p. 629 of printed copy.]
(3) MS. Journal, March 30.   (4) Hubbard's MS. Hist. [p. 630 of printed copy.]   (5) MS. Journal.

or distress them. It cannot therefore be thought strange that the friendly Indians were alienated from their English neighbors, and disposed to listen to the seducing stratagems of the French ; who, in a few years after, made use of them in conjuction with others, sorely to scourge these unhappy people. The English, in reality, had no such design ; but the event proved, that the scheme of engaging the Mohawks in our quarrel, however lawful in itself, and countenanced by the example of Abraham, was a pernicious source of innumerable calamities.

The terror which it was thought this incursion of the Mohawks would strike into the eastern Indians was too small to prevent their renewing hostilities very early in the spring. Some of the garrison who had been left at Kennebeck were surprised by an ambush, as they were attempting to bury the dead bodies of their friends, who had been killed the summer before, and had lain under the snow all winter.[1] The remainder of that garrison were then taken off and conveyed to Pascataqua ; whither a company of fifty men and ten Natick Indians marched, under Captain Swaine, to succor the inhabitants, who were alarmed by scattered parties of the enemy, killing and taking people, and burning houses in Wells, Kittery, and within the bounds of Portsmouth.* A young woman who was taken from Rawling's house, made her escape and came into Cochecho, informing where the enemy lay. Three parties were dispatched to ambush three places, by one of which they must pass. The enemy appearing at $^{\text{Apr. 22.}}$ one of these places, were seasonably discovered ; but by the too great eagerness of the party to fire on them, they avoided the ambush and escaped.

Soon after this, the garrisons at Wells and Black Point were beset, and at the latter place, the enemy lost their leader Mogg, who had proved so treacherous a negotiator. Upon $^{\text{May 16.}}$ his death they fled in their canoes, some to the eastward and others toward York, where they also did some mischief. On a sabbath morning, a party of twenty, under the guidance of Simon, surprised six of our Indians, who lay drunk in the $^{\text{May 27.}}$ woods, at a small distance from Portsmouth. They kept all day hovering about the town, and if they had taken advantage of the people's absence from home, in attending the public worship, they might easily have plundered and burned the outmost houses ; but they were providentially restrained.[2] At night, they crossed the river at the Long Reach, killed some sheep at Kittery, and then

(1) Hubbard's MS. [p. 630 of printed copy.] (2) MS. Letter of Mr. Moodey.

* The following extract from the before mentioned Journal, shews something of the spirit of the times.

" April 16. The house of John Keniston was burnt, and he killed at Green-
" land. The Indians are Simon, Andrew and Peter, those three we had in
" prison, and should have killed. The good Lord pardon us."

went toward Wells; but, being afraid of the Mohawks, let their
prisoners go. Four men were soon after killed at North
June 13. Hill, one of whom was *Edward* Colcord, whose death
was much regretted.[1]

More mischief being expected, and the eastern settlements
needing assistance, the government ordered two hundred Indians
of Natick, with forty English soldiers, under Captain Benjamin
Swett of Hampton, and Lieutenant Richardson, to march to the
falls of Taconick on Kennebeck river; where it was said the Indians had six forts, well furnished with ammunition. The vessels
July. came to an anchor off Black Point; where the captain being
informed that some Indians had been seen, went on shore
with a party; and being joined by some of the inhabitants, so as
to make about ninety in all, marched to seek the enemy; who
shewed themselves on a plain in three parties. Swett divided
his men accordingly, and went to meet them. The enemy retreated till they had drawn our people two miles from the fort,
and then turning suddenly and violently upon them, threw them
into confusion, they being mostly young and inexperienced soldiers. Swett, with a few of the more resolute, fought bravely on
the retreat, till he came near the fort, when he was killed;* sixty
more were left dead or wounded, and the rest got into the fort. [2]
The victorious savages then surprised about twenty fishing vessels, which put into the eastern harbors by night; the crews, not
being apprehensive of danger on the water, fell an easy prey to
them. Thus the summer was spent with terror and perplexity on
our part; whilst the enemy rioted without control, till they had
satiated their vengeance, and greatly reduced the eastern settlements.[3]

At length, in the month of August, Major Andros, governor of
New-York, sent a sloop with some forces to take possession of
the land which had been granted to the Duke of York, and build
a fort at Pemaquid, to defend the country against the encroachment of foreigners. Upon their arrival, the Indians appeared
friendly; and in evidence of their pacific disposition, restored
fifteen prisoners with the fishing vessels. They continued quiet
all the succeeding autumn and winter, and lived in harmony with
the new garrison.

In the spring, Major Shapleigh of Kittery, Captain Champer-

(1) [Hubbard, Hist. N. E. 633. The names of the four persons killed according to the Town records of Hampton, were Abraham Colcord, jun., Abraham Perkins, jun., Benjamin Hilliard and Caleb Towle. Edward in the text
is doubtless a mistake for Abraham. MS. Letter of Rev. Josiah Webster, of 29
January1,830.] (2) MS. Letter of Mr. Gookin of Hampton. (3) Hubbard's MS.
Hist. [p. 634 of printed copy.]

* [Capt. Benjamin Swett had formerly been an inhabitant of Newbury,
where several of his children were born. A record of his death in the Norfolk County records, says, he " was slayn att Black point by the barberus Indians, the 29th of June, 1677."]

noon* and Mr. Fryer† of Portsmouth, were appointed commissioners to settle a formal treaty of peace with Squando and
the other chiefs, which was done at Casco, whither they 1678.
brought the remainder of the captives.[1] It was stipulated in the
treaty that the inhabitants should return to their deserted settlements, on condition of paying one peck of corn annually for each
family, by way of acknowledgment to the Indians for the possession of their lands, and one bushel for Major Pendleton, who was
a great proprietor.‡ Thus an end was put to a tedious and distressing war, which had subsisted three years. The terms of
peace were disgraceful, but not unjust, considering the former
irregular conduct of many of the eastern settlers, and the native
propriety of the Indians in the soil. Certainly they were now
masters of it ; and it was entirely at their option, whether the
English should return to their habitations or not. It was therefore thought better to live peaceably, though in a sort of subjection, than to leave such commodious settlements and forego the
advantages of trade and fishery, which were very considerable,
and by which the inhabitants of that part of the country had
chiefly subsisted.

It was a matter of great inquiry and speculation how the Indians were supplied with arms and ammunition to carry on this
war. The Dutch at New-York were too near the Mohawks for
the eastern Indians to adventure thither. The French in Canada
were too feeble, and too much in fear of the English, to do any
thing which might disturb the tranquillity ; and there was peace
between the two nations. It was therefore supposed that the Indians had long premeditated the war, and laid in a stock before-
hand.[2] There had formerly been severe penalties exacted by the
government, on the selling of arms and ammunition to the Indians ;
but ever since 1657, licenses had been granted to particular persons to supply them occasionally for the purpose of hunting, on

(1) MS. Journal, April 12. (2) Hubbard's printed Narrative, page 82.

* [Francis Champernoon, who was in 1684, appointed a Counsellor. It is
said that he was a cousin of Ferdinando Gorges. He died about the year
1686.]

† [Nathaniel Fryer lived some time at New-Castle. He had been a representative of Portsmouth to the General Court in 1666. He was appointed a
counsellor in 1683, and died 13 August, 1705.]

‡ [Bryan Pendleton was born about the year 1599, and came early to New-
England, and fixed his residence at Watertown, in Massachusetts. He was
admitted a freeman in 1634, and was the deputy or representative of Watertown from 1636 to 1639, 1647 and 1648. He was a member of the Ancient
and Honorable Artillery Company in 1646, and the principal military officer
in the place. He removed to Portsmouth before 1654, and was the deputy
of that town to the Court at Boston in 1654, 1658, 1660, 1661 and 1663. In
1658, he purchased a neck of land at the mouth of Saco river, and removed
thither in 1665, but returned to Portsmouth in 1676. He was appointed a
counsellor under President Danforth in 1680, in which, or the following year,
he died, leaving one son, James, and a daughter who married Seth Fletcher,
minister of Saco.]

paying an acknowledgment to the public treasury.[1] This indulgence, having been much abused by some of the eastern traders,
who, far from the seat of government, were impatient of the restraint of law, was supposed to be the source of the mischief.
But it was afterward discovered that the Baron de St. Castine, a
reduced French officer, who had married a daughter of Madokawando, and kept a trading house at Penobscot, where he considered himself as independent, being out of the limits of any
established government, was the person from whom they had
their supplies; which needed not to be very great as they always
husbanded their ammunition with much care, and never expended
it but when they were certain of doing execution.[2]

The whole burden and expense of this war, on the part of the
colonies, were borne by themselves. It was indeed thought
strange by their friends in England, and resented by those in
power, that they made no application to the king for assistance.
It was intimated to them by Lord Anglesey, 'that his majesty
' was ready to assist them with ships, troops, ammunition or
' money, if they would but ask it;' and their silence was construed to their disadvantage, as if they were proud, and obstinate, and
desired to be considered as an independent state.[3] They had
indeed no inclination to ask favors from thence ; being well aware
of the consequence of laying themselves under obligations to those
who had been seeking to undermine their establishment; and re-
membering how they had been neglected in the late Dutch wars,
when they stood in much greater need of assistance. The king
had then sent ammunition to New-York, but had sent word to
New-England, ' that they must shift for themselves and make
' the best defence they could.'[4] It was therefore highly injurious
to blame them for not making application for help. But if they
had not been so ill treated, they could not be charged with disrespect, since they really did not need foreign assistance. Ships of
war and regular troops must have been altogether useless ; and
no one who knew tho nature of an Indian war could be serious
in proposing to send them. Ammunition and money were necessary, but as they had long enjoyed a free trade, and had coined
the bullion which they imported, there was no scarcity of money,
nor of any stores which money could purchase. The method of
fighting with Indians could be learned only from themselves.
After a little experience, few men in scattered parties were of
more service than the largest and best equipped armies which
Europe could have afforded. It ought ever to be remembered
for the honor of New-England, that as their first settlement, so
their preservation, increase, and defence, even in their weakest

(1) Randolph's Narrative in Hutchinson's col. papers, page 492.   (2) Ibid.
p. 562.   (3) Hutch. History vol. i. p, 309.   (4) Hutch. collection of papers,
p. 506.

infancy were not owing to any foreign assistance, but under God, to their own magnanimity and perseverance.

Our gravest historians have recorded many omens, predictions, and other alarming circumstances, during this and the Pequod war, which in a more philosophical and less credulous age would not be worthy of notice. When men's minds were rendered gloomy by the horrors of a surrounding wilderness, and the continual apprehension of danger from its savage inhabitants; when they were ignorant of the causes of many of the common appearances in nature, and were disposed to resolve every unusual appearance into prodigy and miracle, it is not to be wondered that they should imagine they heard the noise of drums and guns in the air, and saw flaming swords and spears in the heavens,* and should even interpret eclipses as ominous. Some old Indians had intimated their apprehensions concerning the increase of the English, and the diminution of their own people, which any rational observer in a course of forty or fifty years might easily have foretold, without the least pretence to a spirit of prophecy ; yet these sayings were recollected, and recorded, as so many predictions by force of a supernatural impulse on their minds, and many persons of the greatest distinction were disposed to credit them as such. These things would not have been mentioned, but to give a just idea of the age. If mankind are now better enlightened, superstition is the less excusable in its remaining votaries.

CHAPTER VI.

Mason's renewed efforts. Randolph's mission and transactions. Attempts for the trial of Mason's title. New-Hampshire separated from Massachusetts, and made a royal province. Abstract of the commission. Remarks on it.

WHILST the country was laboring under the perplexity and distress arising from the war, measures were taking in England to increase their difficulties and divide their attention. The scheme of selling the provinces of New-Hampshire and Maine to the crown being laid aside, Mason again petitioned the king for the restoration of his property ; and the king referred the matter to his attorney general, Sir William Jones, and his solicitor general, Sir Francis Winnington, who reported, that " John Mason, esq., grandfather to the petitioner, " by virtue of several grants from the council of New-England

1675.

May 17.

---

*[The rays of the rising or setting sun, illuminating the edge of a cloud, frequently produce appearances of this kind. Marginal Note of the Author in the corrected copy.]

" under their common seal was instated in fee in sundry great
" tracts of land in New-England, by the name of New-Hampshire;
" and that the petitioner being heir at law to the said John, had a
" good and legal title to said lands."[1] Whereupon, a letter was
dispatched to the Massachusetts colony, requiring them to
1676.
Mar. 10. send over agents within six months, fully empowered to
answer the complaints, which Mason and the heirs of
Gorges had made, of their usurping jurisdiction over the territories claimed by them; and to receive the royal determination in
that matter. Copies of the complaints were enclosed; and Edward Randolph, a kinsman of Mason, a man of great address and
penetration, resolute and indefatigable in business, was charged
with the letters, and directed by the Lords of Trade to make in-
June 10. quiry into the state of the country. When he arrived,
he waited on Governor Leverett, who read the king's letter, with the petitions of Mason and Gorges, in council, Randolph
being present, who could obtain no other answer than that "they
would consider it."[2]

He then came into New-Hampshire, and as he passed along,
freely declared the business on which he was come, and publicly
July. read a letter which Mason had sent to the inhabitants.—
Some of them he found ready to complain of the government, and desirous of a change ; but the body of the people were
highly enraged against him ; and the inhabitants of Dover, in
public town-meeting, ' protested against the claim of Mason ; de-
' clared that they had bona fide purchased their lands of the In-
' dians ; recognized their subjection to the government of Massa-
' chusetts, under whom they had lived long and happily, and by
' whom they were now assisted in defending their estates and
' families against the savage enemy.' They appointed Major
Waldron " to petition the king in their behalf, that he would in-
" terpose his royal authority and afford them his wonted favor ;
" that they might not be disturbed by Mason, or any other per-
" son, but continue peaceably in possession of their rights under
" the government of Massachusetts."[3] A similar petition was
Sept. 1. sent by the inhabitants of Portsmouth, who appointed
John Cutt and Richard Martyn, Esqrs., Captains Daniel
and Stileman to draught and forward it.[4]

When Randolph returned to Boston, he had a severe reproof
from the governor, for publishing his errand, and endeavoring to
raise discontent among the people. To which he made no other
answer than that ' if he had done amiss, they might complain to
' the king.'[5]

After about six weeks stay, he went back to England and reported to the king, that " he had found the whole country com-

(1) MS. Copy in Superior Court files. (2) Hutch. col. papers, p. 504.—
(3) Dover Records. (4) Portsmouth Records. (5) Hutch. col. papers p. 510.

" plaining of the usurpation of the magistrates of Boston ; earn-
" estly hoping and expecting that his majesty would not permit
" them any longer to be oppressed ; but would give them relief
" according to the promises of the commissioners in 1665."—
With the same bitterness of temper, and in the same strain of
misrepresentation, he inveighed against the government in a long
report to the Lords of Trade ; which farther inflamed the prejudice that had long been conceived against the colony, and prepared the way for the separation which was meditated.

After his departure, a special council being summoned, at
which the elders of the churches were present, the question was
proposed to them, " whether the best way of making answer to
" the complaints of Gorges and Mason about the extent of their
" patent, be by sending agents, or by writing only ?" To which
they answered, " That it was most expedient to send agents, to
" answer by way of information, provided they were instructed
" with much care and caution to negotiate the affair with safety
" to the country, and loyalty to his majesty, in the preservation
" of their patent liberties." Accordingly, William Stoughton, afterward lieutenant-governor, and Peter Bulkley, then speaker of
the house of deputies, were appointed agents and sailed for England.[1]

At their arrival, an hearing was ordered before the lords chief
justices of the King's bench and common pleas ; when   1677.
the agents in the name of the colony disclaimed all title to
the lands claimed by the petitioner, and to the jurisdiction beyond
three miles northward of the river Merrimack, to follow the course
of the river, as far as it extended.[2] The judges reported to the
king, ' that they could give no opinion as to the right of soil, in
' the provinces of New-Hampshire and Maine, not having the
' proper parties before them ; it appearing that not the Massachu-
' setts colony, but the ter-tenants had the right of soil, and whole
' benefit thereof, and yet were not summoned to defend their titles.
' As to Mason's right of government within the soil he claimed,
' their lordships, and indeed his own counsel, agreed he had none ;
' the great council of Plymouth, under whom he claimed, having
' no power to transfer government to any. It was determined
' that the four towns of Portsmouth, Dover, Exeter and Hampton
' were out of the bounds of Massachusetts.'[3] This report was accepted and confirmed by the king in council.

After this, at the request of the agents, Sir William Jones, the
attorney general, drew up a complete state of the case to   1679.
be transmitted to the colony ; by which it seems that he   Sept. 18.
had altered his opinion since the report which he gave to
the king in 1675, concerning the validity of Mason's title.[4] It was

(1) Hutch. Hist. vol. i. p. 311.   (2) Narrative of Allen's Title, p. 5.—
(3) Hutch. vol. i. p. 317.   (4) Hutch. vol. i. p. 317.

also admitted that the title could be tried only on the place, there
being no court in England that had cognizance of it.

It became necessary then to the establishment of Mason's title,
that a new jurisdiction should be erected, in which the king might
direct the mode of trial and appeal at his pleasure. This being
resolved upon, the colony of Massachusetts was informed, by a
letter from the secretary of state, of the king's intention to
July 24. separate New-Hampshire from their government, and required to revoke all commissions which they had granted there,
and which were hereby declared to be null and void.[1] To prevent
any extravagant demand, the king obliged the claimant to declare,
under his hand and seal, that he would require no rents of the
inhabitants for the time passed, before the twenty-fourth of
June, 1679, nor molest any in their possessions for the time to
come ; but would make out titles to them and their heirs forever,
provided they would pay him sixpence in the pound, according
to the yearly value of all houses which they had built and lands
which they had improved.

Things being thus prepared, a commission passed the great
seal on the eighteenth of September, for the government of New-
Hampshire ; which ' inhibits and restrains the jurisdiction exer-
' cised by the colony of Massachusetts over the towns of Ports-
' mouth, Dover, Exeter and Hampton, and all other lands extend-
' ing from three miles to the northward of the river Merrimack
' and of any and every part thereof, to the province of Maine ;
' constitutes a president and council to govern the province ; ap-
' points John Cutt, esq., president, to continue one year, and till
' another be appointed by the same authority ; Richard Martyn,
' William Vaughan, and Thomas Daniel of Portsmouth, John Gil-
' man of Exeter, Christopher Hussey of Hampton and Richard
' Waldron of Dover, esquires, to be of the council, who were au-
' thorised to choose three other qualified persons out of the sev-
' eral parts of the province to be added to them. The said pres-
' ident and every succeeding one to appoint a deputy to preside
' in his absence ; the president or his deputy with any five to be a
' quorum. They were to meet at Portsmouth in twenty days af-
' ter the arrival of the commission, and publish it. They were
' constituted a court of record for the administration of justice,
' according to the laws of England, so far as circumstances would
' permit ; reserving a right of appeal to the king in council for
' actions of fifty pounds value. They were empowered to appoint
' military officers, and take all needful measures for defence a-
' gainst enemies. Liberty of conscience was allowed to all pro-
' testants, those of the church of England to be particularly en-
' couraged. For the support of government, they were to con-
' tinue the present taxes, till an assembly could be called ; to

(1) Hutch. col. pap. 522.

' which end, they were within three months to issue writs under
' the province seal, for calling an assembly, to whom the president
' should recommend the passing such laws as should establish their
' allegiance, good order and defence, and the raising taxes in such
' manner and proportion as they should see fit.   All laws to be
' approved by the president and council, and then to remain in
' force till the king's pleasure should be known, for which purpose,
' they should be sent to England by the first ships.   In case of
' the president's death, his deputy to succeed, and on the death
' of a counsellor, the remainder to elect another, and send over
' his name, with the names of two other meet persons, that the
' king might appoint one of the three.   The king engaged for
' himself and successors to continue the privilege of an assembly,
' in the same manner and form, unless by inconvenience arising
' therefrom he or his heirs should see cause to alter the same.   If
' any of the inhabitants should refuse to agree with Mason or his
' agents, on the terms before mentioned, the president and council
' were directed to reconcile the difference, or send the case stated
' in writing with their own opinions, to the king, that he with his
' privy council might determine it according to equity.'[1]

The form of government described in this commission considered abstractedly from the immediate intentions, characters, and
connections of the persons concerned, appears to be of as simple a
kind as the nature of a subordinate government and the liberty of the
subject can admit.   The people, who are the natural and original
source of power, had a representation in a body chosen by themselves ; and the king was represented by a president and council of
his own appointment ; each had the right of instructing their representative, and the king had the superior prerogative of disannulling
the acts of the whole at his pleasure.   The principal blemish in the
commission was the right claimed by the king of discontinuing the
representation of the people, whenever he should find it inconvenient, after he had solemnly engaged to continue this privilege.
The clause, indeed, is artfully worded, and might be construed to
imply more or less at pleasure.   Herein, Charles was consistent
with himself, parliaments being his aversion.   However, there
was in this plan as much of the spirit of the British constitution
as there could be any foundation for in such a colony ; for here
was no third branch to form a balance between the king or his
representatives, and the people.   The institution of an house of
peers in Britain was the result of the feudal system : the barons
being lords of the soil and enjoying a sovereignty within their own
territories and over their own vassals ; the constitution was formed
by the union of these distinct estates under one common sovereign.
But there was nothing similar to this in New-England.   The settlements began here by an equal division of property among inde-

(1) Commission.

pendent freemen. Lordship and vassalage were held in abhor-
rence. The yeomanry were the proprietors of the soil and the
natural defenders of their own rights and property; and they
knew no superior but the king. A council, whether appointed
by him or chosen by the people could not form a distinct body,
because they could not be independent. Had such a simple form
of colony government been more generally adopted, and perse-
veringly adhered to, and administered only by the most delicate
hands, it might have served better than any other, to perpetuate
the dependence of the colonies on the British crown.

CHAPTER VII.

The administration of the first council. Opposition to the acts of trade.—
Mason's arrival. Opposition to him. His departure. State of trade and
navigation.

THE commission was brought to Portsmouth on the first of
January, by Edward Randolph,[1] than whom there could not be a
more unwelcome messenger. It was received with great
1680. reluctance by the gentlemen therein named ; who, though
they were of the first character, interest and influence, and had
sustained the principal offices civil and military under the colony
government;*[2] yet easily saw that their appointment was not

(1) Council Records.   (2) Fitch's MS.

* The president JOHN CUTT was a principal merchant, of great probity and
esteem in Portsmouth ; but then aged and infirm.

Richard Martyn, was of good character, and great influence. He had been
very active in procuring the settlement of a minister in the town of Portsmouth.

William Vaughan was a wealthy merchant, generous and public spirited,
and of undaunted resolution. He was of Welch extraction, but was bred in
London under Sir Josiah Child, who had a great regard for him, and whose
interest he made use of for the good of the province.

Thomas Daniel, was a person of such note and importance, that when he
died in a time of general sickness and mortality, Mr. Moodey preached his
funeral sermon from 2 Sam. ii. 30. "There lacked of David's servants, nineteen men and Asahel." Fitch's MS.

John Gilman, was a principal man in Exeter, as was *Christopher Hussey,*
in Hampton. [Christopher Hussey was born in Darking, in Surry, came to
New-England as early as 1634, in which year he was admitted a freeman by
the Massachusetts colony. He settled at Hampton in 1638, and represented
that town in the General Court in 1658, 1659 and 1660. In 1685, he was cast
away and lost on the coast of Florida. He had three sons, Stephen, born in
1630, who died in Nantucket in 1718, aged 88; John, who removed to New-
Castle in Delaware, and Joseph, who remained in Hampton, and was the
representative in 1672. Lewis, Hist. Lynn, 29.]

Richard Waldron, was a native of Somersetshire, and one of the first settlers in Dover. He was much respected and eminently useful, having sustained divers important offices civil and military, and approved his courage
and fidelity in the most hazardous enterprises.

from any respect to them or favor to the people; but merely to obtain a more easy introduction to a new form of government, for a particular purpose, which they knew would be a source of perplexity and distress. They would gladly have declined acting in their new capacity; but considering the temper of the government in England, the unavoidable necessity of submitting to the change, and the danger (upon their refusal) of others being appointed who would be inimical to the country, they agreed to qualify themselves, determining to do what good, and keep off what harm they were able. They therefore published the commission, and took the oaths on the twenty-first day of January, which was the utmost time limited, and published the commission the next day. [1] Agreeably to the royal direction, they chose three other gentlemen into the council; Elias Stileman of Great Island, who had been a clerk in the county courts, whom they now appointed secretary, Samuel Dalton of Hampton, and Job Clements of Dover. The president nominated Waldron to be his deputy or vice president; Martyn was appointed treasurer, and John Roberts, marshal.

This change of government gratified the discontented few, but was greatly disrelished by the people in general; as they saw themselves deprived of the privilege of choosing their own rulers, which was still enjoyed by the other colonies of New-England, and as they expected an invasion of their property soon to follow.

When writs were issued for calling a general assembly, the persons in each town who were judged qualified to vote were named in the writs;* and the oath of allegiance was administered to each voter. A public fast was observed, to ask the divine blessing on the approaching assembly, and "the continuance of their precious and pleasant things." The assembly† met at Portsmouth on the sixteenth of March, and was opened with prayer and a sermon by Mr. Moodey.   Feb. 26.

To express their genuine sentiments of the present change, and invalidate the false reports which had been raised against

(1) Council Records.

* The number of qualified voters in each town was,

In Portsmouth	71
Dover	61
Hampton	57
Exeter	20
	209

† The Deputies in this first Assembly were, for

Portsmouth.	Hampton.
Robert Elliot,	Anthony Stanyan,
Philip Lewis,	Thomas Marston,
John Pickering.	Edward Gove.
Dover.	Exeter.
Peter Coffin,	Bartholemew Tippen,
Anthony Nutter,	Ralph Hall.
Richard Waldron, jun.	

them, as well as to shew their gratitude and respect to their former protectors, they wrote to the general court at Boston, " ac-
" knowledging the kindness of that colony in taking them under
" their protection and ruling them well ; assuring them, that it
" was not any dissatisfaction with their government, but merely
" their submission to divine providence and his majesty's com-
" mands, without any seeking of their own, which induced them
" to comply with the present separation, which they should have
" been glad had never taken place ; signifying their desire that
" a mutual correspondence might be continued for defence against
" the common enemy, and offering their service when it should
" be necessary."*1

Their next care was to frame a code of laws, of which the
first, conceived in a style becoming freemen, was " that no act,
" imposition, law or ordinance should be made or imposed upon
" them, but such as should be made by the assembly and approved
" by the president and council." Idolatry, blasphemy, treason,
rebellion, wilful murder, manslaughter, poisoning, witchcraft, sod-
omy, bestiality, perjury, man-stealing, cursing and rebelling against
parents, rape and arson were made capital crimes. The other
penal laws were in their main principles the same that are now
in force. To prevent contentions that might arise by reason of
the late change of government, all townships and grants of land
were confirmed, and ordered to remain as before ; and controversies about the titles of land were to be determined by juries
chosen by the several towns, according to former custom. The
president and council with the assembly were a supreme court of
Judicature, with a jury when desired by the parties ; and three
inferior courts were constituted at Dover, Hampton and Ports-
mouth.2 The military arrangement was, one foot company in
each town, one company of artillery at the fort, and one troop of
horse, all under the command of Major Waldron.

During this administration, things went on as nearly as possible
in the old channel, and with the same spirit, as before the separation. A jealous watch was kept over their rights and privileges,
and every encroachment upon them was withstood to the utmost.
The duties and restrictions established by the acts of trade and

(1) Council Records.   (2) MS. Laws.

* This letter fully shews the absurdity of the reason assigned by Douglass
in his Summary, vol. ii. page 28, for erecting this new government. " The
" proprietors and inhabitants of New-Hampshire not capable of protecting
" themselves against the Canada French and their Indians, desired of the
" crown to take them under its immediate protection."   A random assertion,
unsupported by any proof and contrary to plain fact ! The crown could afford them no protection against Indians. With the French, the crown was in
alliance, and the nation was at peace. [The Letter of the General Assembly
of N. H., addressed " to the honourable Governour and Council of the Massachusetts Colony to be communicated to the General Court," is given entire by Mr. Adams, Annals of Portsmouth, 65—67.]

navigation were universally disgustful, and the more so as Randolph was appointed collector, surveyor and searcher of the customs throughout New-England. In the execution of his commission, he seized a ketch belonging to Portsmouth, but bound from Maryland to Ireland, which had put into this port for a few days. The master, Mark Hunking, brought an action against him at a special court before the president and council, and recovered damages and costs to the amount of thirteen pounds. Randolph behaved on this occasion with such insolence, that the council obliged him publicly to acknowledge his offence and ask their pardon. He appealed from their judgment to the king; but what the issue was doth not appear.[1]   Having constituted Captain Walter Barefoote his deputy at this port, an advertisement was published requiring that all vessels should be entered and cleared with him. Upon which, Barefoote was brought to examination, and afterward indicted before the president and council, for 'having in an high and presumptuous ' manner set up his majesty's office of customs without ' leave from the president and council; in contempt of his majesty's ' authority in this place ; for disturbing and obstructing his majes- ' ty's subjects in passing from harbor to harbor, and town to town ; ' and for his insolence in making no other answer to any question ' propounded to him but "my name is Walter." '   He was sentenced to pay a fine of ten pounds, and stand committed till it was paid.   But though Randolph's authority was denied, yet they made an order of their own for the observation of the acts of trade, and appointed officers of their own to see them executed. They had been long under the Massachusetts government, and learned their political principles from them; and as they had been used to think that all royal authority flowed in the channel of the charter, so they now thought that no authority derived from the crown could be regularly exercised in the province but through their commission. In this, they reasoned agreeably not only to their former principles, but to their fundamental law, to which they steadily adhered, though they had no reason to think it would be allowed by the crown ; and though they knew that a rigid adherence to rights, however clear and sacred, was not the way to recommend themselves to royal favor. But they were not singular in these sentiments, nor in their opposition to the laws of trade. Randolph was equally hated, and his commission neglected at Boston ; where the notary refused to enter his protest against the proceedings of the court ; and he was obliged to post it on the exchange.[2]

In the latter end of the year, Mason arrived from England with a mandamus, requiring the council to admit him to a seat at the board, which was accordingly done. He soon entered on the business he came about ; endeavoring to per-

Mar. 28.

1680.
Mar. 25.

Dec. 30.

1681.

(1) Council Records and Files.   (2) MSS. in files.

suade some of the people to take leases of him, threatening others
if they did not, forbidding them to cut firewood and timber, asserting his right to the province and assuming the title of lord-
protector.   His agents, or stewards as they were called, had rendered themselves obnoxious by demanding rents of several persons and threatening to sell their houses for payment.   These
proceedings raised a general uneasiness ; and petitions were sent
from each town, as well as from divers individuals, to the council
for protection ; who, taking up the matter judicially, published an
order prohibiting Mason or his agents at their peril to repeat such
irregular proceedings, and declaring their intention to transmit the
grievances and complaints of the people to the king.   Upon this,
Mason would no longer sit in council, though desired, nor appear
when sent for ; when they threatened to deal with him as an offender, he threatened to appeal to the king, and published a summons to the president and several members of the council, and
others to appear before his majesty in three months.   This was
Mar. 23. deemed " an usurpation over his majesty's authority here
" established," and a warrant was issued for apprehending
him ; but he got out of their reach and went to England.

   During these transactions, president Cutt died, and Major
April 5. Waldron succeeded him, appointing Captain Stileman for
his deputy, who had quitted his place of secretary upon
the appointment of Richard Chamberlain to that office by royal
Dec. 30. commission.   The vacancy made in the council by the
1680. president's death was filled by Richard Waldron, junior.
On the death of Dalton, Anthony Nutter was chosen.   Henry
Dow was appointed marshal in the room of Roberts who resigned.

   During the remainder of the council's administration, the common business went on in the usual manner, and nothing remarkable is mentioned, excepting another prosecution of Barefoote,
Mar. 10. with his assistants, William Haskins and Thomas Thurton
for seizing a vessel " under pretence of his majesty's name,
" without the knowledge of the authority of the province, and
" without shewing any breach of statute though demanded."
Barefoote pleaded his deputation from Randolph ; but he was
amerced twenty pounds to be respited during his good behaviour,
and his two assistants five pounds each ; the complainant being
left to the law for his damages.   This affair was carried by appeal
to the king ; but the issue is not mentioned.

   It will be proper to close the account of this administration with
a view of the state of the province as to its trade, improvements
and defence, from a representation thereof made by the council
to the lords of trade, pursuant to their order.

   " The trade of the province, (say they) is in masts, planks,
boards and staves and all other lumber, which at present is of
little value in other plantations, to which they are transported ; so

that we see no other way for the advantage of the trade, unless his majesty please to make our river a free port.

" Importation by strangers is of little value ; ships commonly selling their cargoes in other governments, and if they come here, usually come empty to fill with lumber : but if haply they are at any time loaded with fish, it is brought from other ports, there being none made in our province, nor likely to be, until his majesty please to make the south part of the Isles of Shoals part of this government, they not being at present under any.*

" In reference to the improvement of lands by tillage, our soil is generally so barren, and the winters so extreme cold and long that there is not provision enough raised to supply the inhabitants, many of whom were in the late Indian war so impoverished, their houses and estates being destroyed, and they and others remaining still so incapacitated for the improvement of the land, (several of the youth being killed also) that they even groan under the tax or rate, assessed for that service, which is, great part of it, unpaid to this day.†

" There is at the Great Island in Portsmouth, at the harbor's mouth, a fort well enough situated, but for the present too weak and insufficient for the defence of the place ; the guns being eleven in number are small, none exceeding a sacre (six pounder) nor above twenty-one hundred weight, and the people too poor to make defence suitable to the occasion that may happen for the fort.

" These guns were bought, and the fortification erected, at the proper charge of the towns of Dover and Portsmouth, at the beginning of the first Dutch war, about the year 1665, in obedience to his majesty's command in his letter to the government under which this province then was.

" There are five guns more lying at the upper part of Portsmouth, purchased by private persons, for their security and de-

---

* When these islands were first settled is uncertain, but it must have been very early, as they are most commodiously situated for the fishery, which was a principal object with the first settlers. While New-Hampshire was united to Massachusetts, they were under the same jurisdiction, and the town there erected was called Appledore. (Mass. Rec.) They are not named in Cutt's nor Cranfield's commission : but under Dudley's presidency, causes were brought from thence to Portsmouth, which is said to be in the same county. In Allen's and all succeeding commissions, they are particularly mentioned ; the south half of them being in New-Hampshire.

† Taxes were commonly paid in lumber or provisions at stated prices ; and whoever paid them in money was abated one-third part. The prices in 1680, were as follows :

Merchantable white pine boards per m. 30s.
White Oak pine staves per ditto   £3.
Red Oak ditto per ditto   30s.
Red Oak Hhd. ditto per ditto   25s.
Indian Corn per bushel   3s.
Wheat per ditto   5s.
Malt per ditto   4s.

N. B.   Silver was 6s. and 8d. per oz.

fence against the Indians in the late war with them, and whereof the owners may dispose at their pleasure. To supply the foresaid defect and weakness of the guns and fort, we humbly supplicate his majesty to send us such guns as shall be more serviceable, with powder and shot."

By an account of the entries in the port annexed to the above, it appears, that from the fifteenth of June 1680, to the twelfth of April 1681, were entered, twenty-two ships, eighteen ketches, two barks, three pinks, one shallop and one fly-boat; in all forty-seven.[1]

CHAPTER VIII.

The administration of Cranfield. Violent measures. Insurrection, trial and imprisonment of Gove. Mason's suits. Vaughan's imprisonment. Prosecution of Moodey and his imprisonment. Arbitrary proceedings. Complaints. Tumults. Weare's agency in England. Cranfield's removal. Barefoote's administration.

EXPERIENCE having now convinced Mason, that the government which he had procured to be erected, was not likely to be administered in a manner favorable to his views, he made it his business, on his return to England, to solicit a change ; in consequence of which it was determined to commission Edward Cranfield, Esq., lieutenant-governor and commander in chief of New-Hampshire. By a deed enrolled in the court of chancery, Mason

Jan. 25. surrendered to the king one fifth part of the quit-rents, which had or should become due. These, with the fines and forfeitures which had accrued to the crown since the establishment of the province, and which should afterward arise, were appropriated to the support of the governor. But this being deemed too precarious a foundation, Mason by another deed mortgaged the whole province to Cranfield, for twenty-one years, as security for the payment of one hundred and fifty pounds per annum, for the space of seven years.[2] On this encouragement, Cranfield relinquished a profitable office at home, with the view of bettering his fortune here.[3]

By the commission, which bears date the ninth of May, the governor was empowered to call, adjourn, prorogue and dissolve general courts ; to have a negative voice in all acts of government; to suspend any of the council when he should see just cause (and every counsellor so suspended was declared incapable of being elected into the general assembly ;) to appoint a deputy-governor, judges, justices, and other officers, by his sole authority ; and to

(1) Council Records.   (2) MSS. in the files.   (3) Fitch's MS.

execute the powers of vice-admiral. The case of Mason was
recited nearly in the same words as in the former commission,
and the same directions were given to the governor to reconcile differences, or send cases fairly stated to the king in council for his
decision. The counsellors named in this commission were Mason, who was styled proprietor, Waldron, Daniel, Vaughan, Martyn, Gilman, Stileman and Clements : these were of the former
council, and to them were added Walter Barefoote, and Richard
Chamberlain.

Cranfield arrived and published his commission on the fourth
of October, and within six days, Waldron and Martyn were suspended from the council, on certain articles exhibited against them
by Mason.[1] This early specimen of the exercise of power must
have been intended as a public affront to them, in revenge for
their former spirited conduct ; otherwise their names might have
been left out of the commission when it was drawn.

The people now plainly saw the dangerous designs formed a-
gainst them. The negative voice of a governor, his right of suspending counsellors, and appointing officers, by his own authority,
were wholly unprecedented in New-England ; and they had the
singular mortification to see the crown not only appointing two
branches of their legislature, but claiming a negative on the election of their representative, in a particular case, which might
sometimes be essentially necessary to their own security. They
well knew that the sole design of these novel and extraordinary
powers was to facilitate the entry of the claimant on the lands,
which some of them held by virtue of grants from the same authority, and which had all been fairly purchased of the Indians ;
a right which they believed to be of more validity than any other.
Having by their own labor and expense subdued a rough wilderness, defended their families and estates against the savage enemy,
without the least assistance from the claimant, and held possession
for above fifty years ; they now thought it hard and cruel, that
when they had just recovered from the horrors of a bloody war,
they should have their liberty abridged, and their property demanded, to satisfy a claim which was at best disputable, and in
their opinion groundless. On the other hand, it was deemed unjust, that grants made under the royal authority should be disregarded ; and that so great a sum as had been expended by the
ancestor of the claimant, to promote the settlement of the country,
should be entirely lost to him ; especially as he had foregone some
just claims on the estate as a condition of inheritance.[2] Had the
inhabitants by any fraudulent means impeded the designs of the
original grantee, or embezzled his interest, there might have been
a just demand for damages ; but the unsuccessfulness of that adventure was to be sought for in its own impracticability ; or the

(1) Council Records. (2) Mason's Will.

negligence, inability or inexperience of those into whose hands the management of it fell after Captain Mason's death, and during the minority of his successor.

An assembly being summoned, met on the fourteenth of November ; with whose concurrence a new body of laws was enacted, in some respects different from the former ; the fundamental law being omitted and an alteration made in the appointment of jurors, which was now ordered to be done by the sheriff, after the custom in England.[1]

Cranfield, who made no secret of his intention to enrich himself by accepting the government, on the first day of the assembly restored Waldron and Martyn to their places in the council ; having, as he said, examined the allegations against them and found them insufficient.[2] In return for this show of complaisance, and taking advantage of his needy situation, the assembly having ordered an assessment of five hundred pounds, appropriated one half of it as a present to the governor ; hoping thereby to detach him from Mason, who they knew could never comply with his engagements to him. Preferring a certainty to an uncertainty, he Dec. 1. passed the bill, though it was not presented to him till after he had given order for adjourning the court, and after Mason, Barefoote and Chamberlain were withdrawn from the council.[3]

This appearance of good humor was but short-lived ; for at the next session of the assembly, the governor and council having 1683. tendered them a bill for the support of government, which Jan. 20. they did not approve, and they having offered him several bills which he said were contrary to law, he dissolved them ; having previously suspended Stileman from the council and dismissed him from the command of the fort, for suffering a vessel under seizure to go out of the harbor. Barefoote was made captain of the fort in his room.[4]

The dissolution of the Assembly, a thing before unknown, aggravated the popular discontent, and kindled the resentment of some rash persons in Hampton and Exeter ; who, headed by Edward Gove, a member of the dissolved assembly, declared by sound of trumpet for " liberty and reformation." There had been a town meeting at Hampton, when a new clerk was chosen and their records secured. Gove went from town to town proclaiming what had been done at Hampton, carrying his arms, declaring that the governor was a traitor and had exceeded his commission, and that he would not lay down his arms, till matters were set right, and endeavoring to excite the principal men in the province to join in a confederacy to overturn the government. His project appeared to them so wild and dangerous, that they not

(1) MS. Laws.   (2) Vaughan's Journal.   Council Records.   (3) MSS. in the files.   (4) Council Records.

only disapproved of it, but informed against him and assisted in apprehending him. Hearing of their design, he collected his company, and appeared in arms ; but on the persuasion of some of his friends he surrendered. A special court was immediately commissioned for his trial, of which Major Waldron sat as judge, with William Vaughan and Thomas Daniel assistants. The grand jury presented a bill, in which Edward Gove, John Gove, his son, and William Hely, of Hampton ; Joseph, John and Robert Wadleigh, three brothers, Thomas Rawlins, Mark Baker and John Sleeper, of Exeter, were charged with high-treason. Gove, who behaved with great insolence before the court, and pretended to justify what he had done, was convicted and received sentence of death in the usual hideous form ; and his estate was seized, as forfeited to the crown. The others were con- Feb. 1. victed of being accomplices, and respited.[1] The king's pleasure being signified to the governor that he should pardon such as he judged objects of mercy ; they were all set at liberty but Gove, who was sent to England, and imprisoned in the tower of London about three years. On his repeated petitions to the king, and by the interest of Randolph with the Earl of Clarendon, then lord chamberlain, he obtained his pardon and returned home in 1686, with an order to the then president and council of New-England to restore his estate.

Gove in his petitions to the king pleaded " a distemper of mind" as the cause of those actions for which he was prosecuted. He also speaks in some of his private letters of a drinking match at his house, and that he had not slept for twelve days and nights, about that time.[2] When these things are considered, it is not hard to account for his conduct. From a letter which he wrote to the court while in prison, one would suppose him to have been disordered in his mind.* His punishment was by much too severe,

(1) Records of Special Courts.   (2) Gove's papers.

* [The letter alluded to, addressed to the justices of the court of sessions, and found in the Recorder's office, was copied by Dr. Belknap, for the Appendix to the first volume, but it was, with several other papers, excluded for want of room. It is here added, printed from the copy made by the author.

" A Letter from Edward Gove in Prison to the Justices of the Court of Sessions.

From the great Island in Portsmouth in New-Hampshire, 29 Jany. 1682-3. To the much hond. Justices of the Peace as you call yourselfs by your inditement, in which eleven mens names subscribed namely Ed. Gove, John Gove, Jo. Wadly, John Wadly, Rob. Wadly, Ed. Smith, Will. Ely, Tho. Rawlins, John Sleeper, Mark Baker, John Young. Gentlemen excuse me I cannot petision you as persons in authority by the name of Justises of the peace, for now I am upon a serious account for my Life and the Life of those that are with me. Therefore pray consider well and take good advice of persons in Government from whence you came. I pray God that made the Heavens, the Earth, the sease and all that in them is to give you wisdom and corag in your plases to discharg such duty as God requires of you and 2dly I hartyly pray God to direct you to do that which our grasious King Charls the 2d of blessed memory requires of you. Gentlemen, it may be I may be upon a

and his trial was hurried on too fast, it being only six days after the commission of his crime. Had he been indicted only for a riot there would have been no difficulty in the proof, nor hardship in inflicting the legal penalty. Waldron, it is said, shed tears when pronouncing the sentence of death upon him.

On the fourteenth of February, the governor, by advertisement, called upon the inhabitants to take our leases from Mason within one month, otherwise he must, pursuant to his instructions, certify the refusal to the king, that Mason might be discharged of his obligation to grant them. Upon this summons, and within the time set, Major Waldron, John Winget* and Thomas Roberts,

mistake, but according to what I know and believe I am falsly indited and I am abused notwithstanding by another Inditement, by being in Iorns by Cap. Barefoot's order which Iorns are called billbose, exceeding large. Pray consider we are men like yourselves made of the same earth and I know who made the difference.

And I verily believe that the holy righteous just God will have an account of you for your Justis in this matter. Pray consider. When this last change was I writ to one man in this Province, I tould him wee were a hapy people if all was right in the Bottom. Time was that I said all was right in the bottom, I believed it, but now I see otherwise. Who knows what shall be on the morrow. Though it bee appointed a solemn day of fasting, I know that when it was appointed there was not the election of cries and teares that will appear when the day comes. If ever New-England had need of a Solomon, or David, or Moses, Caleb or Joshua it is now. My tears are in my eyes I can hardly see.

Yet will I say I do believe how it will com. You and they with siths and grones must out do the ministry; The Ministry must endeavor to out do you, but if you and they do any thing in hipocrisy, God will find you out and deliverance will com som other way.

We have a hard prison, a good keeper, a hard Captain, iorns an inch over, five foot and several inches long, two men locked together; yet I had I thank God for it a very good nights lodging, beter than I had fourteene or fiveteene nights before. I pray God direct you and let me here from you by a messenger that your honors shall imploy and consider. I am your honors humbel Servant in all duty to be commanded.   EDWARD GOVE.

I know those that will have a blessing from God must endeavor to stand in the way of a blessing. This Doctrin I heard about 32 yeares ago.
                                                         EDWARD GOVE.

Excuse any thing writ amiss for the Lord's sake. I would you all were as I am and as fitt to recieve reward for innosensy. I humbly beg your Prayers to God in our behalfe.   EDWARD GOVE.

If any thing be amiss in what is written, lett the subscriber bear the blame, for the rest are surprized with feare.   EDWARD GOVE.

I humbly and hartily desire some of your honors would speak to Mister Mody to pray to God in the behalfe of all his pore prisoners the world over and espesially for us before named the men of this Province who ly under hevi burdens.   EDWARD GOVE.

The original of this Letter is in ye Recorder's office."
It is now (1830) in the Secretary's office.]

* [He is the ancestor of the Wingate families in New-Hampshire and Maine. He was admitted freeman by the Massachusetts colony in 1666, and died about the year 1689. His children were Ann, born 18 February, 1667; John, born 13 July, 1670; Joshua and Caleb. Joshua married and lived in Hampton, where he died at the age of 90 years or upwards. He was at the conquest of Louisburg in 1745, was afterwards a colonel, and a representative from Hampton in the General Assembly. He wrote his name as in the text, but it seems to have been altered to *Wingate* by his sons, two of whom were educated at Harvard College. Rev. Paine Wingate, the eldest, graduated in 1723, and

three of the principal landholders in Dover, waited on the governor to know his pleasure, who directed them to agree with Mason. They then retired into another room where Mason was, and proposed to refer the matter to the governor, that he might according to his commission, state the matter to the king for his decision. This proposal, Mason rejected, saying that unless they would own his title, he would have nothing to do with them.— Whilst they were in discourse, the governor came in and desired them to depart.[1]

This piece of conduct is difficult to be accounted for, it being directly in the face of the commission. Had the method therein prescribed, and by these men proposed, been adopted, it was natural to expect that the king, who had all along favored Mason's pretensions, would have determined the case as much to his wish as upon an appeal from a judicial court; besides, he had now the fairest opportunity to have it decided in the shortest way, to which his antagonists must have submitted, it being their own proposal. His refusal to accede to it was a capital mistake, as it left both him and Cranfield exposed to the charge of disobedience. But it afforded a powerful plea in behalf of the people; whose confidence in the royal justice would have induced them to comply with the directions in the commission. It being now impossible to have the controversy thus decided they determined to hearken to none of his proposals. As he generally met with opposition and contradiction, he was induced to utter many rash sayings in all companies. He threatened to seize the principal estates, beggar their owners, and provoke them to rebellion, by bringing a frigate into the harbor, and procuring soldiers to be quartered on the inhabitants.[2] These threats were so far from intimidating the people, that they served the more firmly to unite them in their determination not to submit; and each party was now warm in their opposition and resentment.

The governor on some fresh pretence suspended Waldron, Martyn and Gilman from the council. The deaths of Daniels and Clements made two other vacancies. Vaughan held his seat the longest, but was at length thrust out for his non-compliance with some arbitrary measures. So that the governor had it in his power to model the council to his mind, which he did by appointing at various times Nathaniel Fryer, Robert Elliot, John Hinckes,

(1) Weare's MS.   (2) Ibid.

was ordained the minister of Amesbury, in Massachusetts, 15 June, 1726, and died 19 February, 1786, aged 83. John, the youngest, was born at Hampton, 4 January, 1725, graduated in 1744, and died 4 September, 1812, aged 88. A son of the Rev. Paine Wingate, is the Hon. Paine Wingate of Stratham, who was born 14 May, 1739, graduated at Harvard college 1759, and is now the oldest living graduate of that institution. He was one of the first Senators from New-Hampshire under the Federal Constitution, and for many years was Judge of the Supreme Court of the State.]

James Sherlock, Francis Champernoon and Edward Randolph, esquires. The judicial courts were also filled with officers proper for the intended business. Barefoote, the deputy governor, was judge : Mason was chancellor ; Chamberlain was clerk and pro-thonotary ; Randolph was attorney general, and Sherlock provost marshal and sheriff.[1] Some who had always been disaffected to the country, and others who had been awed by threats or flattered by promises took leases from Mason ; and these served for under sheriffs, jurors, evidences, and other necessary persons.

Things being thus prepared, Mason began his law-suits by a writ against Major Waldron, (who had always distinguished him-self in opposition to his claim) for holding lands and felling timber to the amount of four thousand pounds. The major appeared in court, and challenged every one of the jury as interested persons, some of them having taken leases of Mason, and all of them living upon the lands which he claimed. The judge then caused the oath of *voire dire* to be administered to each juror, purport-ing " that he was not concerned in the lands in question, and that " he should neither gain nor lose by the cause." Upon which the major said aloud to the people present, " that his was a lead-" ing case, and that if he were cast they must all become tenants " to Mason ; and that all persons in the province being interested, " none of them could legally be of the jury."[2] The cause how-ever went on ; but he made no defence, asserted no title, and gave no evidence on his part. Judgment was given against him and at the next court of sessions he was fined five pounds for " mutinous and seditious words."

Suits were then instituted against all the principal landholders in the province, who, following Waldron's example, never made any defence. Some, chiefly of Hampton, gave in writing their reasons for not joining issue ; which were, the refusal of Mason to comply with the directions in the commission ; the impropriety of a jury's determining what the king had expressly reserved to himself ; and the incompetency of the jury, they being all inter-ested persons, one of whom had said that " he would spend his " estate to make Mason's right good." These reasons were irri-tating rather than convincing to the court. The jury never hesi-tated in their verdicts. From seven to twelve causes were des-patched in a day, and the costs were multiplied from five to twenty pounds. Executions were issued, of which two or three only were levied ; but Mason could neither keep possession of the premises nor dispose of them by sale, so that the owners still enjoyed them. Several threatened to appeal to the king, but Major Vaughan alone made the experiment.[3]

A suit was also commenced against Martyn who had been treasurer, for the fines and forfeitures received by him, during the

(1) Council Records.   (2) MS. in files.   (3) MS. in files and Weare's MSS.

former administration ; and judgment was recovered for seventy
one pounds, with costs.   Martyn petitioned Mason as chancellor,
setting forth that he had received and disposed of the money according to the orders of the late president and council, and praying that the whole burden might not lie upon him.   A decree
was then issued for the other surviving members of the late council, and the heirs of those who were dead, to bear their proportion.[1]   This decree was afterward reversed by the king in council.

Cranfield with his council had now assumed the whole legislative power.   They prohibited vessels from Massachusetts to enter
the port, because the acts of trade were not observed in that
colony : they fixed the dimensions of merchantable lumber ; altered the value of silver money, which had always passed by weight
at six shillings and eight pence per ounce ; and ordered that
dollars should be received at six shillings each, which was then a
great hardship ; as many of them were greatly deficient in weight.
They also changed the bounds of townships ; established fees
of office ; made regulations for the package of fish, and ordered
the constables to forbear collecting any town or parish taxes till
the province tax was paid, and the accounts settled with the
treasurer.[2]

The public grievances having become insupportable, the people
were driven to the necessity of making a vigorous stand for their
liberties.   The only regular way was by complaint to the king.
Having privately communicated their sentiments to each other,
and raised money by subscription, they appointed Nathaniel
Weare, esq., of Hampton,* their agent ; and the four towns having
drawn and subscribed distinct petitions of the same tenor, Weare
privately withdrew to Boston from whence he sailed for England.
Major Vaughan who accompanied him to Boston, and was appointed to procure depositions to send after him, was upon his
return to Portsmouth, brought to an examination, treated with
great insolence and required to find sureties for his good behaviour ; which, having broken no law, he refused ;† and was by the
governor's own warrant immediately committed to prison ; where
he was kept nine months to the great damage of his health, and
of his own as well as the people's interest.[3]

Amidst these multiplied oppressions, Cranfield was still disap-

(1) MSS. in files.   (2) Council Records.   (3) MSS. in files.

* [Nathaniel Weare is supposed to have been son of Peter Weare.   He was
born about the year 1631, and lived sometime in Newbury, where several of
his children were born.   He was admitted freeman in 1666, at which time he
belonged to Hampton.   He was appointed a counsellor of the province in
1692, and died 13 May, 1718, aged 87.   His son Peter, who was born at Newbury, 15 November, 1660, was also a counsellor of New-Hampshire, being appointed to that office in 1698.]

† In this refusal he is countenanced by the example of the great Selden, and
other members of parliament who were imprisoned by order of Charles I. in
1629.   Macaulay's Hist. Eng. 8vo. vol. 2, page 72.

pointed of the gains he had expected to reap from his office ; and 1684. found to his great mortification, that there was no way of supplying his wants, but by application to the people, through an assembly. He had already abused them so much that he could hope nothing from their favor ; and was therefore obliged to have recourse to artifice. On a vague rumor of a foreign war, he pretended much concern for the preservation of the province from invasion ; and presuming that they would show Jan. 14. the same concern for themselves, he called an assembly at Great-Island, where he resided, to whom he tendered a bill, which in a manner totally unparliamentary, had been drawn and passed by the council, for raising money to defray the expense of repairing the fort, and supplying it with ammunition, and for *other* necessary charges of government. The house* debated a while, and adjourned for the night, and the tide serving, the members went up to the town. In the morning, they returned the bill with their negative ; at which the governor was highly enraged, and telling them that they had been to consult with Moodey, and other declared enemies of the king and church of England, he dissolved them ; and afterward by his influence with the court of sessions, divers of the members were made constables for the following year.[1] Some of them took the oath, and others paid the fine, which was ten pounds. Thus by a mean and execrable revenge, he taxed those whom he could not persuade to tax their constituents for his purpose.

But Moodey was marked as an object of peculiar vengeance. He had for some time rendered himself obnoxious by the freedom and plainness of his pulpit discourses, and his strictness in administering the discipline of the church ; one instance of which merits particular notice. Randolph having seized a vessel, she was in the night carried out of the harbor. The owner, who was a member† of the church, swore that he knew nothing of it ; but upon trial, there appeared strong suspicions that he had perjured himself. He found means to make up the matter with the governor and collector ; but Moodey, being concerned for the purity

(1) Court Records. Vaughan's Journal.

* The Members of this assembly were, for

Portsmouth.	Hampton.
Richard Waldron, jun. speaker,	Anthony Stanyan,
Philip Lewis,	Joseph Smith,
John Pickering.	John Smith.
Dover.	Exeter.
John Gerrish,	Robert Smart,
John Woodman,	Thomas Wiggin.
Anthony Nutter.	Court Records.

† [From Adams, Annals Portsmouth, p. 78, we learn that the name of this member was George Janvrin, but from a letter from Randolph to the Lords of Trade and Plantations, it appears that it was " one Jefferys, a Scotchman," unless there were two similar cases. Jefferys was a member of the church.]

of his church, requested of the governor copies of the evidence, that the offender might be called to account in the way of ecclesiastical discipline. Cranfield sternly refused, saying that he had forgiven him, and that neither the church nor minister should meddle with him ; and even threatened Moodey in case he should. Not intimidated, Moodey consulted the church and preached a sermon against false swearing; then the offender, being called to account, was censured, and at length brought to a public confession.[1] This procedure extremely disgusted the governor, who had no way then in his power to show his resentment. But malice, ever fruitful in expedients to attain its ends, suggested a method, which to the scandal of the English nation, has been too often practised. The penal laws against nonconformists were at this time executing with great rigor in England ; and Cranfield, ambitious to ape his royal master, determined to play off the ecclesiastical artillery here, the direction of which he supposed to be deputed to him with his other powers. He had attempted to impose upon the people the observation of the thirtieth of January as a fast, and to restrain them from manual labor at Christmas ; but his capital stroke was to issue an order in council " that after the first of January, the ministers should ad-" mit all persons of suitable years and not vicious, to the Lord's " supper, and their children to baptism ; and that if any person " should desire baptism or the other sacrament to be administered " according to the liturgy of the church of England, it should be " done in pursuance of the king's command to the colony of " Massachusetts ;* and any minister refusing so to do should suf-" fer the penalty of the statutes of uniformity."

The same week in which he dissolved the assembly, he signified to Moodey in writing, by the hands of the sheriff, that himself, with Mason and Hinckes, intended to partake of the Lord's supper the next Sunday ; requiring him to administer it to them according to the liturgy ; and, as they justly expected, he at once

(1) Portsmouth Church Records.

* This command was conceived in the following terms :
" And since the principle and foundation of that charter was and is freedom and liberty of conscience ; Wee do hereby charge and require you that freedom and liberty be duely admitted and allowed, so that they that desire to use the booke of common prayer and perform their devotion in that manner that is established here be not denyed the exercise thereof, or undergoe any prejudice or disadvantage thereby, they using their liberty peaceably without any disturbance to others ; and that all persons of good and honest lives and conversations be admitted to the sacrament of the Lord's supper according to said booke of common prayer, and their children to baptism." King Charles's Letter in Hutchinson's coll. pap. p. 378.
This command cannot consistently with the acknowledged principle, and strict limitation, be construed any other way, than that the use of the liturgy should be permitted to such ministers and people as desired it. To compel ministers to use it, and leave all others at liberty, was a construction that malice alone could suggest.

denied them.   The way was now opened for a prosecution; and
Feb. 5.   the attorney general Joseph Rayn, by the governor's order,
exhibited an information at the next court of sessions, before
Walter Barefoote, judge, Nathaniel Fryer and Henry Greene, assistants, Peter Coffin, Thomas Edgerly and Henry Robie, justices,
setting forth, " that Joshua Moodey, clerk, being minister of the
" town of Portsmouth, within the dominions of King Charles, was
" by the duty of his place and the laws of the realm, viz. the
" statutes of the fifth and sixth of Edward VI, the first of Eliza-
" beth, and the thirteenth and fourteenth of Charles II, required
" to administer the Lord's supper in such form as was set forth
" in the book of common prayer, and no other.   But that the
" said Moodey, in contempt of the laws, had wilfully and obstin-
" ately refused to administer the same to the honorable Edward
" Cranfield, Robert Mason, and John Hinckes, and did obstinate-
" ly use some other form."[1]   Moodey in his defence pleaded that
he was not episcopally ordained as the statutes required; nor did
he receive his maintenance according to them ; and therefore
was not obliged to the performance of what had been commanded ; that the alleged statutes were not intended for these plantations, the known and avowed end of their settlement being the
enjoyment of freedom from the imposition of those laws ; which
freedom was allowed and confirmed by the king, in the liberty of
conscience granted to all protestants, in the governor's commission.[2] Four of the justices, viz. Greene, Robie, Edgerly and
Fryer were at first for acquitting him ; but the matter being adjourned till the next day, Cranfield found means before morning
to gain Robie and Greene, who then joined with Barefoote and
Coffin, in sentencing him to six months imprisonment, without
bail or mainprize.[3] The other two persisted in their former opinion, and were soon after removed from all their offices.* Moodey

(1) MSS. in files.   (2) Portsmouth Chh. Records.   (3) Vaughan's Journal.

* [In the Records of the Quarter Sessions, in the hand writing of Richard
Chamberlain, clerk of the court, I have found the substance of the debate of
the court, which was in private, on the case of Mr. Moodey. " It was debated among the Justices; and Henry Roby, Justice, did declare his opinion,
that he was very clear that the statutes are clear against the said Mr. Moodey,
if the commission that gives liberty of conscience doth not take away the
force thereof.

"Just. Edgerly—that since his Majesty has been pleased to grant liberty of
conscience to all Protestants here, the said Moodey is not liable to the penalty
of the statutes for refusing to administer the sacraments according to the form
thereof.

" Henry Green, Justice, was of opinion, that the said Moodey is guilty of
the breach of the laws, if the clause in the king's commission giving liberty
of conscience doth not excuse him.

"Nath. Frier, Justice, did affirm his opinion to be, that whereas his gracious
Majesty hath been pleased to grant liberty of conscience to all Protestants in
his royal commission, Mr. Moodey being a Protestant is not liable to the penalty of the acts of Parliament of the first of Queen Elizabeth, and the 13th
and 14th of K. Charles the Second.

was immediately ordered into custody, without being permitted first to see his family ; and he remained under confinement, in company with Major Vaughan, at the house of Captain Stileman, with liberty of the yard, for thirteen weeks ; " his benefice" being declared forfeited to the crown.   The next week after Moody's trial, the governor in a profane bravado sent word to Seaborn Cotton, minister of Hampton, that " when he had prepared his " soul, he would come and demand the sacrament of him as he " had done at Portsmouth."[1]   Upon which Cotton withdrew to Boston.*   The minister of Dover, John Pike, was (as far as I can find) unmolested.†   Exeter had then no settled minister.

(1) Vaughan's Journal.

"Peter Coffin, Justice, did hold that the said Joshua Moodey is guilty of the breach of the said statutes.

"Walter Barefoot, Esquire, was of opinion that the said Joshua Moodey had broken the said laws, and is liable to the penalty thereof."]

* [Rev. Seaborn Cotton was son of Rev. John Cotton, minister of the First Church in Boston, and was born on the Atlantic ocean, while his parents were on their voyage to New-England.   He was baptized at Boston on the 6 of September, 1633, being the second day after the arrival there of his father. He graduated at Harvard college in 1651, in the catalogue of which his name is entered *Marigena*.   He succeeded Rev. John Wheelwright as the minister of Hampton in 1660, and sustained the pastoral office until his death, 19 April, 1686, in the 53d year of his age.   There is scarcely any thing found in contemporary historians respecting his talents and character.   Mather, indeed, in the biography of his father, speaks of him as being " a thorough scholar, and an able preacher," and as condemning the errors of his name-sake Pelagius, a celebrated heresiarch of the fifth century, whose real name was Morgan.

Mr. Cotton was twice married.   His first wife was a daughter of Gov. Bradstreet, named Dorothy, whose mother was the lady so highly esteemed for her poetical powers.   His second wife was the widow of Dr. Anthony Crosby, of Rowley.   Besides a number of daughters, who married reputably, Mr. Cotton had two sons. John and Roland.   John was born 8 May, 1658, and graduated at Harvard college in 1678, in the same class with his cousin, the celebrated Cotton Mather, and with him, was admitted a member of the second church in Boston, then under the care of Rev. Increase Mather, on the 31 August, 1679.   He probably resided some time in Boston, as his name occurs several times after this period in early records.   He was ordained at Hampton as the successor to his father in 1696, and died 27 March, 1710, aged 52, having had one son and two daughters.   Roland, the second son of Rev. Seaborn Cotton, graduated at Harvard college in 1696; went to England, and was a physician in the Isle of Wright.]

† [John Pike was the successor of the second John Rayner.   He was son of Hon. Robert Pike, many years one of the assistants of the colony of Massachusetts, who died 12 December, 1706, at the age of 91.   He was born at Salisbury, 15 May, 1653, and received his education at Harvard college, where he graduated in 1675, in the class of which year, his name is placed at the head. He was ordained the 31 August, 1681, and remained at Dover until the desolation occasioned by the Indians in June, 1689, when he removed to Portsmouth.   The next year he went to Hampton, and from thence to Newbury in 1691.   He returned to Portsmouth, 6 October, 1692, and entered upon their Majesties service for Pemaquid fort, for which place he sailed on the 17 of the same month, and arrived there on the 26th.   He returned to Portsmouth, 13 July, 1695, and removed with his family to Dover, 11 November, 1698, where having remained nearly four years, he removed to his native town, 21 October, 1702, but again returned to Dover after a year or two, and there closed his days, 10 March, 1710, in the 57th year of his age.   (MS. letter of Mr.

During Moodey's imprisonment, Cranfield would neither suffer him to go up to the town to preach, nor the people to assemble at the island to hear, nor the neighboring ministers to supply his place ; only the family where he was confined were permitted to be present with him at sabbath exercises. But whilst the governor was absent on a tour to New-York, Mason gave leave for opening the meeting-house twice, when they obtained a minister to officiate ; he also allowed both Moodey and Vaughan to make a short visit to their families.[1] At length, by the interposition of friends, Moodey obtained a release, though under a strict charge to preach no more within the province, on penalty of farther imprisonment. He then accepted an invitation from the first church in Boston ; where, being out of the reach of his persecutors, he was employed as a preacher, and was so highly esteemed, that upon the death of President Rogers, he was invited to take the oversight of the college,[2] which he modestly declined, and continued his ministrations at Boston, frequently visiting his destitute church at Portsmouth, at their private meetings, till 1692 ; when, the government being in other hands, and the eastern country under trouble by the Indians, at the earnest request of his people, and by the advice of an ecclesiastical council he returned to his charge at Portsmouth, and spent the rest of his days there in usefulness, love and peace.* [3]

Upon a calm review of this prosecution, one can hardly tell which is most detestable, the vindictive temper which gave it birth ; or, the profaneness and hypocrisy with which it was conducted. The pretended zeal of the prosecutors was totally inconsistant with a due regard to those laws, and the principles of that church, for which they made themselves such contemptible champions. For it had been long before this time, a received opinion in the church of England, that the validity of all the sacramental administrations depends on authority derived from the apostles, by *episcopal* ordination, in an uninterrupted succession ; and one of the statutes on which the prosecution was grounded enacts, ' that ' no person shall presume to consecrate and administer the Lord's

(1) Vaughan's Journal.   (2) Harvard College Records.   (3) Original MSS.

Joshua Coffin, 23 April, 1830.)   Rev. Jabez Fitch, in his MSS. speaks of Mr. Pike as " a person of great humility, meekness and patience, much mortified to the world, and without gall or guile."   Dr. Belknap, in the church records of Dover, p. 16, says that Mr. Pike " was esteemed as an extraordinary preacher, and a man of true godliness. He was a grave and venerable person, and generally preached without notes. Those who were well acquainted with him have given him the character of a very considerable divine." Mather, in the Magnalia, ii. 511, says he " was much beholden to him" for communicating many passages which occur in his history. Some of his manuscript sermons were extant when Dr. Belknap wrote. Mr. Pike married in 1681, Sarah, the second daughter of Rev. Joshua Moodey, of Portsmouth.]

* He died at Boston, being there on a visit, July 4, 1697, aged 65. Dr. Cotton Mather preached his funeral sermon from Acts vi. 15. " They saw his face as it had been the face of an angel." Magnalia, lib. 4, cap. 7.

' supper, before he be ordained a priest by episcopal ordination,
' on pain of forfeiting for every offence one hundred pounds.'[1] The
ministers then in the province, being destitute of the grand pre-
requisite, were incapable by the act, of doing what was so peremptorily required of them ; and had they complied with the
governor's order, must have exposed themselves to the penalty,
if he had pleased to exact it from them. But the extending these
penalties to the king's American subjects, who had fled hither
from the rod of prelatic tyranny, was a most unwarrantable stretch
of power ; since the last of these acts, and the only one which
had been made since the settlement of the colonies, was expressly restricted in its operation, to "the realm of England, dominion
" of Wales, and town of Berwick upon Tweed."

Disappointed in all his schemes for raising money by an assembly, Cranfield next ventured on the project of taxing the people
without their consent. The pretext for this was a clause in the
commission, empowering him, with the council, "to continue such
" taxes as had been formerly levied, until a general assembly
" could be called." This had been done, without offence, at the
beginning both of this and the former administration, when the
change of government rendered it necessary. But the council,
though too much devoted to him, were not easily persuaded into
the measure at this time ; till fear at length accomplished what
reason could not approve : for, letters being received from the
eastward, informing of the discovery of a plot among the Indians,
who were instigated by Castine, the Frenchmen, to renew the war
early in the spring, the council were summoned in haste, Feb. 14.
and presently agreed to the governor's proposal, for continuing such taxes as had been formerly laid, which he told them
was necessary for the immediate defence and security of the province. This affair, however, was kept secret for the present ; and
the people were first to be convinced of the governor's paternal
care and kindness in taking the necessary precautions for their
safety. It was ordered that the meeting-houses in each Mar. 18.
town should be fortified, and by-garrisons were established in convenient places : supplies of ammunition were ordered to
be provided ; circular letters were dispatched to the governors of
the neighboring colonies, informing them of the danger ; and, to
crown the whole, Cranfield himself, at the request of the council,
undertook a tour to New-York to solicit the governor, Dongan,
for a number of the Mohawks to come down and destroy the
eastern Indians ; promising to pay them for their services out of
the money which was thus to be raised.[2]

At his return from this excursion, he found himself under some
embarrassment in his favorite views, from a letter of the lords of
trade, which directed him to make use of an assembly, in raising

(1) Stat. 13 and 14, Char. II.   (2) Council Records.   Vaughan's Journal.

money on the people. He could not, therefore, avoid calling
May 27. one, though he immediately dissolved it, because several
of the members were those whom he had formerly ordered to be made constables.   At the same time, in his letters to the
secretary of state, he represented the assembly as persons of such
a mutinous and rebellious disposition, that it was not safe to let
them convene ; that they had never given any thing toward the
support of government ; that he was obliged to raise money without them ; and that it was impossible for him to serve his majesty's interest without a ship of war to enforce his orders ; and finally, he desired leave to go to the West-Indies for the recovery of
his health.   When this business was despatched, warrants were
issued for collecting the taxes ; which caused fresh murmurings
and discontent among the people.

But however disaffected to the governor and his creatures, they
were always ready to testify their obedience to the royal orders ;
an instance of which occurred at this time.   The seas of America and the West-Indies being much infested with pirates, the king
sent orders to all the governors and colony assemblies, directing
acts to made for the suppressing of piracy and robbery on the
July 22. high seas.   Cranfield, having received this order, summoned an assembly ; and though it consisted almost entirely
of the same persons who were in the last ; he suffered them to
pass the act, and then quietly dissolved them :[1] this was the last
assembly that ever he called.

The tax-bills were first put into the hands of the newly made
constables ; who soon returned them, informing the governor that
the people were so averse to the method, that it was impossible to
collect the money.   The provost, Thomas Thurton, was then
commanded to do it, with the assistance of his deputies and the
constables.   The people still refusing compliance, their cattle and
goods were taken by distraint and sold by auction.   Those who
would neither pay nor discover their goods to the officers, were
apprehended and imprisoned ; and some of the constables, who
refused to assist, suffered the same fate.   The more considerate
of the people were disposed to bear these grievances, though
highly irritating, till they could know the result of their applications to the king.   But in a country where the love of liberty had
ever been the ruling passion, it could not be expected but that
some forward spirits would break the restraints of prudence, and
take a summary method to put a stop to their oppressions.   Several persons had declared that they would sooner part with their
lives, than suffer distraints ; and associations were formed for mu-
Dec. 29. tual support.   At Exeter, the sheriff was resisted and
driven off with clubs ; the women having prepared hot
spits and scalding water to assist in the opposition, as Thurton testi-

(1) Council Records and files.

fied in his deposition on the occasion. At Hampton, he was beaten, and his sword was taken from him ; then he was seated on a horse, and conveyed out of the province to Salisbury, with Jan. 22. a rope about his neck and his feet tied under the horse's belly.   Justice Robie attempted to commit some of the rioters ; but they were rescued by the way, and both the justice and the sheriff were struck in the execution of their office.   The Jan. 9. troop of horse, under Mason's command, was then ordered to turn out completely mounted and armed, to assist in suppressing the disorders ; but when the day came, not one trooper appeared.[1]   Cranfield thus finding his efforts ineffectual, and his authority contemptible was obliged to desist.

The agent had been a long time in England, waiting for the depositions, which were to have been transmitted to him, in support of the complaint which he was to exhibit.   Cranfield and his creatures here did all that they could, to retard the business ; first by imprisoning Vaughan, and then by refusing to summon and swear witnesses when applied to by others ; who were obliged to go into the neighboring governments, to get their depositions authenticated ; and after all, the proof was defective, as they had not access to the public records.   The agent, however, July 11. exhibited his complaint against Cranfield in general terms, consisting of eight articles.   ' That he had engrossed the power ' of erecting courts, and establishing fees exclusive of the assem- ' bly : That he had not followed the directions in his commission ' respecting Mason's controversy ; but had caused it to be decided ' on the spot by courts of his own constitution, consisting wholly ' of persons devoted to his interest : That exorbitant charges had ' been exacted and some who were unable to satisfy them had ' been imprisoned : That others had been obliged to submit, for ' want of money to carry on the suits : That he had altered the ' value of silver money : That he had imprisoned sundry persons ' without just cause : That he, with his council, had assumed leg- ' islative authority, without an assembly ; and, That he had done ' his utmost to prevent the people from laying their complaints ' before the king, and procuring the necessary evidence.'[2]

The complaint was, in course, referred to the board of trade ; who transmitted copies of it, and of the several proofs, to July 23. Cranfield, and summoned him to make his defence ; directing him to deliver to the adverse party, copies of all the affidavits which should be taken in his favor ; to let all persons have free access to the records ; and to give all needful assistance to them in collecting their evidence against him.[3]

When he had received this letter, he suspended Mason's suits, till the question concerning the legality of the courts should be decided.   He also ordered the secretary to give copies to those

(1) MSS. in files.   (2) Weare's MSS.   (3) Ibid.

who should apply for them.   At the same time, it was complained
that the people, on their part, had been equally reserved, in se-
creting the records of the several towns; so that Mason, upon
inquiry, could not find where they were deposited ; and the town
clerks, when summoned, had solemnly sworn that they knew
neither where the books were concealed, nor who had taken them
out of their possession.[1]

The necessary evidence on both sides being procured, a new
complaint was drawn up, consisting of twelve articles,
1685. which were, 'That at the first session of the assembly,
' Cranfield had challenged the power of legislation and settlement
' of the affairs to himself, against the words of the commission :
' That he had by purchase or mortgage from Mason, made him-
' self owner of the province, and so was not likely to act impar-
' tially between Mason and the inhabitants : That he had made
' courts, whereof both judges and jurors had agreed with Mason
' for their own lands, and some had taken deeds of him for other
' men's lands, so that they were engaged by their interest to set
' up Mason's title : That Mason had sued forty persons, and cast
' all; and that the governor's interposal to state the cases, as by
' his commission he was directed, had been refused though de-
' sired ; and that the defendants pleas, grounded on the laws of
' England, were rejected : That they could not reconcile the ver-
' dict with the attachment, nor the execution with the verdict, nor
' their practice under color of the execution with either ; that the
' verdict found the lands sued for according to the royal commis-
' sion and instructions, and that commission only gave power to
' state the case, if Mason and the people could not agree ; but
' the execution took land and all : That the charge of every ac-
' tion was about six pounds, though nothing was done in court,
' but reading the commission and some blank grants without hand
' or seal; and these were not read for one case in ten : That
' court charges were exacted in money, which many had not ;
' who though they tendered cattle, were committed to prison for
' non-payment : That ministers, contrary to his majesty's com-
' mission, which granted liberty of conscience to all protestants,
' had their dues withheld from them, even those that were due
' before Cranfield came, and were threatened with six month's
' imprisonment for not administering the sacrament according to
' the liturgy ; that though the general assembly agreed that Span-
' ish money should pass by weight, the governor and council or-
' dered pieces of eight to pass for six shillings, though under
' weight : that men were commonly compelled to enter into bonds
' of great penalty, to appear and answer to what should be ob-
' jected against them, when no crime was alleged : that they had
' few laws, but those made by the governor and council, when his

' commission directed the general assembly to make laws : that
' the courts were kept in a remote corner of the province ; and
' the sheriff was a stranger and had no visible estate, and so was
' not responsible for failures.'[1]

Upon this complaint, an hearing was had before the lords of
trade on Tuesday the tenth of March ; and their lordships reported to the king, on three articles only of the complaint, viz. ' That
' Cranfield had not pursued his instructions with regard to Mason's
' controversy ; but instead thereof, had caused courts to be held
' and titles to be decided, with exorbitant costs ; and that he
' had exceeded his power in regulating the value of coins.' This
report was accepted, and the king's pleasure therein was signified
to him.   At the same time, his request for absence being granted,
he, on receipt of the letters, privately embarked on board a vessel
for Jamaica ; and from thence went to England, where he obtained the collectorship of Barbadoes.[2] *   At his departure, Barefoote, the deputy-governor, took the chair ; which he held till he
was superseded by Dudley's commission, as president of New-
England.

Cranfield's ill conduct must be ascribed in a great measure to
his disappointment of the gains which he expected to acquire, by
the establishment of Mason's title ; which could be his only inducement to accept of the government.   This disappointment in-
flaming his temper, naturally vindictive and imperious, urged him to
actions not only illegal, but cruel and unmanly.   A ruler never de-
grades his character more than when he perverts public justice to
gratify personal resentment ; he should punish none but the enemies of the laws, and disturbers of the peace of the community
over which he presides.   Had there been the least color, either of
zeal or policy, for the severity exercised in the prosecution of
Moodey, candor would oblige us to make some allowance for
human frailty.   His ordering the members of the assembly to be
made constables, was a mode of revenge disgraceful to the character of the supreme magistrate.[3]   From the same base disposition,
he is said to have employed spies and pimps, to find matter of
accusation against people in their clubs, and private discourse.

(1) Weare's MSS.   (2) Neal's Hist. and Fitch's MS.   (3) Neal, vol. 2, p. 39.

* [The following note, from the Appendix of the second volume of the first
edition of this history, may be here introduced. "Since writing the first volume, I have met with a gentleman of Jamaica, who is a great grandson of
Lieut. Governor Cranfield. From him, I learned that Mr. Cranfield was of
the family of Lord Monteagle, who was instrumental of discovering the popish plot in the reign of James I. That after his departure from New-Hampshire, and whilst he resided at Barbadoes, he suggested the expediency of the
4 and an half per cent. duty on sugars to the British government which was
granted by the Assemblies of the islands, and has ever since been continued.
That in the reign of King William III., he procured a ship of war, at his own
expense, and presented it to the crown. That he died about the beginning of
the present century, [the eighteenth] and was buried in the Cathedral Church,
at Bath, in England."]

And his deceit was equal to his malice; for, being at Boston when the charter of that colony was called in question, and the people were solicitous to ward off the danger; he advised them to make a private offer of two thousand guineas to the king, promising to represent them in a favorable light; but when they, not suspecting his intention, followed his advice, and shewed him the letter which they had wrote to their agents for that purpose, he treacherously represented them as " disloyal rogues;" and made them appear so ridiculous that their agents were ashamed to be seen at court.[1]   However, when he had quitted the country, and had time for reflection, he grew ashamed of his misconduct, and whilst he was collector at Barbadoes, made a point of treating the masters of vessels, and others persons who went thither from Pascataqua, with particular respect.[2]

Although the decision of titles in Cranfield's courts had been represented, in the report of the lords, as extrajudicial, and a royal order had been thereupon issued to suspend any farther proceedings in the case of Mason, till the matter should be brought before the king in council, pursuant to the directions in the commission; yet Barefoote suffered executions, which had before been issued, to be extended, and persons to be imprisoned at Mason's suit.   This occasioned a fresh complaint and petition to the king, which was sent by Weare, who, about this time, made a second voyage to England, as agent for the province and attorney to Vaughan, to manage an appeal from several verdicts, judgments, decrees and fines which had been given against him in the courts here, one of which was on the title to his estate.[3] An attempt being made to levy one of the executions in Dover, a number of persons forcibly resisted the officer, and obliged him to relinquish his design.[4] Warrants were then issued against the rioters, and the sheriff with his attendants attempted to seize them, whilst the people were assembled for divine service.   This caused an uproar in the congregation, in which a young heroine distinguished herself by knocking down one of the officers with her bible.   They were all so roughly handled that they were glad to escape with their lives.

That nothing might be wanting to show the enmity of the people to these measures, and their hatred and contempt for the authors of them; there are still preserved the original depositions on oath, of Barefoote and Mason, relating to an assault made on their persons by Thomas Wiggin and Anthony Nutter, who had been members of the assembly.[5] These two men came to Barefoote's house, where Mason lodged, and entered into discourse with him about his proceedings; denying his claim, and using such language as provoked him to take hold of Wiggin, with

Dec. 30.

(1) Hutch. vol. i. p. 337.   (2) Fitch's MS.   (3) Weare's MSS.   (4) MSS. in files.   (5) Ibid.

an intention to thrust him out at the door.   But Wiggin being a
stronger man seized him by his cravat, and threw him into the fire ;
where his clothes and one of his legs were burned.   Barefoote,
attempting to help him, met with the same fate, and had two of
his ribs broken and one of his teeth beaten out in the struggle.
The noise alarmed the servants, who at Mason's command brought
his sword, which Nutter took away, making sport of their misery.*

Nothing else occurred during Barefoote's short administration,
except a treaty of friendship, between the Indians of Penacook
and Saco, on the one part, and the people of New-Hampshire and
Maine, on the other.   The foundation of this treaty seems to have
been laid in Cranfield's project of bringing down the Mohawks on
the eastern Indians ; which had once before proved a pernicious
measure ; as they made no distinction between those tribes which
were at peace with the English, and those which were at war.
Some of the Penacook Indians who had been at Albany after
Cranfield's journey to New-York, reported on their return, that
the Mohawks threatened destruction to all the eastern Indians,
from Narraganset to Pegypscot.   Hagkins, a chief of the tribe,
had informed Cranfield in the spring of the danger he apprehended, and had implored assistance and protection, but had been
treated with neglect.   In August, the Penacook and Saco Indians
gathered their corn, and removed their families ; which gave an
alarm to their English neighbors, as if they were preparing for
war.   Messengers being sent to demand the reason of their
movement, were informed that it was the fear of the Mohawks,
whom they daily expected to destroy them ; and being asked
why they did not come in among the English for protection, they
answered lest the Mohawks should hurt the English on their account.   Upon this, they were persuaded to enter into an agreement ; and accordingly their chiefs being assembled with Sept. 8.
the council of New-Hampshire, and a deputation from the
province of Maine, a treaty was concluded, wherein it was stipulated, that all future personal injuries on either side, should, upon

---

* A farther specimen of the contempt in which these men were held, even
by the lower class of people, expressed in their own genuine language, may
be seen in the following affidavit :

"Mary Rann, aged thirty years or thereabout, witnesseth, that the 21 day
of March, '84. being in company with Seabank Hog,† I heard her say ; it was
very hard for the governor of this province to strike Sam. Seavy before he
spoke ; the said Hog said also that it was well the said Seavy's *mother* was
not there for the governor, for if she had, there had been bloody work for
him. I heard the said Hog say also, that the governor and the rest of the
gentlemen were a crew of pitiful curs, and did they want earthly honor ? if
they did, she would pull off her head clothes and come in her hair to them,
like a parcel of pitiful beggarly curs as they were ; come to undo us both body
and soul ; they could not be contented to take our estates from us, but they
have taken away the gospel also, which the devil would have them for it."

"Sworn in the court of pleas held at Great Island the 7 of Nov. 1684.

R. CHAMBERLAIN, Prothon."

† [This name is *Hodg* in the records of the Quarter Sessions.]

complaint, be immediately redressed ; that information should be given of approaching danger from enemies; that the Indians should not remove their families from the neighborhood of the English without giving timely notice, and if they did, that it should be taken for a declaration of war ; and, that whilst these articles were observed, the English would assist and protect them against the Mohawks, and all other enemies.[1] The danger was but imaginary, and the peace continued about four years.

Though Mason was hitherto disappointed in his views of recovering the inhabited part of the province, he endeavored to lay a foundation for realizing his claim to the waste lands. A purchase having been made from the Indians, by Jonathan Tyng and nineteen others,* of a tract of land on both sides the river Merrimack, six miles in breadth, from Souhegan river to Winnipiseogee lake ; Mason by deed confirmed the same, reserving to himself

Apr. 15. and his heirs the yearly rent of ten shillings. This was called the million acre purchase.[2] About the same time, he farmed out to Hezekiah Usher and his heirs, the mines, min-

May 15. erals, and ores within the limits of New-Hampshire, for the term of one thousand years ; reserving to himself one quarter part of the royal ores, and one seventeenth of the baser sorts,[3] and having put his affairs here in the best order that the times would admit, he sailed for England, to attend the hearing of Vaughan's appeal to the king.†

(1) Original MSS. in files.   (2) Douglass, vol. i. p. 419.   (3) Rec. of Deeds.

* [The other purchasers were Joseph Dudley, Charles Lidget, John Usher, Edward Randolph, John Hubbard, Robert Thompson, Samuel Shrimpton, William Stoughton, Richard Warton, Thomas Hinchman, Thaddeus Maccarty, Edward Thompson, John Blackwell, Peter Bulkley, William Blathwayt, Daniel Cox, and " three other persons to be hereafter named and agreed upon." Douglass, i. 420.]

† [The town of Dunstable having been granted by Massachusetts, and settled for a number of years, ordained a minister at the close of the year 1685. The members who united in forming the church were, Thomas Weld, Jonathan Tyng, John Blanchard, Cornelius Waldo, Samuel Warner, Obadiah Perry and Samuel French. Rev. Thomas Weld, the first named, graduated at Harvard college in 1671 ; was ordained 16 December, 1685, and died 9 June, 1702, in the 50th year of his age. He was son of Thomas Weld, of Roxbury, and grandson of Rev. Thomas Weld, one of the first ministers of that town, who returned to England, and there died. Mr. Weld was succeeded in the ministry at Dunstable by Rev. Nathaniel Prentice, who graduated at Harvard college in 1715. He was ordained in 1718, and died 25 February, 1737. Dunstable suffered much from the Indians, as will appear in the course of this history. In the time of Philip's war, some of the inhabitants were obliged to leave their settlements and take up their residence in the older towns, but I have met with no evidence showing that the town was at any time wholly abandoned by the inhabitants. The early settlers of Dunstable were those above named, with Robert Parris, Thomas Cumings, Isaac Cumings, Joseph Hassell, Christopher Temple, John Goold, Samuel Goold, Christopher Read, John Sollendine, Thomas Lund, Daniel Waldo, Andrew Cook, and Samuel Whiting (son of Rev. Samuel Whiting, of Billerica) who was several years the town clerk, and who died in Billerica, 14 March, 1715, aged 53. On the settlement of the divisional line between the provinces of New-Hampshire

CHAPTER IX.

The administration of Dudley as President, and Andros as governor of New-England. Mason's farther attempt. His disappointment and death. Revolution. Sale to Allen. His commission for the government.

WHEN an arbitrary government is determined to infringe the liberty of the people, it is easy to find pretences to support the most unrighteous claims. King Charles the Second in the latter part of his reign was making large strides toward despotism.— Charters, which obstructed his pernicious views, were by a perversion of the law decreed forfeited. The city of London, and most of the corporations in England, either suffered the execution of these sentences, or tamely surrendered their franchises to the all-grasping hand of power. It could not be expected that in this general wreck of privileges, the colonies of New-England could escape. The people of Massachusetts had long been viewed with a jealous eye.[1] Though the king had repeatedly assured them of his protection, and solemnly confirmed their charter privileges ; yet their spirit and principles were so totally dissonant to the corrupt views of the court, that intriguing men found easy access to the royal ear, with complaints against them. Of these, the most inveterate and indefatigable was Randolph, who made no less than eight voyages in nine years across the Atlantic, on this mischievous business.[2] They were accused of extending their jurisdiction beyond the bounds of their patent ; of invading the prerogative by coining money ; of not allowing appeals to the king from their courts ; and, of obstructing the execution of the navigation and trade laws. By the king's command, agents were sent over to answer these complaints. They found the prejudice against the colony so strong, that it was in vain to withstand it ; and solicited instructions whether to submit to the king's pleasure, or to let the proceedings against them be issued in form of law. A solemn consultation being held, at which the clergy assisted, it was determined " to die by the hands of others rather than by " their own." Upon notice of this, the agents quitted England ; and Randolph, as the angel of death, soon followed them, bringing a writ of *quo warranto* from the king's bench ; 1683. October. but the *scire facias* which issued from the chancery did not arrive till the time fixed for their appearance was elapsed.

(1) Hutch. col. papers. p. 377.   (2) Hutch. vol. i. p. 329.

and Massachusetts, Dunstable was divided into two distinct townships, one in each province. Dunstable in New-Hampshire, which included the ancient settlement, and by far the largest portion of territory, was incorporated by charter, 1 April, 1746.]

This however, was deemed too trivial an error to stop the proceedings ; judgment was entered against them, and the charter declared forfeited.

The king died before a new form of government was settled ; but there could be no hope of favor from his successor, who inherited the arbitrary principles of his brother, and was publicly known to be a bigoted papist.

1685.
Feb. 6.

The intended alteration in the government was introduced in the same gradual manner as it had been in New-Hampshire. A commission was issued, in which Joseph Dudley, esquire, was appointed president of his majesty's territory and dominion of New-England ; William Stoughton, deputy president ; Simon Bradstreet, Robert Mason, John Fitz Winthrop, John Pynchon, Peter Bulkley, Edward Randolph, Wait Winthrop, Richard Warton, John Usher, Nathaniel Saltonstall, Bartholomew Gedney, Jonathan Tyng, Dudley Bradstreet, John Hinckes,* and Edward Tyng, counsellors. Their jurisdiction extended over Massachusetts, New-Hampshire, Maine and the Narraganset, or King's province. These gentlemen were mostly natives of the country, some of them had been magistrates, and one of them, governor under the charter. No house of deputies was mentioned in the commission.

The new form of government took place on the twenty-fifth day of May ; and on the tenth of June, an order of council was issued for settling the county courts, which consisted of such members of the council as resided in each county, and any others of them who might be present ; with such justices as were commissioned for the purpose. These courts had the power of trying and issuing all civil causes, and all criminal matters under life or limb ; from them an appeal was allowed to a superior court, held three times in the year, at Boston, for the whole territory ; and from thence, appeals, in certain cases, might be had to the king in council. Juries were pricked by the marshal and one justice of each county, in a list given them by the selectmen of the towns. A probate court was held at Boston, by the president, and " in the other provinces and remote counties" by a judge and clerk, appointed by the president. The territory was divided into four counties, viz. Suffolk, Middlesex, Essex and Hampshire ; and three provinces, viz. New-Hampshire, Maine, and King's province. By another order of the same date, town-taxes could not be assessed, but by allowance of two justices ; and the members of the council were exempted from paying any part thereof.[1]

1686.

Things were conducted with tolerable decency, and the innova-

(1) Printed orders in the files.

* [Hinckes was the only one of these counsellors who belonged to New-Hampshire. He had been appointed one of the provincial counsellors in 1683, and afterwards, in 1687, was one of Sir Edmund Andros's council.]

tions were rendered as little grievious as possible ; that the people might be induced more readily to submit to the long meditated introduction of a governor-general.

In December following, Sir Edmund Andros who had been governor of New-York, arrived at Boston with a commission, appointing him captain-general and governor in chief **Dec. 30.** of the territory and dominion of New-England, in which the colony of Plymouth was now included.* By this commission, the governor with his council, five of whom were a quorum, were empowered to make such laws, impose such taxes, and apply them to such purposes as they should think proper. They were also empowered to grant lands on such terms, and subject to such quit-rents, as should be appointed by the king.[1] Invested with such powers, these men were capable of the most extravagant actions. Though Andros, like his master, began his administration with the fairest professions, yet, like him, he soon violated them, and proved himself a fit instrument for accomplishing the most execrable designs. Those of his council who were backward in aiding his rapacious intentions were neglected. Seven being sufficient for a full board, he selected such only as were devoted to him, and, with their concurrence, did what he pleased. Randolph and Mason were at first among his confidants ; but afterward when New-York was annexed to his government, the members from that quarter were most in his favor.[2]

To particularize the many instances of tyranny and oppression which the country suffered from these men, is not within the design of this work. Let it suffice to observe, that the press was restrained ; liberty of conscience infringed ; ex- **1687.** orbitant fees and taxes demanded, without the voice or consent of the people, who had no privilege of representation. The charter being vacated, it was pretended that all titles to land were annulled ; and as to Indian deeds, Andros declared them no better than " the scratch of a bear's paw."[3] Landholders were obliged to take out patents for their estates which they had possessed forty or fifty years : for these patents, extravagant fees were exacted, and those, who would not submit to this imposition, had writs of intrusion brought against them, and their land was patented to others. To hinder the people from consulting about the redress of their grievances, town-meetings were prohibited, except one in the month of May, for the choice of town officers ; and to prevent complaints being carried to England, no person was permitted to go out of the country without express leave from the gov-

(1) MS. Copy of the Commission.   (2) Hutch. vol. i. p. 344. Coll. papers, p. 564.   (3) Revolution in New-England justified, p. 21.

* [" There was a great new seal appointed for New-England under the administration of Andros, which was honored with a remarkable motto : *Nunquam libertas gratior extat.*" Chalmers, 463.]

ernor.   But notwithstanding all the vigilance of the governor, his emissaries and his guards, the resolute and indefatigable Increase Mather, minister of the second church in Boston, and president of the college, got on board a ship and sailed for England, with complaints in the name of the people against the governor, which he delivered with his own hand to the king ; but finding no hope of redress, he waited the event of the revolution which was then expected.[1]

When the people groaned under so many real grievances, it is no wonder that their fears and jealousies suggested some that were imaginary.   They believed Andros to be a papist ; that **1688.** he had hired the Indians, and supplied them with ammunition to destroy their frontier settlements ; and that he was preparing to betray the country into the hands of the French.[*2]   At the same time, the large strides that King James the Second was making toward the establishment of popery and despotism, raised the most terrible apprehensions ; so that the report of the landing of the Prince of Orange in England was received here with the greatest joy.   Andros was so alarmed at the news, that he imprisoned the man[†] who brought a copy of the prince's declaration, and published a proclamation commanding all persons to be in readiness to oppose " any invasion from Holland," which met with as much disregard as one he had issued before, appointing a day of thanksgiving for the birth of a Prince of Wales.

The people had now borne these innovations and impositions for about three years :   Their patience was worn out, and their native love of freedom kindled at the prospect of deliver-**1689.** ance.   The news of a complete revolution in England had not reached them ; yet so sanguine were their expectations, so eager were they to prove that they were animated by the same spirit with their brethren at home, that upon the rumor of an intended massacre in the town of Boston by the governor's guards, they were wrought up to a degree of fury.   On the morning of

(1) I. Mather's life, p. 107.   (2) Revolution justified, p. 29, 40.

* [Justice to Sir Edmund Andros requires it to be stated, in reply to these allegations in Revolution in N. E. justified, that he sent a letter to the Justices of the Court of New-Hampshire, concerning trading with the Indians, whereupon it was, probably in pursuance of the instructions contained in it, at a private or special session, holden on the 28 of January, 1688-9, by his Majesty's Justices, " Ordered that no person within this Province (of New-Hampshire) presume to trade with, furnish or supply any Indian, or Indians (particularly those of Pennicook) with any ammunition, instruments of war, goods, provision, or any thing whatsoever.   And whosoever can give any information of any person or persons that have already supplied and furnished the said Indians with ammunition and instruments of war, they are desired forthwith to give notice thereof to the next Justice of the Peace, that they may be secured and proceeded against with all severity." Records of the Quarter Sessions.]

† [John Winslow, of Boston, who, although he offered £2000 security, could not escape imprisonment.]

the eighteenth of April, the town was in arms, and the country flocking in to their assistance. The governor, and those who had fled with him to the fort, were seized and committed to prison. The gentlemen who had been magistrates under the charter, with Bradstreet, the late governor, at their head, assumed the name of a council of safety, and kept up a form of government, in the exigency of affairs, till orders arrived from England ; when Andros and his accomplices were sent home as prisoners of state, to be disposed of according to the king's pleasure.

The people of New-Hampshire had their share of sufferings under this rapacious administration ; and Mason himself did not escape. Having attended the hearing of Vaughan's appeal to the king, which was decided in Mason's favor ; the judg- Nov. 6, ment obtained here, being affirmed ; and having now the 1686. fairest prospect of realizing his claim, he returned hither in the spring of 1687, but found his views obstructed in a manner which he little expected. The government was in the hands of a set of hungry harpies, who looked with envy on the large share of territory which Mason claimed, and were for parcelling it out among themselves.[1] The new judges delayed issuing executions on the judgments which he had formerly recovered, and the attorney-general, Graham,* would not allow that he had power to grant lands by leases. This confirmed the people in their opinion of the invalidity of his claim, and rendered them (if possible) more averse to him than ever they had been. At length, however, he obtained from Dudley, the chief justice, a writ of *certiorari*, directed to the late judges of New-Hampshire, by which, his causes were to be removed to the supreme court of July 18, the whole territory, then held at Boston ;[2] but before this 1688. could be done, death put an end to his hopes and relieved the people for a time of their fears. Being one of Sir Ed- Aug. or mund's council, and attending him on a journey from New- Sept. York to Albany ; he died at Esopus, in the fifty-ninth 1688. year of his age ; leaving two sons, John and Robert, the heirs of his claim and controversy.[3]

The revolution at Boston, though extremely pleasing to the people of New-Hampshire, left them in an unsettled state. They waited the arrival of orders from England ; but none arriving, and the people's minds being uneasy, it was proposed by some of the principal gentlemen, that a convention of deputies from each of the towns should consider what was best to be done. The convention-parliament in England was a sufficient precedent to

(1) Hutch. collection of papers, p. 564.   (2) MS. in Superior Court files. (3) Hutch. vol. i. p. 365.   Coll. papers, p. 566.

* [James Graham was one of the confidants and advisers of Sir Edmund Andros, and his attorney-general.   See Revolution in N. E. justified 21, 31, Hutchinson, Hist. Mass. i. 345.]

authorize this proceeding. Deputies were accordingly chosen,*
and instructed to resolve upon some method of government. At
Jan.   their first meeting, they came to no conclusion ; but after-
1690.   ward, they thought it best to return to their ancient union
        with Massachusetts.[1] A petition† for this purpose being
presented, they were readily admitted till the king's pleasure should
Mar. 12. be known ; and members were sent to the general court,
        which met there in this and the two following years.‡—
The gentlemen who had formerly been in commission for the
peace, the militia and the civil offices, were by town votes, approved by the general court, restored to their places, and ancient
laws and customs continued to be observed.‖

(1) Mass. Records. Portsmouth, Dover and Exeter Records.

* The members of this convention were, for

Portsmouth.	John Tuttle,
Major William Vaughan,	John Roberts,
Richard Waldron,	Thomas Edgerly,
Nathaniel Fryer,	Nicholas Follet.
Robert Elliot,	*Exeter.*
Thomas Cobbet,	Robert Wadley,
Capt. John Pickering.	William Moore,
Dover.	Samuel Leavitt.
Capt. John Woodman,	Portsmouth, Dover and Exeter
Capt. John Gerrish,	Records

It does not appear from Hampton records whether they joined in this convention, or returned immediately to the government of Massachusetts.
[From a letter of Nathaniel Weare of Hampton to Major Robert Pike of
Salisbury, dated 15 March, 1690, printed in the Coll. of the N. H. Hist. Soc.
i. 136, it appears that Hampton was one of the *first* towns in choosing persons
to meet with commissioners of the other towns, if they should see cause to
appoint any, "to debate and conclude of what was necessary at this time to be
done in relation to some orderly way of government, and to make their return
to the several towns for their approbation or otherwise." Afterwards, when
the inhabitants of Portsmouth had met, and " made choice of some persons,
to meet with the commissioners of the other towns to debate and consider of
what was to be done in order to the settlement of some government till their
Majesties should give order in the matter," the town of Hampton, " after
several meetings and debates," chose six persons as commissioners, with power according to the other towns of Portsmouth, Dover and Exeter. But in
the choice of " meet persons" for the *Convention,* it seems that a spirit of
jealousy arose among the people of Hampton, who, being " fearful and suspicious of their neighbor towns ;—that they did not intend to do as was pretended, but to bring them under to their disadvantage," passed a vote that
" they would not choose any person according to the direction of the committee met, and so all proved ineffectual."]

† [The original petition, signed by 372 persons, is among the files in the
Secretary's office of Massachusetts, and a copy of it is in the office of Secretary of State of New-Hampshire.]

‡ [The representatives, during this period, for Portsmouth, were,
1690 Elias Stileman,   1691 Richard Waldron,   1692 Richard Waldron.
    John Foster.   John Pickering.
Waldron was son of the Major who was killed by the Indians in 1689.]

‖ [The Military and Civil officers as presented to the Governor and Council, and approved by them and the deputies of Massachusetts, in March, 1690,
were the following.
                    Military Officers.
              William Vaughan, Major.

Had the inclination of the people been consulted, they would gladly have been annexed to that government. This was 1691. well known to Mather and the other agents, who when soliciting for a new charter, earnestly requested that New-Hampshire might be included in it.[1] But it was answered, that the people had expressed an aversion to it, and desired to be under a distinct government.[2] This could be founded only on the reports which had been made by the commissioners in 1665, and by Randolph in his narrative. The true reason for denying the request was, that Mason's two heirs had sold their title to the lands in New-Hampshire to Samuel Allen of London, merchant, for seven hundred and fifty pounds, the entail having been previously docked by a fine and recovery in the court of king's bench ; and Allen was then soliciting a recognition of his title from the crown, and a commission for the government of the province.[3] When the inhabitants were informed of what was doing, they again assembled by deputies in convention, and sent over a petition to the king, praying that they might be annexed to Massachusetts. The petition was presented to Sir Henry Ashurst, and they were amused with some equivocal promises of success by the earl of Nottingham; but Allen's importunity coinciding with the king's inclination, effectually frustrated their attempt. [4] The claim which Allen had to the lands from Naumkeag to three miles northward of Merrimack, was noticed in the Massachusetts charter; and he obtained a commission for the government of New-Hampshire, in which his son in law, John Usher, then in London, was appointed lieutenant governor, with power to execute the commission in Allen's absence. The counsellors named in the governor's instructions, were, John Usher, lieutenant governor, John Hinckes, Nathaniel Fryer, Thomas Graffort, Peter Coffin, Henry Green, Robert Elliot, John Ger-

Apr. 27.

1692.

Mar. 1.

(1) I. Mather's life, page 136.   (2) Hutch. vol. i. p. 412.   (3) MS. in Superior Court files.   (4) Hutch. vol. ?, p. 6.

Dover.	Exeter.
John Gerrish, Captain.	William Moore, Captain.
John Tuttle, Lieutenant.	Samuel Leavitt, Lieutenant.
William Furber, Ensign.	Jonathan Thing, Ensign.
Oyster River. [Durham.]	*Great-Island.* [New-Castle.]
John Woodman, Captain.	Nathaniel Fryer, Captain.
James Davis, Lieutenant.	Thomas Cobbet, Lieutenant.
Stephen Jones, Ensign.	Shadrach Walton, Ensign.
Portsmouth.	*Hampton.*
Walter Neale, Captain.	Samuel Sherburne, Captain.
John Pickering, Lieutenant.	Edward Gove, Lieutenant.
Tobias Langdon, Ensign.	John Moulton, Ensign.

Civil Officers.

Samuel Penhallow, Treasurer.   John Pickering, Recorder.

Justices of the Peace.

William Vaughan, Portsmouth.	John Gerrish, Dover.
Richard Martyn, do.	Robert Wadleigh, Exeter.]
Nathaniel Fryer, do.	

rish, John Walford and John Love. The governor was instructed to send to the secretary of state, the names of six other persons suitable for counsellors. Three were a quorum, but the instructions were, that nothing should be done unless five were
present, except in extraordinary emergencies. Major Vaughan,
Nathaniel Weare and Richard Waldron were afterward added to
the number.[1]

The council was composed of men, who, in general, had the
confidence of the people ; but Usher was very disagreeable, not
only as he had an interest in Allen's claim to the lands, but as he
had been one of Sir Edmund Andros's adherents, and an active
instrument in the late oppressive government. He arrived with
the commission, and took upon him the command, on the thirteenth
day of August.[2] The people again submitted, with extreme reluctance, to the unavoidable necessity of being under a government distinct from Massachusetts.

The year 1692 was remarkable for a great mortality in Portsmouth and Greenland by the small pox. The infection was
brought in bags of cotton from the West-Indies, and there being
but few people who were acquainted with it, the patients suffered
greatly, and but few recovered.[3]

CHAPTER X.

The war with the French and Indians, commonly called King William's war.

It was the misfortune of this country to have enemies of different kinds to contend with at the same time. Whilst the changes
above related were taking place in their government, a fresh war
broke out on their frontiers, which, though ascribed to divers causes, was really kindled by the rashness of the same persons who
were making havoc of their liberties.

The lands from Penobscot to Nova-Scotia had been ceded to
the French, by the treaty of Breda, in exchange for the island of
St. Christopher. On these lands, the Baron de St.Castine had for
many years resided, and carried on a large trade with the Indians,
with whom he was intimately connected ; having several of their
women, besides a daughter of the sachem Madokawando, for his
wives.[4] The lands which had been granted by the crown of England to the duke of York (now King James the Second) interfered
with Castine's plantation, as the duke claimed to the river St.
Croix. A fort had been built by his order at Pemaquid, and a

(1) MS. Copy of Com. &c. Council minutes.   (2) Council minutes.—
(3) MS. Letter.   (4) Hutch. coll. papers, p. 548.

garrison stationed there to prevent any intrusion on his property. In 1686, a ship belonging to Pascataqua landed some wines at Penobscot, supposing it to be within the French territory. Palmer and West, the duke's agents at Pemaquid, went and seized the wines ; but by the influence of the French ambassador in England, an order was obtained for the restoration of them. Hereupon, a new line was run which took Castine's plantation into the duke's territory. In the spring of 1688, Andros went in the Rose frigate, and plundered Castine's house and fort ; leaving only the ornaments of his chapel to console him for the 1688. loss of his arms and goods. This base action provoked Castine to excite the Indians to a new war, pretences for which were not wanting on their part.[1] They complained that the tribute of corn which had been promised by the treaty of 1678, had been withholden ; that the fishery of the river Saco had been obstructed by seines ; that their standing corn had been devoured by cattle belonging to the English ; that their lands at Pemaquid had been patented without their consent; and that they had been fraudulently dealt with in trade. Some of these complaints were doubtless well grounded ; but none of them were ever inquired into or redressed.

They began to make reprisals at North-Yarmouth by killing cattle. Justice Blackman* ordered sixteen of them to be seized and kept under guard at Falmouth ; but others continued to rob and captivate the inhabitants. Andros, who pretended to treat the Indians with mildness, commanded those whom Blackman had seized to be set at liberty. But this mildness had not the desired effect ; the Indians kept their prisoners, and murdered some of them in their barbarous frolics. Andros then changed his measures, and thought to frighten them, with an army of seven hundred men, which he led into their country in the month of November. The rigor of the season proved fatal to some of his men ; but he never saw an Indian in his whole march. The enemy were quiet during the winter.

After the revolution, the gentlemen who assumed the government took some precautions to prevent the renewal of hostilities. They sent messengers and presents to several 1689. tribes of Indians, who answered them with fair promises ; but their prejudice against the English was too inveterate to be allayed by such means as these.[2]

Thirteen years had almost elapsed since the seizure of the four hundred Indians, at Cochecho, by Major Waldron ; during all

(1) Hutch. coll. pap. p. 562.　　(2) Hutchinson, Neal and Mather.

* [Benjamin Blackman graduated at Harvard College in 1663 ; was sometime a preacher at Malden, which place he left about 1678, and went to Saco. Mather, ii. Magnalia, 508. Hutchinson, i. Hist. Mass. 326. Folsom, MS. Hist. Saco.]

which time, an inextinguishable thirst of revenge had been cher-
ished among them, which never till now found opportunity for
gratification.* Wonolanset, one of the sachems of Penacook,
who was dismissed with his people at the time of the seizure, always observed his father's dying charge not to quarrel with the
English ; but Hagkins, another sachem, who had been treated
with neglect by Cranfield, was more ready to listen to the seducing invitations of Castine's emissaries. Some of those Indians,
who were then seized and sold into slavery abroad, had found
their way home, and could not rest till they had revenge.† Accordingly, a confederacy being formed between the tribes of Penacook
and Pequawket, and the strange Indians (as they were called) who
were incorporated with them, it was determined to surprise the
major and his neighbors, among whom they had all this time been
peaceably conversant.

In that part of the town of Dover, which lies about the first
falls in the river Cochecho, were five garrisoned houses ; three on
the north side, viz. Waldron's, Otis's and Heard's ; and two on the
south side, viz. Peter Coffin's and his son's. These houses were
surrounded with timber-walls, the gates of which, as well as the
house doors, were secured with bolts and bars. The neighboring
families retired to these houses by night ; but by an unaccountable negligence, no watch was kept. The Indians, who were daily
passing through the town, visiting and trading with the inhabitants,
as usual in time of peace, viewed their situation with an attentive
eye. Some hints of a mischievous design had been given out by
their squaws ; but in such dark and ambiguous terms, that no one
could comprehend their meaning. Some of the people were uneasy ; but Waldron, who, from a long course of experience, was
intimately acquainted with the Indians, and on other occasions had
been ready enough to suspect them, was now so thoroughly secure,

* The inveteracy of their hatred to Major Waldron, on account of that
transaction, appears from what is related by Mr. Williams in the narrative of
his captivity, which happened in 1704. When he was in Canada, a jesuit
discoursing with him on the causes of their wars with New-England, "justi-
" fied the Indians in what they did against us ; rehearsing some things done
" by Major Waldron above 30 years ago, and how justly God retaliated
" them." Page 18.

† [In the corrected copy of the author, the following note is inserted. " A
vessel carried away a great number of our surprised Indians in the time of
our Wars, to sell them for slaves, but the nations whither they went would not
buy them. Finally, they were left at Tangier, where they be, so many as
live, or are born there. An Englishman, a Mason, came thence to Boston.
He told me they desire that I would use some means for their return home.
I know not what to do in it, but now it is in my heart to move your honour,
so to mediate, that they may have leave to get home, either from thence hither, or from thence to England, and so to get home. If the Lord shall please
to move your charitable heart therein, I shall be obliged in great thankfulness,
and am persuaded that Christ will at the great day reckon it among your
deeds of charity done to them for his name's sake." Letter from Rev. John
Eliot, of Roxbury to Hon. Robert Boyle, Nov. 27, 1683, in Birch's Life of
Boyle, p. 440.]

that when some of the people hinted their fears to him, he merrily bade them to go and plant their pumpkins, saying that he would tell them when the Indians would break out. The very evening before the mischief was done, being told by a young man that the town was full of Indians and the people were much concerned ; he answered that he knew the Indians very well and there was no danger.

The plan which the Indians had preconcerted was, that two squaws should go to each of the garrisoned houses in the evening, and ask leave to lodge by the fire ; that in the night when the people were asleep, they should open the doors and gates, and give the signal by a whistle ; upon which, the strange Indians, who were to be within hearing, should rush in, and take their long meditated revenge. This plan being ripe for execution, on the evening of Thursday, the twenty-seventh of June, two squaws applied to each of the garrisons for lodging, as they frequently did in time of peace. They were admitted into all but the younger Coffin's, and the people, at their request, shewed them how to open the doors, in case they should have occasion to go out in the night. Mesandowit, one of their chiefs, went to Waldron's garrison, and was kindly entertained, as he had often been before. The squaws told the major, that a number of Indians were coming to trade with him the next day, and Mesandowit while at supper, with his usual familiarity, said, ' Brother Waldron, what ' would you do if the strange Indians should come ?' The major carelessly answered, that he could assemble an hundred men, by lifting up his finger. In this unsuspecting confidence, the family retired to rest.

When all was quiet, the gates were opened, and the signal was given. The Indians entered, set a guard at the door, and rushed into the major's apartment, which was an inner room. Awakened by the noise, he jumped out of bed, and though now advanced in life to the age of eighty years, he retained so much vigor as to drive them with his sword, through two or three doors ; but as he was returning for his other arms, they came behind him, stunned him with a hatchet, drew him into his hall, and seating him in an elbow chair, on a long table, insultingly asked him, " Who shall " judge Indians now ?" They then obliged the people in the house to get them some victuals ; and when they had done eating, they cut the major across the breast and belly with knives, each one with a stroke, saying, " I cross out my account." They then cut off his nose and ears, forcing them into his mouth ; and when spent with the loss of blood, he was falling down from the table, one of them held his own sword under him, which put an end to his misery. They also killed his son in law Abraham Lee :* but

---

* [Abraham Lee was a chymist and probably the first in New-Hampshire. He seemed to have made some trial of his skill in 1685, as the records of the

took his daughter Lee with several others, and having pillaged the
house, left it on fire. Otis's garrison, which was next to the
major's, met with the same fate; he was killed, with several others,
and his wife and child were captivated. Heard's was saved by the
barking of a dog just as the Indians were entering: Elder Wentworth,† who was awakened by the noise, pushed them out, and
falling on his back, set his feet against the gate and held it till he
had alarmed the people; two balls were fired through it, but both
missed him. Coffin's house was surprized, but as the Indians had
no particular enmity to him, they spared his life, and the lives of
his family, and contented themselves with pillaging the house.—
Finding a bag of money, they made him throw it by handfuls on
the floor, whilst they amused themselves in scrambling for it.
They then went to the house of his son who would not admit the
squaws in the evening, and summoned him to surrender, promising him quarter. He declined their offer, and determined to defend his house, till they brought out his father and threatened to
kill him before his eyes. Filial affection then overcame his resolution, and he surrendered. They put both families together into
a deserted house, intending to reserve them for prisoners; but
whilst the Indians were busy in plundering, they all escaped.

Twenty-three people were killed in this surprisal, and twenty-
nine were captivated; five or six houses, with the mills, were
burned; and so expeditious were the Indians in the execution of
their plot, that before the people could be collected from the other
parts of the town to oppose them, they fled with their prisoners
and booty. As they passed by Heard's garrison in their retreat,
they fired upon it; but the people being prepared and resolved
to defend it, and the enemy being in haste, it was preserved. The
preservation of its owner was more remarkable.

Elizabeth Heard, with her three sons and a daughter, and some
others, were returning in the night from Portsmouth. They passed up the river in their boat unperceived by the Indians, who
were then in possession of the houses; but suspecting danger by
the noise which they heard, after they had landed they betook
themselves to Waldron's garrison, where they saw lights, which
they imagined were set up for direction to those who might be

Quarter Sessions show that he was *indicted for coining* that year, but " the
grand jury having found upon the bill of indictment, *ignoramus,*" he was
discharged, " paying the fees." He married Hester Elkins, 21 June, 1686,
and she was probably the daughter of major Waldron named in the text.]

* [The note on Elder Wentworth is transferred from the Appendix to the
first volume of the first edition, to this place. " William Wentworth was one
of the first settlers of Exeter, and after the breaking up of their combination
for government, he removed to Dover, and became a ruling elder in the
church there. In 1689, he was remarkably instrumental of saving Heard's
garrison, as is related in the proper place. After this, he officiated several
years as a preacher at Exeter, and other places, and died at a very advanced
age at Dover, in 1697, leaving a numerous posterity. From him the several
governors of that name are descended. He was a very useful and good man."]

seeking a refuge. They knocked and begged earnestly for admission ; but no answer being given, a young man of the company climbed up the wall, and saw to his inexpressible surprise, an Indian standing in the door of the house, with his gun. The woman was so overcóme with the fright that she was unable to fly ; but begged her children to shift for themselves ; and they with heavy hearts, left her. When she had a little recovered, she crawled into some bushes, and lay there till day-light. She then perceived an Indian coming toward her with a pistol in his hand ; he looked at her and went away ; returning, he looked at her again ; and she asked him what he would have ; he made no answer, but ran yelling to the house, and she saw him no more.— She kept her place till the house was burned, and the Indians were gone ; and then returning home, found her own house safe. Her preservation in these dangerous circumstances was more remarkable, if (as it is supposed) it was an instance of justice and gratitude in the Indians. For at the time when the four hundred were seized in 1676, a young Indian escaped and took refuge in her house, where she concealed him ; in return for which kindness he promised her that he would never kill her, nor any of her family in any future war, and that he would use his influence with the other Indians to the same purpose. This Indian was one of the party who surprised the place, and she was well known to the most of them.*

The same day, after the mischief was done, a letter from Secretary Addington, written by order of the government, directed to Major Waldron, giving him notice of the intention of the Indians to surprise him under pretence of trade, fell into the hands of his son. This design was communicated to Governor Bradstreet by Major Hinchman of Chelmsford, who had learned it of the Indians.†1 The letter was despatched from Boston, the day before, by Mr. Weare ; but some delay which he met with at Newbury ferry prevented its arrival in season.

The prisoners taken at this time were mostly carried to Canada, and sold to the French ; and these, as far as I can learn, were the first that ever were carried thither.‡ The Indians had

(1) Mass. Records.   Original Letter.

* [Elizabeth Heard was the widow of John Heard, and, according to Mather, ii. Magnalia, 512, was the "daughter of Mr. Hull, a reverend minister, formerly living at Pascataqua." She had five sons, viz. Benjamin, born in 1644 ; John, born 1659 ; Joseph, born 1661 ; Samuel, born 1663 ; Tristram, born 1667, and five daughters. Tristram was killed by the Indians as will be seen under the year 1723.]

† [The letter of Major Hinchman, dated 22 June, is published in the Coll. of the N. H. Hist. Soc. i. 222, 223.]

‡ One of these prisoners was Sarah Gerrish, a remarkably fine child of seven years old, and grand-daughter of Major Waldron, in whose house she lodged that fatal night. Some circumstances attending her captivity are truly affecting. When she was awakened by the noise of the Indians in the

been seduced to the French interest by popish emissaries, who
had began to fascinate them with their religious and national prejudices. They had now learned to call the English heretics, and
that to extirpate them as such was meritorious in the sight of
heaven. When their minds were filled with religious phrensy,
they became more bitter and implacable enemies than before ;
and finding the sale of scalps and prisoners turn to good account
in Canada, they had still farther incitement to continue their depredations, and prosecute their vengeance.

The necessity of vigorous measures was now so pressing, that
parties were immediately dispatched, one under Captain Noyes to
Penacook, where they destroyed the corn, but the Indians escaped ; another from Pascataqua, under Captain Wincol,* to Winni-

house, she crept into another bed and hid herself under the clothes to escape
their search. She remained in their hands till the next winter, and was sold
from one to another for several times. An Indian girl once pushed her into
a river ; but, catching by the bushes, she escaped drowning, yet durst not
tell how she came to be wet. Once she was so weary with travelling that she
did not awake in the morning till the Indians were gone, and then found herself alone in the woods, covered with snow, and without any food ; having
found their tracks she went crying after them till they heard her and took her
with them. At another time they kindled a great fire, and the young Indians
told her she was to be roasted. She burst into tears, threw her arms round
her master's neck, and begged him to save her, which he promised to do if she
would behave well. Being arrived in Canada, she was bought by the Inten-
dant's lady, who treated her courteously, and sent her to a nunnery for education. But when Sir William Phips was at Quebec she was exchanged, and
returned to her friends, with whom she lived till she was sixteen years old.

The wife of Richard Otis was taken at the same time, with an infant
daughter of three months old. The French priests took this child under their
care, baptised her by the name of Christina, and educated her in the Romish
religion. She passed some time in a nunnery, but declined taking the veil,
and was married to a Frenchman, by whom she had two children. But her
desire to see New-England was so strong, that upon an exchange of prisoners in 1714, being then a widow, she left both her children, who were not
permitted to come with her, and returned home, where she abjured the Rom
ish faith. M. Siguenot, her former confessor, wrote her a flattering letter,
warning her of her danger, inviting her to return to the bosom of the catholic
church, and repeating many gross calumnies which had formerly been vented
against Luther and the other reformers. This letter being shown to Govern-
or Burnet, he wrote her a sensible and masterly answer, refuting the arguments, and detecting the falsehoods it contained : Both these letters were
printed. She was married afterward to Capt. Thomas Baker, who had been
taken at Deerfield in 1704, and lived in Dover, where she was born, till the
year 1773.

Mr. John Emerson, by declining to lodge at Major Waldron's on the fatal
night, though strongly urged, met with an happy escape. He was afterward
a minister at New-Castle and Portsmouth. [The Mr. John Emerson who declined to lodge at Major Waldron's on the 27 June, 1689, according to Mather,
ii. Magnalia, 511, was " a worthy minister at Berwick," and could not have
been the future minister at New-Castle and Portsmouth, as *he* had not at this
time graduated at college. Alden, both in his Collection of Epitaphs and in
his Account of Religious Societies in Portsmouth, has fallen into the same
error in considering the minister of New-Castle and Portsmouth as the one,
who "met with an happy escape by declining to lodge at Major Waldron's."]

*₊*Some of the circumstances relating to the destruction of Cochecho are
taken from Mather's Magnalia. The others from the tradition of the sufferers and their descendants.

*[Captain John Wincol belonged to Kittery, which he represented in the
General Court of Massachusetts six years, the last time in 1678.]

piseogee, whither the Indians had retired, as John Church, who
had been taken at Cochecho and escaped from them, reported :
one or two Indians were killed there, and their corn was cut down.
But these excursions proved of small service, as the Indians had
little to lose, and could find a home wherever they could find
game and fish.

In the month of August, Major Swaine, with seven or eight
companies raised by the Massachusetts government, marched to
the eastward ; and Major Church, with another party, consisting
of English and Indians, from the colony of Plymouth, soon followed them.   Whilst these forces were on their march, the Indians, who lay in the woods about Oyster river, observed how
many men belonged to Huckin's garrison ; and seeing them all go
out one morning to work, nimbly ran between them and the house,
and killed them all, (being in number eighteen) except one who
had passed the brook.   They then attacked the house, in which
were only two boys, (one of whom was lame) with some women
and children.   The boys kept them off for some time and wounded several of them.   At length, the Indians set the house on fire,
and even then the boys would not surrender, till they had promised them to spare their lives.   They perfidiously murdered three
or four of the children ; one of them was set on a sharp stake, in
the view of its distressed mother, who, with the other women and
the boys, were carried captive.   One of the boys escaped the
next day.   Captain Garner with his company pursued the enemy,
but did not come up with them.

The Massachusetts and Plymouth companies proceeded to the
eastward, settled garrisons in convenient places, and had some
skirmishes with the enemy at Casco and Blue Point.   On their
return, Major Swaine sent a party of the Indian auxiliaries under
Lieutenant Flagg toward Winnipiseogee, to make discoveries.—
These Indians held a consultation in their own language ; and
having persuaded their lieutenant with two men to return, nineteen
of them tarried out eleven days longer ; in which time, they found
the enemy, staid with them two nights, and informed them of every thing which they desired to know ; upon which, the enemy
retired to their inaccessible deserts ; the forces returned without
finding them, and in November, were disbanded.[1]

Nothing was more welcome to the distressed inhabitants of the
frontiers than the approach of winter, as they then expected a
respite from their sufferings.   The deep snows and cold weather
were commonly a good security against an attack from the Indians;
but when resolutely set on mischief, and instigated by popish enthusiasm, no obstacles could prevent the execution of their purposes.

The Count de Frontenac, then governor of Canada, was fond

(1) Magnalia, lib. 7, p. 67.

of distinguishing himself by some enterprises against the American subjects of King William, with whom his master was
at war in Europe. For this purpose, he detached three
parties of French and Indians from Canada in the winter, who
were to take three different routes into the English territories.—
One of these parties marched from Montreal and destroyed Sche-
nectady, a Dutch village on the Mohawk river, in the province of
New-York. This action which happened at an unusual time of
the year, in the month of February, alarmed the whole country ;
and the eastern settlements were ordered to be on their guard.
On the eighteenth day of March, another party which came from
Trois Rivieres, under the command of the Sieur Hertel, an officer of great repute in Canada, found their way to Salmon-falls, a
settlement on the river which divides New-Hampshire from the
province of Maine. This party consisted of fifty-two men, of
whom twenty-five were Indians under Hoophood, a noted warrior.
They began the attack at day-break, in three different places.
The people were surprised; but flew to arms and defended themselves in the garrisoned houses, with a bravery which the enemy
themselves applauded. But as in all such onsets the assailants
have the greatest advantage, so they here proved too strong for
the defendants ; about thirty of the bravest were killed, and the
rest surrendered at discretion, to the number of fifty-four, of whom
the greater part were women and children. After plundering,
the enemy burned the houses, mills and barns, with the cattle*
which were within doors, and then retreated into the woods,
whither they were pursued by about one hundred and forty men,
suddenly collected from the neighboring towns, who came up with
them in the afternoon at a narrow bridge on Wooster's river, in
Berwick. Hertel expecting a pursuit, had posted his men ad-
vantageously on the opposite bank. The pursuers advanced with
great intrepidity, and a warm engagement ensued, which lasted
till night, when they retired with the loss of four or five killed.—
The enemy by their own account lost two, one of whom was Hertel's nephew:[1] his son was wounded in the knee. Another
Frenchman was taken prisoner, who was so tenderly treated that
he embraced the protestant faith, and remained in the country. [2]
Hertel on his way homeward met with a third party who had
marched from Quebec, and joining his company to them attacked
and destroyed the fort and settlement at Casco, the next May.
Thus the three expeditions planned by Count Frontenac proved
successful; but the glory of them was much tarnished by acts of

(1) Charlevoix, lib. 7, p. 74.   (2) Mather, Magnalia, lib. 7, p. 68.

* Charlevoix says they burned "twenty-seven houses and two thousand
head of cattle in the barns."   The number of buildings, including mills,
barns and other out houses, might amount to near twenty ; but the number
of cattle as he gives it, is incredible.

cruelty, which christians should be ashamed to countenance, though perpetrated by savages.*

After the destruction of Casco, the eastern settlements were all deserted, and the people retired to the fort at Wells. The Indians then came up westward, and a party of them under Hoophood, sometime in May, made an assault on Fox Point, in Newington, where they burned several houses, killed about fourteen people, and carried away six. They were pursued by the Captains Floyd and Greenleaf, who came up with them and recovered some of the Captives and spoil, after a skirmish in which Hoophood was wounded and lost is gun.[1] This fellow was soon after killed by a party of Canada Indians who mistook him for one of the Iroquois, with whom they were at war. On the fourth day of July, eight persons were killed as they were mowing in a field near Lamprey river, and a lad was carried captive. The next day, they attacked Captain Hilton's garrison at Exeter, which was relieved by Lieutenant Bancroft, with the loss of a few of his men. One of them, Simon Stone, received nine wounds with shot, and two strokes of a hatchet : when his friends came to bu-

(1) Mag. lib. 7, p. 73.

* The following instances of cruelty exercised towards the prisoners taken at Salmon-falls are mentioned by Dr. [Cotton] Mather.

Robert Rogers, a corpulent man, being unable to carry the burden which the Indians imposed upon him, threw it down in the path and went aside in the woods to conceal himself. They found him by his track, stripped, beat and pricked him with their swords; then tied him to a tree and danced round him till they had kindled a fire. They gave him time to pray, and take leave of his fellow prisoners who were placed round the fire to see his death. They pushed the fire toward him, and when he was almost stifled, took it away to give him time to breathe, and thus prolonged his misery; they drowned his dying groans with their hideous singing and yelling ; all the while dancing round the fire, cutting off pieces of his flesh and throwing them in his face. When he was dead they left his body broiling on the coals, in which state it was found by his friends, and buried.

Mehetabel Goodwin was taken with her child of five months old. When it cried they threatened to kill it, which made the mother go aside and sit for hours together in the snow to lull it to sleep ; her master seeing that this hindered her from travelling, took the child, struck its head against a tree, and hung it on one of the branches ; she would have buried it but he would not let her, telling her that if she came again that way she might have the pleasure of seeing it. She was carried to Canada, and after five years returned home.

Mary Plaisted was taken out of her bed, having lain in but three weeks. They made her travel with them through the snow, and " to ease her of her burden," as they said, struck the child's head against a tree, and threw it into a river.

An anecdote of another kind may relieve the reader after these tragical accounts. Thomas Toogood was pursued by three Indians and overtaken by one of them, who having inquired his name, was preparing strings to bind him, holding his gun under his arm, which Toogood seized and went backward, keeping the gun presented at him, and protesting that he would shoot him if he alarmed the others who had stopped on the opposite side of the hill. By this dexterity, he escaped and got safe into Cochecho ; while his adversary had no recompense in his power but to call after him by the name of *No good*. When he returned to his companions without gun or prisoner, their derision made his misadventure the more grievous.

ry him they perceived life in him, and by the application of cor-
dials he revived, to the amazement of all.[1]

Two companies under the Captains Floyd and Wiswall were
now scouting, and on the sixth day of July, discovered an Indian
track, which they pursued till they came up with the enemy at
Wheelwright's Pond, in Lee, where a bloody engagement ensued for some hours ; in which Wiswall, his lieutenant, Flagg, and
sergeant Walker, with twelve more, were killed, and several
wounded. It was not known how many of the enemy fell, as
they always carried off their dead. Floyd maintained the fight
after Wiswall's death, till his men, fatigued and wounded, drew
off ; which obliged him to follow. The enemy retreated at the
same time ; for when Captain Convers went to look after the
wounded, he found seven alive, whom he brought in by sunrise
the next morning, and then returned to bury the dead. The enemy then went westward, and in the course of one week killed, between Lamprey river and Amesbury, not less than forty people.

The cruelties exercised upon the captives in this war exceeded, both in number and degree, any in former times. The most
healthy and vigorous of them were sold in Canada ; the weaker
were sacrificed, and scalped ; and for every scalp they had a
premium. Two instances only are remembered of their releas-
ing any without a ransom : one was a woman taken from Fox
Point, who obtained her liberty by procuring them some of the
necessaries of life ;[2] the other was at York ; where, after they
had taken many of the people, they restored two aged women
and five children, in return for a generous action of Major Church,
who had spared the lives of as many women and children when
they fell into his hands at Ameriscoggin.[3]

The people of New-England, now looked on Canada as the
source of their troubles, and formed a design to reduce it to
subjection to the crown of England. The enterprise was bold
and hazardous ; and had their ability been equal to the ardor
of their patriotism, it might probably have been accomplished.
Straining every nerve, they equipped an armament in some degree equal to the service. What was wanting in military and naval discipline was made up in resolution ; and the command was
given to Sir William Phips, an honest man, and a friend to his
country ; but by no means qualified for such an attempt. Unavoidable accidents retarded the expedition, so that the fleet did
not arrive before Quebec till October ; when it was more than
time to return. It being impossible to continue there to any purpose ; and the troops growing sickly and discouraged, after some
ineffectual parade, they abandoned the enterprise.*

(1) Mag. lib. 7, p. 74.   (2) Ibid. p. 73.   (3) MS. Letter.

* [1690. The ship Faulkland of 54 guns, was built at Portsmouth. Adams, Annals of Portsmouth.]

This disappointment was severely felt. The equipment of the fleet and army required a supply of money which could not readily be collected, and occasioned a paper currency ; which has often been drawn into precedent on like occasions, and has proved a fatal source of the most complicated and extensive mischief. The people were almost dispirited with the prospect of poverty and ruin. In this melancholy state of the country, it was an happy circumstance that the Indians voluntarily came in with a flag of truce, and desired a cessation of hostilities. A conference being held at Sagadahock, they brought in ten captives, and Nov. 29. settled a truce till the first day of May, which they observed till the ninth of June ; when they attacked Storer's garri- son at Wells, but were bravely repulsed. About the same 1691. time, they killed two men at Exeter,[1] and on the twenty ninth of September, a party of them came from the eastward in canoes to Sandy Beach, (Rye)[2] where they killed and captivated twenty-one persons.* Captain Sherburne of Portsmouth, a worthy officer, was this year killed at Maquoit.[3]

The next winter, the country being alarmed with the destruction of York, some new regulations were made for the general defence. Major Elisha Hutchinson was appointed com- mander in chief of the militia ; by whose prudent conduct 1692. the frontiers were well guarded, and so constant a com- Jan. 25. munication was kept up, by ranging parties, from one post to another, that it became impossible for the enemy to attack in their usual way, by surprise. The good effect of this regulation was presently seen. A young man being in the woods near Cochecho, was fired at by some Indians. Lientenant Wilson immediately went out with eighteen men ; and finding the Indians, killed or wounded the whole party, excepting one. This struck a terror, and kept them quiet the remainder of the winter and spring. But on the tenth day of June, an army of French and Indians made a furious attack on Storer's garrison at Wells, where Capt. Convers commanded ; who after a brave and resolute defence, was so happy as to drive them off with great loss.

Sir William Phips, being now governor of Massachusetts, continued the same method of defence ; keeping out continual scouts under brave and experienced officers. This kept the Indians so quiet that, except one poor family which they took at Oyster river, and some small mischief at Quaboag, there is no mention

(1) Mag. 78.   (2) MS. Letter of Morrill to Prince, [Magnalia.]   (3) Fitch's MS.

* [In the same month, a party made a descent on Dunstable, where they killed Joseph Hassell, sen., his wife Anna, and son Benjamin, Mary Marks, daughter of Peter Marks, Obadiah Perry, one of the founders of the church there, and Christopher Temple. Perry and Temple were killed in the morning of the 28 September ; the others were killed in the evening of the 2d.— MS. Letter of J. B. Hill, Esq.]

of any destruction made by them during the year 1693. Their

1693. animosity against New-England was not quelled; but they needed a space to recruit ; some of their principal men were in captivity, and they could not hope to redeem them without a peace. To obtain it, they came into the Fort at Pemaquid ; and there entered into a solemn covenant ; wherein they acknowledged subjection to the crown of England ; engaged to abandon the French interest ; promised perpetual peace ; to forbear private revenge ; to restore all captives; and even went so far as to deliver hostages for the due performance of their engagements.[1] This peace, or rather truce, gave both sides a respite, which both earnestly desired.*

The people of New-Hampshire were much reduced ; their lumber trade and husbandry being greatly impeded by the war. Frequent complaints were made of the burden of the war, the scarcity of provisions, and the dispiritedness of the people. Once, it is said, in the council minutes, that they were even ready to quit the province. The governor was obliged to impress men to guard the outposts : they were sometimes dismissed for want of provisions, and then the garrison officers were called to account and severely punished : Yet all this time, the public debt did not exceed four hundred pounds. In this situation, they were obliged to apply to their neighbors for assistance ; but this was granted with a sparing hand. The people of Massachusetts were much divided and at variance among themselves, both on account of the new charter which they had received from King William, and the pretended witchcrafts which have made so loud a noise in the world. Party and passion had usurped the place of patriotism ; and the defence, not only of their neighbors, but of themselves was neglected to gratify their malignant humors. Their governor too had been affronted in this province, on the following occasion.

Sir William Phips, having had a quarrel with Capt. Short of the Nonsuch frigate about the extent of his power as vice admiral, arrested Short at Boston, and put him on board a merchant ship bound for England, commanded by one Tay, with a warrant to deliver him to the secretary of state. The ship put into Pascataqua, and the Nonsuch came in after her. The lieutenant, Carey, sent a letter to Hinckes, president of the council, threatening to impress seamen, if Short was not released. Cary was arrested and brought before the council, where he received a rep-

(1) Mag. p. 85.

* [This " Submission and Agreement of the Eastern Indians, at Fort William Henry, in Pemmaquid, the 11th day of August, in the fifth year of our Sovereign Lord and Lady William and Mary, by the grace of God, of England, Scotland, France, and Ireland, King and Queen, Defender of the Faith, &c. 1693," may be found in Mather, ii. Magnalia, p. 542. It is signed by thirteen Indian Chiefs, four Indians, and three English Interpreters.]

rimand for his insolence.   At the same time, Sir William came
hither by land, went on board Tay's ship, and sent the cabin boy
with a message to the president to come to him there ; which
Hinckes highly resented and refused.   Phips then demanded of
Tay his former warrant, and issued another commanding the re-
delivery of Short to him, broke open Short's chest, and seized his
papers.   This action was looked upon by some as an exertion of
power to which he had no right, and it was proposed to cite him
before the council to answer for assuming authority out   Mar.. 30.
of his jurisdiction.   The president was warm ; but a
majority of the council, considering Sir William's opinion that his
vice admiral's commission extended to this province, (though
Usher had one, but was not present) and that no person belonging to the province had been injured, advised the president to
take no farther notice of the matter.[1]   Soon after this, Sir William drew off the men whom he had stationed in this province as
soldiers ; and the council advised the lieutenant governor to apply to the colony of Connecticut for men and provisions ; but
whether this request was granted does not appear.

The towns of Dover and Exeter being more exposed than
Portsmouth or Hampton, suffered the greatest share in the common calamity.   Nothing but the hope of better times kept alive
their fortitude.   When many of the eastern settlements were wholly broken up, they stood their ground, and thus gained to themselves a reputation which their posterity boast of to this day.*

The engagements made by the Indians in the treaty of Pemaquid, might have been performed if they had been left to   1694.
their own choice.   But the French missionaries had been
for some years very assiduous in propagating their tenets among
them, one of which was 'that to break faith with heretics was no
sin.'   The Sieur de Villieu, who had distinguished himself in the
defence of Quebec when Phips was before it, and had contracted a
strong antipathy to the New-Englanders, being then in command
at Penobscot, he with M. Thury, the missionary, diverted Madok-

(1) MS. in files.

* [1693.   New-Castle, formerly Great Island, was incorporated.   This is
now the smallest town in point of territory in the state of New-Hampshire,
containing only 458 acres.   It originally consisted of Great Island, Little
Harbor, and Sandy Beach, (now Rye) all which were once comprehended
within the limits of Portsmouth.   Some of the principal merchants of the
Province resided there—and the principal seat of business for many years
was at Great Island.
     1693.   An act passed the General Assembly of New-Hampshire to estab-
lish a Post-office " in some convenient place within the town of Portsmouth."
The postage on letters from beyond sea was two pence ; on packets equal to
not less than three letters, four pence.   The postage on letters from Boston
was not to exceed six pence, and double for a packet, and " so proportionably
for letters on this side Boston," and " for all other letters beyond Boston,
shall be paid what is the accustomary allowance in the government from
whence they came."]

awando and the other Sachems from complying with their engagements ; so that pretences were found for detaining the English captives, who were more in number, and of more consequence than the hostages whom the Indians had given. Influenced by the same pernicious councils, they kept a watchful eye on the frontier towns, to see what place was most secure and might be attacked to the greatest advantage. The settlement at Oyster river, within the town of Dover, was pitched upon as the most likely place ; and it is said that the design of surprising it was publicly talked of at Quebec two months before it was put in execution. Rumors of Indians lurking in the woods thereabout made some of the people apprehend danger ; but no mischief being attempted, they imagined them to be hunting parties, and returned to their security.[1] At length, the necessary preparations being made, Villieu, with a body of two hundred and fifty Indians, collected from the tribes of St. John, Penobscot and Norridgewog, attended by a French Priest, marched for the devoted place.[2]

Oyster river is a stream which runs into the western branch of Pascataqua : the settlements were on both sides of it, and the houses chiefly near the water. Here, were twelve garrisoned houses sufficient for the defence of the inhabitants, but apprehending no danger, some families remained at their own unfortified houses, and those who were in the garrisons were but indifferently provided for defence, some being even destitute of powder. The enemy approached the place undiscovered, and halted near the falls on Tuesday evening, the seventeenth of July. Here they formed two divisions, one of which was to go on each side of the river and plant themselves in ambush, in small parties, near every house, so as to be ready for the attack at the rising of the sun ; and the first gun was to be the signal. John Dean, whose house stood by the saw-mill at the falls, intending to go from home very early, arose before the dawn of day, and was shot as he came out of his door. This firing, in part, disconcerted their plan ; several parties who had some distance to go, had not then arrived at their stations ; the people in general were immediately alarmed, some of them had time to make their escape, and others to prepare for their defence. The signal being given, the attack began in all parts where the enemy was ready.

Of the twelve garrisoned houses five were destroyed, viz. Adams's, Drew's, Edgerly's Medar's and Beard's. They entered Adams's without resistance, where they killed fourteen persons ; one of them, being a woman with child, they ripped open. The grave is still to be seen in which they were all buried. Drew surrendered his garrison on the promise of security, but was murdered when he fell into their hands. One of his children, a boy

(1) Magnalia, lib. 7, p. 86.   (2) Charlevoix, lib. 15, p. 210.

of nine years old, was made to run through a lane of Indians as a mark for them to throw their hatchets at, till they had dispatched him. Edgerly's was evacuated. The people took to their boat, and one of them was mortally wounded before they got out of reach of the enemy's shot. Beard's and Medar's were also evacuated and the people escaped.

The defenceless houses were nearly all set on fire, the inhabitants being either killed or taken in them, or else in endeavoring to fly to the garrisons. Some escaped by hiding in the bushes and other secret places. Thomas Edgerly, by concealing himself in his cellar, preserved his house, though twice set on fire. The house of John Buss, the minister, was destroyed, with a valuable library. He was absent; his wife and family fled to the woods and escaped.* The wife of John Dean, at whom the first gun was fired, was taken with her daughter, and carried about two miles up the river, where they were left under the care of an old Indian, while the others returned to their bloody work. The Indian complained of a pain in his head, and asked the woman what would be a proper remedy : she answered, *occapee*, which is the Indian word for rum, of which she knew he had taken a bottle from her house. The remedy being agreeable, he took a large dose and fell asleep ; and she took that opportunity to make her escape, with her child, into the woods, and kept herself concealed till they were gone.

The other seven garrisons, viz. Burnham's, Bickford's, Smith's, Bunker's, Davis's, Jones's and Woodman's were resolutely and successfully defended. At Burnham's, the gate was left open : The Indians, ten in number, who were appointed to surprise it, were asleep under the bank of the river, at the time that the alarm was given. A man within, who had been kept awake by the toothache, hearing the first gun, roused the people and secured the gate, just as the Indians, who were awakened by the same noise, were entering. Finding themselves disappointed, they ran to Pitman's defenceless house, and forced the door at the moment, that he had burst a way through that end of the house which was

---

* [John Buss is mentioned in the 3d volume, p. 250, of the first edition, as a practitioner of physic, and as having died in 1736, at the age of 108 years ; but his age is overstated. It should be 96. In a petition from him to Gov. Shute and the General Assembly of Massachusetts, in 1718, he states that he had labored in the work of the ministry at Oyster-River 44 years successively; that he was then advanced to 78 years of age; that he had kept his station there, "even in the time of the terrible Indian war, when many a score fell by the sword, both on the right hand and on the left, and several others forced to flight for want of bread;" that he was then "unable to perform the usual exercise of the ministry," and that "the people had not only called another minister, but stopped their hands from paying to his subsistence, whereupon he was greatly reduced, having neither bread to eat, nor sufficient clothing to encounter the approaching winter." The ministers of Durham from that time down to our own days have not unfrequently complained that they prophesied in sackcloth.]

next to the garrison, to which he with his family, taking advantage of the shade of some trees, it being moonlight, happily escaped. Still defeated, they attacked the house of John Davis, which after some resistance, he surrendered on terms ; but the terms were violated, and the whole family was either killed or made captives. Thomas Bickford preserved his house in a singular manner. It was situated near the river, and surrounded with a palisade. Being alarmed before the enemy had reached the house, he sent off his family in a boat, and then shutting his gate, betook himself alone to the defence of his fortress. Despising alike the promises and threats by which the Indians would have persuaded him to surrender, he kept up a constant fire at them, changing his dress as often as he could, shewing himself with a different cap, hat or coat, and sometimes without either, and giving directions aloud as if he had a number of men with him. Finding their attempt vain, the enemy withdrew, and left him sole master of the house, which he had defended with such admirable address. Smith's, Bunker's and Davis's garrisons, being seasonably apprised of the danger, were resolutely defended. One Indian was supposed to be killed and another wounded by a shot from Davis's. Jones's garrison was beset before day ; Captain Jones hearing his dogs bark, and imagining wolves might be near, went out to secure some swine and returned unmolested. He then went up into the flankart and sat on the wall. Discerning the flash of a gun, he dropped backward ; the ball entered the place from whence he had withdrawn his legs. The enemy from behind a rock kept firing on the house for some time, and then quitted it. During these transactions, the French priest took possession of the meeting-house, and employed himself in writing on the pulpit with chalk ; but the house received no damage.

Those parties of the enemy who were on the south side of the river having completed their destructive work, collected in a field adjoining to Burnham's garrison, where they insultingly showed their prisoners, and derided the people, thinking themselves out of reach of their shot. A young man from the sentry-box fired at one who was making some indecent signs of defiance, and wounded him in the heel : Him they placed on a horse and carried away. Both divisions then met at the falls, where they had parted the evening before, and proceeded together to Capt. Woodman's garrison. The ground being uneven, they approached without danger, and from behind a hill kept up a long and severe fire at the hats and caps which the people within held up on sticks above the walls, without any other damage than galling the roof of the house. At length, apprehending it was time for the people in the neighboring settlements to be collected in pursuit of them, they finally withdrew ; having killed and captivated between ninety and an hundred persons, and burned about twenty houses, of which five were garrisons.*   The main body of them retreated over Winnipiseogee lake, where they divided their prisoners, separating those in particular who were most intimately connected, in which they often took a pleasure suited to their savage nature.†

About forty of the enemy under Toxus, a Norridgewog chief, resolving on farther mischief, went westward and did execution as far as Groton.   A smaller party having crossed the river Pascataqua, came to a farm where Ursula Cutt, widow of the deceased president, resided, who imagining the enemy had done what mischief they intended for that time, could not be persuaded to remove into town till her haymaking should be finished.   As she was in the field with her laborers, the enemy fired from an ambush and killed her, with three others.[1]   Colonel Richard Waldron and his wife, with their infant son, (afterward secretary) had almost shared the same fate.   They were taking boat to go and dine with this lady, when they were stopped by the arrival of some friends at their house; whilst at dinner they were informed of her death.   She lived about two miles above the town of Portsmouth, and had laid out her farm with much elegance.   The scalps taken in this whole expedition were carried to Canada by Madokawando, and presented to Count Frontenac, from whom he received the reward of his treacherous adventure.

There is no mention of any more mischief by the Indians within this province till the next year, when, in the month of July, two men were killed at Exeter.   The following 1695. year, on the seventh day of May, John Church, who had been taken and escaped from them seven years before, was killed and scalped at Cochecho, near his own house.   On 1696. the twenty-sixth of June, an attack was made at Portsmouth plain,

(1) Magnalia, lib. 7, page 86.

* Charlevoix, with his usual parade, boasts of their having killed two hundred and thirty people, and burned fifty or sixty houses.   He speaks of only two forts, both of which were stormed.   [The Rev. John Pike, in his manuscript Journal, says they " killed and carried away 94 persons and burnt 13 houses."   As he then lived in Dover and made a record of the event near the time it occurred, we can probably depend upon the accuracy of his statement.]

† Among these prisoners, were Thomas Drew and his wife, who were newly married.   He was carried to Canada, where he continued two years and was redeemed.   She to Norridgewog, and was gone four years, in which she endured every thing but death.   She was delivered of a child in the winter, in the open air, and in a violent snow storm.   Buing unable to suckle her child, or provide it any food, the Indians killed it.   She lived fourteen days on a decoction of the bark of trees.   Once, they set her to draw a sled up a river against a piercing north-west wind, and left her.   She was so overcome with the cold that she grew sleepy, laid down and was nearly dead, when they returned; they carried her senseless to a wigwam, and poured warm water down her throat, which recovered her.   After her return to her husband, she had fourteen children; they lived together till he was ninety-three, and she eighty-nine years of age; they died within two days of each other, and were buried in one grave.

⁎ These particular circumstances of the destruction at Oyster river were at my desire collected from the information of aged people by John Smith, Esq. a descendant of one of the suffering families.

about two miles from the town. The enemy came from York-nubble to Sandy-beach in canoes, which they hid there among the bushes near the shore. Some suspicion was formed the day before by reason of the cattle running out of the woods at Little-harbor ; but false alarms were frequent, and this was not much regarded. Early in the morning, the attack was made on five houses at once. Fourteen persons were killed on the spot; one was scalped and left for dead, but recovered, and four were taken. The enemy having plundered the houses of what they could carry, set them on fire, and made a precipitate retreat through the great swamp. A company of militia under Captain Shackford* and lieutenant Libbey pursued, and discovered them cooking their breakfast, at a place ever since called Breakfast-hill, in Rye. The Indians were on the farther side, having placed their captives between themselves and the top of the hill, that in case of an attack they might first receive the fire. The lieutenant pleaded to go round the hill, and come upon them below to cut off their retreat ; but the captain fearing in that case that they would, according to their custom, kill the prisoners, rushed upon them from the top of the hill, by which means they retook the captives and plunder, but the Indians, rolling down the hill, escaped into the swamp and got to their canoes. Another party, under another commander, Gerrish, was then sent out in shallops to intercept them as they should cross over to the eastward by night. The captain ranged his boats in a line, and ordered his men to reserve their fire till he gave the watchword. It being a calm night, the Indians were heard as they advanced ; but the captain, unhappily giving the word before they had come within gun-shot, they tacked about to the southward, and going round the Isles of Shoals, by the favor of their light canoes escaped. The watch-word was Crambo, which the captain ever after bore as an appendage to his title.[1] On the twenty-sixth day of July, the people of Dover were waylaid as they were returning from the public worship, when three were killed, three wounded, and three carried to Penobscot, from whence they soon found their way home.[2] †

The next year, on the tenth of June, the town of Exeter was remarkably preserved from destruction. A body of the enemy had placed themselves near the town, intending to make an assault in the morning of the next day. A number of women and children contrary to the advice of their friends went

1697.

(1) Judge Parker.   (2) Magnalia, lib. 7, p. 89.

* [William Shackford was of Dover, and one of the grand jury in 1682.]

† [The persons killed were Nicholas Otis, Mary Downs and Mary Jones; those wounded were Richard Otis, Anthony Lowden and Experience Heard; those captured were John Tucker, Nicholas Otis, jr., and Judith Ricker. On the 25th August following, Lieutenant Lock was slain by the Indians at Sandy Beach, and soon after Arnold Breck, &c. was shot at betwixt Hampton and Greenland. Rev. John Pike, MS. Journal.]

into the fields, without a guard, to gather strawberries. When they were gone, some persons, to frighten them, fired an alarm; which quickly spread through the town, and brought the people together in arms. The Indians supposing that they were discovered, and quickened by fear, after killing one, wounding another, and taking a child, made a hasty retreat and were seen no more there. But on the fourth day of July, they waylaid and killed the worthy Major Frost* at Kittery, to whom they had owed revenge ever since the seizure of the four hundred at Cochecho, in which he was concerned.[1]

The same year, an invasion of the country was projected by the French. A fleet was to sail from France to Newfoundland, and thence to Penobscot, where being joined by an army from Canada, an attempt was to be made on Boston, and the seacoast ravaged from thence to Pascataqua. The plan was too extensive and complicated to be executed in one summer. The fleet came no further than Newfoundland, when the advanced season, and scantiness of provisions obliged them to give over the design. The people of New-England were apprized of the danger, and made the best preparations in their power. They strengthened their fortifications on the coast, and raised a body of men to defend the frontiers against the Indians who were expected to co-operate with the French. Some mischief was done by lurking parties at the eastward; but New-Hampshire was unmolested by them during the remainder of this, and the whole of the following year.†

After the peace of Ryswick, Count Frontenac informed the Indians that he could not any longer support them in a war with the English, with whom his nation was then at peace. He therefore advised them to bury the hatchet and restore their captives. Having suffered much by famine, and being divided in their opinions about prosecuting the war, after a long time they were brought to a treaty at Casco; where they ratified their former engagements; acknowledged subjection to the crown of England; lamented their former perfidy, and

1698.

1699.
Jan. 9.

(1) Mag. lib. 7, page 91.   MS. Journal.

* [Major Charles Frost, was the representative of Kittery in the General Court of Massachusetts in the years 1658, 1660 and 1661, and was long an active and useful officer in the Indian wars. He is named by Hubbard in his Wars with the Eastern Indians, p. 28. Under the charter of William and Mary, at the first election of counsellors, in 1693, he was selected for one of those to be chosen for Maine. He was probably related to the Frosts of New-Hampshire, where the name has continued with reputation from an early period to the present time.]

† [It was in 1697, on the 15 of March, that the town of Haverhill, in Massachusetts, was attacked by the Indians, and some of the prisoners there taken were brought into New-Hampshire, among whom was the intrepid Hannah Duston, whose story is well known. It was on a small island at the mouth of Contoocook river, about six miles above the State House in Concord, that she destroyed her captors. She and her coadjutors killed two men, two women, and six others, and having scalped them, carried their scalps to Boston.]

promised future peace and good behaviour in such terms as the commissioners dictated, and with as much sincerity as could be expected.[1] At the same time, they restored those captives, who were able to travel from the places of their detention to Casco in that unfavorable season of the year; giving assurance for the return of the others in the spring; but many of the younger sort, both males and females, were detained; who, mingling with the Indians, contributed to a succession of enemies in future wars against their own country.[*2]

(1) Mag. lib. 7, page 94.   (2) Hutch. vol. 2, page 110.

* [I have endeavored to collect from various authorities, but principally from a MS. Journal of the Rev. John Pike, of Dover, a summary account of the depredations committed by the Indians in the Eastern part of New-England, during what Cotton Mather calls " Decennium Luctuosum, or the long War with the Indian Salvages," which is presented below in a tabular form, and so far as was practicable, in chronological order. Other depredations doubtless were committed of which no account is preserved.

Time.		Places attacked.	No. Killed.	Wounded.	Capt'd.
1689.	28 June,	Dover,	23	—	29
	August,	Oyster River, (Durham)	18	—	—
	August,	Andover, Ms.	2(1)	—	—
1690.	2 February,	Schenectady, N. Y.	60	—	27
	18 March,	Salmon-Falls,	27	—	52
	22 August,	York, Me.	—	—	1
		Fox Point, (Newington)	14	—	6
	4 July,	Lamprey River,	8	—	1
	5 July,	Exeter,	8	—	—
	6 July,	Wheelwright's pond, (Lee)	16	—	—
	7 July,	Amesbury, Ms.	3	—	—
	July or Aug.	Maquoit, Me.	1	1	—
	21 September,	Maquoit, (near Casco)	8	24	—
1692.	25 January,	York, Me.	48	—	—
	18 July,	Lancaster, Ms.	6	1	—
	1 August,	Billerica, Ms.	6	—	—
	28 September,	Newichwannock,(S.Berwick)	2	—	—
	29 September,	Sandy Beach, (Rye)	21(2)	—	—
1693.	10 May,	Dover,	1(3)	—	—
1694.	18 July,	Oyster River,	94(4)	—	—
	21 July,	Portsmouth,	4	—	—
	27 July,	Groton, Ms.	22	13	—
	20 August,	Spruce Creek and York,	5	—	—
	24 August,	Long Reach, (Kittery)	8(5)	—	—
	4 September,	Pond Plain, Ms. (6)	2	—	—
1695.	28 March,	Saco Fort, Me.	1	1	—
	6 July,	Kittery, Me.	—	1	—
	7 July,	York, Me.	1	—	—
	July,	Exeter,	2	—	—
		Lancaster, Ms.	1	—	—
		Haverhill, Ms.	—	2	—
	5 August,	Billerica, Ms.	10	5	—
	August,	Saco Fort, Me.	1	—	—

(1) Four from Andover died the same year in the war at the Eastward.— Abbot, Hist. Andover, 43.

(2) This number includes those who were killed and carried away. Pike, MS. Journal.

(3) This was Tobias Hanson, who is not named by Dr. Belknap.

(4) Killed and carried away.

(5) Killed and captured.

(6) Between Amesbury and Haverhill, Ms.

A general view of an Indian war will give a just idea of these distressing times, and be a proper close to this narration.

The Indians were seldom or never seen before they did execution. They appeared not in the open field, nor gave proofs of a truly masculine courage; but did their exploits by surprise, chiefly in the morning, keeping themselves hid behind logs and bushes, near the paths in the woods, or the fences contiguous to the doors of houses; and their lurking holes could be known only by the report of their guns, which was indeed but feeble, as they were sparing of ammunition, and as near as possible to their object before they fired. They rarely assaulted an house unless they knew there would be but little resistance, and it has been afterward known that they have lain in ambush for days together, watching the motions of the people at their work, without daring to discover themselves. One of their chiefs, who had got a woman's riding-hood among his plunder, would put it on, in an evening, and walk into the streets of Portsmouth, looking into the windows of houses, and listening to the conversation of the people.

Their cruelty was chiefly exercised upon children, and such aged, infirm, or corpulent persons as could not bear the hardships of a journey through the wilderness. If they took a woman far

Time.		Places attacked.	No. Killed.	Wounded.	Cap't.
1695.	9 September,	Pemaquid, Me.	4	6	—
	7 October,	Newbury, Ms.	—	1	9
1696.	7 May,	Dover, (or near it)	1	—	—
	24 June,	York, Me.	2	1	—
	26 June,	Sagamore's Creek, (Ports.)	24	1	4
	26 July,	Dover,	3	3	3
	13 August,	Andover, Ms.	2	—	—
	15 August,	Haverhill, Ms.	—	—	5
	25 August,	Oxford, Ms.	5	—	—
	25 August,	Sandy Beach,	1	—	—
	27 August,	Lubberland,(1)	1	—	—
	13 October,	Saco Fort, Me.	5	1	—
1697.	15 March,	Haverhill, Ms,	40(2)	—	—
	20 May,	York, Me.	—	—	1
		Groton, Ms.	1	3	—
	10 June,	Exeter,	1	1	1
	10 June,	Salisbury, Ms.	—	—	2
	4 July,	Kittery, Me.	1	—	—
	29 July,	Dover,	3	1	—
	7 August,	Saco Fort, Me.	3	—	3
	9 September,	Damariscotta, Me.	12	12	—
	11 September,	Lancaster, Ms.	21	2	6
	15 November,	Johnson's Creek,	1	—	1
1698.	22 February,	Andover, Ms.	5	—	5
	February,	Haverhill, Ms.	2	—	2
	9 May,	Spruce Creek, Me.	1	—	3
	9 May,	York, Me.	—	1	—

(1) This place was in New-Hampshire.

(2) This was the number killed and taken. Mr. Saltonstall in his Hist. of Haverhill, p. 8, says that, " In 1697, fourteen persons were killed, [in Haverhill] eight of them children." These he makes in addition to the above 40 killed and taken when Mrs. Duston was captured, the time of which he erroneously places under 1698.]

advanced in pregnancy, their knives were plunged into her bowels. An infant, when it became troublesome, had its brains dash-
ed out against the next tree or stone. Sometimes to torment the
wretched mother, they would whip and beat the child till almost
dead, or hold it under water till its breath was just gone, and then
throw it to her to comfort and quiet it. If the mother could not
readily still its weeping, the hatchet was buried in its skull. A
captive wearied with a burden laid on his shoulders was often
sent to rest the same way. If any one proved refractory, or was
known to have been instrumental of the death of an Indian, or related to one who had been so, he was tortured with a lingering
punishment, generally at the stake, whilst the other captives were
insulted with the sight of his miseries. Sometimes a fire would
be kindled and a threatening given out against one or more, though
there was no intention of sacrificing them, only to make sport of
their terrors. The young Indians often signalized their cruelty
in treating captives inhumanly out of sight of the elder, and when
inquiry was made into the matter, the insulted captive must either
be silent or put the best face on it, to prevent worse treatment for
the future. If a captive appeared sad and dejected he was sure
to meet with insult; but if he could sing and dance and laugh
with his masters, he was carressed as a brother. They had a
strong aversion to negroes, and generally killed them when they
fell into their hands.

Famine was a common attendant on these doleful captivities.
The Indians when they caught any game devoured it all at one
sitting, and then girding themselves round the waist, travelled
without sustenance till chance threw more in their way. The
captives, unused to such canine repasts and abstinences, could not
support the surfeit of the one, nor the craving of the other. A
change of masters, though it sometimes proved a relief from misery, yet rendered the prospect of a return to their homes more
distant. If an Indian had lost a relative, a prisoner bought for a
gun, a hatchet, or a few skins, must supply the place of the deceased, and be the father, brother, or son of the purchaser ; and
those who could accommodate themselves to such barbarous
adoption, were treated with the same kindness as the persons in
whose place they were substituted. A sale among the French
of Canada was the most happy event to a captive, especially if
he became a servant in the family; though sometimes, even there,
a prison was their lot, till opportunity presented for their redemption; whilst the priests employed every seducing art to pervert
them to the popish religion, and induce them to abandon their
country. These circumstances, joined with the more obvious
hardships of travelling half naked and barefoot through pathless
deserts, over craggy mountains and deep swamps, through frost,
rain and snow, exposed by day and night to the inclemency of

the weather, and in summer to the venomous stings of those num-
berless insects with which the woods abound ; the restless anxiety
of mind, the retrospect of past scenes of pleasure, the remembrance of distant friends, the bereavements experienced at the
beginning or during the progress of the captivity, and the daily
apprehension of death either by famine or the savage enemy;
these were the horrors of an Indian captivity.

On the other hand, it must be acknowledged that there have
been instances of justice, generosity and tenderness during these
wars which would have done honor to a civilized people. A
kindness shewn to an Indian was remembered as long as an injury ; and persons have had their lives spared, for acts of humanity done to the ancestors of those Indians, into whose hands they
have fallen.* They would sometimes " carry children on their
" arms and shoulders, feed their prisoners with the best of their
" provision, and pinch themselves rather than their captives should
" want food." When sick or wounded, they would afford them
proper means for their recovery, which they were very well able
to do by their knowledge of simples. In thus preserving the lives
and health of their prisoners, they doubtless had a view of gain.
But the most remarkably favorable circumstance in an Indian
captivity, was their decent behaviour to women. I have never
read, nor heard, nor could find by inquiry, that any woman who
fell into their hands was ever treated with the least immodesty ;
but testimonies to the contrary are very frequent.† Whether
this negative virtue is to be ascribed to a natural frigidity of constitution, let philosophers inquire : The fact is certain ; and it
was a most happy circumstance for our female captives, that in

---

* Several instances to this purpose have been occasionally mentioned in the
course of this narrative. The following additional one is taken from Capt.
Hammond's MS. Journal. " April 13, 1677. The Indians Simon, Andrew
" and Peter burnt the house of Edward Weymouth at Sturgeon creek. They
" plundered the house of one Crawley but did not kill him, because of some
" kindness done to Simon's grandmother."

† Mary Rowlandson who was captured at Lancaster, in 1675, has this passage in her narrative, (p. 55.) " I have been in the midst of these roaring
lions and savage bears, that feared neither God nor man nor the devil, by day
and night, alone and in company ; sleeping all sorts together, and yet not one
of them ever offered me the least abuse of unchastity in word or action."

Elizabeth Hanson who was taken from Dover in 1724, testifies in her narrative, (p. 28) that " the Indians are very civil toward their captive women,
not offering any incivility by any indecent carriage."

William Fleming, who was taken in Pennsylvania, in 1755, says the Indians told him " he need not be afraid of their abusing his wife, for they
would not do it, for fear of offending their God (pointing their hands toward
heaven) for the man that affronts his God will surely be killed when he goes
to war." He farther says, that one of them gave his wife a shift and petticoat
which he had among his plunder, and though he was alone with her, yet " he
turned his back, and went to some distance whilst she put them on." (p. 10.)

Charlevoix in his account of the Indians of Canada, says, (letter 7) "There
is no example that any have ever taken the least liberty with the French
women, even when they were their prisoners."

the midst of all their distresses, they had no reason to fear from
a savage foe, the perpetration of a crime, which has too frequently
disgraced, not only the personal, but the national character of
those, who make large pretences to civilization and humanity.

CHAPTER XI.

The civil affairs of the Province during the administrations of Usher, Partridge, Allen, the Earl of Bellomont and Dudley, comprehending the whole
controversy with Allen and his heirs.

JOHN USHER, Esquire, was a native of Boston, and by profession a stationer. He was possessed of an handsome fortune, and
sustained a fair character in trade. He had been employed by
the Massachusetts government, when in England, to negotiate the
purchase of the province of Maine, from the heirs of Sir Ferdinando Gorges, and had thereby got a taste for speculating in landed interest. He was one of the partners in the million purchase,
and had sanguine expectations of gain from that quarter. He
had rendered himself unpopular among his countrymen, by accepting the office of treasurer, under Sir Edmund Andros, and
joining with apparent zeal in the measures of that administration,
and he continued a friendly connexion with that party, after they
were displaced.[1]

Though not illnatured, but rather of an open and generous disposition, yet he wanted those accomplishments which he might
have acquired by a learned and polite education. He had but
little of the statesman, and less of the courtier. Instead of an
engaging affability he affected a severity in his deportment, was
loud in conversation, and stern in command. Fond of presiding
in government, he frequently journeyed into the province, (though
his residence was at Boston, where he carried on his business as
usual,) and often summoned the council, when he had little or
nothing to lay before them. He gave orders, and found fault
like one who felt himself independent, and was determined to be
obeyed. He had an high idea of his authority and the dignity of
his commission ; and when opposed and insulted, as he sometimes was, he treated the offenders with a severity, which he
would not relax, till he had brought them to submission. His
public speeches were always incorrect, and sometimes coarse and
reproachful.[2]

He seems, however, to have taken as much care for the interest and preservation of the province as one in his circumstances

(1) Usher's papers.   (2) Province files.

could have done. He began his administration in the height of
a war, which greatly distressed and impoverished the country,
yet his views from the beginning were lucrative.* The people
perceived these views, and were aware of the danger. The
transfer of the title from Mason to Allen was only a change of
names. They expected a repetition of the same difficulties under
a new claimant. After the opposition they had hitherto made,
it could not be thought strange that men whose pulse beat high
for freedom, should refuse to submit to vassalage; nor, whilst
they were on one side defending their possessions against a savage enemy, could it be expected, that on the other, they should
tamely suffer the intrusion of a landlord. Usher's interest was
united with theirs in providing for the defence of the country, and
contending with the enemy; but when the proprietary of the soil
was in question, they stood on opposite sides; and as both these
controversies were carried on at the same time, the conduct of
the people toward him varied according to the exigency of the
case. They sometimes voted him thanks for his services, and
at other times complained of his abusing and oppressing them.

Some of them would have been content to have held their estates under Allen's title,† but the greater part, including the
principal men, were resolved to oppose it to the last extremity.
They had an aversion not only to the proprietary claim on their
lands, but their separation from the Massachusetts government,
under which they had formerly enjoyed so much freedom and
peace. They had petitioned to be re-annexed to them, at the
time of the revolution; and they were always very fond of applying to them for help in their difficulties, that it might appear
how unable they were to subsist alone. They knew also that the
Massachusetts people were as averse as themselves to Allen's
claim, which extended to a great part of their lands, and was
particularly noticed in their new charter.

Soon after Usher's arrival, he made inquiry for the papers
which contained the transactions relative to Mason's suits. During the suspension of government in 1689, Captain John Pickering,‡ a man of a rough and adventurous spirit, and a lawyer, had
gone with a company of armed men to the house of Chamberlain,
the late secretary and clerk, and demanded the records and files

* In a letter to George Dorrington and John Taylor in London, he writes
thus : " Jan. 29, 1692—3. In case yourselves are concerned in the province
" of New-Hampshire, with prudent management it may be worth money, the
" people only paying 4d and 2d per acre. The reason why the commonalty
" of the people do not agree is because 3 or 4 of the great landed men dissuade
" them from it. The people have petitioned the king to be annexed to Bos-
" ton government, but it will not be for the proprietor's interest to admit of
" that unless the king sends a general governor over all."

† " I have 40 hands in Exeter who desire to take patents for land from you,
" and many in other towns." Usher to Allen, October, 1695.

‡ [He often wrote his name Pickerin.]

which were in his possession. Chamberlain refused to deliver them without some legal warrant for security ; but Pickering took them by force, and conveyed them over the river to Kittery. Pickering was summoned before the governor, threatened and imprisoned, but for some time would neither deliver the books, nor discover the place of their concealment, unless by order of the assembly and to some person by them appointed to receive them. At length, however, he was constrained to deliver them, and they were put into the hands of the secretary, by the lieutenant-governor's order.

Another favorite point with Usher was to have the boundary between New-Hampshire and Massachusetts ascertained. There

1693. were reasons which induced some of the people to fall in with this desire. The general idea was, that New-Hampshire began at the end of three miles north of the river Merrimack ; which imaginary line was also the boundary of the adjoining townships on each side. The people who lived, and owned lands near these limits, pretended to belong to either province, as best suited their conveniency ; which caused a difficulty in the collecting of taxes, and cutting of timber. The town of

1695. Hampton was sensibly affected with these difficulties, and
Oct. 12. petitioned the council that the line might be run. The council appointed a committee of Hampton men to do it, and gave notice to Massachusetts of their intention ; desiring them to join in the affair.[1] They disliked it, and declined to act ; upon which, the lieutenant-governor and council of New-Hampshire caused the boundary line to be run from the sea-shore three miles northward of Merrimack, and parallel to the river, as far as any settlements had been made, or lands occupied.[2]

The only attempt made to extend the settlement of the lands during these times, was, that in the spring of the year 1694, whilst there was a truce with the Indians, Usher granted a charter for the township of Kingston, to about twenty petitioners from Hampton. They were soon discouraged by the dangers and difficulties of the succeeding hostilities, and many of them returned home within two years. After the war, they resumed their enterprise ; but it was not till the year 1725, that they were able to obtain the settlement of a minister. No alterations took place in the old towns, except the separation of Great-Island, Little-

1693. Harbor, and Sandy-Beach, from Portsmouth, and their erection into a town by the name of New-Castle ; together with the annexation of that part of Squamscot patent which now bears the name of Stratham, to Exeter, it having before been connected with Hampton.[3]

The lieutenant-governor was very forward in these transactions,

(1) Prov. files.   (2) Brief of the case of N. H. and Mass. stated by Strange and Hollings, 1738, p. 8.   (3) Prov. files.

thinking them circumstances favorable to his views, and being
willing to recommend himself to the people by seconding their
wishes as far as was consistent with the interest he meaned to
serve.   The people, however, regarded the settling and dividing
of townships, and the running of lines, only as matters of general
convenience, and continued to be disgusted with his administration.   His repeated calls upon them for money were answered
by repeated pleas of poverty, and requests for assistance from the
neighboring province.   Usher used all his influence with that government to obtain a supply of men to garrison the frontiers ; and
when they wanted provisions for the garrisons, and could not readily raise the money, he would advance it out of his own purse
and wait till the treasury could reimburse it.

During the two or three first years of his administration the
public charges were provided for as they had been before, by an
excise on wines and other spirituous liquors, and an impost on
merchandize.   These duties being laid only from year to year,
Usher vehemently urged upon the assembly a renewal of
the act, and an extension of the duty to articles of export ; 1695.
and that a part of the money so raised might be applied to Nov.7-9.
the support of government.   The answer he obtained was, that
‘ considering the exposed state of the province, they were obliged
‘ to apply all the money they could raise to their defence ; and
‘ therefore they were not capable of doing any thing for the sup-
‘ port of government, though they were sensible his honor had
‘ been at considerable expense.   They begged that he would join
‘ with the council in representing to the king, the poverty and
‘ danger of the province, that such methods might be taken for
‘ their support and preservation as to the royal wisdom should
‘ seem meet.’   Being further pressed upon the subject, they passed a vote to lay the proposed duties for one year, ‘ provided he
‘ and the council would join with them in petitioning the king to
‘ annex them to Massachusetts.’

He had the mortification of being disappointed in his expectations of gain, not only from the people, but from his employer.
Allen had promised him two hundred and fifty pounds per annum
for executing his commission ; and when at the end of the third
year, Usher drew on him for the payment of this sum, his bill came
back protested.*   This was the more mortifying, as he had as-
siduously and faithfully attended to Allen’s interest, and acquainted him from time to time with the means he had used, the difficulties he had encountered, the pleas he had urged, the time he
had spent, and the expense he had incurred in defence and support of his claim.   He now desired him to come over and assume
the government himself, or get a successor to him appointed in

* It is probable that Allen was not able to comply with this demand.   The
purchase of the province from the Masons had been made “ with other men's
money.”   Letter of Usher to Sir Matthew Dudley, Sept. 1718.

the office of lieutenant-governor.[1] He did not know that the people were before hand of him in this latter request.

On a pretence of disloyalty he had removed Hinckes, Waldron and Vaughan from their seats in the council.* The former of these was a man who could change with the times; the two latter were steady opposers of the proprietary claim. Their suspension irritated the people, who, by their influence, privately agreed to recommend William Partridge, Esq., as a proper person for their lieutenant-governor in Usher's stead. Partridge was a native of Portsmouth, a shipwright, of an extraordinary mechanical genius, of a politic turn of mind, and a popular man. He was treasurer of the province, and had been ill used by Usher. Being largely concerned in trade he was well known in England, having supplied the navy with masts and timber. His sudden departure for England was very surprising to Usher, who could not imagine he had any other business than to settle his accounts.—

But the surprise was greatly increased, when he returned with a commission appointing him lieutenant-governor and commander in chief in Allen's absence.[2] It was obtained of the lords justices in the king's absence, by the interest of Sir Henry Ashurst, and was dated June 6, 1696.

1697.
Jan.

Immediately on his arrival, his appointment was publicly made known to the people ; though, either from the delay of making out his instructions, or for want of the form of an oath necessary to be taken, the commission was not published in the usual manner. But the party in opposition to Usher triumphed. The suspended counsellors resumed their seats, Pickering was made king's attorney, and Hinkes, as president of the council, opened the assembly with a speech. This assembly ordered the records which had been taken from Pickering to be deposited in the hands of Major Vaughan, who was appointed recorder : in consequence of which they have been kept in that office ever since.[3]

June 8.

Usher being at Boston when this alteration took place, wrote to them, declaring that no commission could supersede his, till duly published ; and intimated his intention of coming hither, " if he could be safe with his life." He also despatched his secretary, Charles Story, to England, with an account of this transaction, which in one of his private letters he styles " the Pascataqua rebellion ;" adding, that " the militia were raised, and forty horse sent to seize him ;" and intimating that the confusion was so great, that " if but three French ships were to appear, he

Feb. 20.

(1) Usher's letter to Allen, July and Oct. 1695.   (2) Ashurst's letters in files.   (3) MS. Laws.

* [The alleged cause of the suspension of Waldron and Vaughan was their refusing to take the oath of allegiance, according to a Law of the Province of July, 1696, requiring all male persons from 16 years old and upwards to take said-oath, and for refusing to sign an association paper according to the form of the statute in England.]

believed they would surrender on the first summons."[1] The extreme imprudence of sending such a letter across the Atlantic in
time of war, was still heightened by an apprehension which then
prevailed, that the French were preparing an armament to invade
the country, and that "they particularly designed for Pascataqua
river."[2]

In answer to his complaint, the lords of trade directed him to
continue in the place of lieutenant-governor, till Partridge should
qualify himself, or till Richard, Earl of Bellomont, should
arrive ; who was commissioned to the government of New-   Aug. 8.
York, Massachusetts Bay and New-Hampshire; but had not yet
departed from England.   Usher received the letter from the lords
together with the articles of peace which had been concluded at Ryswick, and immediately set off for New-   Dec. 10.
Hampshire, (where he had not been for a year) proclaimed the
peace, and published the orders he had received, and
having proceded thus far, "thought all well and quiet."   Dec. 13.
But his opposers having held a consultation at night, Partridge's
commission was the next day published in form ; he took
the oaths, and entered on the administration of govern-   Dec. 14.
ment,[3] to the complete vexation and disappointment of Usher, who
had been so elated with the confirmation of his commission, that
as he passed through Hampton, he had forbidden the minister of
that place to observe a thanksgiving day, which had been appointed by President Hinckes.[4]

An assembly being called, one of their first acts was to write to
the lords of trade, ' acknowledging the favor of the king
' in appointing one of their own inhabitants to the command   1698.
' of the province, complaining of Usher, and alleging that   Jan. 3.
' there had been no disturbances but what he himself had made ; de-
' claring that those counsellors whom he had suspended were loy-
' al subjects, and capable of serving the king ; and informing their
' lordships that Partridge had now qualified himself, and that they
' were waiting the arrival of the Earl of Bellomont.'

They also deputed Ichabod Plaisted to wait on the Earl at
New-York, and compliment him on his arrival. ' If he should
' find his lordship high, and reserved, and not easy of access, he
' was instructed to employ some gentleman who was in his confi-
' dence to manage the business ; but if easy and free, he was to
' wait on him in person ; to tell him how joyfully they received
' the news of his appointment, and that they daily expected Gov-
' ernor Allen, whose commission would be accounted good,
' till his lordship's should be published, and to ask his advice,
' how they should behave in such a case.'[5] The principal design
of this message was to make their court to the earl, and get the

(1) Usher's Letters.   (2) Lt. Gov. Stoughton's letter of Feb. 22, in files.
(3) Usher's papers.   (4) Council files.   (5) Plaisted's instructions, in files.

start of Usher, or any of his friends, who might prepossess him with an opinion to their disadvantage. But if this should have happened, Plaisted was directed ' to observe what reception they ' met with. If his lordship was ready to come this way, he was . ' to beg leave to attend him as far as Boston, and then ask his ' permission to return home ;' and he was furnished with a letter of credit to defray his expenses. This message, which shows the contrivers to be no mean politicians, had the desired effect.

The earl continued at New-York for the first year after his arrival in America ; during which time, Governor Allen came over, Aug. 28. as it was expected, and his commission being still in force, he took the oaths and assumed the command. Upon Sept. 15. which, Usher again made his appearance in council, Nov. 29. where he produced the letter from the lords of trade, claiming his place as lieutenant-governor, and declared that the suspended counsellors had no right to sit till restored by the king's order. This brought on an altercation, wherein Elliot affirmed, that Partridge was duly qualified and in office, that Waldron and Vaughan had been suspended without cause, and that if they were not allowed to sit, the rest were determined to resign. The governor declared Usher to be of the council ; upon which Elliot withdrew.

At the succeeding assembly, two new counsellors appeared ; Joseph Smith, and Kingsly Hall.* The first day passed quietly. 1699.   The governor approved Pickering as speaker of the house ; Jan. 5. told them he had assumed the government, because the Earl of Bellomont had not arrived ; recommended a continuance of the excise and powder money, and advised them to send a congratulatory message to the Earl at New-York. The Jan. 6.   next day, the house answered, that they had continued the customs and excise till November, that they had already congratulated the earl, and received a kind answer, and were waiting his arrival ; *when* they should enter further on business. They complained that Allen's conduct had been grievous in forbidding the collecting of the last tax, whereby the public debts were not paid ; in displacing sundry fit persons, and appointing others less fit, and admitting Usher to be of the council, though superseded by Partridge's commission. These things, they told him, had obliged some members of the council and assembly to apply to his lordship for relief, and, " unless he should manage with a more moderate hand," they threatened him with second application.

The same day, Coffin and Weare moved a question in council, whether Usher was one of that body. He asserted his privilege, and obtained a major vote. They then entered their dissent, and

* [Joseph Smith was of Hampton. Kingsly Hall was of Exeter. The last married a daughter of Rev. Samuel Dudley.]

desired a dismission. The governor forbade their departure.
Weare answered that he would not, by sitting there, put contempt
on the king's commission, meaning Partridge's, and withdrew.
The next day, the assembly ordered the money arising from the
impost and excise to be *kept* in the treasury, till the Earl of Bellomont's arrival; and the governor dissolved them.

These violences on his part were supposed to originate from
Usher's resentment, and his overbearing influence upon Allen,
who is said to have been rather of a pacific and condescending
disposition. The same ill temper continued during the remainder
of this short administration. The old counsellors, excepting Fryer, refused to sit. Sampson Sheafe and Peter Weare made up
the quorum. Sheafe was also secretary; Smith treasurer, and
William Ardell sheriff. The constables refused to collect the
taxes of the preceeding year, and the governor was obliged to
revoke his orders, and commission the former constables to do
the duty which he had forbidden.*[1]

In the spring, the earl of Bellomont set out for his eastern governments. The council voted an address, and sent a committee,
of which Usher was one, to present it to him at Boston; and
preparations were made for his reception in New-Hampshire;
where he, at length, came and published his commission, July 31.
to the great joy of the people, who now saw at the head
of the government, a nobleman of distinguished figure and polite
manners, a firm friend to the revolution, a favorite of King William, and one who had no interest in oppressing them.

(1) MS. in the files.

* [On the 6 January, 1699, the Eastern Indians renewed their submission
to the Crown of England, at Casco Bay, near " Mare's point," (Coll. N. H.
Hist. Soc. ii. 265—267) whereupon lieutenant-governor Stoughton issued a
proclamation, a copy of which was sent to governor Allen, of New-Hampshire,
accompanied with the following letter, lately discovered among secretary.
Waldron's papers.

" *Honble Sir* :—Upon the late submission made by the Eastern Indians
which it's hoped will settle all things in a present quiet, I have thought fit,
with the advice and consent of his Ma: tys Council here, to emit a Proclamation (copy whereof is enclosed) to promote the regular settlement of the Eastern parts of this Province, and for regulating of Trade with the Indians, the
better to secure and preserve his Ma'tys Interests and the future peace and
tranquillity of his subjects, that no just provocation may be given to the Indians, or any abuse or injustice done them therein—the terms whereof the
governmt. here expect an exact compliance with, and conformity unto. And
judge it necessary for his Ma'tys service that your honour be acquainted
therewith, to the end his Ma : tys subjects within your Government may be
notified thereof in such way as you shall think most adviseable, that neither
the good intent of the sd. Proclamation be defeated, nor they suffer any loss
or damage by acting any thing contrary thereunto within the parts of this his
Ma : tys Government. Assuring my selfe nothing will be wanting on your
honor's part to prevent the mischiefes that may ensue upon neglect of the due
observance thereof, I am with much respect, Sir,
                              Your very humble servant,
                                        WM. STOUGHTON."
" Boston, February 16th : 1698."(1)
                  (1) That is 1698–9.]

During the controversy with Allen, Partridge had withdrawn ; but upon this change, he took his seat as lieutenant-governor, and the displaced counsellors were again called to the board. A petition was presented against the judges of the superior court, and a proclamation was issued for justices of the peace and constables only to continue in office, whereby the judges' commissions determined. Richard Jose was made sheriff in the room of Ardell, and Charles Story secretary in the room of Sheafe.

The government was now modelled in favor of the people, and they rejoiced in the change, as they apprehended the way was opened for an effectual settlement of their long continued difficulties and disputes. Both parties laid their complaints before the governor, who wisely avoided censuring either, and advised to a revival of the courts of justice, in which the main controversy might be legally decided. This was agreed to, and the necessary acts being passed by an assembly, (who also presented the earl with five hundred pounds which he obtained the king's leave to accept) after about eighteen day's stay, he quitted the province, leaving Partridge, now quietly seated in the chair, to appoint the judges of the respective courts. Hinckes was made chief justice of the superior court, with Peter Coffin, John Gerrish and John Plaisted for assistants ; Waldron chief justice of the inferior court, with Henry Dow, Theodore Atkinson and John Woodman for assistants.[1]

One principal object of the earl's attention was, to fortify the harbor, and provide for the defence of the country in case of another war. He had recommended to the assembly, in his speech, the building of a strong fort on Great Island, and afterward, in his letters, assured them that if they would provide ma-
1700. terials, he would endeavor to prevail on the king to be at
June 6. the expense of erecting it. Col. Romer, a Dutch Engineer, having viewed the spot, produced to the assembly an estimate of the cost and transportation of materials, amounting to above six thousand pounds. They were amazed at the proposal ; and returned for answer to the governor, that in their greatest difficulties, when their lives and estates were in the most imminent hazard, they were never able to raise one thousand pounds in a year ;* that they had been exceedingly impoverished

(1) Council Records.

* I have here placed in one view such assessments as I have been able to find during the preceding war, with the proportion of each town, which varied according to their respective circumstances at different times.   MS. Laws.

	1692.	1693.	1694.	1695.	Uncert.	1697.
Portsmouth,	70	210	167		129 6	140 1 6
Hampton,	66 13 4	200	230		172 14 6	187 2 4 1-2
Dover,	30	110	90		117 16 6	127 9 7 1-2
Exeter,	33 6 8	80	127		106 16	115 14
New-Castle,			86		73 7	79 12 6
	£200	£600	£700	£400	£600	£650

by a long war, and were now struggling under an heavy debt, besides being engaged in a controversy with " a pretended proprietor ;" that they had expended more " blood and money" to secure his majesty's interest and dominion in New-England than the intrinsic value of their estates, and that the fortifying of the harbor did as much concern Massachusetts as themselves ; but they concluded with assuring his lordship, that if he were " thoroughly acquainted with their miserable, poor and mean cir- " cumstances, they would readily submit to whatever he should " think them capable of doing."[1]   They were also required to furnish their quota of men to join with the other colonies in defending the frontiers of New-York in case of an attack.*   This, they thought extremely hard, not only because they had never received the least assistance from New-York in the late wars, but because an opinion prevailed among them, that their enemies had received supplies from the Dutch at Albany, and that the plunder taken from their desolated towns had been sold in that place. There was, however, no opportunity for affording this assistance, as the New-Yorkers took care to maintain a good understanding with the French and Indians, for the benefit of trade.[2]

But to return to Allen : He had as little prospect of success in the newly established courts, as the people had, when Mason's suits were carried on under Cranfield's government.[3]   On examining the records of the superior court, it was found that twenty-four leaves were missing, in which, it was supposed, the judgments recovered by Mason were recorded. No evidence appeared of his having obtained possession. The work was to begin anew; and Waldron, being one of the principal landholders and most strenuous opposers of the claim, was singled out to stand foremost in the controversy with Allen, as his father had with Mason. The cause went through the courts, and was invariably given in favor of the defendant with costs. Allen's only refuge was in an appeal to the king, which the court, following the example of their brethren in the Massachusetts, refused to admit. He then petitioned the king ; who, by an order in council, granted him an appeal, allowing him eight months to prepare for its prosecution.

The refusal of an appeal could not fail of being highly resented in England. It was severely animadverted on by the lords of trade, who, in a letter to the Earl of Bellomont upon this occasion, say : " This declining to admit ap-

Aug. 18.

1701.
Apr. 24.

(1) MS. in files.   (2) Smith's Hist. New-York, p. 108, 175, 214.   (3) Printed state of Allen's title, p. 9.

* The quotas of men to be furnished by each government for the defence of New-York, if attacked, were as follows, viz.

Massachusetts	350	New-York	200	Pennsylvania	80
New-Hampshire	40	East New-Jersey	60	Maryland	160
Rhode-Island	48	West New-Jersey	60	Virginia	240
Connecticut	120				

" peals to his Majesty in council, is a matter which you ought
" very carefully to watch against in all your governments.
Apr. 29. " It is an humor that prevails so much in proprieties and
" charter colonies, and the *Independency* they thirst after is now
" so notorious, that it has been thought fit those considerations,
" together with other objections against those colonies, should be
" laid before the parliament; and a bill has thereupon been
" brought into the house of lords for re-uniting the right of gov-
" ernment in their colonies to the crown."[1]

Before this letter was written, the earl died at New-York, to the
great regret of the people in his several governments,
Mar. 5. among whom he had made himself very popular.   A copy
of the letter was sent to New-York; but the bill mentioned in it
was not passed into an act of parliament.   For some reasons of
state, it was rejected by the house of lords.

The assembly of New-Hampshire, having now a fair opportunity, endeavoured as much as possible to provide for their own
security; and passed two acts, the one for confirming the
Sept. 13. grants of lands which had been made within their several
townships; the other for ascertaining the bounds of them.[2]   Partridge gave his consent to these acts; but Allen had the address
to get them disallowed and repealed because there was no reserve made in them of the proprietor's right.[3]

The controversy being brought before the king, both sides prepared to attend the suit.   Allen's age, and probably want of cash,
prevented his going in person; he therefore appointed Usher to
act for him, having previously mortgaged one half of the
Oct. 14. province to him, for fifteen hundred pounds.   Vaughan
was appointed agent for the province, and attorney to Waldron.
1702.   It being a general interest, the assembly bore the expense,
May 29. and notwithstanding their pleas of poverty on other occasions, provided a fund, on which, the agent might draw in
case of the emergency.

In the mean time, King William died, and Queen Anne appointed Joseph Dudley, Esq., formerly president of New-England,
to be governor of Massachusetts and New-Hampshire; whose
commission being published at Portsmouth, the assem-
July 13-18. bly, by a well timed present, interested him in their
favor, and afterward settled a salary on him during his administration, agreeably to the queen's instructions, who, about this
time, forbade her governors to receive any but settled salaries.[4]

When Allen's appeal came before the queen in council, it was
found that his attorney had not brought proof that Mason had ever
been legally in possession;[5] for want of this, the judgment recovered by Waldron was affirmed; but the order of council directed
that the appellant ' should be at liberty to begin *de novo* by a writ

(1) MS. in files.   (2) Hutch. vol. 2, p. 131.   (3) MS. Laws.   (4) Council
and Assembly Records.   (5) Printed state of Allen's title, p. 9.

' of ejectment in the courts of New-Hampshire, to try his title to
' the lands, or to quit rents payable for the same ; and that if any
' doubt in law should arise, the jury should declare what titles each
' party did severally make out to the lands in question, and that
' the points in law should be referred to the court; or if any doubt
' should arise concerning the evidence, it should be specially
' stated in writing, that if either party should appeal to her maj-
' esty, she might be more fully informed, in order to a final de-
' termination.'[1]

While this appeal was depending, a petition was presented to
the queen, praying that Allen might be put in possession of the
waste lands.   This petition was referred to Sir Edward Northey.
attorney general, who was ordered to report on three questions,
viz. 1. Whether Allen had a right to the wastes. 2. What
lands ought to be accounted waste. 3. By what method her
majesty might put him into possession.   At the same time, Usher
was making interest to be re-appointed lieutenant-governor of the
province.   Upon this, Vaughan entered a complaint to the queen,
setting forth 'that Allen claimed as waste ground, not only a
' large tract of unoccupied land, but much of that which had been
' long enjoyed by the inhabitants, as common pasture, within the
' bounds of their several townships.   That Usher, by his former
' managements and misdemeanors when in office, had forced
' some of the principal inhabitants to quit the province, and had
' greatly harassed and disgusted all the rest, rendering himself
' quite unacceptable to them.   That he was interested in the suits
' now depending, as on Allen's death, he would, in right of his
' wife, be entitled to part of the estate.   Wherefore, it was hum-
' bly submitted, whether it would be proper to appoint, as lieu-
' tenant-governor, one whose interest and endeavor it would be
' to disseize the people of their ancient estates, and render them
' uneasy ; and it was prayed that no letters might be wrote to put
' Allen in possession of the wastes, till the petitioner should be
' heard by council.'[2]

Usher's interest however prevailed.   The attorney-general
reported, that ' Allen's claim to the wastes was valid ; that   1703.
' all lands *unenclosed and unoccupied* were to be reputed   Jan. 28.
' waste; that he might enter into and take possession of
' them, and if disturbed, might assert his right and prosecute tres-
' passers in the courts there ; but that it would not be proper for
' her majesty to interpose, unless the question should come be-
' fore her by appeal from those courts ; save, that it might be
' reasonable to direct (if Allen should insist on it at the trials)
' that matters of fact be found specially by the juries, and that
' these special matters should be made to appear on an appeal.'[3]

(1) MS. Copy of Lords Trade Report in 1758.   Files of the Superior Court.
(2) Usher's papers.   (3) Superior Court Files.

Soon after this, Usher obtained a second commission as lieutenant-governor ; but was expressly restricted from intermedling
July 26. ' with the appointment of judges or juries, or otherwise, in
' matters relating to the disputes between Allen and the
' inhabitants.' The people did not relish this re-appointment, nor
did his subsequent conduct reconcile them to it. Upon his first
Oct. 27. appearance in council, Partridge took his seat as counsellor ; but the next day, desired a dismission on account of
a ship in the river, which demanded his constant attention. This
request was granted, and he soon after removed to Newbury,
where he spent the rest of his days in a mercantile department,
and in the business of his profession.*

It had always been a favorite point with Usher to get the books
and files, which had been taken from Chamberlain, lodged in the
secretary's office. Among these files, were the original minutes
of the suits which Mason had carried on, and the verdicts, judgments and bills of cost he had recovered. As they were committed to the care of the recorder, who was appointed by the general
court and removable only by them, no use could be made of these
papers, but by consent of the assembly. When Usher produced
Nov. 4. to the council an order from Whitehall that these records
should be deposited with the secretary, Penhallow, the
1704. recorder, who was a member of the council, refused to
deliver them without an act of the general assembly au-
thorising him to do so.

Usher succeeded but little better in his applications for money.
He alleged that he had received nothing for his former services,
though they had given hundreds to Partridge ; and he complained
that no house was provided for him to reside in, which obliged
him to spend most of his time at Boston. The plea of poverty
always at hand was not forgotten in answer to these demands.
But at length, upon his repeated importunity and Dudley's earnest recommendation, after the assembly had refused making any
provision for him, and the governor had expressly directed him
July 7. to reside at New-Castle, and exercise a regular command,
it being a time of war ; the council were prevailed upon to
allow him two rooms in any house he could procure " till the next
meeting of the assembly," and to order *thirty-eight shillings* to
be given him for the expense of his " journey to and from Boston."

When Dudley acquainted the assembly with the royal determination in Allen's suits, they appeared tolerably satisfied with
Feb. 10. the equitable intention discovered therein ; but begged
him to represent to her majesty that ' the province was at
' least sixty miles long and twenty wide, containing twelve hun-

* His son Richard Partridge was an agent for the province in England.
One of his daughters was married to Governor Belcher, and was mother to
the late lieutenant-governor of Nova-Scotia.

' dred square miles, that the inhabitants claimed only the property
' of the lands contained within the bounds of their townships,
' which was less than one third of the province, and had been
' possessed by them and their ancestors more than sixty years;
' that they had nothing to offer as a grievance if the other two
' thirds were adjudged to Allen; but should be glad to see the
' same planted and settled for the better security and defence of
' the whole; withal desiring it might be considered how much
' time, blood and treasure, had been spent in settling and defend-
' ing this part of her majesty's dominion, and that the cost and
' labor bestowed thereon far exceeded the true value of the land,
' so that they hoped it was not her majesty's intention to deprive
' them of all the herbage, timber and fuel, without which they
' could not subsist, and that the lands comprehended within the
' bounds of their townships was little enough to afford these neces-
' sary articles; it not being usual in these plantations to fence in
' more of their lands than would serve for tillage, leaving the rest
' unfenced for the feeding their cattle in common.'[1]

Notwithstanding this plea, which was often alleged, Allen, by
virtue of the queen's permission, had entered upon and Dec. 22.
taken possession by turf and twig of the common land 1703.
in each township, as well as of that which was without their bounds.
He brought his writ of ejectment *de novo* against Waldron, and
when the trial was coming on, informed Governor Dudley of it,
that he might come into court and demand a special verdict
agreeably to the queen's instructions.[2] Dudley, from Boston, informed the court of the day when he intended to be at Portsmouth, and directed the judges to adjourn the court to that day.
Before it came, he heard of a body of Indians above 1704.
Lancaster, which had put the country in alarm, and or- Aug. 10.
dered the court to be again adjourned. At length, he began his journey; but was taken ill at Newbury, with a *seasonable*
fit of the gravel, and proceeded no farther.[3] The jury in the mean
time refused to bring in a special verdict; but found for the defendant with costs. Allen again appealed from the judgment.

Perplexed, however, with these repeated disappointments, and
at the same time being low in purse, as well as weakened with
age, he sought an accommodation with the people, with whom he
was desirous to spend the remainder of his days in peace. It has
been said, that he made very advantageous offers to Vaughan
and Waldron, if they would purchase his title; but that they utterly refused it. The people were sensible that a door was still
open for litigation; and that after Allen's death, they might, perhaps, meet with as much or more difficulty from his heirs, among
whom Usher would probably have a great influence. They well

(1) Records of the Council and Assembly. (2) Usher's papers. (3) Printed state of Allen's title, p. 9.

knew his indefatigable industry in the pursuit of gain; that he
was able to harass them in law, and had great interest in England.   They, therefore, thought it best to fall in with Allen's
views, and enter into an accommodation with him.   A
general meeting of deputies being held at Portsmouth, the
following resolutions and proposals were drawn up, viz:

1705.
May 3.

' That they had no claim or challenge to any part of the prov-
' ince without the bounds of the four towns of Portsmouth, Dover,
' Hampton and Exeter, with the hamlets of New-Castle and
' Kingston, which were all comprehended within lines already
' known and laid out, and which should forthwith be revised; but
' that Allen and his heirs might peaceably hold and enjoy the said
' great waste, containing *forty miles in length and twenty in*
' *breadth*, or thereabouts, at the heads of the four towns afore-
' said, if it should so please her majesty; and that the inhabitants
' of the four towns would be so far from interrupting the settle-
' ment thereof, that they desired the said waste to be planted and
' filled with inhabitants, to whom they would give all the encour-
' agement and assistance in their power.   That in case Allen
' would, for himself and heirs, forever quit-claim, to the present
' inhabitants and their heirs, all that tract of land comprehended
' within the bounds of the several towns, and warrant and defend
' the same against all persons, free of mortgage, entailment and
' every other incumbrance, and that this agreement should be ac-
' cepted and confirmed by the queen; then they would lot and
' lay out to him and his heirs five hundred acres within the town
' of Portsmouth and New-Castle, fifteen hundred in Dover, fif-
' teen hundred in Hampton and Kingston, and fifteen hundred in
' Exeter, out of the commonages of the said towns, in such plac-
' es, not exceeding three divisions in each town, as should best
' accommodate him and be least detrimental to them; and that
' they would pay him or his heirs, two thousand pounds current
' money of New-England at two payments, one within a year after
' receiving the royal confirmation of this agreement, and the other
' within a year after the first payment.   That all contracts made
' either by Mason or Allen with any of the inhabitants, or others,
' for lands or other privileges in the possession of their tenants in
' their own just right, beside the claim of Mason and Allen, and
' no other, should be accounted valid; but that if any of the pur-
' chasers, lessees or tenants should refuse to pay their just part
' of the sums agreed on, according to the lands they held, their
' share should be abated by Allen out of the two thousand pounds
' payable by this agreement.   That upon Allen's acceptance, and
' underwriting of these articles, they would give personal security
' for the aforesaid payment; and that all actions and suits de-
' pending in law concerning the premises should cease till the
' queen's pleasure should be known.'

These articles were ordered to be presented to Allen for his acceptance :[1] But so desirable an issue of the controversy was prevented by his sudden death, which happened on the next day. He left a son and four daughters, and died intestate.

Colonel Allen is represented as a gentleman of no remarkable abilities, and of a solitary rather than a social disposition ; but mild, obliging and charitable. His character, whilst he was a merchant in London, was fair and upright, and his domestic deportment amiable and exemplary. He was a member of the church of England by profession, but constantly attended divine worship in the congregation at New-Castle, and was a strict observer of the christian Sabbath. He died on the fifth of May, 1705, in the seventieth year of his age, and was buried in the fort.[2]

After his death, his only son, Thomas Allen, Esq. of London, renewed the suit, by petitioning the queen, who allowed him to bring a new writ of ejectment, and ordered a revival of the directions given to the governor in 1703, with respect to the jury's finding a special verdict. Accordingly, Allen, having previously conveyed one half of the lands in New-Hampshire, by deed of sale, to Sir Charles Hobby, and appointed his mother Elizabeth Allen, his attorney, brought his writ of ejectment against Waldron in the inferior court of common pleas, where he was cast. He then removed it by appeal to the superior court, where it had been tried three years before. As this was the last trial, and as all the strength of both parties was fullly displayed on the occasion, it will be proper to give as just a view of the case as can now be collected from the papers on file in the office of the superior court.

1706.

May 16.

Aug. 20.

April 15.

On Allen's part, were produced copies of the charter by which King James I, constituted the council of Plymouth ; their grants to Mason in 1629 and 1635 ; his last will and testament ; an inventory of artillery, arms, ammunition, provisions, merchandize and cattle left in the care of his agents here at his death ; depositions of several ancient persons taken in 1685, who remembered the houses, fields, forts, and other possessions of Capt. Mason at Portsmouth and Newichwannock, and were acquainted with his agents, stewards, factors and other servants, who divided the cattle and merchandize among them after his death ; the opinions of Sir Geoffrey Palmer, Sir Francis Winnington and Sir William Jones in favour of the validity of Mason's title ; King Charles' letter to the president and council of New-Hampshire in 1680 ; the paragraph of Cranfield's commission which respects Mason's claim in 1682 ; the writ, verdict, judgment and execution against

(1) MS. Copy of Report of Lords of Trade, 1753.   (2) Atkinson's Letter, MS. Emerson's funeral sermon and letter to Mr Prince, MS.

Major Waldron in 1683 ; the decision of the king in council against Vaughan in 1686 ; Dudley's writ of certiorari in 1688 ; the fine and recovery in Westminster-hall whereby the entail was cut off, and the consequent deed of sale to Allen in 1691 ; Sir Edward Northey's report in 1703 ; and evidence of Allen's taking possession of the wastes, and of his inclosing and occupying some land at Great Island. On this evidence, it was pleaded that the title derived from Mason, and his possession of the province, of which the lands in question were part, was legal ; that the appellee's possession had been interrupted by the appellant and those from whom he derived his title, more especially by the judgment recovered by Robert Mason against Major Waldron ; and a special verdict was moved for, agreeably to the royal directions. The council on this side were James Meinzies and John Valentine.

On Waldron's part, were produced the deed from four Indian sachems to Wheelwright and others in 1629 ; and depositions taken from several ancient persons, who testified that they had lived with Major Waldron, when he began his plantation at Cochecho, about the year 1640, and assisted him in building his houses and mills, and that no person had disturbed him in the possession thereof for above forty years. To invalidate the evidence of the title produced on the opposite side, it was pleaded, that the grant from the council of Plymouth to Mason in 1629, was not signed ; that livery and seizin were not endorsed on it as on other of their grants, and as was then the legal form ; nor was it ever enrolled according to statute : That the sale of part of the same lands in 1628 to the Massachusetts company, by an instrument signed and executed according to law, renders this subsequent grant suspicious ; and that his pretending to procure another grant of part of the same lands in 1635, was an argument that he himself could not rely on the preceeding one, nor was it credible that the same council should grant the same lands twice, and to the same person : That the grant in 1635 was equally defective ; and that he must relinquish one or the other, it being contrary to the reason and usage of law to rely on two several titles at once. It was urged, that Waldron's possession was grounded on a deed from the native lords of the soil, with whom his father had endeavored to cultivate a friendly connexion ; that he had taken up his land with their consent, when the country was a wilderness ; had cultivated it, had defended it in war at a great expense, and at the hazard of his life, which he finally lost in the attempt ; that the Indian deed was legally executed in the presence of the factors and agents of the company of Laconia, of which Mason was one ; that this was done with the toleration of the council of Plymouth, and in pursuance of the great ends of their incorporation, which were to cultivate the

lands, to people the country and christianize the natives, for the
honor and interest of the crown and the trade of England, all
which ends had been pursued and attained by the appellee and
his ancestor. It was also alleged, that the writ against Major
Waldron in 1683 was for " lands and tenements," of which the
quantity, situation and bounds were not described, for want of
which no legal judgment could be given ; that no execution had
ever been levied, nor was the possessor ever disturbed or amoved
by reason thereof ; and that the copies produced were not attested, no book of records being to be found.   To invalidate the evidence of Mason's possession, it was observed, that he himself
was never here in person ; that all the settlement made by his
agents or successors was only a factory for trade with the Indians,
and principally for the discovery of a country called Laconia ;
and that this was done in company with several other merchant-
adventurers in London, who, for the security of their goods erected a fort ; but that this could not amount to a legal possession,
nor prove a title to the country, especially as upon the failure of
trade, the object of their enterprise, they quitted their factory,
after a few years stay in these parts.

As to the motion for a special verdict, it was said that a jury
could not find one, if they had no doubt of the law or fact, for
the reason of a special verdict is a doubt either in point of law
or evidence ; nor was it consistent with the privileges of Englishmen that a jury should be compelled to find specially.   In
addition to these pleas, it was further alleged, that by the statute
law, no action of ejectment can be maintained except the plaintiff, or those under whom he claims, have been in possession within twenty years ; and if they have been out of possession sixty
years, then not only an ejectment, but a writ of right, and all
other real actions are barred in respect of a subject, and that in
such cases the right of the crown is also barred : and that by the
statute of 32 Hen. 8. ch. 9., it is enacted, that no person shall
purchase any lands or tenements, unless the seller, or they, by
whom he claims, have been in possession of the same or the re-
version or the remainder thereof, or have taken the rents or pro-
fits thereof by the space of one whole year next before such bargain is made ; and that the appellee and his ancestor, and no
other person whatever had been in possession of the premises,
nor was it ever pretended by the appellant that the Masons, of
whom the purchase was made, were in possession within one year,
or at any time before the alleged purchase ; that all the mischiefs
provided against by the above statute have been experienced
by the people of New-Hampshire from the purchase made by
the appellant's father, of the bare title of the propriety of the
province.   The council on this side were John Pickering and
Charles Story.

A certificate from the lieutenant-governor respecting the
queen's directions was delivered to the jury who return-
Aug. 12. ed the following verdict : " In the cause depending be-
" tween Thomas Allen, Esq., appellant and Richard Waldron,
" Esq., defendant, the jury finds for the defendant a confirmation
" of the former judgment and costs of courts.   Mark Hunking,
" foreman."

The court then sent out the jury again, with this charge, " Gen-
" men, you are further to consider this case and observe her
" majesty's directions to find specially and your oaths."   They
returned the second time with the same verdict ; upon which,
the court ordered judgment to be entered, and that the defendant
recover costs of the appellant.   The council for the appellant
then moved for an appeal to her majesty in council ; which was
allowed on their giving bond in two hundred pounds to prosecute it.

But the loyalty of the people, and the distresses under which
they labored by reason of the war, prevailed on the queen's ministry to suspend a final decision ; and before the appeal could be
heard, Allen's death, which happened in 1715, put an end to the
suit, which his heirs, being minors, did not renew.[1]

CHAPTER XII.

The war with the French and Indians, called Queen Anne's war.   Conclusion of Dudley's and Usher's administration.

THE peace which followed the treaty of Ryswick was but of
short duration, for the seeds of war were already sown both in
Europe and America.   Louis had proclaimed the pretender king
of England, and his Governor, Villebon, had orders to extend his
province of Acadia to the river Kennebeck, though the English
court understood St. Croix to be the boundary between their territories and those of the French.   The fishery was interrupted
by French men of war, and by the orders of Villebon, who suffered no English vessels to fish on the banks of Nova Scotia.   A
French mission was established, and a chapel erected at Norridgewog, on the upper part of Kennebeck, which served to extend the influence of the French among the Indians.   The governor of Canada, assuming the character of their father and protector, instigated them to prevent the settlement of the English to
the east of Kennebeck, and found some among them ready to
listen to his advice.   The people in those parts were apprehen-

(1) Council and Assembly Records.   Printed state of Allen's title, p. 10.

sive of danger and meditating a removal, and those who had entertained thoughts of settling there were restrained.

Things were in this posture, when Dudley entered on his government. He had particular orders from England to rebuild the
fort at Pemaquid; but could not prevail on the Massachusetts
assembly to bear the expense of it. However, he determined on
a visit to the eastern country, and having notified his intention to
the Indians, took with him a number of gentlemen of both   1703.
provinces,* and held a conference at Casco with delegates June 20.
from the tribes of Norridgewog, Penobscot, Pequawket,
Penacook and Ameriscoggin; who assured him that " as high as
" sun was above the earth, so far distant was their design of ma-
" king the least breach of the peace." They presented him a
belt of wampum in token of their sincerity, and both parties went
to two heaps of stones which had formerly been pitched and called
the *Two Brothers*, where the friendship was further ratified by
the addition of other stones. They also declared, that although
the French emissaries among them had been endeavoring to break
the union, yet it was " firm as a mountain, and should continue
" as long as the sun and moon." Notwithstanding these fair appearances, it was observed that when the Indians fired a salute
their guns were charged with shot; and it was suspected that they
had then formed a design to seize the governor and his attendants,
if a party which they expected from Canada, and which arrived
two or three days after, had come in proper season to their assistance. However this might be, it is certain that in the   Aug. 10.
space of six weeks, a body of French and Indians, five
hundred in number, having divided themselves into several parties,
attacked all the settlements from Casco to Wells, and killed and
took one hundred and thirty people, burning and destroying all
before them.†

The next week, (August 17) a party of thirty Indians under
Captain Tom, killed five people at Hampton village; among
whom was a widow Mussey, a noted speaker among the Friends,
and much lamented by them. They also plundered two houses;
but the people being alarmed, and pursuing them, they fled.‡

The country was now in terror and confusion. The women
and children retired to the garrisons. The men went armed to
their work and posted sentinels in the fields. Troops of horse

---

* Mr. Hutchinson has misplaced this transaction by a year. [In the third
edition of Hutchinson's History, printed in 1795, this transaction is assigned
to the year 1703.]

† Mr. Hutchinson takes no notice of this remarkable devastation, which is
particularly related by Mr. Penhallow in his " Wars of New-England," p. 5.
[See Coll. N. H. Hist. Soc. i. 23.]

‡ [The five who were killed were Jonathan Green, Nicholas Bond, Thomas
Lancaster, Widow Mussey, and a little boy of Will.Hinckley. Lancaster
and the Widow Mussey were Quakers. Town Records of Hampton.]

were quartered at Portsmouth and in the province of Maine.   A
scout of three hundred and sixty men marched toward Pequawket, and another to the Ossipee ponds, but made no discoveries.
Alarms were frequent, and the whole frontier country from Deerfield on the west, to Casco on the east, was kept in continual terror by small parties of the enemy.

In the fall, Col. March, of Casco, made a visit to Pequawket,
where he killed six of the enemy and took six more.   This encouraged the government to offer a bounty of forty pounds for
scalps.

As the winter came on, the frontier towns were ordered to provide a large number of snow-shoes ; and an expedition was planned in New-Hampshire, against the head-quarters of the Indians.
Major Winthrop Hilton, and Captain John Gilman of Exeter,
Captain Chesley and Captain Davis of Oyster river, marched
with their companies on snow-shoes into the woods ; but returned without success.   This is called in the council books " an
honorable service." Hilton received a gratuity of twelve, and
each of the captains, five pounds.

With the return of spring, there was a return of hostilities ; for
notwithstanding the posting a few southern Indians in the garrisons
at Berwick, the enemy appeared at Oyster river, and shot
1704. Nathaniel Medar,* near his own field, and the next day,
Apr. 25. killed Edward Taylor, near Lamprey river, and captivated his wife and son.   These instances of mischief gave color to
a false alarm at Cochecho, where it was said, they lay in wait for
Col. Waldron a whole day, but missing him by reason of his absence from home, took his servant maid as she went to a spring
for water ; and having examined her as to the state of the garrison, stunned her with an hatchet, but did not scalp her. (The
girl invented this story to palliate her too long absence.)†

In May, Col. Church, by Governor Dudley's order, having
planned an expedition to the eastern shore, sailed from Boston
with a number of transports, furnished with whaleboats for going
up rivers.   In his way, he stopt at Pascataqua, where he was
joined by a body of men under Major Hilton, who was of eminent service to him in this expedition,‡ which lasted the whole

* [He was the son of John Medar, and was born at Durham, 14 June, 1671.
Descendants of the family still remain in New-Hampshire.]

† [This sentence is added by the author in the corrected copy.   Rev. Mr.
Pike in his MS. Journal thus notices this affair : " Ap. 28.   Thamsin Me-
sarvey, Mr. Waldron's maid servant was taken by four Indians, betwixt sunset and dark, at a spring in the major's pasture, between his house formerly
burnt, and barn, and after examination was knockt down and left for dead,
but recovered again—the enemy flying away hastily at the outcry of the
watch, by which means Mr. Waldron escaped that was then coming over the
Boom."]

‡ This is called in the council books " an expedition to Port-Royal," and
this was the ostensible object.   But Church in his memoirs says that Dudley would not permit him to go there.   Church, p. 104.   Hutch. ii. 146.

summer, and in which they destroyed the towns of Minas and
Chignecto, and did considerable damage to the French and Indians at Penobscot and Passamaquoddy, and even insulted Port
Royal. While they were at Mount Desert, Church learned from
nine of his prisoners, that a body of six hundred Indians* were
preparing for an attack on Casco, and the head of Pascataqua
river ; and sent an express to Portsmouth which obliged the people to be vigilant. No such great force as this appeared ; but
small parties kept hovering on the outskirts. At Oyster river,
they wounded William Tasker ;† and at Dover, they laid in ambush for the people on their return from public worship, but happily missed their aim. They afterward mortally wounded Mark Giles at that place, and soon after, killed several Aug. 11.
people in a field at Oyster river, whose names are not mentioned.‡

In the former wars, New-Hampshire had received much assistance from their brethren of Massachusetts ; but these now remonstrated to the governor that his other province did not bear
their proportion of the charge for the common defence. The
representatives of New-Hampshire urged, in reply, the different
circumstances of the two provinces ; " most of the towns in
Massachusetts being out of the reach of the enemy, and no otherwise affected by the war than in the payment of their part of
the expense, whilst this province was wholly a frontier by sea and
land, and in equal danger with the county of York, in which four
companies were stationed, and the inhabitants were abated their
proportion of the public charges." They begged that twenty of
the friendly Indians might be sent to scout on their borders, which
request the governor complied with.[1]

In the winter, Col. Hilton with two hundred and seventy men,
including the twenty Indians, were sent to Norridgewog 1705.
on snow shoes. They had a favourable season for

(1) Council Records.

* I suppose this is the party whom Penhallow mentions, p. 23, who quarrelled on their march about dividing the plunder which they might take, and of
whom two hundred returned while the rest pursued their march, and did damage at Lancaster and Groton.

† [This name is Tasket in the records of the court of Quarter Sessions.—
He had been in 1686, " several times summoned to attend this court, or some
justice of the peace, upon complaint made against him for cruelty to his ap-
prentice, Joseph Pitman," who was, in 1686, by the court, discharged from the
service of the said Tasket.]

‡ [From the MS. Journal of the Rev. John Pike, it appears that on the 19
of August, Joseph Pitman was slain by the Indians, as he was guarding some
mowers, not far from Oyster River Meeting house. It is also stated that John
Giles, the son of Mark Giles, was killed at the same time with his father.
The party of Indians who attacked them was seven or eight. Mr. Pike, in
his Journal, has no notice of *William* Tasker, but he records the death
of Samuel Tasker, who was killed on the first day of June, at Oyster
River.]

their march, the snow being four feet deep. When they arrived there, finding no enemy to contend with, they burnt the deserted wigwams, and the chapel. The officers who went on this expedition complained that they had only the pay of private soldiers.*

The late repairs of fort William and Mary at New-Castle were always complained of as burdensome to the people, and a representation thereof had been made to the queen, who instructed Dudley to press the assembly of Massachusetts to contribute to the expense; as the river belonged equally to both provinces. They urged in excuse that the fort was built at first at the sole charge of New-Hampshire, to whom it properly belonged ; that the whole expense of the repairs did not amount to what several of their towns singly paid toward the support of the war for one year ; that all the trade and navigation of the river, on both sides, paid a duty toward maintaining that fortress; and that they had been at great expense in protecting the frontiers of New-Hampshire, and the parties who were employed in getting timber and masts for her majesty's service ; while New-Hampshire had never contributed any thing to the support of the garrisons, forces and guards by sea, which were of equal benefit to them as to Massachusetts. One thing which made New-Hampshire more in favor with the queen was, that they had settled a salary on her governor, which the others never could be persuaded to do. The repairs of the fort, however, went on without their assistance, under the direction of Col. Romer ; and when they were completed, a petition was sent home for a supply of cannon, ammunition and stores.

The next summer was chiefly spent in negotiating an exchange of prisoners ; and Dudley had the address to protract the negotiation, under pretence of consulting with the other governments about a neutrality proposed by the governor of Canada, by which means the frontiers in general were kept tolerably quiet, although the enemy appeared once or twice in the town of Kittery. The line of pickets† which enclosed the town of Portsmouth was repaired, and a nightly patrole established on the sea shore, from Rendezvous Point to the bounds of Hampton, to prevent any

---

* [It was on the 21 January, this year, that the English settlements at Newfoundland were attacked by the French and Indians under M. de Subercase. Rev. John Pike, in his MS. Journal, says that the attack was made by a strong party of French and Indians (Penhallow says 550; Charlevoix, 450) on Sabbath night, and that they " destroyed all excepting the forts. They cut off about seventy families, sparing none save a few young men, that were fit for service. They afterwards besieged the fort at St. John's for divers weeks but could not take it." Pike, MS. Journal.—Penhallow, in Coll. N. H. Hist. Soc. i. 44, 45.—Holmes, Annals of America, i. 492, who quotes Charlevoix, Nouv. France, ii. 298, 299.—Univ. Hist. 155.]

† This line extended from the mill-pond on the south, to the creek on the north side of the town. It crossed the main street a few rods westward of the spot where the State House [in Portsmouth] now stands.

surprise by sea ; the coast being at this time infested by the enemy's privateers.

During this truce, the inhabitants of Kingston who had left the
place, were encouraged to petition for leave to return to their
lands ; which the court granted on condition that they should
build a fort in the centre of the town, lay out a parsonage and
settle a minister, within three years. This last condition was
rendered impracticable by the renewal of hostilities.*

The governor of Canada had encouraged the Indians who inhabited the borders of New-England to remove to Canada, where
being incorporated with the tribe of St. Francis, they have ever
since remained. By this policy, they became more firmly attached to the interest of the French, and were more easily despatched on their bloody business to the frontiers of New-England,
with which they were well acquainted. Dudley, who was generally apprized of their movements, and kept a vigilant eye upon them,
apprehended a rupture in the winter ; and gave orders for a circular scouting march, once a month, round the heads of the towns
from Kingston to Salmon falls ; but the enemy did not appear till
April ; when a small party of them attacked the house of   1706.
John Drew at Oyster river, where they killed eight and
wounded two. The garrison was near, but not a man in it : the
women, however, seeing nothing but death before them, fired an
alarm, and then putting on hats, and loosening their hair that they
might appear like men, they fired so briskly that the enemy, apprehending the people were alarmed, fled without burning or even
plundering the house which they had attacked. John Wheeler,
meeting this party and mistaking them for friendly Indians, unhappily fell into their hands and was killed, with his wife and two
children. Four of his sons took refuge in a cave by the bank of
the Little Bay, and though pursued by the Indians, escaped unhurt.†

In July, Colonel Schuyler, from Albany, gave notice to Dudley

---

* [Kingston had been incorporated in 1694. The charter, granted by Lieut.
Gov. Usher, is dated 6 of August. The first inhabitants were Ebenezer Web-
ster, ancestor of Hon. Daniel Webster, Moses Elkins, Jonathan Sanborn,
Ichabod Robie, who died 15 May, 1757, aged 92, Aaron Sleeper, Thomas
Webster, Thomas Philbrick, and Jabez Colman, who was killed by the Indians, as will be seen, under 1724. Benjamin, son of Thomas and Sarah
Webster, born in 1701, is said to have been the first child born in the place.
Kingston in 1725, contained 81 families. In 1732, it had 164 ratable inhabitants and 115 dwelling houses, of which 64 were two stories high. In 1767,
it numbered 999 inhabitants, but before this time, East-Kingston, Sandown
and Hawke had been detached from it. The first having built a meeting
house as early as 1738, was that year incorporated as a parish. Sandown
was incorporated in 1756 and Hawke in 1760.]

† [This outrage occurred on the 27 of April. On the fourth of June fol-
lowing, George Ricker and Maturin Ricker, of Cochecho, were slain by the
Indians. George was killed while running up the lane, near the garrison.
Maturin was killed in his field, and his son, a boy, was taken captive. Pike's
MS. Journal.]

that two hundred and seventy of the enemy were on their march toward Pascataqua, of which he immediately informed the people, and ordered them to close garrison, and one half of the militia to be ready at a minute's warning. The first appearance of this body of the enemy was at Dunstable;* whence they proceeded to Amesbury and Kingston, where they killed some cattle. Hilton, with sixty four men, marched from Exeter; but was obliged to return without meeting the enemy. The reason he gave to the council for returning so soon was the want of provision, there being none in readiness at the garrisons, notwithstanding a law lately enacted, enjoining it on every town to have stores ready and deposited in the hands of their captains. For the same reason, he had been obliged to discontinue a small scout, which he had for some time kept up. Hilton was so brave and active an officer that the enemy had marked him for destruction; and for this purpose a party of them kept lurking about his house, where they observed ten men to go out one morning with their scythes, and lay aside their arms to mow; they then crept between the men and their guns, and suddenly rushed on them, killed four, wounded one, and took three. Two only of the whole number escaped.† They missed the major for this time, and two of their prisoners escaped; but suffered much in their return, having nothing to subsist on for three weeks, but lily roots and the rinds of trees. After this, they killed William Pearl,‡ and took Nathaniel Tebbets at Dover. It was observed during this war, that the enemy did more damage in small bodies than in larger, and by scattering along the frontiers, kept the people in continual apprehension and alarm; and so very few of them fell into our hands, that in computing the expense of the war it was judged that every Indian killed or taken, cost the country a thousand pounds.‖[1]

August 2.

(1) Penhallow, p. 40.

* [Joseph Kilburn and Jeremiah Nelson of Rowley were killed by the Indians at Dunstable, 10 July 1706, and John Pickard was mortally wounded, and died at Billerica, on the 5 August following. MS. Letter of J. Coffin, S. H. S.]

† [Rev. Mr. Pike says that three escaped, viz. Joseph Hall, John Taylor, who was " sorely wounded, but recovered," and one other. Those captured were Edward Hall, Samuel Mighill and a mulatto. The four persons killed were Richard Mattoon, Hubertas Mattoon, son of Richard, Robert Barber and Samuel Pease. The number of the enemy was about twenty, who attacked the English as they were mowing in a field, between Exeter and Lamprey River. Rev. Mr. Pike.]

‡ [Rev. Mr. Pike says *Nicholas Pearle.* " He was slain by the Indians in the day time in his cave, some miles above Oyster river, where he dwelt night and day, winter and summer, from the last breaking out of the war, precisely three years, though 'twas in the very wake and way where the enemy used to pass. He was a man of strange confidence and would not be persuaded to leave his place." Rev. John Pike, MS. Journal.]

‖ [" Benjamin Fifield, aged about 60 years, was barbarously killed (in his

In the following winter, Hilton made another excursion to the eastward, and a shallop was sent to Casco with stores and provisions for his party, consisting of two hundred and twenty men.   The winter being mild, and the weather unsettled, prevented their marching so far as they intended : cold dry weather and deep snow being most favorable to winter expeditions. However, they came on an Indian track, near Black Point, and pursuing it, killed four, and took a squaw who conducted them to a party of eighteen, whom they surprised as they lay asleep on a neck of land at break of day, and of whom they killed seventeen, and took the other.   This was matter of triumph considering the difficulty of finding their haunts.   It was remarked that on the very morning that this affair happened, it was reported, with but little variation from the truth, at Portsmouth, though at the distance of sixty miles.

1707.

Jan. 21.

When Church went to Nova-Scotia, he very earnestly solicited leave to make an attempt on Port Royal; but Dudley would not consent, and the reason he gave was, that he had written to the ministry in England, and expected orders and naval help to reduce the place.   His enemies however assigned another reason for his refusal; which was, that a clandestine trade was carried on by his connivance, and to his emolument, with the French there.   This report gained credit and occasioned a loud call for justice.   Those who were directly concerned in the illegal traffic, were prosecuted and fined; and the governor suffered much in his reputation.[1]   To wipe off these aspersions, he now determined to make an attack in earnest on Port Royal, even though no assistance should come from England.   It was intended that an armament should be sent to America, and the commander was appointed; but the state of affairs in Europe prevented their coming.*

(1) Hutch. Hist. Mass. vol. 2, p. 154.

pasture not far from his house) by the Indians, August 1, 1706." Town Records of Hampton.

On the 3 of July, the same year, Nathaniel Blanchard, Lydia Blanchard, his wife, Susan Blanchard, their daughter, Mrs. Hannah Blanchard, Mrs. Cummings, the wife of John Cummings, and Rachel Galusha, were killed by the Indians at Dunstable.   Records of Dunstable.

It appears from Penhallow, (Coll. N. H. Hist. Soc. i. 48) that the Indians fell on a garrison in Dunstable, "that had twenty troopers posted in it, who by their negligence and folly, keeping no watch, suffered them to enter, which tended to the destruction of one half of their number.   After that, a small party attacked Jacob Galusha's house, who held them in play for some time, till the old man's courage failed," and he surrendered himself.   "About the same time," says Penhallow, "Joseph English, who was a friendly Indian, going from Dunstable to Chelmsford, with a man and his wife on horseback, was shot dead, the woman taken, but the man made his escape."   See a more particular account of the attack on Dunstable, on the 3 July, 1706, in Coll. of N. H. Hist. Soc. i, 133, and in Pike's MS. Journal.]

* [1707.   On the 23 June, this year, a petition, alleging various instances of misconduct in Governor Dudley was presented to Queen Ann at Windsor.

Early in the spring, the governor applied to the assemblies of both his provinces, and to the colonies of Rhode Island and Connecticut, requesting them to raise one thousand men for the expedition. Connecticut declined; but the other three raised the whole number, who were disposed into two regiments, of which Colonel Wainwright commanded the one, and Colonel Hilton the other. They embarked at Nantasket in twenty three transports furnished with whaleboats, under convoy of the Deptford man of war, Captain Stuckley, and the province galley, Captain Southack. The chief command was given to Colonel March, who had behaved well in several scouts and rencounters with the Indians, but had never been tried in such service as this. They arrived before Port Royal in a few days, and after burning some houses, killing some cattle round the fort, and making some ineffectual attempts to bombard it, a jealousy and disagreement among the officers, and a misapprehension of of the state of the fort and garrison, caused the army to break up and reimbark in a disorderly manner. Some of the officers went to Boston for orders; some of the transports put in at Casco; a sloop with Captain Chesley's company of sixty men arrived at Portsmouth : Chesley suffered his men to disperse, but ordered them to return at the beat of the drum : Being called to account for this conduct, he pleaded that "general orders were given at Port Royal for every man 'to make the best of his way home."[1] The governor, highly chagrined and very angry, sent orders from Boston that if any more vessels should arrive, the men should not be permitted to come on shore "on pain of death." After a while, he ordered Chesley's company to be collected and reimbarked, offering a pardon to those who might voluntarily return, the rest to be severely punished. By the latter end of July, they went on board, and with the rest of the army, returned to the place of action. At the landing, an ambuscade of Indians from among the sedge on the top of a sea-wall, greatly annoyed the troops. Major Walton* and Captain Chesley, being then on shore with the New-Hampshire companies, pushed their men up the beach, flanked the enemy, and after an obstinate struggle put them to

(Marginal dates: May 18. / May 26. / June 6, 7. / June 13.)

(1) Council Records.

The same petition was read before the general assembly of New-Hampshire, when the council and representatives in full assembly, nemine contradicente, voted that some of the charges were scandalous, unheard of, and false reproaches, and drew up an address to the queen in which " they acquit and justify his administration from all those calumnies and pray her majesty's favor to him." Dudley's Defence and Apology in MS. dated 10 Nov. 1707.]

* [Shadrach Walton, son of George Walton (see note to page 94) was born in 1658, and was often engaged in public life. He was appointed by mandamus, one of the counsellors of the province in 1716, and died 3 October, 1741, aged 83 years. Benjamin Walton, who graduated at Harvard college in 1729, is said by Mr. Winthrop to have been a son of Colonel Walton.]

flight. The command was now given to Wainwright, and the army put under the direction of three supervisors; but no means could inspire that union, firmness and skill which were necessary. By the last of August, the whole affair was at an end, and the army returned sickly, fatigued, disheartened, and ashamed; but with no greater loss than sixteen killed and as many wounded.

While this unfortunate expedition was in hand, the frontiers were kept in continual alarm. Two men were taken May 22. from Oyster river, and two more killed* as they were July 3. driving a team between that place and Dover. Captain Sumersby pursued with his troop and recovered the contents of the cart. Stephen and Jacob Gilman, brothers, were ambushed between Exeter and Kingston; their horses were killed, but both of them escaped to the garrison.[1] Kingston, being a new plantation, was much exposed, and was this summer weakened by the desertion of eight men. The remaining inhabitants complained to the government, who ordered the captains of Exeter and Hampton to take them up as deserters, and oblige them to return to the defence of their settlements, or do duty at the fort during the governor's pleasure.[2] They were afterwards bound over to the sessions for contempt of orders. The state of the country at this time was truly distressed; a large quota of their best men were abroad, the rest harassed by the enemy at home, obliged to continual duty in garrisons and in scouts, and subject to severe discipline for neglects. They earned their bread at the continual hazard of their lives, never daring to stir abroad unarmed. They could till no lands but what were within call of the garrisoned houses, into which their families were crowded; their husbandry, lumber trade and fishery were declining, their taxes increasing, their apprehensions both from the force of the enemy and the failure of the Port Royal expedition, were exceedingly dismal, and there was no prospect of an end to the war, in which they were now advanced to the fifth summer. Yet under all these distresses and discouragements, they resolutely kept their ground and maintained their garrisons, not one of which was cut off during the whole of this war, within the limits of New-Hampshire.

In September, one man was killed at Exeter, and two Sept. 15. days after, Henry Elkins at Kingston. But the severest Sept. 17. blow on the frontiers happened at Oyster river, a place which suffered more than all the rest. A party of French Mohawks painted red, attacked with an hideous yell a company who were in the woods, some hewing timber and others driving a team, un-

(1) Penhallow, p. 45. (2) Council Records.

* [John Bunker and Ichabod Rawlins, both of Dover. The enemy were supposed to be from 20 to 30. They slaughtered many cattle at the same time. Rev. John Pike, MS. Journal.]

der the direction of Captain Chesley, who was just returned the
second time from Port Royal. At the first fire, they killed seven
and mortally wounded another. Chesley, with the few who were
left fired on the enemy with great vigor, and for some time checked their ardor ; but being overpowered, he at length fell. He
was much lamented, being a brave officer. Three of the scalps
taken at this time were soon after recovered at Berwick.

The next year, a large army from Canada was destined against
the frontiers of New-England. Dudley received information of
1708. it in the usual route from Albany, and immediately ordered guards in the most exposed places of both his provinces. A troop under Captain Robert Coffin patroled from Kingston to Cochecho, and scouts were kept out continually. Spy-
boats were also kept out at sea between Pascataqua and Winter
harbors. Four hundred Massachusetts soldiers were posted in
this province. The towns were ordered to provide ammunition,
and all things were in as good a state of preparation as could be
Aug. 29. expected. At length, the storm fell on Haverhill ; but the
enemy's force having been diminished by various accidents, they proceeded no farther, and every part of New-Hampshire was quiet. Hilton made another winter march to Pequawket with one hundred and seventy men, but made no discovery.[1]

The next spring, William Moody,* Samuel Stevens, and two
sons of Jeremiah Gilman were taken at Pickpocket-mill in
1709. Exeter, and soon after, Bartholomew Stevenson was kill-
May 8. ed at Oyster river. Colonel Hilton and Captain Davis†
performed their usual tour of duty in scouting, and the people this
June 20. summer kept close in garrison, on a report that two hundred
Indians had marched against them from Montreal. But
the principal object now in view was a desire of wiping off the
disgrace of a former year by an attempt, not on Port Royal, but
on Canada itself. For this purpose, solicitations had been made
in England by Francis Nicholson, Esq., who had been lieutenant-

(1) Penhallow, 45, 48.

* [He was retaken within a month afterwards by some Deerfield men, who,
in their course up French river, met with a body of the enemy in canoes, on
whom they fired, and overset, killing and wounding several of them. In one
of their canoes was William Moody with only one Indian with him. The
English persuaded him to make his escape by killing his adversary. This
he attempted to do, but overset the canoe in the struggle, and then swam towards the shore, and was met on the bank of the river, by several English
who came to his rescue. In the mean time, a number of the enemy arrived at
the bank, re-captured Moody, who was most inhumanly tortured by being
fastened to a stake and roasted alive. His flesh was afterward devoured by
the savages. Penhallow in Coll. N. H. Hist. Soc. i. 60, 61. Pike, MS.
Journal.]

† [James Davis was the son of John Davis of Dover, and was born 23 May,
1662. He was an active and useful officer, and after this period became a
colonel of the militia. He died in 1749, aged 87. He had nine children,
whose ages averaged 87 years each.]

governor of Virginia, and Captain Samuel Vetch, a trader to Nova-Scotia, who was well acquainted with the French settlements
there, and made a full representation of the state of things in A-
merica to the British ministry.   An expedition being determined
upon, they came over early in the spring with the queen's command to the governors of the several provinces, to raise men for
the service.   Vetch was appointed a colonel, and Nicholson, by
nomination of the governor of New-York, and consent of the
other governments, was made commander in chief.   The people
of New-Hampshire were so much exhausted, and their men had
been so ill paid before, that it was with great difficulty, and not
without the dissolution of one assembly and the calling of another,
that they could raise money to levy one hundred men and procure
two transports for conveying them.   After the utmost exertions
had been made by the several governments, and Nicholson with
part of the troops had marched to Wood-creek, and the rest with
the transports had lain at Nantasket three months waiting for a
fleet, news arrived that the armament promised from England was
diverted to another quarter.   Upon which, the commander of the
frigates on the Boston station refused to convey the troops, the
whole army was disbanded, and the expense the colonies had
been at was fruitless.   A congress of governors and delegates
from the assemblies met in the fall at Rhode-Island, who recommended the sending of agents to assist Colonel Nicholson in representing the state of the country, and soliciting an expedition
against Canada the next spring.   The ministry at first seemed to
listen to this proposal, but afterward changed their minds, 1710.
and resolved only on the reduction of Port Royal.   For
this purpose, Nicholson came over in July with five frigates and a
bomb ketch ; the colonies then had to raise their quotas ; Aug. 1.
the New-Hampshire assembly ordered one hundred men,
who were got ready as soon as possible, and put under the command of Colonel Shadrach Walton.   The whole armament sailed
from Boston the eighteenth of September, and on the twenty-
fourth, arrived at the place.   The force now being equal to its
reduction, Subcrease, the governor, waited only the compliment
of a few shot and shells as a decent pretence for a surrender ;
which was completed on the fifth of October, and Vetch was appointed governor of the place which in honor of the queen was
called Annapolis.[1]

Whilst this expedition was in hand, and before the appointment
of the commanders, New-Hampshire sustained an heavy loss in
the death of Colonel Winthrop Hilton.   This worthy offi- July 22.
cer being concerned in the masting business, and having
several large trees felled about fourteen miles from home, went out

(1) Hutchinson and Penhallow.   [The latter spells the name of the French
governor *Supercass*, while the former has it *Subercase*.]

with a party to peel the bark that the wood might not be injured
by worms.   While engaged in this business, they were ambushed
by a party of Indians, who, at the first fire, killed Hilton with two
more, and took two ; the rest being terrified, and their guns being
wet, made no opposition, but escaped.   The next day, one hundred men marched in pursuit, but discovered only the mangled
bodies of the dead.   The enemy in their barbarous triumph had
struck their hatchets into the colonel's brains, and left a lance in
his heart.   He was a gentleman " of good temper, courage and
" conduct, respected and lamented by all that knew him," and
was buried with the honors due to his rank and character.[1] *

Flushed with this success, they insolently appeared in the open
road at Exeter, and took four children who were at their play.
They also took John Wedgwood, and killed John Magoon near
his brother's barn, a place which for three days, he had visited
with a melancholy apprehension arising from a dream that he
should there be murdered.

The same day that Hilton was killed, a company of Indians
who had pretended friendship, who the year before had been
peaceably conversant with the inhabitants of Kingston, and seemed to be thirsting after the blood of the enemy, came into the
town, and ambushing the road, killed Samuel Winslow and Samuel Huntoon.   They also took Philip Huntoon and Jacob Gilman, and carried them to Canada ; where, after some time, they

(1) Penhallow, p. 58.

* [Colonel Hilton was about 39 years of age. He was descended from two
of the most distinguished *fathers of New-England.* His father Edward Hilton, who was son of Edward Hilton, the first settler at Dover, married Ann
Dudley, born 16 October, 1641, who was daughter of Rev. Samuel Dudley
and Mary Winthrop, the son and daughter of governors *Thomas Dudley* and
John Winthrop. Col. Hilton married Ann Wilson, of Exeter, who, after his
death, married Capt. Jonathan Wadleigh, and died 8 March, 1744. The children of Colonel Hilton were five daughters and one son, Winthrop, who was
born 21 Dec. 1710, five months after his father's death. He married widow
Wiggin, originally Martha Weeks, of Greenland. Their children were, 1.
Winthrop, of Newmarket, who was killed by the fall of a tree in January,
1775, (N.H.Gazette) leaving children, Andrew, Winthrop, Sarah and Ichabod ;
2. Ichabod, who died in March, 1822, aged 82, and whose children were
Winthrop, of Newmarket, Susanna and Ann. There is a valuable memoir of
Col. Hilton in the Collections of Farmer and Moore, for 1822, vol. i. 241—
251. At the close of it, it is said, " the colonel, respected and lamented by all
who knew him, was buried with the honors due to his rank and character, in
his own field on the west bank of Lamprey river by the side of his American ancestors, where several of his descendants of four generations have
since been gathered around him. A cluster of wild rose bushes grows rank
over his grave, and the inscription on his moss-covered monument shows
when a brave and a good man died, and where the remains of him who sincerely loved and faithfully served both God and his country, have long since
mouldered into dust." Dudley Hilton, a brother of the colonel, was of the
party, and was never heard of after the attack.
   An elegant silver headed cane which belonged to Colonel Hilton is in possession of John Kelly, Esq., of Northwood, whose children are lineal descendants from the colonel.]

purchased their own redemption by building a saw-mill for the governor after the English mode.[1]

The last that fell this summer was Jacob Garland, who was killed at Cochecho, on his return from the public worship. As the winter approached, Colonel Walton with one hundred and seventy men traversed the eastern shores, which the Indians usually visited at this season for the purpose of gathering clams. On an Island where the party was encamped, several Indians decoyed by their smoke, and mistaking them for some of their own tribe, came among them and were made prisoners. One of them was a sachem of Norridgewog, active, bold and sullen : when he found himself in the hands of enemies, he would answer none of their questions, and laughed with scorn at their threatening him with death. His wife, being an eye witness of the execution of the threatening, was so intimidated as to make the discoveries which the captors had in vain desired of the sachem ; in consequence of which, three were taken at the place of which she informed, and two more at Saco river, where also five were killed. This success, inconsiderable as it may appear, kept up the spirits of the people, and added to the loss of the enemy, who were daily diminishing by sickness and famine.

In the spring, they renewed their ravages on the frontiers in small parties. Thomas Downs, John Church,* and three more were killed at Cochecho ; and on a sabbath day, 1711. several of the people there fell into an ambush as they were returning from public worship. John Horn was wounded, and Humphrey Foss was taken ; but, by the determined bravery of Lieutenant Heard, he was recovered out of the hands of the enemy. Walton, with two companies, marched to the ponds about the fishing season ; but the Indians had withdrawn, and nothing was to be seen but their deserted wigwams.[2]

After the reduction of Port Royal, Nicholson went to England to solicit an expedition against Canada. The tory ministry of Queen Anne, to the surprise of all the whigs in England and America, fell in with the proposal ; and on the eighth of June, Nicholson came to Boston with orders for the northern colonies to get ready their quotas of men and provision at the arrival of the fleet and army from Europe ; which happened within sixteen days ; and whilst the several governors were holding a consultation on the subject of their orders. A compliance with them in so short a time was impossible ; yet every thing that could be done was done ; the nature of the service conspiring with the wishes of the people, made the governments exert themselves to the utmost. New-Hampshire raised one hundred men ; which was more than they could well spare ; one half of the militia be-

(1) MS. Letter of Ward Clark to Prince.   (2) Penhallow, p. 60.

* [He was the son of John Church, who was killed by the Indians, 7 May, 1696. He was 43 years of age..]

ing continually employed in guarding the frontiers. They also voted them subsistence for one hundred and twenty-six days, besides providing for them on shore before their embarkation. Two transports were taken up at eight shillings per month per ton; and artillery stores were issued from the fort. The colony forces formed two regiments under the command of Vetch and Walton. The army which came from England were seven veteran regiments of the Duke of Marlborough's army, and a battalion of marines, under the command of brigadier-general Hill, which, joined with the New-England troops, made a body of about six thousand five hundred men, provided with a fine train of artillery. The fleet consisted of fifteen ships of war from eighty to thirty-six guns, with forty transports and six storeships under the command of Admiral Walker.[1] A force fully equal to the reduction of Quebec.

The fleet sailed from Boston on the thirtieth of July; and a fast was ordered by Dudley to be kept on the last Thursday of that, and each succeeding month, till the enterprise should be finished.[2] This was an imitation of the conduct of the long parliament, during the civil wars in the last century. But the sanguine hopes of success which had been entertained by the nation and the colonies were all blasted in one fatal night. For, the fleet having advanced ten leagues into the river St. Lawrence, in the night of the twenty-third of August, the weather being thick and dark, eight transports were wrecked on Egg-Island near the north shore, and one thousand people perished; among whom there was but one man who belonged to New-England. The next day, the fleet put back, and were eight days beating down the river against an easterly wind which would in two days have carried them to Quebec. After rendezvousing at Spanish river, in the island of Cape-Breton, and holding a fruitless consultation about annoying the French at Placentia, the expedition was broken up: the fleet returned to England, and the New-England troops to their homes. Loud complaints and heavy charges were made on this occasion; the ignorance of the pilots; the obstinacy of the admiral; the detention of the fleet at Boston; its late arrival there; the want of seasonable orders; and the secret intentions of the ministry, were all subjects of bitter altercation;[3] but the miscarriage was never regularly enquired into, Oct. 9. and the voyage was finally settled by the blowing up of the admiral's ship, with most of his papers, and four hundred seamen, at Spithead.

The failure of this expedition encouraged the Indians to harass 1712. the frontiers as soon as the season would permit. In April, one Cunningham was killed at Exeter; Ensign Tuttle at Dover, and Jeremiah Crommet at Oyster river. On

(1) Penhallow, page 64. Hutch. vol. 2, page 190.   (2) Council Records.—
(3) Dummer's defence and letter to a noble lord.

one of the upper branches of this stream, the enemy burned a saw-mill with a large quantity of boards. A scouting party, who went up the river Merrimack, had the good fortune to surprise and kill eight Indians, and recover a considerable quantity of plunder, without the loss of a man. The frontiers were well guarded. One half of the militia did duty at the garrisons and were ready to march at a minute's warning ; a scout of forty men kept ranging on the heads of the towns, and the like care was taken by sea, spy-boats being employed in coasting from Cape Neddock to the Great Boar's head. Notwithstanding this vigilance, small parties of the enemy were frequently seen. Stephen Gilman and Ebenezer Stevens were wounded at Kingston. The former was taken and put to death. In July, an ambush June 3. was discovered at Dover, but the enemy escaped ; and while a party was gone in pursuit of them, two children of John Waldron were taken, and for want of time to scalp them, their heads were cut off. There being no man at that time in Heard's garrison, a woman named Esther Jones mounted guard, and with a commanding voice called so loudly and resolutely, as made the enemy think there was help at hand, and prevented farther mischief.

In the autumn, the news of the peace of Utrecht arrived in America ; and on the 29th of October, the suspension of arms was proclaimed at Portsmouth. The Indians being informed of this event, came in with a flag of truce to Captain Moody at Casco, and desired a treaty ; which the governor, with the council of each province, held at Portsmouth, where the chiefs and deputies of the several belligerent tribes, by a formal wri- 1713. ting* under hand and seal, acknowledged their perfidy, July 11. promised fidelity, renewed their allegiance, submitted to the laws, and begged the queen's pardon for their former miscarriages. [1] The frequent repetition of such engagements and as frequent violations of them, had by this time much abated the sense of obligation on the one part, and of confidence on the other. But it being for the interest of both parries to be at peace, the event was peculiarly welcome.

To preserve the dependence of the Indians, and to prevent all occasions of complaint, private traffic with them was forbidden and ||truck houses established||† at the public expense ; and 1714. the next summer, a ship was fitted out by both provinces, and sent to Quebec, where an exchange of prisoners was effected.

(1) Penhallow, p. 72—80.

* [This "formal writing" or pacification is in Penhallow, in the Coll. of the N. H. Hist. Soc. i. 82.]

† [In the 2d volume p. 39 of the 2d edition, the following note is found : " The reader is desired to correct a mistake in the first volume. Instead of ' truck houses established,' read ' it was in contemplation to establish truck houses.' "]

During the whole of this long war, Usher behaved as a faithful servant of the crown; frequently coming into the province by Dudley's direction, and sometimes residing in it several months, inquiring into the state of the frontiers and garrisons, visiting them in person, consulting with the officers of militia about the proper methods of defence and protection, and offering his service on all occasions : Yet his austere and ungracious manners, and the interest he had in Allen's claim, effectually prevented him from acquiring that popularity which he seems to have deserved. He was solicitous to support the dignity of his commission ; but could never prevail with the assembly to settle a salary upon him. The council generally paid his travelling expenses by a draft on the treasury, which never amounted to more than five pounds for each journey, until he came from Boston to proclaim the accession of King George ; when in a fit of loyalty and good humor, they gave him ten pounds, which served as a precedent for two or three other grants. He often complained, and sometimes in harsh and reproachful terms of their neglect ; and once told them, that his " negro servants were much better accommodated in his house " than the queen's governor was in the queen's fort."[1]

Dudley had the good fortune to be more popular. Beside his attention to the general interest of the province and his care for its defence, he had the particular merit of favoring the views of those who were most strongly opposed to Allen's claim ; and they made him amends, by promoting in the assembly, addresses to the queen, defending his character, when it was attacked and praying for his continuance in office, when petitions were presented for his removal. One of these addresses was in one thousand, seven hundred and six, and another in one thousand, seven hundred and seven, in both which, they represent him as a " prudent, careful and faithful governor," and say, they " are perfectly satis- " fied with his disposal of the people, and their arms and the public " money." Addresses to the crown were very frequent during this female reign. Scarce a year passed without one or two. They either congratulated her majesty on her victories in Europe, or petitioned for arms and military stores for their defence, or for ships and troops to go against Canada, or represented their own poverty or Dudley's merits, or thanked her majesty for her care and protection, and for interposing in the affair of Allen's suit, and not suffering it to be decided against them.[2] A good harmony subsisted between the governor and people, and between the two branches of the Legislature, during the whole of this administration.

On the accession of King George, a change was expected in the government, and the assembly did what they could to prevent it, by petitioning the king for Dudley's continu-

1715.

(1) Council Records.   (2) Ibid.

ance. But it being now a time of peace, and a number of valuable officers who had served with reputation in the late wars being out of employment, interest was made for their obtaining places of profit under the crown. Colonel Eliseus Burges, who had served under General Stanhope, was, by his recommendation, commissioned governor of Massachusetts and New-Hampshire ; and by the same interest, George Vaughan, Esq., then in London, was made lieutenant-governor of the latter province. He arrived and published his commission on the thirteenth of October. Usher had some scruples about the validity of it as he had formerly had of Partridge's, and wrote on the subject to the assembly, who assured him that on inspection, they had found Vaughan's commission " strong and authentic ;" and that his own, was " null and void."[1] Upon his dismission from office, he retired to his elegant seat at Medford, where he spent the rest of his days, and died on the fifth of September, 1726, in the seventy-eighth year of his age.*

Burges wrote a letter to the assembly in July, in which he informed them of his appointment, and of his intention to sail for America in the following month. But Sir William Ashurst, with Jeremy Dummer, the Massachusetts agent, and Jonathan Belcher, then in London, apprehending that he would not be an acceptable person to the people of New-England, prevailed with him for the consideration of one thousand pounds sterling, which Dummer and Belcher generously advanced, to resign his commission ; and Colonel Samuel Shute was appointed in his stead to the command of both provinces.[2] He arrived in New-Hampshire and his commission was published the seventeenth of October, 1716. Dudley being thus superseded, retired to his family-seat at Roxbury, where he died in 1720, in the seventy-third year of his age.

(1) Council and Assembly Records.   (2) Hutch. vol. 2, p. 215.

* [John Usher was son of Hezekiah Usher, who came early to New-England and was admitted freeman in 1638. He settled at Cambridge, from whence he removed to Boston, where the lieutenant-governor was born 27 April, 1648, and was admitted freeman in 1673. In a MS. catalogue of the graduates of Harvard college, by the late William Winthrop, Esq., of Cambridge, it is said that Rev. John Usher, who graduated at that institution in 1719, was a son of lieutenant-governor Usher, and that he was the Episcopal minister of Bristol, R. I., and died 30 April, 1775, aged 76. Rev. John Usher, who graduated at Harvard college in 1743, is said to have been a son of the Rev. Mr. Usher, and his successor at Bristol. He died in July, 1804, aged about 80 years.]

CHAPTER XIII.

The administration of Governor Shute, and his Lieutenants, Vaughan and
Wentworth.

GEORGE VAUGHAN, Esquire, was the son of Major William
Vaughan, who had been so ill used by former governors, and had
suffered so much in the cause of his country, that the advancement of his son, to the office of lieutenant-governor, was esteemed a mark of particular favor, from the crown to the province, and
a singular gratification to the parent, then in the decline of life.
The lieutenant-governor had been employed by the province, as
their agent in England, to manage their defence against Allen.
There he was taken notice of, by some persons of quality and
influence, with whom his father had been connected; and by them,
he was recommended as a candidate for the honor to which he
was now advanced.

After he had arrived, and opened his commission, Dudley,
Oct. 13. though not actually superseded, yet daily expecting Burges
to succeed him, did not think it proper to come into the
province, or perform any acts of government; so that, during a
Nov. 3. year, Vaughan had the sole command. In this time, he
called an assembly, who granted him the product of the
impost and excise, for one year, but refused to establish these
1716. duties for any longer time; upon which he dissolved them,
Aug. 21. and called another; to whom he recommended, in a style
too peremptory, the establishment of a perpetual revenue
to the crown;[1] a matter in which he had been so much engaged,
that while in England, ' he presented a memorial to the king and
' ministry, to bring New-England into the land tax of Great Brit-
' ain; and proposed that a receiver should be appointed by the
' crown.'[2] The assembly was of opinion, that the public charges
might be defrayed in the usual manner, by an equal tax on polls
and estates; and declined laying an impost, or entering on any,
but the common business of the year, till the arrival of a gov
ernor.*

When Governor Shute came to the chair, several of the old
Oct. 17. counsellors were laid aside, and six new ones appointed,
all of whom were inhabitants of Portsmouth. That town,

(1) Assembly Records.   (3) MS. Letter of Sir. W. Ashurst to Dr. Increase
Mather.

* [1716. Stratham was incorporated. This town was included in the
Squamscot patent granted to Edward Hilton. In 1693, it was annexed to
Exeter, it having before that time been connected with Hampton. It was
incorporated by charter, signed by Lieutenant-Governor Vaughan, 20 March,
1716. In 1695, it contained 35 families; in 1767, it had 916 inhabitants.]

at the same time, was unhappily agitated by a controversy, which had for some years subsisted between the two parishes. This had not only embittered the minds of the people, but had prejudiced some of the members of the council and assembly; so as to affect the proceedings of the legislature, and break the harmony, which had been preserved in that body, during the preceding administration. The governor, in his first speech to the assembly, took notice of their division, and advised them to unanimity. They thanked him for his advice, but remonstrated against the removal of the old counsellors, and the confining of the new appointments, both in the council and the judicial courts, to residents in one town, as being contrary to former usage, and giving an advantage, to the trading, above the landed interest. This, they said, was the reason that an impost could not now be obtained, and that the whole burden of taxes was laid on the husbandman, and the laborer, who had been greatly impoverished by the late war. The governor wisely avoided an answer to this remonstrance, by putting it on the council, who were a party in the controversy. The council, in their answer, acknowledged that the province had been much distressed by the war; but had in a great measure recovered; that there would have been no opposition to an impost, if the representatives had agreed to an act of export, according to the practice in England; that the king had a right to appoint his counsellors, from any part of the province; that it was an affront to the prerogative to find fault with the exercise of this right; and that it was most convenient for the affairs of government, especially upon sudden emergencies, that the council should reside near the seat of government. This answer might have appeared decent enough if they had not added, that they were 'gentlemen of the 'best quality, and greatest ability to serve the government, in that 'station; and had as good or better estates in land, and land se-'curities, than any in the house, and not inferior to the gentlemen 'who were laid aside.'

1717.
Jan. 10.

Jan. 23.

Jan. 23.

While these altercations were in hand, there was a great complaint of the scarcity of money, and some expedient was judged necessary to supply the place of current coin. A proposal was made to issue ten thousand pounds in bills, on loan, for twenty-three years, at five per cent. on land security. In this, both houses agreed; but the next day, the council proposed to enlarge the sum to fifteen thousand pounds, to which the house would not consent. The governor then ordered the house to attend a conference with the council. They desired to know on what subject; he gave them no answer, but commanded their attendance. Having conferred about the proposed loan to no purpose, the circumstance of asking on what subject they were to confer was deemed an affront, and served as a pretext for dissolv-

Jan. 24.

ing them. The next assembly was more pliant, and issued fifteen thousand pounds, on loan, for eleven years, at ten per cent.[1]

A controversy also arose between the governor and lieutenant-governor about the power of the latter, in the absence of the former. Vaughan contended, that when the governor was present in his other province, he was absent from New-Hampshire, and consequently that the administration devolved on him. The position was a metaphysical truth, but the inference was to be measured by political rules. Shute alleged that his commissions, being published and recorded, in New-Hampshire and Massachusetts, he had the power of commander in chief over both provinces, during his residence in either ; and thought it an absurdity to suppose, that the king had appointed the governor commander in chief, for five or six weeks only in the year, and the lieutenant-governor during the rest of the time ; and that if the lieutenant-governor should happen, in that time, to step over the province line, the senior counsellor must take the chair ; this he said would make the province ' a monster with three heads.' The controversy was soon brought to an issue ; for Vaughan received an order from Shute, while at Boston, to appoint a fast, which he did not obey. He received another to prorogue the assembly, instead of which he dissolved them, without the advice of council. He required the opinion of the council on the extent of his power, but they declined giving it. Penhallow, the governor's chief friend, was a warm opposer of Vaughan's pretensions, and incurred so much of his displeasure, that he publicly charged him with sowing discord in the government, and suspended him from his seat in council. On hearing this, Shute hastened to Portsmouth, and having summoned the council, ordered the king's instruction to him for suspending counsellors to be read, and demanded of Vaughan whether he had any instruction which superseded it. He answered, No. The governor then asked the council's advice whether the suspension of Penhallow was legal ; they answered in the negative. He then restored him to his seat, and suspended Vaughan.[2]

Sept. 24.

The assembly, which Vaughan had assumed the right to dissolve, met again, and approved the proceedings against him, justifying the construction which the governor had put on his commission, and his opinion of the extent of the lieutenant-governor's power ; which was ' to observe such orders, as he should from ' time to time receive from the king or the governor in chief.' The representatives of Hampton presented a remonstrance ; in which, admitting the lieutenant-governor's opinion, that ' when the ' governor is out of the province, the lieutenant-governor is im-' powered to execute the king's commission,' and asserting that the governor was not in the province when the lieutenant-governor

dissolved the assembly, they declared that they could not act with
the house, unless they were re-elected.[1] This remonstrance was
deemed a libel, and the governor in council having summoned
them before him, laid them under bonds of four hundred pounds
each, for their good behaviour.[2] He then issued a proclamation,
asserting his sole power, as commander in chief; and declaring
that the lieutenant-governor had no right to exercise any acts of
government without his special order.[3]

To maintain a controversy with a superior officer on the extent
of power, equally claimed by both, requires a delicacy and an
address which does not fall to the lot of every man. An aspiring
and precipitate temper may bring on such a contention, but dis-
qualifies the person from managing it with propriety. Had
Vaughan proposed to submit the question to the king, he would
have acted more in character, and might have preserved his reputation, though he had lost his power. But having offended the
governor, and disgusted the council and assembly, he could hope
for no favor from the crown. When the report of the proceedings was sent to England, Sir William Ashurst, who had great interest at court, and was a friend to New-England, and who greatly
disrelished the memorial which Vaughan had formerly presented
to the king, easily found means to displace him ;[4] and in his
room was appointed John Wentworth, Esquire, whose commission
was published on the seventh of December. The celebrated Mr.
Addison, being then secretary of state, this commission is coun-
tersigned by a name particularly dear to the friends of liberty and
literature.[5]

John Wentworth, Esquire, grandson of William Wentworth,
formerly mentioned as one of the first settlers of the country, had
been in the early part of his life, commander of a ship ; and had
acquired a handsome fortune by mercantile industry. Without
any superior abilities or learning, by a steady attention to business,
and a prudent, obliging deportment, he had recommended himself to the esteem of the people. Having been five years in the
council, before his appointment as lieutenant-governor, he had
carried the same useful qualities into public life, and preserved or
increased that respect which he had acquired in a private station.
The rancor of contending parties made moderation a necessary
character in a chief magistrate ; and the circumstances of the
province, at that time, required a person of experience in trade,
at its head.

It being a time of peace, after a long and distressing war, the
improvement of which the province was capable, in regard to its
natural productions, lumber and naval stores, rose into view and
became objects of close attention both here and in England. As

---

(1) Assembly Records. (2) Council Minutes. (3) Penhallow's MSS.—
(4) Ashurst's letter, MS. (5) Original MS.

early as 1668, the government of Massachusetts, under which the province then was, had reserved for the public use all white pine trees of twenty-four inches in diameter, at three feet from the ground.[1] In King William's reign, a surveyor of the woods was appointed by the crown ; and an order was sent to the Earl of Bellomont, to cause acts to be passed in his several governments for the preservation of the white pines.[2] In 1708, a law made in New-Hampshire prohibited the cutting of such as were twenty-four inches in diameter, at twelve inches from the ground, without leave of the surveyor ; who was instructed by the queen, to mark with the broad arrow, those which were or might be fit for the use of the navy, and to keep a register of them.[3] Whatever severity might be used in executing the law, it was no difficult matter for those who knew the woods and were concerned in lumbering, to evade it; though sometimes they were detected and fined.[4] Great complaints were frequently made of the destruction of the royal woods ; every governor and lieutenant-governor had occasion to declaim on the subject, in their speeches and letters ;[5] it was a favorite point in England, and recommended them to their superiors as careful guardians of the royal interest. On the other hand, the people made as loud complaints against the surveyor, for prohibiting the cutting of pine trees, and yet neglecting to mark such as were fit for masts ; by which means many trees, which never could be used as masts, and might be cut into logs for sawing, were rotting in the woods ; or the people who got them were exposed to a vexatious prosecution.[6] When no surveyor was on the spot, the governor and council appointed suitable persons to take care that no waste should be made of the mast trees ; and these officers with a very moderate allowance, performed the duty, to much better purpose, than those who were sent from England and maintained at a great expense to the crown.[7]

As those trees which grew within the limits of the townships were deemed private property, the people were desirous to get other

1718.   townships laid out, that the trees might be secured for their own use. This was a difficult point. The assembly in 1704, during the controversy with Allen, had explicitly disclaimed all title to the waste lands, by which they understood all those without the bounds of their towns. The heirs of Allen kept a jealous eye upon them. Usher, who claimed by mortgage from governor Allen, was still living, and was daily inviting purchasers by advertisements.[8] The heir of Sir Charles Hobby, whose claim was founded on purchase from Thomas Allen, had offered his title to the assembly, but they had refused it. The creditors of Hobby's estate had applied for letters of administration ; and

(1) Mass. Rec.   (2) Council Minutes.   (3) Laws, Chap. 20.   (4) Usher's MSS.   (5) Council and Assembly Records.   (6) Penhallow's MSS.   (7) Assembly Records.   (8) New-England Courants.

though the matter had been, by the judge of probate, submitted to the general court, and by their advice suspended, yet the letters had been granted.[1] Allen's other heirs were in a state of minority in England ; but their guardian was attentive to their interest. [2] The controversy had become more complex than before ; and the claimants, however multiplied in number and discordant in their views, yet had an interest separate from that of the public. The royal determination could not be had, but on an appeal from a verdict at law ; but no suits were now pending ; nor could the lands be granted by royal charter, without seeming to intrench on the property of the claimants. Notwithstanding these difficulties, the necessity of extending the settlements, and improving the natural advantages of the country, was too apparent to be neglected.

Great quantities of iron ore were found in many places ; and it was in contemplation to erect forges on some of the rivers and to introduce foreign artists and laborers to refine it. A law was made laying a penalty of ten pounds per ton on the transporting of it out of the province ; but for the further encouragement of the manufacturer, it was deemed necessary, that some land should be appropriated, to the purpose of supplying with fuel, the iron works which were to be erected, on Lamprey river, and of settling the people who were to be employed in that service.[3] On this occasion, it was recollected, that in 1672, while this province was subject to the Massachusetts government, and after the town of Portsmouth had made a liberal contribution for the rebuilding of Harvard College, a promise had been made by the general court to grant to that town a quantity of ' land for a ' village, when they should declare to the court the place where ' they desired it.'[4] Upon this, a petition was presented to the governor and council praying for a fulfilment of this promise ; and after some hesitation, a grant was made of a slip of land two miles in breadth above the head line of Dover, for the use of the iron works, which was called the ' renewing a grant formerly ' made.'[5] This was known by the name of the two mile slip, and it was afterward included in the township of Barrington.

In some parts of the province, were many pitch-pine trees, unfit for masts, but capable of yielding tar and turpentine. A monopoly of this manufacture had been attempted by a company of merchants ; but when many thousand trees were prepared for use, they were destroyed by unknown hands.[6] Afterwards a law was made providing that tar should be received in lieu of taxes, at twenty shillings per barrel.[7] This encouraged the making of it for some time. Another law laid a penalty on the injuring of trees for drawing turpentine.[8] But, private interest was too strong

1719.

---

(1) Assembly Records. (2) Printed state of Allen's title. (3) Laws, chap. 90. Council Minutes. (4) Mass. Rec. (5) Council Minutes. (6) Ibidem. (7) Laws, chap. 19. (8) Chap. 94.

to be counteracted by a sense of public utility. Too many incisions being made in the trees at once, they were soon destroyed; and those which were near at hand became scarce, the manufacture was gradually discontinued.

Hemp was another object. Some had been sown, and from the specimen of its growth, much advantage was expected. An act was made to encourage it ; and it was allowed to be received at the treasury, in lieu of money, at one shilling per pound.[1] But as there was scarcely land enough in cultivation, for the production of corn, it was vain to think of raising a less necessary commodity.

The parliament of England was attentive to the advantages which might be derived to the nation from the colonies, to which they were particularly incited by the war, which at this time raged between Sweden and Russia, the grand marts for naval stores in Europe. A duty which had been paid on lumber imported from America, was taken off ; and this was esteemed so great favor to New-Hampshire that the assembly thanked Shute for the share he had in obtaining it.[2] About the same time, an act of parliament was made for the preservation of the white pines.— Penalties in proportion to the size of the trees, were laid on the cutting of those which grew without the bounds of townships ; and for the greater terror, these penalties were to be recovered by the oath of one witness, in a court of admiralty ; where a single judge, appointed by the crown, and removable at pleasure, determined the cause without a jury.[3] While this bill was pending, Henry Newman, the agent for New-Hampshire, petitioned against the severity of it, but without effect.[4]

Great inconveniences had arisen for want of a due settlement of the limits of the province. The people who lived near the supposed line, were sometimes taxed in both provinces, and were liable to arrest by the officers of both ; and sometimes the officers themselves were at variance, and imprisoned each other. Several attempts had been made to remove the difficulty, and letters frequently passed between the two courts on the subject, in consequence of petitions and complaints from the borderers. In 1716, commissioners were appointed by both provinces, to settle the line. The New-Hampshire commissioners were furnished by lieutenant-governor Vaughan, with a copy of the report of the lords chief justices in 1677, and were instructed ' to follow the ' course of the river Merrimack, at the distance of three miles ' north as far as the river extends.'[5] The commissioners on the other side complained that this power was not sufficient ; if by sufficient it was meant that they had no power to vary from their

(1) Laws, chap. 94.   (2) Assembly Records.   (3) Statute of George I. chap 12.   (4) MS. Petition.   (5) Original MS. instruction.   MS. Letter of Lt. Governor Wentworth.

instructions, the objection was true, but why this should have been
objected it is not easy to account, since the instructions would have
given Massachusetts all which they could claim by virtue of their
old charter ; or the judgment upon it, on which they always laid
much stress. Three years afterward the affair was agitated again,
in obedience to an order from the lords of trade ; who directed
a map to be drawn and sent to them, in which the boundaries of
the province should be delineated, and the best accounts and
vouchers procured to elucidate it.[1] Commissioners were again
appointed to meet at Newbury ; and those from New-Hampshire
were instructed by lieutenant-governor Wentworth to confer with
the others ; and if they could agree, in fixing the place where to
begin the line, they were to report accordingly ;[2] but if not, they
were to proceed *ex parte*, 'setting their compass on the north side
' of the mouth of Merrimack river at high water mark, and from
' thence measuring three miles on a north line, and from the end
' of the first three miles on a west line into the country, till they
' should meet the great river which runs out of Winnipisiogee
' pond.' To this idea of a west line, the Massachusetts commissioners objected ; and desired that the commission of the govern-
or of New-Hampshire might be sent to Newbury, which was refused, and the conference ended without any agreement. However, a plan was drawn agreeably to these instructions, and sent
to the lords of trade ; and Newman, the agent was instructed to
solicit for a confirmation of it. In these instructions, the ideas of
the gentlemen in government are more fully expressed. The
due west line on the southern side of the province, they supposed,
ought to extend as far as Massachusetts extended.[3] The line on
the northerly side adjoining to the province of Maine, they supposed, ought to be drawn up the middle of the river Pascataqua,
as far as the tide flows in the Newichwannock branch ; and
thence northwestward, but whether two or more points westward
of north was left for further consideration.

While these things were in agitation, the province unexpectedly received an accession of inhabitants from the north of Ireland.
A colony of Scotch presbyterians had been settled in the province
of Ulster, in the reign of James I. They had borne a large share
in the sufferings, which the protestants in that unhappy country
underwent, in the reign of Charles I. and James II. ; and had
thereby conceived an ardent and inextinguishable thirst for civil
and religious liberty.[4] Notwithstanding the peace which Ireland
had enjoyed, since the subjection of the Popish party by King
William, some penal laws were still in force ; which, with the inconvenience of rents and tithes, made these people wish for a
settlement in America ; where they might be free from these

(1) Original MS. order.   (2) Original MS. instructions.   (3) Penhallow's
MSS. (4) Hume.

burthens and have full scope for their industry.   One Holmes, a
young man, son of a clergyman, had been here and carried home
a favorable report of the country,[1] which induced his father, with
three other presbyterian ministers, James Macgregore, William
Cornwell, and William Boyd, and a large number of their congregations, to resolve on an emigration.   Having converted their
substance into money, they embarked in five ships, and about one
Oct. 14. hundred families of them arrived at Boston: Cornwell,
1718. with about twenty families more, arrived at Casco.   They
immediately petitioned the assembly of Massachusetts for a tract
of land ; who gave them leave to look out a settlement of six miles
square, in any of the unappropriated lands at the eastward.   After
a fruitless search along the shore, finding no place that suited
them there ; sixteen families, hearing of a tract of good land,
above Haverhill, called Nutfield (from the great number of chestnut and walnut trees there) and being informed that it was not
appropriated, determined there to take up their grant ; the others
dispersed themselves into various parts of the country.

As soon as the spring opened, the men went from Haverhill,
where they left their families, and built some huts near a
Apr. 11. brook which falls into Beaver river, and which they named
West-running brook.*   The first evening after their arrival, a

(1) MS. of John Harvey.

* [The sixteen families which first removed to the place were the following.

Randel Alexander,	John Barnet,	John Mitchell,	Thomas Steele,
Samuel Allison,	Arch. Clendenin,	John Morrison,	—— Sterrett,
Allen Anderson,	James Clark,	James McKeen,	John Steward,
James Anderson,	James Gregg,	John Nesmith,	Robert Weir.

These were men principally in the middle age of life, robust, persevering,
and adventurous ; such as were well suited to encounter the toils, and endure
the hardships and self denials of commencing a new settlement.   They were
soon followed by many of their countrymen, who had emigrated with them to
America, so that, before the close of the year, the number of families was
considerably increased.   Being industrious and frugal in their habits of life,
and highly favored with the institutions of the gospel, they very soon became
a thriving, wealthy, and respectable settlement.   Rev. Edward L. Parker's
Century Sermon, 11, 13.

From several petitions of the inhabitants of Londonderry, found among the
Waldron papers, deposited two or three years since in the Secretary's office,
I have collected the following list of persons who had settled in Londonderry
before the year 1738, besides those above named.

The names are given, generally, as found in the petitions, having in many
cases the autographs of the first settlers.

James Adams,	John Barr,	Ninin Cochran,
John Adams,	Samuel Barr,	Peter Cochran,(2)
James Aiken,	John Bell,	Robert Cochran,
Nathaniel Aiken,	James Blair,	William Cochran,(2)
William Aiken,	John Blair,	Thomas Cochran,
James Alexander,	James Caldwell,	John Conaghie,
John Anderson,(2)	James Campbell,	Hugh Craige,
Robert Arbuckel,	David Cargill,(2)	John Craig,
John Archbald,	Benja. Chamberlain,	Jesse Cristi,
John Barnett,	Matthew Clark,	John Cromey,
Moses Barnett,	Andrew Clendenin,	John Dinsmore,

sermon was preached to them under a large oak, which, is to this day regarded with a degree of veneration. As soon as they could collect their families, they called Macgregore to be their minister, who since his arrival in the country had preached at Dracut. At the first sacramental occasion, were present two ministers and sixty-five communicants. Macgregore continued with them till his death;* and his memory is still precious among them. He was a wise, affectionate and faithful guide to them, both in civil and religious concerns. These people brought with them the necessary materials for the manufacture of linen; and their spinning wheels, turned by the foot, were a novelty in the country. They also introduced the culture of potatoes, which were first planted in the garden of Nathaniel Walker of Andover. They were an industrious, frugal and consequently thriving people.

They met with some difficulty in obtaining a title to their lands. If the due west line between the provinces had been established, it would have passed through their settlement and divided it be-

Patrick Douglas,
William Eayrs,(2)
James Gillmor,
Robert Gillmor,
John Goffe,
John Goffe, jr.
Samuel Graves,
John Gregg,
Samuel Gregg,
William Harper,
James Harvey,
Jo. Harvey,
William Hogg,
Abraham Holmes,
Jonathan Hollme,
John Hopkins,
Solomon Hopkins,
Thomas Horner,
Samuel Houston,
William Humphrey,
David Hunter,
Alexander Kelsey,
Robert Kennedy,
Benjamin Kidder,
James Leslie,

James Lindsay,
Edward Linkfield,
Daniel Macduffie,
Robert Mcfarlin,
Nathan Mcfarlin,
James MacGregore,
David McGregore,
Robert McKean,
Samuel McKeen,
Archibald Mackmurphy,
John Macmurphy,
Alexander MacNeall,
John McNeill
William Michell,
Hugh Montgomery,
John Moor,
William Moore,
James Morrison,
Robert Morrison,
Samuel Morrison,
David Morrison,
James Nesmith,
Alex. Nickels,
Hugh Ramsey,
James Reid,

Matthew Reid,
Alexander Renkine,
Samuel Renkin,
James Rodgers,
Hugh Rogers,
John Shields,
Archibald Stark,
Charles Stewart,
Thomas Stewart,
John Taggart,
James Thomson,
William Thomson,
Robert Thompson,
Andrew Todd,
Samuel Todd,
Alexander Walker,
James Walles,
Archibald Wear,
Robert Weir,
Benjamin Willson,
James Willson,
Hugh Wilson,
Thomas Wilson.

A few names having become obliterated or not easily decyphered, are omitted. Where (2) is annexed, it shows that there were two persons of the same name, without the addition of any senior or junior. I have been more particular in giving the preceding list on account of the large number of emigrants Londonderry has furnished for several towns in New-Hampshire, and some in Vermont. Among their descendants might be named those who sustained high military stations in the army of the Revolution;—' those who have been members of Congress;—who have presided in our highest seminaries of learning;—who have filled seats in our council and senate,—and who have sustained the chief magistracy of the state; besides a number of eminent and distinguished ministers of the gospel.']

* March 5, 1729, aged 52.

27

tween Massachusetts and New-Hampshire; but the curve line, following the course of Merrimack at three miles distance, would leave them unquestionably in New-Hampshire. This was the idea of the general court of Massachusetts, who, upon application to them for a confirmation of their former grant, declared them to be out of their jurisdiction. Among the many claimants to these lands, they were informed, that Colonel Wheelwright of Wells had the best Indian title, derived from his ancestors. Supposing this to be valid in a moral view, they followed the example of the first settlers of New-England, and obtained a deed of ten miles square, in virtue of the general license granted by the Indian sagamores in 1629. To prevent difficulty from Allen's claim, they applied for leave of settlement to Colonel Usher, who told them that the land was in dispute, and that he could not give them leave, but that he supposed they might settle on it, if they would hold it either of the king or of Allen's heirs, as the case might be determined.[1] They also applied to the lieutenant-governor of New-Hampshire, who declined making them a grant in the king's name; but, by advice of council, gave them a protection, and extended the benefit of the law to them; appointing James M'Keen to be a justice of the peace, and Robert Weir, a deputy sheriff.[2]

Some persons who claimed these lands, by virtue of a deed of about twenty years' date, from John, an Indian sagamore, gave them some disturbance; but, having obtained what they 1720. judged a superior title, and enjoying the protection of government, they went on with their plantation; receiving frequent additions of their countrymen, as well as others, till in 1722, their town was incorporated by the name of Londonderry, from a city in the north of Ireland, in and near to which most of them had resided; and in which some of them had endured the hardships of a memorable siege.[3] *

(1) Usher's MSS.   (2) Council Minutes.   (3) Harvey and Macgregore's MSS.

* John Barr, William Caldwell and Abraham Blair, with several others who had suffered in this siege, and came to America, were by King William's special order made free of taxes through all the British dominions.

This, with several other circumstances relating to these people, I took from a manuscript letter written (1729) by Mr. John Harvey, school-master in Londonderry, to Mr. Prince. In the same letter was the following brief account of the siege above mentioned. ' Londonderry was besieged near half a ' year (1689) by King James's army, when he had all Ireland subdued but ' Derry and a little place hard by. The besieged defended the city, most of ' them being presbyterians, till they were very much pinched by famine, that ' a dog's head was sold cheap enough at half a crown; and yet God supported ' them until King William sent them relief by two ships with men and pro- ' visions from England; at which sight, before the ships got up to the city ' and landed their men, the besiegers moved their camp and fled to the west ' of Ireland, where afterwards two bloody battles were fought and the papists ' subdued.

The settlement of these emigrants, on the waste lands, opened the way for other plantations. Those who had borne the burthens and distresses of war, in defending the country, had long been circumscribed within the limits of the old towns ; but were now multiplied, and required room to make settlements for their children. They thought it hard to be excluded from the privilege of cultivating the lands, which they and their fathers had defended ; while strangers were admitted to sit down peaceably upon them. These were weighty reasons. At the same time no attempt was making, by any of the claimants, to determine the long contested point of property ; and in fact, no person could give a clear and undisputed title to any of the unsettled lands.

In these circumstances, a company of about one hundred persons, inhabitants of Portsmouth, Exeter and Haverhill, petitioned for liberty to begin a plantation, on the northerly part of the lands called Nutfield. These were soon followed by petitioners from the other towns, for the lands which lay contiguous to them. The governor and council kept the petitions suspended for a long time, giving public notice to all persons concerned to make their objections. In this time, the lands were surveyed, and the limits of four proposed townships determined ; and the people were permitted to build and plant upon the lands ' provided that they did not infringe on, or interfere with, ' any former grants, possessions or properties.'[1] Some of these lands were well stocked with pine trees ; which were felled in great abundance ; this occasioned a fresh complaint from the king's surveyor.

1721.

Apr. 21.

At length, charters being prepared, were signed by the gov-

(1) Council Records.

' Two things further, (says he) I have to relate respecting Derry. 1. The ' church of Derry is so strongly built with stone and lime that in the steeple ' they had a cannon fixed, which did more hurt to the Irish army than six ' upon the walls. 2. There was one Col. Murray in the siege. He and a ' party were out against the enemy, and having got the advantage in an en' gagement with them a mile from the walls, the enemy's general, who was a ' Frenchman, and he, met ; and having both fired their pistols, drew their ' swords, and the general having a coat of mail, had the advantage of Murray, ' so that he could not hurt him. At length Murray observing that there was ' no touching him but through the harness in his face, put his sword in through ' the bars of the harness and killed him. They made a great slaughter that ' day.'

Nothing was more offensive to these emigrants than to be called *Irish*. Macgregore in a letter to Governor Shute, (1720) says : ' We are surprised ' to hear ourselves termed Irish people, when we so frequently ventured our ' all for the British crown and liberties against the Irish papists ; and gave ' all tests of our loyalty, which the government of Ireland required and are ' always ready to do the same when demanded.'

The people of this country did not understand the distinction ; nor in fact did they treat these strangers with common decency on their first arrival.— The grudge subsisted a long time, but is now worn out.

ernor; by which four townships, Chester,* Nottingham, Bar-
rington† and Rochester were granted and incorporated.
The grants were made in the name of the king, who was
considered as the common guardian, both of the people

1722.
May 10.

* [In October, 1719, about 80 persons, chiefly from Hampton and Portsmouth, associated for the purpose of obtaining a grant of a township in the
" Chestnut country;"—placed three men on the land to keep possession, and
petitioned for a grant. After some difficulty, they obtained a grant of a tract
of land ten miles square, 26 August, 1720. The settlement was immediately
commenced by several persons from Rye and Hampton, of whom Samuel
Ingalls, Jonathan Goodhue, Jacob Sargent, Ebenezer Dearborn, Robert Smith,
B. and Enoch Colby, John and Samuel Robie seem to have been most active
and useful, and by several families from the north of Ireland, of whom John
Tolford, afterwards a major, and engaged with Col. Lovewell in 1754, in exploring the Coos territory, and who died in July, 1791, aged 90, Thomas
Smith, John Carr, James Wilson, who died in 1739, aged 100, (see vol. iii.
251) William Wilson, Hugh Wilson and James Whiting, seem to have been
among the earliest settlers. From 1722 to 1726, the settlement was retarded
by an Indian war. The Indians, however, did no injury, except that they
took Thomas Smith and John Carr, as related under 1724. Several garrison
houses were maintained in this town till after the peace of 1749. In 1726,
many new settlers arrived from Hampton, Rye and Bradford, (Mass.) among
whom were Samuel Emerson, the first justice of the peace in the town, Francis and Anthony Towle, Sampson Underhill, Nathan Webster, Ephraim
Hazeltine, Sylvanus Smith, Ithamar, Benjamin and John Shackford, and in
1728 and 1730, several emigrants from Ireland, among whom were James
Campbell, Alexander and Andrew Craige, John Shirela, James Shirela (usually written *Shirley*) who died in 1754, aged 105, John and Robert Mills, John
and Charles Moore, John Dickey, John and Samuel Aiken, Thomas Wason,
William Crawford and John Carswell. The first child born in town was a
daughter of Samuel Ingalls. She died a few years since in Candia, over 90
years of age. The first male child born in town was John Sargent, who also
died in Candia, between 70 and 80 years of age. The charter mentioned in
the text included more than 120 square miles of territory. The first meeting
under it was holden, 28 March, 1723. Until 1728, the town meetings were
usually holden in one of the old towns in the province, and almost all the town
officers, though proprietors, were not inhabitants of the town. In 1729, the
town voted to build a meeting house, and in 1731, a church was formed, and
Rev. Moses Hale, H. C. 1722, was ordained. He was dismissed 4 June, 1735.
In 1734, the emigrants from Ireland, who were Presbyterians, formed a society, and settled Rev. John Wilson after the rules of the kirk of Scotland.
He died 1 February, 1779, aged 76. In 1740, the first school house was built.
In 1748, Capt. Abel Morse was chosen the first representative. In 1750, the
inhabitants voted that the S. W. part of the town, should be set off with a
part of Londonderry and the land next to Amuskeag, into a separate parish,
which was incorporated 3 September, 1751, by the name of *Derryfield*, and is
now called Manchester. In 1753, the W. part of the town was set off as a
distinct parish, aud has been since known as the *Long Meadows*. In 1762,
that part of the town called Charmingfare was set off as a parish, and incorporated by the name of *Candia*, 17 December, 1763. In 1763, the N. parish
or Freetown was set off as a parish or town, and incorporated 9 May, 1765,
by the name of *Raymond*. In 1822, a part of Chester was disannexed with
other tracts to form the town of *Hooksett*. MS. Letter of Samuel D. Bell, Esq.]

† [The settlement of Barrington began in 1732. Fourteen of the first planters were living in 1785, who were between 80 and 90 years of age. A congregational church was organized and Rev. Joseph Prince was ordained 18
June, 1755. He was dismissed in 1768. His successors have been Rev. David Tenney from 1771 to 1778, Rev. Benjamin Balch from 1784 to 1815, and
Rev. Cephas H. Kent, from October, 1828 to 1830. The township was divided
in 1820 into two nearly equal parts, and the western division was incorporated
into a new town by the name of Strafford.]

and the claimants; but with a clause of reservation, ' *as far as in us lies*,' that there might be no infringement on the claims.

The signing of these grants was the last act of government performed by Shute in New-Hampshire. A violent party in Massachusetts had made such strenuous opposition to him and caused him so much vexation, as rendered it eligible for him to ask leave to return to England. He is said to have been a man of a humane, obliging and friendly disposition; but having been used to military command, could not bear with patience the collision of parties, nor keep his temper when provoked. Fond of ease, and now in the decline of life, he would gladly have spent his days in America if he could have avoided controversy. The people of New-Hampshire were satisfied with his administration, as far as it respected them; and though they did not settle a salary on him as on his predecessor, yet they made him a grant twice in the year, generally amounting to a hundred pounds, and paid it out of the excise which was voted from year to year.[1] This was more in proportion, than he received from his other government. On his departure for England, which was very sudden and unexpected, lieutenant-governor Wentworth, took the chief command, in a time of distress and perplexity; the country being then involved in another war with the natives.

1723.
June 1.

CHAPTER XIV.

The fourth Indian War, commonly called the three years' war, or Lovewell's war.

To account for the frequent wars with the eastern Indians, usually called by the French, the Abenaquis, and their unsteadiness both in war and peace; we must observe, that they were situated between the colonies of two European nations, who were often at war with each other, and who pursued very different measures with regard to them.

As the lands, on which they lived, were comprehended in the patents granted by the crown of England, the natives were considered by the English, as subjects of that crown. In the treaties and conferences held with them, they were styled the king's subjects; when war was declared against them, they were called rebels; and when they were compelled to make peace, they subscribed an acknowledgment of their perfidy, and a declaration of their submission to the government, without any just ideas of the

(1) Assembly Records.

meaning of those terms; and it is a difficult point to determine what kind of subjects they were.

Beside the patents, derived from the crown, the English, in general, were fond of obtaining from the Indians, deeds of sale for those lands, on which they were disposed to make settlements. Some of these deeds were executed with legal formality, and a valuable consideration was paid to the natives for the purchase; others were of obscure and uncertain original; but the memory of such transactions was soon lost, among a people who had no written records. Lands had been purchased of the Indian chiefs, on the rivers Kennebeck and St. George, at an early period; but the succeeding Indians either had no knowledge of the sales made by their ancestors, or had an idea that such bargains were not binding on posterity; who had as much need of the lands, and could use them to the same purpose as their fathers. At first, the Indians did not know that the European manner of cultivating lands, and erecting mills and dams, would drive away the game and fish, and thereby deprive them of the means of subsistence; afterward, finding by experience that this was the consequence of admitting foreigners to settle among them, they repented of their hospitality, and were inclined to dispossess their new neighbors, as the only way of restoring the country to its pristine state, and of recovering their usual mode of subsistence.

They were extremely offended by the settlements, which the English, after the peace of Utretcht, made on the lands to the eastward, and by their building forts, block houses and mills; whereby their usual mode of passing the rivers and carrying-places was interrupted; and they could not believe, though they were told with great solemnity, that these fortifications were erected for *their* defence against invasion.[1] When conferences were held with them on this subject, they either denied that the lands had been sold, or pretended that the sachems had exceeded their power in making the bargains; or had conveyed lands beyond the limits of their tribe; or that the English had taken advantage of their drunkenness to make them sign the deeds; or that no valuable consideration had been given for the purchase.[2] No arguments or evidence which could be adduced would satisfy them, unless the lands were paid for again; and had this been done once, their posterity after a few years would have renewed the demand.

On the other hand, the French did not in a formal manner declare them subjects of the crown of France; but every tribe, however small, was allowed to preserve its independence.[3] Those who were situated in the heart of Canada kept their lands to themselves, which were never solicited from them; those who dwelt

(1) Governor Shute's conference, 1717.   (2) Waldo's defence of Loveret's title.   (3) Abbe Raynal.

on the rivers and shores of the Atlantic, though distant from the
French colonies, received annual presents from the king of
France; and solitary traders resided with, or occasionally visited
them ; but no attempt was made by any company to settle on
their lands.

It was in the power of the English to supply them with provisions, arms, ammunition, blankets and other articles which they
wanted, cheaper than they could purchase them of the
French. Governor Shute had promised that trading houses 1717.
should be established among them, and that a smith should be
provided to keep their arms and other instruments in repair ; but
the unhappy contentions between the governor and assembly of
Massachusetts prevented a compliance with this engagement.
The Indians were therefore obliged to submit to the impositions
of private traders, or to seek supplies from the French ; who failed
not to join with them in reproaching the English for this breach
of promise, and for their avidity in getting away the land.

The inhabitants of the eastern parts of New-England were not
of the best character for religion, and were ill adapted to engage
the affections of the Indians by their example. The frequent
hostilities on this quarter, not only kept alive a spirit of jealousy
and revenge in individuals, but prevented any endeavors to propagate religious knowledge among the Indians by the government ;
though it was one of the conditions of their charter ; and though
many good men wished it might be attempted. At length, Governor Shute, in his conference with their sachems at Arrowsick,
introduced this important business by offering them in a formal
manner, an Indian bible, and a protestant missionary ; but they
rejected both, saying ' God hath given us teaching already, and if
' we should go from it, we should displease him.' He would
have done much better service, and perhaps prevented a war, if
he had complied with their earnest desire to fix a boundary, beyond which the English should not extend their settlements.[1]

A gentleman, in conversation with one of their sachems, asked
him why they were so strongly attached to the French, from
whom they could not expect to receive so much benefit as from the
English ; the sachem gravely answered, ' because the French
' have taught us to pray to God, which the English never did.'[2]

It has been observed in the former part of this work, that the
Jesuits had planted themselves among these tribes. They had
one church at Penobscot, and another at Norridgewog, where
Sebastian Ralle, a French Jesuit, resided. He was a man of
good sense, learning and address, and by a compliance with their
mode of life, and a gentle, condescending deportment, had gained
their affections so as to manage them at his pleasure. Knowing
the power of superstition over the savage mind, he took advantage

(1) Judge Sewal's memorial.   (2) Penhallow's MSS.

of this, and of their prejudice against the English, to promote the cause, and strengthen the interest of the French among them. He even made the offices of devotion serve as incentives to their ferocity, and kept a flag, in which was depicted a cross, surrounded by bows and arrows, which he used to hoist on a pole, at the door of his church, when he gave them absolution, previously to their engaging in any warlike enterprise.[1] *

With this Jesuit, the governor of Canada held a close correspondence ; and by him was informed of every thing transacted among the Indians. By this means, their discontent with the English, on account of the settlements made at the eastward, was heightened and inflamed ; and they received every encouragement, to assert their title to the lands in question, and molest the settlers, by killing their cattle, burning their stacks of hay, robbing and insulting them. These insolencies discouraged the people, and caused many of them to remove. The garrisons were then reinforced ; and scouting parties were ordered into the eastern quarter, under the command of Colonel Shadrach Walton. By this appearance of force, the Indians, who dreaded the power of the English, were restrained from open hostilities. They had frequent parleys with the commanders of forts, and with commissioners who visited them occasionally ; and though at first they seemed to be resolute in demanding the removal of the English, declaring that ' they had fought for the land three times, and ' would fight for it again ;'[2] yet when they were told that there was no alternative but perfect peace or open war, and that if they chose peace they must forbear every kind of insult, they seemed to prefer peace ; and either pretended ignorance of what had been done, or promised to make inquiry into it ; and as an evidence of their good intentions, offered a tribute of skins, and delivered up four of their young men as hostages.

This proceeding was highly disrelished by the governor of Canada ; who renewed his efforts to keep up the quarrel, and secretly promised to supply the Indians with arms and ammunition ; though as it was a time of peace between the two crowns, he could not openly assist them.[3]

(1) New-England Courant, No. 160.   (2) Captain Penhallow's MSS.— (3) Hutch. Hist. 263.

* [The writer of a biographical memoir of Ralle, published in the 2 Coll. Mass. Hist. Soc. viii. 250—257, has attempted to vindicate his character from this charge, and from several aspersions which appear in works of writers contemporary with the missionary. In relation to the statement in the text, derived from the New-England Courant, the writer says, " How much reliance is to be placed upon newspaper paragraphs, written respecting those with whom hostilities are carried on, the dispassionate will judge. Imputed reasons are not always correct : if they were, the aborigines might infer that the figure of an Indian, with a drawn sword over his head on the flag of the English inhabitants of Massachusetts, implied that it was borne in menace of an exterminating war against all Indians."]

The New-England governments, though highly incensed, were
not easily persuaded to consent to a war. The dispute was between the Indians and the proprietors of the eastern lands, in
which the public were not directly interested. No blood had as
yet been shed. Canseau had been surprised and plundered, and
some people killed there; but that was in the government of Nova-
Scotia. Ralle was regarded as the principal instigator of the Indians; and it was thought, that if he could be taken off they
would be quiet. It was once proposed to send the sheriff of
York county, with a posse of one hundred and fifty men, to seize
and bring him to Boston; but this was not agreed to. The   1721.
next summer, Ralle in company with Castine from Penobscot, and Croisil from Canada, appeared among the Indians, at a
conference held on Arrowsick Island, with Captain Penhallow, the commander of the garrison, and brought a letter, July.
written in the name of the several tribes of Indians, directed to
Governor Shute; in which it was declared, ' that if the English
' did not remove in three weeks, they would kill them and their
' cattle, and burn their houses.' An additional guard was sent
down; but the government, loath to come to a rupture, and desirous if possible to treat with the Indians separately from the
French emissaries, invited them to another conference, which invitation they treated with neglect.

In the succeeding winter, a party under Colonel Thomas Westbrooke was ordered to Norridgewog to seize Ralle. They arrived at the village undiscovered; but before they could surround
his house, he escaped into the woods, leaving his papers in his
strong box, which they brought off without doing any other damage. Among these papers were his letters of correspondence
with the governor of Canada, by which it clearly appeared, that
he was deeply engaged in exciting the Indians to a rupture, and
had promised to assist them.

This attempt to seize their spiritual father, could not long be
unrevenged. The next summer, they took nine families 1722.
from Merrymeeting bay, and after dismissing some of the June 13.
prisoners, retained enough to secure the redemption of
their hostages and sent them to Canada.[1] About the same time,
they made an attempt on the fort at St. George's; but were repulsed with considerable loss. They also surprised some fishing
vessels in the eastern harbors; and at length, made a furious attack on the town of Brunswick, which they destroyed. July 25.
This action determined the government to issue a declaration of war against them, which was published in form at Boston
and Portsmouth.

New-Hampshire being seated in the bosom of Massachusetts,
had the same interest to serve, and bore a proportionable share

(1) Penhallow's Indian wars, p. 85.

of all these transactions and the expenses attending them. Walton, who first commanded the forces sent into the eastern parts, and Westbrooke, who succeeded him, as well as Penhallow, the commander of the fort at Arrowsick, were New-Hampshire men. The two former were of the council. A declaration of war being made, the enemy were expected on every part of the frontiers; and the Assembly were obliged to concert measures for their security, after an interval of peace for about ten years.

The usual route of the Indians, in their marches to the frontiers of New-Hampshire, was by the way of Winnipiseogee lake. The distance from Cochecho falls, in the town of Dover, to the southeast bay of that lake, is about thirty miles. It was thought that if a road could be opened to that place, and a fort built there, the enemy would be prevented from coming that way. Orders were accordingly issued, and a party of two hundred and fifty men were employed in cutting down the woods for a road; but the expense so far exceeded the benefit which could be expected from a fort at such a distance, in the wilderness, to be supplied with provisions and ammunition by land carriage, which might easily be interrupted by the enemy, that the design was laid aside, and the old method of defence by scouts and garrisons was adopted.[1] Lieutenant Governor Wentworth, being commander in chief in Shute's absence, was particularly careful to supply the garrisons with stores, and visit them in person, to see that the duty was regularly performed; for which, and other prudent and faithful services, he frequently received the acknowledgments of the Assembly and grants of money, generally amounting to one hundred pounds at every session, and sometimes more. They also took care to enlist men for two years, and to establish the wages of officers and soldiers at the following rates; a captain, at seven pounds per month; a lieutenant, four pounds; a sergeant, fifty-eight shillings; a corporal, forty-five shillings, and a private, forty shillings. A bounty of one hundred pounds was offered for every Indian scalp. The difference between the currency and sterling, was two and a half for one.*

(1) Assembly Records.

* [1723. On the 24 February, sixty three of the inhabitants "living in that part of New-Castle, called Little-Harbor and Sandy Beach, and at the eastward of the Little River, so called, at the easterly end of Hampton next to Sandy Beach, with sundry persons of Portsmouth living near Sandy Beach," being in all sixty families or upwards, petitioned the governor and council to be set off as " a particular district or precinct for maintaining a minister with the privileges of carrying on the affairs of a town or parish." The petitioners state that by reason of the great distance they live from any meeting house, the " greatest part of their families were deprived of the dispensations of the gospel, and that there had been almost a famine of the word and worship of God amongst them, there being near four hundred souls, whereof not above the sixth or seventh part could attend said worship." MS. Petition.— Their petition was probably granted, as the next year, they built a meeting house, and in 1726, gathered a church, and settled Rev. Nathaniel Morrill for

The first appearance of the enemy in New-Hampshire, was at Dover, where they surprised and killed Joseph Ham, and took three of his children ; the rest of the family escaped to the garrison. Soon after, they waylaid the road, and killed Tristram Heard.* Their next onset was at Lamprey river, where they killed Aaron Rawlins and one of his children, taking his wife and three children captive.[1] †

1723.

Aug. 29.

(1) Penhallow, page 96.

their first minister. The early names in Rye were those of Berry, Seavey, Brackett, Rand, Locke, Wallis and Jenness, most of which are still found there. It had 72 ratable polls in 1727, and 736 inhabitants in 1767. The settlement of this town dates back to the year 1631, perhaps somewhat earlier.]

* [Tristram Heard was son of the widow Elizabeth Heard, who so remarkably escaped in 1689, when Major Waldron and his neighbors were slain. He was born 4 March, 1667, and was consequently 56 years of age when killed. His mother, who is said by Rev. John Pike to have been, " a grave and pious woman, even the mother of virtue and piety," died 30 November, 1706.]

† ' This Aaron Rawlins (whose wife was a daughter of Edward Taylor, who ' was killed by the Indians 1704) lived upon the plantation left by Taylor, ' about half a mile west from Lamprey river landing, at the lower falls on ' Piscasick river. The people there at that time, commonly retired, at night, ' to the garrisoned houses, and returned home in the day time ; but that ' night they neglected to retire as usual. His brother Samuel also lived ' about half a mile distant on the same river. It seems the Indian scout con- ' sisted of eighteen, who probably had been reconnoitering some time, and in- ' tended to have destroyed both the families, and for that purpose divided, and ' nine went to each house ; but the party that went to Samuel Rawlins's, ' beating in the windows, and finding the family gone, immediately joined ' their companions, who were engaged at Aaron's. His wife went out at the ' door, perhaps sooner than they would otherwise have assaulted the house, ' and was immediately seized, and one or two of her children who followed ' her. Her husband being alarmed, secured the door before they could enter, ' and with his eldest daughter, about twelve years old, stood upon his defence, ' repeatedly firing wherever they attempted to enter, and at the same time ' calling earnestly to his neighbors for help ; but the people in the several ' garrisoned houses near, apprehending from the noise and incessant firing, ' the number of the enemy to be greater than they were and expecting every ' moment to be attacked themselves, did not venture to come to his assistance. ' Having for some time bravely withstood such unequal force, he was at last ' killed by their random shots through the house, which they then broke open, ' and killed his daughter. They scalped him, and cut off his daughter's head, ' either through haste, or probably being enraged against her, on account of ' the assistance she had afforded her father in their defence, which evidently ' appeared by her hands being soiled with powder. His wife and two chil- ' dren, a son and a daughter, they carried to Canada : The woman was re- ' deemed in a few years. The son was adopted by the Indians, and lived with ' them all his days ; he came into Penacook with the Indians after the peace, ' and expressed to some people with whom he conversed, much resentment ' against his uncle Samuel Rawlins, on supposing he had detained from his ' mother some property left by his father, but manifested no desire of return- ' ing to Newmarket again. The daughter married with a Frenchman, and ' when she was near sixty years old, returned with her husband to her native ' place, in expectation of recovering the patrimony she conceived was left at ' the death of her father : But the estate having been sold by her grand- ' father Taylor's administrators, they were disappointed, and after a year or ' two went back to Canada.'

This account was collected from some of the surviving sufferers, and other aged persons who were witnesses of the scene, by Wentworth Cheswell, Esq. of Newmarket.

The next spring, they killed James Nock,* one of the elders of the church at Oyster river, as he was returning on horseback

1724. from setting his beaver traps in the woods.[1] Soon after,
May 16. they appeared at Kingston, where they took Peter Col-
cord and Ephraim Stevens, and two children of Ebenezer Stevens.[2] They were pursued by scouts from Kingston and Londonderry, but in vain. Colcord made his escape in about six months, and received a gratuity of ten pounds from the Assembly, for his ' courage and ingenuity, and for the account he gave of the ' proceedings of the enemy.'[3]

On a sabbath day, they ambushed the road at Oyster river, and
May 24. killed George Chesley, and mortally wounded Elizabeth Burnham, as they were returning together from public
June 2. worship.[4] In a few days more, five Indians took Thomas Smith and John Carr at Chester; and after carrying them about thirty miles, bound them and lay down to sleep. The captives escaped, and in three days arrived safe at a garrison in Londonderry.[5]

The settlements at Oyster river being very much exposed, a company of volunteers under the command of Abraham Benwick, who went out on the encouragement offered by the government for scalps, were about marching to make discoveries. It hap-
June 10. pened that Moses Davis,† and his son of the same name, being at work in their corn field, went to a brook to drink, where they discovered three Indian packs. They immediately gave notice of this discovery to the volunteer company, and went before to guide them to the spot. The Indians had placed them-selves in ambush; and the unhappy father and son were both killed. The company then fired, killed one and wounded two others, who made their escape, though they were pursued and tracked by their blood to a considerable distance.[6] The slain Indian was a person of distinction, and wore a kind of coronet of scarlet dyed fur, with an appendage of four small bells, by the sound of which the others might follow him through the thickets. His hair was remarkably soft and fine; and he had about him a devotional book and a muster-roll of one hundred and eighty Indians; from which circumstances it was supposed that he was a natural son of the Jesuit Ralle, by an Indian woman who had served him as a laundress.[7] ‡ His scalp was presented to the lieu-

(1) MS. of Rev. Hugh Adams.   (2) MS. of Rev. Ward Clark.   (3) Assembly Records.   (4) Penhallow and Hugh Adams.   (5) New-England Courant. (6) Penhallow, p. 101.   (7) Hugh Adams's MS.

* [Penhallow says *Sylvanus* Nock.]

† [Moses Davis was son of John Davis, and brother of Captain James Davis, afterwards colonel, who is mentioned under 1703 and 1709. He was born at Dover, 30 December, 1657, and was in the 67th year of his age at the time he was killed.]

‡ [The writer before referred to, (2 Coll. Mass. Hist. Soc. viii. 256) remarks on this statement as follows : " Now, we learn from Charlevoix, T. II. p.

tenant governor in council, by Robert Burnham, and the promised bounty was paid to captain Francis Matthews, in trust for the company.[1]

Within the town of Dover were many families of Quakers; who scrupling the lawfulness of war, could not be persuaded to use any means for their defence ; though equally exposed with their neighbors to an enemy who made no distinction between them. One of these people, Ebenezer Downs, was taken by the Indians, and was grossly insulted and abused by them, because he refused to dance as the other prisoners did, for the diversion of their savage captors. Another of them, John Hanson, who lived on the outside of the town, in a remote situation, could not be persuaded to remove to a garrison, though he had a a large family of children. A party of thirteen Indians, called French Mohawks, had marked his house for their prey ; and lay several days in ambush, waiting for an opportunity to assault it. While Hanson with his eldest daughter were gone to attend the weekly meeting of friends, and his two eldest sons were at work in a meadow at some distance ; the Indians entered the house, killed and scalped two small children, and took his wife, with her infant of fourteen days old, her nurse, two daughters and a son, and after rifling the house, carried them off. This was done so suddenly and secretly, that the first person who discovered it was the eldest daughter at her return from the meeting before her father. Seeing the two children dead at the door, she gave a shriek of distress, which was distinctly heard by her mother, then in the hands of the enemy among the bushes, and by her brothers in the meadow. The people being alarmed, went in pursuit ; but the Indians cautiously avoiding all paths, went off with their captives undiscovered. After this disaster had befallen his family, Hanson removed the remainder of them to the house of his brother ; who, though of the same religious persuasion, yet had a number of lusty sons, and always kept his fire-arms in good order, for the purpose of shooting game.*

(1) Assembly Records, June 12.

107 and 379, that the *Sieur de S.* CASTINE had married an Abnaquis ; that the children lived with their maternal relations ; that the eldest son, *the Baron de* CASTINE, considered himself as belonging on his mother's side to the nation of the Abnaquis, and in 1721, had become acknowledged as their chief. ' From which circumstances, it may be supposed' *with much greater probability*, that the Indian in question was of the family of *Castine*, and not a natural son of the priest. His muster roll imports his being a chieftain ; and his coronet designates his claim to nobility.'']

* This account is given as collected from the information of the family. A narrative of their distresses is in print. The woman, though of a tender constitution, had a firm and vigorous mind, and passed through the various hardships of an Indian captivity, with much resolution and patience. When her milk failed, she supported her infant with water, which she warmed in her mouth, and dropped on her breast, till the squaws taught her to beat the kernel of walnuts and boil it with bruised corn, which proved a nourishing food for her babe. They were all sold to the French in Canada. Hanson

These and other insolencies of the enemy being daily perpetrated on the frontiers, caused the governments to resolve on an
expedition to Norridgewog. The captains Moulton* and Har-
man, both of York, each at the head of company of one
hundred men, executed their orders with great address.
They completely invested and surprised that village ; killed the
obnoxious Jesuit with about eighty of his Indians ; recovered
three captives ; destroyed the chapel, and brought away the plate
and furniture of the altar, and the devotional flag, as trophies of
their victory.† Ralle was then in the sixty-eighth year of his
age, and had resided in his mission at Norridgewog twenty-six
years ; having before spent six years in travelling among the Indian nations, in the interior parts of America.[1] ‡

Aug. 12.

(1) Hutch. Hist. Mass, ii. 309. New-England Courant. MS. of Hugh
Adams.

went the next spring and redeemed his wife, the three younger children and
the nurse but he could not obtain the elder daughter of seventeen years old,
though he saw and conversed with her. He also redeemed Ebenezer Downs.
He made a second attempt in 1727, but died at Crown-point, on his way to
Canada. The girl was married to a Frenchman, and never returned.

* [He was afterwards colonel of a regiment of provincials at the seige of
Louisburg in 1745. He was also a member of the executive council of Massachusetts, and sustained with high reputation, the first civil and military offices in the county of York. He died in the town of York, 20 July, 1765, aged
77. Alden, Coll. of Epitaphs, ii. 118.]

† [From the Memoir before quoted, it may be proper to give an abstract of
the French account of the attack on Narrantsouak or Norridgewog, as given
by Father de la Chasse, superior general of the missions to New France. (See
2 Coll. Mass. Hist. Soc. viii. 254.)
" There were not above fifty fighing men in the village. These took to
their arms, and ran out in confusion, not with any expectation of defending
the place against an enemy already in possession, but to favor the escape of
their wives, their old men and children, and to give them time to gain the other side of the river, of which the English had not then possessed themselves.
" The noise and tumult gave Father Rasles notice of the danger his converts were in. Not intimidated, he went out to meet the assailants in hopes
to draw all his attention to himself and secure his flock at the peril of his own
life. He was not disappointed. As soon as he appeared, the English set up a
shout, which was followed by a shower of shot, and he fell near a cross which
he had erected in the middle of the village, and with him seven Indians, who
had accompanied him to shelter him with their own bodies. The Indians, in
the greatest consternation at his death, immediately took to flight, and crossed
the river, some by fording, and others swimming. The enemy pursued them
until they entered far into the woods ; and then returned, and pillaged and
burnt the church and the wigwams. Notwithstanding so many shot had been
fired, only thirty of the Indians were slain, and fourteen wounded. After
having accomplished their object, the English withdrew with such precipitation that it seemed rather a flight than a victory." 2 Coll. Mass. Hist. Soc.
viii. 254, 255.]

‡ [Sebastian Rasles, or Ralle, was of a respectable family in Franche-Comte,
and was born about the year 1657. Being appointed a missionary from the
Society of Jesuits to the Indians of North America, he embarked at Rochelle,
in France, on the 23d of July 1689, and arrived at Quebec, in October following. He immediately applied himself to learning the language of the *Abna-
kis ;* and went to reside in their village, containing 200 inhabitants and situated about three leagues from Quebec, in the midst of a forest. Among the
various tribes of Indians, he passed the rest of his life, conforming to their
customs, living upon their unpalatable food, in irregular and uncertain sup-

The parties of Indians who were abroad, continued to ravage the frontiers. Two men being missing from Dunstable, a scout of eleven went in quest of them. They were fired upon by thirty of the enemy, and nine of them were killed.[1] The other two made their escape, though one of them was badly wounded.* Afterward another company fell into their ambush   Sept. 5.

(1) New-England Courant.

plies ; taking long journeys through a rugged wilderness, without shelter or comfortable repose by night, and with incessant fatigue by day. He is said to have been a man of superior sense and profound learning ; and particularly skilled in Latin, which he wrote with classical purity. See Memoir of him in 2 Coll. Mass. Hist. Soc. viii. 250—257.]

* [The persons taken were Nathan Cross and Thomas Blanchard, who had been engaged in the manufacture of turpentine on the north side of Nashua river, near where Nashua village now stands. At that time, there were no houses or settlements on that side of the river. These men had been in the habit of returning every night to lodge in a saw mill on the other side. That night they came not as usual. An alarm was given, as it was feared they had fallen into the hands of the Indians. A party consisting of ten of the principal inhabitants of the place started in search of them under the direction of one French, a sergeat of the militia. In this company was Joseph Farwell, who was the next year lieutenant under Lovewell. When this party arrived at the spot where these men had been laboring, they found the hoops of the barrel cut, and the turpentine spread on the ground. From certain marks on the trees made with coal mixed with grease, they understood that the men were taken and carried off alive. In the course of the examination, Farwell perceived the turpentine had not ceased spreading, and called the attention of his comrades to this circumstance. They concluded that the Indians had been gone but a short time, and must be near, and decided upon an instant pursuit. Farwell advised them to take a circuitous route, to avoid an ambush ; but unfortunately, he and French had a short time previous had a misunderstanding, and were then at variance. French imputed this advice to cowardice, and called out, " I am going to take the direct path ; if any of you are not afraid, let him follow me." French led the way, and the whole party followed, Farwell falling in the rear. Their route was up the Merrimack, towards which they bent their course to look for their horses upon the interval. At the brook, near Lutwyche's (now Thornton's) ferry, they were way-laid. The Indians fired upon them, and killed the larger part instantly. A few fled, but were overtaken and destroyed. French was killed about a mile from the place of action, under an oak tree, lately standing in a field belonging to Mr. Lund of Merrimack. Farwell, in the rear, seeing those before him fall, sprung behind a tree, discharged his piece and ran. Two Indians pursued him : the chase was vigorously maintained for some time, without gaining much advantage, till Farwell passing through a thicket, the Indians lost sight of him, and probably fearing he might have loaded again, they desisted. He was the only one of the company that escaped. A company from the neighborhood mustered on the news of this disaster, proceeded to the fatal spot, took up the bodies of their friends and townsmen, and interred them in the burying ground in Dunstable.

My friend J. B. Hill, Esq., of Exeter, Maine, to whom I am indebted for the preceding note, communicated in 1823, informs me, that in the old church yard in Dunstable, on the road to Boston, near the south line of the town, is a monument with the following inscription, copied verbatim et literatim.

" *Memento Mori.*
Here lies the body of Mr. Thomas Lund,
who departed this life, Sept. 5th, 1724, in the
42d year of his age.
This man with seven more that lies in
this grave was slew all in a day by
the Indiens."

and engaged them ; but the enemy being superior in number
Sept. 7. overpowered them, killed one, and wounded four, the rest
retreated.   At Kingston, Jabez Colman* and his son Joseph, were killed as they were at work in the field.[1] The success
of the forces at Norridgewog and the large premium offered for
scalps, having induced several volunteer companies to go out,
they visited one after another of the Indian villages, but found
them deserted.   The fate of Norridgewog had struck such a terror into them, that they did not think themselves safe at any of
their former places of abode, and occupied them as resting places
only, when they were scouting or hunting.

One of these volunteer companies, under the command of
captain John Lovewell of Dunstable, was greatly distinguished,
first by their success and afterwards by their misfortunes.   This
company consisted of thirty.   At their first excursion to the
Dec. 19. northward of Winnipiseogee lake, they discovered an Indian wigwam, in which were a man and a boy.[2] They
killed and scalped the man and brought the boy alive to Boston,
where they received the reward, promised by law, and a handsome gratuity besides.

By this success, his company was augmented to seventy.   They
marched again, and visiting the place where they had killed the
Indian, found his body as they had left it two months before. [3]
1725. Their provision falling short, thirty of them were dismissed
by lot and returned.   The remaining forty continued their
march till they discovered a track, which they followed till they
Feb. 20. saw a smoke just before sunset, by which they judged that
the enemy were encamped for the night.[4] They kept
themselves concealed till after midnight ; when they silently advanced, and discovered ten Indians asleep, round a fire, by the
side of a frozen pond.   Lovewell now determined to make sure
work ; and placing his men conveniently, ordered a part of them
to fire, five at once, as quick after each other as possible, and another part to reserve their fire : he gave the signal, by firing his
own gun, which killed two of them ; the men firing according to
order, killed five more on the spot ; the other three starting up

(1) Penhallow, p. 106.   (2) Ibid. p. 107.   (3) New-England Courant.—
(4) MS. of Hugh Adams.

Blanchard and Cross were carried to Canada. After remaining there some
time, they succeeded by their own exertions in effecting their redemption,
and returned to their native town. The text says that the party who went
after them consisted of eleven; Penhallow says fourteen, but the number
stated in this note is probably correct, it being derived from the late colonel E.
Bancroft of Tyngsborough.]

* [The late venerable Samuel Welch, of Bow, who died 5 April, 1823, in
the 113th year of his age, remembered the death of Colman, as well as the
capture of Colcord and Stevens, mentioned under May, 1724, and related to
the editor some of the circumstances of these attacks of the Indians, less than
a month before his death. It seemed from his account that Colman was shot,
" one ball through his neck and another through his hip."]

from their sleep, two of them were immediately shot dead by the reserve. The other, though wounded, attempted to escape by crossing the pond, but was seized by a dog and held fast till they killed him. Thus in a few minutes the whole company was destroyed, and some attempt against the frontiers of New-Hampshire prevented ; for these Indians were marching from Canada, well furnished with new guns, and plenty of ammunition ; they had also a number of spare blankets, mockaseens and snow-shoes for the accommodation of the prisoners whom they expected to take, and were within two day's march of the frontiers.[1] The pond where this exploit was performed is at the head of a branch of Salmonfall river, in the township of Wakefield, and has ever since borne the name of Lovewell's pond. The action is spoken of by elderly people, at this distance of time, with an air of exultation ; and considering the extreme difficulty of finding and attacking Indians in the woods, and the judicious manner in which they were so completely surprised, it was a capital exploit.

The brave company, with the ten scalps stretched on hoops, and elevated on poles, entered Dover in triumph, and proceeded thence to Boston ; where they received the bounty of one hundred pounds for each, out of the public treasury. Feb. 24.

Encouraged by this success, Lovewell marched a third time ; intending to attack the villages of Pequawket, on the upper part of the river Saco, which had been the residence of a formidable tribe, and which they still occasionally inhabited.[2] His company at this time consisted of forty-six, including a chaplain and surgeon. Two of them proving lame, returned ; another falling sick, they halted and built a stockade fort on the west side of great Ossipee pond ; partly for the accommodation of the sick man, and partly for a place of retreat in case of any misfortune. Here the surgeon was left with the sick man, and eight of the company for a guard. The number was now reduced to thirty-four.* Pursuing their march to the northward, they came to a Mar. 9.

(1) Penhallow, p. 110.   (2) Symmes's Memoirs.

* [The names of this brave company deserve to be transmitted to posterity. They were Capt. John Lovewell, Lieut. Joseph Farwell, Lieut. Jonathan Robbins, Ensign John Harwood, Sergeant Noah Johnson, Robert Usher and Samuel Whiting, all of Dunstable ; Ensign Seth Wyman, Corporal Thomas Richardson, Timothy Richardson, Ichabod Johnson and Josiah Johnson of Woburn ; Eleazar Davis, Josiah Davis, Josiah Jones, David Melvin, Eleazar Melvin, Jacob Farrar and Joseph Farrar of Concord ; Chaplain Jonathan Frye of Andover ; Sergeant Jacob Fulham of Weston ; Corp. Edward Lingfield of Nutfield ; Jonathan Kittredge and Solomon Keyes of Billerica ; John Jefts, Daniel Woods, Thomas Woods, John Chamberlain, Elias Barron, Isaac Larkin and Joseph Gilson of Groton ; Ebenezer Ayer and Abiel Asten of Haverhill ; and one whose name was considered unworthy of being transmitted to posterity. Noah Johnson was the last survivor of this company. He was a native of Woburn, Massachusetts, and one of the first settlers of Pembroke, the town granted to the survivors and the heirs of those who were killed, where he was deacon of the church. He removed to Plymouth in his old age, and there died 13 August, 1798, in the 100th year of his age.]

pond, about twenty-two* miles distant from the fort, and encamped
by the side of it. Early the next morning, while at their devo-
May 8. tions, they heard the report of a gun, and discovered a single
Indian, standing on a point of land, which runs into the pond,
more than a mile distant. They had been alarmed the preceding
night by noises round their camp, which they imagined were
made by Indians, and this opinion was now strengthened. They
suspected that the Indian was placed there to decoy them, and
that a body of the enemy was in their front. A consultation being held, they determined to march forward, and by encompass-
ing the pond, to gain the place where the Indian stood ; and that
they might be ready for action, they disencumbered themselves
of their packs, and left them, without a guard, at the northeast
end of the pond, in a pitch-pine plain, where the trees were thin
and the brakes, at that time of the year, small. It happened that
Lovewell's march had crossed a carrying-place, by which two
parties of Indians, consisting of forty-one men, commanded by
Paugus and Wahwa, who had been scouting down Saco river,
were returning to the lower village of Pequawket, distant about a
mile and a half from this pond. Having fallen on his track, they
followed it till they came to the packs, which they removed ; and
counting them, found the number of his men to be less than their
own. They therefore placed themselves in ambush, to attack
them on their return. The Indian who had stood on the point,
and was returning to the village, by another path, met them, and
received their fire, which he returned, and wounded Lovewell
and another with small shot. Lieutenant Wyman firing again,
killed him, and they took his scalp.† Seeing no other enemy,
they returned to the place where they had left their packs, and
while they were looking for them, the Indians rose and ran toward them with a horrid yelling. A smart firing commenced on
both sides, it being now about ten of the clock. Captain Love-

* The printed accounts say *forty ;* it is probable that the march was circuitous.

† This Indian has been celebrated as a hero, and ranked with the Roman
Curtius, who devoted himself to death to save his country. (See Hutchinson's History, vol. ii. page 315.)
    Having been on the spot where this celebrated action happened, and having
conversed with persons who were acquainted with the Indians of Pequawket,
before and after this battle, I am convinced that there is no foundation for the
idea that he was placed there as a decoy ; and that he had no claim to the
character of a hero. The point on which he stood is a noted fishing place ;
the gun which alarmed Lovewell's company was fired at a flock of ducks ;
and when they met him he was returning home with his game and two fowling
pieces. The village was situated at the edge of the meadow, on Saco river ;
which here forms a large bend. The remains of the stockades were found by
the first settlers, forty years afterward. The pond is in the township of Frye-
burg, [where, on the 19 May, 1825, was holden the first Centennial Celebration of " Lovewell's Fight," and an Address delivered by Charles S. Daveis,
Esquire. The Address, containing 64 pages 8vo. was published at Portland
the same year.]

well and eight more were killed on the spot. Lieutenant Farwell
and two others were wounded. Several of the Indians fell ; but,
being superior in number, they endeavored to surround the party,
who, perceiving their intention, retreated ; hoping to be sheltered
by a point of rocks which ran into the pond, and a few large pine
trees standing on a sandy beach. In this forlorn place, they took
their station. On their right was the mouth of a brook, at that
time unfordable ; on their left was the rocky point ; their front
was partly covered by a deep bog and partly uncovered, and the
pond was in their rear. The enemy galled them in front and
flank, and had them so completely in their power, that had they
made a prudent use of their advantage, the whole company must
either have been killed, or obliged to surrender at discretion ; being destitute of a mouthful of sustenance, and an escape being
impracticable. Under the conduct of Lieutenant Wyman, they
kept up their fire, and shewed a resolute countenance, all the remainder of the day ; during which, their chaplain, Jonathan Frye,*
Ensign Robbins, and one more, were mortally wounded. The
Indians invited them to surrender, by holding up ropes to them,
and endeavored to intimidate them by their hideous yells ; but
they determined to die rather than yield ; and by their well directed fire, the number of the savages was thinned, and their cries
became fainter, till, just before night, they quitted their advantageous ground, carrying off their killed and wounded, and leaving
the dead bodies of Lovewell and his men unscalped. The shat-
tered remnant of this brave company, collected themselves together, found three of their number unable to move from the spot,
eleven wounded but able to march, and nine who had received no
hurt. It was melancholy to leave their dying companions behind,
but there was no possibility of removing them. One of them, ensign Robbins, desired them to lay his gun by him charged, that
if the Indians should return before his death he might be able to
kill one more. After the rising of the moon, they quitted the fatal
spot, and directed their march toward the fort, where the surgeon
and guard had been left. To their great surprise, they found it
deserted. In the beginning of the action, one man, (whose name
has not been thought worthy to be transmitted to posterity) quitted
the field, and fled to the fort ; where, in the style of Job's messengers, he informed them of Lovewell's death, and the defeat of the
whole company ; upon which they made the best of their way
home ; leaving a quantity of bread and pork, which was a seasonable relief to the retreating survivors. From this place, they endeavored to get home. Lieutenant Farwell and the chaplain,
who had the journal of the march in his pocket, and one more,

---

* [He was the son of Capt. James Frye of Andover, where he was born.—
He graduated at Harvard college in 1723. The large elm near the house of
Mr. John Peters in Andover, was set out by him. Abbot, Hist. Andover,
135.]

perished in the woods, for want of dressing for their wounds. The others, after enduring the most severe hardships, came in one after another, and were not only received with joy, but were recompensed for their valor, and sufferings; and a generous provision was made for the widows and children of the slain.[1]

A party from the frontiers of New-Hampshire, were ordered out to bury the dead; but by some mistake, did not reach the place of action. Colonel Tyng, with a company from Dunstable, went to the spot, and having found the bodies of twelve, buried them, and carved their names on the trees where the battle was fought. At a little distance, he found three Indian graves, which he opened; one of the bodies was known to be their warrior Paugus. He also observed tracks of blood, on the ground, to a great distance from the scene of action. It was remarked that a week before this engagement happened, it had been reported in Portsmouth, at the distance of eighty miles, with but little variation from the truth.[2] Such incidents were not uncommon, and could scarcely deserve notice, if they did not indicate that a taste for the marvellous was not extinguished in the minds of the most sober and rational.

This was one of the most fierce and obstinate battles which had been fought with the Indians. They had not only the advantage of numbers, but of placing themselves in ambush, and waiting with deliberation the moment of attack. These circumstances gave them a degree of ardor and impetuosity. Lovewell and his men, though disappointed of meeting the enemy in their front, expected and determined to fight. The fall of their commander, and more than one quarter of their number, in the first onset, was greatly discouraging; but they knew that the situation to which they were reduced, and their distance from the frontiers, cut off all hope of safety from flight. In these circumstances, prudence as well as valor dictated a continuance of the engagement, and a refusal to surrender; until the enemy, awed by their brave resistance, and weakened by their own loss, yielded them the honor of the field. After this encounter, the Indians resided no more at Pequawket, till the peace.*

The conduct of the Marquis de Vaudreuil, governor of Canada, was so flagrant a breach of the treaty of peace, subsisting between the crowns of England and France, that it was thought, a spirited remonstrance might make him ashamed, and produce some beneficial effects. With this view, the general court of

(1) Symmes's Memoirs.   (2) Penhallow's Indian wars.

* This account of Lovewell's battle is collected from the authorities cited, and from the verbal information of aged and intelligent persons. The names of the dead, on the trees, and the holes where balls had entered and been cut out, were plainly visible, when I was on the spot in 1784. The trees had the appearance of being very old, and one of them was fallen.

Massachusetts proposed to the colonies of New-York, Connecticut, Rhode-Island and New-Hampshire, to join in sending commissioners to Canada on this errand. New-Hampshire was the
only one which consented ; and Theodore Atkinson was appointed on their part, to join with William Dudley and Samuel Thax-
ter on the part of Massachusetts.*

The instructions which they received from the lieutenant-gov-
ernors, Dummer and Wentworth, by advice of the council and
assembly of each province, were nearly similar.[1] They were to
demand of the French governor, restitution of the captives who
had been carried into Canada ; to remonstrate to him on his injustice and breach of friendship, in countenancing the Indians in
their hostilities against the people of New-England ; to insist on
his withdrawing his assistance for the future ; and to observe to
him, that if in the farther prosecution of the war, our Indian allies,
should in their pursuit of the enemy commit hostilities against the
French, the blame would be entirely chargeable to himself.[2]   If
the French governor or the Indians, should make any overtures
for peace, they were empowered to give them passports, to come
either to Boston or Portsmouth, for that purpose, and to return ;
but they were not to enter into any treaty with them. The commissioners were also furnished with the original letters of Vaudreuil to the governors of New-England, and to the Jesuit Ralle,
and with copies of the several treaties which had been
made with the Indians. The gentlemen went by the way   Jan. 20.
of Albany, and over the lakes, on the ice, to Montreal, Mar. 2
where they arrived after a tedious and dangerous journey.

The Marquis, who happened to be at Montreal, received and
entertained them with much politeness. Having delivered their
letters, and produced their commissions, they presented their remonstrance in writing, and made the several demands agreeably
to their instructions; using this among other arguments, ‘ Those
‘ Indians dwell either in the dominions of the king of Great-Brit-
‘ ain, or in the territories of the French king. If in the French
‘ king’s dominions, the violation of the peace is very flagrant, they
‘ then being his subjects ; but if they are subjects of the British
‘ crown, then much more is it a breach of the peace, to excite a
‘ rebellion among the subjects of his majesty of Great-Britain.’[3]

The governor gave them no written answer ; but denied that
the Abenaquis were under his government, and that he had either
encouraged or supplied them for the purpose of war. He said
that he considered them as an independent nation, and that the
war was undertaken by them, in defence of their lands, which had

(1) Mass. and N. H. Records.   (2) [Ibid.]   (2) Atkinson’s MS. Journal.

* Mr. Hutchinson in his history, has not said a word respecting this em-
bassy. [The resolve appointing a commissioner in New-Hampshire passed
the General Assembly, 12 December, 1724.]

been invaded by the people of New-England. The commissioners in reply, informed him, that the lands for which the Indians
had quarrelled, were fairly purchased of their ancestors, and had
been for many years inhabited by the English. They produced
his own letters to the governors of New-England, in which he had
(inconsistently, and perhaps inadvertently) styled these Indians
' subjects of the king of France.' They also alleged the several
treaties held with them as evidence that they had acknowledged
themselves subjects of the British crown ; and, to his great mortification, they also produced his own original letters to the Jesuit
Ralle, which had been taken at Norridgewog, in which the evidence of his assisting and encouraging them in the war was too
flagrant to admit of palliation. Farther to strengthen this part of
their argument, they presented to the governor, a Mohawk whom
they had met with at Montreal, who, according to his own voluntary acknowledgment, had been supplied by the governor with
arms, ammunition and provision to engage in the war, and had
killed one man, and taken another, whom he had sold in Canada.

In addition to what was urged by the commissioners in general,
Mr. Atkinson, on the part of New-Hampshire, entered into a
particular remonstrance ; alleging that the Indians had no cause
of controversy with that province, the lands in question being out
of their claim. To this, the governor answered, that New-Hampshire was a part of the same nation, and the Indians could make
no distinction. Atkinson asked him why they did not for the same
reason make war on the people of Albany ? The governor answered, ' The people of Albany have sent a message to pray
' me to restrain the savages from molesting them ; in a manner
' very different from your demands :' To which Atkinson with
equal spirit replied, ' Your lordship then is the right person, for
' our governments to apply to, if the Indians are subject to your
' orders.'

Finding himself thus closely pressed, he promised to do what
lay in his power to bring them to an accommodation, and to restore
those captives who were in the hands of the French, on the payment of what they had cost ; and he engaged to see that no unreasonable demands should be made by the persons who held
them in servitude. As to those who still remained in the hands
of the Indians, he said, he had no power over them, and could
not engage for their redemption. He complained in his turn, of
the governor of New-York, for building a fort on the river Onondago, and said, that he should look upon that proceeding as a
breach of the treaty of peace ; and he boasted that he had the
five nations of the Iroquois so much under his influence, that he
could at any time, cause them to make war upon the subjects of
Great-Britain.

The commissioners employed themselves very diligently in their inquiries respecting the captives, and in settling the terms of their redemption. They succeeded in effecting the ransom of sixteen, and engaging for ten others. The governor obliged the French, who held them, to abate of their demands; but after all, they were paid for at an exorbitant rate. He was extremely desirous, that the gentlemen should have an interview with the Indians, who were at war; and for this purpose, sent for a number of them from the village of St. Francis, and kept them concealed in Montreal. The commissioners had repeatedly told him, that they had no power to treat with them, and that they would not speak to them, unless they should desire peace. At his request, the chief of the Nipissins visited the commissioners, and said that they disapproved the war, which their children the Abenaquis had made, and would persuade them to ask for peace. After a variety of manœuvres, the governor at length promised the commissioners, that if they would consent to meet the Indians at his house, they should speak first. This assurance produced an interview; and the Indians asked the commissioners whether they would make proposals of peace? they answered, No. The Indians then proposed, that ' if the English would demolish all their forts, and re- ' move one mile westward of Saco river; if they would rebuild ' their church at Norridgewog, and *restore to them their priest*, ' they would be brothers again.' The commissioners told them that they had no warrant to treat with them; but if they were disposed for peace, they should have safe conduct to and from Boston or Portsmouth; and the governor promised to send his son with them to see justice done. They answered, that ' this ' was the only place to conclude peace, as the nations were near ' and could readily attend.' The governor would have had them recede from their proposals, which he said were unreasonable, and make others; but father Le Chase, a Jesuit, being present, and acting as interpreter for the Indians, embarrassed the matter so much that nothing more was proposed. It was observed by the commissioners, that when they conversed with the governor alone, they found him more candid and open to conviction, than when Le Chase, or any other Jesuit was present; and, through the whole of their negotiation, it evidently appeared, that the governor himself, as well as the Indians, were subject to the powerful influence of these ecclesiastics; of whom there was a seminary in Canada, under the direction of the Abbe de Belmont.

Having completed their business, and the rivers and lakes being clear of ice, the commissioners took their leave of the governor, and set out on their return, with the redeemed captives, and a guard of soldiers, which the governor ordered to attend them, as far as Crown-point. They went down the river St. Lawrence to the mouth of the Sorel, then up that river to Chamblee, and through the lakes to fort Nicholson. After a pleasant passage, of seven days, they arrived at Albany, [on the first of May.]

Here they found commissioners of Indian affairs for the province of New-York, to whom they communicated the observations which they had made in Canada, and what the Marquis de Vaudreuil* had said respecting the five nations, and the fort at Onondago. There being a deputation from these nations at Albany, they held a conference with them, and gave them belts ; requesting their assistance in establishing a peace with the Abenaquis. From this place, Mr. Atkinson wrote to M. Cavanielle, son of the Marquis, acknowledging the polite reception the commissioners had met with from the family ; subjoining a copy of the information which they had given to the commissioners of New-York ; and promising, that a due representation should be made, to the kings of England and France, on the subject of their negotiation.

The report of the commissioners being laid before the assemblies of Massachusetts and New-Hampshire, it was determined to prosecute the war with vigor. Orders were issued for the defence and supply of the frontiers, and for the encouragement of ranging parties, both volunteers and militia.[1] A petition was sent to the king, complaining of the French governor, and desiring that orders might be given to the other colonies of New-England, and to New-York, to furnish their quotas of assistance, in the further prosecution of the war ; and letters were written to the governor of New-York, requesting that such of the hostile Indians as should resort to Albany, might be seized and secured.

The good effects of this mission to Canada were soon visible. One of the Indian hostages who had been detained at Boston through the whole war, together with one who had been taken, were allowed on their parole, to visit their countrymen ; and they returned with a request for peace. Commissioners from both provinces went to St. George's ; where a conference was held, which ended in a proposal for a farther treaty at Boston. In the mean time, some of the enemy were disposed for further mischief. Those who had been concerned in taking Hanson's family at Dover, in a short time after their redemption and return, came down with a design to take them again, as they had threatened them before they left Canada. When they had come near the house, they observed some people at work in a neighboring field, by which it was necessary for them to pass, both in going and returning. This obliged them to alter their purpose, and conceal themselves in a barn, till they were ready to attack them. Two women passed by the barn, while they were in it, and had just reached the garrison as the guns were fired. They shot Benjamin

Sept. 15.

(1) Assembly Records.

* [He had been the governor of Canada through the war with the French and Indians, called Queen Anne's war, and through Lovewell's war. He died this year (1725) on the 25 of October. He was distinguished for bravery, firmness and vigilance, and gave the English incredible trouble by the long war he maintained against them, by exciting the savages to perpetual inroads on their frontier. Lord, Lempriere, ii. 749.]

Evans dead on the spot ; wounded William Evans and cut his throat.   John Evans received a slight wound in the breast, which bleeding pentifully, deceived them, and thinking him dead, they stripped and scalped him.   He bore the painful operation without discovering any signs of life, though all the time in his perfect senses, and continued in the feigned appearance of death, till they had turned him over, and struck him several blows with their guns, and left him for dead.   After they were gone off, he rose and walked, naked and bloody, toward the garrison ; but on meeting his friends by the way dropped, fainting on the ground, and being covered with a blanket was conveyed to the house.   He recovered and lived fifty years.   A pursuit was made after the enemy, but they got off undiscovered, carrying with them Benjamin Evans, junior, a lad of thirteen years old, to Canada, whence he was redeemed as usual by a charitable collection.

This was the last effort of the enemy in New-Hampshire.   In three months, the treaty which they desired was held in Boston, and the next spring ratified at Falmouth.*   A peace was concluded in the usual form ; which was followed by re- Dec. 15. straining all private traffic with the Indians, and establishing truckhouses in convenient places, where they were supplied with the necessaries of life, on the most advantageous terms.[1]   Though the governments on the whole, were losers by the trade, yet it was a more honorable way of preserving the peace, than if an acknowledgement had been made to the Indians in any other manner.

None of the other colonies of New-England bore any share in the expenses or calamities of this war ; and New-Hampshire did not suffer so much as in former wars ; partly by reason of the more extended frontier of Massachusetts, both on the eastern and western parts, against the former of which the enemy directed their greatest fury ; and partly by reason of the success of the ranging parties, who constantly traversed the woods as far northward as the White Mountains.   The militia at this time was completely trained for active service ; every man of forty years of age having seen more than twenty years of war.   They had been used to handle their arms from the age of childhood, and most of them, by long practice, had become excellent marksmen, and good hunters.   They were well acquainted with the lurking places of the enemy ; and possessed a degree of hardiness and intrepidity, which can be acquired only by the habitude of those scenes of danger and fa-

(1) Hutch. ii. 318.

* [The commissioners sent from New-Hampshire, and who were present at the formation of this treaty, were from the council, John Frost and Shadrach Walton, and from the house, John Gilman and Theodore Atkinson.   Those appointed to attend the ratification of it, were George Jaffrey, Shadrach Walton and Richard Wibird of the council, and Peter Weare, Theodore Atkinson and John Gilman of the house.]

tigue, to which they were daily exposed. They had also imbibed from their infancy a strong antipathy to the savage natives; which was strengthened by repeated horrors of blood and desolation, and not obliterated by the intercourse which they had with them in time of peace. As the Indians frequently resorted to the frontier towns in time of scarcity, it was common for them to visit the families whom they had injured in war ; to recount the circumstances of death and torture which had been practised on their friends ; and when provoked or intoxicated, to threaten a repetition of such insults in future wars. To bear such treatment required more than human patience ; and it is not improbable that secret murders were sometimes the consequence of these harsh provocations. Certain it is, that when any person was arrested, for killing an Indian in time of peace, he was either forcibly rescued from the hands of justice, or if brought to trial, invariably acquitted ; it being impossible to impannel a jury, some of whom had not suffered by the Indians, either in their persons or families.

CHAPTER XV.

Wentworth's administration continued.   Burnet's short administration.   Belcher succeeds him.   Wentworth's death and character.

DURING the war, the lieutenant governor had managed the executive department with much prudence ; the people were satisfied with his administration, and entertained an affection for him, which was expressed not only by words, but by frequent grants of money, in the general assembly. When he returned from Boston, where the treaty of peace was concluded, they presented to him an address of congratulation, and told him that ' his absence had seemed long ; but the service he had ' done them filled their hearts with satisfaction.'[1] This address was followed by a grant of one hundred pounds. He had, just before, consented to an emission of two thousand pounds in bills of credit, to be paid, one half in the year 1735, and the other half in 1736. An excise was laid for three years, and was framed for three hundred pounds.

1726.
Jan. 5.

The divisional line between the provinces of New-Hampshire and Massachusetts was yet unsettled, and in addition to the usual disadvantages occasioned by this long neglect, a new one arose. By the construction which Massachusetts put on their charter, all the lands three miles northward of the river Merrimack were within their limits. On this principle, a grant had formerly been

(1) General Court Records.

made to Governor Endecott, of some lands at Penacook; which had been the seat of a numerous and powerful tribe of Indians. The quality of the land at that place invited the attention of adventurers from Andover, Bradford and Haverhill; to whom a grant was made of a township, seven miles square; comprehending the lands on both sides of the Merrimack, extending southwardly from the branch called Contoocook.[1] This grant awakened the attention of others; and a motion was made in Dec. 21. the Massachusetts assembly, for a line of townships, to extend from Dunstable on Merrimack, to Northfield on Connecticut river; but the motion was not immediately adopted. The assembly of New-Hampshire was alarmed. Newman, their agent, had been a long time at the British court, soliciting the settlement of the line, and a supply of military stores for the fort. Fresh instructions were sent to him to expedite the business, and to submit the settlement of the line to the king. A committee was appointed to go to Penacook, to confer with a committee of Massachusetts, then employed in laying out the lands, and to remonstrate against their proceeding.[2] A survey of other lands near Winnipiseogee lake, was ordered; that it might be known, what number of townships could be laid out, independently of the Massachusetts claim. On the other hand, the heirs of Allen renewed their endeavors, and one of them, John Hobby, petitioned the assembly to compound with him for his claim to half the province; but the only answer which he could obtain was that 'the courts of law ' were competent to the determination of titles,' and his petition was dismissed.

Both provinces became earnestly engaged. Massachusetts proposed to New-Hampshire the appointment of commissioners, to establish the line. The New-Hampshire assembly refused, because they had submitted the case to the king. The Massachusetts people, foreseeing that the result of this application might prove unfavorable to their claim of jurisdiction, were solicitous to secure to themselves the property of the lands in question. Accordingly, the proposed line of townships being surveyed, ' preten- ' ces were encouraged and even sought after, to entitle persons to ' be grantees.'[3] The descendants of the officers and soldiers, who had been employed in expeditions against the Narraganset Indians,* and against Canada,† in the preceding century, were admitted;

(1) Mass. Records.   (2) N. H. Records.   (3) Hutch. ii. 331.

* [Seven townships were finally granted to the officers and soldiers living, and the heirs of those deceased, who were in the Narraganset war of 1675 and 1676. Two of the townships are within the present limits of New-Hampshire, viz. Amherst, which was called Souhegan-West, until incorporated in 1760, and Merrimack, called Souhegan-East, until 1746.]

† [" Nine townships were granted to the heirs of the militia or soldiers, who went against Canada, Anno 1690, and were called Canada Townships." Douglass, Summary, i 424. Six of these townships were in New-Hampshire,

and the survivors of the late Captain Lovewell's company, with
the heirs of the deceased, had a select tract granted to them at
Suncook.[1] There was an appearance of gratitude in making these
grants, and there would have been policy in it, had the grantees
been able to comply with the conditions. New-Hampshire followed the example, and made grants of the townships of
1727. Epsom, Chichester, Barnstead, Canterbury, Gilmanton
May 18, and Bow. All these, excepting the last, were undoubtedly
" 20. within their limits ; but the grant of Bow interfered with
the grants which Massachusetts had made, at Penacook and Suncook, and gave rise to a litigation, tedious, expensive, and of forty
years continuance.

These tracts of land granted by both provinces were too numerous and extensive. It was impracticable to fulfil the conditions,
on which the grants were made. Had the same liberal policy
prevailed here as in Pennsylvania, and had the importation of
emigrants from abroad been encouraged, the country might have
been soon filled with inhabitants; but the people of Londonderry
were already looked upon with a jealous eye, and a farther intrusion of strangers was feared, lest they should prove a burden and
charge to the community. People could not be spared from the
old towns. Penacook was almost the only settlement which was
effected by emigrants from Massachusetts.* A small beginning

(1) Mass. Records.

viz. 1. Canada to Beverly ; 2. Canada to Salem (now Lyndeborough) ; 3.
Canada to Ipswich, all which were situated on Piscataquog, or its branches ;
4. Canada to Rowley (now Rindge) ; 5. Canada to Gallop; and 6. Canada
to Sylvester.]

* [Penacook was very early visited by the first emigrants. The first notice
which I have found of it is in Gov. Winthrop's Hist. N. E. i. 304, from which
it appears that so early as 1639, the government of Massachusetts sent men to
discover the Merrimack, who reported that they found " some part of it about
Penkook to lie more northerly than forty-three and a half." From Felt's
Annals of Salem, p. 358, it appears that the people of Salem had a plantation
granted to them at Penacook in 1663, but that they had never made a settlement there, although some of them had as early as 1674, erected a trading
house there. They petitioned the General Court in 1714, that the grant
might be confirmed to them, and assigned among other reasons for its confirmation, that since the grant was first made, they had been embarrassed by
Indian wars. It would seem that their petition was not granted, as seven
years afterwards, several persons of Haverhill explored the lands in the vicinity, and presented a petition to the General Court of Massachusetts, for a
tract of land " situated on the river Merrymake, at the lower end of Penacook," to contain eight miles square, and in 1725, obtained the grant of a
township about seven miles square. The settlement was commenced in 1726,
by inhabitants from Haverhill, Andover and Salisbury. In 1733, they were
incorporated into a town by the name of Rumford, having settled a minister
in 1730. From 1749 to 1763, there existed a violent and perplexing controversy between the proprietors of Bow and the inhabitants of Rumford, which
was finally decided by the King in Council, 29 December, 1762. On the 17
June, 1765, the charter of the town was granted, by which it received the
name of CONCORD. A church was gathered and Rev. Timothy Walker, who
graduated at H. C. 1725, was ordained 18 Nov. 1730. He died 2 September,
1782, aged 77. His successors have been Rev. Israel Evans, Rev. Asa M'-

was made by the New-Hampshire proprietors, at Bow, on Suncook river; but the most of the intermediate country remained
uncultivated for many years.   Schemes of settlement were indeed
continually forming; meetings of proprietors were frequently
held, and an avaricious spirit of speculation in landed property
prevailed; but the real wealth and improvement of the country
instead of being promoted was retarded.

On the death of King George I., the assembly, which had subsisted five years, was of course dissolved ; and writs for the election
of another were issued in the name of George the Second. [1]
The long continuance of this assembly was principally ^{Nov. 21.}
owing to the absence of Governor Shute, in whose administration
it commenced; and the uncertainty of his return or the appointment of a successor.   It had been deemed a grievance, and an
attempt had been made, in 1724, to limit the duration of assemblies
to three years, in conformity to the custom of England.   At the
meeting of the new assembly, the first business which they _{Dec. 15.}
took up was to move for a triennial act.   The lieutenant
governor was disposed to gratify them.   Both houses agreed in
framing an act for a triennial assembly, in which the duration of
the present assembly was limited to three years, (unless sooner
dissolved by the commander in chief); writs were to issue fifteen
days at least, before a new election ; the qualification of a representative was declared to be a freehold estate of three hundred
pounds value.[2]   The qualification of an elector was a real estate
of fifty pounds, within the town or precinct where the election
should be made ; but habitancy was not required in either case.
The selectmen of the town, with the moderator of the meeting,
were constituted judges of the qualifications of electors, saving an
appeal to the house of representatives.   This act having been
passed, in due form, received the royal approbation, and was the
only act which could be called a constitution or form of government, established by the people of New-Hampshire; all other
parts of their government being founded on royal commissions
and instructions.   But this act was defective, in not determining
by whom the writs should be issued, and in not describing the
places from which representatives should be called, either by name,
extent or population.   This defect gave birth to a long and bitter
controversy, as will be seen hereafter.

The triennial act being passed, the house were disposed to make
other alterations in the government.   An appeal was allowed in
all civil cases from the inferior to the superior court ; if the matter

(1) N. H. Records.   (2) Edition of Laws in 1771, page 166.

Farland, D. D., and Rev. Nathaniel Bouton. A second congregational (uni-
tarian) church was organized and Rev. Moses G. Thomas ordained 25 February, 1829. The population of Concord in 1767, was 752 ; in 1775, 1052; in
1790, 1747 ; in 1800, 2052 ; in 1810, 2393 ; and in 1820, 2838.]

in controversy exceeded one hundred pounds, another appeal was allowed to the governor and council ; and if it exceeded three hundred pounds, to the king in council. The appeal to the governor in council was first established by Cutt's commission, and continued by subsequent commissions and instructions. In Queen Anne's time, it was complained of as a grievance, that the governor and council received appeals and decided causes, without taking an oath to do justice. An oath was then prescribed and taken. The authority of this court had been recognised by several clauses in the laws ; but was disrelished by many of the people ; partly because the judges who had before decided cases, were generally members of the council ; partly because no jury was admitted in this court of appeal ; and partly because no such institution was known in the neighboring province of Massachusetts. The house moved for a repeal of the several clauses in the laws relative to this obnoxious court ; the council non-concurred their vote, and referred them to the royal instructions. The house persisted in their endeavors, and the council in their opposition. Both sides grew warm, and there was no prospect of an accommodation. The lieutenant governor put an end to the session, and soon after dissolved the assembly by proclamation.*

A new assembly was called ; the same persons, with but two or three exceptions, were re-elected, and the same spirit appeared in all their transactions. They chose for their speaker Nathaniel Weare, who had been speaker of the former assembly, and having as usual presented him to the lieutenant governor, he negatived the choice. The house desired to know by what authority ; he produced his commission ; nothing appeared in that, which satisfied them ; and they adjourned from day to day without doing any business. After nine days, they chose another speaker, Andrew Wiggin, and sent up the vote, with a preamble, justifying their former choice. The lieutenant governor approved the speaker, but disapproved the preamble ; and thus the controversy closed, each side retaining their own opinion. The speeches and messages from the chair, and the answers from the house, during this session, were filled with reproaches ; the public business was conducted with ill humor, and the house carried their opposition so far as to pass a vote for addressing the king to annex the province to Massachusetts ; to this vote the council made no answer. But as a new governor was expected, they

1728.

* [1728. Pembroke, originally Suncook, was granted by Massachusetts to 60 persons, of whom 46 were the soldiers, or their legal representatives, who were engaged with Capt. John Lovewell in May, 1725, against the Indians at Pequawket. The settlement began the next year after the grant was made. The first permanent settlement of Rochester was made 28 December, 1728, by Capt. Timothy Roberts. Rev. Amos Main, H. C. 1729, the first minister, was ordained in 1737, at which time the place contained 60 families. (MS. Petition.) Farmington, incorporated in 1798, and Milton, incorporated in 1802, were both taken from Rochester.]

agreed in appointing a committee of both houses to go to Boston, and compliment him on his arrival.

The expected governor was William Burnet, son of the celebrated Bishop of Sarum, whose name was dear to the people of New-England, as a steady and active friend to civil and religious liberty. Mr. Burnet was a man of good understanding and polite literature ; fond of books and of the conversation of literary men ; but an enemy to ostentation and parade. He had been governor of New-York and New-Jersey, and quitted those provinces with reluctance, to make way for another person, for whom the British ministry had to provide. Whilst at New-York, he was very popular, and his fame having reached New-England, the expectations of the people were much raised on the news of his appointment, to the government of Massachusetts and New-Hampshire. Lieutenant Governor Wentworth characterized him in one of his speeches as ' a gentleman of known worth, having justly obtained ' a universal regard from all who have had *the honor* to be under ' his government.' He was received with much parade at Boston, whither the lieutenant-governor of New-Hampshire, with a committee of the council and assembly, went to compliment him on his arrival.*   July 22.

Mr. Burnet had positive instructions from the crown to insist on the establishment of a permanent salary in both his provinces. He began with Massachusetts, and held a long controversy with the general court to no purpose. In New-Hampshire, a precedent had been established in the administration of Dudley, which was favorable to his views. Though some of the assembly were averse to a permanent salary ; yet the lieutenant governor had so much interest with them, by virtue of having made them proprietors in the lately granted townships, that they were induced to consent ; on condition that he should be allowed one third part of the salary, and they should be discharged from all obligations to him.[1]   1729. This bargain being concluded, the house passed a vote,   May 9. with which the council concurred, to pay ' Governor Bur- ' net, for the term of three years, or during his administration, the ' sum of two hundred pounds sterling, or six hundred pounds in ' bills of credit ; which sum was to be in full of all demands from

(1) Belcher's MS. letter.

* Mr. Hutchinson has represented Governor Burnet as a man of humor, and given an anecdote respecting his indifference to the custom of saying grace at meals. The following story of the same kind, perhaps will not be disagreeable to the reader.

One of the committee, who went from Boston, to meet him on the borders of Rhode-Island, and conduct him to the seat of government, was the facetious Col. Tailer. Burnet complained of the long graces which were said by clergymen on the road, and asked Tailer when they would shorten. He answered, ' the graces will increase in length, till you come to Boston ; after that ' they will shorten till you come to your government of New-Hampshire, ' where your Excellency will find no grace at all.'

' this government, for his salary ; and all expenses in coming to,
' tarrying in, or going from this province ; and also for any al-
' lowance to be made to the lieutenant governor ; and that the
' excise on liquors should be appropriated to that use.'[1] To this
vote, six of the representatives entered their dissent.

Sept. 7. The governor came but once into New-England.   His
death, which happened after a few months, was supposed
to be occasioned by the ill effect, which his controversy with
Massachusetts, and the disappointment which he suffered, had on
his nerves.*

When the death of Governor Burnet was known in England,
the resentment against the province of Massachusetts was very
1730. high, on account of their determined refusal to fix a salary
on the king's governor.[2] It was even proposed, to reduce
them to ' a more absolute dependence on the crown ;' but a spirit
of moderation prevailed ; and it was thought that Mr. Jonathan
Belcher, then in England, being a native of the province, and well
acquainted with the temper of his countrymen would have more
influence than a stranger, to carry the favorite point of a fixed
salary.   His appointment, as governor of New-Hampshire, was
merely an appendage to his other commission.

Belcher was a merchant of large fortune and unblemished
reputation.   He had spent six years in Europe ; had been twice
at the court of Hanover, before the protestant succession took
place in the family of Brunswick ; and had received from the
Princess Sophia, a rich golden medal.[3]   He was graceful in his
person, elegant and polite in his manners ; of a lofty and aspiring
disposition ; a steady, generous friend ; a vindictive, but not implacable enemy.   Frank and sincere, he was extremely liberal
in his censures, both in conversation and letters.   Having a high
sense of the dignity of his commission, he determined to support
it, even at the expense of his private fortune ; the emoluments of
office in both provinces being inadequate to the style in which he
chose to live.

Whilst he was in England, and it was uncertain whether he
would be appointed, or Shute would return, Wentworth wrote
letters of compliment to both.   Belcher knew nothing of the letter to Shute, till his arrival in America, and after he had made a

(1) Journal of the House of Representatives.   (2) Letters of Francis Wilkes,
agent.   (3) Belcher's letter to the Bishop of Lincoln, MS.

* [1729.   Litchfield, a small fertile township on Merrimack river, was settled by people from Chelmsford.   Its Indian name was Natticott, and it was
granted by Massachusetts as early as 1656, to a Mr. Brenton, and for many
years was known by the name of *Brenton's Farm.*   It was afterwards included in Dunstable grant, from which it was separated and incorporated by
Massachusetts in 1734.   On the settlement of the boundary line in 1741, it
fell within New-Hampshire, and was incorporated 5 June, 1749.   A church
was organized, and a minister, Rev. Joshua Tufts, H. C. 1736, was ordained
as early as 1741.]

visit to New-Hampshire, and had been entertained at the house
of the lieutenant-governor. He was then informed, that Wentworth had written a letter to Shute, of the same tenor as that to
himself. This he deemed an act of duplicity. How far it was
so, cannot now be determined. The persuasion was so strong in
the mind of Belcher, that on his next visit to Portsmouth, he refused an invitation to Wentworth's house. This was not the only
way in which he manifested his displeasure. When the affair of
the salary came before the assembly, he not only refused   Aug. 31.
to make such a compromise as Burnet had done ; but
obliged the lieutenant-governor under his hand, to ' quit all claim
to any part of the salary, and to acknowledge that he had no expectation from, or dependence on the assembly, for any allowance,
but that he depended wholly on the governor.' The same salary
was then voted, and in nearly the same words, as to his predecessor. He allowed the lieutenant-governor, the fees and perquisites
only which arose from registers, certificates, licenses and passes,
amounting to about fifty pounds sterling. Wentworth and his
friends were disappointed and digusted. He himself did not
long survive ; being seized with a lethargic disorder, he
died within five months ; but his family connections resent-   Dec. 12.
ed the affront, and drew a considerable party into their   Æ. 59.
views. Benning Wentworth, his son, and Theodore Atkinson,
who had married his daughter, were at the head of the opposition.
The latter was removed from his office of collector of the customs,
to make room for Richard Wibird ; the naval office was taken
from him and given to Ellis Huske ;* and the office of high
sheriff, which he had held, was divided between him and Eleazar
Russell. Other alterations were made, which greatly offended
the friends of the late lieutenant-governor ; but Belcher, satisfied
that his conduct was agreeable to his commission and instructions,
disregarded his opponents and apprehended no danger from their
resentment. Atkinson was a man of humor, and took occasion to
express his disgust in a singular manner. The governor, who
was fond of parade, had ordered a troop of horse, to meet him on
the road, and escort him to Portsmouth. The officers of government met him, and joined the cavalcade. Atkinson was tardy ;
but when he appeared, having broken the sheriff's wand, he held
one half in his hand. Being chid by the governor for not appearing sooner, he begged his excellency to excuse him, because he
had but half a horse to ride.

In addition to what has been observed, respecting Lieutenant
Governor Wentworth, the following portrait of his character, by
some contemporary friend, deserves remembrance.

* [His son Ellis Huske was Postmaster in Boston, and the publisher of the
Boston Weekly Post Boy. He was the person, it is said, who recommended
to the British government, the Stamp Act of 1765.]

' He was born at Portsmouth of worthy parents, from whom
' he had a religious education. His inclination leading him to the
' sea, he soon became a commander of note, and gave a laudable
' example to that order, by his sober behaviour, and his constant
' care to uphold the worship of God in his ship. Wherever he
' came, by his discreet and obliging deportment, he gained the love
' and esteem of those with whom he conversed.

' On his leaving the sea, he had considerable business as a
' merchant, and always had the reputation of a fair and generous
' dealer.

' He has approved himself to the general acceptance of his
' majesty's good subjects throughout this province, and under his
' mild administration, we enjoyed great quietness.

' He was a gentleman of good natural abilities, much improved
' by conversation ; remarkably civil and kind to strangers ; re-
' spectful to the ministers of the gospel ; a lover of good men of
' all denominations ; compassionate and bountiful to the poor ;
' courteous and affable to all ; having a constant regard to the du-
' ties of divine worship, in private and public, and paying a due
' deference to all the sacred institutions of Christ.

' He had sixteen children, of whom fourteen yet survive
' him.'[1] *

CHAPTER XVI.

Dunbar's lieutenancy and enmity to Belcher. Efforts to settle the boundary
lines. Divisions. Riot. Trade. Episcopal Church. Throat distemper.

MR. WENTWORTH was succeeded in the lieutenancy by David
Dunbar, Esquire, a native of Ireland, and a reduced colonel in
   the British service ; who was also deputed to be surveyor
1731.
June 24. of the king's woods. This appointment was made by the
   recommendation of the board of trade ; of which Colonel
Bladen was an active member, who bore no good will to Governor
Belcher. Dunbar had been commander of a fort at Pemaquid,
which it was in contemplation to annex to Nova-Scotia.[2] He had
taken upon him to govern the few scattered people in that district,
with a degree of rigor to which they could not easily submit.
This conduct had already opened a controversy, between him and

(1) N. E. Weekly Journal, Dec. 28. (2) Hutch. ii. 224, 379.

* [Lieutenant Governor Wentworth was son of Samuel Wentworth, and
was born 16 June, 1672. One of the fourteen surviving children was Benning Wentworth, the first governor of New-Hampshire after the establishment of the boundary lines.]

the province of Massachusetts; and it was very unfortunate for
Belcher to have such a person connected with both his governments. What were the merits, which recommended Dunbar to
these stations, it is not easy at this time to determine. The only
qualifications, which appear to have pleaded in his favor, were
poverty and the friendship of men in power. He was an instrument of intrigue and disaffection; and he no sooner made his
appearance in New-Hampshire, than he joined the party who
were in opposition to the governor. Belcher perceived the advantage which his enemies would derive from this alliance, and
made all the efforts in his power to displace him. In his letters
to the ministry, to the board of trade, and to his friends in England, he continually represented him in the worst light, and solicited
his removal. It is not improbable, that his numerous letters of
this kind, written in his usual style, with great freedom and without any reserve, might confirm the suspicions, raised by the letters
of his adversaries, and induce the ministry to keep Dunbar in
place, as a check upon Belcher, and to preserve the balance of
parties.[1]

Within a few weeks after Dunbar's coming to Portsmouth, a
complaint was drawn up against Belcher, and signed by
fifteen persons; alleging that his government was grievous,   July 10.
oppressive and arbitrary, and praying the king for his removal.
This roused the governor's friends, at the head of whom was
Richard Waldron,* the secretary who drew up a counter address,
and procured an hundred names to be subscribed.[2] Both addresses reached England about the same time. Richard Partridge,†
Mr. Belcher's brother in law, in conjunction with his son Jonathan Belcher, then a student in the Temple, applied for a copy of
the complaint against him, at the plantation office, and obtained it;

(1) Belcher's MS. letters.   (2) MS. copies of Addresses.

*[He was the son of Colonel Richard Waldron, and grandson of Major Rich-
ard Waldron, who was killed at Dover in 1689. He was born 21 February,
1694, and graduated at Harvard college in 1712. He fixed his residence at
first on his paternal estate at Dover, but removed afterwards to Portsmouth,
and lived at the plains. In 1728, he was appointed a counsellor, and soon after, secretary of the province. In 1737, he was appointed judge of probate.
He retained these offices as long as Governor Belcher was in office; but soon
after Governor Wentworth commenced his administration, he suspended Mr.
Waldron as counsellor, removed him from office, and appointed Theodore Atkinson, secretary, and Andrew Wiggin, judge of probate.
In 1749, he was elected a representative of Hampton, and when the assembly met, was unanimously chosen speaker. Mr. Waldron was a person of
distinguished talents and literary acquirements. A strong friendship existed
between him and Governor Belcher, which continued through life. He was a
professor of religion, and zealously attached to the church, of which he was a
respectable member. He died in 1753, aged 59. Thomas Westbrook Waldron, who died at Dover, 3 April, 1785, aged 64, was his son. Adams, Annals
of Portsmouth, 191, 192.]

† [Richard Partridge, as has been already stated, was son of Lieutenant-Governor William Partridge. He was born 9 December, 1681, and after being
appointed agent, resided in London, where he was living in 1749.]

but could not get sight of the letters which accompanied it, though, on the foundation of those letters, a representation had been made by the board of trade, to the king.[1]

The only effect which Dunbar's letters had at that time, was to procure the appointment of Theodore Atkinson, Benning Wentworth and Joshua Peirce, to be counsellors of New-Hampshire ; and though Belcher remonstrated to the secretary of state against these appointments, and recommended other persons in their room, he could not prevail, any farther than to delay the admission of the two former for about two years ; during which time, they were elected into the house of representatives, and kept up the opposition there. The recommendations, which he made of other persons, were duly attended to when vacancies happened ; and thus the council was composed of his friends, and his enemies. The civil officers, whom he appointed, were sometimes superseded, by persons recommended and sent from England ; and in one instance, a commission for the naval office, in favor of a Mr. Reynolds, son of the bishop of Lincoln, was filled up in England, and sent over with orders for him to sign it ; which he was obliged punctually to obey.

From the confidential letters of the leading men on both sides, which have fallen into my hands in the course of my researches, the views of each party may plainly be seen ; though they endeavored to conceal them from each other. The governor and his friends had projected an union of New-Hampshire with Massachusetts ; but were at a loss by what means to bring it into effect. [2] The most desirable method would have been, a unanimity in the people of New-Hampshire, in petitioning the crown for it ; but as this could not be had, the project was kept out of sight, till some favorable opportunity should present.

The other party contemplated not only the continuance of a separate government, but the appointment of a distinct governor, who should reside in the province, and have no connection with Massachusetts. The greatest obstacle in their way, was the smallness and poverty of the province, which was not able to support a gentleman in the character of governor. To remove this obstacle, it was necessary to have the limits of territory, not only fixed, but enlarged. They were therefore zealous, in their attempts for this purpose ; and had the address to persuade a majority of the people, that they would be gainers by the establishment of the lines ; that the lands would be granted to them and their children ; and that the expense of obtaining the settlement would be so trifling, that each man's share would not exceed the value of a pullet.

The governor's friends were averse to pressing the settlement of the line ; and their reasons were these. The controversy is

(1) Belcher's letters.   (2) Belcher's, Waldron's, Atkinson's and Thomlinson's letters MS.

either between the king and the subjects of his charter government
of Massachusetts ; or else, between the heirs of Mason or Allen
and the people of Massachusetts.   If the controversy be settled
even in favor of New-Hampshire, the lands which fall within the
line, will be either the king's property, to be granted by his governor and council according to royal instructions ; or else the
property of the heirs of Mason or Allen, to be disposed of by
them.   On both suppositions, the people of New-Hampshire can
have no property in the lands, and therefore why should they be
zealous about the division, or tax themselves to pay the expense
of it ?

The governor, as obliged by his instructions, frequently urged
the settlement of the lines in his speeches, and declared, that the
assembly of New-Hampshire had done more towards effecting it,
than that of Massachusetts.   A committee from both provinces met
at Newbury in the autumn of 1731, on this long contested affair ; but the influence of that party in Massachusetts, of Sept. 21.
which Elisha Cooke was at the head, prevented an accommoda-
tion.   Soon after this fruitless conference, the representatives of
New-Hampshire, of whom a majority was in favor of settling the
line, determined no longer to treat with Massachusetts ; but to
represent the matter to the king, and petition him to decide the controversy.[1] Newman's commission, as agent, having expired, Oct. 7.
they chose for this purpose, John Rindge, merchant, of Portsmouth, then bound on a voyage to London.   The appointment of
this gentleman was fortunate for them, not only as he had large
connexions in England ; but as he was capable of advancing
money, to carry on the solicitation.   The council, a majority of
which was in the opposite interest, did neither concur in the appointment, nor consent to the petition.

Mr. Rindge, on his arrival in England, petitioned the king in
his own name, and in behalf of the representatives of New-
Hampshire, to establish the boundaries of the province ; 1732.
but his private affairs requiring his return to America, he Feb. 28.
did, agreeably to his instructions, leave the business in the hands
of Captain John Thomlinson, merchant, of London ; who was
well known in New-Hampshire, where he had frequently been in
quality of a sea commander.   He was a gentleman of great penetration, industry and address ; and having fully entered into the
views of Belcher's opponents, prosecuted the affair of the line,
' with ardor and diligence ;' employing for his solicitor, Ferdinando John Parris ; who being well supplied with money, was indefatigable in his attention.   The petition was of course referred
to the Lords of Trade, and Francis Wilks the agent of Massachusetts, was served with a copy to be sent to his constituents.*

(1) Assembly Records.

* [The province of New-Hampshire at this time (1732) contained 25 incorporated townships and parishes, 2946 ratable inhabitants, 1316 two story dwell-

Whilst the matter of the line was pending on the other side of
the Atlantic, the parties in New-Hampshire maintained their opposition ; and were on all occasions vilifying and abusing each
other, especially in their letters to their friends in England. On
the one side, Belcher incessantly represented Dunbar, as the fo-
menter of opposition ; as false, perfidious, malicious and revengeful ; that he did no service to the crown, nor to himself ;
but was ' a plague to the governor and a deceiver of the people.'
He was also very liberal in his reflections, on his other opposers.
On the other side, they represented him as unfriendly to the royal
interest ; as obstructing the settlement of the lines ; conniving at
the destruction of the king's timber, and partial to his other government, where all his interest lay ; and that he had not even a
freehold in New-Hampshire. As an instance of his partiality, they
1733. alleged, that in almost every session of the assembly of
Massachusetts, he consented to grants of the disputed
lands, to the people of that province ; by which means, their assembly raised money, to enable their agent to protract the controversy, that they might have opportunity to lay out more townships ; while at the same time, he rejected a supply bill of the
New-Hampshire assembly, and dissolved them, because that in it,
they had made an appropriation for their agent. The truth was,
that the council did not consent to the bill, because they had no
hand in appointing the agent, and the bill never came before the
governor. The frequent dissolution of assemblies was another
subject of complaint ; and in fact, this measure never produced
the desired effect; for the same persons were generally re-elected,
and no reconciling measures were adopted by either party.*

ing houses, 606 one story ditto, and 16,434 acres of improved land. This view
of the province embraced the towns of Portsmouth, Greenland, Hampton,
Hampton-Falls, Dover, Durham, Somersworth, Exeter, Newmarket, New-
Castle, Stratham, Kingston, Newington and Londonderry. The remaining
ten townships had been granted but a few years and some of them had not
been settled. We have no data in our records by which the number of polls,
houses, and acres of improved lands in the remaining towns, can be estimated.
1732. Durham, formerly called Oyster River, was incorporated 15 May
this year. The act passed the assembly 13 May, and received the signature
of Governor Belcher on the 15th.]

* [1733. The Plains in the S. W. part of Portsmouth, agreeably to their
petition signed by 72 persons, was set off as a parish 9 March, 1733. It then
contained 80 families besides the families of six widows, 108 ratable polls and
450 souls. They had seven years before erected a meeting house, and from
the month of February, 1725, to March, 1727, had defrayed the charge of constant preaching, paying also their full proportion for the support of the gospel
ministry at the Bank at the same time. MS. Petition among the Waldron
papers in secretary's office.
The towns of Amherst and Boscawen were granted this year, and settled in
1734. The settlement of the first was commenced by Samuel Walton and
Samuel Lampson, from Massachusetts. Others followed from the county of
Essex, so that in 1741, there were fourteen families settled there. A church
was gathered 22 September, 1741, and on the next day, Rev. Daniel Wilkins
was ordained. He died 11 February, 1784, aged 72. The town was called
Souhegan-West until it was incorporated by N. H., 18 January, 1760. See
Hist. Sketch of Amherst, 8vo. pp. 35, published in 1820. Boscawen was

The governor frequently complained, in his speeches, that the public debts were not paid ; nor the fort, prison, and other public buildings kept in repair ; because of their failure in supply- 1734. ing the treasury.   The true reason of their not supplying it was, that they wanted emissions of paper money, to be drawn in, at distant periods.   To this, the governor could not consent, being restrained by a royal instruction, as well as in principle, op-posed to all such practices.   But one emission of paper was made in his administration ; and for its redemption a fund was establish-ed in hemp, iron, and other productions of the country.   When a number of merchants and others had combined to issue notes, to supply the place of a currency, he issued a proclamation against them ; and in his next speech to the assembly, condemned them in very severe terms.   The assembly endeavored to vindicate the character of the bills ; but in a few days he dissolved them, with a reprimand ; charging them with trifling, with injustice and hypoc-risy.   It must be remembered, that his complaints of an empty treasury were not occasioned by any failure of his own salary, which was regularly paid out of the excise.

Belcher revived the idea of his predecessor, Shute, which was also countenanced by his instructions, that he was virtually pres-ent in New-Hampshire, when personally absent, and attending his duty, in his other province ; and therefore, that the lieutenant-governor could do nothing but by his orders.   Dunbar had no seat in the council, and Shadrach Walton being senior member, by the governor's order, summoned them and presided.   He also held the command of the fort, by the governor's commission, granted passes for ships, and licenses for marriage ; and received and executed military orders, as occasion required.   The lieu-tenant-governor contested this point ; but could not prevail ; and finding himself reduced to a state of insignificance, he retired in disgust, to his fort at Pemaquid ; where he resided almost two years.   The governor's friends gave out that he had absconded for debt, and affected to triumph over the opposition, as poor and impotent ; but their complaints, supported by their agent Thom-linson, and the influence of Bladen at the board of trade, made an impression there much to the disadvantage of Mr. Belcher ; though he had friends among the ministry and nobility ; the prin-cipal of whom was Lord Townsend, by whose influence he had obtained his commission.

After Dunbar's return to Portsmouth, the governor thought it good policy to relax his severity ; and gave him the command of the fort, with the ordinary perquisites of office, amounting to about

granted to 91 proprietors, who gave to it the name of Contoocook, its original Indian name.   The settlement commenced early in the year 1734, by people from Newbury and the adjacent towns.   It was incorporated by N. H. 22 April, 1760, when from an English admiral, it received the name of Boscawen, See Rev. Mr. Price's History of Boscawen, 8vo. pp. 116, Concord, 1823.]

fifty pounds sterling. Not content with this, he complained, that the governor did not allow him one third of his salary. The governor's salary was but six hundred pounds currency ; he spent at least one hundred, in every journey to New-Hampshire, of which he made two in a year. At the same time, Dunbar had two hundred pounds sterling, as surveyor general of the woods ; which, with the perquisites, amounting to one hundred more, were divided between him and his deputies. But it must be remembered that he was deeply in debt, both here and in England.

The rigid execution of the office of surveyor general had always been attended with difficulty ; and the violent manner, in which Dunbar proceeded with trespassers, raised a spirit of opposition on such occasions. The statutes for the preservation of the woods empowered the surveyor to seize all logs, cut from white pine trees, without license ; and it rested on the claimant, to prove his property, in the court of admiralty. Dunbar went to the saw mills ; where he seized and marked large quantities of lumber ; and with an air and manner to which he had been accustomed in his military capacity, abused and threatened the people. That class of men, with whom he was disposed to contend, are not easily intimidated with high words ; and he was not a match for them, in that species of controversy, which they have denominated swamp law. An instance of this happened at Dover, whither he came, with his boat's crew, to remove a parcel of boards, which he had seized. The owner, Paul Gerrish, warned him of the consequence : Dunbar threatened with death the first man who should obstruct his intentions : the same threat was returned to the first man who should remove the boards. Dunbar's prudence at this time, got the better of his courage, and he retired.

With the like spirit, an attempt of the same kind was frustrated at Exeter, whither he sent a company in a boat to remove lumber. Whilst his men were regaling themselves at a public house, in the evening, and boasting of what they intended to do the next day ; a number of persons, disguised like Indians, attacked and beat them ; whilst others cut the rigging and sails of the boat, and made a hole in her bottom. The party not finding themselves safe in the house, retreated to the boat, and pushed off; but being there in danger of sinking, they with difficulty regained the shore, and hid themselves till morning, when they returned on foot to Portsmouth.

This was deemed a flagrant insult. Dunbar summoned the council, and complained to them of the riotous proceedings at Apr. 26. Exeter, where there was ' a conspiracy against his life, by ' evil minded persons, who had hired Indians to destroy ' him.' He proposed to the council, the issuing of a proclamation, offering a reward to apprehend the rioters. The major part of the council were of opinion, that no proclamation could be issued but by the governor.* Information being sent to the governor, he issued a proclamation ; commanding all magistrates to assist in discovering the rioters.

This transaction afforded matter for complaint, and a memorial was drawn up by Thomlinson, grounded on letters which he had received. It was suggested, that the governor's pretence to favor the surveyor was deceitful ; that the rioters at Exeter were his greatest friends ; that the council, wholly devoted to him, would not advise to a proclamation till they had sent to Boston ; that the proclamation was delayed ; and when it appeared offered no reward ; though Dunbar had proposed to pay the money himself ; and, that by reason of this delay and omission, the rioters escaped with impunity.[1]

In justice to Mr. Belcher, it must by said, that there was no delay on his part, the proclamation being sent from Boston within six days. It also appears, from the secret and confidential letters of the governor, that he disapproved the riot, and even called it rebellion ; that he gave particular orders to the magistrates, to make inquiry, and take depositions, and do their utmost to discover the rioters. If he did not advertise a reward, it was because there was no money in the treasury ; and if Dunbar had been sincere in his offer to pay it, he might have promised it, by advertisement. The true reason that the rioters were not discovered, was, that their plan was so artfully conducted, their persons so effectually disguised, and their confidence in each other so well placed, that no proof could be obtained ; and the secret remained with themselves, till the danger was over, and the government had passed into other hands.

A law had been made, for holding the inferior court of common pleas, alternately in each of the four old towns ; and the practice had been continued for several years, much to the convenience and satisfaction of the people ; but Dunbar remonstrated against it, to the board of trade, and moved for a disallowance of the act, because the people who had obstructed him in his office deserved not so much favor. The act was in consequence disallowed, and the courts were afterward confined to Portsmouth. 1735.

The order for disallowance, came to the hands of Dunbar, who called a meeting of the council, that they might advise to its publication. A majority of them would not consent, till the original

(1) MS. letters.

* This was also the governor's opinion ; and in his letters he frequently asserts that Dunbar had no command in New-Hampshire whilst he was in either of his governments. To be consistent, he should have maintained, that the lieutenant-governor of Massachusetts had no command whilst he was in New-Hampshire ; but there occurs an instance of a proclamation issued by Lieutenant Governor Phips, (March 25, 1737) on occasion of a riot at Boston, whilst the governor was in New-Hampshire ; and at his return, he issued another, in which he refers to the former, not only without censuring it, but in terms of approbation.

order was sent to Boston, and Governor Belcher directed the publication of it. This transaction served as matter of fresh complaint, and was alleged as an argument for the appointment of a governor, who should reside constantly in the province.

June 13.

To finish what relates to Dunbar. He was caressed by the party in opposition to Belcher, under the idea that he had interest enough in England, to obtain a commission for the government of New-Hampshire. In 1737, he went to England to prosecute his design; where, by his old creditors, he was arrested and thrown into prison. Thomlinson found means to liberate him; but perceived that he had neither steadiness nor ability for the station at which he aimed, nor interest enough to obtain it; though, by his presence in England, he served to keep up the opposition to Belcher, and was used as a tool for that purpose, till the object was accomplished.[1] After which, he was (1743) appointed, by the East India Company, governor of St. Helena.

The trade of the province at this time consisted chiefly in the exportation of lumber and fish to Spain and Portugal, and the Caribbee Islands. The mast trade was wholly confined to Great Britain. In the winter, small vessels went to the southern colonies, with English and West-India goods, and returned with corn and pork. The manufacture of iron within the province, which had been set up by the late Lieutenant Governor Wentworth, and other gentlemen, lay under discouragement, for want of experienced and industrious workmen. The woollen manufacture was diminished, and sheep were scarcer than formerly; the common lands on which they used to feed, being fenced in by the proprietors.[2] The manufacture of linen was much increased by means of the emigrants from Ireland, who were skilled in that business. No improvements were made in agriculture, and the newly granted townships were not cultivated with spirit or success.

There had not been any settled episcopal church in the province from the beginning, till about the year 1732; when some gentlemen who were fond of the mode of divine worship, in the church of England, contributed to the erection of a neat building on a commanding eminence, in Portsmouth, which they called the queen's chapel. Mr. Thomlinson was greatly instrumental of procuring them assistance in England, toward completing and furnishing it. It was consecrated in 1734; and in 1736 they obtained Mr. Arthur Brown for their minister, with a salary from the society for propagating the gospel in foreign parts.

About this time, the country was visited with a new epidemic disease, which has obtained the name of the *throat distemper.*

(1) Thomlinson's letters, MS.   (2) Belcher's letters to the board of trade, MS.

The general description of it was a swelled throat, with white or ash-colored specks, an efflorescence on the skin, great debility of the whole system, and a strong tendency to putridity. Its first appearance was in May, 1735, at Kingston, in New-Hampshire, an inland town, situate on a low plain. The first person seized, was a child,* who died in three days. About a week after, in another family, at the distance of four miles, three children were successively attacked, who also died on the third day. It continued spreading gradually, in that township, through the summer, and of the first forty who had it, none recovered.[1] In August, it began to make its appearance at Exeter, six miles north-eastward; and in September, at Boston,† fifty miles southward, though it was October, before it reached Chester, the nearest settlement on the west of Kingston. It continued its ravages through the succeeding winter and spring, and did not disappear till the end of the next summer.

The most who died of this pestilence, were children ; and the distress, which it occasioned, was heightened to the most poignant degree. From three to six children were lost out of some families. Several buried four in a day, and many lost their all. In some towns, one in three, and in others one in four of the sick were carried off. In the parish of Hampton-Falls, it raged most violently. Twenty families buried all their children. Twenty-seven persons were lost out of five families ; and more than one sixth part of the inhabitants of that place died within thirteen months. In the whole province, not less than one thousand persons, of whom above nine hundred were under twenty years of age, fell victims to this raging distemper.

Since the settlement of this country, such a mortality had not been known. It was observed, that the distemper proved most fatal, when plentiful evacuations, particularly bleeding, were used ; a great prostration of strength being an invariable symptom. The

(1) Douglass's practical history of a new miliary fever. Fitch's Narrative.

* [Abigail Gilman, according to the late Mr. Welch, of Bow, who then lived in Kingston.]

† On its first appearance in Boston, it was supposed to be nothing more than a common cold; but when the report of the mortality in New-Hampshire was received, and a young man from Exeter, whose brother had died of it, was seized (October 1735) the house was shut and guarded, and a general alarm spread through the neighboring towns and colonies. Upon his death, no infection was observed in that house or neighborhood ; but the distemper appeared in other places, which had no communication with the sick. The physicians did not take the infection, nor convey it to their families, nor their other patients. It was therefore concluded, that it was not like the small pox, or the plague, communicable by infection, from the sick or from clothes; and the physicians, having by desire of the selectmen, held a consultation, published their opinion ; that it proceeded entirely from ' some occult quality in the air.' Weekly News Letter, April 29, 1736.

Dr. Douglass computes the number of persons who had the distemper in Boston at 4000 ; of whom 114 died, which is one in 35. The whole number of inhabitants at that time was estimated at 16,000.

summer of 1735, when the sickness began, was unusually wet and cold, and the easterly wind greatly prevailed. But it was acknowledged to be, not ' a creature of the seasons ;' as it raged through every part of the year. Its extent is said to have been ' from Pemaquid to Carolina ;' but with what virulence it raged, or in what measure it proved fatal to the southward of New-England, does not appear. The same distemper has made its appearance at various times since. In 1754 and 1755, it produced a great mortality in several parts of New-Hampshire, and the neighboring parts of Massachusetts. Since that time it has either put on a milder form, or physicians have become better acquainted with it. The last time of its general spreading was in 1784, 5, 6 and 7. It was first seen at Sanford in the county of York ; and thence diffused itself, very slowly, through most of the towns of New-England ; but its virulence, and the mortality which it caused, were comparatively inconsiderable. ' Its remote, or predisposing cause, ' is one of those mysteries in nature, which baffle human inquiry.'1 *

(1) Dr. Hall Jackson's observations, 1786.

* The following Table, drawn from an account published by Mr. Fitch, minister of Portsmouth, July 26, 1736, is a *Bill of Mortality* for 14 months preceding.

Towns.	Under 10.	10 to 20.	Above 20.	Above 30.	Above 40.	Above 90.	Total.
Portsmouth,	81	15	1		2		99
Dover,	77	8	3				88
Hampton,	37	8	8	1		1	55
Hampton-Falls,	160	40	9	1			210
Exeter,	105	18	4				127
New-Castle,	11						11
Gosport,	34	2			1		37
Rye,	34	10					44
Greenland,	13	2	3				18
Newington,	16	5					21
Newmarket,	20	1		1			22
Stratham,	18						18
Kingston,	96	15	1	1			113
Durham,	79	15	6				100
Chester,	21						21
	802	139	35	4	3	1	984

After this account was taken, ' several other children' died of the throat distemper. In the town of Hampton, 13 more within the year 1736. So that the whole number must have exceeded a thousand. In the town of Kittery, in the county of York, died 122.

It appears also, from the church records of Hampton, that from January 1754, to July 1755, fifty-one persons died of the same distemper, in that town.

CHAPTER XVII.

State of parties. Controversy about lines. Commissioners appointed. Their session and result. Appeals. Complaints.

WE have now come to that part of the history of New-Hampshire, in which may be seen, operating in a smaller sphere, the same spirit of intrigue which has frequently influenced the conduct of princes, and determined the fate of nations. Whilst on the one hand, we see Massachusetts stiffly asserting her chartered claims; and looking with contempt, on the small province of New-Hampshire, over which she had formerly exercised jurisdiction; we shall see, on the other hand, New-Hampshire aiming at an equal rank, and contending with her for a large portion of territory; not depending solely on argument; but seeking her refuge in the royal favor, and making interest with the servants of the crown. Had the controversy been decided by a court of law, the claims of Massachusetts would have had as much weight as those of an individual, in a case of private property; but the question being concerning a line of jurisdiction, it was natural to expect a decision, agreeable to the rules of policy and convenience; especially where the tribunal itself was a party concerned.

It must be observed, that the party in New-Hampshire, who were so earnestly engaged in the establishment of the boundary lines, had another object in view, to which this was subordinate. Their avowed intention was to finish a long controversy, which had proved a source of inconvenience to the people who resided on the disputed lands, or those who sought an interest in them; but their secret design was to displace Belcher, and obtain a governor who should have no connexion with Massachusetts. To accomplish the principal, it was necessary that the subordinate object should be vigorously pursued. The government of New-Hampshire, with a salary of six hundred pounds, and perquisites amounting to two hundred pounds more, equal in the whole to about eight hundred dollars per annum, was thought to be not worthy the attention of any gentleman; but if the lines could be extended on both sides, there would be at once an increase of territory, and a prospect of speculating in landed property; and in future, there would be an increase of cultivation, and consequently of ability to support a governor.

The people were told that the lands would be granted to them; and by this bait they were induced to favor the plan; whilst the ministry in England, were flattered with the idea, of an increase of crown influence in the plantations.

The leading men in Massachusetts were aware of the views of those in New-Hampshire, and determined to guard against them. They presumed, that a line of jurisdiction would not affect property ; and therefore endeavored to secure the lands to themselves, by possession and improvement, as far as it was practicable. The same idea prevailed among the governor's friends in New-Hampshire. They perceived, that a tract of wilderness on the north eastern side of Merrimack river, and the ponds which flow into it, must doubtless fall into New-Hampshire. For these lands they petitioned the governor, and a charter was prepared, in which this whole tract, called King's-Wood, was granted to them. It contained all the lands not before granted, between the bounds of New-Hampshire on the south-west and north-east ; which, according to the ideas of those concerned, would have been sufficient for about four large townships.

Governor Belcher had a difficult part to act. He was at the head of two rival provinces ; he had friends in both, who were seeking their own as well as the public interest : He had enemies in both, who were watching him, eager to lay hold on the most trivial mistake, and magnify it to his disadvantage. His own interest was to preserve his commission, and counteract the machinations of his enemies ; but as the settlement of the line, and the removing of him from his office, were carried on at the same time, and by the same persons, it was difficult for him to oppose the latter, without seeming to oppose the former. Besides, Mr. Wilks, the agent of Massachusetts, was well known to be his friend ; and when it was found necessary to increase the number, one of them was his brother, Mr. Partridge. On the other hand, Mr. Rindge and Mr. Thomlinson were his avowed enemies. There was also a difference in the mode of appointing these agents. Those of Massachusetts were constituted by the council and representatives, with the governor's consent. Those of New-Hampshire were chosen by the representatives only, the council nonconcurring in the choice ; which, of course, could not be sanctioned by the governor's signature, nor by the seal of the province.

When the petition which Rindge presented to the king, had been referred to the board of trade, and a copy of it given to 1732. Wilks, to be sent to his constituents, it became necessary that they should instruct him. Their instructions were designedly expressed in such ambiguous terms, that he was left to guess their meaning, and afterward blamed for not observing their directions. His embarrassment on this occasion, expressed in his petition and counter petition, to the board of trade, protracted the business, and gave it a complexion, unfavorable to his constituents, but extremely favorable to the design of New-Hampshire.[1]

(1) Hutch. ii. 385.   Wilks' petitions and report of board of trade, MS.

To bring forward the controversy, Parris, the solicitor of the agents of New-Hampshire, moved a question, ' From what 'part of Merrimack river the line should begin ?' The 1733. board of trade referred this question, to the attorney and solicitor general, who appointed a day to hear council on both sides. [1] The council for New-Hampshire insisted, that the line ought to begin three miles north of the mouth of the Merrimack. The council for Massachusetts declared, that in their opinion, the solution of this question would not determine the controversy, and therefore declined saying any thing upon it. The attorney 1734. and solicitor reported, that ' whether this were so or not, June 5. ' they could not judge ; but as the question had been re- ' ferred to them, they were of opinion, that according to the char- ' ter of William and Mary, the dividing line ought to be taken ' from three miles north of the mouth of Merrimack, where it runs ' into the sea.' Copies of this opinion were given to each 1735. party ; and the lords of trade reported, that the king should June 5. appoint commissioners, from the neighboring provinces, to mark out the dividing line. This report was approved by the lords of council.

Much time was spent in references, messages and petitions, concerning the adjustment of various matters ; and at 1737. length, the principal heads of the commission were deter- Feb. 4-9. mined. The first was, that the commissioners should be appointed, from among the counsellors of New-York, New-Jersey, Rhode-Island and Nova-Scotia. These were all royal governments, except Rhode-Island ; and with that colony, as well as New-York, Massachusetts had a controversy, respecting boundaries. Connecticut, though proposed, was designedly omitted, because it was imagined that they would be partial to Massachusetts, from the similarity of their habits and interests. The other points were, that twenty commissioners should be nominated, of whom five were to be a quorum ; that they should meet at Hampton, in New-Hampshire, on the first of August, 1737 ; that each province should send to the commissioners, *at their first meeting*, the names of two public officers, on whom any notice, summons, or final judgment might be served ; and at the same time should exhibit, in writing, a plain and full state of their respective claims, copies of which should be mutually exchanged ; and that if either province should neglect to send in the names of their officers, or the full state of their demands, at the time appointed, then the commissioners should proceed *ex parte*. That when the commissioners should have made and signed their final determination, they should send copies to the public officers, of each province ; and then should adjourn for six weeks, that either party might enter their appeal.[2]

(1) Printed brief.   MS. report.   (2) Printed brief.

These points being determined ; the board of trade wrote letters to Belcher, enclosing the heads of the proposed commission, and directing him to recommend to the assemblies of each
Feb. 18. province, to choose their public officers, and prepare their demands, by the time when the commissioners were to meet. These were accompanied with letters to the governors of the several provinces, from which the commissioners were elected, informing them of their appointment. The letters were delivered to Parris, and by him to Thomlinson, to be sent by the first ship to America.[1] Those to Massachusetts and New-Hampshire, were directed, the one to Mr. Belcher, by name, as governor of Massachusetts ; the other, to the commander in chief, *resident* in New-Hampshire ; and it was required that the delivery of the letters should be certified by affidavit. The design of this singular injunction was, that Dunbar, if present, should receive the letter, and call the assembly of New-Hampshire immediately ; and that if Belcher should forbid or hinder it, the blame of the neglect should fall on him. At the same time, another letter, respecting a petition of a borderer on the line, and containing a reprimand to Belcher, was sent in the same manner, to be delivered by Dunbar, into Belcher's hands. These intended affronts, both failed of their effect ; Dunbar having, before the arrival of the letters, taken his passage to England.

The anxiety of Thomlinson, to have the earliest notice possible, of the intended commission sent to New-Hampshire, led him not only to forward the public letters ; but to send copies of all the transactions, to his friends there. In a letter to Wiggin
Feb. 15. and Rindge, (the committee who corresponded with him) he advised them, to make the necessary preparations, as soon as possible, to act in conformity to the commission and instructions ; and even went so far as to nominate the persons, whom they should appoint, to manage their cause before the commissioners.[2]

These papers were communicated to the assembly, at their session in March ; and at the same time the governor laid before them, a copy of the report of the board of trade, in favor
Mar. 18. of a commission, which had been made in the preceding December. In consequence of which, the assembly appointed a committee of eight* who were empowered ' to prepare
April 1. ' witnesses, pleas and allegations, papers and records, to ' be laid before the commissioners ; to provide for their reception ' and entertainment, and to draw upon the treasurer for such ' supplies of money as might be needful.'[3] This appointment was

(1) Original letters of Parris.   (2) Original MS. letter.   (3) Assembly Records and printed brief.

* Of the Council.*	*Of the House.*
Shadrach Walton,	Andrew Wiggin,
George Jaffrey,	John Rindge,
Jotham Odiorne,	Thomas Packer,
Theodore Atkinson.	James Jeffrey.

made by the united voice of the council and representatives, and consented to by the governor; and though it was made, three weeks before the reception of the letters, from the lords of trade; directing the appointing of public officers, and preparing a statement of claims; yet it was understood to be a full compliance with the orders and expectations of the government in England.

The same day on which this order passed, the governor prorogued the assembly to the sixth of July; and on the twentieth of June, he prorogued it again, to the fourth of August.

The letters respecting the commission, were delivered to Mr. Belcher, on the twenty-second of April; and he acknowledged the receipt of them, in a letter to the board of trade, on the tenth of May. The commission itself was issued on the ninth of April, and sent to Mr. Rindge; who kept it till the meeting of the commissioners, and then delivered it to them. The expense of it, amounting to one hundred and thirty-five pounds sterling, was paid by the agents of New-Hampshire.

At the spring session of the general court in Massachusetts, the governor laid before them the letter from the lords of trade, inclosing an order from the privy council, and re- _{May 27.} commended to them to stop all processes in law, respecting any disputes of the borderers, till the boundaries should be determined.[1] During the same session, he reminded them of the order, and desired them to consider it; telling them that he had *no advice* of the appointment of commissioners. His _{July 4.} meaning was, that the commission itself, in which they were named, had not been sent to him; nor was he actually informed that it was in America, till after he had prorogued the assemblies of both provinces to the fourth of August. In obedience to the royal order, the assembly of Massachusetts appointed Josiah Willard, secretary, and Edward Winslow, sheriff of Suf- _{July 5.} folk, to be the two public officers; on whom, or at whose place of abode, any notice, summons, or other process of the commissioners, might be served.

On the day appointed, eight of the commissioners met at Hampton.* They published their commission, opened their court, chose William Parker their clerk, and George _{Aug. 1.} Mitchel, surveyor. On the same day, the committee of eight, who had been appointed by the assembly of New-Hampshire, in April, appeared; and delivered a paper to the court, reciting the order of the king, for the appointment of two public officers; al-

(1) Journal of Assembly.

From Nova-Scotia.
William Skene, President,
Erasmus James Phillips,
Otho Hamilton.

From Rhode-Island.
Samuel Vernon,
John Gardner,
John Potter,
Ezekiel Warner,
George Cornel.

leging that the assembly had not been convened since the arrival
of that order ; but, that there should be no failure for want of such
officers, *they* appointed Richard Waldron, secretary, and Eleazar
Russell, sheriff.[1] They also delivered the claim and demand of
New-Hampshire, in the following words. ' That the southern
' boundary of said province should begin at the end of three miles
' north from the middle of the channel of Merrimack river, where
' it runs into the Atlantic ocean ; and from thence should run, on
' a straight line, west, up into the main land (toward the south sea)
' until it meets his majesty's other governments. And that the
' northern boundary of New-Hampshire should begin at the en-
' trance of Pascataqua harbor, and so pass up the same, into the
' river of Newichwannock, and through the same, into the farthest
' head thereof ; and from thence northwestward, (that is, north,
' less than a quarter of a point, westwardly) as far as the British
' dominion extends ; and also the western half of the Isles of
' Shoals, we say, lies within the province of New-Hampshire.'[2]

The same day, Thomas Berry and Benjamin Lynde, counsellors of Massachusetts, appeared and delivered the vote of their
assembly, appointing two public officers, with a letter from the
secretary, by order of the governor, purporting, that ' at the last
' rising of the assembly, there was *no account* that any commission
' had arrived ; that the assembly stood prorogued to the fourth
' of August ; that a committee had been appointed, to draw up a
' state of their demands, which would be reported at the next
' session, and therefore praying that this short delay might not
' operate to their disadvantage.' Upon this, the committtee of
New-Hampshire drew up and presented another paper,
Aug. 2. charging the government of Massachusetts with ' great
' backwardness, and aversion to any measures, which had a ten-
' dency to the settlement of this long subsisting controversy ; and
' also charging their agent, in England, with having used all im-
' aginable artifices, to delay the issue ; for which reason, the
' agent of New-Hampshire had petitioned the king, to give direc-
' tions, that each party might be fully prepared, to give in a state
' of their demands, *at the first meeting* of the commissioners ;
' which direction they had faithfully observed, to the utmost of
' their power ; and as the assembly of Massachusetts had made
' no seasonable preparation, they did, in behalf of New-Hamp-
' shire, except and protest against any claim or evidence being
' received from them, and pray the court to proceed *ex parte*,
' agreeably to the commission.'[3]

It was alleged in favor of Massachusetts, that by the first meeting of the commissioners could not be meant the first day, but the
first session. The court understood the word in this sense, and

(1) MS. original Minutes by Mr. Parker.   (2) MS. Minutes, and Massachusetts Journal, p. 34.   (3) MS. Minutes.

resolved, that Massachusetts should be allowed time, till the eighth of August, and no longer, to bring in their claims; and that if they should fail, the court would proceed *ex parte*. The court then adjourned to the eighth day.

The assembly of New-Hampshire met on the fourth; and the secretary, by the governor's order, prorogued them to the tenth, then to meet at Hampton-Falls. On the same day, Aug. 4. the assembly of Massachusetts met at Boston; and after they had received the report of the committee, who had drawn up their claim, and despatched expresses to New-York and New-Jersey, to expedite the other commissioners; and appointed a committee to support their claims;* the governor adjourned them, to the tenth day, then to meet at Salisbury. Thus the assemblies of both provinces were drawn within five miles of each other; and the governor declared, in his speech, that he would ' act as a ' common father to both.'[1]

The claim of Massachusetts being prepared, was delivered to the court, on the day appointed. After reciting their grant Aug. 8. and charters and the judicial determination in 1677, they asserted their ' claim and demand, still to hold and possess, by a ' boundary line, on the southerly side of New-Hampshire, begin- ' ning at the sea, three English miles north from the Black Rocks, ' so called, at the mouth of the river Merrimack, as it emptied ' itself into the sea sixty years ago; thence running parallel with ' the river, as far northward as the crotch or parting of the river; ' thence due north, as far as a certain tree, commonly known for ' more than seventy years past, by the name of Endecott's tree; ' standing three miles northward of said crotch or parting of Mer- ' rimack river; and thence, due west to the south sea; which, ' (they said) they were able to prove, by ancient and incontestible ' evidence, were the bounds intended, granted, and adjudged to ' them; and they insisted on the grant and settlements as above ' said, to be conclusive and irrefragable.[2]

' On the northerly side of New-Hampshire, they claimed a ' boundary line, beginning at the entrance of Pascataqua harbor; ' passing up the same, to the river Newichwannock; through that ' to the farthest head thereof, and from thence a due north west ' line, till one hundred and twenty miles from the mouth of Pas- ' cataqua harbor be finished.'

(1) Massachusetts Assembly Records.   (2) Journal, p. 6.

* This committee consisted of Edmund Quincy, William Dudley, Samuel Welles, Thomas Berry, and Benjamin Lynde, of the council; and ELISHA COOKE, Thomas Cushing, Job Almy, Henry Rolfe, and Nathaniel Peaslee, of the house. Cooke died while the commissioners were sitting. He had been employed on the same affair at Newbury in 1731, and it was by his means that the business was then obstructed. In reference to this, Belcher, in a private letter says, ' Generations to come will rise up and call him *cursed*.' On account of Cooke's death, and the absence of another member, they appointed John Read and Robert Auchmuty. August 13.

The court ordered copies of the claims of each province, to
be drawn and exchanged ; and having appointed Benjamin Rolfe
of Boston,* an additional clerk, they adjourned to the tenth of
the month.

On that day, both assemblies met at the appointed places.   A
cavalcade was formed from Boston to Salisbury, and the governor
Aug. 10. rode in state, attended by a troop of horse.†   He was
met at Newbury ferry by another troop ; who, joined by
three more at the supposed divisional line, conducted him to the
George tavern, at Hampton-Falls ; where he held a council and
made a speech to the assembly of New-Hampshire.   Whilst
both assemblies were in session ; the governor, with a select company, made an excursion, of three days, to the falls of Amuskeag ;
an account of which was published in the papers, and concluded
in the following manner :   ' His excellency was much pleased
' with the fine soil of Chester, the extraordinary improvements at
' Derry, and the mighty falls at Skeag.'[1]

In the speech, which the governor made to the assembly of
New-Hampshire, he recommended to them to appoint two officers,
agreeably to his majesty's commission.   The assembly appeared
to be much surprised at this speech ; and in their answer, said,
that ' the committee before appointed had already given in the
' names of two officers, which they approved of ; for had it not
' been done, at the first meeting of the commissioners, they might
' have proceeded ex parte.'[2]

Considering the temper and views of Mr. Belcher's opponents,
this was rather unfortunate for him, so soon after his profession of
being ' a common father to both provinces.'   For if the committee had a right to nominate the two officers, then his recommendation was needless ; if they had not, it might justly be asked,

(1) Boston Weekly News Letter, Aug. 25.   (2) Assembly Journal and
printed brief.

* [Benjamin Rolfe was afterwards one of the early settlers of Concord, then
called Rumford, where he died 20 December, 1771. He graduated at Harvard college in 1727, and for some time was the only magistrate in Concord.
He married Sarah, daughter of Rev. Timothy Walker, and she, after the death
of Mr. Rolfe, became the wife of Benjamin Thompson, afterward the distinguished German count, who from his early residence in New-Hampshire, took
the name of Rumford.]

† This procession occasioned the following pasquinade, in an assumed
Hibernian style.
        ' Dear Paddy, you ne'er did behold such a sight,
    As yesterday morning was seen before night.
    You in all your born days saw, nor I didn't neither,
    So many fine horses and men ride together.
    At the head, the lower house trotted two in a row,
    Then all the higher house pranced after the low ;
    Then the governor's coach gallop'd on like the wind,
    And the last that came foremost were troopers behind ;
    But I fear it means no good, to your neck or mine ;
    For they say 'tis to fix a right place for the line.'
                        Collection of Poems, p. 54.

why did he not call the assembly together, on the sixth of July, to which day they had been prorogued ? The excuse was, that he did it, to avoid any objection, which might be made to the regularity of their appointment ; and to give them an opportunity to ratify and confirm it. The truth was, that Mr. Belcher highly resented the conduct of the committee of New-Hampshire, who concealed the commission, and never communicated it to him in form. Had he been aware of the use, which his enemies might make, of his rigid adherence to forms, when he could not but know the contents of the commission, and the time when it must be executed, prudence might have dictated a more flexible conduct. They did not fail, to make the utmost advantage of his mistakes, to serve the main cause which they had in view.

The expresses which were sent by Massachusetts, to call the other commissioners, had no other effect than to add to the number, Philip Livingston, from New-York ; who, being senior in nomination, presided in the court.

To prevent the delay, which would unavoidably attend the taking of plans from actual surveys ; the commissioners recommended, to both assemblies, to agree upon a plan, by which the pretensions of each province should be understood ; but as this could not be done, a plan drawn by Mitchel was accepted, and when their result was made, this plan was annexed to it. They then proceeded to hear the answers, which each party made, to the demands of the other, and to examine witnesses on both sides. Neither party was willing to admit the evidence, produced by the other, and mutual exceptions and protests were entered. The points in debate were, whether Merrimack river, at that time, emptied itself into the sea, at the same place where it did sixty years before ? Whether it bore the same name, from the sea, up to the crotch ? and whether it were possible to draw a parallel line, three miles northward, of every part of a river ; the course of which was, in some places, from north to south ?

With respect to the boundary line, between New-Hampshire and Maine, the controverted points were, whether it should run up the middle of the river, or on its north-eastern shore ; and whether the line, from the head of the river, should be due northwest, or only a few degrees westward of north.

The grand point on which the whole controversy respecting the southern line turned, was, whether the charter of William and Mary granted to Massachusetts, all the lands which were granted, by the charter of Charles the First ? On this question, the commissioners did not come to any conclusion. Reasons of policy might have some weight, to render them indecisive ; but, whether it were really so or not, they made and pronounced their result in the following words. In ' pursuance of his majesty's commission, ' the court took under consideration, the evidences, pleas, and ' allegations offered and made by each party ; and upon mature

' advisement on the whole, a doubt arose in point of law ; and
' the court thereupon came to the following resolution.   That if the
' charter of King William and Queen Mary, grants to the province of
' Massachusetts Bay, all the lands granted by the charter of King
' Charles the First, lying to the northward of Merrimack river ;
' then the court adjudge and determine, that a line shall run, par-
' allel with the said river, at the distance of three English miles,
' north from the mouth of the said river, beginning at the south-
' erly side of the Black Rocks, so called, at low water mark and
' thence to run to the crotch, where the rivers of Pemigewasset
' and Winnipiseogee meet ; and from thence due north three
' miles, and from thence due west, toward the south sea, until it
' meets with his majesty's other governments ; which shall be the
' boundary or dividing line, between the said provinces of Mas-
' sachusetts and New-Hampshire, on that side.   But, if other-
' wise, then the court adjudge and determine, that a line on the
' southerly side of New-Hampshire, beginning at the distance of
' three miles north, from the southerly side of the Black Rocks
' aforesaid, at low water mark, and from thence running due west,
' up into the main land, toward the south sea, until it meets with his
' majesty's other governments, shall be the boundary line between
' the said provinces, on the side aforesaid : Which point in doubt,
' the court humbly submit, to the wise consideration of his most
' sacred majesty, in his privy council ; to be determined accord-
' ing to his royal will and pleasure.

' As to the northern boundary, between the said provinces, the
' court resolve and determine ; that the dividing line shall pass
' through the mouth of Pascataqua harbor, and up the middle of
' the river of Newichwannock, (part of which is now called Sal-
' mon-Falls) and through the middle of the same, to the farthest
' head thereof, and from thence north, two degrees westerly, un-
' til one hundred and twenty miles be finished, from the mouth
' of Pascataqua harbor, aforesaid ; or until it meets with his maj-
' esty's other governments.   And, that the dividing line shall part
' the Isles of Shoals, and run through the middle of the harbor,
' between the islands, to the sea, on the southerly side ; and that
' the southwesterly part of said islands shall lie in, and be account-
' ed part of, the province of New-Hampshire ; and that the north-
' easterly part thereof shall lie in, and be accounted part of, the
' province of Massachusetts Bay ; and be held and enjoyed by
' the said provinces respectively, in the same manner as they now
' do, and have heretofore held and enjoyed the same.

' And the court do further adjudge, that the cost and charge
' arising by taking out the commission, and also of the commis-
' sioners and their officers, viz. the two clerks, surveyor and wait-
' er, for their travelling expenses, and attendance in the execu-
' tion of the same, be equally borne by the said provinces.'[1]

(1) MS. Copy Journal of Massachusetts Assembly, p. 35.

Thus this long depending question, after all the time, expense and argument, which it has occasioned, remained undecided.

When this evasive decree was published, the commissioners adjourned, to the fourteenth of October, to receive appeals ; and the same day, the governor, at the request of the council only, adjourned the assembly of New-Hampshire to the twelfth of October. By this sudden adjournment, it was impossible for them to obtain a copy of the decree, before their dispersion, or to frame an appeal, till two days before the time, when it must have been presented. The assembly of Massachusetts continued their session, at Salisbury, five days longer. On the fifth of September, they obtained copies of the royal commission, and the decree of the commissioners, which they entered on their journal. On the sixth, they agreed upon an appeal ; and on the seventh, at the united request of both houses, the governor adjourned them to the 12th of October.

The sudden adjournment of the assembly of New-Hampshire, when that of Massachusetts continued their session, was unfortunate for Governor Belcher ; and gave his opponents another advantage, to pursue their grand design against him. The reasons assigned for it were, that the report of the commissioners being special, the whole matter would of course come before the king, without any appeal from either province. For this reason, a majority of the council were against an appeal. That as the committee, appointed in April, had the same power to act in the recess, as in the session of the assembly ; and, as the council were against appealing ; so the appeal could not be made, by the whole assembly, and therefore the governor thought, that the best service which he could do to the province, was to adjourn the assembly, and leave the whole business in the hands of the committee. With respect to the short time, between the 12th and 14th of October, it was observed, that the claim of New-Hampshire was contained in a few lines, and their exceptions to the judgment of the commissioners might be prepared in a quarter of an hour.[1]

Both assemblies met again, in the same places, at the appointed time. The representatives of New-Hampshire having, by the help of their committee, in the recess of the assembly, obtained the papers, framed their exceptions and sent a message, to know if the council were sitting ; but the council being determined against an appeal, had met and adjourned, without doing any business. The house therefore was reduced to the necessity of desiring the commissioners to receive their appeal, without the concurrence of the governor and council. The appeal, from the assembly of Massachusetts, was presented in due form, authenticated by the speaker, secretary and governor. Their committee

Oct. 12.

(1) Printed brief.

entered a protest against the appeal of New-Hampshire, because it was not an act of the whole legislature ; nevertheless, the commissioners received it, and entered it on their minutes.   Having received these appeals, the commissioners adjourned their court to the first of August, in the next year, but they never met again.

The assembly of Massachusetts appointed Edmund Quincy and Richard Partridge agents, to join with Francis Wilks, their former agent, in the prosecution of their appeal before the king ; and raised the sum of two thousand pounds sterling, to defray the expense.[1]

When the representatives of New-Hampshire proposed the raising of money, to prosecute their appeal, the council nonconcurred the vote.[2]   Their reasons were, that the appeal was not an act of the council ; that they had no voice in the appointment of the agent ; and, that at the beginning of the affair, the house had declared to the council, that the expense of it would be defrayed by *private subscription.*

At this session of the Massachusetts assembly, Mr. Belcher put them in mind that he had suffered in his interest, by the continually sinking value of their bills of credit, in which his salary was paid ; a point which he had, often before, urged them to consider.   In answer to this message, they made him a grant of £333, 6, 8, in bills of the new tenor.[3]   The same day, they made a grant of the like sum, to the president of Harvard college.   Both these sums appear to have been justly due ; and at any other time, no exception could have been made to either.   But, because the grant to the governor happened to be made, at the same time with the grant of £2000 sterling to the agents, his opponents pretended, that he received it as a bribe, from the assembly of Massachusetts, for favoring their cause.

The appeal of New-Hampshire, from the judgment of the commissioners, was founded on the following reasons.   With respect to the southerly line ; because it made the Black Rocks, lying in a bay of Merrimack river, the point from which the three miles were to be measured ; which point was three quarters of a mile north of the river's mouth ; and, because a line, parallel with the river, was not only impracticable, but founded on the old charter, which had been vacated ; and, if practicable, yet ought not to go farther than the river held a westerly course.   With respect to the northern boundary, they objected to that part of the judgment only, which directed the line to run up the middle of the river ; alleging that the grant to Gorges was only of land, between that river and Kennebeck ; and that New-Hampshire had always been in possession of the whole river, and had maintained a fortress which commanded its entrance.[4]

The appeal of Massachusetts was grounded on the following reasons.   That by the charter of William and Mary, the old colony of Massachusetts was re-incorporated without any exception ; that this charter empowered the governor and general assembly to grant all lands, comprehended in the old colony ; that the committee of New-Hampshire acknowledged, that New-Hampshire lay without the late colony of Massachusetts, by declaring that it was between that and the province of Maine ; that the west line, claimed by New-Hampshire, would cross Merrimack river, thirty miles from its mouth, and exclude forty miles of said said river out of Massachusetts, though declared, by both charters, to be in it.   They objected to extending the line of New-Hampshire till it should meet with his majesty's other governments ; because according to *Mason's grant*, New-Hampshire could extend no farther than sixty miles from the sea.   With respect to the northern boundary, they objected to a line north, two degrees westwardly, alleging that it ought to be on the northwest point ; they also excepted to the protraction of this line, till it should meet with his majesty's other governments ; alleging that it ought to extend no farther than one hundred and twenty miles, the fixed limits of the province of Maine.

It was unfortunate for Massachusetts that their committee had brought Mason's grant, in evidence to the commissioners, and again recited it in their appeal ; for a line of sixty miles from the sea would cross Merrimack river, long before the similar curve line, for which they contended, could be completed.   Besides, Mason's grant extended to Naumkeag ; which was much further southward, than they would have been willing to admit.

It may seem curious and unaccountable to most readers, that the commissioners should determine the northern, or rather eastern bounds of the northern part of New-Hampshire, to be a line drawn *north, two degrees westerly*, from the head of Salmon-fall river ; when the express words of Gorges' patent are ' north westward.'   The agents for Massachusetts, when this claim was put in by New-Hampshire, could hardly think it was seriously meant, when it was alleged that by northwestward must be understood, north *a little* westward.[1]   The only ostensible reason, given for this construction was, that if a northwest line had been intended, then a southeast line, drawn from the mouth of the harbor, would leave all the Isles of Shoals in New-Hampshire; whereas, the dividing line runs between them.[2]   On the other side, it might have been said, with equal propriety, that a line drawn south, two degrees east, from the mouth of the harbor, would leave all these islands in Massachusetts.   For the point where the islands are divided bears south, twenty-nine degrees east, from the middle of the harbor's mouth; the variation of the needle being six degrees west.[3]

(1) Hutch. ii. 389.   (2) MS. minutes of the commissioners.   (3) [As] observed 1781.

When this affair was again agitated in England, the agents of Massachusetts obtained a certificate from the learned Dr. Halley, that a line northwestward ought to run forty-five degrees westward of the north point. This was demonstratively true; but there were political reasons for dissenting from mathematical demonstration. One of them is thus expressed, in a private letter, from a committee of the assembly, to their agent Thomlinson. ' We ' hope that the northern line will be but a few degrees to the west- ' ward of north, that his majesty's province may include the great- ' est number, and best mast trees for the royal navy.' Though this thought might never have occurred to a mathematician, yet some of the commissioners were doubtless acquainted with it; and it was too important, not to have been communicated to the king's ministers. Another political reason of dissent was, that by enlarging New-Hampshire, there would be a better prospect of obtaining a distinct governor, which was the grand object in view.

The new agent of Massachusetts, Edmund Quincy, died of the small pox, soon after his arrival in London. The affair was then

1738. left in the hands of Wilks and Partridge, neither of whom understood so much of the controversy as Thomlinson; who was also far superior to them in address. In his letters, to his friends in New-Hampshire, he frequently blames them for their negligence, in not sending to him the necessary papers in proper season; and when sent, for the want of correctness and regularity in them. But their deficiency was abundantly compensated by the dexterity of his solicitor, Parris; who drew up a long ' petition of appeal;' in which, all the circumstances, attending the whole transaction, from the beginning, were recited, and colored, in such a manner, as to asperse the governor and assembly of ' the vast, opulent, overgrown province of Massachusetts;' while ' the poor, little, loyal, distressed province of New-Hamp- ' shire' was represented as ready to be devoured, and the king's own property and possessions swallowed up, by the boundless rapacity of the charter government. Concerning the manner in which this masterly philippic was framed, and the principal object at which it was directed, there can be no better evidence, than that which is contained in a letter, written by Parris to Thomlinson, and by him sent to New-Hampshire. ' Two nights ago, I

Feb. 4. ' received a heap of papers from you, about the lines; ' and have been four times to the colony office, and board ' of trade, to discover what I could in this imperfect affair; but ' cannot see the case, till after Tuesday next. Notwithstanding ' which, I have, as well as I can, *without proper materials*, drawn ' up a long petition of appeal, to his majesty; and as the Massa- ' chusetts have not yet presented theirs, I send you the draught ' of it, and hope we shall have our appeal, as well as the petition, ' from the New-Hampshire assembly, in, before the Massachusetts ' get theirs in. Had your principals considered the great conse-

' quence of being first, surely, in all this time, they would have
' sent you a copy of their proceedings, in order to have enabled
' us to be first ; but, as it is, I am forced to *guess* at matters, and
' *affirm facts at adventure*, or upon dubious passages in letters ;
' which is a sad way of proceeding, and I wish we do not mistake
' some facts. They oblige us to make bricks without straw.—
' Above all, why did they not send a copy of their own appeal ?
' For want of it, I have been forced to *guess* what that appeal
' was, from loose passages in Mr. A.'s letters. Beg them, im-
' mediately to order, an exact copy to be made of all their votes,
' from March to October last. Had these votes come over regu-
' larly and authentically, his *Excellency* would have been *shaken*
' *quite down*, in a few weeks by them. You'll observe, I have
' *laid it on him* pretty handsomely, in my petition to the king.'*

Thus the petition of appeal became a petition of complaint,
against the governor and assembly of Massachusetts. Copies
were delivered to their agents, and the governor was ordered to
make answer to the allegations against him. At the same time,
Thomlinson advised his friends in New-Hampshire, to prepare
their proofs, as *silently* as possible ; and by no means to give any
offence to the governor ; assuring them of the favorable disposition
of several lords of the privy council, as well as the board of trade,
toward their cause ; and that they had need to be in no pain,
about the event.[1]

The death of Mr. Quincy at this critical moment, and the length
of time necessary to prepare and send over answers, to the complaint which Parris had thus artfully drawn up, obliged the agents
of Massachusetts to suspend the presenting of their appeal for
several months.

CHAPTER XVIII.

Revival of Mason's claim. Accusations against Belcher, real and forged.
Royal censure. Final establishment of the lines. Hutchinson's agency.
Spanish war. Belcher's zeal and fidelity. His removal. Examination of
his character.

THE spirit of intrigue was not confined to New-Hampshire ;
for the politicians of Massachusetts, by bringing into view the long
dormant claim of Mason, had another game to play, besides proving
the small extent of New-Hampshire. They perceived that the

(1) Thomlinson's MS. letters.

* This petition is printed at large, in the Journal of the Massachusetts assembly for 1738, with their vindication annexed, in which they call the petition ' a chain of blundering, if not malicious falsehood.'

line, whether settled according to their own demand or that of
New-Hampshire, would cut off a considerable part of several of
their townships; and though they had, by their agent, obtained a
promise, that private property should not be affected by the line
of jurisdiction, yet they thought it best to have some other security.

For what reason the government of Massachusetts did not
purchase the province of New-Hampshire, from Robert Mason,
at the same time (1677) that they purchased the province of
Maine, from the heirs of Gorges, we are not now able precisely
to determine. It is probable that the purchase might then have
been easily made, and much controversy prevented. When it
was sold, by John and Robert Mason, to Samuel Allen (1691)
the bargain was made in England; and the lands were, by fiction
of law, supposed to be there;* by which means, the process respecting the fine and recovery was carried on in the court of king's
bench. During the lives of the two Masons, no notice was taken
of the supposed flaw; and the sale to Allen was not disputed.
The brothers returned to America. John, the elder, died
without issue. Robert married in New-England, and had a son;
who, after the death of his father, conceived hopes of invalidating
Allen's purchase, and regaining his paternal inheritance; which
it was supposed could not have been transferred by his father and
uncle, for any longer term, than their own lives. It was also said
that the fiction, by which the lands were described, to be within
the jurisdiction of the courts of Westminster hall, rendered the
proceedings void; and therefore that the entail was still good.
Filled with these ideas, he made strenuous exertions, to acquire
money, to assist him in realizing his expectations; but died in the
midst of his days, (1718) at the Havana, whither he had made a
voyage with this view. His eldest son, John Tufton, was bred to
a mechanical employment in Boston; and came of age, about the
time in which the controversy between the two provinces was in
agitation. He inherited the enterprising spirit of his ancestors,
and the public controversy called his attention to his interest. On
this young man, the politicians cast their eyes; and having consulted counsel on the validity of his claim, and the defect of the
transfer, they encouraged him to hope, that this was the most
favorable time to assert his pretensions.[1] Had they purchased his
claim at once; they might doubtless have obtained it for a trifle,
and have greatly embarrassed the views of their antagonists. Instead of such a stroke of liberal policy, they treated with him,

(1) MS. copy of Read's and Auchmuty's opinions.

* In the process by which the entail was then docked, the situation of the
land is expressed in these words :
‘ In New-Hampshire, Main, Masonia, Laconia, Mason-hall and Mariana,
in New-England, in America, in the parish of Greenwich.’ MS. in Proprietary Office.

concerning the release all of those lands, in Salisbury, Amesbury, Haverhill, Methuen and Dracut, which the line would cut off; and, for five hundred pounds currency, obtained a quit-claim of twenty-three thousand six hundred and seventy-five acres. They also admitted his memorial to the assembly; in which he represented to them, that his interest might probably be affected, by the final determination of the line, and praying that the province would be at the expense of his voyage to England, to take proper measures for securing it.[1] To this, they consented, on condition that he should prove his descent from Captain John Mason, the original patentee.* Depositions were accordingly taken in both provinces, to which the public seals were affixed; and they put him under the direction of their agents, ordering his expenses to be paid, as long as they should judge his presence in England serviceable to their views.[2]

July 1.

The agents stated his case to their counsel, the king's solicitor; and asked his opinion how they should proceed; but he advised them, not to bring him into view, lest the lords should think it an artifice, intended to perplex the main cause. On this consideration, they dismissed him from any farther attendance; and paid his expenses, amounting to above ninety pounds sterling.† [3]

(1) Journal of Assembly. (2) MS. copies in the proprietary office.—
(3) Agent's letters in Secretary's office of Massachusetts.

* [His descent from the original proprietor of New-Hampshire will appear from the following:

Capt. John Mason was born at Lynn-:::Anne, his wife, who survived him. Regis, in Norfolk, and died in Nov. |
1635.
                    Jane Mason:::Joseph Tufton, (see p. 16.]
                        |

John Tufton, who took the name of Mason and died sine prole.	Robert Tufton, who took::: —— the name of Mason and | died in 1688, aged 56.	Anne Tufton, who died 1677, sine prole.
John Tufton Mason, who died in Virginia, sine prole.	Robert Tufton Mason, who:::Catharine Wiggin. lived in Portsmouth, and was lost at sea in 1696.	
John Tufton Mason,::: —— who died at Havana, in 1718.	Elizabeth Mason, and several others	
John Tufton Mason, mariner of Boston, born about 1713, in whom the title was revived in 1738.	Thomas Tufton Mason, who was a minor in 1738.]	

† Mr. Hutchinson, in his history of Massachusetts, has passed over this whole transaction in silence; though it is well known that he was one of the managers of it. See Journal of Mass. Rep. June 2, 1738, p. 11.

Such a transaction, though conducted as privately as the nature of the thing would admit, did not escape the vigilance of Thomlinson ; who, on finding Mason detached from the agents of Massachusetts, entered into an agreement with him, for the release of his whole interest, to the assembly of New-Hampshire ; in consideration of the payment of one thousand pounds, currency of New-England. This manœuvre served to strengthen the interest of New-Hampshire, and Thomlinson was much applauded for his dexterity. He had the strongest inducement, to continue his efforts in their favor ; for no less than twelve hundred pounds sterling had been already expended, in prosecuting the affair of the line ; which sum had been advanced by himself and Rindge. There was no prospect of repayment, unless the province could be put under a separate governor ; and this point could not be obtained, till the removal of Belcher.

The agents of Massachusetts, after a long delay, presented their appeal ; and followed it with a petition, for the benefit of their former protests, against the New-Hampshire appeal ; objecting also to its regularity, as it contained matters of personal complaint, against the governor ; which had been no part of the records of the commissioners.[1] Thomlinson finding this new petition thrown in his way, applied for its being immediately heard ; and at the Nov. 30. hearing, it was dismissed, but without prejudice to the agents of Massachusetts being permitted, to object against the regularity of the New-Hampshire appeal, when it should come to a hearing. Such were the complaints against the governor, and the importunity of his adversaries to prosecute them, that it was necessary to hear and despatch them, before the appeal respecting the lines could be brought forward.

It must be remembered, that Mr. Belcher had enemies, in his government of Massachusetts as well as New-Hampshire, who united their efforts to obtain his removal from both ; but as they supposed him more vulnerable in his capacity of governor of New-Hampshire, so they joined in strengthening the complaints, from that quarter, as a preparatory step, to effect his complete removal. Whilst he was engaged, in preparing for his defence, against the charges, in the petition of appeal, other attacks were meditating, which were conducted with such *silence* that it was impossible for him to guard against their effects. One of 1739. these was a letter, purporting to have been written at Ex-May 5. eter, subscribed by five persons, said to be inhabitants of that town, and directed to Sir Charles Wager, first lord of the admiralty. In this letter, it was said, that ' finding his lordship ' had ordered the judge advocate of the court of admiralty to in-' quire into the riot, which had been committed there, (1734) and

(1) July 18–October 9. Printed brief and MS. letters.

' the assault of the surveyor and his officers ; and fearing to be
' brought into trouble on that account, they would confess the
' whole truth.   That they had been indulged, by former survey-
' ors, in cutting all sorts of pine trees, till the appointment of
' Colonel Dunbar to that office ; who had restrained and prose-
' cuted them ; but that Governor Belcher had privately given
' them encouragement to go on ; by assuring them that they had
' the best right to the trees ; that the laws were iniquitous, and
' ought not to be regarded ; that although he must make a shew
' of assisting that Irish dog of a surveyor ; yet he would so man-
' age it with the council and justices, who were under his influ-
' ence, that they should not suffer ; and further to encourage
' them, he had made several of them justices of the peace, and
' officers of militia.   That he had also told them not to fear any
' inquiry into their conduct ; for that he would write to the board
' of admiralty, in their favor ; and boasted that he had such an
' influence over their lordships, that they would believe every
' thing which he should say.   That as they had now confessed
' the truth, they hoped to be forgiven, and not prosecuted in the
' admiralty court ; and begged that this information might be kept
' secret till the governor's removal, which they hoped would soon
' be effected.   That whatever might have been said to the con-
' trary, they could assure him that the province of New-Hamp-
' shire contained the largest number of pine trees, and of the best
' quality, in all his majesty's American dominions ; and, for fur-
' ther information, they referred his lordship to several persons
' then in London, particularly to Mr. Wentworth and Mr. Waldo ;
' the latter of whom, was agent to Mr. Gulston, for procuring
' masts for the royal navy.'[1]

On the receipt of this letter, Sir Charles, with the candor of a
gentleman, sent a copy of it to Mr. Belcher ; who immediately
ordered an inquiry ; and it was proved to be an entire forgery ;
four of the persons whose names were subscribed utterly disclaimed it, and the fifth was not to be found ; no such person being known in the town of Exeter.   The evidence of this forgery
was transmitted to England, with all possible expedition ; but not
till it had made an impression, to the disadvantage of the governor.

Another artifice used against him, was a memorial of Gulston,
the navy agent, and others ; complaining of the defenceless state
of the province ; that the fort lay in ruins, and that the militia
were without discipline ; notwithstanding the probability of a war.
This memorial was so artfully drawn, as to throw the blame of the
neglect on the governor, without mentioning his name ; which
was intended, to prevent his obtaining a copy, and being allowed
time to answer.   Another complaint was made in the form of a
letter, respecting the grant of the tract called Kingswood ; in

(1) MS. copy of Exeter letter.

which he was represented, as partial to his friends, in giving them an exclusive right, to the whole of that territory, which they deemed, the unappropriated lands of the province. Several parts of his administration were also complained of ; and in particular, the infrequency of his visits to New-Hampshire.[1] This letter was signed by six members of the council, and a majority of the representatives.

Gulston's memorial was presented to the lords of council ; and by them referred to the board of trade, accompanied by the letter ; and though Mr. Belcher's brother and son applied for copies, and time to answer, the request was evaded ; and a report was framed, in favor of putting New-Hampshire under a separate governor. When this report came before the privy council, Lord Wilmington, the president, ordered it back again ; that the governor might have that justice which his agents had asked. By this means, he had opportunity to answer in his defence ; that without money, the fort could not be repaired ; that it was not in his power to tax the people ; that he had frequently applied to the assemblies for money, to repair the fort ; to which they had constantly answered, that the people were too poor to be taxed ; and had solicited him to break through his instructions, and allow them to issue paper money, without any fund for its redemption ; that the militia had always been trained according to law ; and that he had constantly visited New-Hampshire, and held an assembly, twice in the year, unless prevented by sickness ; for which he appealed to the journals. To corroborate these pleas, the governor's friends procured five petitions, in his favor, and praying for his continuance, signed by about five hundred people. The petitions, however, did not express the sense of the majority ; who had been persuaded into a belief, that they should receive much benefit by a separate governor ; and accordingly, a counter petition being circulated, was signed by about seven hundred of the inhabitants.*

Things being thus prepared, the complaints were brought to a hearing, before the lords of council ; who reported to the king,

Nov. 21. ' that Governor Belcher had acted with great partiality, ' by proroguing the assembly of New-Hampshire, from the ' sixth of July, 1737, to the fourth of August following ; in dis- ' obedience to his majesty's order in council ; which had been ' transmitted to him by the lords of trade, and which was proved ' to have been delivered to him, in due time ; and, also by farther ' proroguing the said assembly, from the second of September, ' 1737, to the thirteenth of October ; whereby the province were

(1) Belcher's letters, MS.

* [The whole number was 662. They belonged to the towns of Hampton, Hampton-Falls, Kingston, Chester, Stratham, Exeter and Kensington. A list of their names is in the Secretary's office of New-Hampshire.]

' deprived of the time, intended by his majesty's said order, to be
' allowed them, to prepare a proper and regular appeal; thereby
' endeavoring to frustrate the intention of his majesty's commis-
' sion.'[1] This report was approved by the king; and from
this time, it may be concluded, that Mr. Belcher's removal ^{Dec. 27.}
from the government of New-Hampshire was seriously contemplated. The grant of Kingswood was also annulled; and he was
prohibited from making any other grants of land, till the lines
should be determined.

This censure being passed on the governor, and the complaints
being at an end, the way was prepared for a hearing of the appeals, from both provinces, respecting the lines; which
being had, the determination of this long controversy was ^{1740. Mar. 5.}
made on a plan entirely new. The special part of the
decree of the commissioners was set aside, and no regard was
had to their *doubt*, whether the new charter granted all the lands
comprehended in the old. It was said, that when the first grant
was made, the country was not explored. The course of the
river, though unknown, was supposed to be from west to east;
therefore it was deemed equitable, that as far as the river flowed
in that course, the parallel line at three miles distance should
extend. But as on the one hand, if by pursuing the course of
the river, up into the country, it had been found to have a southern bend, it would have been inequitable to have contracted the
Massachusetts grant; so, on the other hand, when it appeared to
have a northern bend, it was equally inequitable to enlarge it.
Therefore it was determined, ' That the northern boundary of
' the province of Massachusetts be, a similar curve line, pursuing
' the course of Merrimack river, at three miles distance, on the
' north side thereof, beginning at the Atlantic ocean, and ending
' at a point due north of Pawtucket falls; and a straight line
' drawn from thence due west, till it meets with his majesty's other
' governments.'[2] The other parts of the decree of the commissioners, respecting the northern line, and the payment of expenses,
were affirmed.

This determination exceeded the utmost expectation of New-
Hampshire; as it gave them a tract of country, fourteen miles in
breadth, and above fifty in length, more than they had ever claimed. It cut off from Massachusetts, twenty-eight new townships,
between Merrimack and Connecticut rivers; besides large tracts
of vacant land, which lay intermixed; and districts from six of
their old towns, on the north side of the Merrimack; and if, as
was then supposed, the due west line were to extend, to twenty
miles east of Hudson's river, the reputed boundary of New-York;
a vast tract of fertile country, on the western side of Connecticut
river, was annexed to New-Hampshire; by which an ample

(1) Printed brief.   (2) Council Records.

scope was given, first for landed speculation, and afterward for
cultivation, and wealth.

When this determination was known, the politicians of Massachusetts were chagrined and enraged. They talked loudly of
injustice ; and some of the more zealous proposed trying the merits
of the cause, upon the words of the charter, before the judges in
Westminster hall ; who, it was expected, would upon their oath
and honor reverse the judgment, and tell the king that he had
mistaken the meaning of the royal charter.[1] This would indeed
have been a bold stroke. But a more moderate and pusillanimous
scheme was adopted ; which was to send over a new agent, to
petition the king, that he would re-annex to their government, the
twenty-eight new townships, which had been cut off, and the districts of the six old towns. It was also thought prudent, that the
whole province should not openly appear, in the affair ; but that
petitions should be drawn, by the inhabitants of these towns, and
that the agent should be chosen by them.[2] Accordingly town
meetings were held ; petitions were prepared and subscribed ;
and Thomas Hutchinson was appointed their agent, and sent over
to England ; where he formed those connexions, which afterwards served to raise him, to the chair of government in his native province.

About the same time, Governor Belcher procured a petition,
from his six friends, of the council of New-Hampshire, to the
king ; praying that the *whole* province might be annexed to the
government of Massachusetts.[3] This matter had been long in
contemplation, with these gentlemen ; but was now produced at
the most unfortunate time, which could have been chosen. Their
petition was at once rejected. But that from the towns was kept
in suspense a long time ; till Thomlinson was prepared, to answer
all the pleas, which Hutchinson could advance, and proved too hard
an antagonist for him. It was finally dismissed,* because it was
thought ' that it never could be for his majesty's service, to annex
' any part of his province of New-Hampshire, as an increase of
' territory, to Massachusetts ; but rather, that it would be for the
' benefit of his subjects there, to be under a distinct government.'[4]

Though Belcher's removal was seriously feared, by his best
friends ; yet he had so much interest with some of the lords in high
office, that they could not be prevailed with to give him up. The
war, which had commenced between Britain and Spain, afforded
him an opportunity, to signalize his zeal for the king's service ;
and he determined to prove himself, a faithful servant to the
crown, in every instance ; in hope that a course of time and fidel-

(1) Belcher's letters.   (2) Thomlinson's observations on Massachusetts petition, MS.   (3) Thomlinson's MS. letters.   (4) Bow brief.

* The ill success of this agency was probably the reason, that Mr. Hutchin
son took no notice of it, in his history of Massachusetts.

ity might efface the impressions, which had been made, to his disadvantage.

It being resolved by the British court, to undertake an expedition to the island of Cuba, Governor Belcher, agreeably to the orders which he had received from the Duke of Newcastle, issued a proclamation, for the encouragement of men who would enlist in the service ; ' that they should be supplied ^{Apr. 29.} ' with arms and clothing ; be in the king's pay ; have a share of ' the booty which should be taken ; and be sent home, at the ex- ' piration of their time of service ; and that his majesty would ' order a number of blank commissions, to be filled up by the ' governor, and given to the officers, who should command the ' troops, to be raised in the provinces.' He afterwards pressed this matter, closely, in his speech to the assembly ; ^{Aug. 1.} and urged them, to make provision, for one hundred men, and a transport, to convey them to Virginia ; where all the colony troops were to rendezvous ; and thence to proceed, under the command of Colonel Gooch, to the place of their destination. The assembly voted, as much as they judged sufficient for this purpose ; and the governor appointed a captain, and gave him beating orders ; but the commissions and arms not being sent, according to the royal promise, no men could be enlisted in New-Hampshire. The governor received commissions and arms for four companies to be raised in Massachusetts ; where he could easily have enlisted ten, had he been furnished according to the engagement.[1] To this failure and not to any want of exertion, on his part, in either of his governments, may be ascribed the paucity of troops raised in them ; and yet his enemies failed not of blaming him on this account. The representatives of New-Hampshire took this occasion to frame a vote, disapproving his administra- ^{August.} tion ; and upon this vote, their agent founded another battery, to attack his character.[2]

In conformity to the royal determination of the boundaries, orders were given to Belcher, to apply to both his govern- ments, to join in appointing surveyors, to run out, and mark ^{1741.} the lines ; and that if either should refuse, the other should proceed *ex parte.* The assembly of Massachusetts delayed giving an answer in season, which was construed a denial. The assembly of New-Hampshire appointed three surveyors, to execute the service, who were commissioned by the governor. They were directed to allow ten degrees, for the westerly variation of the needle ; and the work was performed in the months of February and March. George Mitchell surveyed and marked the similar curve line, from the ocean, three miles north of Merrimack river, to a station north of Pawtucket falls, in the township of Dracut. Richard Hazzen began at that station and marked the west line, across

(1) Belcher's letters.   (2) Thomlinson's letters.

Connecticut river, to the supposed boundary line of New-Hampshire. Walter Bryent began the line, from the head of Salmonfalls river, and marked it about thirty miles ; but was prevented from proceeding farther, partly by the breaking up of the rivers, which rendered travelling impracticable ; and partly by meeting a company of Indians who were hunting, and took his men for a scouting party. In their return, they found on one of the trees, which they had marked, ' the figure of a man's hand grasping a ' sword ;' which they interpreted, as a signal of defiance, from the Indians.[1]

The return of these lines to the board of trade was one of the last acts of Mr. Belcher's administration. His enemies in both governments were indefatigable in their endeavors to remove him ; and by their incessant applications to the ministry ; by taking every advantage of his mistakes ; by falsehood and misrepresentation ; and finally, by the diabolical arts of forgery and perjury, they accomplished their views.[2] He was succeeded in the government of Massachusetts, by William Shirley ; and in New-Hampshire, by Benning Wentworth.

At this distance of time, when all these parties are extinct, and every reader may be supposed impartial ; it may seem rather strange, that Governor Belcher should meet with such treatment, from the British court, in the reign of so mild and just a prince, as George the Second. That Mr. Belcher was imprudent and unguarded, in some instances, cannot be denied. He was indeed zealous to serve his friends, and hearken to their advice ; but, by this means, he laid himself open, to the attacks of his enemies ; to whom he paid no court, but openly treated them with contempt. His language to them was severe and reproachful, and he never spared to tell the world, what he thought of them.

This provoked them ; but they had the art to conceal their resentment, and carry on their designs, in silence, till they were ripe for execution. He had by far too mean an opinion of their abilities, and the interest which they had at court ; and when he knew that they had the ear of the lords of trade, he affected to think them, ' not very mighty lords, nor able to administer life and death.' He had a consciousness of the general integrity of his own intentions ; and appears to have been influenced, by motives of honor and justice ; but he was not aware of the force of his own prejudices. It may admit of doubt, whether, considering the extreme delicacy of his situation, it were within the compass of human policy, to have conducted so as to give offence to neither of his provinces, in the management of such a controversy ; but it is certain, that his antagonists could not fairly fix but one real stigma, on his character ; and that when impartially examined, can

(1) MS. returns in the files. Bryent's Journal. (2) Douglass, i. 481.—
Hutch. ii. 397.

amount to no more than an imprudent step, at a critical time, grounded on an undue resentment of an affront; for to suppose that his *intention* was to frustrate the commission, is inconsistent with the whole tenor of his public declarations, and private correspondence. When his enemies met him on fair and open ground, he was always prepared to answer; but it was impossible to guard against their secret attacks. If the cause which they meant to serve was a good one, why did they employ the basest means to effect it?

The cruelty and hardship of his case may appear from the following considerations. He had been one of the principal merchants of New-England; but, on his appointment, to the chair of government, quitted every other kind of business, that he might attend with punctuality, and dignity to the duties of his station. [1] By the royal instructions, he was restrained from giving his assent, to any grant of money, to himself; unless it should be a permanent salary. What he received from New-Hampshire was fixed, and paid out of the excise; but the assembly of Massachusetts could not be persuaded, to settle any salary upon him. They made him a grant of three thousand pounds, (worth about seven or eight hundred sterling) generally once in a year, at their session in May. He was then obliged to solicit leave from the king, to accept the grant, and sign the bill; and sometimes could not obtain this leave till the end of the year; once not till five days before the dissolution of the assembly. In the mean time, he was obliged to subsist on his own estate; and had he died within the year, the grant would have been wholly lost, to his family. He was earnest to obtain a general permission to sign these grants; but in that case, the clerks of offices, in England, through whose hands the permission must have passed, would have lost their fees. He was now in the sixtieth year of his age; he had a family of children and grand children, whose sole dependence was on him; and he thought with reason, that if his course of faithful service, and the unworthy arts of his enemies had been duly considered; the censure of his superiors would have been less severe, than ' to deprive him of his bread and honor.'

Whilst he entertained the worst opinion possible of the characters of his enemies, he had a strong confidence, in the justice of the government, before which he was accused. In one of his letters to his son, he says, ' I must expect no favor while Bladen ' is at the board of trade; but where the devil there, I should ex- ' pect justice, under the British constitution, corroborated by the ' Hanover succession.' The event proved, that his confidence was not ill founded. For, on being superseded, he repaired to court; where, though his presence was unwelcome to some, yet he had opportunity to bring the most convincing evidence of his

(1) Belcher's letter to Doddington, MS.

integrity, and of the base designs of his enemies. He was so far restored to the royal favor, that he obtained a promise, of the first vacant government in America, which would be worthy of his acceptance. This proved to be the province of New-Jersey; where he spent the remaining years of his life; and where his memory has been treated with deserved respect.*

CHAPTER XIX.

The beginning of Benning Wentworth's administration. War opened in Nova Scotia. Expedition to Cape-Breton; its plan, conduct and success, with a description of the island, and of the city of Louisburg.

BENNING WENTWORTH, Esquire, son of the deceased lieutenant governor, was a merchant of good reputation in Portsmouth, and well beloved by the people. He had represented his native town in the assembly for several years, where he distinguished himself in the opposition to Belcher. He afterward obtained a seat in council; where, sensible of the popularity of his family, and feeling the pride of elevation, he continued the opposition, and joined in the measures which were pursued for obtaining a distinct governor, without any apprehension that himself would be the person; till a series of incidents, at first view unfortunate, prepared the way for his advancement to the chair.

In the course of his mercantile dealings, he had entered into a contract with an agent of the court of Spain, and supplied him with a large quantity of the best oak timber; to procure which, he borrowed money in London. When he delivered the timber at Cadiz, the agent with whom he had contracted, was out of place, and the new officer declined payment. In returning to America, the ship foundered, and he was saved with the crew in

* [JONATHAN BELCHER died at Elizabeth-Town, 31 August. 1757. In a letter to Secretary Waldron, dated 7 January, 1740, he says, " This day entered the fifty-ninth year of my age." He was therefore at the time of his death in his 76th year. His father Andrew Belcher was born at Cambridge, 1 January, 1647, and removed to Boston about 1707. He was one of the council of safety on the deposition of Andros in 1689, and a member of the council of the province of Massachusetts, from May, 1702, to the time of his death, 31 October, 1717, at the age of 70. The grandfather of Governor Belcher was Andrew Belcher, who came from England as early as 1640, and settled at Cambridge. He married a sister of Deputy Gov. Thomas Danforth, of Cambridge, and died as early as 1680. Two sons of Gov. Belcher were educated at Harvard college, viz. Andrew, who graduated in 1724, and died at Milton, Massachusetts, 24 January, 1771, aged 65, and Jonathan, who graduated in 1728, chief justice and governor of Nova Scotia, and died 29 March, 1776, aged 65, leaving an only son, Andrew, who resides in England, and one daughter, who lives in Cambridge, Massachusetts.]

a boat.   These misfortunes deranged his affairs and reduced him
to a state of bankruptcy.   Afterward, he went again to Spain,
hoping by the interest of Sir Benjamin Keene, the British minister, to obtain his due, but his suit was ineffectual.   About that time,
Thomlinson, despairing of Dunbar's advancement to the government of New-Hampshire, turned his thoughts toward Wentworth ;
and having procured him a letter of license from his creditors in
London, invited him thither.[1] Wentworth represented his case to
the British court, complained of the injustice of Spain, and petitioned for redress.   Many British merchants, who had suffered
by the insolence of the Spaniards, were, at the same time, clam-
orous for reparation.   The ministry were studious to avoid a war.
A negociation was begun, and the court of Spain promised restitution ; but failed in the performance.[2] War was then determined
on, and all negociation ended.   Disappointed in his plea for justice, Wentworth made his suit for favor ; and by the aid of Thomlinson, who understood the ways of access to the great, he obtained
a promise from the Duke of Newcastle, that when New-Hampshire should be put under a distinct governor, he should have the
commission.   The expense of the solicitation and fees, amounting to three hundred pounds sterling, was advanced by his friends
in England, and repaid by his friends in New-Hampshire.[3]

He was received in Portsmouth after a long absence, with great
marks of popular respect.   Among the compliments
which were paid to him on that occasion, one was, that   1741.
he had been instrumental of 'rescuing New-Hampshire Dec. 12.
from contempt and dependence.'   In his first speech to the assembly, he reflected on the conduct of his predecessor, not by
name, but by implication ; for not having taken early measures to
raise men for the expedition against the Spanish West-Indies ; and
intimated his apprehension, that the good intention of the
province in raising money for that purpose, would be frus-   1742.
trated, since the men who were willing to enter into the service had
enlisted in the other provinces.[4]   He also complimented them, on
their good faith in regard to the several emissions of paper money ;
all of which were to be called in within the present year.   He did not
forget to recommend a fixed salary for himself, not subject to depreciation ; nor the payment of expenses which had arisen on account
of the boundary lines.   He informed them of the king's indulgence, in giving him leave to consent to a farther emission of bills
of credit, to enable them to discharge their obligations to the
crown ; provided that no injury should be done to the trade of the
mother country.   He also recommended to their attention the
faithful services of their agents, one of whom, Rindge, was dead,
and the payment of the debt due to his heirs.

(1) Thomlinson's letter, MS.   (2) Gentleman's Magazine, for 1739.—
(3) MS. letters of Thomlinson and Atkinson.   (4) Journal Assembly, Jan. 14

The assembly, in their answer, acknowledged the wisdom and justice of the king in determining the long controversy between them and Massachusetts; but as to payment of the expense, they reminded him that one half ought to be paid by Massachusetts, and desired him to use his influence for that purpose. With respect to the failure of raising men for the expedition, they set him right by ascribing it to the true cause; there being no commissions sent to the province for that service. Concerning the salary, they said, that as soon as they could know what number of inhabitants would be added to them by the settlement of the lines, and how the money could be raised, they should make as ample provision for his honorable support as their circumstances would admit. They acknowledged the fidelity and industry of their agents, and professed a good will to reward them; but could not then promise adequate compensation.

The assembly voted a salary of two hundred and fifty pounds, proclamation money, to the governor, funded as usual on the excise; and having obtained the royal license for emitting twenty-five thousand pounds on loan for ten years, they granted the governor two hundred and fifty pounds more, to be paid annually out of the interest of the loan.[1] When this fund failed, they made annual grants for his ' further and more ample support,' and generally added something for house rent. They presented their agent, Thomlinson, one hundred pounds sterling, for his faithful services; but what they did for the heirs of Rindge does not appear.

After Mr. Wentworth was quietly seated in the chair of government, an opportunity presented to advance his interest still farther. 1743. For the sum of two thousand pounds sterling, Dunbar was prevailed on to resign the surveyorship of the woods, and Thomlinson negotiated an appointment in favor of Wentworth, with a salary of eight hundred pounds sterling, out of which he was to maintain four deputies. But to obtain this office, he was obliged to ' rest his claim on the crown of Spain for fifty-six thousand dollars.'

These appointments of Mr. Wentworth gave the opposers of the former administration great cause of triumph; but the spirit of opposition had only changed sides. It was hoped and expected by some, that Mr Belcher, by going to England, would not only remove the ill impressions, which the malice of his enemies had made, but return to his former station. Others, who had no predilection for Belcher, looked with envy on the good fortune of Wentworth, and aimed to undermine him; at the same time courting the friends of the former administration to join in their measures. These things were managed with secrecy, and a few hints only are left as evidence of the existence of designs, which were never brought to maturity.

(1) MS. Acts.

It was one of the royal instructions to governors, that in any cases of difficulty or sudden emergency, they should communicate with each other. Mr. Wentworth had a high opinion of the abilities of the new governor of Massachusetts, and there being a strict friendship between them, consulted him on all occasions. Shirley was gratified by this deference, and knew how to make his advantage of it. Thus, though New-Hampshire was under a governor distinct from'that of Massachusetts, a point which had long been contended for ; yet the difference was not so great in reality as in appearance. This was a circumstance not much known at that time. The advice which Shirley gave him was, in general, salutary and judicious.[1]

The war which had been kindled between Britain and Spain, extended its flames over a great part of Europe; and when France became involved in it, the American colonies were more nearly interested, because of the proximity of the French, and of the Indians, who were in their interest. War is so natural to savages, that they need but little to excite them to it. An Indian war was a necessary appendage of a war with France. The scene of both was opened in Nova-Scotia.

That province had been alternately claimed and possessed by the English and French for more than a century. Ever since the peace of Utrecht, it had been subject to the crown of Britain, and the French inhabitants who were under a kind of patriarchal government of their priests, and devoted to the French interest, were kept in awe, partly by the fear of having their dikes destroyed, which they had erected to prevent the sea from overflowing their fields ; and partly by a British garrison at Annapolis where a governor and council resided.[2] The Indian tribes maintained their native independence, though they were attached to the French by religious, as well as interested obligations. Canseau, an island on the northeastern part of Nova-Scotia, was in possession of the English. It was resorted to by the fishermen of New-England. It was defended by a block-house and garrisoned by a detachment of troops from Annapolis. The island of Cape-Breton was possessed by the French, and lay between the English of Canseau and those of Newfoundland. This was too near a neighborhood for enemies, especially when both were pursuing one object, the fishery.

The French at Cape-Breton, having received early intelligence of the declaration of war, immediately resolved on the Mar. 15. destruction of the English fishery at Canseau. Duquesnel, the governor, sent Duvivier with a few small armed May. 13. vessels, and about nine hundred men, who seized and took possession of the island, burned the houses, and made prisoners of the garrison and inhabitants. This was done, before the news of

(1) MS. letters of Wentworth and Shirley.   (2) MS. of Charles Morris.

war had arrived in New-England. It was followed by an attempt upon Placentia, in Newfoundland, which miscarried. An attack was also made upon Annapolis, the garrison of which was reinforced by several companies of militia and rangers from Massachusetts, and the enemy were obliged to retire. The Indians of Nova-Scotia assisted the French in this attack ; which, with some other insolencies committed by them, occasioned a declaration of war, by the government of Massachusetts, against them, with a premium for scalps and prisoners.[1]

Oct. 19.

These proceedings of the French were rash and precipitate. They were not prepared for extensive operations; nor had they any orders from their court to undertake them. What they had done, served to irritate and alarm the neighboring English colonies, and shew them their danger in the most conspicuous manner. Their sea coast, navigation and fishery lay exposed to continual insults. Their frontier, settlements, on the western side, were but eighty miles distant from the French fort on Lake Champlain. The Indians who lay between them, had not yet taken up the hatchet; but it was expected that encouragement would be given them by the governor of Canada, to insult the frontiers. Several new settlements were wholly broken up ; and many of the women and children of other frontier places retired to the old towns for security.

In the autumn, Duquesnel the French governor of Cape-Breton, died, and was succeeded in the command by Duchambon, who had not so good a military character.[2] Duvivier went to France to solicit a force to carry on the war in Nova-Scotia in the ensuing spring. The storeships, expected from France at Cape-Breton, came on the coast so late in the fall ; and the winter there set in so early and fierce, as to keep them out of port, and drive them off to the West-Indies. The captive garrison of Canseau, with other prisoners, who had been taken at sea, and carried into Louisburg, were sent to Boston. From them, as well as from other informants, Governor Shirley obtained such intelligence of the state of that island and fortress, as induced him to form the project of attacking it. But before we open this romantic and hazardous scene, it is necessary to give some account of the place which was to be the theatre of operations.

The island of Cape-Breton, so denominated from one of its capes, lies between the forty-fifth and forty-seventh degrees of north latitude ; at the distance of fifteen leagues from Cape Ray, the southwestern extremity of Newfoundland.[3] It is separated from the main land of Nova-Scotia by a narrow strait, six leagues in length, the navigation of which is safe for a ship of forty guns. The greatest length of the island, from north-east to south-west is about fifty leagues and its greatest breadth thirty-three. It is

(1) Douglass, i. 318.   (2) Prince and Douglass.   (3) Charlevoix.

about eighty-eight leagues in circuit as seamen estimate distances. Its general form is triangular, but it is indented by many deep bays.[1]

The soil of this island is by no means inviting. It is either rocky and mountainous, or else cold and boggy ; and much less capable of improvement than Nova-Scotia. Its only valuable productions are of the fossil kind, pit-coal and plaster. Its atmosphere in the spring and summer is an almost continual fog, which prevents the rays of the sun from perfecting vegetation. Its winter is severe and of long continuance ; and as the island forms an eddy to the current which sets through the gulf of St. Lawrence, its harbors are filled with large quantities of floating ice, with which its shores are invironed till late in the spring.[2]

Much has been said by French and English writers on the great importance and advantage of this island, and some political and temporary purposes were doubtless to be answered by such publications ; but in fact the only real importance of Cape-Breton was derived from its central situation, and the convenience of its ports. On the north and west sides, it is steep and inaccessible ; but the southeastern side is full of fine bays and harbors, capable of receiving and securing ships of any burden ; and, being situated between Canada, France and the West-Indies, it was extremely favorable to the French commerce. It was not so good a station for the fishery as several parts of Nova-Scotia and Newfoundland. The greater part of the French fishery was prosecuted elsewhere ; and they could buy fish at Canseau, cheaper than they conld cure it at Cape-Breton.[3]

Whilst the French held possession of the coasts of Nova-Scotia and Newfoundland, this island was neglected ; but after they had ceded these places to the crown of England, and the crown of England had ceded this island to them by the treaty of Utrecht, (1713) they began to see its value. Instead of giving so much attention to the fur trade of Canada, as they had before done, they contemplated building a fortified town on this island, as a security to their navigation and fishery. For this purpose, they chose a fine harbor on the south-east side of the island, formerly called English Harbor ; where they erected their fortifications, and called the place Louisburg.[4]

The harbor of Louisburg lies in latitude 45° 55'. Its entrance is about four hundred yards wide. The anchorage is uniformly safe, and ships may run ashore on a soft muddy bottom. The depth of water at the entrance is from nine to twelve fathoms. The harbor lies open to the south-east. Upon a neck of land on the south side of the harbor was built the town, two miles and a quarter in circumference ; fortified in every accessible part with

(1) MS. of Sir William Pepperell.   (2) State of Trade by Otis Little, p. 18, 30.   (3) Hutchinson.   (4) Charlevoix, Douglass, Rolt, Prince.

a rampart of stone, from thirty to thirty-six feet high, and a ditch eighty feet wide. A space of about two hundred yards was left without a rampart, on the side next to the sea; it was enclosed by a simple dike and a line of pickets.[1] The sea was so shallow in this place that it made only a narrow channel, inaccessible from its numerous reefs to any shipping whatever. The side fire from the bastions secured this spot from an attack. There were six bastions and three batteries, containing embrasures for one hundred and forty-eight cannon, of which sixty-five only were mounted, and sixteen mortars. On an island, at the entrance of the harbor, was planted a battery of thirty cannon, carrying twenty-eight pounds shot; and at the bottom of the harbor, directly opposite to the entrance, was the grand or royal battery of twenty-eight cannon, forty-two pounders, and two eighteen pounders. On a high cliff, opposite to the island battery, stood a light-house; and within this point, at the north-east part of the harbor, was a careening wharf, secure from all winds, and a magazine of naval stores.

The town was regularly laid out in squares. The streets were broad; the houses mostly of wood, but some of stone. On the west side, near the rampart, was a spacious citadel, and a large parade; on one side of which were the governor's apartments. Under the rampart were casements to receive the women and children during a siege. The entrance of the town on the land side was at the west gate, over a draw bridge, near to which was a circular battery, mounting sixteen guns of twenty-four pounds shot.

These works had been twenty-five years in building; and though not finished, had cost the crown not less than thirty millions of livres. The place was so strong as to be called 'the Dunkirk of America.' It was, in peace, a safe retreat for the ships of France bound homeward from the East and West-Indies; and in war, a source of distress to the northern English colonies; its situation being extremely favorable for privateers to ruin their fishery and interrupt their coasting and foreign trade; for which reasons, the reduction of it was an object as desirable to them, as that of Carthage was to the Romans.

In the autumn, Shirley wrote to the British ministry, representing the danger of an attack on Nova-Scotia, from the French, in the ensuing spring; and praying for some naval assistance.[2] These letters he sent by Captain Ryal, an officer of the garrison, which had been taken at Canseau, who, 'from his particular knowledge ' of Louisburg, and of the great consequence of the acquisition ' of Cape-Breton, and the preservation of Nova-Scotia, he hop- ' ed would be of considerable service to the northern colonies, ' with the lords of the admiralty.' Thus early did Shirley con-

(1) Abbe Raynal.   (2) Nov. 10—Shirley's letters to Wentworth, MS.

ceive and communicate to Wentworth his great design ; and the
most prudent step which he took in this whole affair was to solicit
help from England. His petition, supported by that worthy officer, was so favorably received by the ministry, that as early as the
beginning of January, orders were despatched to Commodore
Warren, then in the West-Indies, to proceed to the northward in
the spring, and employ such a force as might be sufficient to protect the northern colonies in their trade and fishery, and distress
the enemy ; and for this purpose to consult with Governor Shirley.[1] Orders of the same date were written to Shirley, inclosed
to Warren, directing him to assist the king's ships with transports,
men and provisions. These orders, though extremely favorable
to the design, were totally unknown in New-England, till the middle of April following, before which time the expedition was completely formed.

It has been said, that a plan of this famous enterprise, was first
suggested by William Vaughan, a son of Lieutenant Governor
Vaughan of New-Hampshire.[2] Several other persons have
claimed the like merit. How far each one's information or advice, contributed toward forming the design, cannot now be determined. Vaughan was largely concerned in the fishery on the
eastern coast of Massachusetts. He was a man of good understanding, but of a daring, enterprising and tenacious mind, and
one who thought of no obstacles to the accomplishment of his
views. An instance of his temerity is still remembered. He had
equipped, at Portsmouth, a number of boats to carry on his fishery
at Montinicus. On the day appointed for sailing, in the month
of March, though the wind was so boisterous that experienced
mariners deemed it impossible for such vessels to carry sail, he
went on board one, and ordered the others to follow. One was
lost at the mouth of the river, the rest arrived with much difficulty, but in a short time, at the place of their destination. Vaughan
had not been at Louisburg ; but had learned from fishermen and
others, something of the strength and situation of the place ; and
nothing being in his view impracticable, which he had a mind to
accomplish, he conceived a design to take the city by surprise ;
and even proposed going over the walls in the winter on the drifts
of snow. This idea of a surprisal forcibly struck the mind of
Shirley, and prevailed with him to hasten his preparations, before
he could have any answer or orders from England.

In the beginning of January, he requested of the members of
the general court, that they would lay themselves under
an oath of secresy, to receive a proposal from him, of very   1745.
great importance. This was the first request of the kind which
had ever been made to a legislative body in the colonies. They

(1) MS. copy of the Duke of Newcastle's letter, Jan. 3.   (2) Douglass, Bollan, Hutchinson.

readily took the oath, and he communicated to them the plan which he had formed of attacking Louisburg. The secret was kept for some days; till an honest member, who performed the family devotion at his lodgings, inadvertently discovered it by praying for a blessing on the attempt. At the first deliberation, the proposal was rejected; but by the address of the governor and the invincible perseverance of Vaughan, a petition from the merchants concerned in the fishery, was brought into court, which revived the affair; and it was finally carried in the affirmative by a majority of *one* voice, in the absence of several members Jan. 26. who were known to be against it. Circular letters were immediately despatched to all the colonies, as far as Pennsylvania, requesting their assistance, and an embargo on their ports.

Feb. 1. With one of these letters, Vaughan rode express to Portsmouth, where the assembly was sitting. Governor Wentworth immediately laid the matter before them, and proposed a conference of the two houses to be held on the next day. The house of representatives having caught the enthusiasm of Vaughan, were impatient of delay, and desired that it might be held immediately. It was accordingly held, and the committee reported in

Feb. 2. favor of the expedition; estimated the expense at four thousand pounds, and desired the governor to issue a proclamation for enlisting two hundred and fifty men, at twenty-five shillings per month, one month's pay to be advanced. They also recommended that military stores and transports should be provided, and that such preparations should be made as that the whole might be ready by the beginning of March.[1] All this was instantly agreed to, on condition that proper methods could be found to pay the charges. This could be done in no other way than by a new emission of bills of credit, contrary to the letter of royal instructions. But, by the help of Shirley, a way was found to surmount this difficulty; for on the same day, he wrote to Wentworth, informing him that he had, in answer to repeated solicitations, obtained a relaxation of his instructions relative to bills of credit, so far, as to have leave to consent to such emissions as the exigencies of war might require; and advising him, that considering the occasion, it was probable, his consenting to an emission would rather be approved than censured by his superiors.[2] The

Feb. 5. next day, he wrote again, assuring him that he might safely do it, provided that the sum to be emitted, were solely appropriated to the service of the expedition. He also sent him a copy of the instruction, enjoining him to let no person know that he had sent it. Shirley himself had consented to an emission of fifty thousand pounds, to be drawn in by a tax in the years 1747 and 1748.

The house of representatives passed a vote for an emission of

(1) Printed Journal of this session.   (2) Private MS. letters of Shirley.

ten thousand pounds toward defraying the charge of the expedition and farther carrying on the war, and the support of government ; to be drawn in by taxes in ten annual payments, to begin in 1755. The council objected and said, that the grant should be wholly appropriated to the expedition and the payments should begin in 1751. The house adhered to their vote. The governor interposed, and an altercation took place, which continued several days. The governor adjourned the assembly till he could again ask Shirley's advice and receive his answer. At length, the house altered their vote, and appointed the year 1751 for drawing in the money ; augmenting the sum to thirteen thousand pounds, and at the governor's express desire, they publicly assured him, that they ' could not find out any other way to carry on the expedition, or ' in any degree shorten the period for bringing in the money.' This was done to serve as an apology for the governor's consenting to the bill, notwitstanding he had no liberty to recede from his instructions ; and thus, the matter being compromised, he gave his consent. Feb. 13.

During this tedious interval, a report was spread, that the house had refused to raise men and money for the expedition ; and the author of the report was sought out and called to account by the house for his misbehaviour. The next day, they altered their terms of enlistment, conformably to those offered in Massachusetts, and by the 17th of February, two hundred and fifty men were enlisted for the service.

The person appointed to command the expedition was William Pepperrell, Esq., of Kittery, colonel of a regiment of militia ; a merchant of unblemished reputation and engaging manners, extensively known both in Massachusetts and New-Hampshire, and very popular. These qualities were absolutely necessary in the commander of an army of volunteers, his own countrymen, who were to quit their domestic connexions and employments, and engage in a hazardous enterprise, which none of them, from the highest to the lowest, knew how to conduct. Professional skill and experience were entirely out of the question ; had these qualities been necessary, the expedition must have been laid aside ; for there was no person in New-England, in these respects qualified for the command. Fidelity, resolution and popularity must supply the place of military talents ; and Pepperrell was possessed of these. It was necessary that the men should know and love their general, or they would not enlist under him.*

* The following private note was sent from Boston to Pepperrell, whilst at Louisburg, and found among his papers.

' You was made general, being a popular man, most likely to raise soldiers
' soonest. The expedition was calculated to *establish* Sh——, and make his
' creature W. governor of Cape-Breton, which is to be a place of refuge to
' him from his creditors. Beware of snakes in the grass, and mark their
' hissing.'

After this appointment was made, and while it was uncertain whether the assembly of Massachusetts would agree with the governor in raising money for the expedition, Shirley proposed to Wentworth, the raising of men in New-Hampshire, to be in the pay of Massachusetts, and in the letter which he wrote on that occasion paid him the following compliment. ' It would have ' been an infinite satisfaction to me, and done great honor to the ' expedition, if your limbs would have permitted you to take the ' chief command.' Wentworth was charmed with the idea, and forgetting his gout, made an offer of his personal service ; but not till after the assembly had agreed to his terms and the money bill was passed. Shirley was then obliged to answer him thus :— ' Upon communicating your offer to two or three gentlemen, in ' whose prudence and judgment I most confide, I found them ' clearly of opinion, that any alteration of the present command ' would be attended with great risk, both with respect to the as- ' sembly and the soldiers being entirely disgusted.'[1]

Before Pepperrell accepted the command, he asked the opinion of the famous George Whitefield, who was then itinerating and preaching in New-England. Whitefield told him, that he did not think the scheme very promising ; that the eyes of all would be on him ; that if it should not succeed, the widows and orphans of the slain would reproach him ; and if it should succeed, many would regard him with envy, and endeavor to eclipse his glory ; that he ought therefore to go with ' a single eye,' and then he would find his strength proportioned to his necessity.[2] Henry Sherburne, the commissary of New-Hampshire, another of Whitefield's friends, pressed him to favor the expedition and give a motto for the flag ; to which, after some hestitation, he consented. The motto was, ' *Nil desperandum Christo duce*.' This gave the expedition the air of a crusade, and many of his followers enlisted. One of them, a chaplain, carried on his shoulder a hatchet, with which he intended to destroy the images in the French churches.

There are certain latent sparks in human nature, which, by a collision of causes, are sometimes brought to light ; and when once excited, their operations are not easily controled. In undertaking any thing hazardous, there is a necessity for extraordinary vigor of mind, and a degree of confidence and fortitude, which shall raise us above the dread of danger, and dispose us to run a risk which the cold maxims of prudence would forbid. The people of New-England have at various times shewn such an enthusiastic ardor, which has been excited by the example of their ancestors and their own exposed situation. It was never more apparent, and perhaps never more necessary, than on occasion of this expedition. Nor ought it to be forgotten, that several cir-

(1) Shirley's private letters, MS.   (2) Whitefield's letters, No. 572.

cumstances, which did not depend on human foresight, greatly favored this undertaking.

The winters in this country are often severe, but the winter in which this expedition was planned, and particularly the month of February, was very mild. The harbors and rivers were open, and the weather was in general so pleasant, that every kind of labor could be done abroad. The fruitfulness of the preceding season had made provisions plenty. The Indians had not yet molested the frontiers ; and though some of them had heard that an expedition against Cape Breton was in hand, and carried the news of it to Canada, such an attempt was so improbable, that the French gave no credit to the report, and those in Nova-Scotia did not receive the least intelligence of the preparations. Douglass observes, that ' some guardian angel preserved the troops from ' taking the small pox,' which appeared in Boston about the time of their embarkation, and was actually imported in one of the ships which was taken into the service. A concurrence of happy incidents brought together every British ship of war from the ports of the American continent and islands, till they made a formidable naval force, consisting of four ships of the line and six frigates, under the command of an active, judicious and experienced officer. On the other hand, the garrison of Louisburg was discontented and mutinous ; they were in want of provisions and stores ; they had no knowledge of the design formed against them ; their shores were so environed with ice, that no supplies could arrive early from France, and those which came afterward, were intercepted and taken by our cruisers. In short, ' if any one circumstance ' had taken a wrong turn on our side, and if any one circumstance ' had not taken a wrong turn on the French side, the expedition ' must have miscarried.'[1]

In the undertaking and prosecuting of an enterprise so novel to the people of New-England, it is amusing to see how many projects were invented ; what a variety of advice was given from all quarters, and what romantic expectations were formed by advisers and adventurers. During the enlistment, one of the officers was heard to say with great sobriety, that he intended to carry with him three shirts, one of which should be ruffled, because he expected that the general would give him the command of the city, when it should be taken. An ingenious and benevolent clergyman, presented to the general a plan for the encampment of the army, the opening of trenches and the placing of batteries before the city.[2] To prevent danger to the troops from subterraneous mines, he proposed, that two confidential persons, attended by a guard, should, during the night, approach the walls ; that one should with a beetle strike the ground, while the other should lay his ear to it, and observe whether the sound was hollow,

(1) Douglass, i. 336.   (2) Private MS. letters.

and that a mark should be set on all places suspected.   Another
gentleman of equal ingenuity, sent the general a model of a flying
bridge, to be used in scaling the walls of Louisburg.   It was so
light, that twenty men could carry it on their shoulders to the wall,
and raise it in a minute.   The apparatus for raising it consisted
of four blocks, and two hundred fathoms of rope.   It was to be
floored with boards, wide enough for eight men to march abreast ;
and to prevent danger from the enemy's fire, it might be covered
with raw hides.   This bridge, it was said, might be erected against
any part of the wall, even where no breach had been made ; and
it was supposed that a thousand men might pass over it in four
minutes.

But the most extraordinary project of all, was Shirley's scheme
for taking the city by surprise, in the first night after the arrival
of the troops, and before any British naval force could possibly
come to their assistance.   It is thus delineated in a confidential
letter which he wrote to Wentworth, when he urged him to send
the New-Hampshire troops to Boston, to proceed thence with
the fleet of transports.   ' The success of our scheme for sur-
' prising Louisburg will entirely depend on the execution
Mar. 2.   ' of the first night, after the arrival of our forces.   For
' this purpose, it is necessary, that the whole fleet should make
' Chappeau-rouge point just at the shutting in of the day, when
' they cannot easily be discovered, and from thence push into the
' bay, so as to have all the men landed before midnight ; (the
' landing of whom, it is computed by captain Durell and Mr. Bas-
' tide, will take up three hours at least.)   After which, the form-
' ing of the four several corps, to be employed in attempting to
' scale the walls of Louisburg, near the east gate, fronting the
' sea, and the west gate, fronting the harbor ; to cover the retreat
' of the two beforementioned parties in case of a repulse ; and,
' to attack the grand battery ; (which attack must be made at the
' same time with the two other attacks) will take up two hours
' more at least.   After these four bodies are formed, their march
' to their respective posts from whence they are to make their at-
' tacks and serve as a cover to the retreat, will take up another
' two hours ; which, supposing the transports to arrive in Chap-
' peau-rouge bay at nine o'clock in the evening, and not before,
' as it will be necessary for them to do, in order to land and march
' under cover of the night, will bring them to four in the morning,
' being day break, before they begin the attack, which will be full
' late for them to begin.   Your excellency will from hence per-
' ceive how critical an affair, the time of the fleet's arrival in
' Chappeau-rouge bay is, and how necessary it is to the success
' of our principal scheme, that the fleet should arrive there, in a
' body, at that precise hour.'

It is easy to perceive that this plan was contrived by a person totally unskilled in the arts of navigation and of war.   The coast of Cape-Breton was dangerous and inhospitable ; the season of the year rough and tempestuous, and the air a continual fog ; yet, a fleet of an hundred vessels, after sailing nearly two hundred leagues (for by this plan they were not to stop) must make a certain point of land ' at a precise hour,' and enter an unknown bay, in an evening.   The troops were to land in the dark, amidst a violent surf, on a rocky shore ; to march through a thicket and bog three miles, to the city, and some of them a mile beyond it to the royal battery.   Men who had never been in action, were to perform services, which the most experienced veteran would think of with dread ; to pull down pickets with grapling irons, and scale the walls of a regular fortification, with ladders, which were afterward found to be too short by ten feet ; all in the space of twelve hours from their first making the land, and nine hours from their debarkation.   This part of the plan was prudently concealed from the troops.

The forces which New-Hampshire furnished for this expedition, were three hundred and fifty men, including the crew of an armed sloop which conveyed the transports and served as a cruiser. They were formed into a regiment, consisting of eight companies, and were under the command of colonel Samuel Moore.   The sloop was commanded by captain John Fernald ; her crew consisted of thirty men.   The regiment, sloop and transports, were, by governor Wentworth's written instructions to the general, put under his command.   Besides these, a body of one hundred and fifty men was enlisted in New-Hampshire and aggregated to the regiment in the pay of Massachusetts.   Thus New-Hampshire employed five hundred men ; about one eighth part of the whole land force.*   In these men, there was such an ardor for action, and such a dread of delay, that it was impracticable to put them so far out of their course, as to join the fleet at Boston.[1]   Shirley therefore altered the plan, and appointed a rendezvous at Canseau ; where the forces of New-Hampshire arrived, Mar. 31. two days before the general and his other troops from Boston.

The instructions which Pepperrell received from Shirley, were conformed to the plan which he had communicated to Wentworth, but much more particular and circumstantial.   He was ordered to proceed to Canseau, there to build a block-house and battery,

(1) Wentworth's letters, MS.

* In the introductory part of Dr. Ramsay's elegant history of the American Revolution, (page 34) it is said, that ' this enterprise was undertaken by the ' sole authority of the legislature of Massachusetts.'   This is not sufficiently accurate.   It originated in Massachusetts ; but the colonies of New-Hampshire, Rhode-Island and Connecticut, by their legislative authority, furnished troops and stores.   New-York sent a supply of artillery, and Pennsylvania of provisions ; but the troops from Rhode-Island, and the provisions from Pennsylvania, did not arrive till after the surrender of the city.

and leave two companies in garrison, and to deposite the stores which might not immediately be wanted by the army. Thence he was to send a detachment to the village of St. Peters, on the island of Cape-Breton and destroy it ; to *prevent* any intelligence which might be carried to Louisburg; for which purpose also, the armed vessels were to cruise before the harbor.[1] The whole fleet was to sail from Canseau, so as to arrive in Chappeau-rouge bay about nine o'clock in the evening. The troops were to land in four divisions, and proceed to the assault before morning. If the plan for the surprisal should fail, he had particular directions where and how to land, march, encamp, attack and defend ; to hold councils and keep records ; and to send intelligence to Boston by certain vessels retained for the purpose, which vessels were to stop at Castle William, and there receive the governor's orders. Several other vessels were appointed to cruise between Canseau and the camp, to convey orders, transport stores, and *catch fish* for the army. To close these instructions, after the most minute detail of duty, the general was finally ' left to act upon unforeseen ' emergencies according to his discretion ;' which, in the opinion of military gentlemen, is accounted the most rational part of the whole. Such was the plan, for the reduction of a regularly constructed fortress, drawn by a lawyer, to be executed by a merchant, at the head of a body of husbandmen and mechanics ; animated indeed by ardent patriotism, but destitute of professional skill and experience. After they had embarked, the hearts of many began to fail. Some repented that they had voted for the expedition, or promoted it ; and the most thoughtful were in the greatest perplexity.[2]

The troops were detained at Canseau, three weeks, waiting for the ice which environed the island of Cape-Breton, to be dissolved. They were all this time within view of St. Peters, but were not discovered.[3] Their provisions became short ; but they were supplied by prizes taken by the cruisers. Among others, the New-Hampshire sloop took a ship from Martinico, and retook one of the transports, which she had taken the day before. At length, to their great joy, commodore Warren, in the Superbe, of sixty guns, with three other ships of forty guns each, arrived at Canseau, and having held a consultation, with the general, proceeded to cruise before Louisburg. The general having sent the New-Hampshire sloop, to cover a detatchment which destroyed the village of St Peters, and scattered the inhabitants, sailed with the whole fleet ; but instead of making Chappeau-rouge point in the evening, the wind falling short, they made it at the dawn of the next morning ; and their appearance in the bay, gave the first notice to the French, of a design formed against them.[3]

Apr. 23.

Apr. 29.

(1) Original instructions, in MS.   (2) Prince's thanksgiving sermon, p. 25.
(3) Pepperrell's letters to Shirley.

The intended surprisal being thus happily frustrated, the next thing after landing the troops, was to invest the city.—Vaughan, the adventurer from New-Hampshire, had the rank and pay of a lieutenant-colonel, but refused to have a regular command. He was appointed one of the council of war, and was ready for any service which the general might think suited to his genius. He conducted the first column through the woods, within sight of the city, and saluted it with three cheers. He headed a detatchment, consisting chiefly of the New-Hampshire troops, and marched to the northeast part of the harbor, in the night ; where they burned the ware-houses, containing the naval stores, and staved a large quantity of wine and brandy. May 1.

The smoke of this fire being driven by the wind into the grand battery, so terrified the French, that they abandoned it and retired to the city, after having spiked the guns and cut the halliards of the flag-staff. The next morning as Vaughan was return- May 2. ing, with thirteen men only, he crept up the hill which overlooked the battery, and observed, that the chimneys of the barrack were without smoke, and the staff without a flag. With a bottle of brandy, which he had in his pocket, (though he never drank spirituous liquors) he hired one of his party, a Cape Cod Indian, to crawl in at an embrasure and open the gate. He then wrote to the general, these words, ' May it please your honor, to ' be informed, that by the grace of God, and the courage of thir- ' teen men, I entered the royal battery, about nine o'clock, and ' am waiting for a reinforcement, and a flag.'[1] Before either could arrive, one of the men climbed up the staff, with a red coat in his teeth, which he fastened by a nail to the top. This piece of triumphant vanity alarmed the city, and immediately an hundred men were despatched in boats to retake the battery. But Vaughan, with his small party, on the naked beach, and in the face of a smart fire from the city and the boats, kept them from landing, till the reinforcement arrived. In every duty of fatigue or sanguine adventure, he was always ready ; and the New-Hampshire troops, animated by the same enthusiastic ardor, partook of all the labors and dangers of the siege. They were employed for fourteen nights successively, in drawing cannon from the landing place to the camp, through a morass ; and their lieutenant-colonel Meserve, being a ship carpenter, constructed sledges, on which the cannon were drawn, when it was found that their wheels were buried in the mire. The men, with straps over their shoulders, and sinking to their knees in mud, performed labor beyond the power of oxen ; which labor could be done only in the night or in a foggy day; the place being within plain view and random shot of the enemy's walls. They were much disappointed and chagrined, when they found that these meritorious services were

(1) Original MS.

not more distinctly acknowledged in the accounts which were sent
to England, and afterwards published.[1]

In the unfortunate attempt on the island battery by four hundred volunteers from different regiments, the New-Hampshire
troops were very active. When it was determined to erect
May 26. a battery on the light-house cliff; two companies of them
(Mason's and Fernald's) were employed in that laborious service,
under cover of their armed sloop; and when a proposal was made
for a general assault by sea and land, colonel Moore, who had
been an experienced sea commander, offered to go on board the
Vigilant, with his whole regiment, and lead the attack, if in case
of success he might be confirmed in the command of the ship;
but when this was denied, most of the men who were fit for duty,
readily went on board the Princess Mary, to act as marines on
that occasion.

It has been said, that ' this siege was carried on in a tumultua-
' ry, random manner, resembling a Cambridge commencement.' [2]
The remark is in a great measure true. Though the business of
the council of war was conducted with all the formality of a legislative assembly; though orders were issued by the general, and
returns made by the officers at the several posts; yet the want
of discipline was too visible in the camp.* Those who were
on the spot, have frequently in my hearing, laughed at the recital
of their own irregularities, and expressed their admiration when
they reflected on the almost miraculous preservation of the army
from destruction. They indeed presented a formidable front to
the enemy; but the rear was a scene of confusion and frolic.
While some were on duty at the trenches, others were racing,
wrestling, pitching quoits, firing at marks or at birds, or running
after shot from the enemy's guns, for which they received a
bounty, and the shot were sent back to the city. The ground
was so uneven and the people so scattered, that the French could
form no estimate of their numbers; nor could they learn it from
the prisoners, taken at the island battery, who on their examination, as if by previous agreement, represented the number to be
vastly greater than it was. The garrison of Louisburg had been
so mutinous before the siege, that the officers could not trust the
men to make a sortie, lest they should desert; had they been
united and acted with vigor, the camp might have been surprised
and many of the people destroyed.

Much has been ascribed, and much is justly due to the activity
and vigilance of Commodore Warren, and the ships under his

(1) Wentworth's letters, MS.   (2) Douglass, i. 352.

* [There is in the library of the New-Hampshire Historical Society, a manuscript volume of about 260 pages, in folio, which contains a record of the
" General Courts Martial and Courts of Inquiry, held in the city of Louisburg, in the island of Cape-Breton, in the years 1746, 1747 and 1748." It appears to be the original.]

command ; much is also due to the vigor and perseverance of
the land forces, and the success was doubtless owing, under God,
to the joint efforts of both. Something of policy, as well as bravery, is generally necessary in such undertakings ; and there was
one piece of management, which, though not mentioned by any
historian, yet greatly contributed to the surrender of the city.

The capture of the Vigilant, a French sixty-four gun ship,
commanded by the Marquis de la Maison forte, and richly
laden with military stores for the relief of the garrison, May 19.
was one of the most capital exploits performed by the navy.
This ship had been anxiously expected by the French ; and it
was thought that the news of her capture, if properly communicated to them, might produce a good effect ; but how to do it
was the question. At length, the commodore hit on this
expedient, which he proposed to the general, who ap- June 1.
proved, and put it into execution.[1] In a skirmish on the island,
with a party of French and Indians, some English prisoners had
been taken by them and used with cruelty. This circumstance
was made known to the marquis, and he was requested to go on
board of all the ships in the bay where French prisoners were
confined, and observe the condition in which they were kept.
He did so, and was well satisfied with their fare and accommodations. He was then desired to write to the governor of the city,
and inform him how well the French prisoners were treated, and
to request the like favor for the English prisoners. The
humane marquis readily consented, and the letter was sent June 7.
the next day by a flag, intrusted to the care of Captain Mac-
donald. He was carried before the governor and his chief officers; and by pretending not to understand their language, he had
the advantage of listening to their discourse; by which he found,
that they had not before heard of the capture of the Vigilant,
and that the news of it, under the hand of her late commander,
threw them into visible perturbation. This event, with the erection of a battery on the high cliff at the light house, under the direction of lieutenant colonel Gridley, by which the island battery
was much annoyed, and the preparations which were
evidently making for a general assault, determined Du- June 15-17.
chambon to surrender ; and accordingly, in a few days he capitulated.

Upon entering the fortress and viewing its strength, and the
plenty and variety of its means of defence, the stoutest hearts
were appalled, and the impracticability of carrying it by assault,
was fully demonstrated.

No sooner was the city taken, and the army under shelter,
than the weather, which during the siege, excepting eight or nine
days after the first landing, had been remarkably dry for that cli-

(1) MS. letters of Warren and Pepperrell.

mate, changed for the worse ; and, an incessant rain of ten days succeeded.[1] Had this happened before the surrender, the troops who had then begun to be sickly, and had none but very thin tents, must have perished in great numbers. Reinforcements of men, stores and provisions arrived,* and it was determined in a council of war to maintain the place and repair the breaches. A total demolition might have been more advantageous to the nation ; but in that case, individuals would not have enjoyed the profit of drawing bills on the navy and ordnance establishments. The French flag was kept flying on the ramparts ; and several rich prizes were decoyed into the harbor. The army supposed that they had a right to a share of these prizes ; but means were found to suppress or evade their claim ; nor did any of the colony cruisers, (except one) though they were retained in the service, under the direction of the commodore, reap any benefit from the captures.

The news of this important victory filled America with joy, and Europe with astonishment. The enterprising spirit of New-England gave a serious alarm to those jealous fears, which had long predicted the independence of the colonies. Great pains were taken in England to ascribe all the glory to the navy, and lessen the merit of the army. However, Pepperrell received the title of a baronet, as well as Warren. The latter was promoted to be an admiral ; the former had a commission as colonel in the British establishment, and was empowered to raise a regiment in America, to be in the pay of the crown. The same emolument was given to Shirley, and both he and Wentworth acquired so much reputation as to be confirmed in their places. Vaughan went to England to seek a reward for his services, and there died of the small pox.† Solicitations were set on foot for a parliamentary reimbursement, which, after much difficulty and delay, was obtained ; and the colonies who had expended their substance were in credit

(1) Pepperrell's letters, MS.

* Of the reinforcements, New-Hampshire sent 115 men. The loss which the New-Hampshire troops suffered was but eleven, of whom five were killed and six died of sickness. This was before the surrender. More died afterwards in garrison. Shirley's letter to Wentworth, from Louisburg, September 2.

† [He died in London " about the middle of December 1746." (Interleaved almanack of Eleazar Russell, Esq.) He was born at Portsmouth, 12 September, 1703, and graduated at Harvard college in 1722. For several years, he was a merchant in his native town ; but, possessing an enterprising disposition, accompanied by a few hardy adventurers from the neighboring towns, he left Portsmouth, emigrated to the eastern country, and formed a settlement at a place called Damariscotta, about 13 miles below fort Pemaquid. He died a disappointed man ; for while the successful commander of the expedition was soon after knighted and otherwise distinguished, the intrepid Vaughan remained more than a year in England, in the vain expectation of receiving some compensation from the sovereign whom he had so signally served. See the Collections of Farmer and Moore, ii. 161—165. iii. 35, 36.]

at the British treasury.*[1] The justice and policy of this measure must appear to every one, who considers, that excepting the suppression of a rebellion within the bowels of the kingdom, this conquest was the only action which could be called a victory, on the part of the British nation, during the whole French war, and afforded them the means of purchasing a peace.

CHAPTER XX.

Projected Expedition to Canada.   Alarm by the French fleet.   State of the Frontiers.   Peace.

WHILST the expedition to Cape-Breton was in hand, the active mind of Governor Shirley contemplated nothing less than the conquest of all the French dominions in America ; and he consulted with Governor Wentworth and Mr. Atkinson on the practicability of such a design.   After Louisburg was taken, he made a visit thither, and held a consultation with Sir Peter Warren and Sir William Pepperell ; and from that place wrote pressingly to the British ministry on the subject.[2]   His solicitations, enforced by the brilliant success at Louisburg, and the apparent danger in which Nova-Scotia and the new conquest were involved, had such an effect, that in the spring of the following year, a circular letter was sent from the Duke of Newcastle, secretary of state, to all the governors of the American colonies, as far southward as Virginia ; requiring them to raise as many men as they could spare, and form them into companies of one hundred ; to be ready to unite and act according to the orders which they should afterwards receive.[3]   The plan was, that a squadron of ships of war, and a body of land forces, should be sent from England against Canada ; that the troops raised in New-England should join the British fleet and army at Louisburg, and proceed up the river St. Lawrence ; that those of New-York and the other provinces at the southward, should be collected at Albany, and march against Crown-Point and Montreal.   The management of this expedition was committed to Sir John St. Clair, in conjuction with Sir Peter Warren and governor Shirley.   St. Clair did not come to America.   Warren and Shirley gave the orders, while Warren was here ; and afterward commodore Knowles, who succeeded him, was joined with Shirley ; but as Knowles was part of the time at Louisburg, most of the concern devolved on Shirley alone.

1746.
April 6.

(1) Bollan's MS. letters.   (2) Shirley's MS. letters.   (3) Douglass, i. 315.

* The reimbursement to New-Hampshire was sixteen thousand, three hundred and fifty-five pounds sterling.   Thomlinson's MS. letter.

Beside the danger of losing Nova-Scotia and Cape-Breton, there were other reasons for undertaking this expedition. The Indians, instigated by the governor of Canada, were ravaging the frontiers, destroying the fields and cattle, burning houses and mills, killing and carrying away the inhabitants.[1] Though scouts and garrisons were maintained by the governments ; yet to act altogether on the defensive, was thought to be not only an ineffectual, but a disgraceful mode of carrying on the war ; especially after the success which had attended the arms of the colonists in their attempt against Louisburg. The continuance of such a mode of defence, would neither dispirit the enemy, nor secure the frontiers from their depredations.

The design was pleasing, and the colonies readily furnished their quotas of men. In New-Hampshire the same difficulty occurred as on occasion of the Louisburg expedition. The governor had no authority to consent to the emission of bills of credit, but Shirley removed that obstacle, by suggesting to him, that as the ministry did not disapprove what he had done before, so there was no reason to fear it now ; and that the importance of the service, and the necessity of the case, would justify his conduct. The demand at first, was for levy money and victualing. The arms and pay of the troops were to be furnished by the crown ; but it was afterward found necessary that the several governments should provide clothing, transports and stores, and depend on a reimbursement from the British parliament.[2]

The assembly was immediately convened, and voted an encouragement for enlisting a thousand men, or more, if they June. could be raised ; with a bounty of thirty pounds currency, and a blanket to each man, besides keeping two armed vessels in pay. Colonel Atkinson was appointed to the command of the troops.[3] Eight hundred men were inlisted and ready for embarkation by the beginning of July. Transports and provisions were prepared, and the men waited, impatiently, all summer for employment. Neither the general nor any orders arrived from England ; the fleet, which was said to be destined for the expedition, sailed seven times from Spithead, and as often returned. Two regiments, only, were sent from Gibraltar, to Louisburg, to relieve the New-England men, who had garrisoned it since the conquest. It is much easier to write the history of an active campaign, than to trace the causes of inaction and disappointment ; and it is in vain to supply the place of facts by conjecture.*

In this time of suspense, Sir Peter Warren, and Sir William Pepperell, having arrived at Boston, from Louisburg, Shirley had

(1) Shirley's speech, June 28.   (2) Shirley's MS. letters.   (3) Atkinson's MS. letters.

* ' The last war was ruinous in the expense, and unsuccessful in the end, ' for want of consideration, and a reasonable plan at the beginning.' Doddington's Diary, May 27, 1775, page 330.

an opportunity of consulting them, and such other gentlemen as
he thought proper, on the affair of the Canada expedition.   The
season was so far advanced, that a fleet could hardly be expected
from England ; or if it should arrive, it would be too late to attempt the navigation of the river St. Lawrence. But, as a sufficient body of the troops might be assembled at Albany, it was
judged prudent to employ them in an attempt against the French
fort at Crown-Point.[1] At the same time, Clinton, governor of
New-York, solicited and obtained the friendly assistance of the Six
Nations of Indians, on the borders of his province. It was thought,
that if this attempt should be made, the alliance with these Indians would be strengthened and secured ; and the frontiers
would be relieved from the horrors of desolation and captivity,
to which they were continually exposed. In pursuance of this
plan, the forces of New-Hampshire were ordered to hold themselves in readiness, to march to Albany ; but, it being discovered
that the small-pox was there, the rendezvous was appointed at
Saratoga and the adjacent villages.[2]

No sooner was this plan resolved on, and preparations made to
carry it into execution, than accounts were received of danger
which threatened Annapolis, from a body of French and Indians
at Minas, and the probable revolt of the Acadians. It was thought
that Nova-Scotia would be lost, if some powerful succor were
not sent thither.[3] Orders were accordingly issued, for the troops
of Massachusetts, Rhode-Island and New-Hampshire, to embark
for that place, and ' drive the enemy out of Nova-Scotia.' But,
within a few days more, the whole country was alarmed, and
thrown into the utmost consternation, by reports of the arrival   Sept. 20.
of a large fleet and army from France, at Nova-Scotia, under the
command of the Duke D'Anville. It was supposed that their object was to recover Louisburg ; to take Annapolis ; to break up
the settlements on the eastern coast of Massachusetts ; and to
distress, if not attempt the conquest of the whole country of New-
England.   On this occasion, the troops destined for Canada found
sufficient employment at home, and the militia was collected to
join them ; the old forts on the sea coast were repaired, and new
ones were erected. A new battery, consisting of sixteen guns,
of thirty-two and twenty-four pounds shot, was added to fort William and Mary, at the entrance of Pascataqua harbor ; and another, of nine thirty-two pounders, was placed at the point of
Little-Harbor. These works were supposed to be sufficient to
prevent a surprisal. Military guards were appointed ; and in this
state of fear and anxiety, the people were kept for six weeks,
when some prisoners, who had been released by the   Oct. 25.
French, brought the most affecting accounts of the dis-

(1) Shirley's and Warren's MS. letters, Aug. 25.   (2) MS. letter of Secretary Willard, Sept. 1.   (3) Shirley's and Warren's MS. letters, Sept. 12.

tress and confusion on board the fleet. It was expected, by the
people in New-England, that an English fleet would have followed them to America. This expectation was grounded on some
letters from England, which Shirley had received and which he
forwarded by express to admiral Townsend, at Louisburg. The
letters were intercepted by a French cruiser, and carried into
Chebucto, where the fleet lay. They were opened in a council
of war, and caused a division among the officers ; which, added
to the sickly condition of the men, and the damage which the
fleet had sustained by storms, and their loss by shipwrecks,
dejected their commander to that degree, that he put an end to
his life by poison ; and the second in command fell on his sword.
These melancholy events disconcerted their first plan. They
then resolved to make an attempt on Annapolis ; but when they
had sailed from Chebucto, they were overtaken by a violent tem-
pest, off Cape Sable ; and those ships which escaped destruction,
returned singly to France. Never was the hand of divine Providence more visible, than on this occasion. Never was a disappointment more severe, on the side of the enemy ; nor a deliverance more complete, without human help, in favor of this country.*

Nova-Scotia was not out of danger. The French and Indians,
who, during the stay of the fleet at Chebucto, had appeared before Annapolis, but on their departure retired, were still in the
peninsula ; and it was thought necessary to dislodge them. For
this purpose, Shirley sent a body of the Massachusetts forces, and
Nov. 10. pressed the governors of Rhode-Island and New-Hampshire to send part of theirs. Those from Rhode-Island,
and one transport from Boston, were wrecked on the passage.
The armed vessels of New-Hampshire, with two hundred men,
went to Annapolis ; but the commander of one of them, instead
of landing his men, sailed across the bay of Fundy, into St. John's
river ; where, meeting with a French snow, and mistaking her for
one of the Rhode-Island transports, he imprudently sent his boat
with eight men on board, who were made prisoners, and the snow
escaped. The sloop, instead of returning to Annapolis, came back
to Portsmouth.[1] These misfortunes and disappointments had very
1747. serious ill consequences. The Massachusetts forces, who
Jan. 31. were at Nova-Scotia,being inferior in number to the French,
and deceived by false intelligence, were surprised in the
midst of a snow storm at Minas ; and after an obstinate resistance,
were obliged to capitulate. Their commander, Col. Arthur Noble,

(1) Dec. 13—Shirley's MS. letters, and affidavits of the crew.

* [1746. The towns of Dunstable, Merrimack, Hollis, Nottingham-West,
(whose name was altered to Hudson at the session of the legislature in June,
1830,) and Pelham were incorporated by the province of New-Hampshire.—
MS. volume of charters in Secretary's office.]

and about sixty men, were killed, and fifty were wounded.[1] The
enemy being provided with snow-shoes, made forced marches ;
and ours being destitute of them were unable to escape.

When the alarm occasioned by the French fleet had subsided,
Atkinson's regiment marched into the country to cover the lower
part of the frontiers, and encamped near the shore of Winnipiseogee lake ; where they passed the winter and built a slight fort.
They were plentifully supplied with provisions, and had but little
exercise or discipline. Courts martial were not instituted, nor
offences punished. The officers and men were tired of the service ; but were not permitted to enter on any other business, lest
orders should arrive from England. Some were employed in
scouting ; some in hunting or fishing, and some deserted.[2]

Shirley was so intent on attacking Crown-Point, that he even
proposed to march thither in the winter, and had the address to
draw the assembly of Massachusetts into an approbation of this
project. He enlarged his plan, by proposing that the New-
Hampshire troops should at the same time go, by the way of
Connecticut river, to the Indian village of St. Frances, at the distance of two hundred miles and destroy it ; while the troops from
Massachusetts, Connecticut and New-York, should go by the way
of the lakes to Crown-Point.[3] The governor of New-York
would have consented to this wild projection, on account of the
Indian allies, who were impatient for war ; but it was happily
frustrated, by the prudence of the Connecticut assembly ; who
deemed the winter an improper season for so great an undertaking, and deferred their assistance till the ensuing spring.[4] At the
same time, the small pox prevailed in the settlements above Albany, through which the forces must have marched ; and that
distemper was then an object of much greater dread, than the
storms of winter, or the face of an enemy.

To finish what relates to the Canada forces, it can only be
said, that excepting some who were employed on the frontiers,
they were kept in a state of military indolence, till the
autumn of the ensuing year ; when by order from the   Oct. 1747.
Duke of Newcastle they were disbanded, and paid at the same
rate as the king's troops. The governors drew bills on the British treasury ; which were negotiated among the merchants at sev-
en and eight hundred per cent. and the parliament granted money,
to reimburse the charges of the equipment and subsistence of
these forces.[5]

The state of the frontiers now demands our attention. By the
extension of the boundaries of the province, several settlements which had been made by the people of Massachu-   1745.
setts, and under the authority of grants from their general court,

---

(1) Boston Evening Post. (2) Atkikson's MS. letters. (3) Shirley's MS.
letters. (4) MS. copy of Conn. Resolves—Jan. 28. (5) Bollan's MS. letters.

had fallen within New-Hampshire. In one of them stood Fort
Dummer, on the west side of Connecticut river, and within the
lately extended line of New-Hampshire. This fort had been
erected and maintained, at the expense of Massachusetts ; but
when it was found to be within New-Hampshire, the governor was
instructed by the crown to recommend to the assembly, the future
maintenance of it. In the same assembly, which had so zealously
entered upon the expedition against Cape-Breton, this matter was
introduced ; but a considerable majority of the lower house declined making any grant for this purpose, and adduced the following reasons, viz.[1] That the fort was fifty miles distant from any
towns which had been settled by the government or people of New-
Hampshire ; that the people had no right to the lands which, by the
dividing line, had fallen within New-Hampshire ; notwithstanding
the plausible arguments which had been used to induce them to
bear the expense of the line ; namely, that the land would be given
to them or else would be sold to pay that expense ; that the charge
of maintaining that fort, at so great a distance, and to which there
was no communication by roads, would exceed what had been
the whole expense of government before the line was established ;
that the great load of debt contracted on that account, and the
yearly support of government, with the unavoidable expenses of
the war, were as much as the people could bear ; that if they
should take upon them to maintain this fort, there was another
much better and more convenient fort at a place called Number-
Four, besides several other settlements, which they should also be
obliged to defend ; and finally that there was no danger that these
forts would want support, since it was the interest of Massachusetts, by whom they were erected, to maintain them as a cover to
their frontier.

When these reasons were given, the governor dissolved the assembly and called another, to whom he recommended the same
June 7. measure in the most pressing terms ; telling them, ' that it
       ' was of the last consequence to the present and future
' prosperity of the government ; that their refusal would lessen
' them in the esteem of the king and his ministers, and strip the
' children yet unborn of their natural right ; and deprive their
' brethren who were then hazarding their lives before the walls
' of Louisburg of their just expectations, which were to sit down
' on that valuable part of the province.' But his eloquence had
no effect. They thought it unjust to burden their constituents
with an expense which could yield them no profit, and afford
them no protection.

When it was determined, that New-Hampshire would make no
provision for Fort-Dummer, the assembly of Massachusetts continued its usual support, and also provided for the other posts on

(1) Printed Journal, May 3.

Connecticut river and its branches, which were within the limits of
New-Hampshire.   They afterwards petitioned the king, to de-
duct that charge out of the reimbursement, which the parliament
had granted to New-Hampshire, for the Canada expedition ; but
in this, they were defeated, by the vigilance and address of Thomlinson, the agent of New-Hampshire.

Most of the frontier towns of New-Hampshire, at that time,
were distinguished by no other than by Indian or temporary names.
It may be convenient to compare them with their present names.
On Connecticut river, and its eastern branches, were

Number-Four,		Charlestown,
Great-Meadow,		Westmoreland,
Great-Fall,	which	Walpole,
Fort-Dummer,	are now called	Hinsdale,
Upper-Ashuelot &		Keene and
Lower-Ashuelot,		Swanzey.

On Merrimack river and its branches, were

Penacook,		Concord,
Suncook,		Pembroke,
Contoocook,	which	Boscawen,
New-Hopkinton,	are now called	Hopkinton,
Souhegan-East and		Merrimack and
Souhegan-West,		Amherst.

On the Pascataqua river, and its branches, were the townships of
Nottingham,* Barrington and Rochester.

Besides the forts which were maintained at the public expense,
there were private houses enclosed with ramparts, or palisades of
timber ; to which the people who remained on the frontiers retired ;
these private garrisoned houses were distinguished by the names
of the owners.   The danger to which these distressed people
were constantly exposed, did not permit them to cultivate their
lands to any advantage.   They were frequently alarmed when
at labor in their fields, and obliged either to repel an attack, or
make a retreat.   Their crops were often injured, and sometimes
destroyed, either by their cattle getting into the fields where the
enemy had broken the fences, or because they were afraid to venture out, to collect and secure the harvest.   Their cattle and
horses were frequently killed by the enemy ; who cut the flesh
from the bones, and took out the tongues, which they preserved
for food, by drying in smoke.   Sometimes they were afraid even
to milk their cows ; though they kept them in pastures as near as
possible to the forts.   When they went abroad, they were always
armed ; but frequently they were shut up for weeks together in a
state of inactivity.

* [Nottingham was settled about the year 1727, by Capt. Joseph Cilley and
others.   Rev. Stephen Emery, the first minister, was ordained in 1742; dismissed about 1749.   The population in 1767, was 703.]

The history of a war on the frontiers can be little else than a recital of the exploits, the sufferings, the escapes and deliverances of individuals, of single families or small parties. The first appearance of the enemy on the western frontier was at the Great-Meadow, sixteen miles above Fort-Dummer. Two Indians took William Phips, as he was hoeing his corn. When they had carried him half a mile, one of them went down a steep hill to fetch something which had been left. In his absence, Phips, with his own hoe, knocked down the Indian who was with him ; then seizing his gun, shot the other as he ascended the hill.[1] Unfortunately, meeting with three others of the same party, they killed him. The Indian whom he knocked down died of his wound. The same week they killed Josiah Fisher of Upper-Ashuelot.

July 5.

July 10.

No other damage was done for three months ; when a party of twelve Indians approached the fort at Great-Meadow, and took Nehemiah How, who was at a little distance from the fort, cutting wood. The fort was alarmed, and one Indian was killed by a shot from the rampart ; but no attempt was made to rescue the prisoner. As they were leading him away, by the side of the river, they espied a canoe coming down, with two men, at whom they fired, and killed David Rugg ; but Robert Baker got to the opposite shore and escaped. Proceeding farther, they met three other men, who, by skulking under the bank, got safe to the fort. One of them was Caleb How, the prisoner's son. When they came opposite to Number-Four, they made their captive write his name on a piece of bark, and left it there. Having travelled seven days westward, they came to a lake, where they found five canoes, with corn, pork and tobacco. In these canoes they embarked ; and having stuck the scalp of David Rugg on a pole, proceeded to the fort at Crown-Point; where How received humane treatment from the French. He was then carried down to Quebec, where he died in prison.[2] He was a useful man, greatly lamented by his friends and fellow captives.

Oct. 11.

The next spring, a party of Indians appeared at Number-Four, where they took John Spafford, Isaac Parker and Stephen Farnsworth, as they were driving a team.[3] Their cattle were found dead, with their tongues cut out. The men were carried to Canada, and, after some time, returned to Boston, in a flag of truce.

1746.

Within a few days, a large party, consisting of fifty, laid a plan to surprise the fort at Upper-Ashuelot. They hid themselves in a swamp, in the evening ; intending to wait till the men had gone out to their work, in the morning, and then rush in. Ephraim Dorman, who was abroad very early, discovered

Apr. 23.

(1) Doolittle's Memoirs, p. 2.   (2) How's Narrative.   (3) April 19—Doolittle's Memoirs.

them and gave the alarm. He bravely defended himself against
two Indians, and stripped one of his blanket and gun, which he
carried into the fort. John Bullard, and the wife of Daniel Mc-
Kenny were killed. Nathan Blake was taken and carried to
Canada, where he remained two years. They burned several
houses and barns ; and from the human bones found among the
ashes, it was thought that some of the enemy fell and were concealed in the flames.[1]

About the same time, a party came down to New-Hopkinton,
where they entered a garrisoned house, and found the people
asleep ; the door having been left open by one who had
risen early and gone out to hunt. Eight persons were $^{Apr.\,27.}$
thus taken ; Samuel Burbank and his two sons, David Woodwell,
his wife, two sons, and a daughter. Burbank and the wife of
Woodwell, died in captivity. Woodwell and three of the children returned in a flag of truce to Boston.[2] *

The enemy were scattered in small parties, on all the frontiers.
At Number-Four, some women went out to milk their cows, with
major Josiah Willard† and several soldiers, for their guard :
eight Indians who were concealed in a barn, fired on them, $^{May\,2.}$
and killed Seth Putnam ; as they were scalping him, Willard and
two more fired on them, and mortally wounded two, whom their
companions carried off.[3]

At Contoocook, five white men and a negro were fired at.—
Elisha Cook and the negro were killed. Thomas Jones was
taken and died in Canada.[4]

At Lower-Ashuelot, they took Timothy Brown and Robert Moffat, who were carried to Canada and returned. At the
same time, a party lay about the fort at Upper-Ashuelot. $^{May\,6.}$
As one of them knocked at the gate in the night, the sentinel fired
through the gate and gave him a mortal wound.[5]

(1) Doolittle's Memoirs, and Sumner's MS. letter.   (2) How's Narrative,
and Norton's Narrative. Boston Post Boy. [Collections of Farmer and
Moore for 1822, vol. i. 284—287.]   (3) Doolittle's Narrative.   (4) May 4—
Norton's and How's Narratives. [Price, Hist. Boscawen, 112.]   (5) Doolittle's Narrative.

* [The names of those captured were Samuel Burbank, his sons Caleb and
Jonathan, David Woodwell, his wife, and sons Benjamin and Thomas, and
daughter Mary. Jonathan Burbank, after his redemption, became an officer,
and was killed by the Indians in the French war, being supposed by them to
have been Major Rogers, their avowed enemy. Mary Woodwell, after a detention of six months among the French at Montreal, returned to Albany, and
soon after, to Hopkinton, Mass. her native place. She was twice married,
and died a widow, among the Shakers at Canterbury, N. H. in October, 1829,
in the 100th year of her age.]

† [Of Fort-Dummer, afterwards Colonel Willard. He was probably the
same who was one of the first settlers of Winchester, and one to whom the
charter of that town was granted in 1753. He was son or grandson of Capt.
Simon Willard of Salem, whose father was the Simon Willard, mentioned
page 56.]

The danger thus increasing, a reinforcement was sent by the
Massachusetts assembly, to these distressed towns. Cap-
May 24. tain Paine, with a troop, came to Number-Four; and about
twenty of his men, going to view the place where Putnam was
killed, fell into an ambush. The enemy rose and fired, and then
endeavored to cut off their retreat. Captain Phinehas Stevens,
with a party, rushed out to their relief. A skirmish ensued ; in
which, five men were killed on each side, and one of ours was
taken.* The Indians left some of their guns and blankets behind.

In about a month after this, another engagement happened at
the same place. As Captain Stevens and Captain Brown were
June 19. going into the meadow, to look for their horses, the dogs
discovered an ambush, which put the men into a posture
for action, and gave them the advantage of the first fire.[1] After a
sharp encounter, the enemy were driven into a swamp, drawing
away several of their dead. In this action, one man only was
lost. Several blankets, hatchets, spears, guns and other things,
were left on the ground, which were sold for forty pounds old
tenor. This was reckoned ' a great booty from such beggarly
' enemies.'

At Bridgman's fort, near Fort-Dummer, William Robbins and
James Baker were killed in a meadow. Daniel How
June 24. and John Beatman were taken. How killed one of the
Indians before he was taken.

When the people wanted bread, they were obliged to go to
the mills, with a guard; every place being full of danger. A
July 3. party who went to Hinsdale's mill, with Colonel Willard
at their head, in searching round the mill, discovered an
ambush. The enemy were put to flight with the loss of their
packs.

At Number-Four, one Phillips was killed ; and as some of the
people were bringing him into the fort, they were fired upon ; but
Aug. 3. none were hurt. Having burned some buildings, and
killed some cattle, the enemy went and ambushed the
Aug. 6. road near Winchester, where they killed Joseph Rawson.

Whilst the upper settlements were thus suffering, the lower
towns did not escape. A party of Indians came down to Roch-
June 27. ester, within twenty miles of Portsmouth. Five men
were at work in a field, having their arms at hand. The
Indians concealed themselves. One of them fired, with a view
to induce the men to discharge their pieces, which they did. The
enemy then rushed upon them before they could load again.
They retreated to a small deserted house and fastened the door.

(1) Doolittle's Narrative.   Boston Evening Post.

* [The names of the English killed were Samuel Farnsworth, Joseph Allen, Peter Perrin, Aaron Lyon and Joseph Massey.]

The Indians tore off the roof, and with their guns and tomahawks despatched Joseph Heard, Joseph Richards, John Wentworth and Gershom Downs.   They wounded and took John Richards; and then crossing over to another road, came upon some men who were at work in a field, all of whom escaped; but they took Jonathan Door, a boy, as he was sitting on a fence.   Richards was kindly used, his wounds were healed, and after eighteen months, he was sent to Boston in a flag of truce.   Door lived with the Indians and acquired their manners and habits ; but, after the conquest of Canada, returned to his native place.[1]

Soon after this, another man was killed at Rochester.*   Two men were surprised and taken at Contoocook ; and a large party of Indians lay in ambush at Penacook, with an intention to attack the people, while assembled for public worship ; but seeing them go armed to their devotions, they waited till the next morning, when they killed five and took two.†   Aug. 6.

In these irritating skirmishes, the summer was spent ; till a large body of French and Indians attacked Fort Massachusetts, at Hoosuck.[2]   This fort was lost for want of ammunition to defend it.   After this success, the enemy remained quiet during the rest of the summer.   Aug. 20.

The prospect of an expedition to Canada had induced many of the soldiers who were posted on the frontiers to enlist into the regiments, because they preferred active service to the dull routine of a garrison.   The defence of the western posts was not only hazardous, but ineffectual ; and some persons in the northwestern part of Massachusetts thought it inexpedient, to be at the

(1) Haven's MS. letter.   (2) Norton's Narrative.

* [This man was Moses Roberts. He was not killed by the Indians as might be inferred in the text. He had been stationed as a sentinel, and having become alarmed, retreated from his post into the woods, when another sentinel, hearing a noise in the bushes, and seeing them wave, supposed the Indians were approaching, fired his gun and shot Roberts, who died the next morning, blaming himself and justifying the man who shot him. MS. Communication from Rev. Thomas C. Upham.]

† [These men were killed and captured on the road leading from Concord to Hopkinton, within about a mile of the seat of Judge Green. There is a full account of the massacre in Moore's Annals of Concord, 23—25, and in the Coll. of the N. H. Hist. Soc. i. 171—173. There has been lately erected near the scene of destruction by a descendant of one of the victims of Indian cruelty, a durable monument, on which is the following inscription : "This Monument is erected in Memory of SAMUEL BRADLEY, JONATHAN BRADLEY, OBADIAH PETERS, JOHN BEAN and JOHN LUFKIN, who were massacred August 11th, 1746, by the Indians near this spot. Erected by Richard Bradley, son of the late Hon. John Bradley and grandson of Samuel Bradley." The names of those who were taken were Alexander Roberts and William Stickney. Roberts returned from captivity, but Stickney was drowned when he was within about one day's journey of the white settlements. The loss sustained by the Indians was four killed and several wounded, and two of them mortally. On the 10 November following, the Indians killed a Mr. Estabrook on the road between the principal settlement and the place of the former massacre.]

charge of defending a territory, which was out of their jurisdiction.
November. Their petitions prevailed with the assembly, to withdraw
their troops from the western parts of New-Hampshire.
The inhabitants were then obliged to quit their estates. They
deposited in the earth, such furniture and utensils as could be
saved by that means; they carried off on horseback such as were
portable ; and the remainder, with their buildings, was left as a
prey to the enemy, who came and destroyed or carried away what
they pleased. Four families, who remained in Shattack's fort,
(Hinsdale) defended it against a party of Indians, who attempted
to burn it.[1] Six men only were left in the fort at Number-Four,
who, in the following winter deserted it ; and it was wholly destitute for two months. In this time, some gentlemen, who understood the true interest of the country, prevailed on the assembly
of Massachusetts, to resume the protection of those deserted
places ; and to employ a sufficiency of men, not only to garrison
them, but to range the woods and watch the motions of the
enemy.

In the latter end of March, Captain Phinehas Stevens, who
commanded a ranging company of thirty men, came to Number-
1747. Four; and finding the fort entire, determined to keep
possession of it. He had not been there many days, when
April 4. he was attacked by a very large party of French and Indians, commanded by M. Debeline. The dogs, by their barking, discovered that the enemy were near ; which caused the gate
to be kept shut, beyond the usual time. One man went out to
make discovery and was fired on ; but returned with a slight
wound only. The enemy, finding that they were discovered,
arose from their concealment and fired at the fort on all sides.
The wind being high, they set fire to the fences and log-houses,
till the fort was surrounded by flames. Capt. Stevens took the
most prudent measures for his security ; keeping every vessel
full of water and digging trenches under the walls in several places ; so that a man might creep through, and extinguish any fire,
which might catch on the outside of the walls. The fire of the
fences did not reach the fort ; nor did the flaming arrows which
they incessantly shot against it take effect. Having continued
this mode of attack for two days, accompanied with hideous
shouts and yells ; they prepared a wheel carriage, loaded with
dry fagots, to be pushed before them, that they might set fire to
the fort. Before they proceeded to this operation, they demanded a cessation of arms till the sun-rising, which was granted. In
the morning, Debeline came up with fifty men, and a flag of
truce, which he stuck in the ground. He demanded a parley,
which was agreed to. A French officer, with a soldier and an
Indian, then advanced ; and proposed that the garrison should

(1) Sumner's and Olcott's MS. letters.

bind up a quantity of provisions with their blankets, and having laid down their arms should be conducted prisoners to Montreal. [1] Another proposal was that the two commanders should meet, and that an answer should then be given. Stevens met the French commander, who, without waiting for an answer, began to enforce his proposal, by threatening to storm the fort, and put every man to death, if they should refuse his terms, and kill one of his men. Stevens answered, that he could hearken to no terms till the last extremity ; that he was intrusted with the defence of the fort, and was determined to maintain it, till he should be convinced that the Frenchman could perform what he had threatened. He added, that it was poor encouragement to surrender, if they were all to be put to the sword for killing one man, when it was probable they had already killed more. The Frenchman replied, ' Go and ' see if your men dare to fight any longer, and give me a quick ' answer.' Stevens returned and asked his men, whether they would fight or surrender. They unanimously determined to fight. This was immediately made known to the enemy, who renewed their shouting and firing all that day and night. On the morning of the third day, they requested another cessation for two hours. Two Indians came with a flag, and proposed, that if Stevens would sell them provisions they would withdraw. He answered, that to sell them provisions for money was contrary to the law of nations ; but that he would pay them five bushels of corn for every captive, for whom they would give a hostage, till the captive could be brought from Canada. After this answer, a few guns were fired, and the enemy were seen no more.[2]

In this furious attack from a starving enemy, no lives were lost in the fort, and two men only were wounded. No men could have behaved with more intrepidity in the midst of such threatening danger. An express was immediately despatched to Boston, and the news was received there with great joy. Commodore Sir Charles Knowles was so highly pleased with the conduct of Captain Stevens, that he presented him with a valuable and elegant sword, as a reward for his bravery. From this circumstance, the township when it was incorporated, took the name of Charlestown.*

Small parties of the enemy kept hovering, and sometimes discovered themselves. Sergeant Phelps killed one, near the fort, and escaped unhurt, though fired upon and pursued by two others.

Other parties went farther down the country ; and at Rochester, they ambushed a company who were at work in a field. The

(1) Stevens's letter, in Boston Evening Post, April 27.   (2) [Ibid.]

* [Commodore Knowles was afterwards an admiral in the British Navy, and in 1770, being invited by the empress of Russia, went into her service.— Hutchinson, ii. 390.]

ambush was discovered by three lads, John and George Place, and Paul Jennens. The Indians fired upon them. John Place returned the fire and wounded an Indian. Jennens presented his gun but did not fire ; this prevented the enemy from rushing upon them, till the men from the field came to their relief and put the Indians to flight.[1]

At Penacook, a party of the enemy discovered themselves by firing at some cattle. They were pursued by fifty men ; and retreated with such precipitation, as to leave their packs and blankets, with other things behind. One man had his arm broken in this conflict.[2] About the same time, a man was killed there,† who had just returned from Cape-Breton, after an absence of two years. Another was killed at Suncook ; and at Nottingham, Robert Beard, John Folsom and Elizabeth Simpson, suffered the same fate.[3]

In the autumn, Major Willard and Captain Alexander, wounded and took a Frenchman near Winchester, who was conducted to Boston and returned to Canada. Soon after, the enemy burned Bridgman's fort ; (Hinsdale) and killed several persons, and took others from that place, and from Number-Four, in the ensuing winter. No pursuit could be made, because the garrison was not provided with snow-shoes, though many hundreds had been paid for by the government.

The next spring, Captain Stevens was again appointed to command at Number-Four, with a garrison of an hundred men ; Captain Humphrey Hobbs being second in command.[4] A scouting party of eighteen, was sent out under Captain Eleazer Melvin. They discovered two canoes in Lake Champlain, at which they fired. The fort at Crown-Point was alarmed, and a party came out to intercept them. Melvin crossed their track, and came back to West River ; where, as his men were diverting themselves by shooting salmon, the Indians suddenly came upon them and killed six.[5] The others came in at different times to Fort-Dummer.

1748.
May 25.

On a Sabbath morning, at Rochester, the wife of Jonathan Hodgdon was taken by the Indians, as she was going to milk her cows. She called aloud to her husband. The Indians would have kept her quiet, but as she persisted in calling, they killed her, apparently contrary to their intentions. Her husband heard her cries, and came to her assistance, at the instant of her death. His gun missed fire, and he escaped. The alarm, occasioned by this action, prevented greater mischief.[6]

May 1.

(1) June 7—Haven's MS. letters.   (2) July 28—Boston Evening Post.—
(3) Upham's MS. letter.   (4) Olcott's MS. letter.   (5) Doolittle's Narrative.
(6) Haven's MS. letter.

† [Perhaps a Mr. Estabrook, who was killed at Penacook, on the 10 November, that year. Moore, Annals of Concord, 25.]

The next month, they killed three men belonging to Hinsdale's fort, Nathan French, Joseph Richardson and John Frost. Seven were taken ; one of whom, William Bickford, died of his wounds. Captain Hobbs, and forty men, being on a scout near West River, were surprised by a party of Indians, *June 16.* with whom they had a smart encounter, of three hours continuance. Hobbs left the ground, having had three men killed and four wounded. The same party of the enemy killed two *July 14.* men and took nine, between Fort Hinsdale and Fort-Dummer.

The cessation of arms between the belligerent powers did not wholly put a stop to the incursions of the enemy; for after it was known here, and after the garrison of Number- *1749.* Four was withdrawn, excepting fifteen men, Obadiah Sartwell was killed, and a son of Captain Stevens was taken and carried to Canada ; but he was released and returned.[1]

During this affecting scene of devastation and captivity, there were no instances of deliberate murder nor torture exercised on those who fell into the hands of the Indians ; and even the old custom of making them run the gauntlet, was in most cases omitted. On the contrary, there is a universal testimony from the captives who survived and returned, in favor of the humanity of their captors. When feeble, they assisted them in travelling ; and in cases of distress from want of provision, they shared with them an equal proportion. A singular instance of moderation deserves remembrance. An Indian had surprised a man at Ashuelot. The man asked for quarter, and it was granted. Whilst the Indian was preparing to bind him, he seized the Indian's gun, and shot him in one arm. The Indian, however, secured him ; but took no other revenge than, with a kick, to say, ' You dog, how ' could you treat me so ?' The gentleman from whom this information came, has frequently heard the story both from the captive and the captor. The latter related it as an instance of English perfidy ; the former of Indian lenity.[2]

There was a striking difference between the manner in which this war was managed, on the part of the English and on the part of the French. The latter kept out small parties continually engaged in killing, scalping and taking prisoners ; who were sold in Canada and redeemed by their friends, at a great expense. By this mode of conduct, the French made their enemies pay the whole charge of their predatory excursions, besides reaping a handsome profit to themselves. On the other hand, the English attended only to the defence of the frontiers ; and that in such a manner, as to leave them for the most part insecure. No parties were sent to harass the settlements of the French. If the whole country of Canada could not be subdued, nothing less could be attempted. Men were continually kept in pay, and in expectation of service ; but spent their time either in garrisons, or camps, or in guarding provisions when sent to the several forts. Though large rewards were promised for scalps and prisoners, scarcely any were obtained unless by accident. A confusion of councils, and a multiplicity of directors, caused frequent changes of measures, and delays in the execution of them. The forts were ill supplied with ammunition, provisions, clothing and snow-shoes.

1747. When an alarm happened, it was necessary, either to bake bread, or dress meat, or cast bullets, before a pursuit could be made. The French gave commissions to none but those who had distinguished themselves by some exploit. Among us, persons frequently obtained preferment, for themselves or their friends, by making their court to governors, and promoting favorite measures in town meetings, or general assemblies.

A community recovering from a war, like an individual recovering from sickness, is sometimes in danger of a relapse. This war was not decisive, and the causes which kindled it were not removed. One of its effects was, that it produced a class of men, who, having been for a time released from laborious occupations, and devoted to the parade of military life, did not readily listen to the calls of industry. To such men, peace was burdensome, and the more so, because they had not the advantage of half pay. The interval between this and the succeeding war was not long. The peace took place in 1749, and in 1754 there was a call to resume the sword.

CHAPTER XXI.

Purchase of Mason's claim. Controversy about Representation. Plan of extending the settlements. Jealousy and resentment of the savages.

WHILST the people were contending with an enemy abroad, an attempt was making at home, to revive the old claim of Mason, which their fathers had withstood, and which for many years had lain dormant, till recalled to view by the politicians of Massachusetts, as already related. After Thomlinson had engaged with Mason, for the purchase of his title, nothing more was heard of it, till the controversy respecting the lines was

1744. finished, and Wentworth was established in the seat of government, and in the office of surveyor of the woods. The agreement which Thomlinson had made, was in behalf of

Oct. 30. the Representatives of New-Hampshire ; and the instrument was lodged in the hands of the governor, who sent it to the house for their perusal and consideration. It lay on their

table a long time, without any formal notice.[1] Quickening messages were sent time after time ; but the affairs of the war, and
Mason's absence at sea, and in the expedition to Louisburg, where
he had a company, together with a disinclination in the house,
which was of a different complexion from that in 1739, prevented
any thing from being done.

In the mean time, Mason suffered a fine and recovery, by
which the entail was docked, in the courts of New-Hampshire,
and he became entitled to the privilege of selling his in-   1745.
terest. He also presented a memorial to the assembly, in
which he told them that he would wait no longer ; and Feb. 22.
unless they would come to some resolution, he should take their
silence as a refusal. Intimations were given, that if they would
not ratify the agreement, a sale would be made to other   1746.
persons, who stood ready to purchase. At length, the
house came to a resolution, ' that they would comply with the a-
' greement, and pay the price ; and that the waste lands should
' be *granted by the general assembly*, to the inhabitants, as Jan. 29.
' they should think proper.' A committee was appointed
to treat with Mason, about fulfilling his agreement, and to draw
the proper instruments of conveyance ; but he had on the same
day, by deed of sale, for the sum of fifteen hundred   Jan. 30.
pounds currency, conveyed his whole interest to twelve
persons, in fifteen shares. When the house sent a message to the
council to inform them of this resolution, the council objected to
that clause of the resolve, ' that the lands be granted by the gen-
' eral assembly,' as contrary to the royal commission and instructions ; but if the house would address the king, for leave to dispose of the lands, they said that they were content.

These transactions raised a great ferment among the people.
Angry and menacing words were plentifully thrown out against
the purchasers ; but they had prudently taken care to file in the
recorder's office a deed of quit-claim to all the towns which had
been settled and granted within the limits of their purchase.*—

(1) Assembly records.

* The purchasers of this claim were,
Theodore Atkinson, (three fifteenths) Thomas Packer,
M. H. Wentworth, (two fifteenths)   Thomas Wallingford,
Richard Wibird,   Jotham Odiorne,
John Wentworth, son of the Governor, Joshua Peirce,
George Jaffrey,   Samuel Moore,
Nathaniel Meserve,   John Moffat, (one fifteenth each.)

The towns quitclaimed were,

Portsmouth,	Londonderry,	Bow,
Dover,	Chester,	Chichester,
Exeter,	Nottingham,	Epsom,
Hampton,	Barrington,	Barnstead,
Gosport,	Rochester,	and afterward
Kingston,	Canterbury,	Gilmantown.

In this quit-claim, they inserted a clause in the following words,
' excepting and reserving our respective rights, titles, inheritance
' and possessions, which we heretofore had, in common or sever-
' alty, as inhabitants or proprietors of houses or lands, within any
' of the towns precincts, districts or villages aforesaid.'[1]   This
precaution had not at first its effect.   A committee of both houses
was appointed to consider the matter, and they reported that ' for
' quieting the minds of the people, and to prevent future diffi-
' culty, it would be best for the province to purchase the claim,
' for the use and benefit of the inhabitants ; provided that the pur-
' chasers would sell it for the cost and charges.'[2]   This report
was accepted, concurred and consented to, by every branch of
the legislature.   A committee was appointed to consult counsel,
Aug. 4. and agree on proper instruments of conveyance.   The
same day, this committee met with the purchasers, and
conferred on the question whether they would sell on the terms
proposed ?   At the conference, the purchasers appeared to be
divided, and agreed so far only, as to withdraw their deed from
Aug. 12. the recorder's office.   The committee reported that they
could make no terms with the purchasers ; in consequence
Aug. 28. of which, the deed was again lodged in the office and
recorded.

Much blame was cast on the purchasers, for clandestinely taking
a bargain out of the hands of the assembly.   They said in their
Sept. 4. vindication, ' that they saw no prospect of an effectual
' purchase by the assembly, though those of them who
' were members, voted for it, and did what they could to encourage
' it ; that they would have gladly given Mason as much money,
' for his private quit-claim to their several rights in the townships
' already granted and settled ; that Mason's claim had for many
' years hung over the province, and that on every turn, they had
' been threatened with a proprietor ; that Mason's deed to a com-
' mittee of Massachusetts, in behalf of that province, for a tract of
' land adjoining the boundary line, had been entered on the records,
' and a title under it set up, in opposition to grants made by the
' governor and council; that it was impossible to say where this
' evil would stop, and therefore they thought it most prudent to
' prevent any farther effects of it, by taking up with his offer,
' especially as they knew that he might have made a more advan-
' tageous bargain, with a gentleman of fortune in the neighboring
' province ; but that they were still willing, to sell their interest to
' the assembly, for the cost and charges; provided that the land
' be *granted by the governor and council;* and that the agreement
' be made within one month from the date of their letter.'[3]

Within that month, the alarm caused by the approach of D'An-

(1) Records of deeds.   (2) Assembly records.   (3) MS. letter in Proprietary office.

ville's fleet, put a stop to the negotiation. After that danger was over, the affair was revived ; but the grand difficulty subsisted. The purchasers would not sell, but on condition that the lands should be granted, by the governor and council. The assembly thought that they could have no security that the land would be granted to the people ; because the governor and council might grant it to themselves, or to their dependents, or to stran- 1747. gers, and the people who had paid for it, might be excluded from the benefit which they had purchased. A proposal Aug. 20. was afterward made, that the sale should be to feoffees in trust for the people; and a form of a deed for this purpose was drawn. To this proposal, the purchasers raised several objections ; and as the assembly had not voted any money to make the purchase, they declined signing the deed; and no farther efforts being made by the assembly, the purchase rested in the hands of the proprietors. In 1749, they took a second deed, comprehending all the Masonian grants, from Naumkeag to Pascataqua ; whereas the former deed was confined to the lately established boundaries of New-Hampshire.   This latter deed was not recorded till 1753.[1]

After they had taken their first deed, the Masonians began to grant townships, and continued granting them to petitioners, 1748. often without fees, and always without quit-rents. They quieted the proprietors of the towns, on the western side of the Merrimack, which had been granted by Massachusetts, before the establishment of the line ; so that they went on peaceably with their settlements. The terms of their grants were, that the grantees should, within a limited time, erect mills and meeting-houses, clear out roads and settle ministers. In every township, they reserved one right for the first settled minister, another for a parsonage, and a third for a school. They also reserved fifteen rights for themselves, and two for their attorneys; all of which were to be free from taxes, till sold or occupied. By virtue of these grants, many townships were settled, and the interest of the people became so united with that of the proprietors, that the prejudice against them gradually abated ; and, at length, even some who had been the most violent opposers, acquiesced in the safety and policy of their measures, though they could not concede to the validity of their claim.

The heirs of Allen menaced them by advertisements, and warned the people against accepting their grants. They depended on the recognition of Allen's purchase, in the charter of Massachusetts, as an argument in favor of its validity ; and supposed, that because the ablest lawyers in the kingdom were consulted, and employed in framing that charter, they must have had evidence of the justice of his pretensions, before such a reservation

(1) Records of deeds.

could have been introduced into it.   So strong was the impression, which this argument had made, on the minds of speculators in England, that large sums had been offered, to some of Allen's heirs, in that kingdom; and, Thomlinson himself, the first mover of the purchase from Mason, in, behalf of New-Hampshire, had his doubts; and would have persuaded the associates to join in buying Allen's title also, even at the price of two thousand pounds sterling, to prevent a more expensive litigation, the issue of which would be uncertain.[1]   But they, being vested with the principal offices of government; being men of large property, which was also increased by this purchase; and having satisfied themselves, of the validity of their title, by the opinions of some principal lawyers, both here and in England, contented themselves with the purchase which they had made; and by maintaining their possession, extended the cultivation of the country within their limits.

The words of the original grants to Mason, describe an extent of sixty miles, from the sea, on each side of the province, and a line to *cross over* from the end of one line of sixty miles, to the end of the other.   The Masonian proprietors pleaded, that this cross line should be a *curve*, because, no other line would preserve the distance of sixty miles from the sea, in every part of their western boundary.   No person had any right to contest this point with them, but the king.   It was not for the interest of his governor and council to object; because several of them, and of their connections, were of the Masonian propriety; and no objection was made by any other persons, in behalf of the crown.   Surveyors were employed, at several times, to mark this curve line; but on running, first from the southern, and then from the eastern boundary, to the river Pemigewassett, they could not make the lines meet.   Controversies were thus engendered, between the grantees of crown lands and those of the Masonians, which subsisted for many years.   In some cases, the disputes were compromised, and in others, left open for litigation; till, by the revolution, the government fell into other hands.

This was not the only controversy, which, till that period, remained undetermined.   When the extension of the boundary lines gave birth to a demand, for the maintenance of Fort-Dummer, the governor had the address, to call to that assembly, into which he introduced this demand, six new members; who appeared as representatives for six towns and districts, some of which had been, by the southern line, cut off from Massachusetts.[2]   It was supposed that his design, in calling these members, was to facilitate the adoption of Fort-Dummer.   Other towns, which ought to have had the same privilege extended to them, were neglected.   When the new members appeared in the house, the secretary, by the governor's order, administered to them the usual oaths; after

(1) MS. letters of Thomlinson.   (2) Printed Journal, Jan. 1744.

which, they were asked, in the name of the house, by what authority they came thither? They answered, that they were chosen by virtue of a writ, in the king's name, delivered to their respective towns and districts, by the sheriff. The house remonstrated to the governor, that these places had no right, by law, nor by custom, to send persons to represent them, and then debarred them from the privilege of voting, in the choice of a speaker; two only dissenting, out of nineteen. Several sharp messages passed, between the governor and the house, on that occasion; but the pressing exigencies of the war, and the proposed expedition to Cape-Breton, obliged him, for that time, to give way, and suffer his new members to be excluded, till the king's pleasure could be known.

The house vindicated their proceedings, by appealing to their records; from which it appeared, that all the additions, which had been made to the house of representatives, were, in consequence of their own votes, either issuing a precept themselves, or requesting the governor to do it; from which they argued, that no town, or parish, ought to have any writ, for the choice of a representative, but by a vote of the house, or by an act of the assembly. On the other side, it was alleged, that the right of sending representatives was originally founded on the royal commission and instructions, and therefore, that the privilege might, by the same authority, be lawfully extended to the new towns, as the king, or his governor, by advice of council, might think proper. The precedents on both sides were undisputed; but neither party would admit the conclusion drawn by the other. Had this difficulty been foreseen, it might have been prevented when the triennial act was made in 1727. The defects of that law, began now to be severely felt; but could not be remedied.

The dispute having thus subsided, was not revived during the war; but as soon as the peace was made, and the king had gone on a visit to his German dominions, an additional instruction was sent from the lords justices, who presided in the king's absence, directing the governor to dissolve the assembly then subsisting; and when another should be called, to issue the king's writ June 30. to the sheriff, commanding him to make out precepts to the towns and districts, whose representatives had been before excluded; and that when they should be chosen, the governor should support their rights.[1]

Had this instruction extended to all the other towns in the province, which had not been before represented, it might have been deemed equitable; but as it respected those only, which had been the subject of controversy, it appeared to be grounded on partial information, and intended to strengthen the prerogative of the crown, without a due regard to the privileges of the people at large.

(1) Douglass ii. 35.

The party in opposition to the governor became more acrimo-nious than ever. Richard Waldron, the former secretary, and 1749. the confidential friend of Belcher, appeared in the new Jan. 3. assembly and was chosen speaker. The governor nega-tived him ; and ordered the house to admit the new mem-bers, and choose another speaker. They denied his power of negativing their speaker and of introducing new members. The style of his messages was peremptory and severe ; their answers and remonstrances were calm, but resolute, and in some instances satirical. Neither party would yield. No business was trans-acted ; though the assembly met about once in a month, and was kept alive, by adjournments and prorogations, for three years. Had he dissolved them, before the time for which they were chosen had expired, he knew, that in all probability, the same persons would be re-elected.

The effect of this controversy was injurious to the governor, as well as to the people. The public bills of credit had depreciated since this administration began, in the ratio of thirty to fifty-six ; and the value of the governor's salary had declined in the same proportion. The excise could neither be farmed nor collected ; and that part of the governor's salary, which was funded upon it, failed. The treasurer's accounts were unsettled. The soldiers, who had guarded the frontiers in the preceding war, were not paid ; nor were their muster-rolls adjusted. The public records of deeds were shut up ; for the recorder's time having expired, and the appointment being by law vested in the assembly, no choice could be made. No authenticated papers could be ob-tained, though the agent was constantly soliciting for those which related to the controversy about Fort-Dummer, at that time before the king and council.*

When the situation of the province was known in England, an 1750–51. impression to its disadvantage was made on the minds of its best friends ; and they even imagined that the governor's conduct was not blameless.† The language at court

---

* [1749. Plaistow, Litchfield, Newtown, and Hampstead were incorporat-ed. The settlement of Walpole commenced.

1750. Salem and Bedford were incorporated. The last was one of the Narraganset townships. The settlement of it commenced in the winter of 1737, by Robert and James Walker, and in the year following, by John Goffe, afterwards colonel, Matthew Patten, afterwards judge of probate, and captain Samuel Patten, and soon after by many others. See Coll. N. H. Hist. Soc. i. 288—296.

1751. Derryfield, now called Manchester, was incorporated.]

† August 10, 1749, Mr Thomlinson wrote thus to Mr. Atkinson. ' I am ' sorry to find by your letters, and by every body from your country, the con-' fusion your Province is in. I wish I could set you right. I cannot help ' thinking that the governor has done some imprudent things ; but the other ' party is fundamentally wrong, and the governor will always be supported as ' long as he conducts himself by his majesty's instructions, and in his right ' of negativing a speaker. Notwithstanding this, I am surprised that he, or ' any other governor, should not think it their interest, to behave so to all ' sorts of people under their government, as to make all their enemies their ' friends, rather than to make their friends their enemies.'

was totally changed. The people of New-Hampshire who had
formerly been in favor, as loyal and obedient subjects, were now
said to be in rebellion. Their agent was frequently reproached
and mortified on their account, and was under great apprehension,
that they would suffer, not only in their reputation, but in their
interest.[1] The agent of Massachusetts was continually soliciting
for repayment of the charges of maintaining Fort-Dummer, and
is was in contemplation, to take off a large district from the western part of New-Hampshire, and to annex it to Massachusetts, to
satisfy them for that expense. Besides this, the paper money of
the colonies was under the consideration of parliament ; and the
province of Massachusetts was rising into favor for having abolished that system of iniquity. The same justice was expected of
New-Hampshire, since they had the same means in their power
by the reimbursement granted to them by parliament for the
Cape-Breton and Canada expeditions. This money, amounting
to about thirty thousand pounds sterling, clear of all fees and commissions, had lain long in the treasury ; and when it was paid to
the agent, he would have placed it in the funds, where it might
have yielded an interest of three per cent ; but having no directions from the assembly, he locked it up in the bank.. This was
a clear loss to them of nine hundred pounds per annum. There
were some who reflected on the agent, as if he had made an advantage to himself of this money. Had he done it, his own capital was sufficient to have answered any of their demands ; but it
was also sufficient to put him above the necessity of employing
their money, either in trade or speculation.

It had also been suggested, that Thomlinson, at the governor's
request, had solicited and procured the instruction, which had
occasioned this unhappy stagnation of business. When this suggestion came to his knowledge, he exculpated himself from the
charge, in a letter which he wrote to a leading member of the
assembly ; and gave a full account of the matter as far as it had
come to his knowledge. He said, that the governor himself had
stated the facts in his letters to the ministry ; concerning his calling of the new members, in 1745, and their exclusion from the
assembly, with the reasons given for it ; and had desired to know

(1) Thomlinson's MS. letters.

October 19, 1749, Mr. Atkinson wrote thus in answer. ' I am supposed
' by many people to be privy to all the governor's transactions here, which is
' totally without foundation. I never saw a letter which he wrote home, nor
' any he received, only, when any of them were communicated to the council
' or assembly ; nor any of his speeches or messages. So that, really I cannot
' be said to advise. Neither do I see what reason the people have to complain.
' His greatest enemies are now of the assembly, and in all the controversy,
' not one particular instance of injustice or oppression hath been mentioned
' by them ; and when you read over their several messages, and votes, you
' will not discover any inclination to conceal the least failing he had been the
' author of.'

the king's pleasure, and to have directions how to act.[1] That the
ministry, without any exception or hesitation, had pronounced his
conduct conformable to his duty. That nevertheless, the board
of trade had solemnly considered the matter, and consulted counsel, and had summoned him, as agent of the province, to attend
their deliberation. Their result was, that as the crown had an
indisputable right to incorporate any town in England, and qualify
it to send members to parliament, so the same right and power
had been legally given to all the governors in America ; by means
of which, all the assemblies in the king's governments, had increased in number, as the colonies had increased in settlements.
That any other usage in calling representatives was wrong ; although it might have been indulged, when the province was under
the same governor with Massachusetts. This was all which passed before the additional instruction came out, which was sent
through the hands of the agent. As it was founded on a question
concerning the rights and prerogatives of the crown ; he argued
the absurdity of supposing, either that it had been solicited, or that
any attempt to have it withdrawn could be effectual. His advice
was, that they should submit to it ; because, that under it, they
would enjoy the same rights and privileges with their fellow subjects in England, and in the other colonies ; assuring them, that
the then reigning prince had never discovered the least inclination
to infringe the constitutional rights of any of his subjects.

This advice, however salutary, had not the intended effect.
Instead of submitting, the party in opposition to the governor,
framed a complaint against him, and sent it to London, to be
presented to the king. If they could have prevailed, their next
measure would have been, to recommend a gentleman, Sir William
Pepperrell, of Massachusetts, for his successor. This manoeuvre
came to the ears of Thomlinson ; but he was under no necessity
to exert himself on this occasion ; for the person to whose care
the address was intrusted, considering the absurdity of complaining
to the king, against his governor, for acting agreeably to his instructions, was advised not to present it.[2] This disappointment
vexed the opposition to such a degree, that they would have gladly
dissolved the government, and put themselves under the jurisdiction of Massachusetts, had it been in their power. But, finding
all their efforts ineffectual, either to have the instruction withdrawn, or the governor removed, they consoled themselves with
this thought, that it was ' better to have two privileges taken from
' them, than voluntarily to give up one.'*

(1) MS. letter of Thomlinson to H. Sherburne, Nov. 13, 1749.   (2) MS.
letters of Thomlinson.

* [1750. A singular and splendid appearance in the heavens was noticed
in the eastern part of New-Hampshire, of which I find the following account
in an interleaved almanack, kept by a gentleman of Portsmouth.
   " 26 August. This evening I was suddenly surprised by an explosion in

The time for which the assembly was elected having expired, a new one was called in the same manner. They came together with a spirit of moderation, and a disposition to transact the long neglected business. The members, from the new towns, quietly took their seats. An unexceptionable speaker, Meshech Weare, was elected. A recorder was appointed. A committee was chosen to settle the treasurer's accounts, and a vote was passed for putting the reimbursement money into the public funds in England.[1] The governor's salary was augmented, and all things went on smoothly. The party which had been opposed to the governor, declined, in number and in virulence. Some had been removed by death; others were softened and relaxed. A liberal distribution of commissions, civil and military, was made, and an era of domestic reconciliation commenced.

1752. Jan. 2.

The controversy respecting Fort-Dummer, and the fear of losing a district in that neighborhood, quickened the governor to make grants of several townships in that quarter, on both sides of Connecticut river ; chiefly to those persons who claimed the same lands, under the Massachusetts title. The war being over, the old inhabitants returned to their plantations, and were strengthened by additions to their number. It was in contemplation, to extend the settlements, farther up Connecticut river, to the rich meadows of Cohos. The plan was, to cut a road to that place ; to lay out two townships, one on each side of the river, and opposite to each other; to erect stockades, with lodgments for two hundred men, in each township, enclosing a space of fifteen acres ; in the centre of which was to be a citadel, containing the public buildings and granaries, which were to be large enough to receive all the inhabitants, and their moveable effects, in case of necessity. [2] As an inducement to people to remove to this new plantation ; they were to have courts of judicature, and other civil privileges among themselves, and were to be under strict military discipline. A large number of persons engaged in this enterprise ; and they were the rather stimulated to undertake it, because it was feared, that the French, who had already begun to encroach on the territory claimed by the British crown, would take possession of this valuable tract, if it should be left unoccupied.

In pursuance of this plan, a party was sent up in the spring of 1752, to view the meadows of Cohos, and lay out the proposed townships.[3] The Indians observed them, and suspected their

(1) Records of assembly. Atkinson's MS. letters.   (2) Atkinson's MS. letters.   (3) MS. letters of Col. Israel Williams.

the air. It was a quarter after nine, and the sky as free from clouds and thick of stars as I ever saw it. It appeared as if the sky opened in the South about half way from the horizon, as large as the broad side of a house, and the flame as deep a color as any fire I ever saw. It closed up gradually, and was near two minutes before it disappeared.''']

intentions. The land was theirs, and they knew its value. A party of the Aresaguntacook, or St. Francis tribe was deputed, to remonstrate against this proceeding. They came to the fort at Number-Four, with a flag of truce; pretending that they had not heard of the treaty of peace, which had been made with the several Indian tribes. They complained to Captain Stevens, of the encroachment which was meditating on their land; and said, that they could not allow the English to settle at Cohos, when they owned more land already than they could improve; and, that if this settlement were pursued, they should think the English had a mind for war, and would resist them. This threatening being communicated to the governor of Massachusetts, and by him to the governor of New-Hampshire, threw such discouragement on the project that it was laid aside.

The Indians did not content themselves with remonstrating and threatening. Two of the same tribe named Sabatis and Christi, April. came to Canterbury; where they were entertained in a friendly manner for more than a month. At their departure, they forced away two negroes; one of whom escaped and returned; and the other was carried to Crown-Point and sold to a French officer.[1] A party of ten or twelve of the same tribe, May. commanded by Captain Moses, met with four young men who were hunting on Baker's river. One of these was John Stark.[2] When he found himself surprised and fallen into their hands, he called to his brother William Stark, who being in a canoe, gained the opposite shore, and escaped. They fired at the canoe, and killed a young man who was in it.[3] John received a severe beating from the Indians for alarming his brother. They carried him and his companion, Eastman, up Connecticut river, through several carrying places, and down the lake Memphremagog to the head quarters of their tribe. There they dressed him in their finest robes and adopted him as a son. This early captivity, from which he was redeemed, qualified him to be an expert partisan, in the succeeding war; from which station, he afterward rose to the rank of brigadier-general in the armies of the United States.*

The next year, Sabatis, with another Indian named Plausawa, came to Canterbury; where, being reproached with the misconduct respecting the negroes, he and his companion behaved
1753. in an insolent manner. Several persons treated them very
June. freely with strong liquor.[4] One followed them into the woods, and killed them, and by the help of another, buried them; but so shallow, that their bodies were devoured by beasts of prey,

(1) MS. depositions.   (2) Shirley's printed conference, 1754.   (3) Information of W. Stark.   (4) MS. depositions.

* [1752. The towns of Chesterfield, Westmoreland, Walpole and Richmond were incorporated.]

and their bones lay on the ground.* By the treaties of peace,
it had been stipulated, on the one part, that if any of the Indians
should commit an act of hostility against the English, their young
men should join with the English in reducing such Indians to submission; and on the other hand, that if an Englishman should
injure any of them, no private revenge should be taken; but application should be made to the government for justice. In the
autumn of the same year, a conference being held, with the eastern Indians, by the government of Massachusetts, a present was
made to the Aresaguntacook tribe, expressive of an intention to
wipe away the blood. They accepted the present, and ratified
the peace which had been made in 1749.[1] †

(1) Printed conference, 1753.

* [The names of the persons concerned in the death of these Indians, it
appears from the Rev. Mr Price's History of Boscawen, p. 44, were Bowen
and Morril. The circumstances of their death are particularly narrated in an
article entitled *Indian Bridge*, in the Coll. of Farmer and Moore, iii. 27—29.
It appears from *that* account, that the person who killed them was Peter Bow-
en, to whose house in Contoocook, (Boscawen) he invited them to stay during the night. "They had been in a surly mood and had used some threats
to two persons who offered to trade with them that day, but became in better
humor on being freely treated with rum by their host. The night was spent
in a drunken Indian frolic, for which Bowen had as good a relish as his
guests. As they became intoxicated, he fearing that they might do mischief,
took the precaution to make his wife engage their attention, while he drew
the charges from their guns. The next morning, they asked Bowen to go
with his horse, and carry their baggage to the place where their canoe was left
the evening before. He went and carried their packs on his horse. As they
went, Sabatis proposed to run a race with the horse. Bowen suspecting mischief was intended, declined the race, but finally consented to run. He however, took care to let the Indian outrun the horse. Sabatis laughed heartily
at Bowen, because his horse could run no faster. They then proceeded apparently in good humour. After a while, Sabatis said to Bowen—" Bowen
walk woods,"—meaning "go with me as a prisoner." Bowen said, "No walk
woods, all one brothers." They went on until they were near the canoe,
when Sabatis proposed a second race, and that the horse should be unloaded
of the baggage and should start a little before him. Bowen refused to start
so, but consented to start together. They ran, and as soon as the horse had
got a little before the Indian, Bowen heard a gun snap. Looking round, he
saw the smoke of powder, and the gun aimed at him. He turned and struck
his tomahawk in the Indian's head. He went back to meet Plausawa, who
seeing the fate of Sabatis, took aim with his gun at Bowen. The gun flash-
ed. Plausawa fell on his knees and begged for his life. He pleaded his in-
nocence, and former friendship for the English; but all in vain. Bowen
knew there would be no safety for him while the companion and friend of
Sabatis was living. To secure himself, he buried the same tomahawk in the
skull of Plausawa. This was done in the road on the bank of Merrimack river, near the northerly line of Boscawen. Bowen hid the dead bodies under
a small bridge in Salisbury. The next spring the bodies were discovered and
buried."]

† [1753. Keene, Charlestown, Swanzey, Winchester and Hinsdale were
incorporated. Swanzey was first granted by Massachusetts in 1734, to 64
proprietors, whose first meeting was holden at Concord, Mass., 27 June, that
year. Until its incorporation by New-Hampshire, it was called *Lower-Ashuelot*, from the Indian name of the river, which was originally *Ashaelock*. From
1741 to 1747, this town suffered much from Indian depredations. Several of
the inhabitants were killed and some were made prisoners. The province of
Massachusetts, under whose jurisdiction this town had remained thirteen

The two men who killed Sabatis and Plausawa, were apprehended and brought to Portsmouth. A bill was found against them by the grand jury, and they were confined in irons. In the night, before the day appointed for their trial, an armed mob from the country, with axes and crows, forced the prison, and carried them off in triumph. A proclamation was issued, and a reward offered by the governor for apprehending the rioters ; but no discovery was made, and the action was even deemed meritorious.[1] The next summer, another conference was held at Falmouth, at which commissioners from New-Hampshire assisted. The Aresaguntacooks did not attend ; but sent a message purporting that the blood was not wiped away. The commissioners from New-Hampshire made a handsome present, to all the Indians, who appeared at this conference ; which ended as usual, in the promise of peace and friendship.[2]

1754.

CHAPTER XXII.

The last French and Indian war, which terminated in the conquest of Canada. Controversy concerning the lands westward of Connecticut river.

By the treaty of Aix la Chapelle, in 1748, it was stipulated, that ' all things should be restored, on the footing they were ' before the war.'[3] The island of Cape-Breton was accordingly restored to France ; but the limits of the French and English territories on the continent, were undetermined ; and it was the policy of both nations to gain possession of important passes, and to which each had some pretensions, to hold them, till the limits should be settled by commissioners mutually chosen. These commissioners met at Paris ; but came to no decision. By the construction of charters and grants from the crown of England, her colonies extended indefinitely westward. The French had settlements in Canada and Louisiana, and they meditated to join these distant colonies, by a chain of forts and posts, from the St. Lawrence to the Mississippi ; and to extend the limits of Canada, as far eastward, as to command nav-

(1) MS. letters of Governor Wentworth.   (2) Printed conference.—
(3) Printed treaty.

years, having withdrawn her protection, and left the people in a defenceless state, and exposed to the fury of the savages, the settlers abandoned the place, and many of them returned to their former places of residence in Massachusetts. The Indians very soon set fire to their forts, which, with every house except one, they reduced to ashes. They returned about three years afterwards, when nothing but desolation and ruin was to be seen about their former habitations. They recommenced their settlements, and were not afterwards molested by the Indians. N. H. Gazetteer, 248.

1755. Madbury was incorporated. 1756. Sandown was incorporated.]

igation in the winter, when the great river St. Lawrence is impassable. These claims of territory, extending on the one part from east to west, and on the other from north to south, necessarily interfered. The colonies of Nova-Scotia, New-York and Virginia, were principally affected by this interference ; and the encroachments made on them by the French, were a subject of complaint, both here and in Europe.

It was foreseen that this controversy could not be decided but by the sword ; and the English determined to be early in 1754. their preparations. The Earl of Holderness, secretary of state, wrote to the governors of the American colonies, recommending *union* for their mutual protection and defence. A meeting of commissioners from the colonies, at Albany, having been appointed, for the purpose of holding a conference with the Six Nations, on the subject of French encroachments, within their country ; it was proposed, by Governor Shirley, to the several governors, that the delegates should be instructed on the subject of union.[1]

At the place appointed, the congress was held ; consisting of delegates from Massachusetts, New-Hampshire, Rhode- June 19. Island, Connecticut, Pennsylvania and Maryland ; with the lieutenant-governor and council of New-York. They took their rank in geographical order, beginning at the north. One member from each colony was appointed to draw a plan of union ; Hutchinson of Massachusetts, Atkinson of New-Hampshire, Hopkins of Rhode-Island, Pitkin of Connecticut, Smith of New-York, Franklin of Pennsylvania, and Tasker of Maryland.[2] The substance of the plan was, that application be made, for an act of parliament, to form a grand council, consisting of delegates from the several legislative assemblies, subject to the control of a president-general, to be appointed by the crown, with a negative voice. That this council should enact general laws ; apportion the quotas of men and money, to be raised by each colony ; determine the building of forts ; regulate the operations of armies ; and concert all measures for the common protection and safety. The delegates of Connecticut alone, entered their dissent to the plan, because of the negative voice of the president-general. It is worthy of remark, that this plan, for the union of the colonies, was agreed to, on the *fourth day of July ;* exactly twenty-two years before the declaration of American Independence, and that the name of FRANKLIN appears in both.*†

(1) Shirley's letters and speeches.   (2) Atkinson's MS. Journal.

* [The plan of a proposed union of the several colonies of Massachusetts-Bay, New-Hampshire, Connecticut, Rhode-Island, New-York, New-Jersey, Pennsylvania, Maryland, Virginia, North-Carolina, and South-Carolina, for their mutual defence and security, and for extending the British settlements in North-America, with the reasons and motives for each article of the plan, (as far as could be remembered) is given entire in the Works of Franklin, Philadelphia edition, 1809, vol. iv. p. 5—38.]

With the plan of union, a representation was made to the king, of the danger in which the colonies were involved. Copies of both were laid before the several assemblies. They were fully sensible of their danger from the French ; but they apprehended greater danger from the plan of union. Its fate was singular. It was rejected in America, because it was supposed to put too much power into the hands of the king ; and it was rejected in England, because it was supposed to give too much power to the assemblies of the colonies. The ministry made another proposal ; that the governor, with one or two members of the council, of each colony, should assemble, and consult for the common defence, and draw on the British treasury for the sums expended ; which should be raised by a general tax, laid by parliament, on the colonies. [1]— But this was not a time to push such an alarming innovation ; and when it was found impracticable, the ministry determined to employ their own troops, to fight their battles in America, rather than to let the colonists feel their own strength, and be directed by their own counsels.

To draw some aid, however from the colonies was necessary. Their militia might serve as guards, or rangers, or laborers, or do garrison duty, or be employed in other inferior offices ; but British troops, commanded by British officers, must have the *honor* of reducing the French dominions in North America.

The savage nations in the French interest were always ready, on the first appearance of a rupture, to take up the hatchet. It was the policy of the French government, to encourage their depredations, on the frontiers of the English colonies, to which they had a native antipathy. By this means, the French could make their enemies pay the whole expense of a war ; for all the supplies, which they afforded to the Indians, were amply compensated, by the ransom of captives. In these later wars, therefore, we find the savages more dextrous in taking captives, and more tender of them when taken, than in former wars ; which were carried on with circumstances of greater cruelty.

No sooner had the alarm of hostilities, which commenced between the English and French, in the western part of Virginia, spread through the continent ; than the Indians renewed their attacks on the frontiers of New-Hampshire.* A party of them

(1) Franklin's Examination, 1766.

† At this congress, a present from the crown was distributed to the Indians. The commissioners of New-Hampshire, Atkinson, Wibird, Sherburne and Weare, by direction of the assembly, made them a separate present. It is a custom among the Six Nations to give a *name* to their benefactors on such occasions. The name which they gave to the province of New-Hampshire was *So-saguax-owane.* I have inquired of the Rev. Mr. Kirkland, the meaning of this name : He informed me that *So* signifies, AGAIN; *saguax*, a DISH ; and *owane*, LARGE.

* [On the 16 May, Nathaniel Meloon, who had recently removed his family from the fort in Contoocook to Stevens-town, now the west part of Salisbury, was captured by the Indians, together with his wife and four children,

made an assault, on a family at Baker's-town, on Pemigewasset river ; where they killed a woman, and took several cap- Aug. 15. tives.* Within three days, they killed a man and woman at Steven's-town in the same neighborhood ; upon which Aug. 18. the settlements were broken up, and the people retired to the lower towns for safety, and the government was obliged to post soldiers in the deserted places.[1] After a few days more, Aug. 29. they broke into the house of James Johnson, at Number-Four, early in the morning, before any of the family were awake ; and took him, with his wife and three children, her sister Miriam Willard, and two men, Peter Laboree and Ebenezer Farnsworth. The surprisal was complete and bloodless, and they carried them off undisturbed. The next day, Johnson's wife was delivered of a daughter, who from the circumstance of its birth was named *Captive*. The Indians halted one day, on the woman's account, and the next day resumed their march ; carrying her on a litter, which they made for the purpose, and afterwards put her on horse-back. On their march, they were distressed for provision ; and killed the horse for food. The infant was nourished, by sucking pieces of its flesh. When they arrived at Montreal, Johnson obtained a parole, of two months, to return and solicit the

(1) Council minutes.

viz. Rachel, John, Daniel and Sarah. Nathaniel his eldest son escaped.— They were carried to Canada, and upon their arrival there, the children were separated, and sold to the French. Mr. Meloon and wife were permitted to live together, and their son Joseph, lately living in Salisbury, in this state, was born in their captivity in 1755. After a servitude of more than three years in Canada, the parents, with their three sons, were shipped for France ; but on their voyage, near the Grand Banks, were taken by the British, and safely landed at Portland, in Maine, from whence they travelled by land, and returned home after an absence of four years, of tedious captivity. Their daughter Rachel, who was nine years when taken, returned after nine years, though much against her inclination. She had become much attached to the Indians, had learned their language and could sing their songs, and ever after retained a partiality for their manners and habits. Sarah the youngest child is supposed to have died soon after their arrival in Canada. Rachel the mother was the second woman who moved into the town of Salisbury. She lived until 1804, when she died at the age of 94. Price, Hist. of Boscawen, 113.—Coll. of N. H. Hist. Soc. ii. 26.—Coll. of Farmer and Moore, ii. 376.— Gazetteer of N. H. by do. 233.—Hough's Concord Courier, 1804.—MS. letter Moses Eastman, Esq.]

* [The woman killed was the wife of Philip Call. Timothy Cook, son of Elisha Cook who was killed in 1746 (see page 289.) was killed at the same time. The captives were Samuel Scribner and Robert Barber of Salisbury, whowere both sold to the French, and Enos Bishop of Boscawen, who arrived in thirteen days at St. Francois, and within eight weeks, was sold to a French gentleman at Montreal for 300 livres. On the 26 September, the next year, he, with two others escaped from Montreal, and after travelling twenty-six days, eighteen of which were without any food other than what the wilderness afforded them, he arrived at Charlestown, and from thence returned to their friends. A sum of money had been raised for his ransom, but the person by whom it was sent, converted it to his own use. After his return, Bishop represented his sufferings to the general court, and received £50 from the public treasury. Price, Hist. Boscawen, 113, 114.—Farmer and Moore, Hist. Coll. i. 62, 63.—Gazetteer of N. H. 233.—Papers in Secretary's office.]

means of redemption.[1] He applied to the assembly of New-
Dec. 19. Hampshire, and after some delay obtained one hundred
and fifty pounds sterling.[2] But the season was so far advanced, and the winter proved so severe, that he did not reach
Canada till the spring. He was then charged with breaking his
parole ; a great part of his money was taken from him by violence ;
and, he was shut up with his family in prison ; where they took
the small pox, which they happily survived. After eighteen
months, the woman, with her sister, and two daughters, were sent
in a cartel ship to England ; and thence returned to Boston.—
Johnson was kept in prison three years ; and then, with his son,
returned and met his wife in Boston ; where he had the singular
ill fortune, to be suspected of designs unfriendly to his country,
aad was again imprisoned ; but no evidence being produced
against him, he was liberated. His eldest daughter was retained
in a Canadian nunnery.[3]

The fort and settlement at Number-Four, being in an exposed
situation, required assistance and support. It had been built by
Massachusetts when it was supposed to be within its limits. It
was projected by Colonel Stoddard of Northampton, and was well
situated, in connection with the other forts, on the western frontier,
to command all the paths by which the Indians travelled from
Canada to New-England. It was now evidently in New-Hampshire ; and Shirley, by advice of his council, applied to Wentworth, recommending the future maintenance of that post, to the
care of his assembly ; but they did not think themselves interested
in its preservation, and refused to make any provision for it.[4]
The inhabitants made several applications for the same purpose ;
but were uniformly disappointed. They then made pressing remonstrances to the assembly of Massachusetts, who sent soldiers
for the defence of that post, and of Fort-Dummer, till 1757 ;[5]
when they supposed that the commander in chief of the king's
forces would take them under his care, as royal garrisons. It
was also recommended to the assembly of New-Hampshire to
build a fort at Cohos ; but this proposal met the same fate.

The next spring, three expeditions were undertaken against
the French forts. One against Fort du Quesne, on the Ohio,
1755. was conducted by General Braddock ; who was defeated
and slain. Another against Niagara, by Governor Shirley,
which miscarried ; and a third against Crown-Point, by General
Johnson. For this last expedition, New-Hampshire raised five
hundred men, and put them under the command of Colonel Joseph Blanchard.* The governor ordered them to Connecticut

(1) Olcott's MS. letter.   (2) Assembly records.   (3) [Narrative of the captivity of Mrs. Johnson, in the Collections of Farmer and Moore for 1822, vol.
i. 177—239.]   (4) Shirley's MS. letters.   (5) Massachusetts Records.

* [Colonel Blanchard was of Dunstable, where he was born 11 February,
1705. He was appointed by mandamus, one of the counsellors of New-Hamp-

river, to build a fort at Cohos, supposing it to be in their way to Crown-Point. They first marched to Baker's town, where they began to build batteaux, and consumed their time and provisions to no purpose. By Shirley's advice, they quitted that futile employment, and made a fatiguing march through the woods, by the way of Number-Four, to Albany. Whilst Johnson lay encamped at Lake George, with his other forces, he posted the New-Hampshire regiment at Fort Edward. On the eighth of September, he was attacked in his camp, by Baron Dieskau, commanding a body of French regular troops, Canadians and savages. On the morning of that day, a scouting party from Fort Edward discovered wagons burning in the road; upon which Captain Nathaniel Folsom was ordered out, with eighty of the New-Hampshire regiment, and forty of New-York under Captain McGennis. When they came to the place, they found the wagoners and the cattle dead: but no enemy was there. Hearing the report of guns, toward the lake, they hasted thither; and having approached within two miles, found the baggage of the French army, under the care of a guard, whom they attacked and dispersed. When the retreating army of Dieskau appeared, about four of the clock in the afternoon, Folsom posted his men among the trees, and kept up a well directed fire, till night; the enemy retired, with great loss, and he made his way to the camp, carrying his own wounded, and several French prisoners, with many of the enemy's packs.[1] This well-timed engagement, in which but six men on our side were lost, deprived the French army of their ammunition and baggage; the remains of which were brought into camp the next day.[2] After this, the regiment of New-Hampshire joined the army. The men were employed in scouting, which service they performed in a manner so acceptable, that no other duty was required of them. Parties of them frequently went within view of the French fort at Crown-Point; and at one time they brought off the scalp of a French soldier, whom they killed near the gate.[3]

After the engagement on the 8th of September, when it was found necessary to reinforce the army, a second regiment, of three hundred men, was raised in New-Hampshire, and put under the command of Colonel Peter Gilman. These men were as alert, and indefatigable as their brethren, though they had not opportunity to give such convincing evidence of it. The expedition was no farther pursued; and late in autumn the forces were disbanded and returned home.

(1) Folsom's information.   (2) Johnson's printed letter.   (3) Atkinson's MS. letters.

shire in 1740, and sustained the office until his death, 7 April, 1758. He was distinguished as a land surveyor, and in conjunction with Rev. Samuel Langdon, prepared a map of New-Hampshire, which was published in 1761, being inscribed to the Hon. Charles Townsend, his majesty's secretary at war, and one of the privy council.]

The exertions made for the reduction of Crown-Point, not only failed of their object, but provoked the Indians, to execute their mischievous designs, against the frontiers of New-Hampshire ; which were wholly uncovered, and exposed to their full force. Between the rivers Connecticut and St. Francis, there is a safe and easy communication by short carrying-places, with which they were perfectly acquainted. The Indians of that river, therefore, made frequent incursions, and returned unmolested with their prisoners and booty.

At New-Hopkinton, they took a man and a boy ; but perceiving the approach of a scouting party, they fled and left their captives. At Keene, they took Benjamin Twitchel, and at Walpole they killed Daniel Twitchel, and a man named Flint.*[1] At the same place, Colonel Bellows, at the head of twenty men met with a party of fifty Indians ; and having exchanged some shot, and killed several of the enemy, he broke through them and got into the fort ; not one man of his company being killed or wounded.† After a few days, these Indians, being joined by others to the number of one hundred and seventy, assaulted the garrison of John Kilburn, in which were himself, John Peak, two boys and several women ; who bravely defended the house and obliged the enemy to retire, with considerable loss. Peak was mortally wounded.[2] ‡ Some of these Indians joined Dieskau's army, and

(1) Sumner's MS. letter.   (2) Fessenden's MS. letter.

* [They had gone back to the hills, about a mile east from the settlement, to procure some timber for oars. One of them was scalped ; the other they cut open and took out his heart, cut it in pieces and laid them on his breast. Their bodies were buried near where they were found ; and a ridge of land, the west side of the road, about two miles north of Walpole village, towards Drewsville, points out the spot hallowed by the remains of the first victims of Indian massacre in the town of Walpole. Coll. N. H. Hist. Soc. ii. 51, 52.]

† [It appears that Colonel Bellows and his men were returning home, each having a bag of meal on his back. From the motions of the dogs, they suspected the near approach of the enemy. The colonel ordered all his men to throw off the meal, advance to an eminence before them, carefully crawl up the bank, spring upon their feet, give one whoop, and then drop into the sweet fern. This manœuvre had the desired effect ; for as soon as the whoop was given, the Indians all arose from their ambush in a semicircle around the path Bellows was to follow. His men immediately fired which so disconcerted the plans and expectations of the Indians, that they darted away into the bushes without firing a gun. Finding their number too great for his, the colonel ordered his men to file off to the south and make for the fort. Ibid. ii. 55, 56.]

‡ [The defence of Kilburn's garrison, of which a particular account is given in the Coll. N. H. Hist. Soc. ii. 55—57, was one of the most heroic and successful efforts of personal courage and valor recorded in the annals of Indian warfare. The number of Indians was about 200, some accounts say 400, against whom, John Kilburn, his son John, in his 18th year, John Peak (whose name was erroneously printed Pike in the former editions) and his son, and the wife and daughter of Kilburn, were obliged to contend for their lives.— The leader of the Indians, named Philip, was well acquainted with Kilburn, and having approached near the garrison and secured himself behind a tree, called out to those in the house to surrender. "Old John, young John," said he, "I know you, come out here :—We give you good quarter." "Quarter,"

were in the battle at Lake George.   At Number-Four, they killed
a large number of cattle, and cut off the flesh.   At Hinsdale,
they attacked a party, who were at work in the woods ; killed
John Hardiclay and John Alexander, and took Jonathan Colby.
The others escaped to the fort.   Within a few days afterward,
they ambushed Caleb Howe, Hilkiah Grout, and Benja- July 27.
min Gaffield, as they were returning from their labor in
the field.   Howe was killed ; Gaffield was drowned in attempting
to cross the river ; and Grout made his escape.   The Indians
went directly to Bridgman's fort, where the families of these unfortunate men resided.   They had heard the report of the guns,
and were impatient to learn the cause.   By the sound of feet
without, it being in the dusk of the evening, they concluded that
their friends had returned, and too hastily opened the gate to receive them ; when to their inexpressible surprise, they admitted
the savages, and the three families, consisting of fourteen persons,
were made captives.*1

After the defeat and death of Braddock, the chief command
of the operations against the enemy fell into the hands of Shirley ;

(1) Gay's MS. letter.

vociferated Kilburn, with a voice of thunder, " you black rascals, begone, or
we'll quarter you."   The Indians soon rushed forward to the attack, but were
repulsed by Kilburn and his men, who were aided by the females in running
bullets and in loading their guns, of which they had several in the house.
All the afternoon, one incessant firing was kept up till near sundown, when
the Indians began to disappear ; and as the sun sunk behind the western hills,
the sound of the guns, and the cry of the war whoop died away in silence.—
Peak, by an imprudent exposure before the port hole, received a ball in his
hip, which, for want of surgical aid, proved fatal on the 5th day.   Kilburn
lived to see the town of Walpole populous and flourishing, and his fourth
generation on the stage.   On a plain unpolished stone in Walpole burying
ground is the following inscription :

" In Memory
of
JOHN KILBURN,
who departed this life for a better, April 8th, 1789,
in his 85th year of his age.   He was the first
settler of this town in 1749."

His son John spent the last years of his life in the town of Shrewsbury,
Vermont, and died in 1822, at the same age of his father.   Ibid. ii. 55—58.
Rev. Mr. Fessenden in the letter referred to, says, " but four families settled
in town until after the reduction of Canada."]

* One of these, the wife of Caleb Howe, was the *fair captive*, of whom such
a brilliant account is given in the life of General Putnam, published by Colonel Humphreys.   She is still living at Hinsdale, and has obliged the author
with a particular narrative of her sufferings and deliverance.   This account,
drawn up by the Rev. Mr. Gay, is too long to be here inserted, and too entertaining to be abridged ; but will probably be published at some future time.
[It appeared in the appendix to the iii. volume.]   As to that part of the story,
that the people of Hinsdale chose her to go to Europe, as their agent in a case
of disputed lands ; it was never known or thought of by them till the life of
Putnam appeared in print.   Gay's MS. letter.   [Eunice, the wife of Benjamin Gaffield, after having been carried to Canada and sold to the French, was
sent to France, from thence to England, and from England to Boston.   (Newspaper.)   She afterwards married a Mr. Pratt, and lived until the present year
(1839) when she died at Dana, in Massachusetts, at the age of 97.]

who called another congress, at New-York, and planned another
expedition against Crown-Point; for which purpose, he called on
the several governments to raise men and provide stores. A regiment was raised in New-Hampshire, the command of which was
given to Colonel Nathaniel Meserve.[1] They also appointed two
commissioners, Peter Gilman and Thomas Westbrooke Waldron,
who resided at Albany, to take care of the stores, whilst the regiment, with the other troops, assisted in building forts and batteaux.
In the midst of this campaign, Shirley was superseded by the
Earl of Loudon ; but the summer passed away in fruitless labor ;
whilst the French, by their superior alertness, besieged and took
the English fort at Oswego ; and the regiments of Shirley and
Pepperell, who garrisoned it, were sent prisoners to France. [2]
During this summer, the Indians killed Lieutenant Moses Willard,
and wounded his son at Number-Four ; and took Josiah Foster,
with his wife and two children, from Winchester. They also
wounded Zebulon Stebbins, of Hinsdale, who, with Reuben
Wright, discovered an ambush, and prevented the captivity of
several persons for whom the Indians were lying in wait.[3]

The soldiers of New-Hampshire were so expert, in every service which required agility, and so habituated to fatigue and danger ; that, by the express desire of Lord Loudon, three ranging
companies were formed of them ; who continued in service during
the winter as well as the summer.[4] The command of these companies was given to Robert Rogers, John Stark, and William
Stark. They were eminently useful in scouring the woods, procuring intelligence, and skirmishing with detached parties of the
enemy. These companies were kept during the war, in the pay
of the crown ; and after the peace, the officers were allowed half
pay on the British establishment.*

(1) Shirley's letters.   (2) July 25—Loudon's MS. letters.   (3) Gay, Sumner and Olcott's MS. letters.   (4) Lord Loudon's MS. letters.

* [1756. From this period is to be dated the first introduction of printing in
the province of New-Hampshire. A printing press was set up at Portsmouth in
August, this year, by Daniel Fowle, from Boston, and the New-Hampshire
Gazette was issued by him on the seventh of October following. Dr. Thomas in his History of Printing, vol. ii. p. 280, thus speaks of the establishment
of the Gazette. " A Press having been established at Portsmouth, by Daniel Fowle, from Boston, he, in August, 1756, began the publication of a public journal, entitled the New-Hampshire Gazette." From the circumstance
that the head of the first number of the Gazette, with the date, (August) is
given by Dr. Thomas, it might be supposed he had seen that number, or that
some one who had seen it, had copied the head of it for him, with the true
date. But the time given by him is evidently wrong, as will appear from the
following printed note from Ames's Almanack for 1757, which was issued
from the same press the same year the Gazette commenced. " The first
PRINTING PRESS set up in PORTSMOUTH, NEW-HAMPSHIRE, was on August
1756 ; The GAZETTE published the 7th October ; and this ALMANACK November
following." This paper is still continued and is the oldest in New-England.
The number for 12 October, 1830, is marked Vol. LXXV. No. 48. About
eighty different newspapers have been published in New-Hampshire. Some
of them have had a very brief existence, while others have attained a respect-

The next year, another Crown-Point expedition was projected by Lord Loudon. The crown was at the expense of stores and provisions, and required of the colonies, to raise, arm, clothe, and pay their quotas of men. Another regiment 1757. was raised in New-Hampshire, of which Meserve was commander ; who went to Halifax with part of his regiment, a body of one hundred carpenters, and three companies of rangers, to serve under Lord Loudon, whilst the other part of the regiment under Lieutenant-Colonel Goffe, was ordered by General Webb, who commanded at the westward, in the absence of the Earl of Loudon, to rendezvous 'at Number-Four. Before their arrival, a large party of French and Indians attacked the mills in that place, and took Sampson Colefax, David Farnsworth and Thomas Adams.[1] The inhabitants, hearing the guns, advanced to the mills ; but finding the enemy in force, prudently retreated. The enemy burned the mills ; and in their retreat, took two other men, who were coming in from hunting, viz. Thomas Robbins and Asa Spafford. Farnsworth and Robbins returned ; the others died in Canada.

Goffe with his men marched through Number-Four and joined General Webb at Albany ; who posted them at Fort William Henry, near Lake George, under the command of Colonel Munroe, of the thirty-fifth British regiment. The French General Montcalm, at the head of a large body of Canadians and Indians, with a train of artillery, invested this fort ; and in six days, the garrison, after having expended all their ammunition, ca- Aug. 3. pitulated ; on condition that they should not serve against the French for eighteen months. They were allowed the honors of war, and were to be escorted by the French Aug. 9. troops to Fort Edward, with their private baggage. The Indians, who served in this expedition, *on the promise of plunder*, were enraged at the terms granted to the garrison ; and, as they marched out unarmed, fell upon them, stripped them naked, and murdered all who made any resistance. The New-Hampshire regiment happening to be in the rear, felt the chief fury of the enemy. Out of two hundred, eighty were killed and taken.[2]

(1) Olcott's MS. letters. (2) New-Hampshire Gazette, No. 49.

able age. The three oldest, next to the Gazette, now published, are the *Portsmouth Journal*, marked on the 3 July, 1830, No. 27, Vol. XLI ; the *New-Hampshire Sentinel*, printed at Keene, which commenced in March, 1799 ; and the *Farmer's Cabinet*, published at Amherst, which commenced 11 November, 1802. The number of newspapers now (1830) printed in the state amounts to nineteen.

1756. Ezekiel Flanders and Edward Emery were killed by the Indians, when hunting beaver by New-found pond, between Bristol and Hebron, in the county of Grafton. The Indians afterwards informed, that one of them was shot when skinning a beaver in a camp, and the other shot at the same time, in sight of the camp, bringing in a beaver on his back. The next year, Moses Jackman, of Boscawen, who it is believed is still living, was taken captive while on a visit at Mr. Clough's in Canterbury. He returned after a captivity of four years. Price, Hist. of Boscawen, 114, 115.]

This melancholy event threw the whole country into the deepest consternation. Webb, who remained at Fort Edward, expecting to be there attacked, sent expresses to all the provinces for reinforcements. The French, however, did not pursue their advantage, but returned to Canada. A reinforcement of two hundred and fifty men was raised in New-Hampshire, under the command of Major Thomas Tash ;* which, by the orders of General Webb, was stationed at Number-Four. This was the first time that the troops of New-Hampshire occupied that important post.[1]

Hitherto the war had been, on our part, unsuccessful. The great expense, the frequent disappointments, the loss of men, of forts, and of stores, were very discouraging. The enemy's country was filled with prisoners, and scalps, private plunder, and public stores and provisions, which our people, as beasts of burden, had conveyed to them. These reflections were the dismal entertainment of the winter. The next spring called for fresh exertions ; and happily for America, the British ministry had been changed, and the direction of the war, in answer to the united voice of the people of England, was put into the hands of that decisive statesman, William Pitt.

In his circular letter to the American governors, he assured them ; that to repair the losses and disappointments of the last inactive campaign, it was determined to send a formidable force, to operate by sea and land, against the French in America ; and he called upon them to raise ' as large bodies of ' men, within their respective governments, as the number of in- ' habitants might allow ;' leaving it to them, to form the regiments and to appoint officers at their discretion.[2] He informed them that arms, ammunition, tents, provisions, and boats would be furnished by the crown ; and he required the colonies to levy, clothe and pay their men ; assuring them that recommendations would be made to parliament ' to grant them a compensation.'

1758.

Notwithstanding their former losses and disappointments, the assembly of New-Hampshire, on receiving this requisition, cheerfully voted eight hundred men for the service of the year.[3] The regiment commanded by Colonel John Hart, marched to the westward, and served under General Abercrombie. A body of one hundred and eight carpenters, under the conduct of Colonel Meserve, embarked for Louisburg, to serve at the second siege of that fortress, under General Amherst. Unhappily the small pox broke out among them, which disabled them from service ; all but six-

(1) MS. letters of Governor Wentworth.   (2) Original MS.   (3) Governor's proclamation, April 1.

* [Major Thomas Tash was born in Durham in 1722. He was a brave officer in both the French and Revolutionary wars. At the close of the latter, he removed to New-Durham, where he died at the age of 87. Gazetteer of New-Hampshire, 195.]

teen were seized at once, and these attended the sick.[1] Meserve*
and his eldest son died of this fatal disorder. This year was remarkable for the second surrender of Louisburg ; the unfortunate
attack on the lines of Ticonderoga, where Lord Howe was killed ;
the taking of Fort Frontenac by Colonel Bradstreet, and the destruction of Fort du Quesne on the Ohio, the contention for
which, began the war.†

In the course of this year, the Indians continued to infest the
frontiers. At Hinsdale, they killed Captain Moore, and his son ;
took his family and burned his house. At Number-Four, they
killed Asahel Stebbins, and took his wife, with Isaac Parker and
a soldier. The cattle of this exposed settlement, which fed
chiefly in the woods, at a distance from the fort, often served the
enemy for provisions.[2]

The next year, a similar requisition being made by Secretary
Pitt, New-Hampshire raised a thousand men for the ser- 1759.
vice, who were regimented under the command of Colonel Zaccheus Lovewell, son of the famous partisan, who lost his
life at Pequawket.‡ This regiment joined the army at the westward, and served under General Amherst in the *actual* reduction
of Ticonderoga and Crown-Point, and in building a new fortress
at the last place. The success of this summer was brilliant, beyond former example. The French fort at Niagara surrendered
to General Johnson ; and the strong city of Quebec was taken by
the British troops under General Wolfe, who, with the French
General Montcalm, was slain in the decisive battle.

When the British arms had obtained a decided superiority over
the French, it was determined to chastise the Indians who had
committed so many devastations on the frontiers of New- Sept. 13.
England. Major Robert Rogers§ was despatched from

(1) Amherst's printed journal, June 28.   (2) Gay's and Olcott's MS. letters.

* Colonel Meserve, was a gentleman of a fine mechanical genius. Being a
shipwright by profession, he attained to eminence in his business, and acquired
a handsome fortune. His moral and social character was unblemished, and
in the military line, he was highly respected. The Earl of Loudon had such
a sense of his merit, as to present him a piece of plate, with an inscription,
acknowledging ' his capacity, fidelity, and ready disposition, in the service of
his country.' New-Hampshire Gazette, No. 97.

† [This important fortress was taken by the English on the 25 November,
and in compliment to the popular minister of England at that time, was called
Pittsburg.]

‡ [Colonel Zaccheus Lovewell was a *brother* of Captain John Lovewell, the
hero of Pequawket. See Collections of Farmer and Moore, ii. 64.]

§ [Major Rogers after the peace went to England, and published his journals of this war, in London in 1765. He also published a Concise Account
of North America in 8vo. London 1765. In the Revolution he espoused the
side of the British, and was included in the act passed by the General Court
of New-Hampshire, 19 November, 1778, " to prevent the return to this State
of certain persons therein named, and of others who have left, or shall leave
this State, or either of the United States of America, and have joined, or shall
join the enemies thereof."]

Crown-Point by Gen. Amherst, with about two hundred rangers, to destroy the Indian village of St. Francis. After a fatiguing march of twenty-one days, he came within sight of the place, Oct. 3. which he discovered from the top of a tree, and halted his men at the distance of three miles. In the evening, he entered the village in disguise with two of his officers. The Indians were engaged in a grand dance, and he passed through them undiscovered. Having formed his men into parties, and posted them to advantage ; he made a general assault, just before day, whilst the Indians were asleep. They were so completely surprised that little resistance could be made. Some were killed in their houses ; and of those who attempted to flee, many were shot or tomahawked by parties placed at the avenues. The dawn of day disclosed a horrid scene ; and an edge was given to the fury of the assailants by the sight of several hundred scalps of their countrymen, elevated on poles, and waving in the air. [1] This village had been enriched with the plunder of the frontiers and the sale of captives. The houses were well furnished, and the church was adorned with plate. The suddenness of the attack, and the fear of a pursuit, did not allow much time for pillage ; but the rangers brought off such things as were most convenient for transportation ; among which were about two hundred guineas in money, a silver image weighing ten pounds, a large quantity of wampum and clothing. Having set fire to the village, Rogers made his retreat up the river St. Francis, intending that his men should rendezvous at the upper Cohos, on Connecticut river. They took with them five English prisoners, whom they found at St. Francis, and about twenty Indians ; but these last they dismissed. Of the rangers, one man only was killed ; and six or seven were wounded. In their retreat, they were pursued, and lost seven men. They kept in a body for about ten days, passing on the eastern side of lake Memphremagog, and then scattered. Some found their way to Number-Four, after having suffered much by hunger and fatigue. Others perished in the woods, and their bones were found near Connecticut river, by the people, who after several years began plantations at the upper Cohos.

After the taking of Quebec, the remainder of the season was too short to complete the reduction of Canada. The next summer, General Amherst made preparations to approach 1760. Montreal, by three different routes ; intending, with equal prudence and humanity, to finish the conquest, without the effusion of blood. For the service of this year, eight hundred men were raised in New-Hampshire, and put under the command of Colonel John Goffe. They marched, as usual, to Number-Four ; but instead of taking the old route, to Albany, they cut a

(1) New-Hampshire Gazette, No. 165.

road* through the woods, directly toward Crown-Point. In this work, they made such despatch, as to join that part of the army which Amherst had left at Crown-Point, twelve days before their embarkation. They proceeded down the lake, under the command of Colonel Haviland. The enemy made some resistance at Isle au Noix, which stopped their progress for some days, and a few men were lost on both sides.[1] But this post being deserted, the forts of St. John and Chamblee became an easy conquest, and finally Montreal capitulated. This event finished the campaign, and crowned Amherst with deserved laurels.†

July 31.

Aug. 11.

Sept. 8.

Whilst the New-Hampshire regiment was employed in cutting the new road, signs of hovering Indians were frequently discovered, though none were actually seen. But they took the family of Joseph Willard, from Number-Four, and carried them into Montreal just before it was invested by the British army.[2]

The conquest of Canada, gave peace to the frontiers of New-Hampshire, after a turbulent scene of fifteen years ; in which, with very little intermission, they had been distressed by the enemy. Many captives returned to their homes ; and friends who had long been separated, embraced each other in peace. The joy was heightened by this consideration, that the country of Canada, being subdued, could no longer be a source of terror and distress.

The expense of this war, was paid by a paper currency.—Though an act of parliament was passed in 1751, prohibiting the governors, from giving their assent to acts of assembly, made for such a purpose ; yet by a proviso, extraordinary emergencies were excepted. Governor Wentworth was slow to take advantage of this proviso, and construed the act in a more rigid sense than others ; but his friend Shirley helped him out of his difficulties. In 1755, paper bills were issued under the denomination of new tenor ; of which, fifteen shillings were equal in value to one dollar. Of this currency, the soldiers were promised thirteen pounds ten shillings per month ; but it depreciated so much in the course of the year, that in the muster rolls, their pay was made

(1) Macclintock's MS. journal.   (2) Olcott's MS. letter.

* This new road began at Wentworth's ferry, two miles above the fort at No. 4, and was cut 26 miles ; at the end of which, they found a path, made the year before ; in which they passed over the mountains, to Otter-Creek ; where they found a good road, which led to Crown-Point. Their stores were brought in wagons, as far as the 26 miles extended ; and then transported on horses over the mountains. A drove of cattle for the supply of the army went from No. 4, by this route, to Crown-Point.

† [1760. The towns of Amherst, Peterborough, Hawke, Boscawen, and Bath were incorporated. Peterborough had been settled as early as 1739, by a small number of Scotch Presbyterians. See an account of this town in Farmer and Moore's Collections, i. 129—140. Amherst, Peterborough and Boscawen had many years before been *granted* by Massachusetts.]

up at fifteen pounds. In 1756, there was another emission from the same plates, and their pay was eighteen pounds. In 1757, it was twenty-five pounds. In 1758, they had twenty-seven shillings sterling. In the three succeeding years, they had thirty shillings sterling, besides a bounty at the time of their enlistment, equal to one month's pay.[1] At length, sterling money became the standard of all contracts ; and though the paper continued passing as a currency, its value was regulated by the price of silver, and the course of exchange.

It ought to be remembered as a signal favor of divine providence, that during this war, the seasons were fruitful, and the colonies were able to supply their own troops with provisions, and the British fleets and armies with refreshments of every kind 1761. which they needed. No sooner were the operations of the war in the northern colonies closed, than two years of scarcity succeeded; (1761 and 1762) in which the drought of summer was so severe, as to cut short the crops, and render supplies from abroad absolutely necessary. Had this calamity attended any of the preceding years of the war, the distress must have been extreme, both at home and in the camp. During the drought of 1761, a fire raged in the woods, in the towns of Barrington and Rochester, and passed over into the county of York, burning with irresistible fury for several weeks, and was not extinguished till a plentiful rain fell, in August. An immense quantity of the best timber was destroyed by this conflagration.*

For the succeeding part of the war, a smaller body of men was required to garrison the new conquests ; whilst the British troops 1762. were employed in the West India islands. The success which attended their operations in that quarter, brought the war to a conclusion ; and by the treaty of peace, though many of the conquered places were restored, yet, the whole continent of North-America remained to the British crown, and the colonies received a reimbursement of their expenses.

The war being closed, a large and valuable tract of country, situated between New-England, New-York and Canada, was secured to the British dominions ; and it became the interest of the governors of both the royal provinces of New-Hampshire and New-York, to vie with each other, in granting this territory and receiving the emoluments arising from this lucrative branch of their respective offices. The seeds of a controversy on this subject had been already sown. During the short peace which

(1) Atkinson's MS. letters.

* [1761. The towns of Campton, Canaan, Dorchester, Enfield, Goffstown, Grantham, Groton, Hanover, Holderness, Lebanon, Lempster, Lyman, Lyme, Marlow, Newport, Orford, Plainfield and Rumney were incorporated by separate charters.
1762. Wilton, New-Ipswich and New-Durham were incorporated.]

followed the preceding war, Governor Wentworth wrote to Governor Clinton, that he had it in command from the king, to grant the unimproved lands within his government; that the war had prevented that progress, which he had **1749. Nov. 17.** *hoped for* in this business; but that the peace had induced many people, to apply for grants in the western parts of New-Hampshire, which might fall in the neighborhood of New-York.[1] He communicated to him a paragraph of his commission, describing the bounds of New-Hampshire, and requested of him a description of the bounds of New-York.[2] Before he received any answer to this letter, Wentworth, presuming that New-Hampshire ought to extend as far westward as Massachusetts; that is, to the distance of twenty miles east from Hudson's river, granted a township, six miles square, called Bennington; situate twenty-four miles east of Hudson's river, and six miles north of the line of **1750.** Massachusetts. Clinton having laid Wentworth's letter before the council of New-York; by their advice answered him, that the province of New-York was bounded easterly by Connecticut river.[3] This claim was founded on a grant of King Charles the Second; in which, ' all the land from the west side of Connecti-' cut river, to the east side of Delaware bay,' was conveyed to his brother James, duke of York; by whose elevation to the throne, the same tract merged in the crown of England, and descended at the revolution to King William and his successors. The province of New-York had formerly urged this claim against the colony of Connecticut; but for prudential reasons had conceded that the bounds of that colony should extend, as far as a line drawn twenty miles east of Hudson's river. The like extent was demanded by Massachusetts; and, though New-York affected to call this demand ' an intrusion,' and strenuously urged their right to extend eastward to Connecticut river; yet the original grant of Massachusetts, being prior to that of the duke of York, was a barrier which could not easily be broken. These reasons, however, it was said, could be of no avail to the cause of New-Hampshire, whose first limits, as described in Mason's patent, did not reach to Connecticut river; and whose late extent, by the settlement of the lines in 1741, was no farther westward than ' till it meets with ' the king's other governments.' Though it was agreed, between the two governors, to submit the point in controversy to the king; yet the governor of New-Hampshire, continued to make grants, on the western side of Connecticut river, till 1754; when the renewal of hostilities not only put a stop to applications; **1754.** but prevented any determination of the controversy by the crown.

During the war, the continual passing of troops through those lands, caused the value of them to be more generally known;

(1) Council Minutes.   (2) New-York printed Narrative. Appendix, No. 3.
(3) New-Hampshire book of Charters.

and when by the conquest of Canada, tranquillity was restored, they were eagerly sought by adventurers and speculators. Wentworth availed himself of this golden opportunity, and by advice of his council, ordered a survey to be made of Connecticut river for sixty miles, and three lines of townships on each side, to be laid out. As applications increased, the surveys were extend- 1761. ed. Townships of six miles square were granted to va- July 1. rious petitioners; and so rapidly did this work go on, that during the year 1761, not less than sixty townships were granted on the west, and eighteen on the east side of the river. Besides the fees and presents for these grants, which were undefined, a reservation was made for the governor, of five hundred acres in each township; and of lots for public purposes.* These reservations were clear of all fees and charges.[1] The whole number of grants on the western side of the river, amounted to one 1763. hundred and thirty-eight; and the extent was from Connecticut river to twenty miles east of Hudson, as far as that river extended northerly; and after that, westward to lake Champlain. The rapid progress of these grants filled the coffers of the governor. Those who had obtained the grants were seeking purchasers in all the neighboring colonies; whilst the original inhabitants of New-Hampshire, to whom these lands had formerly been promised, as a reward for their merit in defending the country, were

(1) Atkinson's MS.

* [In most of the townships there was a reservation of a glebe of 350 acres, although there were but few Episcopalians in the province. From a letter of Rev. Ranna Cossit, written about the year 1773, some opinion may be formed respecting the condition of the Episcopal church in the western part of New-Hampshire at that period. He says there were " church people settled scattering for above 150 miles on Connecticut river. The nearest of these to any clergyman is more than 130 miles. There are four towns in which the church people have met together the summer past, and read prayers and the best printed sermons they could get. The first of these towns is *Alstead*, where I assisted them two Sundays. They were very poorly furnished with prayer books and all others, and begged me to ask the society to give them some ; they being newly settled, were unable to buy. The next is *Claremont*, about 30 miles above, where Esq. [Samuel] Cole, the society's schoolmaster hath instructed so well in the church service, and likewise in singing, that I must say I never was at any place, where I thought divine service was performed with greater decency and sincerity. Seven miles west of this is *Springfield*, in New-York government, where sundry families of the establishment meet and read prayers, but are very poorly furnished with books. Twenty-four miles above, Dr. Wheelock hath a college, and informs the church people that he will supply them with ministers. There is a considerable number of church people opposite Dr. Wheelock on N. York side of the river, and some on the same side with him, who constantly meet and read prayers among themselves. Forty miles above this is *Haverhill*, where the summer past they read prayers, and here, Gov. Wentworth intended I should make my head quarters, if it pleased the society to make me their missionary in those parts. Here they are poorly furnished with books and desired me to beg the society to give them some." Mr. Cossit sailed for England for holy orders in December, 1772, and was ordained the next year by the bishop of London. He settled at Claremont as the first Episcopal minister of that place, from whence he was recalled by the bishop to the island of Cape-Breton in 1785. He died at Yarmouth in Nova-Scotia in 1815, aged 75.]

overlooked in the distribution; unless they were disposed to apply
in the same manner, as persons from abroad; or unless they
happened to be in favor. When remonstrances were made to the
governor on this subject, his answer was, that the people of the
old towns had been formerly complimented with grants in Chichester, Barnstead and Gilmanton,* which they had neglected to
improve; and that the new grantees were better husbandmen and
would promote the cultivation of the province.[1]

The passion for occupying new lands rose to a great height.
These tracts were filled with emigrants from Massachusetts and
Connecticut. Population and cultivation began to increase with
a rapidity hitherto unknown; and from this time may be dated
the flourishing state of New-Hampshire; which before had been
circumscribed and stinted in its growth, by the continual danger
of a savage enemy.†

The grants on the western side of Connecticut river, alarmed
the government of New-York; who, by their agent, made application to the crown, representing ' that it would be greatly to the
' advantage of *the people* settled on those lands, to be annexed to
' New-York;' and submitting the cause to the royal decision. [2]
In the mean time, a proclamation was issued by Lieuten- Dec. 28.
ant-Governor Colden, reciting the grant of King Charles
to the duke of York; asserting the jurisdiction of New-York as
far eastward as Connecticut river; and enjoining the sheriff of
the county of Albany, to return the names of all persons, who,
under color of the New-Hampshire grants, held possession of
lands westward of that river. This was answered by a 1764.
proclamation of Governor Wentworth, declaring the grant Mar. 13.
to the duke of York to be obsolete, and that the western
bounds of New-Hampshire were co-extensive with those of Massachusetts and Connecticut; encouraging the grantees to maintain
their possessions, and cultivate their lands; and commanding civil
officers to execute the laws and punish disturbers of the peace.

The application from New-York was referred to the board of
trade; and upon their representation, seconded by a report of a
committee of the privy council, an order was passed, by July 20.
the king in council; declaring ' the western banks of Con-
' necticut river, from where it enters the province of Massachu-
' setts-Bay, as far north as the forty-fifth degree of latitude, TO BE

(1) Information of the late P. Gilman and M. Weare. (2) Ethan Allen's
Narrative, 1774, p. 1.

* [This town was granted in 1727 to 24 persons of the name of Gilman and
152 others. Its permanent settlement did not commence until 27 December,
1761. See Coll. of Farmer and Moore, i. 72—79.]

† [1763. The towns of New-Boston, Haverhill, Croydon, Cornish, Thornton, Warren, Plymouth, Lancaster, Alstead, Peeling, Sandwich, Candia, Gil-
sum and Wentworth were incorporated.
1764. Claremont, Unity, Lincoln, Coventry, Franconia, Poplin, Lyndeborough, Weare, Piermont and Newington were incorporated.]

' the boundary line, between the two provinces of New-Hamp-
' shire and New-York.'[1]

This decree, like many other judicial determinations, while it
closed one controversy, opened another. The jurisdiction of the
governor of New-Hampshire, and his power of granting land,
were circumscribed by the western bank of Connecticut river ;
but the grantees of the soil, found themselves involved in a dispute
with the government of New-York. From the words TO BE, in
the royal declaration, two very opposite conclusions were drawn.
The government supposed them to refer to the time past, and
construed them as a declaration that the river always *had been*
the eastern limits of New-York ; consequently, that the grants
made by the governor of New-Hampshire, were invalid, and that
the lands might be granted again. The grantees understood the
words in the future tense, as declaring Connecticut river from that
time *to be* the line of jurisdiction only, between the two provinces ;
consequently that their grants, being derived from the crown,
through the medium of one of its governors, were valid. To the
jurisdiction, they would have quietly submitted, had no attempt
been made to wrest from them their possessions. These opposite opinions, proved a source of litigation for ten succeeding
years ; but, as this controversy belongs to the history of New-
York, it is dismissed, with one remark only. That though it was
carried on with a degree of virulence, unfriendly to the progress
of civilization and humanity, within the disputed territory ; yet it
called into action, a spirit of vigorous self-defence, and hardy enterprise, which prepared the nerves of that people for encounter-
ing the dangers of a revolution, more extensive and beneficial.

CHAPTER XXIII.

Beginning of the controversy with Great-Britain. Stamp act. Resignation
of Benning Wentworth.

FROM the earliest establishment of the American colonies, a
jealousy of their independence had existed among the people of
Great-Britain. At first, this apprehension was perhaps no more
than a conjecture founded on the vicissitude of human affairs, or
on their knowledge of those emigrants who came away from
England, disgusted with the abusive treatment which they had
endured at home. But from whatever cause it arose, it was
strengthened by age ; and the conduct of the British government

(1) Original MS.

toward America, was frequently influenced by it. In the reign
of James the First, ' speculative reasoners raised objections to
' the planting of these colonies ; and foretold, that after draining
' the mother country of inhabitants, they would shake off her yoke
' and erect an independent government.'[1] Some traces of this
jealousy appeared in every succeeding reign, not excepting that
of William, whom America, as well as Britain, was proud to style
' our great deliverer.' But it became most evident, and began
to produce its most pernicious effects, at a time when there was
the least reason for indulging the idea.

During the administration of Pitt, a liberal kind of policy had
been adopted toward the colonies ; which being crowned with
success, had attached us* more firmly than ever, to the kingdom
of Britain. We were proud of our connexion with a nation
whose flag was triumphant in every quarter of the globe ; and by
whose assistance we had been delivered from the danger of our
most formidable enemies, the French in Canada. The 1760.
accession of George the Third, at this critical and important era, was celebrated here, with as true a zeal and loyalty, as
in any part of his dominions. We were fond of repeating every
plaudit, which the ardent affection of the British nation bestowed
on a young monarch, rising to the throne of his ancestors, and
professing to ' glory in the name of Briton.' At such a time,
nothing could have been more easy, than by pursuing the system
of commercial regulation, already established, and continuing the
indulgencies which had been allowed, to have drawn the whole
profit of our labor and trade, into the hands of British merchants
and manufacturers. This would have prevented a spirit of enterprise in the colonies, and kept us in as complete subjection and
dependence, as the most sanguine friend of the British nation
could have wished.

We had, among ourselves, a set of men, who, ambitious of
perpetuating the rank of their families, were privately seek- 1763.
ing the establishment of an *American Nobility;* out of
which, an intermediate branch of legislation, between the royal and
democratic powers, should be appointed.[2] Plans were drawn, and
presented to the British ministry, for new modeling our governments
and reducing their powers ; whilst the authority of parliament should
be rendered absolute and imperial. The military gentlemen of
Britain, who had served here in the war, and on whom, a pro-
fusion of grateful attention had been bestowed, carried home reports of our wealth ; whilst the sons of our merchants and plant-

(1) Hume. (2) Bernard's select letters. Oliver's letters.

* Though it may be accounted a deviation from the proper style of history,
for the author to speak in the first person ; yet he hopes to be excused in expressing the feelings of an American, whilst he relates the history of his own
time, and his own country.

ers, who went to England for their education, exhibited specimens of prodigality which confirmed the idea. During the war, there had been a great influx of money; and at the conclusion of it, British goods were largely imported; by which means, the cash went back again with a rapid circulation.

In no age, perhaps, excepting that in which Rome lost her liberty, was the spirit of venality and corruption so prevalent as at this time, in Britain. Exhausted by a long war, and disgraced by a peace which deprived her of her most valuable conquests, the national supplies were inadequate to the continual drain of the exchequer.[1] A new ministry, raised on the ruin of that by which America was conquered and secured, looked to this country as a source of revenue. But, neglecting the ' principles of ' law and polity,' which had been early suggested to them by an officious correspondent; and by which they might have gradually and silently extended their system of corruption into America; they planned measures by which they supposed an addition to the revenues of Britain might be drawn from America; and the pretence was, ' to defray the expenses of protecting, defending ' and securing it.'[2] The fallacy of this pretence was easily seen. If we had not done our part toward the protection and defence of our country, why were our expenditures reimbursed by parliament? The truth is, that during the whole war, we had exerted ourselves beyond our ability; relying on a promise from a secretary of state, that it should be recommended to parliament to make us compensation. It was recommended; the compensation was honorably granted, and gratefully received. The idea of drawing that money from us again by taxes to repay the charges of our former defence, was unjust and inconsistent. If the new conquests needed protection or defence, those who reaped the gain of their commerce, or enjoyed the benefit of grants and offices within those territories, might be required to contribute their aid. Notwithstanding this pretext, it was our opinion, that the grand object was to provide for dependents, and to extend the corrupt and venal principle of crown influence, through every part of the British dominions. However artfully it was thrown out, that the revenue to be drawn from us would ease the taxes of our brethren in Britain, or diminish the load of national debt; it was not easy for us to believe that the ministry had either of these objects sincerely in contemplation. But if it had been ever so equitable that we should contribute to discharge the debt of the nation, incurred by the preceding war; we supposed that the monopoly and control of our commerce, which Britain enjoyed, was a full equivalent for all the advantages, which we reaped from our political connexion with her.

(1) History of the minority, 1765, page 286.   (2) Bernard's select letters.

The same gazette, which contained the definitive treaty of peace, announced the intentions of the British ministry to quarter troops in America, and support them at our expense.[1] The money was to be raised by a duty on foreign sugar and molasses, and by stamps on all papers legal and mercantile. These intentions were at first thrown out in the form of resolves, and afterward digested into acts of parliament. The first of these acts, restricting the intercourse which the American colonies had enjoyed with the West-India islands, caused a general uneasiness and suspicion, but was viewed as a regulation of trade, and was submitted to, though with reluctance. The effect of this act was to call forth a spirit of frugality, particularly in the introduction of a less expensive mode of conducting funerals. Petitions and remonstrances were sent to England by some of the colonies; but instead of any redress, a new act of parliament was made for raising a revenue by a general stamp duty through all the American colonies. The true friends of constitutional liberty now saw their dearest interests in danger; from an assumption of power in the parent state to give and grant the property of the colonists at their pleasure. Even those who had been seeking alterations in the colonial governments, and an establishment of hereditary honors, plainly saw that the ministry were desirous of plucking the fruit, before they had grafted the stock on which it must grow.[2] To render the new act less odious to us, some of our fellow citizens were appointed to distribute the stamped paper, which was prepared in England and brought over in bales. The framers of the act boasted that it was so contrived as to execute itself; because no writing could be deemed legal without the stamp; and all controversies which might arise, were to be determined in the courts of admiralty, by a single judge, entirely dependant on the crown.

This direct and violent attack on our dearest privileges at first threw us into a silent gloom; and we were at a loss how to proceed. To submit, was to rivet the shackles of slavery on ourselves and our posterity. To revolt, was to rend asunder the most endearing connexion, and hazard the resentment of a powerful nation. In this dilemma, the house of burgesses in Virginia, passed some spirited resolves, asserting the rights of their country, and denying the claim of parliamentary taxation. The assembly of Massachusetts proposed a congress of deputies from each colony, to consult upon our common interest, as had frequently been practised in times of common danger. Several speeches made in parliament by opposers of the stamp-act were reprinted here; in one of which the Americans were styled ' sons of liberty,' and the speaker[3] ventured,

1764.

1765.
May 28.

June 6.

(1) New-Hampshire Gazette, May 27.   (2) Bernard's select letters.—
(3) Colonel Barre.

from his personal knowledge of this country, to foretel our opposition to the act.

The spirit of the Virginian resolves, like an electric spark,
diffused itself instantly and universally ; and the cautious proposal
of Massachusetts was generally approved. The anxious mind,
resting on the bold assertion of constitutional rights, looked forward
with pleasure, to the time when an American congress would
unite in a successful defence of them. The title ' sons of liberty,'
was eagerly adopted by associations in every colony ; determining
to carry into execution the prediction of him, who with such noble
energy, had espoused the cause of our freedom. They began the
opposition at Boston ; by publicly exhibiting effigies of the enemies
of America, and obliging the stamp-officer to resign his employment. The popular commotions in that town were afterward
carried to an unjustifiable excess ; but the spirit of opposition
animated the body of the people in every colony.

The person appointed distributor of stamps for New-Hampshire, was George Meserve, son of the late colonel, who died at
Louisburg. He received his appointment in England, and soon
after embarked for America, and arrived at Boston. Before he
Sept. 9. landed, he was informed of the opposition which was
making to the act; and that it would be acceptable to the
people if he would resign, which he readily did, and they wel-
Sept. 12. comed him on shore. An exhibition of effigies at Portsmouth had prepared the minds of the people there for his
Sept. 18. reception ; and at his coming to town, he made a second
resignation, on the parade, before he went to his own house.
Sept. 30. This was accepted with the usual salutation ; and every
one appeared to be satisfied with the success of the popular measures. Soon after, the stamped paper destined for New-
Hampshire arrived at Boston in the same vessel with that intended
for Massachusetts ; but there being no person in either province
who had any concern with it, it was, by the order of Governor
Bernard, lodged in the castle.

The stamp-act was to commence its operation on the first day
of November ; previously to which, the appointed congress was
formed at New-York, consisting of delegates from the assemblies
of Massachusetts, Rhode-Island, Connecticut, New-York, New-
Jersey, Pennsylvania, the Delaware counties, Maryland and
South-Carolina. Having, like the congress at Albany in 1754,
formed themselves in geographical order ; they framed a bill of
rights, for the colonies ; in which the sole power of taxation was
declared to be in their own assemblies. They prepared three
distinct addresses to the king, lords and commons, stating their
grievances, and asking for redress. These were subscribed by
the delegates of six colonies ; the others who were present were
not empowered to sign ; but reported their proceeding to their

constituents, who approved them in assembly, and forwarded their petitions. No delegates went from New-Hampshire to this Congress; but the assembly at their next meeting adopted the same measures, and sent similar petitions to England, which they committed to Barlow Trecothick, their agent, and John Wentworth, a young gentleman of Portsmouth, who was then in England, to be by them presented to the king and parliament.[1] These measures were the most respectful and prudent which could be devised; and were attended with some prospect of success from a change which had been made in the British ministry.

In the mean time, the newspapers were filled with essays, in which every plea for and against the new duties was amply discussed. These vehicles of intelligence were doomed to be loaded with a stamp; and the printers felt themselves interested in the opposition. On the last day of October, the New-Hampshire Gazette appeared with a mourning border. A body of people from the country approached the town of Portsmouth, under an apprehension that the stamps would be distributed; but being met, by a number from the town, and assured that no such thing was intended, they quietly returned. The next day, the bells tolled, and a funeral procession was made for the Goddess of Liberty; but on depositing her in the grave, some signs Nov. 1. of life were supposed to be discovered, and she was carried off in triumph. By such exhibitions, the spirit of the populace was kept up; though the minds of the most thoughtful persons were filled with anxiety.

It was doubtful, whether the courts of law could proceed without stamps; and it was certain that none could be procured. Some licentious persons began to think that debts could not be recovered, and that they might insult their creditors with impunity. On the first appearance of this disorderly spirit, associations were formed at Portsmouth, Exeter and other places, to support the magistrates and preserve the peace. The fifth of November had always been observed as a day of hilarity, in remembrance of the powder-plot. On the following night, a strong guard was kept in Portsmouth. By these precautions, the tendency to riot was seasonably checked, and no waste of property or personal insult was committed; though some obnoxious characters began to tremble for their safety.*

When Meserve arrived, the people supposed that he had brought his commission with him, and were content that it should remain iu his own hands, being rendered void by his resignation. But,

(1) Assembly Records.

* [1765. Raymond, Conway, Concord, the seat of government, and formerly *Penacook*, Dunbarton and Hopkinton were incorporated.
1766. Deerfield, Burton, Eaton, Lee, Tamworth and Acworth were incorporated.]

in fact, he did not receive it till after the time fixed for the operation of the act. Having shown his instructions to the governor, and some other public officers, it was suspected that he intended ' to commence the execution of his office.' The sons of liberty were alarmed; they assembled by beat of drum, and obliged him publicly to deliver up his commission and instructions; which they mounted on the point of a sword, and carried in triumph through the town. An oath was administered to him by Justice Clagett,* purporting that he would neither directly nor indirectly attempt to execute his office. The master of a ship, then ready to sail for England, was also sworn to deliver the packet containing the commission and instructions, as it was directed. It was first addressed to the commissioners of the stamp-office in London; but afterward it was enclosed in a letter to the agents of the province, referring the disposal of it to their discretion. It happened to arrive, when great exertions were making, and a strong probability existed, of the repeal of the stamp-act. The agents therefore concealed the packet, and had the good fortune to suppress the intelligence of all these proceedings; that no irritation might ensue to prevent the expected repeal.

During all these commotions, Governor Wentworth was silent. The ministry, either by accident or design, had neglected to send authentic copies of the stamp-act, to some of the American governors, and to him among others. There had been no tumults, which rendered his interposition necessary. He was in the decline of life, and his health was much impaired. His fortune was made, and it lay chiefly in his native country. One of the reasons given, for the removal of his predecessor, was, that he had enjoyed his office ten years. Mr. Wentworth had been twenty-five years in the chair, and expected soon to be superseded. It was therefore his interest, not to put himself forward in support of unpopular measures. His example was followed by most of the gentlemen in the province, who held offices under the crown. If any of them were secretly in favor of the act, they were restrained by fear, from contradicting openly the voice of the people.

The popular spirit was sufficiently roused to join in any measures which might be necessary for the defence of liberty. All fear of the consequence of proceeding in the public business without stamps, was gradually laid aside. The courts of law, and custom houses were kept open. Newspapers circulated, and

1766.
Jan. 9.

---

* [Wyseman Clagett, who then resided at Portsmouth. He was born and educated in England, and admitted a barrister at law in the court of the king's bench. He came soon after to this country; was admitted to the bar of the superior court of New-Hampshire, and was some time the king's attorney general; was one of the council in the time of the revolution, and a representative in the general court from Litchfield, where he died 4 December, 1784, aged 63 years and 4 months. A valuable memoir of this gentleman, written by the Hon. Charles H. Atherton, of Amherst, is among the files of the N. H. Hist. Society.]

licenses for marriage, without stamps, were publicly advertised. As it was uncertain, what might be the event of the petitions to the king and parliament, it was thought best, to awaken the attention of the merchants and manufacturers of England, by an agreement to import no goods, until the stamp-act should be repealed. To provide for the worst, an association was formed by the ' sons of liberty' in all the northern colonies, to stand by each other, and unite their whole force, for the protection and relief of any who might be in danger, from the operation of this, or any other oppressive act. The letters which passed between them, on this occasion, are replete with expressions of loyalty and affection to the king, his person, family and authority.[1] Had there been any disaffection to the royal government, or desire to shake off our allegiance, where would the evidence of it be more likely to be found, than in letters which passed between bodies of men, who were avowedly endeavoring, to form a union, to resist the usurped authority of the British lords and commons ?*

The idea which we entertained of our political connexion with the British empire, was, that the king was its supreme head ; that every branch of it was a perfect state, competent to its own internal legislation, but subject to the control and negative of the sovereign ; that taxation and representation were correlative, and therefore, that no part of the empire could be taxed, but by its own representatives in assembly. From a regard to the general interest, it was conceded, that the parliament of Great-Britain, representing the first and most powerful branch of the empire, might regulate the exterior commerce of the whole. In Britain, the American governments were considered as corporations, existing by the pleasure of the king and parliament, who had a right to alter or dissolve them. Our laws were deemed by-laws ; and we were supposed to be, in all cases of legislation and taxation, subject to the supreme, undefined power of the British parliament. Between claims so widely different, there was no arbitrator to decide. Temporary expedients, if wisely applied, might have preserved peace ; but the most delicate and judicious management was necessary, to prevent irritation.

When the commotions which had happened in America, were known in England, a circular letter was written to the several governors, by Secretary Conway,[2] in which it was ' hoped that ' the resistance to the authority of the mother country, had only

(1) MS. letters of the sons of liberty. (2) October 24, 1765.

* From an intimate acquaintance with many persons, of all ranks, who were instrumental of conducting the American revolution, through all its stages ; and from a perusal of many of their confidential letters ; the author of these sheets is fully satisfied, that the public professions of loyalty, made by his countrymen, were sincere ; and that the most determined opposers of the claims of parliament, were very far from desiring a disunion of the British empire, till they were driven to it by necessity.

'found place among the lower and more ignorant of the people.'
To the constitutional authority (as we understood it) of the king
and parliament, there had been no resistance ; but to the assumed
authority, of our fellow subjects in Britain, over our property, the
resistance began, and was supported by the representatives of the
people, in their assemblies. Those who appeared under the
name of ' the sons of liberty' were chiefly tradesmen of reputation, who were occasionally assisted by lawyers, clergymen, and
other persons of literary abilities. The writings of Sidney and
Locke were produced, in evidence of the justice of our claims ;
and the arguments which had formerly been used in England,
against the usurpations of the house of Stuart, were adopted and
repeated by us, in favor of our rights and liberties. Political
inquiries were encouraged, and the eyes of the people were opened. Never was a sentiment more generally adopted, on the full-
est conviction, than that we could be constitutionally taxed by
none but our own representatives ; and that all assumption of this
power, by any other body of men, was usurpation which might be
lawfully resisted.

The petitions of the American assemblies, enforced by the
agreement for non-importation, and aided by the exertions of the
British merchants and manufacturers, induced the new ministry
to recommend to parliament, a repeal of the odious stamp-act.
Mar. 18. It was accordingly repealed ; not on the true principle of
its repugnancy to the rights of America ; but on that of
political expediency. Even on this principle, the repeal could be
obtained by no other means ; than by passing, at the same time,
a declaratory act, asserting the right and power, of the British
parliament, ' to bind America, in all cases whatsoever,' and an-
nulling all the resolutions of our assemblies, in which they had
claimed the right of exemption from parliamentary taxation.

The rejoicings which were occasioned by the repeal of the
stamp-act, in this country, were extravagantly disproportioned to
the object. We felt a transient relief from an intolerable burden ;
but the claim of sovereign power, in our fellow subjects, to take
our property, and abridge our liberty at their pleasure, was established by law. Our only hope was, that they would profit by
their recent experience ; and whilst they enjoyed the pride of
seeing their claim exist on paper, would suspend the exercise of
it in future.

With the repealing and declaratory acts, a circular letter came
from Secretary Conway ; in which, ' the lenity and tenderness,
' the moderation and forbearance of the parliament toward the
' colonies' were celebrated in the language of panegyric, and we
were called upon, to show our 'respectful gratitude and cheerful
' obedience,' in return for such a ' signal display of indulgence and

' affection.' This letter enclosed a resolution of parliament, that those persons who had ' suffered any injury or damage,' in consequence of their assisting to ' execute the late act, ought to be ' compensated by the colonies, in which such injuries were sus- ' tained.'

When Governor Wentworth laid this letter before the assembly, he told them ' with pleasure and satisfaction, that he had ' no requisition of this kind to make.' Meserve, however, June 25. applied to the assembly to grant him a compensation for the injuries which he said he had suffered. A committee, being appointed to inquire into the ground of his petition, reported, ' that ' he had suffered no real damage either in person or property ; ' but that when any danger had been expected, guards had been ' appointed to protect him.' Upon this report, his petition was dismissed. He afterwards went to England and obtained the office of collector of the customs.

At this session the assembly prepared a respectful address to the king and both houses of parliament, on account of the repeal ; which was sent to England, at the same time that the stamped paper and parchment, which had been deposited at the castle in Boston, were returned.

Complaints had been made in England against some of the American governors, and other public officers, that exorbitant fees had been taken for the passing of patents for land ; and a proclamation had been issued by the crown and published in the colonies, *threatening* such persons with a removal from office. [1] Governor Wentworth was involved in this charge. He had also been accused of negligence in corresponding with the king's ministers; of informality and want of accuracy in his grants of land ; and of passing acts of assembly respecting private property, without a suspending clause ' till his majesty's pleasure could ' be known.' In his office of surveyor-general, he had been charged with neglect of duty, and with indulging his deputies in selling and wasting the king's timber. By whom these complaints were made, and by what evidence they were supported, I have not been able to discover. Certain it is, that such an impression was made on the minds of the ministry, that a resolution was taken to remove him ; but the difficulties attending the stamp-act, caused a delay in the appointment of a successor. When the ferment had subsided, the attention of the ministry was turned to this object. John Wentworth, son of Mark Hunking Wentworth, and nephew of the governor, was then in England. He had appeared at court, as a joint agent with Mr. Trecothick in presenting the petition of the province against the stamp-act. He had become acquainted with several families of high rank and of his own name in Yorkshire, and in particular, with the marquis of

(1) New-Hampshire Gazette, Aug. 29, 1764.

Rockingham, then at the head of the ministry. By his indulgence, Mr. Wentworth prevailed to soften the rigor of government against his uncle. Instead of being censured and removed from office, he was allowed opportunity to *resign*, and the appearance of resigning in favor of his nephew, who was destined by the marquis, to be his successor. Having received his commissions, as governor of New-Hampshire, and surveyor of the king's woods in North-America, Mr. Wentworth sailed from England, and arrived at Charlestown, in South-Carolina. Thence he travelled through the continent, registering his commission of surveyor in each of the colonies, and was received at Portsmouth, with every mark of respect and affection. This appointment, made by a popular ministry, was peculiarly grateful to the people of New-Hampshire, by whom Mr. Wentworth was well known and much esteemed.

Aug. 11.

1767. March.

June 13.

In addition to what has been said, of the superseded governor, it may be observed; that his natural abilities were neither brilliant nor contemptible. As a private gentleman, he was obliging, and as a merchant, honorable. He was generous and hospitable to his friends; but his passions were strong and his resentments lasting. He was subject to frequent and long continued visits of the gout; a distemper rather unfriendly to the virtue of patience. In his deportment, there was an appearance of haughtiness, contracted by his residence in Spain, where he learned the manners of the people of rank; as well as the maxims of their government. He thought it best that the highest offices, should be filled with men of property; and though in some instances he deviated from this principle, yet, in others, he adhered to it so closely, as to disregard more necessary qualifications.*

In the former part of his administration, he was scrupulous in obeying his instructions, and inflexible in maintaining the prerogative. In conducting the operations of two successive wars, his attention to the service was very conspicuous; and he frequently received letters of thanks, from the generals, and other officers of the British troops employed in America.

* [Mr. Adams in his Annals of Portsmouth, p. 230, says, " It has been objected against him, that all the important offices in the government, were filled by his particular friends." A scrap found among Secretary Waldron's papers, headed *Family Government*, seems to establish the fact, although the cause of it is not particularly assigned. The following is a copy of it :

" *George Jaffrey*, brother-in-law, president of the council, treasurer, chief justice and justice of the admiralty. *Jotham Odiorne*, brother married his grand daughter, second judge and justice. *Henry Sherburne*, cousin, &c. counsellor, &c. *Theodore Atkinson*, brother-in-law, secretary, chief justice of inferior court, &c. *Richard Wibird*, governor's brother married his sister, a counsellor. *Ellis Huske*, wife's brother married governor's sister, a counsellor. *Samuel Solley*, who married George Jaffrey's daughter, a counsellor. *Thomas Packer*, a brother-in-law, high sheriff. *John Downing* and *Samuel Smith*, counsellors, related by their cash. FRIENDS, *Wiggin*, justice and judge of probate, *Clarkson, Gage, Wallingford, Gilman, Palmer, Roby, Jenness, Odiorne, Walton* and *Stevens*, justices."]

He was closely attached to the interest of the church of England; and in his grants of townships, reserved a right for the society for propagating the gospel of which he was a member. A project was formed during his administration, to establish a college in New-Hampshire. When he was applied to for a charter, he declined giving it, unless the college were put under the direction of the bishop of London. But, when a grant was made by the assembly, of three hundred pounds sterling, to Harvard college, where he had received his education, to repair the destruction which it had suffered by fire; he consented to the vote, and his name is inscribed on an alcove of the library, as a benefactor, in conjunction with the name of the province.

In his appointment of civil and military officers, he was frequently governed by motives of favor, or prejudice to particular persons. When he came to the chair, he found but twenty-five justices of the peace in the whole province; but in the first commission which he issued, he nominated as many in the town of Portsmouth only. In the latter part of his time, appointments of this kind became so numerous, and were so easily procured, that the office was rendered contemptible.*

* The following pasquinade was published in the Portsmouth Mercury of October 7, 1765. It was supposed to have been written by the late Judge Parker,† and was entitled

THE SILVER AGE.

In days of yore, and pious times,
Great care was had to punish crimes;
When conservators *pacis* sought
To keep good order as they ought.
This office then, was no great booty,
Small were the fees, though great the duty.
But when a law, the old restriction
Dock'd—and enlarg'd the jurisdiction;
His worship had a right to hold,
In civil plea, a pound twice told.
The post was then thought worth possessing,
For 'twas attended with a blessing.
But still, in after times it grew
Much better, as our tale will shew;

† [Judge William Parker was a native of Portsmouth, and was born 9 December, 1703. His father was William Parker, whose wife was Zerviah Stanley, daughter, as the late Nathaniel Adams, Esquire, of Portsmouth, informed me, of the Earl of Derby. The judge had not a liberal education, but received in 1763 the honorary degree of Master of Arts, "*pro meritis suis.*" In his diploma, it is expressed, " licet non Academiæ instructum, Generosum, nihil ominus in rebus literariis scil: Classicis Philosophicis, &c. egregie eruditum." He pursued the study of law, and was admitted to the bar in 1732. He was esteemed as a well read and accurate lawyer. In August, 1771, he was appointed one of the justices of the superior court, which office he held until the revolution commenced. He died 29 April, 1781, aged 77. Adams, Annals Portsmouth, 272—274. Judge Parker left four sons, *William* of Exeter, who graduated at H. C. 1751, was a judge of the C. C. P. and register of probate, and died in 1811 ; *John,* sheriff of the province and marshal of the district of N. H. ; *Samuel,* who graduated at H. C. in 1764, was bishop of the Episcopal church and D. D., and died at Boston, 6 December, 1804, in his 60th year; and *Matthew Stanley,* who settled in Wolfeborough.]

Notwithstanding some instances, in which a want of magnanimity was too conspicuous, his administration was, in other respects, beneficial. Though he was highly censured, for granting the best lands of the province to the people of Massachusetts and Connecticut, with views of pecuniary reward ; yet, the true interest of the country was certainly promoted ; because the grantees in general, were better husbandmen than the people of New-Hampshire.

In those cases, where dissatisfaction appeared, it was chiefly owing to the nature of a royal government, in which the aristocratic feature was prominent, and the democratic too much depressed. The people of New-Hampshire, though increasing in numbers, had not the privilege of an equal representation. The aim of most of those gentlemen, who received their appointments from abroad, was rather to please their masters, and secure the emoluments of their offices, than to extend benefits to the people, or condescend to their prejudices. They did not feel their dependence on them, as the source of power ; nor their responsibility to them for its exercise. And, the people themselves had not that just idea of their own weight and importance, which they acquired, when the controversy with the British government called up their attention to their native rights.*

When, as it goes by common fame,
Two pounds and forty were the same.   [By depreciation.]
Then civil suits began to thrive,
And claims grown obsolete revive.
But when their worships, manifold,
Like men divinely bless'd of old,
Were bid ' t'increase and multiply,'
Obsequious rose a num'rous fry,
Who, ever prompt, and nigh at hand,
Could scatter justice through the land.
Then, with important air and look,
The sons of Littleton and Coke
Swarming appear'd, to mind the Squires ;
What honors such a post requires !
These skilful clerks, always attending,
Help'd to despatch all matters pending ;
Took care that judgment (as it should)
Was render'd for the man that sued ;
Aided their honors to indite,
And sign'd for those who could not write.
Who but must think these, happy times,
When men, adroit to punish crimes
Were close at hand ? and what is better,
Made every little tardy debtor
Fulfil his contract, and to boot,
Pay twice his debt in costs of suit.
This was the happy silver age
When magistrates, profoundly sage,
O'erspread the land ; and made, it seems,
' Justice run down the streets in streams.'

* [1767.   Chatham was incorporated.
1768.   Seabrook, Meredith, Henniker, Salisbury, Mason and Rindge were incorporated.]

CHAPTER XXIV.

Administration of John Wentworth the second. New attempt to force a revenue from America. Establishment of Dartmouth college. Division of the province into counties. Death of Benning Wentworth. Complaint of Peter Livius against the governor. Its issue. Progress of the controversy with Great Britain. War. Dissolution of British government in New-Hampshire.

THE genius, as well as the interest of the new governor, led him to cultivate the good will of the people. He was grandson, by his mother, to the late agent John Rindge, 1767. who had been instrumental of establishing the boundaries of the province, and had advanced a large sum for that purpose. His family, who had long complained of ingratitude and neglect, were now amply gratified, not only by the advancement of the new governor, but by his recommending several other gentlemen, who were connected with it, to fill vacant seats at the council board, and other offices of government. Several gentlemen of other respectable families, who had been treated with neglect, in the preceding administration, were also taken into favor ; and a spirit of conciliation, among those who had formerly been at variance, seemed to mark the beginning of this administration with fair omens of peace and success.

Being in the prime of life, active and enterprising in his disposition, polite and easy in his address, and placed in the chair by the same minister who had procured the repeal of the stamp-act, to which event his own agency had contributed ; Mr. Wentworth enjoyed a great share of popular favor ; which was much heightened when his conduct was viewed in contrast with that of some other governors in the neighboring provinces. Though bred a merchant, he had a taste for agriculture, and entered vigorously into the spirit of cultivation. He frequently traversed the forests ; explored the ground for new roads ; and began a plantation for himself in the township of Wolfeborough, on which he expended large sums, and built an elegant house. His example was influential on other landholders, who also applied themselves in earnest to cultivate the wilderness.

The improvement of the country at this time occupied the minds of the people of New-Hampshire, and took off their attention, in a great measure, from the view of those political difficulties, which were occasioned by a new act of parliament, laying duties on paper, glass, painters' colors, aad tea ; and the establishment of a board of commissioners for collecting the American revenue. In the other colonies, particularly in Massachusetts, these duties had become a subject of altercation and serious alarm, being grounded on the right which the parliament had assumed of ' binding America in all cases whatsoever.' The only remedy was to be found in frugality, non-importation, and domestic manufactures. These things were recommended, and, in some measure, complied with ; and by means of these exertions, the revenue fell short of the sanguine expectations which its advocates had formed.

The popularity of the governor of New-Hampshire, and the influence of his numerous friends and connexions, who were of the principal families and the richest merchants in the province, prevented the adoption of a non-importation agreement in Portsmouth,* till the merchants in some of the other colonies threatened to withhold any mercantile intercourse with them. A plan of the same kind was then (1770) formed ; and the union of so many colonies, in this measure, caused the manufacturers in Great-Britain to experience distresses of the same nature with those occasioned by the stamp-act ; and to exert their influence for a repeal of the new revenue law, which was in part effected. All the duties, excepting that on tea, were taken off. This relaxation, on the other side of the Atlantic, produced a relaxation here.— The ministry in Great-Britain was frequently changed ; and no uniform system either of coercion or lenity was adopted. The opposition on this side languished for want of unanimity. The more candid among us were willing to suppose that Britain would never lay any more duties ; and there was some foundation for this supposition, as far as letters from ministers of state, and speeches from provincial governors might be depended on. The tax on *tea* was reserved as a latent spark to rekindle the controversy.

When the governor, at his first meeting the assembly, according to the custom on such occasions, recommended to them the establishment of an ' adequate, honorable and permanent salary,' they made some hesitation, on account of a report, that the salaries of the American governors were to be paid out of the revenue. On being assured, that if such a general establishment should take place, it would be so guarded as to prevent his receiving any reward from the assembly ; they framed a vote, granting Sept. 30. seven hundred pounds per annum during his administration (dollars being then fixed at six shillings.) The fund appropriated to the salary was the excise, and in case of its insufficiency, other provision was made. But the vote was limited with an exception, ' unless provision shall be made by parliament.'—

* ' We cannot depend on the countenance of many persons of the first rank ' here ; for royal commissions and family connexions influence the principal ' gentlemen among us, at least *to keep silence* in these evil times. The press ' here has never been openly attacked ; but the printer remembers what he ' once suffered, at Boston; and is easily kept in awe by more private rebukes.' —MS. letter of the sons of liberty, in Portsmouth, to those in Boston.

When the question was put, the house was equally divided, and the speaker, Peter Gilman, turned it against a permanent salary. It was therefore voted from year to year, and generally amounted to seven hundred pounds ; besides which an allowance was made for house-rent, from sixty or seventy to one hundred pounds.[1] *

Among the improvements, which during this administration, were made in the province, one of the most conspicuous, was the establishment of a seminary of literature. It was founded on a projection of Doctor Eleazar Wheelock, of Lebanon, in Connecticut, for the removal of his Indian charity school.

1769.

The first design of a school of this kind was conceived by Mr. John Sergeant, missionary to the Indians, at Stockbridge. A rambling mode of life, and a total want of letters, were ever unfriendly to the propagation of religious knowledge among the savages of America.[2] That worthy missionary, intent on the business of his profession, and having observed the progress made by some of the younger Indians, who resided in the English families, in reading and other improvements, conceived the benevolent idea of changing their whole habit of thinking and acting ; and raising them from their native indolence to a state of civilization ; and at the same time, by introducing the English language, instead of their own barren dialect, to instil into their minds the principles of morality and religion.

To accomplish this design, he procured benefactions from many well disposed persons both here and in England ; and began a school at Stockbridge ; where the Indian youth were to be maintained, under the instruction of two masters; one to oversee their studies, and the other their field labor ; whilst a matron should direct the female children in acquiring the arts of domestic life.   Death put an end to the labors of this excellent man (1749) before his plan could be accomplished.

This design was revived by Wheelock. Having made some experiments, he was encouraged to proceed, (1754) by the tractable disposition of the Indian youths, and their proficiency in learning ; but especially, by the numerous benefactions, which he received from the friends of religion and humanity. Among which, a donation of Joshua Moor, of Mansfield, being the largest, in the infancy of the institution, determined its name ' Moor's school.'[3]

To increase the means of improvement, charitable contributions were solicited in different parts of America, in England, and in Scotland. The money collected in England, was put into the

(1) Journal of Assembly.   (2) Hopkins' memoirs of the Housatoonock Indians, 1736.   (3) Wheelock's printed narrative.

* [1769. Raby, now Brookline, Temple, Surry and Concord, now Lisbon, were incorporated. Sanbornton and Wolfeborough were incorporated the next year.]

hands of a board of trustees, of whom the Earl of Dartmouth was at the head ; and that collected in Scotland was committed to the society for promoting christian knowledge.

As an improvement on the original design, a number of English youths were educated with the Indians, both in literary and agricultural exercises ; that their example might invite the Indians to the love of those employments, and abate the prejudice which they have universally imbibed, that it is beneath the dignity of man to delve in the earth.

As the number of scholars increased, it became necessary to erect buildings, and extend cultivation. That part of the country in which the school was first placed, being filled with inhabitants, a removal was contemplated. When this intention was publicly known, offers were made by private and public persons in several of the neighboring colonies. The wary foresight of the founder, aided by the advice of the board of trustees, in England, led him to accept an invitation made by the governor, and other gentlemen of New-Hampshire. The township of Hanover, on the eastern bank of Connecticut river, was finally determined on, as the most convenient situation for the school ; to which the governor annexed a charter of incorporation for a university, which took the Dec. 13. name of Dartmouth College, from its benefactor, the Earl of Dartmouth. Of this university, Doctor Wheelock was declared the founder and the president ; with power to nominate his successor, in his last will. A board of twelve trustees was constituted, with perpetual succession ; and the college was endowed with a large landed estate, consisting of one whole township (Landaff) besides many other tracts of land in different situations, amounting in the whole, to forty-four thousand acres. One valuable lot, of five hundred acres, in the township of Hanover, given by the late governor, Benning Wentworth, was fixed upon as the site of the school and college. Besides these donations of land, the amount of three hundred and forty pounds sterling, was subscribed, to be paid in labor, provisions, and materials for building. With these advantages, and the prospect of a rapidly increasing neighborhood, in a fertile soil, on both sides of Connecticut river, Doctor Wheelock removed his family and school into the wilderness. 1770. At first, their accommodations were similar to those of Sept. other settlers, on new lands. They built huts of green logs, and lived in them, till a proper edifice could be erected. The number of scholars, at this time, was twenty-four ; of which eighteen were white, and the rest Indians.

Experience had taught Doctor Wheelock, that his Indian youths, however well educated, were not to be depended on for instructors of their countrymen. Of forty, who had been under his care, twenty had returned to the vices of savage life ; and some, whom he esteemed ' subjects of divine grace, had not kept their garments

' unspotted.'[1] It was, therefore, in his view, necessary that a greater proportion of English youths should be educated, to serve as missionaries, and oversee the conduct of the Indian teachers. This was given as the grand reason, for uniting the college with the Indian school, and placing it under the same government ; though the appropriations were distinctly preserved. That the general concerns of the institution might be better regulated, and the intrusion of vicious persons within the purlieus of the college prevented ; a district of three miles square was put under its jurisdiction, and the president was invested with the office of a magistrate. In 1771, a commencement was held, and the first degrees were conferred, on four students ;* one of whom was John Wheelock, the son and successor of the founder.

Another improvement was made about the same time, by dividing the province into counties. This had been long sought, but could not be obtained. The inconvenience to which the people in the western parts of the province were subject, by reason of their distance from Portsmouth, where all the courts were held, was extremely burdensome ; whilst the convenience and emoluments of office were enjoyed by gentlemen in that vicinity. Some attemps to divide the province had been made in the former administration ; but without effect. The rapid increase of inhabitants for several years, made a division so necessary, that it had become one of the principal subjects of debate, in the assembly, from the time of the governor's arrival. Several sessions passed before all points could be adjusted. The number of counties, and the lines of division, were not easily agreed to, and a punctilio of prerogative about the erecting of courts, made some difficulty ; but it was finally determined, that the number of counties should be five ; and the courts were established by an act of the whole legislature. It was passed with a clause, suspending its operation, till the king's pleasure should be known. The royal approbation being obtained, it took effect in 1771. The five counties were named by the governor, after some of his friends in England, Rockingham, Strafford, Hillsborough, Cheshire

(1) Narrative No. 5, p. 20, 21.

* [These students were *Levi Frisbie*, afterwards minister of Ipswich, who died 25 February, 1806, aged 58 ; *Samuel Gray*, a native and resident of Windham, Connecticut, the only survivor of the class ; *Sylvanus Ripley*, afterwards professor of divinity at the college, who died in July, 1787 ; and *John Wheelock*, the president of the college from 1779 to 1815, who died 4 April, 1817, aged 63. The number of graduates since the foundation of the institution is 1637. The presidents who have successively presided over it have been Eleazar Wheelock, D. D., who died 24 April, 1779, Æt. 68 ; John Wheelock, LL. D., from 1779 to 1815, died 4 April, 1817, Æt. 63 ; Francis Brown, D. D., from 1815 to his death, 27 July, 1820, Æt. 36 ; Daniel Dana, D. D., part of the years 1820 and 1821 ; Bennet Tyler, D. D., from 1822 to 1828; and Nathan Lord, D. D., who was inducted into office, 28 October, 1828.]

and Grafton. The counties of Strafford and Grafton being much less populous, than the others, were to remain annexed to the county of Rockingham, till the governor, by advice of council, should declare them competent to the exercise of their respective jurisdictions; which was done in 1773.*

The year 1771 was also distinguished by the abolition of paper currency. Silver and gold had been gradually introduced, and the paper had for several years been called in by taxes. The time limited for its existence being now come, it totally disappeared.†

The death of the late governor[1] produced consequences which materially affected his successor. This family had been for many years of the first rank in the province, and some of its members and connexions had held the principal offices. In such a case, domestic union may be considered as necessary to preserve public honor. The late governor, though superseded, had been treated with every mark of respect; and having no children, it was expected his successor would be his principal heir. A later will, made in favor of his young widow, and unknown till after his death, caused a sudden disappointment; which, if it had evaporated in private reflections only, might have passed among the infirmities incident to humanity, and with them might have been consigned to oblivion; for it is beneath the dignity of history, to record the altercations of families, unless they are connected with public transactions, or events.

Antiquated claims upon the late governor's estate were revived; and law-suits were commenced, which probably would not have been agitated, if the expected disposition had been made. But the most alarming effect of this unhappy disappointment was a question, which the governor moved in council, ' whether the ' reservation of five hundred acres, in the several townships, made ' by the late governor, Benning Wentworth, in the charter grants, ' conveyed the title to him ?' The council determined this question in the negative. The governor then asked, whether they would advise him to grant the said tracts, to such of his majesty's subjects, as should settle and cultivate the same ? To this they gave their assent.[2] Seven of the counsellors present on this occasion were the governor's relations. The eighth was Peter Livius, a gentleman of foreign extraction, who entered his dissent.

(1) Oct. 14, 1770, Ætat. 75. (2) March 19—MS. deposition of seven of the council.

* [Three other counties have since been incorporated, viz. Cohos, formed of the north part of Grafton, 24 December, 1803; Merrimack, taken from the counties of Rockingham and Hillsborough, 3 July, 1823; and Sullivan, being the north division of Cheshire, 5 July, 1827.]

† [1771. The towns of Wakefield, Dublin, Maynesborough and Paulsburg were granted by charter. Paulsburg was incorporated by the name of Milan, 16 December, 1824, and Maynesborough by the name of Berlin, 1 July, 1829.]

He had for several years served as a justice of the common pleas ;
but on the division of the province into counties, it was necessary
to issue new commissions. Finding himself overlooked
in the appointment of officers, and his private affairs calling him abroad, he sailed for England, and there exhibited to the lords of trade, articles of complaint against the governor
and his council.

1772.
July 9.

The first was, that the governor and council, without any legal
process, or the intervention of a jury, had deprived the grantees
under the crown of their lands, on suggestion only that the conditions had not been fulfilled.[1]

The second was, that the duty paid by foreign shipping, commonly called powder money, had not been accounted for, since
the year 1741 ; and that the council had refused to join with the
representatives in an inquiry into this matter in the year 1768.

The third was, that the governor had moved in council, that
the lands reserved to the late governor, in the charters of townships, should be regranted to himself, through the medium of
another person ; and that the protest of the complainant, against
the legality of this proceeding, was rejected.

The fourth was, that in consequence of the opposition, which
he was in duty bound thus to make, he had been injuriously
treated, and had received personal abuse from the governor.

The fifth was, that pending an action in the common pleas,
brought by the governor, though in other names, the judges had
several times been changed, till a question on a point of law was
determined in favor of the governor.

The sixth article stated, that the complainant had expected to
prove several of the above facts, by referring to copies of the
council records in their lordship's office ; but was surprised to
find that the governor had disobeyed his instructions in not
sending them.

The memorial concluded with a general charge of partiality
arising from the family connexions of the governor and council.

Copies of this memorial were sent to the governor and council,
who separately prepared and returned distinct answers to the
several articles of complaint.[2]

To the first, it was said, that the resumption of grants forfeited
by non-compliance with the conditions of settlement was supported by the opinion of the attorney and solicitor general, given in
1752 ; that the invariable usage in these cases, had been to issue
notice to delinquent proprietors, that they should appear on a set
day, and shew cause why their shares should not be forfeited and
regranted ; that their allegations had been always treated with
proper respect, and that no complaint of injustice had been made
by any persons whose grants had been thus resumed.

(1) Printed complaint.   (2) MS. copies.

To the second, it was answered, that the amount of powder-money, during the former administration, though long neglected had been lately recovered; and that since 1768, it had been regularly accounted for. The reason for the non-concurrence of the council, with the vote for inquiring into this matter, was their respect to the royal prerogative, conceiving that the house had no concern with the matter.

To the third article, it was said, that the late governor, conscious of the insufficiency of his title, had solicited his successor for grants of these reservations, which he had declined giving, unless a mandamus from the king could be procured; that this uncertainty had prevented his alienating them; that in consequence, they were uncultivated and forfeited; that some of these lands had been regranted to other persons; but that the present governor had no interest directly or indirectly in them. The council denied, that the governor had ever proposed the granting of these lands to himself, through another person. They also denied that the dissent of the memorialist had been refused.

The charge of personal abuse, in the fourth article, was contradicted and retorted; but it was conceded, that the governor had told him that his reasons of dissent were not founded in truth.

In answer to the fifth article, it was acknowledged, that the action was brought for the governor's benefit; but that any unfair means were used to influence the court was denied. This denial was corroborated by the depositions of the judges themselves, and of the attorneys who were concerned in the suit. It was also proved that the judgment of the court on the question of law, was of no moment, being reversed by the superior court, before which the cause was carried by appeal.

To the sixth article, it was answered, that the governor had directed the secretary to furnish him with copies of all the public transactions which had usually been sent to England, and that he had regularly transmitted them. But it appeared from the affidavit of the secretary, that in June 1760, the late governor had ordered him not to transcribe the minutes of the council, when sitting without the assembly, unless specially directed; and since that time it had been usual to send the journal of the council when sitting as a house of assembly, and not as a council of state.

In fine, the council denied that they had ever acted in their public capacity, from any private or family interest; but asserted, that they had frequently given their judgment directly against it; and they concluded with very severe reflections on the complainant.*

* [1772. Franconia, Hillsborough and Bretton-Woods were incorporated. 1773. Northwood, Loudon, Fitzwilliam, Jaffrey, Cambridge, Dummer, Shelburne, Stratford and Success were incorporated.]

With these answers, were transmitted a great number of depositions, from persons of all ranks and professions, testifying in favor of the governor.[1] These being laid before the lords of trade, and the memorialist being heard in reply, the board represented to the king, that the complaint against the governor 'had been fully verified.'[2] At the same time, they thought it their duty to represent, ' that the reports which they ' had received, through different channels, of the situation of af-' fairs within New-Hampshire, did all concur in representing the ' colony to have been, since Mr. Wentworth's appointment, in a ' state of peace and prosperity ; that its commerce had been ex-' tended, and the number of its inhabitants increased ; and that ' every attempt made to excite the people to disorder and disobe-' dience, had been, by the firm and temperate conduct of Mr. ' Wentworth, suppressed and restrained.'

1773.
May 10.

When the cause was reheard before a committee of the privy council, it was observed by the governor's advocate, that ' peace, prosperity and obedience, were not compatible ' with oppression and injustice ; and that however the lords of trade ' had in the beginning of their report condemned the governor, ' they had, by the praise bestowed upon him, in the end contra-' dicted themselves.'

July 29.

The lords of the committee reported to the king in council, their judgment upon several articles of the complaint, in substance as follows.[3]

' That by the law of England, when lands were granted, upon condition, the breach of that condition must be found by a jury under a commission from the court of chancery ; but that no such court existed in New-Hampshire ; and though the general rule was, that the law of England extended to the colonies, yet it must be understood to mean, such part of the law as is adapted to the state and constitution of them. That though the governor had resumed and regranted lands, yet there was no evidence that such resumptions had been made without proof or public notoriety, that the conditions of former grants had not been complied with ; and that no complaint had been made by any person supposed to be injured. That it had not been proved that resumptions had been made without notice to the proprietors ; and it had not even been suggested, in cases where time had been allowed, that grants were resumed before the expiration of it. That the lands granted to the late governor were granted in the name of the king, which was sufficient to convey a title ; and that the council was mistaken in thinking otherwise. That the governor, by their advice, did resume and regrant several tracts of land which had been granted to the late governor ; but it had not been proved that the said lands were regranted in trust for himself ; and in many instances such

(1) MS. copies.   (2) Printed representation.   (3) Aug. 26—Printed report.

lands were regranted to different inhabitants for their own use
and benefit ; and that the late governor's widow had not complained of any injury, by such resumption. That it appeared to
have been the constant practice when any standing justice of a
court was interested in a suit, for a special justice to be appointed ;
that other causes were depending at the same inferior court of
common pleas, in which the standing justices were interested, and
there was no proof that special justices were appointed on account
of that particular cause in which the governor was concerned ;
but that the commission was solicited in the common form ; and
that the defendant himself had testified that he had no objection
to the commission or to the special justices. With respect to the
transmission of the records of council, it was their opinion that it
might be proper to revive that practice, as it had been conducted
previously to the year 1760. But upon the whole, they submitted
their judgment that there 'was no foundation for any censure
' upon the said governor, for any of the charges contained in the
' complaint, and that the general conduct of his administration had
' tended greatly to the peace and prosperity of the said province.'

This report was approved by the king in council, and the complaint was dismissed. But the governor was strictly en-
Oct. 8. joined to transmit to the lords of trade, authentic copies of
the journals of the council, as a council of state.

In this controversy, Mr. Livius met with great support, from
the interest of those who wished to displace the governor ; and
they became so deeply engaged to him, as to procure for him an
appointment to be the chief justice of New-Hampshire ; but,
upon more mature consideration, this was thought too likely to
produce discord and confusion, and he obtained an appointment
to a more lucrative office in the province of Quebec.

When the final issue of the complaint was known in New-
Hampshire, a general satisfaction appeared among the people.
At the next session of the assembly, the house of representatives
presented to the governor, an address of congratulation, in the
name of their constituents ; and the citizens of Portsmouth gave
a splendid ball, to which the governor and both houses of assembly
were invited.

Hitherto the governor had preserved his popularity ; and the
people, in general, were satisfied with his administration. But,
the obligation which lay on him to support the claims of Britain,
and aid the plans of her ministry, rendered his situation extremely
delicate, and his popularity very precarious. The controversy
between Britain and the colonies was drawing to a crisis. By
the reservation of the duty on tea, the parliament insisted on it as
their right, to tax their American brethren without their consent ;
and the Americans, by withholding the importation of tea from
Britain, made use of the only peaceable mode, in their power,

effectually to oppose that claim. The revenue failed, and the
warehouses of the East India company were filled with an un-
saleable commodity. The ministry and the company, thus severely disappointed, formed a plan, by which it was expected, that
the one would enforce their claim, and the other secure their
traffic.

It was therefore enacted in parliament, that the duty on the
exportation of tea, from Britain, should be taken off; and the
East India company be enabled to send tea, on their own account,
to America, subject to a duty only of three pence on the pound ;
by which means it would come to us, cheaper than before, or than
it could be procured by illicit trade.

This measure caused a general alarm, through the colonies;
and united the interest of the merchants, with the views of the
politicians, and the general sense of liberty in the people. The
trading towns set the example, which the others followed, of
passing resolves, not to permit tea, freighted by the East India
company, to be landed or sold. These resolutions were effectual.
In some places, the consignees were obliged to relinquish their
appointments, and the tea was returned unladen. In other places,
it was deposited in stores, till it could be reshipped. In Boston,
where the obstinacy of Governor Hutchinson drove the people to
desperation, it was destroyed. In New-Hampshire, the prudence
of Governor Wentworth, the vigilance of the magistrates and the
firmness of the people were combined, and the hateful commodity
was sent away without any damage, aud with but little tumult.

The first cargo of tea, consisting of twenty-seven chests, 1774.
was landed and stored at the custom house, before any
people could assemble to obstruct it. A town meeting June 25.
was called, and a proposal was made to Mr. Parry, the consignee,
to reship it. To this, he consented. A guard was appointed
by order of the town, to watch the custom house. The tea having been entered, it was necessary that the duty should be paid ;
which was done openly, by the consignee. The governor convened the council, and kept the magistrates and peace officers in
readiness to suppress any riotous appearances ; but there was no
need of their exertion. The tea was peaceably reshipped and
sent to Halifax.

A second cargo of thirty chests, which came consigned to the
same person, raised a small ferment ; and the windows of Sept. 8.
his lodgings were broken. He applied to the governor
for protection. The governor, as before, summoned the council
and magistrates. The town, by their committee, prevailed on
the consignee to send the tea to Halifax, after having paid the
duty, without which the ship could not legally be cleared at the
custom house.

A general detestation of the measures, pursued by the British
ministry, to rivet the chains on America, universally prevailed.

The towns had severally passed resolves, asserting their right of exemption from all taxation by parliament; condemning the importation and use of tea; and appointing committees of inspection to carry their resolutions into effect. The committees were vigilant; and being aided by the general sentiment of the people, their exertions were successful.

The controversy had now advanced, to a stage, which excited the most serious apprehensions. The parliament had assumed *judicial*, as well as legislative powers; and directed their vengeance against Boston. Its port was shut, and guarded by ships of war; its commerce was interdicted; its tradesmen were without employment; and its poor without bread. A military governor presided there, and was drawing together all the British troops from every part of America; that he might be prepared, to make any sanguinary experiment, which, in the ministerial plan of coercion, might be judged necessary.

The sympathy of their American brethren, raised contributions, for the relief of the numerous poor in Boston, who were regarded as suffering in the common cause. But, to guard ourselves effectually against the gathering storm, a *union of the colonies* was thought absolutely necessary; and recourse was had to the same measure which had formerly been tried in cases of common danger, to hold a CONGRESS of delegates from each colony.

The enemies of America have uniformly censured this measure as unprecedented, illegal and dangerous. That it was dangerous to the designs of the British administration, is admitted; but for that reason, it was to us the means of safety. Though it was not supported by any written law, yet it was evidently founded on self preservation, the first law of nature. But that it was unprecedented, is a very great mistake. From the middle of the preceding century, the united colonies of New-England, held annual, or semiannual meetings of commissioners, on their common concerns, for above forty years. From the reign of Queen Anne, to that of George the Second, governors, and delegates from councils and assemblies, occasionally met in central places, to hold conferences relative to the operations of war, or treaties with the Indian tribes.* These meetings, usually called by the name of Congresses, though unknown, or disregarded in Britain, were familiar to the people of America; and what could be a more natural or obvious step, in a time of common danger, than to assemble by deputies, and confer on the means of safety? Precedents were numerous, that governors and delegates had

* 'May 6, 1754. A question was moved in council by the governor, 'Whether it be not an infringement of the prerogative for the house to join 'with the council, in appointing delegates to the congress at Albany? To 'which the council answered; that the house had no inherent right; but 'it had been long the custom, at such interviews, for the lower house to nom-'inate persons, to be joined with such as the council should appoint.' Council Minutes.

held these assemblies, when their interests were united ; what
then should hinder the people from following the example, when
their interest required them to meet, without their governors, who
were endeavoring to maintain a separate interest ?

At the meeting of the assembly of New-Hampshire, in the
spring, the house of representatives, conformably to the May 10.
proceedings of the assemblies in the other colonies, appointed a committee of correspondence. The governor, who had
in vain labored to prevent this measure, adjourned the as- July 8.
sembly, and after a few days, dissolved it ; hoping, by
this means, to dissolve the committee also. But they were not
restricted by forms. On a summons issued by the committee,
the representatives met again, in their own chamber. The July 6.
governor, attended by the sheriff of the county, went
among them. They rose at his entrance. He declared their
meeting illegal, and directed the sheriff to make open proclamation, for all persons to disperse, and keep the king's peace. When
he had retired, they resumed their seats ; but, on further consideration, adjourned to another house ; and after some conversation, wrote letters to *all the towns* in the province ; requesting
them to send deputies, to hold a convention at Exeter, who
should choose delegates for a general congress ; and to pay their
respective quotas of two hundred pounds, agreeably to the last
proportion of the provincial tax. They also recommended a day
of fasting and prayer, to be observed by the several congregations,
on account of the gloomy appearance of public affairs. The day
was observed, with religious solemnity. The money was collected. Eighty-five deputies were chosen and met at Exe- July 14.
ter, where they delegated Nathaniel Folsom and John
Sullivan, Esquires, to attend the proposed congress, at July 21.
Philadelphia, in September, and delivered to them the money
which had been collected, to defray their expenses. They also
recommended the distressed state of Boston, to the commiseration of their brethren in New-Hampshire ; and contributions
were raised in many of the towns for their relief.

The governor was now convinced, and in his letters to the
ministry acknowledged, that ' the union of the colonies would not
' be lost in New-Hampshire.'[1] At the same time, he did the
people the justice to say, that they had abstained from violence
and outrage, and that the laws had their course. In his letters,
which were published by the ministry, there appears a spirit of
candor toward the people, as well as a desire to recommend
himself to the approbation of his superiors. Though he saw
another authority rising in the province, founded on the broad
basis of public opinion, and unrestrained representation, an authority over which he had no influence or control ; yet he en-

(1) Parliamentary register, 1775, vol. i. p. 61, &c.

deavored to preserve the shadow of the royal government, and keep up its forms as long as possible.

But it was impracticable for a person, circumstanced as he was, to withstand the spirit of the people.* That his wish was to prevent a rupture, there is sufficient evidence, for candor to believe. But it cannot be thought strange, that in his endeavors to comply with the expectations of the ministry, and their instruments, which he conceived to be his duty, he should fall into such a snare, as to lose the affections of the people; for it was impossible to please both.

The troops in Boston wanted barracks, to secure them against the approaching winter. The artificers of the town, were, by the popular voice, restrained from working in the service of government. General Gage was therefore obliged to send for assistance to the neighboring governors, and, among others, to Governor Wentworth. Instead of convening his council for their advice, or issuing a proclamation, inviting help and promising a reward, he privately employed a person to hire carpenters to go to Boston. It was impossible that the secret should be kept, and when it was known, his best friends reprobated his conduct. The committee of Portsmouth, at the head of which, was his uncle, Hunking Wentworth, bore their public testimony against it; and censured him, not by name, but by implication, as ' an enemy to the community,' and the men whom he had employed, as ' unworthy of society.' The agent in this secret business, was brought on his knees before the committee of Rochester, and made an humble acknowledgment. This prudent step of the committee, disarmed the popular rage, and prevented any injury to his person or property.

The transactions of the congress which met at Philadelphia, were universally approved. The spirit of them was firm, but Sept. 4. pacific. The mode of opposition, to the arbitrary claims of Britain, which they recommended, was non-importation and non-consumption. But in the close of their address, to their constituents, they advised them to ' extend their views to the most ' unhappy events, and to be in all respects prepared for every ' contingency.' Not long after this advice was made public, a contingency presented itself, in which the people of New-Hampshire gave an example of that spirit, by which the whole country was animated.

An order having been passed by the king in council, prohibiting the exportation of gunpowder and other military stores, to Ameri-

* The following paragraph, of one of his private letters, written at that time, to a confidential friend, deserves to be remembered.
' Our hemisphere threatens a hurricane. I have in vain strove, almost to ' death, to prevent it. If I can, at last, bring out of it, safety to my country, ' and honor to our sovereign, my labors will be joyful. My heart is devoted ' to it, and you know its sincerity.' MS. letter to T. W. W.

ca ; a copy of it was brought by express to Portsmouth, a ta time, when a ship of war was daily expected from Boston, with a party of troops, to take possession of Fort William and Mary, at the entrance of the harbor.   The committee of the town, with all possible secrecy and despatch, collected a company, from that and some of the neighboring towns ; and before the governor had any suspicion of their intentions, they proceeded to Newcastle, and assaulted the fort.   The captain and his five men (which was the whole garrison) were confined, and one hundred barrels of powder were carried off.   The next day, another company went and removed fifte en of the lightest cannon, and all the small arms, with some other warlike stores ; which they distributed in the several towns, under the care of the committees. Major John Sullivan, and Captain John Langdon, distinguished themselves, as leaders in this affair.   It was transacted with great expedition and alacrity, and in the most fortunate point of time ; just before the arrival of the Scarborough frigate, and Canseau sloop, with several companies of soldiers ; who took possession of the fort, and of the heavy cannon which had not been removed.

Dec. 13.

The governor put the five men, who belonged to the fort, on board the ships of war, to be reserved as evidences in case of a prosecution of the offenders for high treason ; and having consulted counsel in this and the neighboring province, thought it his duty ; that he might prevent any charge of misprision of treason against himse``; to dismiss from public trust, all those persons concerned in the assault of the fort, who had held any office under the government, and concerning whose proceedings he had authentic testimony.   He also issued a proclamation,* command-

---

* [The following is a copy of the proclamation :
  PROVINCE OF NEW-HAMPSHIRE.—*A Proclamation by the Governor.*
Whereas, several bodies of men did, in the day time of the 14th, and in the night of the 15th of this instant December, in the most daring and rebellious manner invest, attack, and forcibly enter into his majesty's castle William and Mary in this province, and overpowering and confining the captain and garrison, did, besides committing many treasonable insults and outrages, break open the magazine of said castle and plunder it of above one hundred barrels of gunpowder, with upwards of sixty stand of small arms, and did also force from the ramparts of said castle and carry off sixteen pieces of cannon, and other military stores, in open hostility and direct oppugnation of his majesty's government, and in the most atrocious contempt of his crown and dignity ;—

I DO, by advice and consent of his majesty's council, issue this proclamation. ordering and requiring, in his majesty's name, all magistrates and other officers, whether civil or military, as they regard their duty to the king and the tenor of the oaths they have solemnly taken and subscribed, to exert themselves in detecting and securing in some of his majesty's goals in this province the said offenders, in order to their being brought to condign punishment ; And from motives of duty to the king and regard to the welfare of the good people of this province : I do in the most earnest and solemn manner, exhort and injoin you, his majesty's liege subjects of this government, to beware of suffering yourselves to be seduced by the false arts or menaces of abandoned men, to abet, protect, or screen from justice any of the said high handed offenders, or to withhold or secrete his majesty's munition forcibly ta-

ing all officers, civil and military, to assist in detecting and securing the offenders ; and exhorting all people to beware of being
seduced, by the false arts and menaces of abandoned men.*

It was thought proper by the governor and some of his friends,
to form an association, for the support of the royal government,
and for their mutual defence. They boasted, that an hundred
men could be procured, from the ships, at a minute's warning.
This transaction exposed the weakness of the cause, which
1775. they meant to support ; for what could an hundred men
do against the whole country ?

A second convention of deputies met at Exeter, to consult on
the state of affairs, and appoint delegates for the next general
congress, to be holden on the tenth of May, at Philadel-
Jan. 25. phia. Major Sullivan and Captain Langdon were chosen ;
and the sum of two hundred and fifty pounds, were ordered to
defray their expenses. This convention issued an address to the
people, warning them of their danger ; exhorting them to union,
peace and harmony, frugality, industry, manufactures, and learning the military art ; that they might be able, if necessary, to defend the country against invasion. They appointed a committee
of correspondence, with power to call another convention, when
they should judge it necessary.

The winter passed away in gloomy apprehension and anxiety.
Men of consideration saw that a wide breach was made, and that
it could not easily be closed. Some happy genius was wanting
to plan, and wisdom on both sides to adopt, a constitution for
Britain and America. Royal charters and instructions, acts of
parliament and precedents of all kinds, were at best but a rotten

ken from his castle ; but that each and every of you will use your utmost
endeavors to detect and discover the perpetrators of these crimes to the civil
magistrate, and assist in securing and bringing them to justice, and in recovering the king's munition ; This injunction it is my bounded duty to lay
strictly upon you, and to require your obedience thereto, as you value individually your faith and allegiance to his majesty, as you wish to preserve that
reputation to the province in general ; and as you would avert the dreadful
but most certain consequences of a contrary conduct to yourselves and posterity.

Given at the council-chamber in Portsmouth, the 26th day of December, in
the 15th year of the reign of our sovereign lord George the Third, by the
grace of God, of Great-Britain, France and Ireland, king, defender of
the faith, &c. and in the year of our Lord Christ, 1774.
                                                      J. WENTWORTH.
    By his excellency's command,
        with advice of council,
            THEODORE ATKINSON, Sec'ry.
                GOD save the King.]

    * [1774. Warner, Deering, Nelson, Stoddard, Erroll, Kilkenny, Mills-
field, Piercy and Whitefield were granted or incorporated. During the revolutionary war, the following towns were incorporated : viz. in 1776, Washington and Marlborough ; 1777, Antrim, Moultonborough and New-Hampton ;
1778, Fishersfield and New-Chester ; 1779, Andover, Hancock, New-London
and Northumberland ; 1780, Orange and Northfield ; 1781, Thornton ; and
1782, Pittsfield.]

foundation. The store of temporary expedients was exhausted.
It was doubtful whether force could generate submission, or
whether resistance could enervate force. Neither country was
sensible of the strength and resources of the other. The press
teemed with arguments on both sides ; but no plan of conciliation
was adopted. A fair and candid representation of our grievances
could not be received, in the court of Britain. Each side was
tenacious of its claims, and there appeared no disposition to relax.
When two independent nations are in such a state, they generally
find among their friends and allies, some mediating power, to bring
them to terms and prevent a rupture. Between Britain and
America, no mediator could be found. The controversy could
be decided only by the supreme arbiter of nations.

The first ships, which arrived in the spring, brought us news
that the petition of congress was graciously received by the king ;
and that the merchants of England were petitioning in our favor.
This revived our hopes. Soon after, we were informed, that the
parliament had *voted* the existence of a rebellion in Massachusetts ; and that the other colonies were aiding and assisting :
That the lords and commons had addressed the king, to enforce
the revenue-acts, and had assured him, that they would stand by
him, with their lives and fortunes : That the king had demanded
an augmentation of his forces, by sea and land : That the commerce of the New-England colonies was to be restrained, and
their fishery prohibited ; and that an additional number of troops,
horse and foot, were ordered to America. These tidings threw
us into distress. A war seemed inevitable ; and a gloom over-
spread the whole country. The people of Boston began to remove from the town ; and those, who could not remove, were
solicitous to secure their most valuable effects. In the midst of
this distress, a frigate arrived express from England ; with Apr. 14.
an account of a proposal made and voted in parliament,
which was called Lord North's conciliatory proposition. It was
this ; ' that when any colony by their governor, council and as-
' sembly, shall engage to make provision, for the support of civil
' government, and administration of justice, in such colony ; it
' will be proper, if such proposal be approved by the king and
' parliament, for so long time as such provision shall be made, to
' forbear to levy any duties or taxes in such colony, except for
' the regulation of commerce ; the neat proceeds of which shall
' be carried to the account of such colony respectively.' The
troops, however, were to remain ; and the refractory colonies were
to be punished. This proposition was said to be founded on some
advice, received from New-York, that if concessions were made
by parliament, they would censure the proceedings of congress,
and break the union of the colonies. The proposal was evidently
a bait thrown out to divide us, and tempt us to desert the colony

of Massachusetts; who could not comply, without submitting to the alteration, lately made by parliament in their charter.

What might have been the effect of this proposition in the other colonies, if it had been allowed time to operate, is uncertain. The conduct of General Gage, on receiving this news, was in the highest degree absurd and inconsistent. He had been blamed in parliament for his inactivity. He had *friends* in Boston, who constantly assured him, that the people in the country would not dare to face his troops. He had been informed of a magazine of provisions and stores, at Concord, laid up by the provincial congress, in case of extremity. With the news of the conciliatory proposition, he received orders to make an experiment of its success. On the eighteenth day of April, he issued writs for calling a general assembly, to comply with the proposed terms of reconciliation; and in the night following, he privately despatched a body of his troops, to destroy the magazine at Concord; and to seize some of the leaders of opposition, who had retired from the town. He was induced to believe, that if between the issuing of his writs, and the meeting of the assembly, he could strike a bold stroke; it would so intimidate the people, and unfit them for defence, that they would easily comply with the terms proposed. But he totally mistook the genius of the people of New-England. Nor were his designs carried on so secretly as he imagined. The popular leaders were seasonably apprised of their danger, and kept themselves out of his reach. The country was alarmed, by expresses sent off in the night, before he had taken the precaution to shut the avenues of the town. A company of armed citizens kept guard at Lexington, on the road to Concord. The British troops, when they appeared in the morning, having ordered them to disperse, fired upon them, as they were retiring, and killed several on the spot. They then proceeded to Concord, Apr. 19. and destroyed such of the stores as had not been removed; and having accomplished their object, as far as they were able, they retreated through showers of musquetry from the people, who suddenly collected from all quarters to oppose them.

On the alarm of this act of hostility, the people of New-Hampshire, and of the other colonies, took arms, and flew to the assistance of their brethren.

Notwithstanding this ill-advised and unsuccessful attempt of Gage, Governor Wentworth had very sanguine hopes of the good effect of the ' conciliatory proposition;' and determined, as he said, ' to plant the root of peace in New-Hampshire.' He summoned a new assembly; and in his speech, entreated them, as May 4. ' the only legal and constitutional representatives of the ' people, to direct their counsels to such measures, as ' might tend to secure their peace and safety; and effectually ' lead to a restoration of the public tranquillity; and an affection-

' ate reconciliation with the mother country.' The house desired a short recess, that they might advise with their constituents on so momentous a question ; and the governor reluctantly consented to adjourn them to the twelfth day of June.

In the mean time, the officers and men of the Scarborough began to dismantle the fort ; they also stopped two vessels laden with provisions, which were coming into the harbor ; and notwithstanding the most pressing remonstrances of the inhabitants, and solicitation of the governor, refused to release them. Upon this, a body of armed men, went to a battery on Jerry's May 26. point, at Great-Island, and took away eight cannon of twenty-four and thirty-two pound shot, which they brought up to Portsmouth ; and whilst they were engaged in this work, the Canseau sloop convoyed the two provision vessels to Boston, for the supply of the fleet and army.

A new convention was at this time sitting at Exeter ; in which the province was more fully and equally represented, than it ever had been before. They passed votes of thanks to those who had taken the powder and guns from the fort, in the preceding winter, and to those who had removed-the cannon from the battery. They also instructed the representatives, how to act at the next meeting of the assembly; and the voice of the convention was regarded by the house, as the voice of their constituents.

At the adjournment, the governor again recommended ' the conciliatory proposition.' The first step which the house June 12. took, was in obedience to the voice of the convention, to expel three members whom the governor had called by the king's writ, from three new townships ; whilst many other towns, of much older standing, and more populous, were neglected, and never enjoyed the privilege of representation, but in the newly established conventions. The governor then adjourned the assembly to the eleventh of July. One of the expelled members, having spoken his mind freely without doors, was ussaulted by the populace, and took shelter in the governor's house. The people demanded him, and brought a gun, mounted on a carriage, to the door ; upon which the offender was delivered up, and conveyed to Exeter. The governor, conceiving himself insulted, retired to the fort ; and his house became a scene of pillage.

When the assembly met again, he sent a message from the fort, and adjourned them to the twenty-eighth of September ; but they never met any more. He continued under the July 11 protection of the Scarborough, and another ship of war, till all the remaining cannon of the fort were taken on board, and then Aug. 24. sailed for Boston. In September, he came to the Isles of Shoals, and there issued a proclamation, adjourning the assembly to the next April. This was the last act of his administration, and the last time that he set his foot in the province. Thus an end was put to the British government in New-Hampshire, when it had subsisted ninety-five years.

From this view of the administration of Governor Wentworth, it is easy to conclude, that his intentions were pacific ; and whilst the temper of the times allowed him to act agreeably to his own principles, his government was acceptable and beneficial ; but when matters had come to the worst, his faults were as few, and his conduct as temperate, as could be expected from a servant of the crown. If a comparison be drawn, between him and most of the other governors on this continent, at the beginning of the revolution, he must appear to advantage. Instead of widening the breach, he endeavored to close it ; and when his efforts failed, he retired from a situation, where he could no longer exercise the office of a governor ; leaving his estate and many of his friends ; and preserving only his commission, as surveyor of the king's woods ; the limits of which were much contracted by the succeeding revolution.*

CHAPTER XXV.

War with Britain. Change of government. Temporary constitution. Independence. Military exertions. Stark's expedition. Employment of troops during the war.

WHEN the controversy with Britain shewed symptoms of hostility, and the design of the ministry and parliament to provoke us to arms became apparent, the people of New-Hampshire began seriously to meditate the defence of their country. It was uncertain in what manner the scene would open ; for this and other reasons no regular plan of operations could be formed. By the old militia law, every male inhabitant, from sixteen years old to sixty, was obliged to be provided with a mus-

1775.

* [JOHN WENTWORTH, was son of Mark Hunking Wentworth, and was the fifth in descent from elder William Wentworth, mentioned under the year 1689. He was born about 1736, and graduated at Harvard college in 1755, and his name stands as the fifth in the class, being preceded by the names of Cushing, Appleton, Brown and Livingston. He received the appointment of governor when he was but 31 years of age, being advanced to that station at an earlier age than any of his predecessors, or any who has succeeded him. After leaving New-Hampshire in 1775, he was appointed governor of Nova-Scotia, and resided at Halifax, where he died 8 April, 1820, aged 84. He received the title of baronet from George III., and was honored by the universities of Oxford, in England, and Aberdeen, in Scotland, with the degree of Doctor of Laws. He received a similar honor from Dartmouth college.— The late Dr. Dwight in speaking of his character, describes him as " a man of sound understanding, refined taste, enlarged views, and a dignified spirit ; and as retiring from the chair with a higher reputation than any other man who held the same office he did in the country."]

ket and bayonet, knapsack, cartridge-box, one pound of powder, twenty bullets and twelve flints. Every town was obliged to keep in readiness one barrel of powder, two hundred pounds of lead and three hundred flints, for every sixty men ; besides a quantity of arms and ammunition for the supply of such as were not able to provide themselves with the necessary articles. Even those persons who were exempted from appearing at the common military trainings, were obliged to keep the same arms and ammunition. In a time of peace, these requisitions were neglected, and the people in general were not completely furnished, nor the towns supplied according to law. The care which the governor had taken to appoint officers of militia and review the regiments, for some years before, had awakened their attention to the duties of the parade ; which were performed with renewed ardor, after the provincial convention had recommended the learning of military exercises and manœuvres. Voluntary associations were formed for this purpose, and the most experienced persons were chosen to command on these occasions. To prevent false rumors and confusion, the committees of inspection in each town were also committees of correspondence, by whom all intelligence concerning the motions of the British, were to be communicated ; and proper persons were retained to carry expresses when there should be occasion.

In this state of anxiety and expectation ; when an early spring had invited the husbandman to the labor of the field ; General Gage thought it proper to open the drama of war. The alarm was immediately communicated from town to town ^{Apr. 19.} through the whole country, and volunteers flocked from all parts ; till a body of ten thousand men assembled in the neighborhood of Boston, completely invested it on the land side, and cut of all communication with the country.

On the first alarm, about twelve hundred men marched from the nearest parts of New-Hampshire, to join their brethren, who had assembled in arms about Boston. Of these, some returned ; others formed themselves into two regiments, under the authority of the Massachusetts convention. As soon as the provincial congress of New-Hampshire met, they voted to raise ^{May 17.} two thousand men, to be formed into three regiments ; those which were already there to be accounted as two, and another to be enlisted immediately. These men engaged to serve till the last day of December, unless sooner discharged. The command of these regiments was given to the Colonels John Stark, James Reed and Enoch Poor. The two former were present in the memorable battle on the heights of Charlestown, being ^{June 17.} posted on the left wing, behind a fence ; from which they sorely galled the British as they advanced to the attack, and cut them down by whole ranks at once. In their retreat, they lost

several men, and among others, the brave Major Andrew McClary, who was killed by a cannon shot after he had passed the isth-
mus of Charlestown.* On the alarm occasioned by this battle, the
June 20. third regiment collected and marched to the camp ; and with
the other New-Hampshire troops, was posted on the left
wing of the army at Winter-Hill, under the immediate command of
Brigadier-General Sullivan, who with the other general officers,
received his appointment from congress.

It had been a common sentiment among the British troops, that
the Americans would not dare to fight with them. This battle
effectually convinced them of their mistake. They found that
fighting with us was a serious thing ; and the loss which they sustained in this battle, evidently had an influence on their subsequent operations.

Whilst the Scarborough frigate remained in the harbor of Pascataqua, frequent bickerings happened between her crew and the
inhabitants. Captain Berkeley seized all inward bound vessels, and sent them to Boston. He also prevented the boats belonging to the river from going out to catch fish. This conduct
was conformable to the orders which he had received to execute
the restraining act. In return, his boats were not permitted to
fetch provisions from the town ; and one of them was fired upon
in the night, by some of the guards stationed on the shore. A
compromise, at length, was made between him and the committee
of the town ; open boats were permitted to pass, to catch fish for
the inhabitants ; and his boats were allowed to take fresh provisions for the use of the ship. This agreement subsisted but a short
time, and finally all intercourse was cut off.

After the departure of the ship, the people went in volunteer
parties, under the direction of Major Ezekiel Worthen, whom the
Aug. 24. convention appointed engineer, and built forts on the points
of two islands, which form a narrow channel, about a mile
below the town of Portsmouth. One of these was called Fort
Washington, and the other Fort Sullivan. The cannon which
had been saved from the old fort and battery were mounted here,
and the town was thought to be secure from being surprised by
ships of war.

The tenth of September was the last day of exportation
fixed by the general congress. Most of the vessels which sailed

* [ANDREW McCLARY was son of Andrew McClary of Epsom, who with
his brother John were early inhabitants of that town. The male line of the
family name has become extinct. Major McClary was an active and efficient
officer. Swett, Hist. of Bunker Hill Battle, 2d edit. p. 48.
In a letter from Colonel Stark to Matthew Thornton, written two days after the battle of Bunker Hill, (see Coll. of N. H. Hist. Soc. ii. 145) it appears
that the number lost from Stark's regiment, was 15 killed and missing, and
60 wounded ; the number from Colonel Reed's regiment was 3 killed, 1 missing and 29 wounded. The number in Swett's History, where the names of
the killed are given, is different from the account given in this letter.]

out of the harbor were seized by the British cruisers, and carried into Boston. One was retaken by a privateer of Beverly, and carried into Cape-Anne.

In the following month, several British armed vessels were sent to burn the town of Falmouth ; which was in part effect- Oct. 18. ed, by throwing carcases and sending a party on shore, under cover of their guns. It was suspected that they had the same design against Portsmouth. General Washington despatched Brigadier-General Sullivan from the camp at Cambridge, with orders to take the command of the militia and defend the harbor of Pascataqua. On this occasion, the works on the islands were strengthened ; a boom, constructed with masts and chains, was thrown across the Narrows, which was several times broken by the rapidity of the current, until it was impossible to secure the passage by such means ; an old ship was scuttled and sunk in the northern channel of the river ; a company of rifle-men, from the camp, was posted on Great-Island ; and fire-rafts were constructed to burn the enemy's shipping. These preparations served to keep up the spirits of the people ; but many families, not thinking themselves safe in Portsmouth, removed into the country, and there remained till the next spring.

A spirit of violent resentment was excited against all who were suspected of a disposition inimical to the American cause. Some persons were taken up on suspicion and imprisoned ; some fled to Nova-Scotia, or to England, or joined the British army in Boston. Others were restricted to certain limits and their motions continually watched. The passions of jealousy, hatred and revenge were freely indulged, and the tongue of slander was under no restraint. Wise and good men secretly lamented these excesses ; but no effectual remedy could be administered. All commissions under the former authority being annulled, the courts of justice were shut, and the sword of magistracy was sheathed. The provincial convention directed the general affairs of the war ; and town committees had a discretionary, but undefined power to preserve domestic peace. Habits of decency, family government, and the good examples of influential persons, contributed more to maintain order than any other authority. The value of these secret bonds of society was now more than ever conspicuous.

In the convention which met at Exeter, in May, and continued sitting with but little interruption till November, one hundred and two towns were represented, by one hundred and thirty-three members.[1] Their first care was to establish post offices ; to appoint a committee of supplies for the army, and a committee of safety. To this last committee, the general instruction was similar to that, given by the Romans, to their dictators, ' to take un- ' der consideration, all matters in which the welfare of the prov-

(1) MS. Records of Convention.

48

' ince, in the security of their rights, is concerned ; and to take
' the utmost care, that the public sustain no damage.'* Particu-
ar instructions were given to them, from time to time, as occasion required. They were considered as the supreme executive ;
and during the recess of the convention, their orders and recommendations had the same effect as the acts and resolves of that
whole body.

By an order of the convention, the former secretary, Theodore
Atkinson, Esquire, delivered up the province records, to a committee which was sent to receive them, and Ebenezer Thompson,
Esquire, was appointed in his place. The records of deeds, and
of the probate office, for the county of Rockingham, were also
removed to Exeter, as a place of greater safety than Portsmouth.
The former treasurer, George Jaffrey, Esquire, was applied to
for the public money in his hands, which, to the amount of one
thousand five hundred and sixteen pounds, four shillings and eight
pence, he delivered ; and Nicholas Gilman, Esquire, was appointed treasurer in his room.†

During this year, three emissions of paper bills were made.
The first, of ten thousand and fifty pounds ; the second, of ten
thousand pounds ; and the third, of twenty thousand pounds.
For the amount of those sums, the treasurer gave his obligation
in small notes, which passed for a time, as current money, equal
in value to silver and gold. But as emissions were multiplied, as
the redemption of the bills was put off to distant periods, and the
bills themselves were counterfeited, it was impossible for them
long to hold their value.

Beside the three regiments which made part of the American
army at Cambridge, a company of artillery was raised to do duty
at the forts. A company of rangers was posted on Connecticut
river ; and two companies more were appointed, to be ready to
march wherever the committee of safety should direct. The
whole militia was divided into twelve regiments ; the field officers
were appointed by the convention, and the inferior officers were
chosen by the companies. Out of the militia were inlisted four
regiments of minute-men, so called, because they were to be
ready at a minute's warning. They were constantly trained to
military duty, and when called to service were allowed the same

* ' Ne quid detrimenti respublica capiat.'

† [NICHOLAS GILMAN was son of Daniel Gilman, of Exeter, a grandson of
the Hon. John Gilman, one of the first council under President Cutt, in 1680.
(See page 90.) He was born 31 October, 1731, and received a common
school education. He was elected a counsellor under the temporary constitution of New-Hampshire in 1777, and, by annual elections, continued in office until his death, 7 April, 1783. Three of his sons enjoyed some of the
first offices in the state. Nicholas, the eldest, died while a senator in congress, in 1814. John Taylor, after having been governor of the state fourteen
years, died 31 August, 1828, æ. 75. Nathaniel, now living, has been senator
in the state legislature and state treasurer.]

pay as the regiments in the continental army. In the succeeding
winter, when the Connecticut forces had withdrawn from the camp,
because their time of service was expired, sixteen companies of
the New-Hampshire militia, of sixty-one men each, supplied their
place, till the British troops evacuated Boston.

The convention having been appointed for six months only;
before the expiration of that time, applied to the general congress
for their advice, respecting some mode of government for the
future. In answer to which, the congress recommended   Nov. 3.
to them, ' to call a full and free representation of the
' people ; that these representatives, if they should think it neces-
' sary, might establish such a form of government, as, in their
' judgment, would best conduce to the happiness of the people,
' and most effectually tend to secure peace and good order in the
' province, during the continuance of the dispute between Great-
' Britain and the colonies.' On receiving this advice, the convention took into their consideration the mode in which a   Nov. 14.
full and free representation should be called ; and finally
agreed, that each elector should possess a real estate of twenty
pounds value, and every candidate for election, one of three hundred pounds ; that every town, consisting of one hundred families,
should send one representative ; and one more for every hundred
families ; and that those towns which contained a less number than
one hundred should be classed.   They had before ordered a survey to be made of the number of people in the several counties ;
and having obtained it, they determined, that the number of representatives to the next convention, should bear the following proportion to the number of people, viz.

Rockingham,	37850 people	38 representatives.
Strafford,	12713	13
Hillsborough,	16447	17
Cheshire,	11089	15
Grafton,	4101	6
In all,	82200	89

These representatives were to be empowered, by their constituents, to assume government as recommended by the general
congress, and to continue for one whole year from the time of such
assumption.   The wages of the members were to be paid by
the several towns, and their travelling expenses out of the
public treasury. Having formed this plan, and sent cop-   Nov. 16.
ies of it to the several towns, the convention dissolved.

This convention was composed chiefly of men who knew nothing of the theory of government, and had never before been concerned in public business.   In the short term of six months, they
acquired so much knowledge by experience, as to be convinced,

that it was improper for a legislative assembly to consist of one house only. As soon as the new convention came together, they Dec. 21. drew up a temporary form of government; and, agree- ably to the trust reposed in them by their constituents, 1776. having assumed the name and authority of the house of Jan. 5. representatives, they proceeded to choose twelve persons, to be a distinct branch of the legislature, by the name of a coun- cil. Of these, five were chosen from the county of Rockingham, two from Strafford, two from Hillsborough, two from Cheshire and one from Grafton. These were empowered to elect their own president, and any seven of them were to be a quorum. It was ordained, that no act or resolve should be valid, unless pass- ed by both branches of the legislature; that all money bills should originate in the house of representatives; that neither house should adjourn for more than two days, without the consent of the other; that a secretary, and all other public officers of the colony, and of each county, for the current year, all general and field officers of militia, and all officers of the marching regiments, should be appointed by the two houses; all subordinate militia officers by their respective companies; that the present assembly should subsist one year, and if the dispute with Britain should continue longer, and the general congress should give no directions to the contrary, that precepts should be issued annually to the several towns on or before the first day of November, for the choice of counsellors and representatives, to be returned by the third Wednesday in December.

In this hasty production, there were some material defects. One was the want of an executive branch of government. To remedy this, the two houses, during their session, performed ex- ecutive as well as legislative duty; and at every adjournment appointed a committee of safety, to sit in the recess, with the same powers, as had been given in the preceding year, by the conven- tion. The number of this committee varied from six to sixteen. The president of the council was also president of this executive committee. The person chosen to fill this chair was an old, tried, faithful servant of the public, the honorable Meshech Weare, Esquire, who was also appointed chief justice of the superior court. So great was the confidence of the people in this gentleman, that they scrupled not to invest him, at the same time, with the highest offices, legislative, executive, and judicial; in which he was con- tinued by annual elections during the whole war.*

* [Of a character so beloved and esteemed as President Weare, a note more extended than this, should be given, but the want of suitable materials, will permit only the following notice.

The family of *Weares* was an early one in New-England, although not among the earliest. Peter Weare, probably the first ancestor of the President who came hither, died 12 October, 1653, at Newbury, Massachusetts, in which place he had resided some time. His son, Nathaniel Weare, resided in

This constitution was prefaced with several reasons for adopting government, viz. That the British parliament had, by many grievous and oppressive acts, deprived us of our native rights ; to enforce obedience to which acts, the ministry of that kingdom had sent a powerful fleet and army into this country, and had wantonly and cruelly abused their power, in destroying our lives and property ; that the sudden and abrupt departure of our late governor, had left us destitute of legislation ; that no judicial courts were open to punish offenders ; and that the continental congress had recommended the adoption of a form of government. Upon these grounds, the convention made a declaration in these words, ' We conceive ourselves *reduced to the necessity* of establishing a ' form of government, to continue during the present unhappy ' and unnatural contest with Great-Britain ; protesting and de- ' claring, that we never sought to throw off our dependence on ' Great-Britain ; but felt ourselves happy under her protection, ' whilst we could enjoy our constitutional rights and privileges ; ' and that we shall rejoice, if such a reconciliation between us and ' our parent state can be effected, as shall be approved by the

that place several years, and afterwards removed to Hampton, as intimated in a note, p. 103. Peter Weare, the son of Nathaniel, was born at Newbury, 15 Nov. 1660, and was appointed a counsellor of N. H. in 1698. The father of the President was Nathaniel Weare, who was probably son of Peter Weare, the counsellor. He had four sons and eight daughters. MESHECH WEARE was the youngest of the sons, and was born at what was then Hampton, in 1714. He graduated at Harvard college, then under President Wadsworth, in the year 1735, and devoted some time to theological studies, which he relinquished for the calls of civil and political life. He was chosen speaker of the house of representatives in 1752 ; and in 1754, was appointed a commissioner to the congress at Albany, and was afterwards one of the justices of the superior court of New-Hampshire. In 1776, he was chosen president of the state under the new constitution, adopted that year to continue during the war, and was annually elected to the same office during the contest with Great-Britain. He was also appointed to the office of chief justice in 1777, which he held at the same time he sustained the office of chief magistrate. In 1784, he was elected the first president under the constitution which was adopted in 1783, and which went into operation the following year ; but on account of his declining health, he resigned his office before the expiration of the political year. He enjoyed not only civil honors, but was complimented with those of a literary kind. In 1782, he was elected a fellow of the American academy of arts and sciences, which two years before had gone into operation in Massachusetts, under very favorable auspices. His election was announced to him by the corresponding secretary, Rev. Joseph Willard, the president of Harvard college.

Being worn out with public service and the infirmities of age, President Weare departed this life at his residence at Hampton-Falls, on the twenty-fifth of January, 1786, having entered on the 73d year of his age.

In speaking of his character, Dr. Belknap, who personally knew him, says, " he was not a person of an original inventive genius, but had a clear discernment, extensive knowledge, accurate judgment, calm temper, a modest deportment, an upright and benevolent heart, and a habit of prudence and diligence in discharging the various duties of public and private life. He did not enrich himself by his public employment, but was one of those good men, ' who dare to love their country and be *poor*.' "

The two last paragraphs have been transferred from a note in the Appendix to the 2d vol. of the former editions, to this place.]

' continental congress, in whose prudence and wisdom we con-
' fide.'*

Such was the language, and such were the sentiments of the
people at that time ; and had the British government, on the removal of their troops from Boston, treated with us, in answer to
our last petition, upon the principle of reconciliation ; and restored
us to the state in which we were before the stamp-act was made,
they might even then, have preserved their connexion with us.
But in the course of a few months, we not only found our petitions
disregarded, and our professions of attachment to the parent state
treated as hypocritical ; but their hostile intentions became so apparent, and our situation was so singular, that there could be no
hope of safety for us, without dissolving our connexion with them,
and assuming that equal rank among the powers of the earth for
which nature had destined us, and to which the voice of reason
and providence loudly called us.   Britain had engaged foreign
mercenaries to assist in subjugating us ; justice required that we
should in our turn court foreign aid ; but this could not be had,
whilst we acknowledged ourselves subjects of the crown against
whose power we were struggling.   The exertions which we had
made, and the blood which we had shed, were deemed too great
a price for reconciliation to a power which still claimed the right
' to bind us in all cases whatsoever,' and which held out to us un-
conditional submission, as the only terms on which we were to
expect even a pardon.   Subjection to a prince who had thrown
us out of his protection ; who had ruined our commerce, destroyed our cities and spilled our blood ;   and who would not govern
us at all, without the interposition of a legislative body, in whose
election we had no voice, was an idea too absurd to be any longer
entertained.   These sentiments, being set in their just light by various publications and addresses, had such force as to produce a
total change of the public opinion.   Independence became the
general voice of the same people, who but a few months before
had petitioned for reconciliation.   When this could not be had,
but on terms disgraceful to the cause which we had undertaken
to support, we were driven to that as our only refuge.   The
minds of the people at large in most of the colonies being thus in-

* [This was the first constitution, it has been said, which was adopted by
any of the colonies, after the revolution commenced.   It met with a small
opposition from some of the delegates, and from the inhabitants of Portsmouth.
Twelve of the former entered their protest against it, and the following among
other reasons are given for their dissent.   " Because the colonies of New-
York and Virginia, which are in similar circumstances with us, are much
larger and more opulent, and, we presume, much wiser, (to whom we would
pay all due deference) have not attempted any thing of this kind, nor, as we
can learn, ever desired it."   The *ninth* reason was " Because it appears to
us too much like setting up an INDEPENDENCY of the Mother Country."—
Portsmouth sent in a remonstrance 12 January, 1776, but the new government went into operation with much energy, and but little complaint was
made by the people after the first year.]

fluenced, they called upon their delegates in congress to execute the act which should sever us from foreign dominion, and put us into a situation to govern ourselves.*

It ought ever to be remembered, that the declaration of our independence was made, at a point of time, when no royal governor had even the shadow of authority in any of the colonies; and when no British troops had any footing on this continent. The country was then absolutely our own. A formidable

July 4.

* On the 11th of June, 1776, a committee was chosen by the assembly of New-Hampshire ' to make a draught of a declaration of the general assembly ' for the INDEPENDENCE of the united colonies on Great Britain, to be trans-' mitted to our delegates in congress.' [The proceedings of the assembly, and the declaration are here introduced, copied from the records in the secretary's office.

DECLARATION OF INDEPENDENCE BY NEW-HAMPSHIRE IN 1776.

In the House of Representatives, June 11, 1776.

"*Voted,* That Samuel Cutts, Timothy Walker and John Dudley, Esquires, be a committee of this house to join a committee of the honorable board, to make a draft of a declaration of this general assembly for INDEPENDENCE of the united colonies, on Great-Britain."

June 15, 1776.

" The committee of both houses, appointed to prepare a draft setting forth the sentiments and opinion of the council and assembly of this colony relative to the united colonies setting up an independent state, make report as on file —which report being read and considered, *Voted unanimously,* That the report of said committee be received and accepted, and that the draft by them brought in be sent to our delegates at the continental congress forthwith as the sense of the house."

" The draft made by the committee of both houses, relating to independency, and voted as the sense of this house, is as follows, viz.

" Whereas it now appears an undoubted fact, that notwithstanding all the dutiful petitions and decent remonstrances from the American colonies, and the utmost exertions of their best friends in England on their behalf, the British ministry, arbitrary and vindictive, are yet determined to reduce by fire and sword our bleeding country, to their absolute obedience; and for this purpose, in addition to their own forces, have engaged great numbers of foreign mercenaries, who may now be on their passage here, accompanied by a formidable fleet to ravish and plunder the sea-coast; from all which we may reasonably expect the most dismal scenes of distress the ensuing year, unless we exert ourselves by every means and precaution possible; and whereas we of this colony of New-Hampshire have the example of several of the most respectable of our sister colonies before us for entering upon that most important step of disunion from Great-Britain, and declaring ourselves FREE and INDEPENDENT of the crown thereof, being impelled thereto by the most violent and injurious treatment; and it appearing absolutely necessary in this most critical juncture of our public affairs, that the honorable the continental congress, who have this important object under immediate consideration, should be also informed of our resolutions thereon without loss of time, we do hereby declare that it is the opinion of this assembly that our delegates at the continental congress should be instructed, and they are hereby instructed, to join with the other colonies in declaring the thirteen united colonies a free and independent state—solemnly pledging our faith and honor, that we will on our parts support the measure with our lives and fortunes—and that in consequence thereof they, the continental congress, on whose wisdom, fidelity and integrity we rely, may enter into and form such alliances as they may judge most conducive to the present safety and future advantage of these American colonies : *Provided,* the regulation of our own internal police be under the direction of our own assembly.

Entered according to the original,

Attest,   NOAH EMERY, *Clr. D. Reps.*]

force was indeed collected on our coasts, ready to invade us ; and in the face of that armament, this decisive step was taken. The declaration was received with joy by the American army then assembled at New-York. Within fourteen days, it was published by beat of drum in all the shire towns of New-Hampshire. It relieved us from a state of embarrassment. We then knew the ground on which we stood, and from that time, every thing assumed a new appearance. The jargon of distinctions between the limits of authority on the one side, and of liberty on the other, was done away. The single question was, whether we should be conquered provinces, or free and independent states. On this question, every person was able to form his own judgment ; and it was of such magnitude that no man could be at a loss to stake his life on its decision.[1] *

It is amusing to recollect, at this distance of time, that one effect of independence was an aversion to every thing which bore the name and marks of royalty. Sign boards on which were painted the king's arms, or the crown and sceptre, or the portraits of any branches of the royal family, were pulled down or defaced. Pictures and escutcheons of the same kind in private houses were inverted or concealed. The names of streets, which had been called after a king or queen were altered ; and the half-pence, which bore the name of George III., were either refused in payment, or degraded to farthings. These last have not yet recovered their value.

The new assembly began their administration by establishing judicial courts, on the same system as before, excepting that the court of appeals, which had long been esteemed a grievance, was abolished, and all appeals to Great-Britain were prohibited. Appeals from the probate courts, which formerly came before the governor and council, were transferred to the superior court, whose judgment was now made final. Encouragement was given to fit out armed vessels, and a maritime court was established for the trial of captures by sea. A law was made to punish the counterfeiting of the paper bills of this and of the United States ; and to make them ' a tender for any money due by deed or simple ' contract.' After the declaration of independence the style of

(in margin:) July 18.

(1) Observations on the American Revolution, p. 57, 58.

* [The delegates from New-Hampshire in congress, who signed the declaration of independence, were Josiah Bartlett, William Whipple and Matthew Thornton, of each of whom a memoir is given in the national work, *Biography of the Signers of the Declaration of Independence.* As the editor of this work furnished the biographer of these men all the facts and materials in his possession, he can add nothing new to their history, but refers the reader to the work mentioned. The most important information contained in this work has been condensed by N. Dwight of the city of New-York, and published in a duodecimo volume.]

Colony was changed for that of the STATE of New-Hampshire. A new law was enacted to regulate the militia. More paper bills were issued to pay the expenses of the war ; and provision was made for drawing in some of the bills by taxes. Doubts had arisen, whether the former laws were in force ; a special act was therefore passed, reviving and re-enacting all the laws which were in force, at the time when government was assumed ; as far as they were not repugnant to the new form, or to the independence of the colonies, or not actually repealed.*

The congress having ordered several frigates to be built in different places ; one of thirty-two guns, called the Raleigh, May 21. was launched at Portsmouth, in sixty days from the time when her keel was laid ; but for want of guns and ammunition, and other necessaries, it was a long time before she was completely fitted for the sea. The making of salt-petre was encouraged by a bounty ; and many trials were made before it was produced in purity. Powder mills were erected, and the manufacture of gunpowder was, after some time, established ; but notwithstanding all our exertions, foreign supplies were necessary.

For the service of this year, two thousand men were raised, and formed into three regiments, under the same commanders as in the former year. Three hundred men were posted at the forts in the harbor. Supplies of fire arms and ammunition were sent to the western parts of the state, and a regiment was raised in that quarter, under the command of Colonel Timothy Bedel, to be ready to march into Canada.

The three regiments went with the army under General Washington to New-York ; and thence were ordered up the Hudson, and down the lakes into Canada, under the immediate command of Brigadier-General Sullivan. The design of this movement was to succor and reinforce the army, which had been sent, the preceding year, against Quebec ; and which was now retreating before a superior force, which had arrived from Britain, as early as the navigation of the St. Lawrence was opened. Our troops having met the retreating army at the mouth of the Sorel, threw up some slight works round their camp. General Thomas, who had commanded the army after the fall of the brave Montgomery, was dead of the small-pox.† Arnold was engaged in stripping

---

* [1776. The towns of Washington, formerly *Cambden*, and Marlborough, formerly *New-Marlborough*, were incorporated on the 13 December, this year. Acts and Laws of the state of New-Hampshire, folio 57, 58.]

† [General JOHN THOMAS was from Massachusetts, and was descended from one of the most ancient and respectable families in the county of Plymouth. His death was deplored as a great public calamity. · He was distinguished by great prudence and judgment, as well as resolution and intrepidity. He was appointed a major-general on the continental establishment in March, 1776 ; but had been second in command in the provincial army in the summer of 1775, till General Washington arrived at Cambridge. He had also served with reputation as a field officer in the war of 1756, between England and

the merchants of Montreal, under pretence of supplying the army ; and Thompson was taken prisoner in an unsuccessful attack on the village of Trois Rivieres.   The command therefore devolved on Sullivan, who, finding a retreat necessary, conducted it with great prudence.   At this time, the American troops, and in particular the regiments of New-Hampshire, had taken the infection of the small-pox.   The sick were placed in batteaux, and with the cannon and stores, were drawn against the rapid current, by the strength of men on shore, or wading in the water ; and so close was the pursuit of the enemy, that they could scarcely find time to kindle a fire to dress their victuals, or dry their clothes.   At St. John's, the pursuit ceased.   On the arrival of our army at July 1. Ticonderoga, Sullivan, being superseded by Gates, returned to the main army at New-York.   The troops in the northern department being reinforced by the militia of the neighboring states, fortified the posts of Ticonderoga and Mount Independence.   Besides the small pox, a dysentery and putrid fever raged among them ; and it was computed, that of the New-Hampshire regiments, nearly one third part died this year by sickness.

When the danger of an attack on Ticonderoga for that season, was passed, the remaining part of the New-Hampshire troops marched by the way of the Minisinks, into Pennsylvania.   There they joined General Washington, and assisted in the glorious capture of the Hessians at Trenton, and afterward in the battle of Princeton.   Though worn down with fatigue, and almost destitute of clothing, in that inclement season, (December and January,) they continued in the service six weeks after the term of their enlistment had expired ; and two regiments of the militia which were sent to reinforce the army remained till March.

By this time, the inconvenience of maintaining an army, by annual enlistments and temporary levies, was severely felt, and generally reprobated ; and the congress, though slow in listen-
1777. ing to remonstrances on this head, were obliged to adopt a more permanent establishment.   In recruiting the army for the next year, the officers were appointed by congress, during the war ; and the men enlisted either for that term, or for three years.   The commanders of the three regiments of New-Hampshire, were the Colonels Joseph Cilley,* Nathan Hale and Alex-

France.   Bradford, Hist. of Mass. ii. 104.   He died at Chamblee.   It has been said that from some scruples, he refused to be inoculated for the small-pox himself, and would not suffer his troops to receive inoculation.]

* [JOSEPH CILLEY was of Nottingham, where his father was one of the early settlers.   He was distinguished for his bravery and patriotism during the whole revolutionary contest.   After the liberties of the country were secured, he was several times elected a representative to the legislature of New-Hampshire, and in 1797 and 1798, was chosen one of the executive council. He was appointed major-general of the militia, 22 June, 1786, in which office he remained a number of years.   He died at Nottingham in August, 1799, aged 65.]

ander Scammell. These regiments were supplied with new French arms; and their rendezvous was at Ticonderoga, under the immediate command of Brigadier-General Poor. There they remained, till the approach of the British army under _{July 6.} General Burgoyne, rendered it eligible to abandon that post. On the retreat, Colonel Hale's battalion was ordered to cover the rear of the invalids, by which means, he was seven miles behind the main body. The next morning, he was attacked, by an advanced party of the enemy at Hubberton.* In this engagement, Major Titcomb of the New-Hampshire troops, was wounded. Colonel Hale, Captains Robertson, Carr, and Norris, Adjutant Elliot, and two other officers were taken prisoners, with about one hundred men. The main body of the army continued their retreat to Saratoga. On their way, they had a skirmish with the enemy at Fort Anne, in which Captain Weare, son of the president, was mortally wounded, and died at Albany.

Immediately after the evacuation of Ticonderoga, the committee of the New-Hampshire grants (who had now formed themselves into a new state) wrote in the most pressing terms, to the _{July 8.} committee of safety at Exeter for assistance, and said that if none should be afforded to them, they should be obliged to retreat to the New-England states for safety.[1] When the news of this affair reached New-Hampshire, the assembly had finished their spring session and returned home. A summons from _{July 17.} the committee brought them together again; and in a short session of three days only, they took the most effectual and decisive steps for the defence of the country. They formed the whole militia of the state into two brigades; of the first, they gave the command to William Whipple,† and of the second, to John Stark. They ordered one fourth part of Stark's brigade, and one fourth of three regiments of the other brigade, to march immediately under his command, ' to stop the progress of the enemy on ' our western frontiers.' They ordered the militia officers, to take

(1) Original letters in files.

* [In the county of Rutland in Vermont. It is often written Hubbardton, which is probably the correct orthography.]

† [WILLIAM WHIPPLE was a native of Kittery, in Maine, where he was born in 1730. Before he was 21 years of age, he obtained the command of a vessel, and performed a number of voyages to the West Indies, and to Europe. In 1759, he abandoned the sea, and went into business at Portsmouth; was a delegate from that town to the convention at Exeter, in 1775; was one of the first council of New-Hampshire after the war with Great-Britain commenced; was a delegate to the general congress at Philadelphia, and one of the signers of the declaration of independence. In 1777, he changed his political for a military character, and received the appointment above named. His services to the American cause were important. After the war closed, he was appointed judge of the superior court of judicature, in which office he remained about three years. He died at Portsmouth, 10 November, 1785, aged 54. Adams, Annals of Portsmouth, 281—284.—Biography of the Signers of the Declaration of Independence, V. 73—98.]

away arms, from all persons, who scrupled or refused to assist, in defending the country ; and appointed a day of fasting and prayer, which was observed with great solemnity.

The appointment of Stark, to this command, with the same pay as a brigadier in the continental service, was peculiarly grateful to the people, as well as to himself. In an arrangement of general officers, in the preceding year, Poor, a junior officer, had been promoted, whilst he was neglected. He had written on this subject to congress, and his letters were laid on the table. He therefore quitted the army, and retired to his own state.* He was now by the unanimous voice of his fellow citizens, invested with a separate command, and received orders to ' repair to ' Charlestown on Connecticut river ; there to consult with a com- ' mittee of New-Hampshire grants, respecting his future opera- ' tions and the supply of his men with provisions ; to take the ' command of the militia and march into the grants to act in con- ' junction with the troops of that new state, or any other of the ' states, or of the United States, or separately, as it should appear ' expedient to him ; for the protection of the people and the an- ' noyance of the enemy.'[1]

In a few days, he proceeded to Charlestown, and as fast as his men arrived, he sent them forward, to join the forces of the new state, under Colonel Warner, who had taken post at Manchester, twenty miles northward of Bennington.[2] Here, Stark joined him, and met with General Lincoln, who had been sent from Stillwater, by General Schuyler, commander of the northern department, to conduct the militia to the west side of Hudson's river. Stark informed him of his orders, and of the danger which the inhabitants of the grants apprehended from the enemy, and from their disaffected neighbors ; that he had consulted with the committee, and that it was the determination of the people, in case he should join the continental army and leave them exposed, that they would retire to the east of Connecticut river ; in which case New-Hampshire would be a frontier. He therefore determined to remain on the flank of the enemy, and to watch their motions. For this purpose, he collected his force at Bennington, and left Warner with his regiment at Manchester. A report of this determination was transmitted to congress, and the

Aug. 9.

(1) MS. copy of orders on file.   (2) Aug. 17—MS. copy of Lincoln's letter.

* [Upon his resignation, the council and house of delegates of New-Hampshire, on the 21 March, 1777, passed the following vote : " Voted that the thanks of both houses in convention be given to Colonel Stark, for his good services in the present war, and that from his early and steadfast attachments to the cause of his country, they make not the least doubt that his future conduct in whatever state of life providence may place him, will manifest the same noble disposition of mind." Whereupon the thanks of both houses were presented to Colonel Stark by the honorable the president. Records of the House of Reps. vol. ii. 120.]

orders on which it was founded were by them disapproved ; but the propriety of it was evinced by the subsequent facts.

General Burgoyne, with the main body of the British army lay at fort Edward. Thence he detached Lieutenant Colonel Baum, with about fifteen hundred of his German troops, and one hundred Indians, to pervade the grants as far as Connecticut river, with a view to collect horses to mount the dragoons, and cattle, both for labor and provisions ; and to return to the army with his booty. He was to persuade the people among whom he should pass, that his detachment was the advanced guard of the British army, which was marching to Boston. He was accompanied by Colonel Skeene, who was well acquainted with the country ; and he was ordered to secure his camp by night.[1]

The Indians who preceeded this detachment, being discovered about twelve miles from Bennington ; Stark detached Colonel Gregg,* with two hundred men, to stop their march. In the evening of the same day, he was informed that a body of regular troops, with a train of artillery, was in full march for Bennington. [2] The next morning, he marched with his whole brigade, Aug. 14. and some of the militia of the grants, to support Gregg, who found himself unable to withstand the superior number of the enemy. Having proceeded about four miles, he met Gregg retreating, and the main body of the enemy pursuing, within half a mile of his rear. When they discovered Stark's column, they halted in an advantageous position ; and he drew up his men on an eminence in open view ; but could not bring them to an engagement. He then marched back, about a mile, and encamped ; leaving a few men to skirmish with them ; who killed thirty of the enemy and two of the Indian chiefs. The next day was Aug. 15. rainy. Stark kept his position, and sent out parties to harass the enemy. Many of the Indians took this opportunity to desert ; because, as they said, ' the woods were full of yankees.'

On the following morning, Stark was joined by a company of militia from the grants, and another from the county of Berkshire, in Massachusetts. His whole force amounted to about sixteen hundred. He sent Colonel Nichols,† with two Aug. 16.

(1) MS. copy of Burgoyne's orders.   (2) Aug. 13—Stark's MS. letters in files.

* [Col. William Gregg was born at Londonderry, 21 October, 1730. He was son of Capt. John Gregg, and grandson of Capt. James Gregg, who was one of the first sixteen who settled that town, as mentioned page 192. There is a short memoir of Colonel Gregg's revolutionary services in the Coll. of Farmer and Moore, iii. p. 311. At the close of the war, he retired to his farm, and employed himself in the pursuits of husbandry till within a few years of his death. He died at Londonderry on the 16 September, 1824, having almost completed his 94th year.]

† [Col. Moses Nichols was of Amherst, where he died 23d May, 1790, aged 50 years. He was appointed a colonel of the 6th regiment of N. H. militia, 6 Dec. 1776; was a delegate to the convention, which met in 1778 to form a

hundred and fifty men, to the rear of the enemy's left wing; and Colonel Hendrick, with three hundred, to the rear of their right. He placed three hundred to oppose their front and draw their attention. Then sending Colonels Hubbard and Stickney,* with two hundred to attack the right wing, and one hundred more to reinforce Nichols in the rear of their left, the attack began in that quarter precisely at three of the clock in the afternoon. It was immediately seconded by the other detachments; and at the same time, Stark himself advanced with the main body. The engagement lasted two hours; at the end of which he forced their breastworks, took two pieces of brass cannon and a number of prisoners; the rest retreated.

Just at this instant, he received intelligence that another body of the enemy was within two miles of him. This was a reinforcement for which Baum had sent, when he first knew the force which he was to oppose. It was commanded by Colonel Breyman. Happily Warner's regiment from Manchester came up with them and stopped them. Stark rallied his men and renewed the action; it was warm and desperate; he used, with success, the cannon which he had taken; and at sunset obliged the enemy to retreat. He pursued them till night, and then halted, to prevent his own men from killing each other, in the dark. He took from the enemy two other pieces of cannon, with all their baggage, wagons and horses. Two hundred and twenty-six men were found dead on the field. Their commander, Baum, was taken and died of his wounds; beside whom, thirty-three officers, and above seven hundred privates, were made prisoners. Of Stark's brigade, four officers and ten privates were killed and forty-two were wounded.

In the account of this battle, which Stark sent to the committee of New-Hampshire, he said, ' our people behaved with the great-
Aug. 18. ' est spirit and bravery imaginable. Had every man been
' an Alexander, or a Charles of Sweden, they could not
' have behaved better.' He was sensible of the advantage of keeping on the flank of the enemy's main body; and therefore sent for one thousand men to replace those whose time had expired; but intimated to the committee that he himself should re-

new constitution, and a representative from Amherst in 1781 and 1782, and subsequently a brigadier-general. He was register of deeds of Hillsborough county from 1776 to his death. He was bred a physician and practised with much success. He left several sons, the eldest of whom was Moses Nichols, Esq. a physician, who resided in Thornton, in Canada, in Amherst, and afterwards again in Canada, to which place he removed in 1811, and where he lately sustained the office of judge of some court.]

* [Col. THOMAS STICKNEY, son of Lieut. Jeremiah Stickney, was a native of Bradford, Massachusetts, but spent nearly his whole life in Concord, in this state, where his father removed about the year 1731, and where the colonel died 26 January, 1809, in the 80th year of his age. Moore, Annals of Concord, 63.]

turn with the brigade.   They cordially thanked him ' for the very
' essential service which he had done to the country,' but earnestly pressed him to continue in the command ; and sent him a reinforcement, ' assuring the men that they were to serve under
' General Stark.'   This argument prevailed with the men to
march, and with Stark to remain.

The prisoners taken in this battle were sent to Boston.   The
trophies were divided between New-Hampshire and Massachusetts.   But congress heard of this victory by accident.   Having
waited some time in expectation of letters, and none arriving ; inquiry was made why Stark had not written to congress ?   He
answered, that his correspondence with them was closed, as they
had not attended to his last letters.   They took the hint ; and
though they had but a few days before resolved, that the instructions which he had received were destructive of military subordination, and prejudicial to the common cause ; yet they presented their thanks to him, and to the officers and troops under his
command, and promoted him to the rank of a brigadier-general,
in the army of the United States.*

This victory gave a severe check tó the hopes of the enemy,
and raised the spirits of the people after long depression.   It
wholly changed the face of affairs in the northern department.
Instead of disappointment and retreat, and the loss of men by
hard labor and sickness ; we now were convinced, not only that
our militia could fight without being covered by intrenchments ;
but that they were able, even without artillery, to cope with regular troops in their intrenchments.   The success thus gained was
regarded as a good omen of farther advantages.   ' Let us get
them into the woods,' was the language of the whole country.
Burgoyne was daily putting his army into a more hazardous situation ; and we determined that no exertion should be wanting on
our part to complete the ruin of his boasted enterprise.   The
northern army was reinforced by the militia of all the neighboring
states.   Brigadier Whipple marched with a great part of his brigade ; besides which, volunteers in abundance from every part of
New-Hampshire flew to the northern army now commanded by
General Gates.   Two desperate battles were fought, the one at Stillwater, and the other at Saratoga ; in both of which, the troops of
New-Hampshire had a large share of the honor due to the Amer-

---

* [General JOHN STARK was a native of Londonderry, and died at Manchester, (formerly Derryfield) 8 May, 1822, having nearly completed his 94th
year.   Excepting Gen. Sumpter of South-Carolina, he was the last surviving
general who had a command in the war of the American revolution.   It is
only necessary to refer the reader for a biography of him to the Coll. of Farmer and Moore, i. 92—116, and the sketch of his life published in the Boston
Statesman, in 1829, and copied into various papers the same year.   In the
392d number of Sir Richard Phillips's London Magazine, there is an account
of him which is very erroneous and ridiculous.   The editor of that work however afterwards received more correct information respecting General Stark.]

ican army. In the former action, two lieutenant-colonels, Adams
and Colburn,* and Lieutenant Thomas, were slain in the field ; and
several other brave officers were wounded, one of whom, Captain
Bell, died in the hospital. In the latter, Lieutenant-Colonel Con-
ner and Lieutenant McClary were killed, with a great number of
their men ; and Colonel Scammell was wounded. The consequence of these battles was the surrender of Burgoyne's army.
This grand object being attained, the New-Hampshire regiments
performed a march of forty miles, and forded the Mohawk river,
below the falls, in the space of fourteen hours. The design of
this rapid movement was to check the progress of a detachment,
commanded by the British general, Clinton ; who threatened Albany with the same destruction which he had spread in the country
below ; but on hearing the fate of Burgoyne, he returned quietly
to New-York. The regiments then marched into Pennsylvania
and passed the winter in huts at Valley-Forge. Besides those
officers slain at the northward, we sustained a loss in the death of
Major Edward Sherburne, aid de camp to General Sullivan, who
was killed in a bold, but unsuccessful action at Germantown.†

After the capture of Burgoyne's army, all danger of invasion
from Canada ceased ; and the theatre of the war was removed to
the southward. The troops of New-Hampshire, being formed
into a distinct brigade, partook of all the services and sufferings,
to which their brethren were exposed. In the battle of Monmouth,
a part of them were closely engaged, under the conduct of Colonel
1778.   Cilley and Lieutenant-Colonel Dearborn ; and behaved
with such bravery as to merit the particular approbation of
their illustrious general. They continued with the main body, all
that campaign, and were hutted, in the following winter, at Reading.

In the summer of 1778, when a French fleet appeared on our
coast, to aid us in the contest with Britain ; an invasion of Rhode-
Island, then possessed by the British, was projected, and General
Sullivan had the command. Detachments of militia and volunteers, from Massachusetts and New-Hampshire, formed a part of
his troops. But a violent storm having prevented the co-operation
of the French fleet and driven them to sea ; the army, after a
few skirmishes, was under the disagreeable necessity of quitting
the island ; and the retreat was conducted by Sullivan with the
greatest caution and prudence.‡

* [Lieut. Colonel ANDREW COLBURN belonged to Marlborough, and received the appointment of lieutenant-colonel of the third battalion, raised in
New-Hampshire in 1776. He was a brave meritorious officer.]

† [1777. Antrim, being part of a place called Society-Lands, was incorporated 22 March. Acts and Laws of the state of New-Hampshire, folio, p. 76.
The towns of Moultonborough and New-Hampton were incorporated 27 November. Ibid. 93, 94.]

‡ [1778. The towns of Grafton, New-Chester and Fishersfield were incorporated on the 11, 20 and 27 of November respectively. Acts and Laws of
the state of New-Hampshire, folio 127, 131, 137.]

When an expedition into the Indian country was determined
on, General Sullivan was appointed to the command, and the New-
Hampshire brigade made a part of his force. His route
was up the river Susquehanna into the country of the Sen- 1779.
ecas; a tract imperfectly known, and into which no troops had
ever penetrated. The order of his march was planned with
great judgment, and executed with much regularity and perseverance. In several engagements with the savages, the troops of
New-Hampshire behaved with their usual intrepidity. Captain
Cloyes and Lieutenant McAulay were killed, and Major Titcomb
was again badly wounded. The provisions of the army falling
short, before the object of the expedition was completed, the troops
generously agreed to subsist on such as could be found in the Indian country. After their return, they rejoined the main army,
and passed a third winter in huts, at Newtown in Connecticut.
In the latter end of this year, Sullivan resigned his command and
retired.*

In the following year, the New-Hampshire regiments did duty
at the important post of West-Point, and afterward marched into New-Jersey, where General Poor died.† Three 1780.
regiments of militia were employed in the service of this year.
The fourth winter was passed in a hutted cantonment, at a place
called Soldier's Fortune, near Hudson's river. In the close of
this year, the three regiments were reduced to two, which were
commanded by the colonels, Scammell and George Reid.‡

The next year, a part of them remained in the state of New-
York, and another part marched to Virginia, and were 1781.
present at the capture of the second British army, under
Earl Cornwallis. Here the brave and active Colonel Scammell
was killed.§ In the winter, the first regiment, commanded by

* [1779. The towns of Andover, formerly *New-Bretton*, New-London, formerly *Addition of Alexandria*, Hancock, formerly part of the Society-Land,
Northumberland, and Stratford were incorporated. Acts and Laws of the
state of New-Hampshire, folio, 156, 157, 163, 165, 166.]

† [ENOCH POOR was son of Thomas Poor, of Andover, Massachusetts. He
received his appointment as colonel of one of the New-Hampshire regiments
in 1775. In 1779, he accompanied General Sullivan in the wilderness as far
as the Gennesee, and defeated the savage enemy. In 1780, he commanded
a brigade under Major General La Fayette. He died in New-Jersey, 8 September, 1780, aged 43. See Rev. Israel Evans's oration, at his interment, at
Hackinsack, N. J.—Abbot, Hist. of Andover, 26, 27.—Coll. of Farmer and
Moore, ii. 165, 166.]

‡ [GEORGE REID was of Londonderry. He was appointed a brigadier-general of the militia of N. H. 10 August, 1785, and received the appointment of
sheriff of the county of Rockingham, 22 October, 1791. He died in October,
1815, aged 81.]

§ [ALEXANDER SCAMMELL was born in that part of Mendon, now Milford,
in the county of Worcester, Massachusetts. He graduated at Harvard college in 1769, and after having been engaged in instructing a school at Kingston, Massachusetts; in the study of law under General Sullivan; in assisting
Captain Holland in making surveys for his map of New-Hampshire, and in

Lieutenant-Colonel Dearborn,* was quartered at Saratoga, and the second on Mohawk river; in which places they were stationed, till the close of the following year; when the approach of peace relaxed the operations of war. In a few months, the negotiations were so far advanced, that a treaty was made; and the *same* royal lips, which from the throne had pronounced us ' re-' volted subjects,' now acknowledged us as ' FREE AND INDEPEN-' DENT STATES.'

CHAPTER XXVI.

Paper money.   Confiscations.   State constitution.   Controversy with Vermont.

THE war in which we became involved with Britain, found us not destitute of resources, but unskilled in the art of finance. Former wars had been maintained by a paper currency; which, though it depreciated in some measure, yet was finally redeemed by the reimbursements which we received from the British treasury. We had been also used to issue bills on loan, and receive landed property as security for its redemption. To the same mode we had recourse on this occasion, without either of the foundations on which our former currencies had been supported. Bills of credit were emitted with no other fund for their redemption than taxation, and that deferred to distant periods. It was imagined that the justice of our cause, and the united ardor and patriotism of the people, would preserve the value of these bills

exercising the office of surveyor of the royal forests of New-Hampshire and Maine, was, in 1775, appointed brigade major, and in 1776, received the appointment of colonel of the third battalion of continental troops raised in this state. In 1777, he commanded the third regiment from New-Hampshire, and was wounded in the desperate battle of Saratoga, as stated under the year 1777. In 1780, the levy of this state being reduced to two regiments, he commanded the first. He was afterwards appointed adjutant general of the American armies, in which office he was deservedly popular, and secured the esteem of the officers of the army generally. On the 30 September, 1781, at the memorable and successful siege at Yorktown, he was the officer of the day; and while reconnoitering the situation of the enemy, was surprised by a party of their horse; and after being taken prisoner, was inhumanly wounded by them. He was conveyed to the city of Williamsburg, Virginia, where he died on the 6 of October, and where there is a monumental tablet to his memory. 2 Coll. Mass. Hist. Soc. iii. 176. iv. 90, 95. Coll. of Farmer and Moore, i. 125. ii. 166, 179, 222. iii. 253, 285—289, 388.]

* [Afterwards, secretary of war during President Jefferson's administration, and in the second war between Great Britain and the United States, the senior major general in the U. S. service. He was born at North-Hampton in this state, 12 February, 1751, and died at Roxbury, Massachusetts, 7 June, 1829, aged 78. A biographical memoir of him was published in the Boston Patriot and other papers of the day.]

during the contest which we were very sanguine would be short;
and in fact the circulation of them for the first year was   1776.
supported by no other means.   But being counterfeited,
they began to depreciate, and then it was thought necessary to
enact a law against forging them, and to make them a legal   July 3.
tender in all payments.   In some of the states, these bills
were made a tender for the interest, but not for the principal of
former debts; but in New-Hampshire, if the creditor should refuse them when offered in payment, the whole debt was cancelled.
Had this law regarded future contracts only, every man would
have known on what terms to make his engagements; but to declare it legal to pay debts, already contracted, with money of an
inferior value, was altogether unjust.   It was not in human power to prevent a depreciation of the bills; and the enforcing of
their currency accelerated the destruction of their value.   The
fraudulent debtor took advantage of this law to cheat his creditor,
under color of justice; whilst the creditor had no other refuge,
than in some cases privately to transfer the written obligation; and
in other cases to refuse the tender, at the risk indeed of losing
the debt; but in hope that justice would at some future time have
its course.   Husbandmen, who lived remote from the scene of
hostilities, and who had the produce of the earth at their command, were able to keep their property good.   Hawkers and
monopolizers, who crept from obscurity and assumed the name
of merchants, could even increase their substance in these perilous
times.   But those persons whose property was in other men's
hands; or whose living depended on stated salaries; or whose
honest minds could not descend to practise knavery, though established by law, were doomed to suffer.

   To palliate these evils, at one time, a law was enacted against
monopoly and extortion; and when found impracticable,   1777.
it was repealed.   At other times, the prices of different
articles were stated under severe penalties; but ways were soon
found to evade these establishments; and when found ineffectual,
the laws were repealed.   It is not consistent with the nature of
commerce to bear such restrictions; and the laws increased the
evils which they pretended to cure.   At another time, public
sales by auction were prohibited, because it was said that they
were the means of depreciating the currency; but in fact they
served only to demonstrate its real value.   There was a disposition in the governing part of the people to keep out of sight the
true cause of this growing mischief.   Even the general congress,
in a public address which they ordered to be read in the congregations, assembled for religious worship, after saying much in praise
of paper money, told us, that it was ' the *only* kind of money
' which could not make to itself wings and fly away.'[1]   Had this

(1) Circular letter of Sept. 13, 1779.

been intended as the language of burlesque, it might have been received with a smile ; in any other sense, it was an insult to the feelings of honest men.

In the midst of these distresses, frequent meetings of different bodies of men were held, to consult on some practicable modes of relief. Committees of counties, and of different states, at various times, formed projects, and issued public addresses ; but palliatives in this, as in all other cases, soon lost their efficacy. From one of these conventions, holden at Springfield, and composed of delegates from the New-England states and New-York ; a letter was addressed to the general congress, which put them on devising means to surmount the existing difficulties.[1] Among other expedients they recommended effectual taxation, the opening of loan-offices, and that the states individually should emit no more bills of credit. These were salutary proposals ; but the most notable effect of this letter was a recommendation from congress to the several states ' to confiscate and make sale of all the real and ' personal estates of such of their inhabitants and other persons as ' had forfeited the same, and the right to the protection of their ' respective states ; and to invest the money arising from the sales ' in continental loan certificates, to be appropriated as the respec- ' tive states should direct.'[2]

This was a delicate point, and required the most critical discussion. It involved a question of national law ; and some persons who were acquainted with the subject, thought such a step not only illegal, but impolitic and dangerous. In cases of war between independent nations, acknowledging no common superior, the acquisition of immovable property is not complete till confirmed by a treaty of peace.[3] The war between America and Britain was so far a war between two independent nations, that the common laws of war ought to have been observed. Had the estates of absentees been taken into possession, and the income arising from them been applied to the support of the war ; and had the question of property remained undecided till the conclusion of a peace, there is no doubt that the state would have been a gainer both in reputation and interest ; but when we were daily cheating and deceiving ourselves with a fraudulent paper medium, it is not strange that the voice of justice toward those whom we deemed our enemies could not be heard.

The first step toward executing this recommendation of congress, was an act proscribing certain persons, to the number of seventy-six, who had at various times, and for various reasons, quitted this state.* These were forbidden to return

1778.

(1) July and August—MS. minutes of convention. (2) Journal of congress, Nov. 27. (3) Vattel.

* [The names of these proscribed persons were *John Wentworth*, Peter Livius, John Fisher, *Geo. Meserve*, Robert Trail, George Boyd, John Fenton,

without leave, under the penalty of transportation; and in case of a second return, they were to suffer death.

The next step, was to confiscate the whole estate, real and personal, of twenty-eight of the proscribed; of whom it was declared that they had ' justly forfeited all right to protection from the ' state; and also their right to any farther enjoyment of their in-' terest and property within it.'

In these acts, no distinction was made between those persons who had withdrawn themselves from the state, by a sense of their duty; those who were in fact British subjects, but occasionally resident here; those who had absconded through timidity; and those who had committed crimes against express law, and had fled from justice. No conditional offer of pardon was made; no time was allowed for any to return and enter into the service of the country; but the whole were put indiscriminately into one *black list,* and stigmatised as ' having basely deserted the cause of lib-' erty, and manifested a disposition inimical to the state, and a ' design to aid its enemies in their wicked purposes.'

Some persons who had legal demands on these estates, had for the security of their debts laid attachments on them; but by another act, all attachments which had been made since the commencement of hostilities, were declared null and void, and the courts were required to dismiss them.

Trustees were appointed in each county to take possession of all these estates, real and personal; and to sell the personal immediately at public auction; with a discretionary power to leave out of the sale such articles as they should deem necessary to the support of the families of the proscribed. To preserve some farther appearance of justice, the creditors of these estates, though they were not allowed to bid at the auctions without payment, were ordered to exhibit their claims to the trustees, and in cases of insolvency, all claims were to be settled by the judges of probate.

Whilst the settlement of these estates was going on, the money was rapidly depreciating. After the year 1777, the state issued no more bills, and the former were called in and exchanged for treasurer's notes on interest, of a value not less than five pounds. The continental bills continued passing and depreciating till the spring of 1781, when suddenly, and by general consent, they went out of circulation, and solid coin succeeded in their place. Then a scale of depreciation for the preceding years of the war was framed, and all past payments were regulated by it. The treaty of peace obliged us to proceed no farther in the matter of confiscations. By a subsequent act,* the judges of probate were empowered to liquidate by the scale of depreciation, the sums paid into the treasury by the trustees ; to receive claims against the estates, and to adjust and certify the same to the president, who was authorised to order the treasurer, to issue notes, bearing interest from the time when the said sums were paid into the treasury ; which notes the creditors were to receive in payment ; but if any of the estates should prove insolvent, then the creditors were to receive their average. In this manner, some of these estates have been settled and the creditors paid ; others remain unsettled. Some of them barely paid the expenses of their management ; others were rendered insolvent. The estate of the late governor paid all the demands upon it excepting that of his father ; who generously withdrew his claim that the other creditors might be paid in full.† The clear profit to the state from

* March 1, 1783.

† The following papers are taken from the registry of probate for the county of Rockingham.

'Rockingham, ss. Feb. 16, 1786. I hereby certify, that the sums against
' each person's name herein set down, were respectively due to them the last
' day of July, 1782, from the estate of the late governor, John Wentworth,
' Esq. at which time it appears there had been received into the treasury, a
' sufficiency to pay all the demands, exhibited against him, except his father's ;
' who has withdrawn his, that the others might be paid in full.
                                   ' P. White, Judge of Probate.'

'Portsmouth, Feb. 6, 1785. Sir,—After considering the great delays in
' settling the demands against the estate of my son, Governor Wentworth,
' and the probability, from the ill management thereof, before it fell under
' your direction, that it will be greatly insolvent; and feeling for the distress
' of many of the creditors, and wishing that all may have their just demands
' paid, I have determined to remove their embarrassment as far as I can, by
' withdrawing my account and claim, until theirs be fully adjusted and dis-
' charged, by you or other proper officers. Reserving to myself still the right
' of claiming, if there should be found a surplus or balance in his favor. For
' as proved by my account and authentic vouchers ready to be produced, that,
' exclusive of my account before, I have paid off several creditors to a con-
' siderable amount, since he left this government; and had also greatly aug-
' mented the value of his estate at Wolfeborough, by my advances and care
' thereof, all to the benefit of his present creditors. I shall therefore be great-
' ly obliged, by your directing that my account be sent me ; and I shall hope

all these confiscations, as far as it had been ascertained, is inconsiderable.

Power when delegated without restrictions, and for the abuse of which the delegate is not held accountable, has a strong tendency toward despotism. The temporary constitution which we had adopted at the beginning of the war, was found, by experience, to have many imperfections; and the necessity of checks and exclusions became every day more evident. Other states were forming constitutions on certain established principles, and defining their rights as a preliminary to the delegation of power. An attempt of the like kind was made in New-Hampshire. A convention of delegates, chosen for the purpose, drew up and sent abroad a system of government; but so deficient was it in its principles, and so inadequate in its provisions, that being proposed to the people, in their town-meetings, it was rejected. Another convention was appointed, which had more advantage than the former, the neighbouring state of Massachusetts having digested and adopted a constitution, which was supposed to be an improvement on all which had been framed in America. This convention had no less than nine sessions, and continued for more than two years.* In the first plan of government which they composed, they distinctly stated the alienable and unalienable rights of the people. They divided the government into three branches, legislative, executive and judicial, and defined the limits of each. The legislative branch was composed of a senate and house of representatives. The senate was to consist of twelve persons, five for the county of Rockingham, two for Strafford, two for Hillsborough, two for Cheshire and one for Grafton. These were to be voted for in town-meetings, and the votes sealed and returned to the secretary's office. The number of representatives was limited to fifty, and apportioned among the counties, thus; twenty for Rocking-

1779.

1781.

' for your future friendly interposition, if it should be found necessary; be-
' ing, with the highest esteem and respect, your most humble servant,
'MARK H. WENTWORTH.†
' Phillips White, Esq.'

A general statement of the claims against the confiscated estate of the late Governor John Wentworth, and the neat proceeds from the sale of it; the account being not yet settled. April, 1791.

Dr. The claim of M. H. Wentworth, proved by authentic vouchers,	£13680	10	11
Amount of other claims proved as above,	3877	15	3¾
Paid to the several other creditors, since the governor's absence, by M. H. Wentworth,	819	11	6
	£18377	17	8¾
Cr. Paid into the treasury by the trustee for said estate,	10435	8	6

† [He was appointed by mandamus one of the counsellors of the province in 1759. He died 19 December, 1785. Adams, Annals of Portsmouth, 285.]

* From June, 1781, to October, 1783.

ham ; eight for Strafford ; ten for Hillsborough ; eight for Cheshire ; and four for Grafton. These were to be elected by the
county conventions, consisting of one delegate for every fifty rate-
able polls. This mode was recommended, to prevent those interested views and that party spirit, which too often appear in
single towns in the election of representatives. The executive
power was vested in a governor, whom the convention, in their
address to the people, described in the following terms : ' They
' have arrayed him with honors, they have armed him with pow-
' er and set him on high ; but still he is only the right hand of
' your power, and the mirror of your majesty.' But though armed with power and liable to be impeached for misconduct, he
was shrouded from responsibility, by a council, without whose
advice he could not take one step of any importance. The judicial department was to be appointed by the executive and supported by the legislative ; but the judges were removable for misconduct, by the governor and council, on the address of both
houses of the legislature. Justices of the peace were to hold
their commissions five years only. Provision was made for the
exclusion of persons from holding several offices at the same
time ; the reason of which was thus expressed. ' Besides the
' interference of several offices held by the same person in point
' of time, which we have seen, and the difficulty of one man's
' giving his attention to many matters sufficiently to understand
' them all, which we have too often felt ; there is a still stronger
' reason, which is, the difficulty of a man's preserving his integ-
' rity in discharging the duties of each.' The encouragement
of literature was also recommended as essential to the preservation of a free government, and it was declared to be the duty of
legislators to cherish its interests.

This plan was printed and sent to every town. The inhabitants were requested to state their objections distinctly to
Sept. 14. any particular part, and return them at a fixed time.
The objections were so many and so various, that it became necessary to alter the form and send it out a second time. The
name of governor, and most of his powers, were still retained ;
1782. but the mode of representation was altered. Instead of
being elected, by county conventions, the representatives
Aug. 21. were to be chosen immediately by the towns ; every incorporated township containing one hundred and fifty
ratable polls, having the privilege of choosing one ; and every one
containing four hundred and fifty, of choosing two. Particular
attention was given to the mode of appointing officers of militia.
Instead of superior officers being chosen by their inferiors, and
inferior officers by the privates, as had been practised since the
beginning of the war, the order of appointment was reversed, and
the privates had no power of choice at all. This was said to

be necessary to the preservation of harmony, subordination and discipline.   The second plan being sent out was generally approved ;
but it was not completed at the time when the news of peace   1783.
arrived.   The old form having expired with the war, it was,   March.
by the votes of the people in their town-meetings, revived   April.
and continued for one year longer. In the following autumn,   Oct. 31.
the new form was finished ; and the name of governor being
changed to president, it was a third time printed and declared to
be 'the civil constitution for the state of New-Hampshire.'   It
took place on the second day of the following June, and   1784.
was introduced at Concord by a religious solemnity,
which has since been repeated at every annual election.

To the convention which formed this constitution, several towns
in the western part of the state did not send delegates.   The cause
of this omission, and of some other eccentricities in the conduct of
the people in that quarter must now be explained.

The inhabitants of the district on the western side of Connecticut river, which was severed from New-Hampshire in 1764, had
been engaged in a long and bitter controversy with the government of New-York.   They had even been obliged to have recourse
to arms in defence of their estates ; and frequent acts of violence
had been committed.   There was among them a set of intrepid
men, ready to encounter dangers, and trained to hardy enterprise.
At the commencement of hostilities, by the advice of some principal opposers of the British government, in the other colonies, a
company of those people styling themselves Green Mountain Boys,
marched to Ticonderoga, and wrested that fortress, to-   1775.
gether with Crown-Point, out of the hands of the British
garrisons.   A regiment of them was embodied by order and in
the pay of the general congress.   Their exertions in the common
cause were meritorious and their services were acceptable.

Soon after the declaration of independence, the inhabitants of
that territory assembled in convention to consider their   1776.
peculiar situation and concert measures for their safety.
The opportunity which then presented for a change in their political connexions, was too precious to be lost.   By the dissolution of the bonds which had held America in subjection to the
crown of Britain, they conceived themselves free from the government of New-York, to which the most of them had never
voluntarily submitted ; and, being as they said, reduced to ' a
state of nature,' they thought that they had a right to form such
connexions as were agreeable to themselves.   Accordingly, they
made and published a declaration ; ' that they would at   1777.
' all times consider themselves as a free and independent
' state ; capable of regulating their own internal police ;   Jan. 15.
' that they had the sole exclusive right of governing themselves,
' in such manner as they should choose, not repugnant to the re-

51

' solves of congress ; and that they were ready to contribute their ' proportion to the common defence.' Under the influence of these principles, they formed a plan of government and a code of laws, and petitioned congress to receive them into the union.

The inhabitants on the eastern side of Connecticut river were very conveniently situated to unite with those on the western side, and many of them had the same principles and views.— They argued that the original grant of New-Hampshire to Mason was circumscribed by a line drawn at the distance of sixty miles from the sea ; that all the lands westward of that line, being royal grants, had been held in subjection to the government of New-Hampshire by force of the royal commissions, which were vacated by the assumed independence of the American colonies ; and therefore that the inhabitants of all those lands had ' reverted to a ' state of nature.'[1] By this expression, however, they did not mean that each individual was reduced to such a state ; but that each town retained its corporate unity, unconnected with any superior jurisdiction. They distinguished between commissions derived from the king, which were revocable at his pleasure, and incorporations held on certain conditions, which being performed, the powers and privileges granted by the incorporations were perpetual. They asserted, that jurisdictions, established by royal commissions, could bind a people together no longer than the force which first compelled continues to operate ; but when the coercive power of the king was rejected, and its operation had ceased, the people had a right to make a stand at the first legal stage, viz. their town incorporations.[2] These, by universal consent, were held sacred ; hence they concluded that the major part of each one of those towns had a right to control the minor part ; and they considered themselves as so many distinct corporations, until they should agree to unite in one aggregate body.

In these sentiments, the people were not all united. The majority of some towns was in favor of their former connexion, and

(1) Observations on the right of jurisdiction over N. H. Grants. Printed 1778. (2) Public defence of the right of N. H. Grants, &c. Printed 1779.— [There were several publications relative to the New-Hampshire Grants, of which I have seen—1. " A Defence of the New-Hampshire Grants, &c." (title page missing) printed probably in 1778 or 1779, in small 12 mo. containing 56 pages, to which are added, " Resolves of a Convention held on the N. Hampshire Grants," 4 pages ; 2. " Observations on the Right of Jurisdiction claimed by the States of New-York and New-Hampshire over the New-Hampshire Grants (so called) lying on both sides of Connecticut river. In a Letter to the Inhabitants on said Grants." 12 mo. pp. 15. Danvers, 1778 ; 3. " A Vindication of the Conduct of the General Assembly of the State of Vermont, held at Windsor in October 1778, against Allegations and Remark of the Protesting Members ; with Observations on their Proceedings at a Convention held at Cornish, on the 9th of Day of December, 1778. By Ira Allen. Arlington, 9th Jan. 1779." 12 mo. pp. 48. Dresden, printed by Alden Spooner, 1779. " A Concise Refutation of the Claims of New-Hampshire and Massachusetts-Bay, to the Territory of Vermont ; with occasional Remarks on the long disputed claim of New-York to the same. Written by Ethan Allen and Jonas Fay, Esqrs." 12 mo. pp, 29. Hartford, 1780.]

in those towns where the majority inclined the other way, the minority claimed protection of the government.

They supposed that the existence of their town incorporations, and of the privileges annexed to them, depended on their union to New-Hampshire; and that their acceptance of the grants was in effect an acknowledgment of the jurisdiction, and a submission to the laws of the state; from which they could not fairly be disengaged without its consent; as the state had never injured or oppressed them.

Much pains were taken by the other party, to disseminate the new ideas. Conventions were held, pamphlets were printed, and at length, a petition was drawn in the name of sixteen towns* on the eastern side of Connecticut river, requesting the new state, which had assumed the name of VERMONT, to receive them into its union, alleging, ' that they were not connected with any state, ' with respect to their internal police.'₁ The assembly at first appeared to be against receiving them; but the members from those towns which were situated near the river on the west side, declared that they would withdraw and join with the people on the east side, in forming a new state. The question was then referred to the people at large, and means were used to influ- June 11. ence a majority of the towns to vote in favor of the union, which the assembly could not but confirm. The sixteen towns were accordingly received; and the Vermont assembly resolved, that any other towns on the eastern side of the river might be admitted on producing a vote of a majority of the inhabitants, or on the appointment of a representative. Being thus admitted into the state of Vermont, they gave notice to the government June 22. of New-Hampshire, of the separation which they had made, and expressed their wish for an amicable settlement of a jurisdictional line, and a friendly correspondence.

The president of New-Hampshire, in the name of the assembly, wrote to the government of Vermont, claiming the Aug. 23. sixteen towns as part of the state, the limits of which had been determined prior to the revolution; reminding him that those towns had sent delegates to the convention in 1775; that they had applied to the assembly for arms and ammunition, which had been sent to them; that their military officers had accepted

(1) MSS. in New-Hampshire files.

* 1 Cornish,
2 Lebanon,
3 Dresden, { a name given to the district belonging to Dartmouth College; but now disused.
4 Lime,
5 Orford,
6 Piermont,
7 Haverhill,
8 Bath,
9 Lyman,
10 Apthorp, { now divided into Littleton and Dalton.
11 Enfield,
12 Canaan.
13 Cardigan, now Orange,
14 Landaff,
15 Gunthwaite, now New-Concord,
16 Morris-town, now Franconia.

commissions and obeyed orders from the government; that the minority of those towns was averse to a disunion, and had claimed protection of the state, which the assembly thought themselves bound to afford; and beseeching him to use his influence with the assembly of Vermont to dissolve the newly formed connexion.

At the same time, the president wrote to the delegates of the state in congress; desiring them to take advice and endeavor to obtain the interposition of that body; intimating his apprehension, that without it, the controversy must be decided by the sword, as every condescending measure had been used from the beginning and rejected.

Aug. 19.

The governor and council of Vermont sent a messenger to congress to see in what light the new state was viewed by them. On his return, he reported, that the congress was unanimously opposed to the union of the sixteen towns with Vermont; otherwise they (excepting the delegates of New-York) had no objection to the independence of the new state.

At the next session of the Vermont assembly at Windsor, when the representatives of the sixteen towns had taken their seats, a debate arose on a question, whether they should be erected into a new county, which passed in the negative. Conceiving that they were not admitted to equal privileges with their brethren, the members from those towns withdrew; and were followed by several others belonging to the towns adjoining the river on the west side. They formed themselves into a convention, and invited all the towns on both sides of the river to unite, and set up another state by the name of New-Connecticut. This secession had nearly proved fatal to the state of Vermont. A ridge of mountains which extends from south to north through that territory, seemed to form not only a natural, but a political line of division. A more cordial union subsisted between the people on the eastern side of the Green Mountains, and the eastern side of Connecticut river, than between the latter and those on the western side of the mountains; but these alone were insufficient, without the others, to make a state. The governor, and other leading men of Vermont, who resided on the west side of the mountains, wrote letters to the assembly of New-Hampshire, informing them of the separation, and expressing their disapprobation of a connexion with the sixteen towns. The assembly regarded these letters as ambiguous, and as not expressing a disinclination to any *future* connexion with them. Jealousy is said to be a republican virtue; it operated on this occasion, and the event proved that it was not without foundation.

October.

A convention of delegates from several towns on both sides of the river assembled at Cornish and agreed to unite, without any regard to the limits established by the king in 1764; and to make the following proposals to New-Hampshire,

Dec. 9.

viz. either to agree with them on a dividing line, or to submit the dispute to congress, or to arbitrators mutually chosen.   If neither of these proposals were accepted, then, in case they could agree with New-Hampshire on a form of government, they would consent that ' the whole of the grants on both sides of the river ' should connect themselves with New-Hampshire, and become ' one entire state, as before the royal determination in 1764.'— Till one or other of these proposals should be complied with, they determine ' to trust in providence and defend themselves.'

An attempt was made in the following year to form a a constitution for New-Hampshire, in which the limits of the state were said to be the same as under the royal government   1779. ' reserving nevertheless our claim to the New-Hampshire Grants, ' west of Connecticut river.'   Though this form of government was rejected by a majority of the people ; yet there was a disposition in a great part of the assembly to retain their claim to the whole of the grants westward of the river.   At the same time, the state of New-York set up a claim to the same lands, and it was suspected, perhaps not without reason, that intrigues were forming to divide Vermont between New-Hampshire and New-York, by the ridge of mountains which runs through the territory.   Certain it is, that the Vermonters were alarmed ; and, that they might have the same advantage of their adversaries, they extended their claim westward into New-York, and eastward into New-Hampshire ; and thus not only the sixteen towns, but several other towns in the counties of Cheshire and Grafton, became incorporated with Vermont by ' articles of union and con- ' federation.'

It is not easy to develope the intrigues of the several parties, or to clear their transactions from the obscurity which surrounds them.*   He who looks for consistency in the proceedings of the conventions and assemblies which were involved in this controversy, will be disappointed.   Several interfering interests conspired to perplex the subject.   The people on the western side of the Green Mountains, wished to have the seat of government among them.   Those adjoining Connecticut river, on both sides, were desirous of bringing the centre of jurisdiction to the verge of the river.   The leading men in the eastern part of New-Hampshire, were averse to a removal of the government from its old seat : Vermont had assumed independence, but its limits were not defined.   New-York had a claim on that territory as far as Connecticut river, from which there was no disposition to recede. That state had been always opposed to the independence of

* The author has spared no pains to gain as perfect a knowledge of these things as the nature of them will admit.   If he has not succeeded in obtaining materials, for a just and full account, it is his request that those who are better acquainted with the subject would oblige the public with more accurate information.

Vermont. New-Hampshire at first seemed to acquiesce in it; and some letters which the President wrote to the Governor of Vermont, when threatened with invasion in 1777, were understood as an acknowledgment of it. Had there been no attempt to unite with the towns on the eastern side of the river, New-Hampshire would perhaps never have opposed the independence of Vermont. But the Assembly was afterward induced to claim all that territory, which before the year 1764, had been supposed to be within the limits of the state. This interfered with the claim of New-York; and at the same time, Massachusetts put in a claim to a part of Vermont. The controversy had become so intricate, that it was thought necessary to be decided by congress; and Sept. 24. application being made to that body, they recommended to the three States of New-York, Massachusetts and New-Hampshire, to pass acts which should authorise congress to determine their boundaries; and at the same time, they advised the people of Vermont to relinquish jurisdiction over all *persons* on the west or east sides of Connecticut river, who had not denied the authority of New-York and New-Hampshire; and to abstain from granting lands, or confiscating estates, within their assumed limits, till the matter should be decided. The states of New-York and New-Hampshire passed these acts; but Massachusetts did not. The Vermont assembly proceeded in granting lands and confiscating estates; and congress could only resolve that their proceedings were unwarrantable.

It was necessary that nine states should be present in congress, beside those whose claims were to be heard. A deficiency in the representation caused a long delay; but after the expiration of another year, the question was brought on. The claims of 1780. New-York and New-Hampshire were put in; and both Sept. 20. pleaded that Vermont had no right to independence. The agents of the New-State asserted their right, and offered to become part of the Union; intimating, that if they could not be admitted, they should be reduced to the necessity of making the best terms which the British government.*

* How far intrigues of this kind were carried on, it may be difficult to ascertain; but that the British government had some dependence on the defection of Vermont appears from the following paragraph of an intercepted letter from Lord George Germaine, to Sir Henry Clinton, dated Whitehall, Feb. 7, 1781.
' The return of the people of Vermont to their allegiance, is an event of ' the utmost importance to the King's affairs; and at this time, if the French ' and Washington really meditate an irruption into Canada, may be consider-' ed as opposing an insurmountable bar to the attempt. General Haldiman, ' who had the same instructions with you to draw over those people, and ' give them support, will, I doubt not, push up a body of troops, to act in con-' junction with them, to secure all the avenues, through their country into ' Canada; and when the season admits, take possession of the upper parts of ' the Hudson's and Connecticut rivers, and cut off the communication between ' Albany and the Mohawk country. How far they may be able to extend ' themselves southward and eastward, must depend on their numbers, and the ' disposition of the inhabitants.' Pennsylvania Packet, Aug. 4, 1781.

The cause was further perplexed by a constitutional question, whether congress had any power to form a new State within the limits of the union ?   The decision was defer-red ; and after eleven months, congress had proceeded no farther, than to lay it down as an indispensable preliminary, to the recognition of Vermont, as a member of the union ; that they should ' explicitly relinquish all demands of land and jurisdiction ' on the east side of Connecticut river, and on the west side of a ' line drawn twenty miles eastward of Hudson's river to Lake ' Champlain.'

1781. Aug. 20.

When this resolution was laid before the assembly of Vermont, which met at Charlestown, they determined to ' remain ' firm in the principles on which they first assumed govern- ' ment, and to hold the articles of union inviolate, that they would ' not submit the question of their independence to the arbitrament ' of any power whatever ; but they were willing at present to ' refer the question of their jurisdictional boundary to commission- ' ers mutually chosen, and when they should be admitted into the ' American union, they would submit any such disputes to con- ' gress.'[1]

Oct. 19.

The state of society within the seceding towns, at this time, was very unhappy.   The majorities attempted to control the mi-norities ; and these were disposed not to submit, but to seek pro-tection of the government with which they had been connected. At the same time, and in the same place, justices, sheriffs and constables, appointed by the authority of both states, were exer-cising jurisdiction over the same persons.   Party rage, high words and deep resentment, were the effect of these clashing interests. An affray which began in the town of Chesterfield, threatened a scene of open hostility, between the states of New-Hampshire and Vermont.

A constable, appointed by the authority of Vermont, had a writ, in an action of debt against a man who was in the interest of New-Hampshire.   He found the man in company with a number of people of his own party, and attempted to arrest him. The owner of the house interposed.   The constable produced a book, which he said contained the laws of Vermont, and began to read.   The owner of the house forbade him. Threatening words were used ; and the officer was compelled to retreat.   By a warrant from a Vermont justice, the householder, and another of the company, were committed to prison, in Charles-town.   They sent a petition to the assembly of New-Hampshire for relief.   The assembly empowered the committee of safety to direct the sheriff of Cheshire to release the prisoners ; they farther empowered the committee to cause to be apprehended and committed to prison, in any of the counties, all

Nov. 14.

Nov. 28.

(1) MS. copy of Vermont resolves in New-Hampshire files.   (2) MS. depo sitions and letters in the files.

persons acting under the pretended authority of the state of Vermont, to be tried by the courts of those counties where they might be confined ; and for this purpose, the sheriffs were empowered to raise the *posse Comitatus*.

In attempting to release the two prisoners from Charlestown goal, the sheriff himself was imprisoned by the Vermont sheriff, under the authority of a warrant from three Justices. The imprisoned sheriff applied to a brigadier-general of New-Hampshire, to raise the militia for his liberation. This alarmed the Vermonters ; and orders were issued by the governor for their militia to oppose force with force. A committee of Vermont was sent to Exeter, 'to agree on measures to 'prevent hostilities.' One of this committee was the Vermont sheriff; he was immediately arrested and thrown into prison at Exeter, and there held as a hostage for the release of the sheriff of Cheshire. The assembly issued a proclamation, allowing forty days for the people in the revolted towns to repair to some magistrate of New-Hampshire, and subscribe a declaration, that they acknowledged the extent of New-Hampshire to Connecticut river ; and that they would demean themselves peaceably as good citizens of the State. They also ordered the militia of all the counties to hold themselves in readiness to march against the revolters.

(margin: 1782. Jan. 12.)

While affairs wore such a threatening aspect between the two States, means were used at congress to take up the controversy on more general ground. A committee, who had under consideration the affair of admitting Vermont into the union and determining its boundaries, prevailed on General Washington, then at Philadelphia, to write to the governor of Vermont, advising to a relinquishment of their late extension, as an ' indispensable preliminary,' to their admission into the union ; intimating also, that upon their non-compliance, they must be considered as having a hostile disposition toward the United States, in which case *coercion* on the part of congress, however disagreeable, would be necessary.*

(margin: Jan. 1.)

---

* The following is the letter from Washington alluded to.

PHILADELPHIA, 1st January, 1782.

SIR,—I received your favor of the 14th of November, by Mr. Brownson. You cannot be at a loss to know why I have not heretofore, and why I cannot now, address you in your public character or answer you in mine : But the confidence which you have been pleased to repose in me, gives me an opportunity of offering you my sentiments, as an individual, wishing most ardently to see the peace and union of his country, preserved, and the just rights of the people of every part of it fully and firmly established.

It is not my business, neither do I think it necessary now, to discuss the origin of the right of a number of inhabitants to that tract of country formerly distinguished by the name of the New-Hampshire Grants, and now known by that of Vermont. I will take it for granted that their right was good, because congress, by their resolve of the 7th of August, imply it; and by that of the 21st, are willing fully to confirm it, provided the new state is confined to certain described bounds. It appears, therefore, to me, that the dispute of

This letter had the desired effect.   The assembly of Vermont, taking advantage of the absence of the members from the _{Feb. 22.} eastern side of the river, obtained a majority for complying with the preliminary, and resolved, ' that the western bank of ' Connecticut river on the one part, and a line drawn from the ' north-west corner of Massachusetts, north-ward, to Lake Cham ' plain on the other part, be the eastern and western boundaries ' of the state of Vermont, and that they relinquished all claim of ' jurisdiction without those limits.'   When the members from the eastern side of Connecticut river arrived, they found themselves excluded from a seat in the assembly, and took their leave with some expressions of bitterness.

After this compliance, it was expected that Vermont would be admitted into the union, and the question was solemnly put in congress ; but a majority decided against it, to the no _{Apr. 14.} small disappointment of many persons, beside the inhabi tants of the disputed territory.   The pretence for this decision was, that they had exceeded the limited time ; but they had com plied with the ' indispensable preliminary ;' and the order of congress, requiring it, stood unrepealed.

Though cut off from their connexion with Vermont, the re volted towns did not at once return to a state of peace ; but the divisions and animosities which had so long subsisted, continued

boundary is the only one that exists, and that that being removed, all further difficulties would be removed also, and the matter terminated to the satisfac tion of all parties.   Now I would ask you candidly, whether the claim of the people of Vermont, was not, for a long time, confined solely, or very nearly, to that tract of country which is described in the resolve of congress of the 21st of August last ; and whether, agreeable to the tenor of your own letter to me, the late extension of your claim upon New-Hampshire and New-York, was not more a political manœuvre, than one in which you conceived yourselves justifiable.   If my first question be answered in the affirmative, it certainly bars your new claim.   And if my second be well founded, your end is answered, and you have nothing to do but withdraw your jurisdiction to the confines of your old limits, and obtain an acknowledgment of indepen dence and sovereignty, under the resolve of the 21st of August, for so much territory as does not interfere with the ancient established bounds of New-York, New-Hampshire and Massachusetts.   I persuade myself you will see and acquiesce in the reason, the justice, and indeed the necessity of such a decision.

You must consider, sir, that the point now in dispute is of the utmost po litical importance to the future union and peace of this great country.   The state of Vermont, if acknowledged, will be the first new one admitted into the confederacy ; and if suffered to encroach upon the ancient established boundaries of the adjacent ones, will serve as a precedent for others, which it may hereafter be expedient to set off, to make the same unjustifiable demands. Thus, in my private opinion, while it behoves the delegates of the states now confederated, to do ample justice to a body of people sufficiently respectable by their numbers, and entitled by other claims to be admitted into that con federation, it becomes them also to attend to the interests of their constitu ents, and see, that under the appearance of justice to one, they do not mate rially injure the rights of others.   I am apt to think this is the prevailing opinion of congress, and that your late extension of claim has, upon the prin ciple I have above mentioned, rather diminished than increased your friends ; and that, if such extension should be persisted in, it will be made a common

to produce disagreeable effects. The judicial courts of New-Hampshire had sat without much interruption, in the county of Cheshire and Grafton, whilst the officers of Vermont held jurisdiction also ; but when the latter were excluded by the act of the Vermont assembly, a spirit of opposition began to arise against the sitting of the former.

When the inferior court was holden at Keene, a number of persons appeared, to oppose its proceedings, and effected their Sept. purpose so far as to make an adjournment necessary ; but three of the leaders of the opposition were arrested and bound over to the superior court. In the mean time, efforts were made to raise a party who should oppose the superior court ; and it was reported that two hundred men had associated and armed themselves Oct. for that purpose. On the morning before the court was opened, several of the leaders came to the judges' chambers and presented a petition, praying, ' that the court might ' be adjourned, and that no judicial proceedings might be had, ' whilst the troubles in which the country had been involved still ' subsisted.' They were told that the judges could come to no determination on the subject but in open court. When the court was opened, their petition was publicly read ; and the consideration of it was postponed to the next day. The court then pro-

cause, and not considered as only affecting the rights of those states immediately interested in the loss of territory ; a loss of too serious a nature not to claim the attention of any people. There is no calamity within the compass of my foresight, which is more to be dreaded than a necessity of *coercion* on the part of congress ; and consequently every endeavor should be used to prevent the execution of so disagreeable a measure. It must involve the ruin of that state against which the resentment of the others is pointed.

I will only add a few words upon the subject of the negotiations, which have been carried on between you and the enemy in Canada and in New-York. I will take it for granted, as you assert it, that they were so far innocent, that there never was any serious intention of joining Great-Britain in their attempts to subjugate your country ; but it has had this certain bad tendency, it has served to give some ground to that delusive opinion of the enemy, and upon which they, in a great measure, found their hopes of success ; that they have numerous friends among us, who only want a proper opportunity to shew themselves openly ; and that internal disputes and feuds will soon break us in pieces. At the same time, the seeds of distrust and jealousy are scattered among ourselves by a conduct of this kind. If you are serious in your professions, these will be additional motives for accepting the terms which have been offered, (and which appear to me equitable) and thereby convincing the common enemy, that all their expectations of disunion are vain, and that they have been worsted at their own weapon—deception.

As you unbosom yourself to me, I thought I had the greater right of speaking my sentiments openly and candidly to you. I have done so, and if they should produce the effect which I most sincerely wish, that of an honorable and amicable adjustment of a matter, which, if carried to hostile lengths, may destroy the future happiness of my country, I shall have attained my end, while the enemy will be defeated of theirs.

Believe me to be, with great respect,
Sir,
Your most obedient servant,
GEORGE WASHINGTON.

THOMAS CHITTENDEN, Esquire.

ceeded to its common business. The grand jury being impan-
nelled, the doors of the house where they met were kept open,
whilst the attorney general laid before them the case of the rioters at the inferior court. A bill was found against them. They
were arraigned, they pleaded guilty, and cast themselves on the
mercy of the court. The court remitted their punishment on
condition of their future peaceable behaviour. This well judged
combination of firmness and lenity disarmed the insurgents ; and
they quietly dispersed. From that time, the spirit of opposition
to government in that quarter gradually abated ; and the people
returned to their connexion with New-Hampshire.

CHAPTER XXVII.

Popular discontent.   Efforts for paper currency.   Tender acts.   Insurrection.
Dignity and lenity of government.   Federal constitution.

THE American revolution had been crowned with success, as
far as it respected our emancipation from foreign jurisdiction,
the establishment of forms of government among ourselves, and
our deliverance from war. It remained, to accommodate the
minds and manners of the people under the new administration,
to a regular course of justice, both public and private ; to perfect
the union of the states ; and to establish a system of finance.
These things were necessary to make the revolution complete.

The extremes of despotism on the one hand, and of li-
centiousness on the other, are equally to be avoided. In a
just medium between these, a government well balanced and
executed with vigor, is capable of producing the most valuable benefits. To this point it was necessary to conduct our
revolution. But it was equally necessary, that it should proceed
by slow degrees ; that errors in principle should be gradually reformed ; and that men should be taught by their own experience,
the folly of relying on any system of politics, which however supported by popularity, is not founded in rectitude.

A large debt accumulated by the war, remained to be discharged. For this purpose, requisitions were made by congress, as
well as by the state governments. Silver and gold, which had
circulated largely in the latter years of the war, were returning,
by the usual course of trade, to those countries, whence large
quantities of necessary and unnecessary commodities had been
imported. Had any general system of impost been adopted,
some part of this money might have been retained, and some part

of the public debt discharged; but the power of congress did not extend to this object; and the states were not united in the expediency of delegating new and sufficient powers to that body.—— The partial imposts, laid by some of the states, were ineffectual, so long as others found their interest in omitting them. Recourse therefore, was had to the usual mode of taxation on polls and estates; by which means, a heavy burden was laid on the husbandman and the laborer. Those who were punctual in their payments, saw no probable end of their exertions, whilst the negligence of others occasioned repeated demands. Private creditors, who had suffered by long forbearance, were importunate for their dues; and the courts of law were full of suits.

The people who felt themselves distressed, held conferences with a view to devise means of redress. The remedy which appeared to many of them most easy, was a new emission of paper bills, funded on real estate, and loaned on interest. To effect 1785. this, petitions were addressed to the legislature; and to Feb. 24. remedy the grievance, as far as it was occasioned by a debt of the state, an act was passed, to draw into the treasury all notes issued by the state, and give certificates for the interest, and for fifteen per cent. of the principal, annually; which certificates were to be received by the treasurer for taxes, ' in ' lieu of, and equal to silver and gold.' By this means, it was expected that the debt would gradually be extinguished; and that the people would easily be enabled to pay at least one species of their taxes.

This was far from satisfying the complainants. The public securities, they said, were engrossed by rich speculators, and the poor were distressed for the means of paying their taxes and their private debts. The cry for paper money was incessant; and the people were called upon in the public papers, 'to assert their own ' majesty, as the origin of power, and to make their governors ' know, that they are but the executors of the public will.'

To this clamor, the voice of reason and justice calmly answered; that it was not in the power of the legislature to establish any fund, which should secure paper money from depreciation; that there was so much paper then in circulation, and the time of its redemption was so distant, that the notes passed at a discount of sixty, and the certificates of twenty per cent; that if the quantity were increased, the depreciation would increase in proportion; that if bills were issued and made a tender in all payments, it would never be in the power of government to redeem them by silver and gold, because none could be collected; and in that case, no part of the continental or foreign debt could be discharged; that if bills were loaned on land security, it would be in the power of the public debtor to purchase the bills at a reduced value, and with them to make his payment at the treasury, in which

case, though the public chest might be filled with paper, yet the
government would suffer all the embarrassment of poverty. It
was added, that the legislature were by the constitution expressly
forbidden to make retrospective laws, and had no right to alter
the nature of private contracts; and that should the majority of
the people petition the government to make paper a lawful tender,
it would be their duty to reject the petition as unconstitutional.—
When it was proposed, that the paper should not be a tender for
past but only for future contracts; it was answered, that this would
not relieve the debtor, who was suffering for his past engagements,
and the difficulties which it pretended to cure would still exist.

In vain were agriculture and manufactures, industry and frugality recommended as the only adequate sources of relief; the
complainants had no disposition to apply a remedy so slow in its
operation; and indeed it was doubtful whether the utmost exertions in that way would have been sufficient, completely to extri-
cate us out of these difficulties, without some alteration in our
confederated government.

Similar difficulties, at the same time, existed in the neighboring
state of Massachusetts; to remedy which, among other palliatives,
a law was passed called a *tender-act*, ' by which it was provided
' that executions issued for private demands, might be satisfied by
' cattle and other enumerated articles, at an appraisement of im-
' partial men under oath.'[1] For such a law, the discontented
party in New-Hampshire petitioned; and to gratify them, the legislature enacted, that ' when any debtor shall tender to his Nov. 8.
' creditor, in satisfaction of an execution for debt, either
' real or personal estate sufficient, the body of the debtor shall be
' exempt from imprisonment, and the debt shall carry an interest
' of six per cent; the creditor being at liberty either to receive
' the estate, so tendered, at a value estimated by three appraisers,
' or to keep alive the demand by taking out an alias, within one
' year after the return of any former execution, and levying it on
' any estate of the debtor which he can find.' At the same time,
an act was made, enlarging the power of justices of the peace, to
try and determine actions of debt and trespass to the value of ten
pounds. These laws were complained of as unconstitutional;
the former as being retrospective, and changing the nature of contracts; the latter as depriving the creditor, in certain cases, of a
right to trial by jury. But so strong was the clamor for redress
of grievances; and so influential was the example of the neighboring state, that some of the best men in the legislature found it
necessary to comply; whilst another part were secretly in favor
of worse measures.

The tender-act, at first, was made for two years only; before
the expiration of which it was revived, with some alterations, and

(1) Minot's History of the Insurrections, p. 15.

continued for three years longer.   The effect of this law, in cases
where an attempt was made to execute it, was, that the most valuable kinds of property were either concealed or made over to a
third person ; and when the sheriff came with an execution, it was
levied on such articles as were of little use to the creditor.   But
the most general effect of the law was to prevent any demand on
the part of the creditor, and to encourage the debtor in neglecting payment.

The scarcity of money was still a grievance which the laws had
not remedied, but rather had a tendency to increase.   To encourage its importation into the country, the legislature
1786.   exempted from all port duties, except light-money, every
vessel which should bring gold and silver only ;   and from one
half of the duties, if a sum of money equal to one half of the cargo should be imported.   But it was to no purpose to import money, unless encouragement were given for its circulation, which
could not be expected whilst the tender-act was in force ;   for
every man who owned money thought it more secure in his own
hands, than in the hands of others.

The clamor for paper currency increased, and, like a raging
fever, approached toward a crisis.   In every town, there was a
party in favor of it, and the public papers were continually filled
with declamations on the subject.   It was said that an emission of
bills of credit would give a spring to commerce and encourage
agriculture ; that the poor would be able to pay their debts and
taxes ; that all the arguments against issuing paper were framed
by speculators, and were intended to serve the wealthy part of the
community, who had monopolized the public securities, that they
might raise their value and get all the good bargains into their
own hands ; that other states in the union had issued paper bills,
and were rejoicing in the happy effects of their currency, *without
any depreciation ;* that the people had a right to call upon their
representatives to stamp a value on paper, or leather, or any
other substance capable of receiving an impression ; and that to
prevent its depreciation, a law should be enacted to punish with
banishment and outlawry, every person who should attempt by
any means to lessen its value.*

The same party who were so zealous in favor of paper cur-

* A specimen of the language used on this occasion is as follows :—' Seven
' states are now blessed with harmony, plenty and happiness.   Worthy, in-
' dustrious men can go to market with a penny in their pockets; their benev-
' olent friends, the farmers, meet them half way with cheerfulness, and are
' as ready to receive as they to offer ; now one greets the other with social
' benedictions, trade flourishes, agriculture increases, mutual confidence is
' restored, and harmony reigns triumphant.   Elysian fields these ! when con-
' trasted with the bondage of the inhabitants of New-Hampshire ; for ' in the
' midst of life, they are in death,' death of the worst kind, penury and want of
' the common blessings of providence.   How long, freemen of New-Hamp-
' shire, can ye bear the yoke of oppression !'   New-Hampshire Gazette, July
20, 1786.

rency, and against laws which obliged them to pay their debts, proceeded to inveigh against courts and lawyers. The inferior courts were represented as sinecures for judges and clerks; the defaulting, appealing, demurring, abatements, fees and bills of cost, without any decision, were complained of as burdens, and an abolition of these courts became a part of the popular cry.— But the party did not content themselves with writing in the public papers. An attempt was made to call a convention, at Concord, whilst the assembly were sitting there, who should petition the legislature in favor of the plan ; and it was thought, that the presence of such a body of men, convened at the same time and place, would have great weight. The attempt was defeated in a manner singular and humorous.

At the first sitting of the assembly, when five only of the members of the proposed convention were in town, some wags, June. among whom were several young lawyers, pretended to have been chosen by the towns in which they lived for the same purpose. In conference with the five, they penetrated their views, and persuaded them to post an advertisement, for all the members who were in town to assemble immediately ; it being of the utmost importance to present their petition as early in the session as possible. By this means, sixteen pretended members, with the five real ones, formed themselves into a convention, choosing one of the five their president, and one of the sixteen their clerk. They carried on their debates and passed votes with much apparent solemnity. Having framed a petition, complaining in the most extravagant terms of their grievances ; praying for a loan of *three millions* of dollars, funded on real estate ; for the abolition of inferior courts, and a reduction of the number of lawyers, to two only in a county ; and for a free trade with all the world ; they went in procession to the assembly, (some of whom had been previously let into the secret) and with great formality presented their petition, which was suffered to lie on the table, and was afterwards withdrawn. The convention then dissolved ; and when others who had been really chosen by the towns arrived, they were exceedingly mortified on finding their views for that time so completely frustrated.

The next effort of the party was to call county conventions.— Of what class of people these were composed, some idea may be formed from this circumstance. An innholder, at whose house one of these conventions first met, refused to take their promise for lumber to pay the expense of their meeting ; upon which they adjourned to a ware-house, belonging to one of the party, and were treated with liquor, gratis.

From two of these conventions, and from several towns in different parts of the state, petitions were presented to the Sept. 13. legislature, at their session in Exeter. On calm deliberation, these petitions appeared to be inconsistent with each other, with the constitution, with justice and public faith. But to still the clamor and collect the real sense of the people on the subject of paper currency ; the assembly formed a plan for the emission of fifty thousand pounds, to be let at four per cent. on land security ; to be a tender in payment of state taxes, and for the fees and salaries of public officers. This plan was immediately printed, and sent to the several towns ; and the people were desired to give their opinions in town meetings for and against it, and to make return of their votes to the assembly at their next session.

This way of proceeding did not coincide with the views of the party ; the principal directors of which endeavored to conceal themselves, whilst they persuaded a considerable number of persons of various characters, to appear openly in support of the petitions. They took pains to spread false reports through the country ; and among other things, it was said that the assembly had passed an act, to refund the value of the confiscated estates, which was to be immediately assessed on the people.

It must be observed, that at this time, causes of a similar nature had excited numbers of people in some counties of Massachusetts, to assemble in arms and prevent the judicial courts from sitting.* This example, aided by false reports, and a sense of grievances, partly real and partly imaginary, operated so powerfully on the minds of a number of people, in the western part of the county of Rockingham ; that on the morning of the twentieth of September, about two hundred men assembled at Kingston, six miles from Exeter, where they chose leaders and procured a drum. By the help of some militia officers, they formed themselves into military order, and in the afternoon, marched to Exeter ; about one third of them being armed with muskets, and the others with swords and clubs. Having entered the confines of the town, they halted ; and sent a paper to the assembly, signed by one of them who styled himself moderator, demanding an answer to their former petition immediately. They then marched through the town, and paraded before the meeting-house, where both houses of assembly were holding a conference. The doors were open, and as many of them as were disposed, entered.— The president, in a cool and deliberate speech, explained the

* [The insurrection in Massachusetts assumed such a threatening aspect, that the governor of that state wrote to President Sullivan, requesting him to offer a reward for apprehending any of the rebels who should flee to this state, and to take measures for preventing their receiving any supplies.— " The government of New-Hampshire, pursued every measure, which it was thought the powers vested in the president and council would authorize.— They did not think proper, to admit armed parties from another state into that ; but the existing laws permitted civil officers of other states, to pursue offenders there, and by application to a magistrate to have them apprehended and sent into the state having jurisdiction of the offence. They, therefore directed a major-general, to secure all armed parties, who might come into their state ; and a proclamation was issued by their president, agreeably to the request of the governor of the commonwealth." Minot, Hist. of the Insurrection in Mass. 154.]

reasons on which the assembly had proceeded in rejecting the petitions; exposed the weakness, inconsistency and injustice of their request; and said, that if it were ever so just and proper in itself, and if the whole body of the people were in favor of it, yet the legislature ought not to comply with it, while surrounded by an armed force. To do this, would be, to betray the rights of the people, which they had all solemnly sworn to support. He concluded by declaring, that no consideration of personal danger would ever compel them to violate the rights of their constituents.

This speech being ended, the drum beat to arms; as many as had guns were ordered to load them with balls; sentries were placed at the doors, and the whole legislature were held prisoners; the mob threatening death to any person who should attempt to escape, till their demands were granted. The assembly went on with their business, taking no farther notice of the rioters, till the approach of evening; when the president attempted to go out, but was stopped by an impenetrable column. He then reasoned with them, and warned them of the fatal tendency of their conduct, assuring them, that the force of the country would support the government. Their answers to him were insolent and reproachful. They raised a cry for paper money, an equal distribution of property, and a release from debts. The inhabitants of Exeter had all this time beheld with silence the insult offered to the legislature. Having no orders to take arms, they restrained their indignation, till the dusk of the evening; when some of them beat a drum at a distance, and others cried, ' Huzza for ' government ! Bring up the artillery !' At the sound of these words, the mob were struck with a panic, and began to disperse. Their moderator ordered them to meet again, at nine of the clock the next morning, and they scattered in every direction.*

* [The president of New-Hampshire at this time was John Sullivan, of whom through the kindness of the Hon. William Plumer, I am enabled to add the following note.

JOHN SULLIVAN was the son of John Sullivan, and was born in Berwick, Maine. Without an academic education, he commenced the practice of law at Durham, in this state, where he lived till his death. He was in the times in which he lived, considered a distinguished lawyer. In 1772, he was appointed a major in the militia. In 1774, he was appointed a delegate to the general congress; and in December, he, with others, seized the British fort William and Mary, at New-Castle, and took more than a hundred barrels of gunpowder from thence, and removed it into the country. In 1775, he was re-appointed delegate to congress; and by that body on the 22 June, was appointed brigadier-general in the revolutionary army. He commanded the troops stationed on Winter Hill, in the vicinity of Boston.

He received from congress the appointment of major-general, 29 July, 1776. The 26th August, he was taken prisoner on Long-Island, New-York, and in October, was exchanged; sent to the army in Canada, where after the death of General Thomas, he commanded; but was soon superseded, and returned to the main army. In 1777, he was distinguished for his bravery and good conduct in the battles of Brandywine and Germantown. In August, 1778, he commanded the army at Newport, Rhode-Island, but was obliged to retreat, on which occasion his conduct met the approbation of congress. In 1779, he commanded an expedition against the Indians, where he suffered

The assembly being thus at liberty, requested the president to call out the force of the state to quell the insurrection. In the evening, he issued his orders, and before morning companies of militia, well armed, began to come in from the neighboring towns. By ten of the clock in the morning, a sufficient body of horse and foot, with field-pieces and military music, having arrived ; the president put them in motion against the insurgents, who were then parading, about a mile distant. Having by their spies obtained intelligence of the motion of the militia, the unarmed part of the insurgents retreated to a hill beyond the river ; the others kept their ground till a party of light-horse appeared in view, and then the whole body retired. Some of them were taken by the pursuers ; others recovered the bridge at King's fall, and being met by those who had first retreated, made an appearance as if they would dispute the passage. Orders were given by one of their leaders to fire ; but the force of the government appeared so formidable that they dared not to obey. The officers of the militia rushed in among them, seized their moderator and others, to the number of forty. The rest fled with precipitation, and no farther pursuit was made. The prisoners were disarmed and conducted to the town ; where they were brought to an examination before the president and council. Had these men been engaged in a good cause, and commanded by proper officers, they would have maintained the honor of their country, and fought her battles with ardor and perseverance ; but, conscious of their inconsistency in opposing a government of their own establishing, their native fortitude forsook them ; and they gave an example of the most humiliating submission. Most of them professed to be ashamed of their conduct, and their shame appeared to be sincere.

The dignity of government being thus vindicated, its lenity

Sep*t*. 21.

great fatigue, but destroyed many Indians, and laid their country waste. On the 30th November, congress accepted his resignation, which he had previously requested.

In February, 1780, the legislature of the state appointed him an agent to settle the line between New-Hampshire and New-York ; and June 21st, a delegate to the congress of the United States, and on the 19 January following, re-appointed him to that office. In January, 1782, the legislature appointed him commander of their troops to Vermont, and on the 21 June, attorney general of New-Hampshire.

After the establishment of the state constitution, he was re-appointed attorney general, 25 December, 1784, and major-general of the militia, both of which he held till 28 February, 1786, when he resigned them both. In 1785, he was member and speaker of the house of representatives and counsellor. In 1786 and 1787, he was elected president of the state. In 1788, he was a member and speaker of the house of representatives ; member and president of the convention which ratified the constitution of the United States.

In 1789, he was an elector of president and vice president of the United States, and in March, was elected president of the state for the third time.— In September, the same year, the president and senate of the U. S. appointed him judge of the district court of New-Hampshire, which office he held as long as he lived. He died 23 January, 1795, aged 54 years.]

was equally conspicuous. Six only of the prisoners were detained, and a party of light-horse was sent to apprehend two others of the most culpable. They were taken out of their beds and brought to Exeter. This manœuvre had an excellent effect, for some, who knew themselves equally guilty, were afraid to sleep in their own houses. The superior court being then Sept. 25. in session at Exeter, these eight prisoners were arraigned on an indictment for treason. One dropping on his knees, pleaded guilty. Others hesitated when they pronounced the words ' not guilty.' They were ordered to recognize for their appearance at the next superior court, when their bonds were discharged. Some of them, who belonged to the presbyterian churches, were cited before the ecclesiastical session, and there censured, as opposers of just government. Others, being military officers, were tried by a general court martial ; of these, some were cashiered, but not incapacitated for future service ; some were reprimanded, and others were acquitted. The whole opposition was completely subdued ; wavering minds became settled; converts were made to the side of government ; and the system of knavery received a deep wound, from which it has not since recovered.

The plan which had been issued by the assembly, for emitting paper money, was in course referred to the people, in 1787. their town meetings ; and at the next session, the returns Jan. 4. were made, when a majority appeared against it. To finish the whole matter, two questions were put in the assembly. The first was ' whether the legislature can, consistently with the ' constitution, and their oaths, pass an act making paper bills of ' credit, a tender to discharge private contracts, made prior to the ' passing such act ?' The other was, ' whether paper money be ' emitted on any plan which has been proposed ?' Both these questions were determined in the negative.

To observe the progress of wisdom and virtue, and the obstacles which are laid in the way of vice, is a most pleasing entertainment to the philanthropist ; and it is but just, in such a contemplation, to acknowledge that superintending influence, which brings good out of evil. It was feared by many, that the American revolution would not produce that sum of political happiness which its warmest advocates had fondly predicted. The efforts of faction in several of the states were very alarming. In New-Hampshire, the assault being made directly at the supreme head of the government, the force of the state immediately rose and crushed it. In Massachusetts, the attacks were made on the judicial courts, which of themselves had no power effectually to oppose them. The disaffection there rose to a higher degree ; it was more extensively diffused, and with more difficulty quelled. But at length, the constitutional powers of government being exerted with vigor, the spirit of anarchy was suppressed. In another neighboring state, the same spirit reigned triumphant. A depreciating currency was established by law, aud pertinaciously adhered to by the government.

The imbecility of the confederation by which the states were united, had long been felt, and some attempts had been making to strengthen it ; but the view of our situation at this time demonstrated the total inefficacy of that constitution, to bind together thirteen distinct sovereignties, over which no coercive power was established, which could prevent or cure such evils as threatened the destruction of all public and private credit. Happily for the American union, the remedy existed within itself. The good sense and public virtue of the great body of our citizens readily adopted the idea of a CONVENTION OF THE STATES. The first proposal came from Virginia, where American liberty was first publicly asserted, when it was flagrantly violated by the stamp act. The name of *Patrick Henry* will ever be illustrious in the American annals for moving the resolves of 1765 ; and the name of *James Madison* will be equally distinguished for proposing the convention of 1787.

To this convention, which was holden at Philadelphia, all the states, except *one*, sent their delegates. After a close and particular investigation, they produced a new federal constitution ; containing adequate remedies for those political disorders, which had threatened with extinction, the liberty and independence of the American states.

Among other wise provisions, to establish justice and secure the blessings of liberty, those which respect public and private credit are not the least conspicuous. To support the former, the congress has a power which, by the first confederation, was not delegated, ' to lay and collect taxes, duties, imposts, and excises, to ' pay the debts and provide for the common defence and general ' welfare of the United States.' For the latter, it is declared, that ' no state shall coin money, emit bills of credit, make any thing ' but gold and silver coin a tender in payment of debts, pass any ' bill of attainder or *expost facto* law, or any law impairing the ' obligation of contracts.'

When this new constitution was proposed to the people, conventions were called in each state to consider it. In these bodies, composed of persons who represented impartially every class and description of the people, and who were themselves equally various in their principles, habits and views, the constitution underwent the most critical and severe discussion. Whilst it was in debate, the anxiety of all parties was extended to the utmost degree, and the efforts of its friends and its opposers were unremitted.

After the constitution had been, with the help of some proposed amendments, adopted by Massachusetts, a convention was called at Exeter in New-Hampshire. At its first meeting, a debate which continued ten days ended in an adjournment for four months; at the expiration of which term, in a short session of three days only at Concord, the question for adopting and ratifying the constitution, was, with the same help as in Massachusetts, carried in the affirmative, by a majority of eleven; the whole number present being one hundred and three. This was the *ninth* state in the union which accepted the constitution; and thus the number was completed which was necessary to put in motion the political machine.* In about a

1788.
Feb. 13.
June 21.

* [1788. JOHN LANGDON was elected president of New-Hampshire for the second time. A note, detailing the services of this early patriot of the revolution, will conclude the editor's annotations on this part of the labors of the historian of New-Hampshire. John Langdon was a native of Portsmouth, and was born in 1740. His father, of the same name, was the sixth son of Tobias Langdon, and lived at Sagamore's creek in Portsmouth, where his house was burned, about the year 1740. Tobias is supposed to have been son of Tobias Langdon, who lived in New-Hampshire in 1662.

He received his education at the public grammar school, under the tuition of Samuel Hale. From school, he went into the counting house of the honorable Daniel Rindge, where he became well acquainted with mercantile transactions. At the close of his apprenticeship, he entered upon a seafaring life, which business he continued to follow, until the troubles between the country and Great-Britain commenced. He took an early and active part in the opposition to the British government, and was one of the leaders of that party, which removed the powder and military stores from the fort at Newcastle, in December, 1774. In 1775, he was appointed a delegate to the general congress, and in January, 1776, was re-appointed to the same office.—Soon after the beginning of the revolutionary war, he had the command of an independent company of cadets, and at the time of the surrender of the British army under Burgoyne, went to Bennington as a volunteer. He was likewise at Rhode-Island with a detachment of his company, at the time the British troops were in possession of the island, and when General Sullivan brought off the American troops.

He was representative and speaker of the house of representatives in this state in 1776 and 1777, and in the former year, judge of the court of common pleas, which office he resigned in April, 1777. In 1778, he had the agency under congress of building several public ships of war, and was appointed continental agent in New-Hampshire. In 1779, he was a member and president of the New-Hampshire convention for regulating the currency; and from 1777 to 1782 member and speaker of the house of representatives of New-Hampshire. In 1780, he was a commissioner to raise men and procure provisions for the army; and on the 13 June, 1783, was appointed delegate to the congress of the United States.

In 1784 and 1785, he was elected a member of the New-Hampshire senate, and the latter year, president of the state, being the successor of Meshech Weare. In 1788, he was a delegate to the convention which formed the constitution of the United States. In March, the same year, was elected representative of the legislature, and speaker of the house in June, when on counting the votes for president, he was found to be elected. In November, the legislature elected him senator to the congress of the United States, and was there elected the first president *pro tem.* of that body, they ever appointed. In 1794, he was re-elected for another term of six years.

From 1801 to 1805, inclusive, he was representative in the N. H. legislature, and in 1804 and 1805, was elected speaker of the house. From 1805 to 1808, and in 1810 and 1811, he was elected governor of the state. In 1805, the government of Dartmouth college conferred on him the degree of Doctor of Laws. Governor Langdon died at Portsmouth, 18 September, 1819, aged 79. Adams, Annals of Portsmouth, 370—373.—MS. Amer. Biography by Hon. W. Plumer.—Gazetteer of N. Hamp. 222.]

month, two more states were added.   Then a congress was formed, and the illustrious WASHINGTON, by the unanimous
1789. suffrage of the people, was placed in the first seat of government.   Three other states, of which one is Vermont, have
since been admitted into the union ; and there is now in opera-
1790. tion a general system of energetic government, which
pervades every part of the United States, and has already
produced a surprising alteration for the better.   By the funding
of the continental debt, and the assumption of the debts of the individual states, into one general mass, a foundation is laid for the
support of public credit ; by which means, the American revolution appears to be completed.   Let it be the sincere prayer and
endeavor of every thoughtful citizen, that such harmony may prevail between the general government, and the jurisdiction of each
state, as the peculiar delicacy of their connexion requires ; and
that the blessings of ' peace, liberty and safety,' so dearly obtained, may descend inviolate to our posterity.

APPENDIX.

TABLES.

Chief Magistrates of New-Hampshire and Massachusetts from 1641 to 1830 ; with the Kings of England from the first settlement of N. H. in 1623, until the separation of this country from Great-Britain, and the Presidents of the United States from the adoption of the Federal Constitution.

COLONIAL GOVERNMENT.

A.D.	Kings of England.	Governors of New-Hampshire and Massachusetts, while united.
1623	James I.	
1625	Charles I.	
1641	"	Richard Bellingham.
1642	"	John Winthrop.
1644	"	John Endecott.
1645	"	Thomas Dudley,
1646	"	John Winthrop.
1649	The Commonwealth.	John Endecott.
1650	"	Thomas Dudley.
1651	"	John Endecott.
1654	"	Richard Bellingham.
1655	"	John Endecott.
1660	Charles II.	"
1665	"	Richard Bellingham.
1673	"	John Leverett.
1679	"	Simon Bradstreet.

PROVINCIAL GOVERNMENT.

A.D.	Kings of England.	Chief Magistrates of New-Hampshire.	Chief Magistrates of Massachusetts.*
1680	Charles II.	John Cutt	Simon Bradstreet
1681	"	Richard Waldron	"
1682	"	Edward Cranfield	"
1685	James II.	Walter Barefoote	"
1686	"	Joseph Dudley	Joseph Dudley
1687	"	Edmund Andros	Edmund Andros
1689	William III.	Simon Bradstreet	Simon Bradstreet

* Massachusetts did not become a Province until the charter of William and Mary was granted in 1691.

1692	William III.	John Usher	William Phips
1697	"	William Partridge	"
1698	"	Samuel Allen	"
1699	"	Earl of Bellomont	Earl of Bellomont
1702	Anne.	Joseph Dudley	Joseph Dudley
1714	George I.	"	"
1716	"	Samuel Shute	Samuel Shute
1727	George II.	"	"
1728	"	William Burnet	William Burnet
1730	"	Jonathan Belcher	Jonathan Belcher
1741	"	Benning Wentworth	William Shirley
1757	"	"	Thomas Pownal
1760	George III.	"	Francis Bernard
1767	"	John Wentworth	"
1770	"	"	Tho. Hutchinson
1774	"	"	Thomas Gage
1775	The British government terminated.		

REPUBLICAN GOVERNMENT.

A.D.	United States.	Pres. & Gov's. N.H.	Governors of Mass.
1776		Meshech Weare	
1780		"	John Hancock
1785	Continental	John Langdon	James Bowdoin
1786	Congress.	John Sullivan	"
1787		"	John Hancock
1788		John Langdon	"
	Presidents U. S.		
1789	G. Washington	John Sullivan	"
1790	"	Josiah Bartlett*	"
1794	"	John T. Gilman	Samuel Adams
1797	John Adams.	"	Increase Sumner
1800	"	"	Caleb Strong
1801	Tho. Jefferson	"	"
1805	"	John Langdon	"
1807	"	"	James Sullivan
1809	James Madison	Jeremiah Smith	Christopher Gore
1810	"	John Langdon	Elbridge Gerry
1812	"	William Plumer	Caleb Strong
1813	"	John T. Gilman	"
1816	"	William Plumer	John Brooks
1817	James Monroe	"	"
1819	"	Samuel Bell	"
1823	"	Levi Woodbury	William Eustis
1824	"	David L. Morril	"
1825	John Q. Adams	"	Levi Lincoln
1827	"	Benjamin Pierce	"
1828	"	John Bell	"
1829	A. Jackson	Benjamin Pierce	"
1830	"	Matthew Harvey	"

* From 1793, the chief magistrate of N. H. has been styled *Governor*.

DEATH AND AGES OF THE PRECEDING.

KINGS OF ENGLAND.

James I.	8 April,	1625,	58.
Charles I.	30 January,	1648,	47.
Charles II.	6 Feb.	1685,	54.
James II.	16 Sept.	1701,	68.
William III.	16 March,	1702,	52.
Anne	1 August,	1714,	50.
George I.	11 June,	1727,	67.
George II.	25 October,	1760,	77.
George III.	29 January,	1820,	81.

GOVERNORS,
WHILE MASSACHUSETTS AND NEW-HAMPSHIRE WERE UNITED.

Richard Bellingham,	7 December,	1672,	80.
John Winthrop,	26 March,	1649,	61.
John Endecott,	15 March,	1665,	76.
Thomas Dudley,	31 July,	1653,	77.
John Leverett,	16 March,	1679.	
Simon Bradstreet,	27 March,	1697,	94.

CHIEF MAGISTRATES,
WHILE NEW-HAMPSHIRE WAS A SEPARATE PROVINCE.

John Cutt,	27 March,	1681.	
Richard Waldron,	27 June,	1689,	80.
Edward Cranfield,	about	1700.	
Walter Barefoote,	about	1688,	53.
Joseph Dudley,	2 April,	1720,	72.
Edmund Andros,	February,	1714.	
John Usher,	5 September,	1726,	78.
William Partridge,	3 January,	1729,	74.
Samuel Allen,	4 May,	1705,	69.

GOVERNORS OF MASSACHUSETTS AND NEW-HAMPSHIRE,
UNTIL THE REVOLUTION.

William Phips,	18 February,	1695,	44.
Earl of Bellomont,	5 March,	1701.	
Samuel Shute,	15 April,	1742,	80.
William Burnet,	7 September,	1729,	41.
Jonathan Belcher,	31 August,	1757,	75.
William Shirley,	24 March,	1771.	
Benning Wentworth,	14 October,	1770,	75.
Thomas Pownall,	25 February,	1805,	83.
Francis Bernard,	June,	1779.	
John Wentworth,	8 April,	1820,	84.
Thomas Hutchinson,	3 June,	1780,	69.
Thomas Gage,	April,	1787.	

54

GOVERNORS OF MASSACHUSETTS AND NEW-HAMPSHIRE,
SINCE THE REVOLUTION, WHO HAVE DECEASED.

Meshech Weare,	15 January,	1786,	73.
John Hancock,	8 October,	1793,	56.
John Langdon,	18 September,	1819,	79.
John Sullivan,	28 January,	1795,	54.
James Bowdoin,	6 November,	1790,	64.
Josiah Bartlett,	19 May,	1795,	65.
John T. Gilman,	31 August,	1828,	75.
Samuel Adams,	2 October,	1803,	81.
Increase Sumner,	7 June,	1799,	52.
Caleb Strong,	7 November,	1820,	75.
James Sullivan,	8 December,	1808,	64.
Christopher Gore,	1 March,	1827,	69.
Elbridge Gerry,	23 November,	1814,	70.
John Brooks,	1 March,	1825,	73.
William Eustis,	6 February,	1825,	75.

PRESIDENTS OF THE UNITED STATES,
WHO HAVE DECEASED.

George Washington,	14 December,	1799,	67.
John Adams,	4 July,	1826,	91.
Thomas Jefferson,	4 July,	1826,	83.

A CATALOGUE OF THE COUNSELLORS OF NEW-HAMPSHIRE,
FROM 1680 TO 1830.

UNDER THE ROYAL GOVERNMENT.

[The ages of those with this mark † are conjectured. Where a dash precedes a name, the time of appointment is uncertain.]

App.	Counsellors.	Residence.	Died.		Age
1680	John Cutt	Portsmouth	27 March,	1681	⎫
	Richard Martyn	Portsmouth		1693	⎪
	William Vaughan	Portsmouth		1719	⎬ 1
	Thomas Daniel	Portsmouth		1683	⎭
	John Gilman	Exeter	24 July,	1708	84†
	Christopher Hussey	Hampton		1685	75†
	Richard Waldron	Dover	27 June,	1689	80†
	Elias Stileman	New-Castle	19 Dec.	1695	78†
	Samuel Dalton	Hampton	22 August,	1681	
1681	Job Clements	Dover		1717	
	Robert Mason[2]	New-Castle		1688	58
	Richard Waldron	Portsmouth	30 Nov.	1730	80
	Anthony Nutter	Dover	19 Feb.	1686	

(1) These four would probably average 70 years each. (2) He died at Esopus, in New-York.

App.	Counsellors.	Residence.	Died.	Age.
1682	Walter Barefoote	New-Castle	1688 or 1689	53
	Richard Chamberlain			
1683	Nathaniel Fryer	New-Castle	13 August, 1705	
	Robert Elliot[1]	New-Castle		
	John Hinkes[2]	New-Castle		
	Edward Randolph[3]	Portsmouth	ret. to England.	
1684	James Sherlock			
	Francis Champernoon[4]		about 1686	
	Robert Wadleigh	Exeter		
1685	Henry Greene	Hampton	5 August, 1700	80
1692	John Usher	Boston	5 Sept. 1726	78
	Thomas Graffort[5]	Portsmouth	6 August, 1697	
	John Walford	Portsmouth		
	John Love			
	Peter Coffin[6]	Dover		
	John Gerrish	Dover	1714	68
	Nathaniel Weare	Hampton	13 May, 1718	87
1697	William Partridge	Portsmouth	3 Jan. 1729	74
1698	Joseph Smith	Hampton	9 Nov. 1717	64
	Kingsley Hall	Exeter	about 1736	
	Sampson Sheafe[5]	New-Castle	1724	76
	Peter Weare	Hamp.-Falls		
1702	Samuel Penhallow	Portsmouth	2 Dec. 1726	61
	John Plaisted	Portsmouth	about 1707	
	Henry Dow	Hampton	6 May, 1707	73
	George Jaffrey[7]	New-Castle	13 Feb. 1707	69
1710	Mark Hunking	Portsmouth		
1712	John Wentworth	Portsmouth	12 Dec. 1730	59
1715	George Vaughan	Portsmouth	Dec. 1725	49
1716	Richard Gerrish	Dover	1717	
	Theodore Atkinson	New-Castle	6 May, 1.19	50
	Shadrach Walton	New-Castle	3 Oct. 1741	83
	George Jaffrey	New-Castle	8 May, 1749	66
	Richard Wibird	Portsmouth	Oct. 1732	
	Thomas Westbrook	Portsmouth	1735	
1719	Thomas Packer	Portsmouth	1723	
1722	Archibald Macpheadris	Portsmouth	1728	
1724	John Ffrost[8]	New-Castle	25 Dec. 1732	51

(1) Living in 1745. (2) Living in 1707, and probably in 1722, when there is a deed from John Hinkes on record in Rockingham county.

(3) Randolph returned to England. (4) Champernoon was cousin to Sir Ferdinando Gorges. He lived sometime in York, Maine.

(5) Graffort and Sheafe removed to Boston and died there.

(6) Living in 1714 at the age of 83. (7) Died at Col. Appleton's in Ipswich.

(8) He was son of Major Charles Ffrost, who is noticed page 143. It might have been there stated that the major was born 20 July, 1631, the son of Nicholas Ffrost of Kittery, who was born at Tiverton, in England, in 1589, came very early to New-England, and died 20 July, 1663, aged 74. John, the grandson above mentioned, was born 1 March, 1682.— His wife was Mary, sister of Sir William Pepperell. After his death, she married successively Rev. Benjamin Colman, D. D., of Boston, and Rev.

App.	Counsellors.	Residence.	Died.		Age
1724	Jotham Odiorne	New-Castle	16	Aug.	1748 73
1728	Henry Sherburne	Portsmouth	29	Dec.	1757 83
1732	Richard Waldron	Portsmouth	23	Aug.	1753 60
	Joshua Peirce[1]	Portsmouth	7	Feb.	1743 72
	Benning Wentworth[2]	Portsmouth	14	Oct.	1770 75
	Benjamin Gamling	Portsmouth			1737 57
	Ephraim Dennet	Portsmouth			
	Theodore Atkinson[2]	New-Castle	22	Sept	1779 81
1733	Ellis Huske	Portsmouth			1755
	Joseph Sherburne	Portsmouth	3	Dec.	1744 64
1739	Richard Wibird	Portsmouth	25	Sept.	1765 63
1740	John Rindge	Portsmouth	6	Nov.	1740 45
———	John Downing		16	Sept.	1745 85
———	Samuel Smith		2	May,	1760 74
———	Joseph Blanchard	Dunstable	7	April,	1758 53
———	Sampson Sheafe	New-Castle			1772 91
———	Samuel Solley	Portsmouth			
1753	Daniel Warner	Portsmouth			1778
1754	Joseph Newmarch	Portsmouth			1765
1759	Mark H. Wentworth	Portsmouth	19	Dec.	1785
	James Nevin	Portsmouth	6	Feb.	1769 60
1761	John Nelson[3]	Portsmouth			1787
1762	William Temple	Portsmouth			1789
	Theodore Atkinson		28	Oct.	1769 33
	Nathaniel Barrell	Portsmouth			
1765	Peter Livius[4]	Portsmouth			1795 68†
1766	Jonathan Warner	Portsmouth	15	May,	1814 87
	Daniel Rindge	Portsmouth	12	Jan.	1799 68
	Daniel Peirce	Portsmouth	4	Dec.	1773
	Daniel Rogers	Portsmouth			
	George Jaffrey	Portsmouth	25	Dec.	1802 86
	Henry Sherburne	Portsmouth	30	March,	1767 58
———	Paul Wentworth	Somerswo'th			
1772	Peter Gilman	Exeter	1	Dec.	1788 84
	Thomas W. Waldron	Portsmouth	3	April,	1785 63
1774	John Sherburne	Portsmouth	10	March,	1797 76
	John Phillips	Exeter		April,	1795 76
1775	George Boyd[5]	Portsmouth			1787

Benjamin Prescott, of Danvers, Mass. She died in 1766. Mr. Ffrost had seventeen children. George, the 11th child and the sixth son, was a counsellor three years in the time of the Revolution, and a delegate to the old Congress. To his son George Ffrost, Esq., of Durham, the editor is indebted for the facts contained in this note.

(1) Sworn into office 18 January, 1733.
(2) Not sworn into office until 12 Oct. 1734. Gov. Belcher, in a letter, dated 15 Aug, 1734, speaking of the expense of their mandamuses, says, " I am told W. and A.'s mandamuses have already cost them about 100 guineas a piece."
(3) He went to Grenada, where it is believed he died about 1795.
(4) Died in England. W. Winthrop.
(5) He left the state, and was included in the act proscribing 76 persons, passed in 1778, and died on his return from England to this country.

App.	Counsellors.	Residence	In office.	Died.		Age.
1778	Meshech Weare	Hamp.-Falls	8	15 Jan.	1786	72
	Matthew Thornton	Londonderry	1	24 June,	1803	89
	William Whipple	Portsmouth	1	10 Nov.	1785	54
	Josiah Bartlett	Kingston	8	19 May,	1795	65
	Nathaniel Folsom	Exeter	1	26 May,	1790	64
	John ‡ Wentworth	Dover	8	10 Jan.	1787	40
	Ebenezer Thompson	Durham	5	15 Aug.	1~02	65
	Wyseman Clagett	Litchfield	1	4 Dec.	1784	63
	Jonathan Blanchard	Dunstable	3	16 July,	1788	50
	Samuel Ashley	Winchester1	4	18 Feb.	1792	71
	Benjamin Giles	Newport	1	9 Dec.	1787	70
	John Hurd	Haverhill	1			
1777	Nicholas Gilman	Exeter	7	7 April,	1782	52
	George Atkinson2	Portsmouth	3	13 Jan.	1805	66
	Timothy Walker	Concord	3	5 May,	1822	85
	Matthew Patten	Bedford	2	27 Aug.	1795	76
	Benjamin Bellows	Walpole	3	4 June,	1802	62
1779	Moses Nichols	Amherst	1	23 May,	1790	50
	Jacob Abbot3	Wilton	2	5 March,	1820	74
1780	George Atkinson	Portsmouth	1	See 1777.		
	John M'Clary	Epsom	4	16 June,	1801	82
	Timothy Farrar	New-Ipswich	1			
	Samuel Hunt	Charlestown	1	24 August,	1799	66
	Enoch Hale	Walpole	2			
	Charles Johnston	Haverhill	1	5 March,	1813	76
1781	Woodbury Langdon	Portsmouth	3	13 Jan.	1805	66
	George Ffrost	Durham	3	21 June,	1796	76
	John Hale	Hollis	1		1791	60
	Wyseman Clagett	Litchfield	2	See 1776		
	Benjamin Bellows	Walpole	3	See 1777		
	Francis Worcester	Plymouth	1			
1782	Timothy Farrar	See 1780	2			
	Jacob Abbot	Wilton	2	See 1779		
	Thomas Sparhawk	Walpole	2	31 Oct.	1802	64
	Charles Johnston	Haverhill	1	See 1780		
1783	Francis Worcester	See 1781.	1			

App.	Counsellors.	Residence	In office.	Died.		Age.
1784	John M'Clary	Epsom	1	16 June,	1801	82
	Joseph Badger	Gilmanton	1	14 Jan.	1809	61
	Francis Blood	Temple	1	Nov.	1814	79
	Moses Chase	Cornish	1	18 Oct.	1799	73
	Nathaniel Peabody	Atkinson	1	29 June,	1823	81
1785	John Sullivan	Durham	1	23 Jan.	1795	54
	Matthew Thornton	Merrimack	1	See 1776		
	Amos Shepard	Alstead	2	1 Jan.	1812	

(1) Afterwards of Claremont, where he died. (2) His name was originally George King. (3) Died at Brunswick, Maine.

App.	Counsellors.	Residence.	In office.	Died.	Age.
1785	Moses Dow	Haverhill	2	31 March, 1811	64
1786	Christopher Toppan	Hampton	1	28 Feb. 1818	83
	Joshua Wentworth	Portsmouth	1	19 Oct. 1809	67
	Robert Means	Amherst	1	24 Jan. 1823	80
1787	Joseph Gilman	Exeter	1	1806	68
	Ebenezer Thompson	Durham	1	See 1776	
	Daniel Emerson	Hollis	1	4 Oct. 1821	75
	Moses Chase	Cornish	1	See 1784	
	John Pickering	Portsmouth	1	11 April, 1805	67
1788	Peter Green	Concord	1	27 March, 1798	52
	Ebenezer Smith	Durham	1		
	Robert Wallace	Henniker	1	Jan. 1815	66
	Josiah Richardson	Keene	1	25 Feb. 1820	74
	William Simpson	Orford	1	1823	81
1789	John Pickering	Portsmouth	1	See 1787	
	Ichabod Rollins	Somersworth	1	31 Jan. 1800	
	Charles Barrett	New-Ipswich	1	21 Sept. 1808	63
	Sandford Kingsbury	Claremont	1		
	Jonathan Freeman	Hanover	8	20 August, 1808	63
1790	Christopher Toppan	Hampton	1	See 1786	
	Joseph Badger	Gilmanton	3	See 1784	
	Robert Wallace	Henniker	13	See 1788	
	Lemuel Holmes	Surry	4	died in Vermont	
1791	Nathaniel Rogers	Exeter	1	May, 1829	83
1792	Phillips White	S. Hampton	2	24 June, 1811	82
1793	Ebenezer Smith	See 1788	3		
1794	Christopher Toppan	Hampton	3	See 1786	
	Thomas Bellows	Walpole	5		
1795	Joseph Badger	Gilmanton	2	See 1784	
1797	Joseph Cilley	Nottingham	2	Aug. 1799	65
	Aaron Wingate	Farmington	6	24 Feb. 1822	78
	Russell Freeman[1]	Hanover	5	27 Dec. 1805	57
1799	James Sheafe	Portsmouth	1	6 Dec. 1829	74
	Samuel Stevens	Charlestown	6	17 Nov. 1823	88
1800	Joseph Blanchard	Chester	2		
1802	Levi Bartlett	Kingston	6	30 Jan. 1828	64
	David Hough	Lebanon	1		
1803	William Hale	Dover	2		
	Benjamin Pierce	Hillsborough	6		
	Daniel Blaisdell	Canaan	5		
1805	Joseph Badger	Gilmanton	4	See 1784	
	Nahum Parker	Fitzwilliam	2		
1807	Amasa Allen	Walpole	2	1 July, 1821	69
	Daniel Gookin	N. Hampton	1		
	William Tarleton	Piermont	2	26 March, 1819	68
1809	Elijah Hall	Portsmouth	8	22 June, 1830	87
	Richard Dame	Rochester	2	19 Sept. 1828	72
	Samuel Bell	Amherst	1		

(1) Murdered by Josiah Burnham.

App.	Counsellors	Residence.	In office.	Died	Age.
1809	Caleb Ellis	Claremont	2	9 May, 1816	49
	Benjamin J. Gilbert	Hanover	2		
1810	Jedidiah K. Smith	Amherst	4	17 Dec. 1828	58
1811	Nathaniel Upham	Rochester	2	10 July, 1829	56
	Ithamar Chase	Cornish	5	August, 1817	55
	Jonathan Franklin	Lyme	2		
1813	Nathan Taylor	Sanbornton	1		
	Enoch Colby	Thornton	5		
1814	Samuel Quarles	Ossipee	3		
	Benjamin Pierce	See 1803	2		
1816	Levi Jackson	Chesterfield	2	30 August, 1821	49
1817	John M. Page	Tamworth	3	May, 1826	48
	John Bell, jr.	Chester	5		
1818	Richard H. Ayer	Hooksett	5		
	Samuel Grant	Walpole	1		
	Jeduthun Wilcox	Orford	2		
1819	Aaron Matson	Stoddard	2		
	John French	Landaff	3		
1820	Richard Odell	Conway	3		
1821	Samuel Dinsmoor	Keene	1		
1822	Hunking Penhallow	Portsmouth	2	24 Sept. 1826	60
	Elijah Belding	Swanzey	2		
	Ezra Bartlett	Haverhill	3		
1823	Daniel C. Atkinson	Sanbornton	2		
	Jonathan Harvey	Sutton	2		
1824	Thomas C. Drew	Walpole	2		
	Daniel Hoit	Sandwich	2		
1825	Langley Boardman	Portsmouth	2		
	John Wallace	Milford	3		
	Caleb Keith	Wentworth	4		
1826	Jotham Lord	Westmorela'd	3		
1827	Francis N. Fisk	Concord	1		
	Andrew Peirce	Dover	2		
1828	Langley Boardman	See 1825	1		
	Matthew Harvey	Hopkinton	2		
1829	Francis N. Fisk	See 1827			
	Benning M. Bean	Moultonboro'	1		
	Joseph Healey	Washington			
	Stephen P. Webster	Haverhill			
1830	Thomas E. Sawyer	Dover			
	Jesse Bowers	Dunstable			

SECRETARIES OF STATE OF NEW-HAMPSHIRE,
FROM 1680 TO 1830.

[This list may not be complete, as the Council Records are missing for a number of years from the Secretary's office.]

App.	Names.	Discont'd	Died.	Age.
1680	Elias Stileman		1695	
1682	Richard Chamberlain			
1692	Thomas Davis			
1696	Henry Penny		1709	
1699	Sampson Sheafe		1724	76
1669	Charles Story	1714		
——	Samuel Penhallow		1726	61
——	Richard Waldron		1753	60
——	Theodore Atkinson		1779	81
——	Theodore Atkinson, jr.		1769	33
——	Theodore Atkinson		as above	
1775	Ebenezer Thompson		1802	68
1786	Joseph Pearson	1805	1822	85
1805	Philip Carrigain	1809		
1809	Nathaniel Parker	1810	1810	
1810	Samuel Sparhawk	1814		
1814	Albe Cady	1816		
1816	Samuel Sparhawk	1825		
1825	Richard Bartlett	1829		
1829	Dudley S. Palmer			

TREASURERS OF NEW-HAMPSHIRE,
SINCE THE REVOLUTION.

App.	Names.	Residence.	Dis.
1775	Nicholas Gilman	Exeter	1783
1783	John Taylor Gilman	Exeter	1794
1794	Oliver Peabody	Exeter	1805
1805	Nathaniel Gilman	Exeter	1813
1813	William Austin Kent	Concord	1816
1816	William Pickering	Greenland	1829
1828	Samuel Morril	Concord	1829
1829	William Pickering	Concord	1830
1830	Abner Bayley Kelly	Warner	

DELEGATES TO CONGRESS,
DURING THE CONFEDERATION OF THE STATES.*

Name.	Residence.	Death.		Age.
John Sullivan	Durham	22 Jan.	1795	54
Nathaniel Folsom	Exeter		1789	
Josiah Bartlett	Kingston	19 May,	1795	65
John Langdon	Portsmouth	18 Sept.	1819	79

* Some of the following were elected a second and third time. The records show that several others were elected, who declined the appointment.

Name.	Residence.	Death.	Age.
William Whipple	Portsmouth	28 Nov. 1785	54
Matthew Thornton	Londonderry	24 June, 1803	89
George Ffrost	Durham	21 June, 1796	76
Nathaniel Peabody	Atkinson	29 June, 1823	81
Woodbury Langdon	Portsmouth	13 Jan. 1805	66
Paine Wingate	Stratham		
Samuel Livermore	Portsmouth	May, 1803	71
Abiel Foster	Canterbury.	Feb. 1806	71
Nicholas Gilman	Exeter	7 April, 1782	52
John Wentworth		10 Jan. 1787	42
Phillips White	S. Hampton	24 June, 1811	82
John Taylor Gilman	Exeter	31 Aug. 1828	75
Jonathan Blanchard	Dunstable	16 July, 1788	50
Peirce Long	Portsmouth	31 March, 1789	

DELEGATES TO THE CONVENTION OF THE UNITED STATES, IN 1787.

John Langdon,   Portsmouth.
Nicholas Gilman,   Exeter.

SENATORS AND REPRESENTATIVES IN CONGRESS
UNDER THE FEDERAL CONSTITUTION.

SENATORS.

Commenced.		In office.	Commenced.		In office.
1789	John Langdon	12	1813	Jeremiah Mason	4
1789	Paine Wingate	4	1814	Tho. W Thompson	3
1793	Samuel Livermore	8	1817	Clement Storer	2
1801	Simeon Olcott	4	1817	David L. Morril	6
1801	James Sheafe	1	1819	John F. Parrott	6
1802	William Plumer	5	1823	Samuel Bell	–
1805	Nicholas Gilman	9	1825	Levi Woodbury	6
1807	Nahum Parker	3	1831	Isaac Hill	–
1810	Charles Cutts	3			

REPRESENTATIVES.

Commenced.		In office.	Commenced.		In office.
1789	Samuel Livermore	4	1811	John A. Harper	2
1789	Abiel Foster	2	1811	Samuel Dinsmoor	2
1789	Nicholas Gilman	8	1811	Obed Hall	2
1791	Jeremiah Smith*	6	1813	Samuel Smith‡	1
1793	John S. Sherburne	4	1813	Daniel Webster	4
1793	Paine Wingate	2	1813	Bradbury Cilley	4
1795	Abiel Foster	8	1813	William Hale	4
1797	Jonathan Freeman	4	1813	Roger Vose	4
1797	William Gordon	3	1813	Jeduthun Wilcox	4
1797	Peleg Sprague	2	1815	Charles H. Atherton	2
1800	James Sheafe†	1	1817	John F. Parrott	2
1800	Samuel Tenney	7	1817	Salma Hale	2
1801	George B. Upham	2	1817	Clifton Clagett	4
1801	Joseph Pierce	1	1817	Arthur Livermore	4
1802	Samuel Hunt	1	1817	Josiah Butler	6
1803	Silas Betton	4	1817	Nathaniel Upham	6
1803	David Hough	4	1819	Joseph Buffum, jr.	2
1803	Clifton Clagett	2	1819	William Plumer, jr.	6
1805	Thomas W Thompson	2	1821	Matthew Harvey	4
1805	Caleb Ellis	2	1821	Aaron Matson	4
1807	Daniel M. Durell	2	1821	Thomas Whipple	8
1807	Clement Storer	2	1823	Arthur Livermore§	2
1807	Jedidiah K. Smith	2	1823	Ichabod Bartlett	6
1807	Francis Gardner	2	1823	Titus Brown	4
1807	Peter Carleton	2	1823	Joseph Healey	4
1809	William Hale	2	1823	Jonathan Harvey	
1809	Nathaniel A. Haven	2	1827	David Barker, jr.	2
1809	James Wilson	2	1829	John Brodhead	
1809	John C. Chamberlain	2	1829	Joseph Hammons	
1809	Daniel Blaisdell	2	1829	Thomas Chandler	
1811	Josiah Bartlett	2	1829	Henry Hubbard	
1811	George Sullivan	2	1829	John W. Weeks	

* Mr. Smith resigned his seat after attending the May session of 1797, and Mr. Sprague was elected to supply the vacancy.

† Mr. Sheafe was elected in the place of Mr. Sprague, resigned, and took his seat in January, 1800.

‡ Mr. Smith resigned in 1814, and the vacancy was not filled.

§ Mr. Livermore was chosen in March, 1830.

TABLE shewing the Officers of Government in New-Hampshire in 1773; the authority by which they held their places; their annual salary or compensation; and the mode of their appointment.

Office.	Names of Officers.	The authority by which they held their places.	The annual value in proclamation or current money.	Mode of their appointment.
Governor & Commander in Chief.	JOHN WENTWORTH.	By the King's commission under the great seal of England.	£700 salary, voted annually by the assembly, and about £100 fees.	By the King.
Counsellors.	Theodore Atkinson, Daniel Warner, Mark H. Wentworth, Peter Livius, Jonathan Warner, Daniel Rindge, George Jaffrey, Daniel Rogers, Peter Gilman, Thomas W. Waldron, Paul Wentworth, (one vacancy.)	By the King's Mandamus.	7s. per diem, while they set as part of the Assembly, and nothing when they set as a Council of State, which was near as often as in their former capacity.	By the King.
Court of Appeals, and also of Supreme Probate.	The Governor and Council.	By President Cutt's commission and by laws of the Province.	22s. to the Gov. and 6s. to each Counsellor actually sitting in the case, for each action. About 5 entries in a year.	By the King's Counsellor in Mandamus as Counsellors.
Justices and Clerk of the Superior Court.	Theodore Atkinson, Meshech Weare, Leverett Hubbard and William Parker. Clerk, George King.	By Laws of the Province. By ditto.	£60 salary, annually voted by the Assembly, and about £24 each. £5 more to Chief Justice.	By the Governor with adv. council. App. by Court.
Justices and Clerks of the Inferior Court of Common Pleas.	Rockingham. Daniel Warner, Clement March, Jno. Phillips & Chris. Toppan. Clerk, Isaac Rindge.	By Laws of the Province.	£60, arising out of fees established by law. £100 ditto.	By the Gov. with advice Council. Elect. by Court.
	Strafford. John Wentworth, George Ffrost, Otis Baker & John Plummer. Clerk, Ebenezer Thompson.	By Laws of the Province.	£25 per annum, as above. 50 per annum, as above.	As above.
	Hillsboro'. Matth. Thornton, Sam'l Hobart, John Shepard & Samuel Blodget. Clerk, Stephen Holland.	By Laws of the Province.	£30 per annum. £50 per annum.	As above.

Office.	Names of Officers.	The authority by which they held their places.	The annual value in proclamation or current money.	Mode of their appointment.
Che-shire.	Daniel Jones, Samuel Ashley, Elisha Marsh, Benja. Bellows. Clerk, Simeon Jones.	By Laws of the Province.	£50 per annum.	As above.
Graf-ton.	John Hurd, Asa Porter, David Hobart, Bazaleel Woodward. Clerk, John Fenton.	By Laws of the Province.	£10 per annum.	As above.
Sheriffs.	Rockingham, John Parker. Strafford, Theopilus Dame. Hillsborough, Benjamin Whiting. Cheshire, Josiah Willard. Grafton, William Simpson.	By Laws of the Province.	£100 per annum. £ 70 per annum. £ 65 per annum. £ 70 per annum. £ 50 per annum.	By the Governor and Council, appointed and commissioned.
Judges of Probate.	Rockingham, John Sherburne. Strafford, Henry Rust. Hillsborough, John Goffe. Cheshire, Simeon Olcott. Grafton, John Fenton.	By the Governor's commission and Laws.	£ 65 per annum. £ 30 per annum. £ 25 per annum. £ 24 per annum. £ 18 per annum.	As above.
Registers of Probate.	Rockingham, William Parker. Strafford, John Wentworth. Hillsborough, Joshua Atherton. Cheshire, Thomas Sparhawk. Grafton, Jona. M. Sewall.	As above.	£ 65 per annum. £ 30 per annum. £ 25 per annum. £ 24 per annum. £ 18 per annum.	As above.
Admiralty { Judge. Register. Marshal.	Robert Auchmuty. Charles Russel. John Beck.	By Lords Com'rs Admiralty. By ditto. By com'n from the Judge.	£600 sterling. Fees on causes tried. Fees on business.	By the King. do. By Judge Adm.
Recorders of Deeds.	Rockingham, Joseph Peirce. Strafford, Thomas W. Waldron. Hillsborough, Samuel Hobart. Cheshire, Josiah Willard. Grafton, John Hurd.	By the Laws of the Province.	£ 65 per annum. £ 25 per annum. £ 30 per annum. £ 40 per annum. £ 30 per annum.	Elected annually by the Governor, Council and Assembly.

Office		Name	Method of appointment	Salary	How appointed
County Treasurers.	Rockingham,	Peter Gilman.	Justices of the Quarter Sessions.	£50 per annum.	By warrant.
	Strafford,	Thomas W. Waldron.		£20 per annum.	
	Hillsborough,	Samuel Hobart.		£20 per annum.	
	Cheshire,	Daniel Jones.		£20 per annum.	
	Grafton,	John Hurd.		£20 per annum.	
Prov. Judge Admiralty.		William Parker.	The Gov's com'n as Vice-Ad.	Generally about 8 guineas, arising from fees.	By commission from Governor.
Register do.		John Sherburne.	do.		
Advocate.		Samuel Livermore.	do.		
Marshal.		John Beck.	do.		
Secretary of Province.		Theodore Atkinson.	By mandamus from the King.	£100 per ann. including office, fire, candles, &c. £60 salary, granted annually by the Assembly, and £40 fees.	By commission from Governor.
Treasurer.		George Jaffrey.	By com'n from Governor.	£125 granted by Assembly, ann.	As above.
Attorney General.		Samuel Livermore.	By ditto.	£25, as above, and 45l. fees.	As above.
Surveyor Gen. of Lands.		George Sproule.	By ditto.	About 20 guineas, fees.	As above.
Receiver of Quit Rents.		John Hurd.	By ditto.	L.100 sterling per annum.	As above.
Receiver Powder Money.		Theodore Atkinson.	By ditto.	5 per centum on the amount.	As above.
Master of the Harbor.		John Briard.	By warrant from the Gov.	12l. s. per ann. from powder money.	As above.
Collector of the Customs.		George Meserve.	By com'n from the Com'rs of his Majesty's revenue.	About 600l. sterling.	Warrant com'rs.
Comptroller.		Robert Trail.	By ditto.	About 180l. sterling.	As above.
Naval Officer.		John Fisher.	By com'n from the Gov.	200l. per annum, by fees.	King's mandam.
Post-Master.		Eleazar Russel.	By com'n dep. P.M.G. Amer.	50l. per annum, salary	By dep. P. M.G.
Notaries Public.		Wyseman Clagett, John Wendell.	Licensed by the Archbishop of Canterbury.	14l. per annum, in fees.	By commission issued.
Major General.		Theodore Atkinson.	By the Governor.	Nothing.	By commission.
Brigadier General.		Peter Gilman.	ditto.	"	As above.

ORIGINAL PAPERS,

AND COPIES OF PUBLIC DOCUMENTS.

———

[This portion of the Appendix, excepting the articles numbered 14, 15, 23, 33, 54, 55 and 62, is printed from the *original manuscript copy* of Dr. BEL-KNAP, from which the first edition of the first volume was printed at Phil-adelphia in the year 1784. It was preserved by the late EBENEZER HAZ-ARD, Esquire, who superintended that volume while in the press, and was transmitted by him to the author or his family at Boston. It will be seen that sixteen of the articles, viz. Nos. 12, 13, 14, 15, 17, 18, 19, 20, 21, 26, 30, 33, 34, 50, 51 and 53, have never before appeared in the work. Those three numbered 14, 15 and 33, have been added by the editor. The others were prepared for the history by the author, but they were not published for want of room. The Wheelwright Indian deed of 1629, as it is indis-putably a forgery, is omitted, although the number and title of it are given to preserve the numerical arrangement of the papers. Excepting the numbers from No. 2 to No. 11, inclusive, the ancient spelling, being ex-ceedingly variable, and in many instances uncouth, has not been followed. As some doubts have rested on the genuineness of some of the early pa-pers, the former orthography has been retained in the numbers just men-tioned. It has also been retained in Nos. 55 and 59 merely as a curiosity.]

———

No. 1.   *Copy of a Deed from four Indian Sagamores to John Wheel-wright and others.*   17 *May*, 1629.

No. 2.   *An original letter from Thomas Eyre, one of the adventurers or company of Laconia, to Mr. Gibbins, their factor.*

LONDON, the last of May, 1631.

Mr. Gibbins,—Yours of the 8th April, 1630, from Plymouth I received and thereby took notice of your entertaining Roger Knight ; and here I present his wife 20s. pr. quarter at your de-sire and 3l. per quarter to yours. I hope by this they are both with you according to your desire. I wish all your wives with you, and that so many of you as desire wives had such as they desire ; for the adventurers desire not to be troubled with quarterly pay-ments.

Your next to me is dated the 21st of July last at Pascataquacke, I take notice of your complaints for want of the trade goods, and so much as lieth in me it shall be otherwise, especially if you send us returnes, doubt you not but that you shall be supplied from time to time unto your owne contents.

Your 3d lre to me is dated the 14th of August, by which I per-ceive divers of the commodities and provisions which you carried with you in the barke Warwicke, were not to your liking for which I am sorry. You know the trouble we had. I could not looke to Mr. Olden's and all besides. I hope by the Pide-Cowe you find it otherwise. I pray write me how you like the hatchetts sent you by that ship and how all goeth.

I like it well that your governor will have a stocke of boards at all times readie. I hope you will find something to relade both the Pide-Cowe and the Warwicke. I will now put on the sending of you the moddell of a saw-mill that you may have one going.

Your wife and children, Roger Knight's wife and one wife more we have already sent you, and more you shall have as you write for them.

Another lre I have from you of the 14th August, in which you write for another Mason. Wee have had enough to doe to goe so farre forwards as we have, as Capt. Keyes can tell you, yet now we begine to take hearte agayne, but the sight of returnes will be that which will indeede put life into us.

Among my New-England records I find your lre unto Capt. Mason of the 14th August last, wherein you give a good account of your times spent from the first of June until then, as also of the manner of your trade which was to Capt. Mason's liking. *We hope you will find out some good mines, which will be welcome newes unto us.*

By Mr. Glover we recd. lres from Capt. Neale, written as we think about the end of March last, write me I pray, what winter you had, and how you had your healthes and why Capt. Neale went not in Septem. last to discover the lakes, as he wrote he would, and why you did not write by that conveyance.

By the barke Warwicke we send you a factor to take charge of the trade goods ; also a soldier for discovrie &c.

Thus I commend you, and your wife, who by this I hope is with you to the protection of the almightie.

Your loving friend,
THO. EYRE.

Kept untill the 7th of June.

No. 3. *An original letter from the company to Ambrose Gibbins.*

LONDON, 5th Decemb. 1632.

Mr. Ambrose Gibbins,—Your sundrie letters we have received. Wee doe take notice of your care and paines in our plantation and doe wish that others had bine that way the same that you are and will wee hope soe continew. The adventures here have bine soe discouraged by reason of John Gibbes ill dealing in his fishing voiage, as alsoe by the small returnes sent hither by Capt. Neal, Mr. Herbert or any of their factors as that they have noe desire to proceed any farther, until Capt. Neale come hither to confer with them, that by conferrence with him they may settle things in a better order. Wee have written unto Capt. Neale to dismise the household, onlie such as will or canne live of themselves may stay upon our plantation in such convenient places as Capt. Neale, Mr. Godfrie and you shall think fitt ; and after conferrence had with Capt. Neale they shall have a reasonable quantity of land granted unto them by deed.

Wee praie you to take care of our house at Newichwannick and *to looke well to our vines,* also you may take some of our swine and goates, which wee pray you to preserve. Wee have committed the cheife care of our house at Pascattaway to Mr. Godfrie and written unto Mr. Warnerton to take care of our house at Straw-berry-bancke. Our desire is that Mr. Godfrie, Mr. Warnerton and you should joyne loveinglie together in all things for our good, and to advise us what our best course will be to doe another yeare.

You desire to settle yourself upon Sanders Point. The adven-turers are willing to pleasure you not only in this, in regard of the good report they have heard of you from tyme to tyme, but alsoe after they have conferred with Capt. Neale, they determyne some further good towards you for your further incouridgment.

Wee desire to have our fishermen increased, whereof we have written unto Mr. Godfrye. Wee thank you for assisting John Raymond, wee pray you still to be helpful to him that so he may dispatch and come to us with such returne as he hath, and if he hath any of his trade goods remayning unsold wee have willed him to leave them with you and wee doe hereby pray you to re-ceive them into your custody and to put them off with what con-veniency you canne, and to send us the retournes by the first shipp that comes. Thus we commend you and your wife to the protec-tion of the almightye.

Your loving friends,

JOHN MASON,	THO. WARNERTON,
HENRY GARDINER,	THO. EYRE, for my
GEO. GRIFFITH,	children.

No. 4. *Copy of a letter from Ambrose Gibbins to the company.*

After my umble duty remembred unto your worships, I pray for your good health and prosperity. These are certifying your wor-ship for the goods I have received from you. I have delivered unto Mr. John Raymon 76lb and 4 ounses of beaver, 10 otters, 6 musquashes and on martin more, that Captain Neale had 358lb and ii ounses of beaver and otter, 17 martins, on black fox skin, on other fox skin, 3 racoon skins, 14 musquashes two of them with stones. Mr Raymon's present departing and the intermixing of all the trade goods in my care until Mr. Vaughan com I cannot give you any satisfaction for the account of trade. I did advise Mr. Raymon to returne with all speede unto you. Your letters I received the 7th of June. At larg I will write if God wil by the next. Thus taking my leave I comit your worship to Almighty God.

Your worship's at command,

AMBROSE GIBBINS.

From Newichwanicke,
this 24th of June, 1633.

No. 5.   *Copy of another from Gibbins to the company.*

Newichwanicke, July 13, 1633.

Right honourable, right worshippful and the rest, my humble servis rembred. Your letter dated the 5th of December and Mr. Ares letter third of April I received the seventh of June. The detaining of the former letter hath put you to a great charge in the plantation. For my care and paines I have not thought it much although I have had very little encouradgement from you and here. I do not doubt of your good will unto mee. For your fishing, you complain of Mr. Gibbes : A Londoner is not for fishing, neither is there any amity betwixt the West countrimen and them. Bristo or Barnstable is very convenient for your fishing shipes. It is not enough to fit our shipes to fish but they must be sure (God will) to be at their fishing place the beginning of February and not to come to the land when other men have half their viage.

Mr. Warnerton hath the charge of the house at Pascatawa and hath with him William Cooper, Rafe Gee,* Roger Knight, and his wife, William Dermit and on boy. For your house at Newichwannicke, I seeing the necessity will doe the best I can there and elsewhere for you until I hear from you againe. Advise I have sent but not knowing your intentes I cannot wel enlarge but I refer you to Mr. Herbert and Mr. Vaughan. For my settlement at Sanders-Point and the further good you intend me I humbly thank you I shall do the best I can to be grateful. I have taken into my handes all the trade goods that remains of John Raymon's and Mr. Vaughan's and will with what convenience I may put them of. *You complain of your returnes ; you take the coorse to have little ; a plantation must be furnished with cattle and good hir'd hands, and necessaries for them and not thinke the great lookes of men and many words will be a meanes to raise a plantation.* Those that have been here this three year some of them have neither meat, money nor clothes, a great disparagement. I shall not need to speak of this, you shall hear of it by others. For myself, my wife and child and four men we have but half a barrel of corne; beefe and porke I have not had but on peese this three months, nor beare this four months ; for I have for two and twenty months had but two barrels of beare and two barrels and four booshel of malt, our number commonly hath bin ten. I nor the servantes have neither money nor clothes, I have been as sparing as I could, but it will not doe. These four men with me is Charles Knell, Thomas Clarke, Steven Kidder, and Thomas Crockitt, three of them is to have for their wages until the first of March four pounds per peese and the other for the year six pounds which in your behalf I have promised to satisfy in money or beaver at ten shillings per pound, If there were necessarys for them for clothing there would not bee much for them to receive. You may perhaps think that fewer men would serve me but I have sometimes on C [*one hundred*] or more Indians and far from neybors : These that I have I can set to pale

* [Probably the same as Ralph Goe, mentioned in Adams' Annals, p. 18, as of Pascataqua in 1631.]

in ground for corne or garden. I have digged a wel within the palizado, where is good water, I have that to close with timber. More men I could have and more employ, but I rest thus until I hear from you. *The vines that were planted will come to little, they prosper not in the ground they were set,* them that groo natural are veri good of divers sorts. I have sent you a note of the beaver taken by me at Newichwanick, and how it hath gon from me. George Vaughan hath a note of all the trade goodes in my custody of the old store John Ramon's and George Vaughan's accomtes, but the beaver beinge disposed of before I could make the divident I cannot see but it must be all onpackt and be divided by you. The governor departed from the plantation the fifteenth of July in the morning. So for this time I end, committing you to the protection of the Almighty and ever rest your loving servant.

AMBROSE GIBBINS.

No. 6.   *Copy of a letter from Walter Neal and Thomas Wiggin, to the Company, relating to a division of the lands of Pascataqua,* 1633.

[The following is the letter supposed to be spurious. See note on it, pages 12 and 13 of this volume.]

Much honoured,—In obediance to your commands have survaied the river from the mouth of the harbor to Squamscutt falls, and liquise from the harbor's mouth by the sea side to the Massachusetts bounds, and find that the bounds of your pattents will not aford more than for two towns in the river of Piscataway and the remainder will make another good towne having much salt marsh in it. And because you would have foure townes named as you desired wee have treated with a gentleman who has purchased a trackt of land of the Indyans at Squamscutt falls, and your land running up to the said falls on one side of the river from the falls about a mile downward, said gentlemen having a mind to said land on your side to a certain crike and one mile backward from the river which we agreed on and the crike is called Weelewright's, the gentleman's name being Weelewright and he was to name said plantation (when settled) *Exeter.* And the other two towns in the river, the one *North-ham* and *Portsmouth* the other. Bounded as followeth, viz. Portsmouth runes from the harbor's mouth by the sea aide to the entrance of a little river between two hed lands which we have given the names of Little Bore's-hed, and the Grate Bore's-hed, and from the mouth of that little river to go on a strait line to the aforesaid creeke which we have named Weeleright's creeke and from thens down the river to the harbor's mouth where it began. And North-ham is the bounds of all the land of Hilton's Point side. And the other land from the little river between the two Boores-Heds to run by the sea till it meets with the line between the Massachusets and you, and so to run from the sea by said Massathusets line into the woods eight miles and from thence atwart the woods to meet with Portsmouth line neere

Wheleright's creek and that tracte of land to be called *Hampton.* So that their is foure towns named as you desired but Exeter is not within the bounds of your pattents. But the grete dificulty is the agreement about the dividing line between the pattent of the twenty thousand acres belonging to the company of Laconyah and the pattent of Bluddy poynt the river running so intrycate, and Bluddy poynt patent bounds from thence to Squamscutt falls to run three miles into the woods from the water side. But for your better understanding thereof wee have sent you a draft of it according to our best skill of what we know of it at present, and have drawn a dividing line between the two pattents, so that Portsmouth is part of both pattents and Hampton we apprehend will be holly in the twenty thousand acres pattent, and North-ham is the bounds of Hilton's point pattent. If what we have don be to your likinge wee shall think our time well spent and what further commands you will please to lay on us we shall readily obeye to the utmost of our power. Wee humbly take leve and subscribe ourselves, Your devoted and most humble servants,

North-ham on Piscataway river, in ⎱ WALTER NELE,
New-England, 13 Augst 1633. ⎰ THOMAS WIGGIN.

Superscribed, To John Mason Esq. governor of Portsmouth to be communicated to the pattentes of Laconiah and Hilton's point, humbly present in London.

Wee under written being of the government of the province of Maine doe affirm that the above letter written and sent by Walter Nele and Thomas Wiggin and directed to John Mason Esq. governor of Portsmouth to be communicated to the pattentes of Laconiah and Hilton's point, is a trew copia compared with the originall. And further wee doe affirm that there was foure grete gunes brought to Piscataqua which ware given by a marchant of London for the defence of the river, and at the same time the Earle of Warwicke, Sr Ferdenando Gorges, Capt. John Mason and the rest of the pattentees sent an order to Capt. Walter Nele and Captn. Thomas Wiggin ther agents and governor at Piscataway to make choise of the most convenient place in the said river to make a fortefecatyon for the defence thereof, and to mount those foure gunes giveen to the place, which accordingly was done by Capt. Walter Nele and Capt. Thomas Wiggin and the pattentes servants, and a draft was sent of the place that they had made choice of to the said Earle and company, and the draft did containe all the necke of land in the north este side of the grete island that makes the grete harbor, and they gave it the name of Fort-poynt, and alloted it so far backe into the island about a bow-shoat to a grete high rocke whereon was intended in time to set the principall forte.

That the above is all truth wee affirme, and by the desire of Capt. Walter Nele and Capt. Thos. Wiggen wee have ordered this wrighting to ly in our files of records of their doings therein. In witness whereof wee have hereunto sett our hands and seles at Gorgeana, in the province of Maine, in New-England, 20th August 1633.

RICH. VINES, (Seal.)
HENRY JOCELYN, (Seal.)

No. 7. *An original letter from Sir Ferdinando Gorges and Capt. John Mason to Messrs. Wannerton and Gibbins.*

Mr. Wannerton and Mr. Gibbins,—These are to let you know that wee with the consent of the rest of our partners have made a division of all our land lying on the north east side of the harbor, and river of Pascataway ; of the quantities of which lands and bounds agreed upon for every man's part we send you a coppie of the draft, desiring your furtherance with the advice of Capt. Norton and Mr Godfrey to set out the lynes of division betwixt our lands and the lands of our partners next adjoining, because we have not onlie each of us shipped people present to plant upon our owne landes at our own charge, but have given direction to invite and authoritie to receive such others as may be had *to be tenants,* to plant and live there for the more speedie peopling of the countrie. And whereas there is belonging unto me Sri Ferdnando Gorges, and unto Capt. Mason for himself and for Mr. John Cotton and his deceased brother Mr. William Cotton, both whose interests Capt. Mason bath bought, the one halfe of all matters mentioned in the inventorie of houshold stuffe and implements left in trust with you by Capt. Neale, whereunto you have subscribed your names and whereof a coppie is herewith sent, we desire you to cause an equal division as neere as possible may to be made of all the saied matters menconed in the inventorie inkinde, or if some of them cannot be so divided then the on halfe to be made equall to the other in valew of all the saied matters, except the cattell and suites of apparell and such other things as belong perticularly to Capt. Mason, and to deliver the said one halfe of all the saied matters soe to be divided, unto Mr Henry Jocelyn for the use of our plantations, taking an inventory thereof under his hand of all you shall soe deliver hime, and making certificate to us thereof. And for your soe doeing this shall be you suffitient warrant and discharge. And so wee rest,

Your verie lovinge friends,

Portsmouth, Maye 5, 1634.

FERDIN. GORGE, JOHN MASON.

No. 8. *An original letter from Capt. John Mason to Ambrose Gibbins.*

Mr. Gibbins,—These people and provisions which I have now sent with Mr. Jocelyne are to sett upp two mills upon my own division of lands lately agreed upon betwixt our adventurers ; but I thinke not any of them will adventure this yeare to the plantation besides Sr Ferdinando Gorges and myself, for which I am sorrye in that so good a business (albeit hitherto it hath bene unprofitable) should be subject to fall to the ground. Therefore I have strayned myself to doe this at this present, and could have wished that the rest would have joyned to have sent you some provisions for trade and support of the place, but that failieing I have directed to you as a token from myselfe one hogshead of mault to make

you some beare. The servants with you and such others as re-
maine upon the companies chardge are to be discharged and payed their wages out of the stocke of beaver in your hands at the
rate of 12s. the pound, whereof I thinke the company will write
you more at large. And wee have agreed to devide all our mova-
bles mentioned in the inventory that Capt. Neale brought home,
which were left in trust with you and Mr Wannerton. I bought
Mr. Cotton's and his brother's parte of all their adventures ; so
that the halfe of all belongs to Sr Ferdinando Gorges and myselfe,
and of that halfe three quarters will be due to me and one quarter
to Sr Ferdinando. These things being equally divided they are
to be delivered to Mr. Jocelyne, my three partes of the halfe, and
the other fourth to whom Sr Ferdinando shall appointe. And you
must afford my people some house roome in Newichewannocke
house, and the cowes and goates which are all mine, and 14 swine
with their increase, some ground to be upon till we have some
place provided upon new divided land, or that you receive my
further order. A copie of the division of the lands is herewith
sent unto you.

The stockinges and the mault and the suites of cloathes and
suggar and raysinges and wine that was delivered by Mr. Bright
and Mr. Lewes I have not received any satisfaction for, wherein I
must crave your helpe and such satisfaction as may be sent by this
shipp.

*The christall stoanes you sent are of little or no valew unless they
were so great as to make drinking cuppes or some other workes, as pil-
lers for faire lookeinge glasses or for garnishinge of rich cabinets.
Good iron or lead oare I should like better of if it could be found.*

I have disbursed a great deal of money in your plantation and
never received one penny, but *hope if there were once a discoverie
of the lakes that I should in some reasonable time be reimbursed again.*
I pray you helpe the mr. what you can to some of the best iron
stoane for ballast, and in case he want other ladeinge to fill the
shipp upp with stockes of cypress wood and cedar. Let me hear
from you of all matters necessary, and wherein I may doe you
any pleasure I shall be reddie, and so with my heartie commendations, I rest your verie loveing friend,

Portsmouth, May 5th, 1634.   JOHN MASON.
(Received 10th July, 1634.)

No. 9.   *Answer to the foregoing.*

Sir,—Your worship have done well in setting forward your
plantaçon, and for your milles they will prove beneficial unto you
by God's assistance. I would you had taken this coorse sooner,
for the marchants I shall be very cautyouse how I deale with any
of them while I live. But God's will be done. I and the world
doth judge that I could not in these my days have spent my time
for noethinge. For their sending trade and support I desire it
not. I have supported but now sonke under my burthen, the
more I thinke on this, the more is my griefe.

I have received the hogsd. of mault that you sent me, giveing you humble thanks for the same. The servants that were with me are discharged and payed their wages for the yeare past and I have delivered unto Mr. Wannerton 43lb. of beaver to pay those that were with him for the year past. For the paying of the servants there old wages or the dividing of the goods I expect a general letter, if not then to heare further from your worshippe. Your carpenters are with me and I will further them the best I can. Capt. Neale appoynted me two of your goats to keepe, at his departinge, I praise God they are 4. Of the goods that Mr. Bright left I only recd. of Capt. Neale 4 bushells of mault and at several times 8 gallons of sacke, and from Mr. Wannerton 7 bushels and 1 peck of mault, 5 lb. and halfe of sugar and 3 pr of children stockings and 97 lb. of beefe which was of an old cow that Mr. Wannerton killed, being doubtful that she would not live over the winter. For these I will pay Mr. Jocelyn for you.

I perceive you have a great mynd to the lakes, and I as great a will to assist you. If I had 2 horses and 3 men with me I would by God's helpe soon resolve you of the situation of it, but not to live there myselfe.

The Pide-Cow arrived the 8th Julie, the 13th day she cast anchor some halfe a mile from the fall, the 18th day the shippee unladen, the 19th fell down the river, the 22d day the carpenters began about the mill, the 5th of August the *iron stoane* taken in the shipe. There is of 3 sorts, on sorte that the myne doth cast fourth as the tree doth gum, which is sent in a rundit. On of the other sortes we take to be very rich, there is great store of it. For the other I know not; but may it please you to take notice of the waight and measure of every sort, before it goeth into the furnace and what the stone of such waight and measure will yeeld in Iron. This that 'e take to be the best stone is one mile to the southward of the great house* it is some 200 rodd in length, 6 foote wide, the depth we know not, for want of tooles for that purpose we tooke onely the surface of the mine.

I have paled in a piece of ground and planted it. If it please God to send us a drie time, I hope there will be 8 or 10 quarters of corne. You have heare at the great house 9 cowes, 1 Bull, 4 Calves of the last yeare, and 9 of this yeare they prove very well, farre better than ever was expected, they are as good as your ordinary cattle in England and the goates prove some of them very well both for milk and breed. If you did send a shippe for the westerne Islands of 6 score tunne or thereabouts for cowes and goates it would be profitable for you. A stocke of iron worke to be put away with your boardes from the mill will be good, nayles, spikes, lockes, hinges, iron workes for boats and pinaces, twine, canvis, needles and cordage, pitch and tarr, graples, ankers, and necessarys for that purpose.

Sr I have written unto Mr. John Round to repaire unto your worship, he is a silver smith by his trade but hath spent much time and means about iron, may it please you to send for him, he

---

* The great house stood opposite to the house of Mr. Temple Knight.

dwelleth in Mogull street, if you are acquainted with any finer or mettle man enquire of him and as you see cause send for him, he is well seene in all myneralls if you deale with him he will give you a good light for your proceedings.

The 6th of August, the shippe ready to set sayle for Saco to load cloave boardes and pipe staves. A good husband with his wife to tend the cattle and to make butter and cheese will be profitable ; for maides they are soon gone in this country. For the rest I hope Mr. Jocelyn for your own particulars will satisfie you for I have not power to examen it. This with my humble service to your worship, I rest your ever lovinge servant,

AMBROSE GIBBINS.

Newichwannock,
the 6th of August 1634.

No 10. *An original Letter from George Vaughan to Mr. Ambrose Gibbins.*

Boston, August 20, 1634.

Mr. Gibbins,—We only waite for a faire wind. I shall acquaint Mr. Mason and the rest of the owners fully of what you and I have formerly discourst and if they give me incouradgment hope shall see you againe the next yere. Lookeing over my papers found the inclosed, it being the division of the Townes and the copia of what Capt. Nele and Capt. Wiggins wroate hoome to the Patentees of Laconiah and Hilton's poynt. It may be of som use to you hereafter, therefore sent it you, *leste Capt. Wiggins should make another Bluster.* Which with my kind Love to you & your spouse and little Beck, I am your assured frend,

GEORGE VAUGHAN.

No. 11. *Another from the same.*

London, 10th April, 1636.

Loving frend Gibbens,—Wee put into Ireland goinge home, and there was taken sike and lefte behind, and laye so long before I got well that it was the latter end of December laste before I got to London, and *Mr. Mason was ded.* But I spoke with Sr Ferdinando Gorges and the other owners, but they gave me no incouradgment for New-England. I acquainted them fully of what you and I discoursed, but they were quite could in that matter, Mr. Mason being ded and Sr Ferdinando minding only his one divityon.— He teles me he is geting a pattente for it *from the king* from Piscataqua to Sagadehocke, and that betwene Meremacke and Piscataqua he left for Mr. Mason, *who if hee had lived would a tooke a pattent for that also,* and so I suppose the affairs of Laconia is ded also. I intend to goe for the Este Indyes, a frend of mine have made mee a very good proffer and I thinke to take up with it. Which is what offers at present. Thus with my kind love to you and your wife and daughter, I am your loving friend,

GEORGE VAUGHAN.

(The ten preceding papers are in the Recorder's office for Rockingham county.)

No. 12. *Combination for government at Exeter, with the forms of oaths for rulers and people.*

[Not inserted in the former editions.]

Whereas it hath pleased the Lord to move the heart of our dread sovereign Charles, by the grace of God, King, &c. to grant license and liberty to sundry of his subjects to plant themselves in the western parts of America :—We his loyal subjects, brethren of the church in Exeter, situate and lying upon the river Pascataqua, with other inhabitants there, considering with ourselves the holy will of God and our own necessity, that we should not live without wholesome laws and civil government among us, of which we are altogether destitute, do in the name of Christ and in the sight of God combine ourselves together to erect and set up among us such government as shall be to our best discerning agreeable to the will of God, professing ourselves subjects of our Sovereign Lord King Charles, according to the liberties of our English colony of Massachusetts, and binding of ourselves solemnly by the grace and help of Christ, and in his name and fear, to submit ourselves to such godly and christian laws as are established in the realm of England to our best knowledge, and to all other such laws which shall upon good grounds be made and enacted among us according to God, that we may live quietly a peaceably together in all godliness and honesty. Mo. 8. D. 4. 1639.

John Wheelwright,
Augustine Storer,
Thomas Wright,
William Wentworth,
Henry Elkins,
George Walton,
Samuel Walker,
Thomas Petit,
Henry Roby,
William Winborne,
Thomas Crawley,
Christopher Helme,

Darby Field,
Robert Read,
Edward Rishworth,
Francis Matthews,
Godfrey Dearborne,
William Wardhall,
Robert Smith,
Ralph Hall,
Robert Seward,
Richard Bulgar,*
Christopher Lawson,
George Barlow,

Richard Morris,
Nicholas Needham,
Thomas Wilson,
George Rawbone,
William Cole,
James Wall,
Thomas Leavit,
Edmund Littlefield,
John Cramme,
Philemon Purmot,
Thomas Wardhall.

The Elder's or Ruler's Oath.

You shall swear by the great and dreadful name of the high God, maker and governor of heaven and earth, and by the Lord Jesus Christ, the prince of the kings and rulers of the earth, that in his name and fear you will rule and govern his people according to the righteous will of God, ministering justice and judgment on the workers of iniquity, and ministering due encouragement and countenance to well doers, protecting of the people so far as in you lieth, by the help of God from foreign annoyance and inward disturbance, that they may live a quiet and peaceable life in all godliness and honesty. So God be helpful and gracious to you and yours in Christ Jesus.

* This name is erroneously *Biellyer* in Hazard's Collections and in Coll. N. H. Hist. Soc. i. 322.

The Oath of the People.

We do here swear by the great and dreadful name of the high God, maker and governor of heaven and earth, and by the Lord Jesus Christ, the king and saviour of his people, that in his name and fear, we will submit ourselves to be ruled and governed according to the will and word of God, and such wholesome laws and ordinances as shall be desired therefrom by our honored rulers, and the lawful assistants, with the consent of the people, and that we will be ready to assist them by the help of God, in the administration of justice and preservation of the peace, with our bodies and goods and best endeavors according to God. So God protect and save us and ours in Jesus Christ.

(Taken from the Town Records of Exeter.)

No. 13. *The Combination for Government at Dover.*

Whereas sundry mischiefs and inconveniences have befallen us, and more and greater may, in regard of want of civil government, his most gracious Majesty having settled no order for us to our knowledge—We, whose names are underwritten, being inhabitants upon the river Pascataqua, have voluntarily agreed to combine ourselves into a body politic, that we may the more comfortably enjoy the benefit of his Majesty's laws, together with all such laws as shall be concluded by a major part of the freemen of our society, in case they be not repugnant to the laws of England and administered in behalf of his Majesty. And this we have mutually promised and engaged to do, and so to continue till his excellent Majesty shall give other orders concerning us. In witness whereof, we have hereunto set our hands, October 22, [1640] in the 16th year of the reign of our Sovereign Lord Charles, by the grace of God, King of Great Britain, France and Ireland, defender of the faith, &c.

THOMAS LARKHAM,
RICHARD WALDRON,
WILLIAM WALDRON,*
with 38 more.†

(From Hubbard's History of New-England.)

No. 14. *Petition of the Inhabitants of Portsmouth.*

To the honored General Court, assembled at Boston this present month of May, 1653.

The humble petition of the inhabitants of the town at present called *Strawberry-Bank*, sheweth :

That whereas your petitioners petitioned to the last General

---

* William Waldron was their recorder. He afterward removed to Saco and was drowned in Kennebunk river, in September, 1646. [Hubbard.]
Edward Colcot was sometime governor of this plantation. Ibid.

† [The names of these 38 cannot be found.]

Court to grant unto the said inhabitants a competent portion of land to make us a township, whereby we may be enabled to subsist and be useful to the church and commonwealth, our desire is, that this honored court will be pleased to shew their favor and good will towards us and willingness to accommodate us to the uttermost. And for that purpose, hath desired the honored Captain Wiggin to bring his patent to this present court.

Now may it please this honored court to take our case into consideration and consider of our extreme necessities : First, in respect of the number of families which are between 50 and 60, of which some are constrained to move for want of land to accommodate them with their stock : Secondly, the quality of the land we live on is so bad, it's incredible to believe, except those which have seen it : Thirdly, the place being settled a plantation the first of any in these parts, and our willingness in submitting to your government : Fourthly, that all the neighboring plantations about us which were settled since we, have their townships settled and bounded; only we as yet have none: Fifthly, that whereas there is much benefit by saw mills in other towns in this river and adjacent towns, there is none in this town, but only one which was never perfected, nor like to be.

We humbly entreat this honored court to take into their view this neck of land which we live upon, which nature itself hath bounded with the Maine sea and river, as may be seen by the draft of the river, which was presented to the last General Court and now presented again by our deputy, which neck of land is far less than any neighboring town about us.

The desire of your humble petitioners is, that this honored court would grant us the neck of land, beginning in the great bay at a place called Cotterill's Delight, and running to the sea according to our former petition presented to the last General Court.

And whereas the name of this plantation at present being STRABERY BANKE, accidentally so called by reason of a bank where strawberries *was* found in this place. Now your petitioners humbly desire to have it called *Portsmouth*, being a name most suitable for this place, it being the river *mouth* and *good harbor as any in this land*—And your petitioners shall humbly pray.

> BRIAN PENDLETON,
> RENALD FERNALD,
> RICHARD CUTT,
> SAMUEL HAINES,
> JOHN SHERBURNE,
> In behalf of the rest.

On this petition, it was first proposed to postpone, " because of Mr. Mason's claim to the land;" afterwards granted 28 May, 1653, and allowed to be called PORTSMOUTH, " and the line of the township of Portsmouth to reach from the sea, by Hampton line to Winnicowett river leaving the proprietors to their just rights."

(From the Massachusetts Colony Files.)

No. 15. *Declaration of John Allen, Nicholas Shapleigh and Thomas Lake respecting the Dover and Swampscot Patents.*

The General Court ordering that the petitioners, John Allen, Nicholas Shapleigh and Thomas Lake, might make a brief declaration of their right in the two patents, Swampscot and Dover, (November, 1654.)

We humbly present to this honored court as followeth :

1. That Mr. Edward Hilton was possessed of this land about the year 1628, which is about 26 years ago.

2. Mr. Hilton sold the said land to some merchants of Bristol, who had it in possession for about 2 years.

3. The Lord Say, the Lord Brook, Sir Richard Saltonstall, Sir Arthur Haslerigg, Mr. Bosville, Mr. Wyllys, Mr. Whiting, Mr. Hewett and others bought the said land of Bristol merchants and they have paid £2150. They being writ unto by the governor and magistrates of the Massachusetts, who encouraged them to purchase the said lands of the Bristol men, in respect they feared some ill neighborhood from them, as some in this honored court may please to remember.

4. The lords and gentlemen engaged the said land (so purchased) about 9 years, and placed more inhabitants at Dover, some of which came over at their cost and charges, and had their several letters set forth unto them.

5. The 14th of ye 4 mo. 1641, Mr. Wyllys, Mr. Saltonstall, Mr. Holyoke, and Mr. Makepeace, for themselves and partners, put the said patent under the government of the Massachusetts, reserving 1-3 of Dover patent, and the whole of the south part of the river, to the lords and gentlemen, and the said court confirmed the lands on them, their heirs and assigns forever, as by the said contract fully appears, the 14th 4th mo. 1641, and the 2-3 of Dover patent should remain to the inhabitants of Dover.

6. The 7 mo. 1642, Mr. Samuel Dudley and others were appointed by the court to lay out the limits of Dover according to the agreement with Mr. Whiting and company, and that nothing be done to the prejudice of Mr. Whiting and company appears per the court record 7 mo. 1642.

7. The 7 mo. 1643, the marsh and meadows in the great bay and 400 acres of upland was granted to Dover, reserving the right to the proprietors.

Now we humbly pray this honored court to take into consideration that, this conditional grant to Dover was 2 years and 3 months after your contract with Mr. Whiting and company, and 15 years after the owners had purchased and possessed it, during which time, the whole patent was twice sold and several parts also, and also it was enjoyed by the owners 13 years before the honored court challenged any interest in the said land by the extent of your patent. And that this honored court will be pleased to grant a division of the said lands according as you have formerly ordered.

[Copied from the Massachusetts files and communicated to the editor by Mr. Joshua Coffin.]

No. 16. *Copy of a report of a Committee of Reference on the petition of Robert Mason, Edward Godfrey, and others to the king,* (in 1661.)

To the King's most excellent Majesty,

According to your majesty's reference upon the petition of Robert Mason, Edward Godfrey, and others, hereunto annexed, bearing date at Whitehall, the seventeenth of November, 1660, we have heard the claims and complaints of the petitioners, and also summoned by process publicly executed at the exchange on the 21st day of January last against all persons interested in that business, but none appeared but Capt. John Leverett, who acknowledged that formerly he was commissionated as an agent of the corporation of Boston in New-England, but that now he had no authority to appear or act on their behalf.

Upon producing of divers letters patents and examination of witnesses, we find, That Capt. John Mason, grandfather to Robert Mason, one of the petitioners, and Edward Godfrey, another of the petitioners, by virtue of several letters patents under the great seal of England granted unto them and others by your majesty's late royal father, by themselves and their assigns have been in actual and quiet possession of several tracts, parcels and divisions of land in New-England, as in and by the said letters patents is particularly expressed, and that the said Capt. John Mason and the said Edward Godfrey did expend and lay out considerable sums of money in settling plantations and colonies there; That the said Edward Godfrey has lived there for five and twenty years, having undergone and discharged the office of governor of the province of Maine with much reputation of integrity and justice, endeavoring the regulation and government of those parts, where he lives according to the known and settled laws of this kingdom; That notwithstanding, the said Edward Godfrey has not only been turned out of his said place of governor, but has been utterly outed and dispossessed of his lands and estate in that country, which the inhabitants of the Massachusetts have forcibly seized and still do detain the same from him; That it appears as well by testimony of witnesses as by a copy of the letters patents that they were not to act any thing repugnant to the laws of England, nor to extend their bounds and limits of the said corporation farther than three miles northward of Merrimack river, and as a memorial and evidence thereof, the governor of the Massachusetts did set up a house about thirty years since, which is called *the bound house,* and is known by that name to this day, and with this division and assignment or lot of land the inhabitants and patentees of the said corporation of the Massachusetts rested content for the space of sixteen years together, until about the year 1652, they did enlarge and stretch their line about threescore miles beyond their known and settled bounds aforesaid; and have thereby not only invaded and encroached upon the plantations and inheritances of the petitioners and other your majesty's subjects, but by menaces and armed forces compelled them to submit to their usurped and arbitrary government, which they have declared to be independent of this your majesty's crown of England, and not subordinate thereunto.

It appears further by the witnesses, that the colony of Massachusetts has for these many years past endeavored to model and contrive themselves into a free state or commonwealth without any relation to the crown of England, assuming on themselves the name and style of a commonwealth, issuing of writs in their own name, imposing of oaths to be true unto themselves contrary to that of allegiance, coining of money with their own stamps and signatures, exercising an arbitrary power over the estates and persons of all such as submit not unto their government, allowing them no appeals to England, and some have been so bold as publicly to affirm, that if his majesty should send them a governor, that the several towns and churches throughout the whole country under their government did resolve to oppose him, and others have said that before they of New-England would or should submit to any appeal to England, they would sell that country or plantation to the king of Spain.*

That by reason of the premises the said Robert Mason and Edward Godfrey have been damnified in their plantations and estates to the value of five thousand pounds, according to the judgment and estimation of several witnesses, examined in that behalf. But by what pretence of right or authority the Massachusetts have taken upon them to proceed and act in such manner doth not appear to us.

All which we most humbly represent to your majesty in duty and obedience to your commands, not presuming to offer any opinion in a business of so high importance, wherein the public interest and government of your majesty appears so much intermixt and concerned with the private interest of the petitioners.

ROBT. MASON,	G. SWEIT,
JA. BUNCE,	RICHARD FOXE,
TH. EXTON,	JO. MYLLES,
THO. POVEY.	

([Without date] in the recorder's office for Rockingham county.)

No. 17. *Copy of a Commission granted by the Massachusetts General Court in 1665, for settling the eastern parts, when disturbed by the King's Commissioners.*

[Not inserted in the former editions.]

The General Court of the Massachusetts Jurisdiction in New-England,—

To Thomas Danforth, Eleazar Lusher
    and John Leverett, Esquires,—
You or any two of you are hereby fully authorized and impowered to repair in person to the counties of Norfolk, Pascataqua and Isle of Shoals and York, and to call before you any or every person or persons that have or shall act in the disturbance or reviling of the

* Vide Hutchinson's collection papers, page 339.

government there settled according to his majesty's royal charter
to this colony under the broad seal of England and to proceed against
them according to their demerits and the laws here established,
and to do any act for the settling the peace of the said places by
declaration or otherwise according to your good and sound discretion, appointing of constables and associates for the courts, and
keeping of the same, according to the articles of agreement made
with said people of said counties respectively. And for the better
enabling you herein, all officers military and civil and all others
the inhabitants of this jurisdiction are required to be aiding and
assisting to you for the ends aforesaid, as you shall see meet to require; and in case you shall find it more expedient you may send
for any delinquents as abovesaid, by warrant, directed to any of the
officers of this jurisdiction, or such other as you shall appoint for
the apprehending of their persons and causing them to appear before you in such places as you shall appoint, where after examination you shall further proceed as the matter shall require, and what
you shall do herein to make return to the next General Court, &c.

No. 18.   *Copy of an address of the town of Dover to the General Court of Massachusetts.*

[Not inserted in the former editions.]

To the honored General Court of the Massachusetts in Boston,
     these presents shew this 9th day of October, 1665,

May it please the honored Court,—

Whereas we the inhabitants of Dover have received credible
information that the inhabitants of the towns bordering upon the
river of Pascataqua have petitioned his majesty, our dread sovereign with respect to wrongs and usurpations they sustain in the
present government, under which they reside, for an alienation to
be made among them in the government as his majesty shall please
to order the same. We thought it necessary, being orderly assembled in a town meeting, to clear ourselves for our own part by these
presents, from having any hand in any such petition or remonstrance ; and in case any such act hath passed, we look at it as an
unworthy misrepresentation of us the inhabitants of Dover to his
majesty, as being done without any either consent or meeting or
cognizance of the town or the major part thereof. Furthermore,
as it is our bounden duty, so upon this occasion we, profess the same
that God assisting, we shall continue in our faith and allegiance to
his majesty by adhering to the present government, established by
his royal charter in the colony of the Massachusetts, being well
contented with the privileges thereof, and willing to perform what
is required of us therein according to the articles of agreement.

We beseech the Lord for his presence in the midst of you, and
his blessing upon all your public and weighty occasions, and humbly take leave.

It was voted in a public town meeting, October 10, 1665, that
the contents thereof be presented to the General Court as the

town's act, and that it be presented to all the rest of our neighbors to subscribe their hands as they are willing.   This is a true copy taken from the original, per me.

WM. POMFRET, *Town Clerk.*

[Subscribed also by 25 others.]

RICH'D WALDRON,
WM. WENTWORTH,
JOHN ROBERTS,
JOHN DAVIS, } *Selectmen.*

No. 19.   *Copy of a similar address from Portsmouth.*
[Not inserted in the former editions.]

To the honored General Court of the Massachusetts.

May it please you,—

That whereas there was a bruit or fame of a petition drawn up by us the inhabitants of Portsmouth and sent to his majesty ; the contents of which is to charge the government of the Massachusetts with usurpation upon us, and to supplicate an alteration of governors and government that his majesty hath at present established among us,—We, the selectmen for the prudential affairs of the said town, and sundry other inhabitants, do certify the honored court that we are innocent and clear of any such act, and do disclaim the same as any of our town act, and do account ourselves abused by any that have fathered such a thing upon us.

In testimony whereof, we subscribe our names the 9th day of October, 1665.

[Subscribed by 16 others.]

RICHARD CUTT,
JOHN CUTT,
NATH'L FRYER,
ELIAS STILEMAN, } *Selectmen.*

No. 20.   *Copy of a certificate of the same matter from Rev. Samuel Dudley, minister of Exeter.*

[This certificate is inserted as a note to page 61 of this volume.]

No. 21.   *Copy of an address of the town of Portsmouth relating to the College.*

[This address was not inserted in the former editions.]

To the much honored the General Court of the Massachusetts Colony assembled at Boston the 20th of May, 1669.

The humble address of the inhabitants of the town of Portsmouth, humbly sheweth,—

That seeing by your means under God, we enjoy much peace and quietness, and very worthy deeds are done to us by the favorable aspect of the government of this colony upon us, we accept it always and in all places with thankfulness.   And though we have articled with yourselves for exemption from public charges, yet we never articled with God and our own consciences for exemption from gratitude, which to demonstrate while we were studying the loud groans of the sinking college in its present low estate came to our ears, the relieving of which we account a good work for the house of our God, and needful for the perpetuating of knowledge both religious and civil among us and our posterity after us, and therefore grateful to yourselves whose care and study is to seek the welfare of our Israel.

The premises considered,we have made a collection in our town of sixty pounds per annum,(and hope to make it more) which said sum is to be paid annually for these seven years ensuing, to be improved at the discretion of the honored overseers of the college for the behoof of the same, and the advancement of good literature there ; hoping withal that the example of ourselves (which have been accounted no people) will provoke the rest of the country to jealousy ; we mean an holy emulation to appear in so good a work, and that this honored court will in their wisdom see meet vigorously to act for the diverting the sad omen to poor New-England. If a college begun and comfortably upheld while we were little should sink now we are grown great, especially after so large and profitable an harvest that this country and other places have reaped from the same.

Your acceptance of our good meaning herein will further oblige us to endeavor the approving ourselves to be your thankful and humble servants.

JOHN CUTT,   ) In the name and behalf of the rest
RICH'D CUTT,   } of the subscribers in the town
JOSHUA MOODY,) of Portsmouth.

The address from the inhabitants of the town of Portsmouth was presented by Mr. Richard Cutt and Mr. Joshua Moodey, 20th May, 1669, and gratefully accepted ; and the Governor, in the name of the whole court, met together, returned them the thanks of this court for their pious and liberal gift to the college herein mentioned.

Attest,—   EDWARD RAWSON, *Secretary.*

(The four preceding papers are taken from the Mass. Records.)

No. 22. *Copy of Robert Mason's Petition to the King.*

To the King's most excellent majesty—The humble petition of Robert Mason, proprietor of the province of New-Hampshire, in New-England, sheweth,

That your majesty's royal grandfather king James, of ever blessed memory, did by his highness' letters patents under the great seal of England, bearing date at Westminister, the third day of November, in the eighteenth year of his reign, give, grant and confirm unto several of the principal nobility and gentry of this kingdom by the name of the council of New-England, their successors and assigns forever, all the land in America lying between the degrees of 40 and 48 north latitude, by the name of New-England, to be held in fee, with many royal privileges and immunities, only paying to his majesty, his heirs and successors, one fifth part of all the ore of gold and silver that should at any time be found upon the said lands, as by the said letters patents doth at large appear.

That John Mason, Esq., your petitioner's grandfather, by virtue of several grants from the said council of New-England, under their common seal, bearing date the 9th of March, 1621, the 10th of August, 1622, the 7th of November, 1629, and the 22d of April, 1635, was instated in fee in a great tract of land in New-England, by the name of New-Hampshire, lying upon the sea-coast between the rivers of Naumkeak and Pascataqua, and running up into the land westward threescore miles, with all the islands lying within five leagues distance of any part thereof, and also the south half of the Isles of Shoals ; and also the said John Mason, together with Sir Ferdinando Gorges, knt. was enfeoffed by the aforesaid council of New-England in other lands by the name of Laconia, by their deed bearing date the 27th day of November, 1629, the said lands lying and bordering upon the great lakes and rivers of the Iroquois and other nations adjoining. All which said lands to be held as fully, freely, in as large, ample and beneficial manner and form to all intents and purposes whatsoever as the said council of New-England by virtue of his majesty's said letters patents might or ought to hold and enjoy the same, as by the said several grants appears.

Whereupon your petitioner's said grandfather did expend upwards of twenty-two thousand pounds in transporting people, building houses, forts, and magazines, furnishing them with great store of arms of all sorts, with artillery great and small, for defence and protection of his servants and tenants, with all other necessary commodities and materials for establishing a settled plantation.

That in the year 1628, in the fourth year of the reign of your majesty's royal father, some persons did surreptitiously and *unknown to the said council*, get the seal of the said council affixed to a grant of a certain lands, whereof the greatest part were solemnly past unto your petitioner's grandfather and others long before, and soon after did the same persons *by their subtile practices* get a confirmation of the said grant under the great seal of England, as a corporation by the name of THE CORPORATION OF THE MASSACHUSETTS BAY IN NEW-ENGLAND, *your majesty's royal father being unwitting thereof*, and having thus *by fraud* obtained a grant and confirmation, they compelled the rightful inhabitants to desert their plantations, and by many outrageous actions they became possessed of that part of the country, declaring themselves to be a free people, framing to themselves new laws, with new methods in religion absolutely contrary to the laws and customs of this your majesty's realm of England, punishing divers that would not approve thereof, some by whipping, others by burning their houses, and some by banishing, and the like.

At last the complaints of the oppressed subjects reaching the

ears of your royal father, his majesty caused the whole matter to
be examined before his most honorable privy council and all being
fully proved, his majesty did command the council of New-England to give an account, by what authority, or by whose procurement those people of the Massachusetts Bay were sent over, his
majesty conceiving the said council to be guilty thereof.

But the said council of New-England made it plainly to appear
to his majesty that they were ignorant of the whole matter and
that they had no share in the evils committed and wholly disclaim
the same, and the said council finding they had not sufficient means
to give redress and rectify what was brought to ruin, they humbly
referred it to his majesty to do therein as he pleased, and thereupon
the said council of New-England resolved to resign, and did
actually resign, the great charter of New-England into his
majesty's royal hands, seeing there was an absolute necessity
for his majesty to take the management of that country to himself, it being become a business of high consequence and only
to be remedied by his sovereign power, all which appears by
the declaration of the council of New-England dated the 25th of
April, 1635, together with the act of surrender of the great charter
of New-England dated the 7th day of June, the same year.

That immediately thereupon, his majesty in trinity term, 1635,
caused a quo warranto to be brought up by Sir John Banks, his
majesty's then attorney general, against the governor, deputy governor, and every of the assistants of the said corporation of Massachusetts in New-England severally, according to their names mentioned in the said patents of incorporation, being twenty-six persons, whereof two being dead, of the remaining twenty-four persons, there did fourteen at several times appear at the king's bench
bar and there disclaimed the charter, the remaining ten persons
were outlawed, and thereupon judgment given for the king, that
the liberties and franchises of the said corporation of Massachusetts Bay should be seized into the king's hands and the body of
the governor to be taken into custody for usurping the said liberties, all which appears by the rolls in the crown office, and office
of custos brevium for the king's bench of the proceedings in the
several terms from the year 1635 to 1637.

That thereupon his said royal majesty on the 3d day of May,
1637, did order in council that the attorney general be required
to call for the said patent and present the same to the board, and
his majesty by his declaration of the 23d of July, 1637, in the 13th
year of his reign declared his royal pleasure for establishing a general government in his territory of New-England for the prevention of the evils that otherwise might ensue for default thereof,
thereby declaring Sir Ferdinando Gorges to be governor general
of the whole country and requiring all persons to give their obedience accordingly.

That the wars and troubles immediately ensuing in Scotland
and presently after here in England, did hinder his said majesty
from settling that country or prosecuting the right which he intended his subjects, however the proceedings of his majesty caused

some restraint to the further violences and oppressions of the said Massachusetts, and they contained themselves for a time within their pretended bounds, but no sooner was that king of blessed memory, your royal father, become a sacrifice, but they renewed their former violences by oppressing all the other colonies and designing by encouragement from some in England to erect themselves into a commonwealth, and in order to lay a foundation for this power and dominion which they now aspired unto, they thought it necessary to extend their bounds and spread into a larger territory than as yet they had usurped, and that this work might not be done without a mask or color of right, they do in an assembly held at Boston, the 19th of October, 1652, seriously peruse the grant (which had been procured as aforesaid) and therein weighing the words, and trying what new sense they might bear more suitable to their increase of power, they thought fit at length to declare themselves mistaken in what they had done in the year 1631, when they erected bound-houses and had for so many years confined themselves thereunto, whereas now by the help of an imaginary line, or rather by a new reason of state, there is *a sense imposed by themselves upon their own words*, and they stretch their rights to near two hundred miles of land northward and as much southward more than they were satisfied withal before, swallowing up your majesty's petitioner as well as others, whose properties were established long before the said people had any being. And that they might give execution to this righteous sentence they presently invade and *by force of arms seize upon the province of New-Hampshire*, and other lands of right belonging to your petitioner, besides what they did to others, compelling the inhabitants to swear to be true to them and to cast off their lawful lords, and such as refused were either ruined, banished or imprisoned, and any appeals to England utterly denied unto them, then they proceed to coining of money with their own impress, raising the coin of England, and acting in all matters in a most absolute and arbitrary way. And although your petitioner by his agent Joseph Mason did demand redress of the general court of Massachusetts setting at Boston in 1652, offering to make out the right and title of your petitioner to the province of New-Hampshire and other lands against all persons whatsoever, yet no restitution could be obtained without a submission to their authority, and to hold the lands from them which the petitioner then did refuse and hath always refused, choosing rather to wait for more happy times wherein to expect relief than by a legal resignation of his rights to those who had none at all divest himself of what his ancestors had purchased at so dear a rate : Your petitioner having as equal a *right to the government* in the said province as he hath to the land itself, all which appears by a report made to your majesty the 15th of February, 1661, when your petitioner first exposed to your majesty the oppressions under which he had so long groaned, in the evil times, and which grieves him now much more to bear while he has the protection of so just and gracious a sovereign to resort to.

Wherefore your petitioner most humbly implores your majesty to take notice, that (by a plain discovery of what fraud in the beginning and the length of troubled times has helped to conceal) the Bostoners have no patent of incorporation at all, that yet they have under color of right and authority from the crown devoured your petitioner and other proprietors whose titles are by your majesty's learned council allowed as strong as the law can make them.

That all ways have been tried and methods used to obtain justice from the Bostoners, but all have proved ineffectual, that your petitioner's losses have been so many and great, and his sufferings so continued, that he cannot any longer support the burthen of them. And when your majesty will but consider how small the respect has been wherewith those people have treated your majesty since your happy restoration, and what daily breaches are by them made upon your majesty's acts of navigation, which turns so greatly to the detriment of this kingdom in general, these losses and sufferings of a particular subject cannot much be questioned, so that your petitioner humbly hopes that your majesty will think it high time to stretch forth your royal hand of justice to assist your petitioner, that he may have the quiet possession of his province, and reparation made him for the losses sustained, in such ways and methods as the importance of the case requires, and your majesty in your royal wisdom shall think most fit.

And your petitioner shall ever pray.

ROBT. MASON.

(From a copy in the possession of the Masonian proprietors.)

No. 23. *Copy of the answer of Massachusetts to Mason's and Gorges' complaints.*

A brief declaration of the right and claim of the governor and company of the Massachusetts Bay in New-England, to the lands now in their possession, but pretended to by Gorges and Mr. Mason, together with an answer to their several pleas and complaints in their petitions exhibited : Humbly presented and submitted by the said governor and company to the king's most excellent majesty, as their defence.

In the year of our Lord 1628, in the third year of his late majesty Charles the First, of happy memory, several loyal and piously disposed gentlemen obtained of the great council of New-England, a grant of a certain tract of land lying in New-England, described and bounded as therein expressed; which was in all respects fairly and openly procured and with so good an intent of propagating the gospel among the natives, and to advance the honor and dignity of his late majesty, of happy memory, that they were bold to supplicate his said majesty to superadd his royal confirmation thereto, which accordingly in an ample royal charter was passed and remains under the broad seal of England, March the 4th, 1629, in the fourth year of his majesty's reign, with further additions and enlargements well becoming so royal a majesty, and suitable for the encouragement of so hazardous and chargeable an adventure. In pursuance whereof many of the said patentees and other adventurers transported themselves and estates, and settled in the most known and accommodable parts of those lands contained in the said charter, neither time, estate, nor power suffering them speedily to survey the just extent of their limits. Not many years different in time, several others also of his majesty's subjects obtained other grants, and made several settlements in the more northern and eastern parts of the country, with whom for several years we had neighborly correspondence, being as they supposed without the limits of our patent, amongst whom the present claimers and petitioners were. These grants partly by reason of the smallness of some of them, and partly by reason of dark involved and dubious expression of their limits, brought the inhabitants under many entanglements and dissatisfactions among themselves, which there being no settled authority to be applied to, being deserted and forsaken of all such as by virtue of said grants did claim jurisdiction over them and had made a successless essay for the settlement of government among them proved of some continuance, unto the great disquiet and disturbance of those his majesty's subjects that were peaceable and well disposed amongst them; to remedy which inconvenience they betook themselves to the way of combinations for government, but by experience found it ineffectual. In this time ignorance of the northerly running of Merrimack river, hindered our actual claim and extention of government, yet at length being more fully settled, and having obtained further acquaintance and correspondency with the Indians possessing the uppermost parts of that river, encouraging an adventure, as also frequent solicitations from the most considerable inhabitants of those eastern parts, earnestly desiring us to make proof of, and ascertain our interest, we employed the most approved artists that could be obtained, who upon their solemn oaths made returns, that upon their certain observation our northern patent line did extend so far north as to take in all those towns and places which we now possess ; which when the inhabitants as well as ourselves were satisfied in, (urged also with the necessity of government amongst them) they peaceably and voluntarily submitted to the government of the Massachusetts, (viz.) Dover, Squamscot and Portsmouth, anno 1641, Kittery, York and Wells, anno 1652 and 1653, from which times until the year 1662, when there was a small interruption by a letter of Mr. Gorges, and afterwards in the year 1665, (when his majesty's commissioners, Colonel Nicolls and others, came over) the inhabitants of those parts lived well satisfied and uninterrupted under the Massachusetts government. But when the said commissioners neither regarding the Massachusetts' just right nor the claims of Mr. Gorges and Mr. Mason, settled a new form of government there, but this hardly outlived their departure, the people impatient of innovations, and well experienced and satisfied in their former settlement, quickly and quietly returned to order again and so continue unto this time. This is in a few words the true state of the matter ; for the further illustration whereof and justification of our proceedings therein, and vindication of ourselves from the reproachful imputation of usurping authority over his majesty's subjects in the eastern parts pretended to, with other scandals cast upon us by the petitioners, we humbly present the following pleas by way of demonstration, and argue that our extension of government to those eastern parts claimed is agreeable to our indubitable patent right; our patent according to the express term therein contained without any ambiguity or color of other interpretation, lies *between two east and west parallel lines drawn from the most southerly part of Charles river and the most northerly part of Merrimack, with three miles advantage upon each,* which upon the observation of men of approved and undoubted truth upon oath, are found distant one degree and forty-nine minutes north latitude, being to extend in full latitude and breadth from sea to sea (ut in terminis) and therefore cannot be bounded by many hundreds or infinite numbers of lines, as the river Merrimack maketh bends or angles in two hundred miles passage from Winnipiseogee lake to the mouth thereof, which to imagine, as it is irrational, so would it involve us and any borderer into so many inextricable disputes as are by no ways to be admitted by a prince seeking his subjects' peace. Besides were such a construction allowable, (which with uttermost straining is) yet all favorable interpretation is to be offered the patentees by the gracious expression of the charter. Now according to the aforementioned observation, (so confirmed) all those eastern plantations challenged by our opponents (ut supra) are comprehended within our northerly line. We deny not but the artists of theirselves, and if any question thence arise, we fear not to submit to trial to the most exact and rigorous test that may be. The invincible strength of this our first plea, may further appear by the consideration of the frivolous and insignificant allegations of the petitioners in opposition thereunto, viz. 1st. The nonextension of our line or assertion of our right to those eastern parts for some years, ignorance, as our case was circumstanced, debarring no man of his just right, neither can it reasonably be supposed that the exact survey of so large a grant, in so hideous a wilderness, possessed by an enemy, would be the work of a few years, our own poverty not affording means, and our weakness (allowing no deep adventure into the country) permitting us not to view the favorable running of the river, which none can imagine altered its course by our delay; we may as well be deprived of far more than we possess or ever saw on our western parts to the south sea (which none will deny) because we have not surveyed it or are soon like to be able, as be taken from our northern right so obvious to the meanest artist.

2dly. The possession-house in Hampton of so little signification and so long since disused, that Mr. Mason hath forgot the name thereof and calleth it Bound-house, erected to give the world to know that we claimed considerably to the northward of our then habitations upon the bay, though we did not know the utmost extent of our right, our fathers not being so ignorant of the law of the realm to which they did appertain as to suppose the taking possession of part did debar them of the remainder but the contrary ; and we challenge Mr. Mason or any on his behalf, promising our records shall be open to the most scrutinous search to prove it, either called or intended according to his abuse thereof.

3dly. That notorious falsehood of stretching our right to near four hundred miles north and south more than formerly we were satisfied with, our whole breadth being but one hundred and nine miles which is not much more than a quarter part of what he would have the world believe our new claim and (as he would insinuate) usurped territory doth contain, arising (we would charitably believe) partly from ignorance of the coasting of the country, Mr. Mason accounting by the sea-side, and we suppose coasting in the measure of every harbour and cove to make up that calculation, which lies much of it due east and not to the north, but we fear malevolently suggested (as many other things as of little credit) to introduce into his majesty's royal breast a belief that we are unreasonable in our pretensions, and so unworthy of his majesty's favor, which we hope such unlawful endeavours will never be so prosperous as to obtain. What may be further added to this our first plea, may be supplied from the reasons formerly presented. We urge secondly, The invalidity of those grants pretended to by the petitioners, which are of two sorts ; 1st. Such as bear date after ours, which we see no reason to fear any interruption from. Secondly, Such as are pretended to bear date before ours, against which we object that they are not authentic, wanting a sufficient number of grantors to make them so, none of them as we presume will appear upon trial having above six hands and seals annexed to them, the said council of New-England consisting of forty, and his majesty's grant to them expressly requiring (as we are informed) seven at the least to sign to make any valid act ; and indeed Mr. Mason's own often unwearied renewal of his grants in 1621, sixteen hundred twenty-two, sixteen hundred twenty-nine and 1635, (as he saith) tacitly confesseth the same invalidity, in the former putting him to charge for the latter, till at last he fell into such a trade of obtaining grants that his last and most considerable was six years after the grant of our charter from his majesty, and but three days before the said council's declaration of their absolute resolution to resign, and but a few days before their actual surrender, as he asserts ; which of what value and consideration it is from the said council's circumstanced under a necessity of resignation of their great charter, procured rather by the clamor of such ill affected persons as the present complaint than by any true account of dissettlement or ill management here, is not difficult to judge. Hence it appears, first, how little reason Mr. Mason hath to brand us with fraud or surreptitiousness in obtaining our charter ; which hath most show of fraud and surreptitious procuration, a sufficient number of those honorable persons subscribing ours and fewer his pretended antedated grants, is easy to determine. In which assertion is to be observed the high reflection cast upon the members of his late majesty and ministers of state, groundlessly rendering the council's seal, yea the great seal of England, exposed to fraud and deceitful clandestine practices; yea upon his present majesty, insinuating himself better acquainted with matters of state than he who allows and confirms our grant as authentic by his gracious letter of sixteen hundred sixty-two, which intolerable boldness how unbecoming (not to say more) in a subject, it is not easy for us to say. To all which we may add Sir Ferdinando Gorges' application to the authority here to interpose in his affair, which he, being one of the great council, would have been far from acknowledging, had Mr. Mason's allegations been founded upon truth.

Secondly, That articles of charge depending upon such illegal and post-dated grants cannot take place against us were their disburse as great as it is affirmed, which by eye witnesses upon the place and still living are proved comparatively very inconsiderable.

3dly. We affirm that the whole management of the affair respecting our government of those eastern parts was in an orderly and peaceable way, and not without the reiterated and earnest solicitation of most of the people there inhabiting, sufficiently appearing by their several petitions ; and we challenge Mr. Gorges and Mr. Mason by any living evidence or record to shew any sign of a forcible entrance : Some magistrates upon the clearing of our right to them and acceptance of the tender of themselves to us, being sent thither without any other force than each of them a servant to attend them. Indeed some years after Capt. Bonython for mutinous carriage was seized and brought to justice ; concerning which and many other cases many inhabitants yet living and eye witnesses can give the most impartial evidence.

4thly. We offer to consideration that the deserted and ungoverned state of the people of those places had we not had that patent right so clearly evinced, might warrant our actions ; especially considering the obligation upon us to secure his majesty's honour and maintain the public peace, so hazarded by the total want of government amongst them. Our first exercise of jurisdiction being in the year 1641, eight years after Capt. Neal, agent for Mr. Mason, had wholly deserted the improvement of land and the government of the country, which indeed he never used but one year, for in the year 1630 he first came over, and in the year 1634 he quitted the place ; and in the interim, neglected the same in making a voyage for England, the short time of his tarriance not admitting of settlement of government or improvement. We may hereto subjoin that Mr. Joseph Mason, agent for Mrs. Anne Mason, when here and all things were fresh in memory, made no demand contrary to what is affirmed, but petitioned our justice against his debtors there and elsewhere, and that Sir Ferdinando Gorges his grant being so mean and uncertainly bounded that he knew not well how to find, much less to improve, to considerable advantage, by his letter bearing date ——— doth devolve the whole charge and care of his pretended province upon the authority here established. Lastly, That the exercise of jurisdiction in those eastern parts hath been and is his majesty's honour, the people's great benefit, and our charge without profit, which had it not been, the ruin of those parts would have unavoidably ensued in the want of all government, and their seizure by the French, who ever waited a fit opportunity for the same. They have part of them for thirty-five years and others twenty years (some small interruption intervening producing the stronger inclination and resolution in them to be constant to his majesty's authority here, lived under the government of the Massachusetts a quiet, well ordered and thriving people. And as for any complaint from ill affected persons, it is well known that the best and wisest government is not without disquiet from some such ; and no wonder if silly people are soon affected with such fair glossing promises as Mr. Mason hath made and published, as it were determining the case before trial by his late letters to the inhabitants in those parts, and that our government in those places have been no gain, is so unquestionable a truth, that never was any levy laid upon them for the supply of the public treasury, though much hath been and is further like to be expended for their security, who otherwise will inevitably become an easy prey to the heathen, now in hostility with us, and at this present time raging in those parts.

The before written, is a true copy transcribed from the records of the general court of the late colony of the Massachusetts Bay, held by the governor and company of the said colony, at Boston, the 6th of September, 1676.

Examd. per ISA. ADDINGTON, Sec'y.

No. 24. *Copy of the Report of the Lords Chief Justices, and the King's confirmation thereof.*

At the Court at Whitehall, July 20, 1677.

(L. S.) Present the King's most excellent majesty.

Lord Chancellor,	Earl of Craven,
Lord Treasurer,	Lord Bishop of London,
Lord Privy Seal,	Lord Maynard,
Duke of Ormond,	Lord Berkley,
Marquis of Worcester,	Mr. Vice Chamberlain,
Lord Chamberlain,	Mr. Secretary Coventry,
Earl of Northampton,	Mr. Secretary Williamson,
Earl of Peterborough,	Mr. Chancellor of the Exche-
Earl of Stratford,	quer,
Earl of Sunderland,	Master of Ordnance,
Earl of Bath,	Mr. Speaker.

Whereas the right honorable the lords of the committee for trade and plantations, did, in pursuance of an order of the 7th of February last, make report to the board, of the matters in controversy, between the corporation of the Massachusetts Bay, in New-England, and Mr. Mason and Mr. Gorges, touching the right of the soil and government, claimed by the said parties in certain lands there, by virtue of several grants from his majesty's royal father and grandfather, as followeth, in these words,

May it please your majesty,—Having received your majesty's order in council, of the 7th of February last past, whereby we are directed to enter into the examination of the bounds and limits, which the corporation of the Massachusetts Bay, in New-England, on the one hand, and Mr. Mason and Mr. Gorges on the other, do pretend by their several grants and patents to have been assigned unto them, as also to examine the patents and charters which are insisted on by either side, in order to find out and settle how far the rights of soil and government do belong unto any of them. In consideration whereof, the lords chief justices of your majesty's courts of king's bench and common pleas, were appointed to give us their assistance, we did, on the 5th of April last, together with the said lords chief justices, meet in obedience to your majesty's commands, and having heard both parties by their counsel, learned in the law, we did recommend unto their lordships to receive a state of the claims made by both parties, and to return their opinions upon the whole matter unto us, which their lordships have accordingly performed, in the words following :

In obedience to your lordships' order, we appointed a day for the hearing of all parties, and considering the matters referred, having received from them such papers of their cases as they were pleased to deliver ; at which time all parties appearing, the respondents did disclaim title to the lands claimed by the petitioners, and it appeared to us that the said lands are in the possession of several other persons, not before us, whereupon we thought not fit to examine any claims to the said lands, it being (in our opinion) improper to judge of any title of land, without hearing of the ter tenants, or some other persons on their behalf; and if there be any course of justice upon the place, having jurisdiction, we esteem it most proper to direct the parties to have recourse thither, for the decision of any question of property, until it shall appear that there is just cause of complaint, against the courts of justice there, for injustice or grievance.

We did, in the presence of said parties, examine their several claims to the government, and the petitioners having waived the pretence of a grant of government from the council of Plymouth, wherein they were convinced, by their own counsel, that no such power or jurisdiction could be transferred or assigned by any color of law ; the question was reduced to the province of Maine, whereto the petitioner, Gorges, made his title, by a grant from king Charles the First, in the 15th year of his reign, made to Sir Ferdinando Gorges, and his heirs, of the province of Maine and the government thereof. In answer to this, the respondents alleged, that long before, viz. in quarto Caroli primi, the government was granted to them, and produced copies of letters patents, wherein it is recited, that the council of Plymouth, having granted to certain persons a territory thus described, viz. " all that part of New-" England in America, which lies and extends between a great " river that is commonly called Monomack alias Merrimack, and a " certain other river there, called Charles river, being in the bot-" tom of a certain bay there, called the Massachusetts bay, and

" also all and singular the lands and hereditaments whatsoever,
" lying and being within the space of three English miles on the
" south part of the said Charles river, or any or every part thereof;
" and also all and singular the lands and hereditaments whatsoev-
" er, lying and being within the space of three English miles to
" the southermost part of the said bay, called Massachusetts bay;
" and all those lands and hereditaments whatsoever, which [*lie*]
" within the space of three English miles to the northward of the
" said river, called Monomack alias Merrimack, or the northward
" of any and every part thereof, and all lands and hereditaments
" whatsoever, lying within the limits aforesaid, north and south in
" latitude and breadth, and in length and longitude of and within
" all the breadth aforesaid, throughout the main lands there, from
" the Atlantic and western sea and ocean on the east part, to the
" south sea on the west." By the said letters patents, the king
confirmed that grant, made them a corporation, and gave them
power to make laws for the governing of the lands and the people
therein. To which it was replied, that the patent of 4° Caroli. 1^{mi}
is invalid. 1. Because there was a precedent grant 18° Jacobi, of
the same thing, then in being, which patent was surrendered afterwards, and before the date of the other 15° Car. 1^{mi}. 2. The
grant of the government can extend no farther than the ownership
of the soil, the boundaries of which, as recited in that patent, wholly excludes the province of Maine, which lies northward more
than three miles beyond the river Merrimack.

We having considered these matters, do humbly conceive as to
the first matter, that the patent of 4° Caroli 1^{mi} is good, notwithstanding the grant made in the 18° Jac : for it appeared to us by
the recital in the patent 4° Caroli 1^{mi} that the council of Plymouth
had granted away all their interest in the lands the year before,
and it must be presumed they then deserted the government;
whereupon it was lawful and necessary for the king to establish
a suitable frame of government, according to his royal wisdom,
which was done by that patent, 4° Caroli 1^{mi} making the adventurers a corporation upon the place. As to the second matter it
seems to us to be very clear that the grant of the government
4° Caroli 1^{mi} extends no farther than the boundaries expressed in
the patent, and those boundaries cannot be construed to extend
further northwards along the river Merrimack than three English
miles, for the north and south bounds of the lands granted so far
as the river extends, are to follow the course of the river, which
make the breadth of the grant, the words describing the length to
comprehend all the lands from the Atlantic ocean, to the South
sea, of, and in all the breadth aforesaid, do not warrant the over
reaching those bounds by imaginary lines or bounds, other exposition, would (in our humble opinion) be unreasonable and against
the interest of the grant. The words ' of, and in all the breadth
aforesaid,' shew, that the breadth was not intended an imaginary
line of breadth, laid upon the broadest part, but the breadth respecting the continuance of the boundaries by the river, as far as
the rivers go, but when the known boundary of breadth determine*

it must be carried on by imaginary lines to the South sea. And if the province of Maine, lies more northerly than three English miles from the river Merrimack, the patent of 4º Caroli 1^{mi} gives no right to govern there, and thereupon the patent of the same 15º Car. 1^{mi} to the petitioner Gorges, will be valid. So that upon the whole matter, we are humbly of opinion, as to the power of government, that the respondents, the Massachusetts and their successors, by their patent of 4º martis 4º Caroli 1^{mi} have such right of government as is granted them by the same patent within the boundaries of their land expressed therein, according to such description and exposition, as we have thereof made as aforesaid, and the petitioner, Sir Ferdinando Gorges, his heirs and assigns, by the patent 3d April, have such right of government, as is granted them by the same patent, within (*the territory*) called the province of Maine, according to the boundaries of the same expressed in the same patent. RI. RAINSFORD,
FRA. NORTH.

All which being the opinion of the lords chief justices, and fully agreeing with what we have to report unto your majesty upon the whole matter referred unto us by the said order, we humbly submit the determination thereof unto your majesty.

ANGLESEY,	CRAVEN,	J. WILLIAMSON,
ORMOND,	H. LONDON,	THO. CHICKLEY,
BATH,	G. CARTERET,	EDW. SEYMOUR.

Which having been read at the board the 18th instant, it was then ordered that the said Mr. Mason and Mr. Gorges, as also that the agents of the corporation of the Massachusetts Bay, should be this day heard upon the said report, if they had any objections to make thereunto. In pursuance whereof, all parties attending with their counsel, who not alleging any thing so material as to prevail with his majesty and the board to differ in judgment from the said report; his majesty was thereupon pleased to approve of and confirm the same, and did order that all parties do acquiesce therein, and contribute what lies in them to the punctual and due performance of the said report, as there shall be occasion.
JOHN NICHOLAS.

(The above paper, of which the copy is attested by Edward Rawson, secretary of Massachusetts, and John Penhallow, clerk of the superior court of New-Hampshire, is in the files of the said superior court, and in the Masonian proprietary office.)

No. 25. *Copy of that part of President Cutt's commission, in which the claim of Robert Mason is recited.*

" And whereas the inhabitants of said province of New-Hampshire, have many of them been long in possession of several quantities of lands, and are said to have made considerable improvements thereupon, having no other title for the same than what has been derived from the government of the Massachusetts Bay, virtue of their imaginary line; which title, as it hath by the opinion of our judges in England been altogether set aside, so the agents from the said colony have consequently disowned any right, either in the soil or government thereof, from the three mile line aforesaid ; and it appearing to us, that the ancestors of Robert Mason, Esq. obtained grants from our great council of Plymouth, for the tract of land aforesaid, and were at very great expense upon the same, until molested and finally driven out, which hath occasioned a lasting complaint for justice, by the said Robert Mason, ever since our restoration. However, to prevent in this case any unreasonable demands which might be made by the said Robert Mason, for the right he claimeth in the said soil, we have obliged the said Robert Mason under his hand and seal, to declare that he will demand nothing for the time past, until the 24th of June last past, nor molest any in their possession for the time to come, but will make out titles to them and their heirs forever, provided they will pay to him upon a fair agreement in lieu of all other rents, sixpence in the pound, according to the just and true yearly value of all houses built by them, and of all lands, whether gardens, orchards, arable, or pasture, which have been improved by them, which he will agree shall be bounded out unto every of the parties concerned, and that the residue may remain unto himself to be disposed of, for his best advantage.

" But if, notwithstanding this overture from the said Robert Mason, which seemeth to be fair unto us, any of the inhabitants. of the said province of New-Hampshire, shall refuse to agree with the agents of said Robert Mason upon the terms aforesaid, our will and pleasure is, that the president and council of New-Hampshire aforesaid, for the time being shall have power, and are hereby impowered to interpose and reconcile all differency, if they can, that shall or may arise between the said Robert Mason and the said inhabitants, but if they cannot, then we do hereby command and require the said president and council to send into England such cases, fairly and impartially stated, together with their own opinions upon such cases, that we, our heirs and successors, by and with the advice of our and their privy council, may determine therein according to equity."

(The same mutatis mutandis is inserted in Cranfield's commission.)

No. 26. *The General Laws and Liberties of the Province of New-Hampshire.*

[Not inserted in the former editions.]

The general laws and liberties of the province of New-Hampshire, made by the General Assembly, in Portsmouth, the 16th of March, 1679–80, and approved by the President and Council.

Forasmuch as it hath pleased our sovereign lord, the king, out of his princely grace and favor to take us, the inhabitants of New-Hampshire, into his immediate government and protection, the which, as we are ever bound to acknowledge with great thankfulness, so we have great reason to hope and believe that his majesty will still continue to countenance and encourage us with the enjoyment of such liberties, immunities and pp'ties [properties] as belong to free born Englishmen.

And whereas, his majesty hath been pleased by his letters patents, sent to us to confer such power upon the General Assembly as to make such laws and ordinances as may best suit with the good government and quiet settlement of his majesty's subjects within this province :—

It is therefore *ordered and enacted,* by this General Assembly and the authority thereof, That no act, imposition, law, or ordinance be made or imposed upon us, but such as shall be made by the said assembly, and approved by the president and council from time to time ; and, that justice and right be equally and impartially administered unto all, not sold, denied or causelessly deferred unto any.

9 Hen. 3. Ch. 29.—Stat. 2. Edw'd 3. Ch. 8.—Stat. 5. Edw'd 3—9.—Stat. 14. Edw'd 28.—Edw'd 3, 3.—Stat. 11. R. 2—10.— 17 Caro. 1—10.

CAPITAL LAWS.

1. It is enacted by this assembly and the authority thereof, That if any person having had the knowledge of the true God, openly and manifestly have or worship any other God but the Lord God, he shall be put to death. Ex. 22. 20. Deut. 13. 6 and 10.

2. If any person within this province, professing the true God, shall wittingly and willingly presume to blaspheme the holy name of God, Father, Son or Holy Ghost, with direct, express, presumptuous or high-handed blasphemy, either by wilful or obstinate, denying the true God, or his creation or government of the world, or shall curse God, Father, Son or Holy Ghost—such person shall be put to death. Levit. 24. 15, 16.

3. Treason against the person of our sovereign, the King, the state and commonwealth of England, shall be punished with death.

4. If any man conspire and attempt any invasion or insurrection, or public rebellion against this his majesty's proving, or shall endeavor to surprise any town or towns, fort or forts therein, or shall treacherously or perfidiously attempt the alteration or subversion of the fundamental frame of this government according to his majesty's constitution by his letters patents, every such person shall be put to death or otherwise grievously punished.

5. If any person shall commit wilful murder by killing any man, woman or child, upon premeditated malice, hatred or cruelty, not in a way of necessary and just defence, nor by casualty against his will, he shall be put to death.

6. If any person slayeth another person suddenly in his anger and cruelty of passion, he shall be put to death.

7. If any person shall slay another through guile either by poisoning or other such devilish practice, he shall be put to death.

8. If any christian, so called, be a witch, that is, hath or consulteth with a familiar spirit, he or they shall be put to death.

9 If any person lie with a beast or brute creature by carnal copulation, they shall surely be put to death, and the beast shall be slain and buried, and not eaten.

10. If any man lieth with mankind as he lieth with a woman, both of them hath committed abomination, they both shall surely be put to death, unless the one party were forced or be under fourteen years of age, and all other Sodomitical filthiness shall be severely punished according to the nature of it.

11. If any person rise up by false witness wittingly and of purpose to take away a man's life, he shall be put to death.

12. If any man stealeth mankind, he shall be put to death or otherwise grievously punished.

13. If any child or children, above sixteen years old and of competent understanding, shall curse or smite their natural father or mother, he or they shall be put to death, unless it can be sufficiently testified, that the parents have been very unchristianly negligent in the education of such children, or so provoked them by extreme and cruel correction, that they have been forced thereunto to preserve themselves from death or maiming.

14. If a man have a rebellious or stubborn son, of sufficient years and understanding, viz.—sixteen years of age or upward, which shall not obey the voice of his father or the voice of his mother, that when they have chastened him will not hearken unto them, then shall his father and mother, being his natural parents, bring him before the magistrates assembled in court, and testify unto them, that their son is rebellious and stubborn, and will not obey their voice and chastisement, but lives in sundry notorious crimes, such a son shall be put to death or otherwise severely punished.

15. If any man shall ravish a maid or women, by committing carnal copulation with her that is above ten years of age, or if she were under ten years of age, though her will was gained by him, he shall be punished with death or some other grievous punishment, as the fact may be circumstanced.

16. Whosoever shall wilfully, or on purpose, burn any house, ship or barque, or any other vessel of considerable value, such person shall be put to death or otherwise grievously punished, as the case may be circumstanced.

(The two preceding papers are in the first book of MS. Laws of New-Hampshire.)

No. 27. *Address of the General Court of New-Hampshire to the King.*

To his most excellent majesty, Charles the 2d, by the grace of God, of England, Scotland, France and Ireland, king, defender of the faith, &c. :

The humble address and petition of the President and Council of his majesty's province of New-Hampshire, in New-England, humbly sheweth,—

That, it having pleased your most excellent majesty to separate us, the inhabitants of this province, from that shadow of your majesty's authority and government under which we had long found protection, especially in the late war with the barbarous natives, who (this divine protection) proved a heavy scourge to us, and had certainly been the ruin of these poor weak plantations, (being few in number, and otherwise under great disadvantages,) if our brethren and neighbors had not, out of pity and compassion, stretched forth their helping hand, and with their blood and treasure defended us, our lives and estates ; nevertheless, upon the receipt of your majesty's pleasure, delivered by Edward Randolph, Esquire, upon the first of January last, directing unto and commanding the erecting of a new government in and over these four towns, (the government of the Massachusetts yielding readier obedience to your majesty's commands with reference to our relation formerly to them,) although deeply sensible of the disadvantages likely to accrue to your majesty's provinces and ourselves, more especially by the multiplying of small and weak governments, unfit either for offence or defence, (the union of these neighbor colonies having been more than a little instrumental in our preservation.) We have taken the oaths prescribed us by your majesty, and administered to your subjects of these four towns the oath of allegiance, and convened a general assembly for regulating the common affairs of the people and making of such laws as may be of more peculiar use to ourselves, having special regard to the acts for trade and navigation set forth in the book of rates commonly printed and sold, *and if some obstruction occasioned by such as make greater pretences of your majesty's favour and authority had not hindered* we might have brought matters to a greater maturity, yet hope to perfect something by the first opportunity of shipping from hence, but feared it might be too long to defer our humble acknowledgment of your majesty's grace and favor, in committing the power into such hands as it pleased your majesty to nominate, not imposing strangers upon us, and it much comforts us against any *pretended claimers* to our soil, or any *malevolent spirits,* which may misrepresent us (as they have done others) unto your majesty or honorable council, while, beside the known laws of the realm, and the undoubted right of English men, we have the favor of a gracious prince to fly to. We do therefore most humbly beg the continuance of your majesty's royal favor and protection, without which, we are daily *liable to disturbance if not ruin.*

And, as in duty bound, we shall humbly pray, &c.

March 29, 1680.

No. 28. *Address of the same to the same.*

To the king's most excellent majesty,—

We, the president and council of your province of New-Hampshire, having (according to the royal pleasure) given an account of our allegiance and observance of your commission, by Mr. Jowles, in March last, and therefore shall not give you the trouble of repetition. According to your majesty's command, we have with our general assembly, been considering of such laws and orders, as do by divine favor, preserve the peace, and are to the satisfaction of your majesty's good subjects here, in all which, we have had a special regard to the statute book your majesty was pleased to honor us with, for which, together with the seal of your province, we return most humble and hearty thanks ; but such has been the hurry of our necessary occasions, and such is the shortness of the summer, (the only season to prepare for a long winter,) that we have not been capable of sitting so long, as to frame and finish aught that we judge worthy to be presented to your royal view, but shall, as in duty bound, give as speedy a despatch to the affair as we may. In the mean time, your subjects are at quiet under the shadow of your gracious protection, *fearing no disturbance, unless by some pretended claimers to our soil,* whom we trust your majesty's clemency and equity will guard us from injury by ; and, *considering the purchase of our lands from the heathen, the natural proprietors thereof, and our long quiet possession, not interrupted by any legal claim, our defence of it against the barbarous adversary, by our lives and estates, we are encouraged, that we shall be maintained in our free enjoyment of the same, without being tenants to those who can show no such title thereunto.* Further, we do gratefully acknowledge the mark of your princely favor in sending us your royal effigies and imperial arms, and lament, when we think that they are, through the loss of the ship, miscarried by the way. And, seeing your majesty is graciously pleased to license us to crave what may conduce to the better promoting of our weal and your majesty's authority, we would humbly suggest, *whether the allowance of appeals, mentioned in the commission, may not prove a great occasion, by means of malignant spirits, for the obstructing of justice among us.* There are also sundry other things that a little time and experience may more evidently discover a great convenience in, which, upon the continuance of the same liberty from your majesty, we shall with like humility present. Thus craving a favorable construction of what is above suggested, and praying for your majesty's long and prosperous reign, begging also the continuance of your majesty's favor, out of which, if any of our adversaries, under a pretence of loyalty or zeal for your majesty's interest, should endeavor to eject us, we hope, upon liberty granted us, to speak for ourselves, we shall abundantly demonstrate that we do truly and sincerely subscribe,

Your majesty's most loyal and dutiful subjects.

JOHN CUTT, President,

with the consent of the council.

Portsmouth, in the Province of
New-Hampshire, June 11, 1680.

No. 29. *Copy of the Mandamus by which Robert Mason, Esq., was admitted to a seat in the council, December 30, 1680.*

Trusty and well beloved, we greet you well.

Whereas, we have thought it fit to take into our special care and protection our province of New-Hampshire, and provide for its prosperity and good government, and the settlement of the estates and possessions of our good subjects there : And that *for the avoiding any suits or contentions in matters of title*, and the determining any demands, which might be made by our well beloved subject, Robert Mason, Esq., as proprietor under us, of that province, by virtue of a grant derived from our royal grandfather, king James, under the great seal of England :* We have so composed all matters with him, that for the time past, until the 24th day of June, 1679, he shall not claim or demand any rent, dues, or arrears, whatsoever ; And for the future, he, his heirs or assigns, shall receive only six pence in the pound yearly of every tenant, by way of quit rent, according to the true and just yearly value of what is improved by any of the inhabitants ; as is more fully expressed in our commission under our great seal, bearing date, the 18th day of September, in the 31st year of our reign. And whereas, the said Robert Mason hath humbly signified to us, that he is preparing to transport himself, for the taking care of his affairs and interest in the said province, and for the giving a secure and legal confirmation of the estates of such persons as are now in possession, but *without any right or legal title* to the same. And he being a person whom we have esteemed useful to our service, as he is chiefly concerned in the welfare of that our province ; we have further thought fit to constitute and appoint him to be one of our council therein, and we do hereby order and require you, our president and council, that immediately after his arrival, you do admit him one of our council of our province of New-Hampshire, he first taking the oaths mentioned in our said commission. And we do further require you and him, that you do betake yourselves to such discreet and equitable ways and methods in your proceedings, agreements and settlements for the future, that there may be no occasion of complaint to our royal person and authority here. We being resolved to discountenance all such as shall wilfully or unnecessarily avoid or delay your submitting to those determinations which may be reasonably decreed according to justice and good conscience. Which you are to signify to all our good subjects within our said province, that they may govern themselves accordingly. And so we bid you heartily farewell. Given at our court, at New-Market, the first day of October, 1680, in the two and thirtieth year of our reign. By his majesty's command,

SUNDERLAND.

To our trusty and well beloved, the president and council }
of our province of New-Hampshire, in New-England. }

No. 30. *The order of the Council and General Assembly, for a Fast, made in March, 1681, and published under the seal of the Province.*

[Not inserted in the former editions.]

Upon serious consideration of the manifold sinful provocations among us, as of the sundry tokens of divine displeasure evident to

* This must mean the charter to the council of Plymouth.

us, both in the present dangerous sickness of the honorable president of the council for New-Hampshire, in the continuance of whose life is wrapt up much blessing, whose death may occasion much trouble; as also in respect of that *awful portentous blazing star*, usually foreboding sore calamity to the beholders thereof; and in regard of the great need that we have of *more than ordinary presence of Almighty God* with us, in our necessary applications to his royal majesty, our sovereign lord the king; as also having a real sympathy with the great thoughts of heart in our brethren and neighbors, as they are circumstanced; ever seriously and loyally imploring the divine favor for the continuance of his majesty's life and prosperous reign, as the protection of God's cause and church against the popish party throughout the world; humbly craving covenant mercy to be continued to us, and ours after us in their generations, as also God's crowning the several seasons of the year with suitable goodness: The council and general assembly for the province of New-Hampshire, have appointed the next Thursday, being the 17th day of this instant March, a day of public fasting and prayer, to be solemnly kept by all the inhabitants thereof, hereby strictly inhibiting all servile labor thereon. Commending the same to all elders, churches, ministers, and people, that they fervently wrestle with the Lord, that he may turn from the fierceness of his anger, and cause his face to shine upon us in all our concerns.

(The four preceding papers are in the Council Minutes, first book.)

[The Council Minutes from 1680 to 1698, are not to be found in the Secretary's office.]

No. 31. *Answer to the claim made by Mr. Mason to the house and lands of New-Hampshire.*

(In Mr. Weare's hand writing, but without date or signature.)

It does not legally appear, that Mr. Mason can lay any just claim to any of the lands in New-Hampshire, for what right he pretends, is either derived from Capt. John Mason, (whom he says was his grandfather) or from his majesty's commission : but presume from neither of these has he any right. Not from Capt. John Mason; for 1. It does not legally appear that ever he had any right to the province of New-Hampshire. It is true there is a copy of a patent or deed from the council of Plymouth, which he brings over without attestation of public notary, or any other authority. Besides, in said copy there is not the least intimation of any hand or seal to the original, and there is two men that swear this is a true copy of the original, which plainly demonstrates that the original is but a blank; the truth whereof we are the more confirmed in, because it is not rational to imagine, that Mr. Mason would come from England to prosecute a right, and not bring with him what he had to make good his claim, but having nothing but blank copies, he could bring no better than he had, which cannot be looked upon as authentic, in any court.

2. If it should be supposed that ever Capt. John Mason had a right by patent, yet it does not appear how Robert Tufton Mason (as the plaintiff calls himself) derives a title from him, either as his heir, executor, or administrator, or by deed of gift ; all that we can hear in court is, that the plaintiff calls himself Capt. Mason's heir.

3. If the plaintiff, or his ancestors, ever had a title to the lands he claims, by patent from the council of Plymouth, yet they have lost it by non-use, for they never attended the ends of granting patents, by king James, of blessed memory, in his highness' patent to the great council of Plymouth, which was the peopling of the land, enlarging the king's dominions, propagating the gospel, conversion of the heathen—the native proprietors, &c. Now, the plaintiff, nor ancestors, never planted this province, nor expended any thing upon it, to the upholding of it, in peace nor war, but the present inhabitants did, either by themselves or predecessors, purchase their possessions from the natives, and by their permission did sit down upon the land, and manured, to the vast expence of above 50 years time, in hard labor, and expending upon it their whole estate. And in the late Indian war, did defend it against the enemy, to the loss of many of their lives, and considerable part of their estates, without any assistance from Mr. Mason, who now claims not only what poor people have purchased and labored hard upon, but also conquered or relieved from cruel attempts of the barbarous heathen, and we conceive we were under no obligation to run such adventures to make ourselves slaves to Mr. Mason.

4. It does not appear that there was a quorum of the great council of Plymouth, to the making of Capt. Mason's deed, according to the patent granted to the great council of Plymouth, which renders his claim unvalid, if ever any thing in that kind was done, which we question.

From what is said, we humbly conceive Mr. Mason has no right from Capt. John Mason.

And that his majesty's commission does neither give nor confirm any title to the lands claimed, we prove ;

(1) We humbly conceive that his royal majesty, who is so prudent a prince, and so solicitous for the peace of his subjects, would not have left that matter doubtful, to his subjects of this province, but rather have told us, that he had given all the lands to Mr. Mason, but there is nothing of gift, to him, in the commission, and *if his majesty had*, (which we cannot believe he would) we should crave the benefit of the statue in the 17º of Charles the first, which says, No king and council can alienate lands but by due course of law. But we were never yet heard, and when it comes to legal trial, we presume the law of possessions will confirm our lands to us, seeing we have had peaceable possession 50 years.

(2) If his majesty had given the lands in the province to Mr. Mason, what can be understood by that clause in the commission, ' That in case the inhabitants shall refuse to agree with Mr. Mason, then the governor shall interpose and reconcile all differences,

if he can, but if he cannot, then to send the case, fairly stated to England, that his majesty and privy counsel, might determine according to right ;' which we humbly conceive puts a bar to any legal proceedings, until his majesty's mind be further known therein. The inhabitants have offered their reasons to the governor according to commission, which he will not admit of, only did take of one, viz. Capt. Stileman, and promised to send them to England, but we can hear of no answer, and much fear his neglect.

(3) His majesty in his commission, says, ' To prevent unreasonable demands, that may be made by Mr. Mason, for the right he claims,' which claim may prove good or bad, when it comes to trial. We understand, to claim and to have, are different things.

(4) His majesty intimates in his royal commission, by what title Mr. Mason does claim, viz. by a grant to his ancestors, ' who improved and possessed the province with great expence, until molested and finally driven out ;' but this province cannot be concluded to be the place he claims, until he make these circumstances appear, which we are sure he never can do.

Now, Mr. Mason, not producing any original deed for any of the lands of this province, nor authentic copies, the inhabitants cannot make any compliance with him, both, because we see no right he ever had, or believing if ever any was, he hath mortgaged it already in England, and so alienated what right he had.

Although upon the former grounds, we have good plea against Mr. Mason's claim, yet we did not see cause to join issue, not only because judges and jurors were not qualified according to law, all of them being picked for espousing Mr. Mason's interest, by the governor's order, who has a mortgage for 21 years from Mr. Mason, for all the lands in the province ; but also because we were willing to attend the methods, prescribed by his majesty, in his royal commission.

No. 32. *The Answer of Elias Stileman to Mason's Claim.*

The answer of Elias Stileman, to the summons from the Hon. Edward Cranfield, Esquire, governor of his majesty's province of New-Hampshire, in N. E. in pursuance of the method which his majesty hath been gratiously pleased to prescribe in his commission.

PORTSMOUTH, the 15th of November, 1682.

May it please your Honor,—In obedience to your command, that I should render a reason why I refuse to pay quit-rent unto Robert Mason, Esq., (as he titles himself) for my house and lands, and take deeds from him for the confirming of the same, I answer as followeth :

1stly. Because my said land I bought and paid for. The title unto which is successively derived unto me from those that have possessed it, without any claim for at least these 50 years, upon which I have built at my own charge without any interruption, and am in the possession thereof, as my own. As to what is said in the commission, concerning Mr. Mason's proprietors, with all due submission to his majesty, I conceive it implies rather his claim than a positive determination of his title.

2dly. I humbly conceive, that, being in possession of what I have bought and built upon, it rests upon the claimer to make out his title, (if he have any by law) begging the favor of an English subject therein, that it may be first tried upon the place, according to the statute law, and the opinion of his majesty's judges in England, and this before I am liable to pay quit-rent, and take deeds of confirmation from him.

3dly. Should Mr. Mason obtain his demands, myself and the rest of the inhabitants would be undone forever, for then all his, granted to him, which he calls commons, being out of fence, which yet hath been bounded out by the several towns, and possessed by them for these 50 years, and improved for the maintenance of their cattle both winter and summer, and for timber and fire wood, without which there is no living for us, it being impossible for us to subsist upon that, which, in the commission is called gardens, orchards, if he may have the disposal of the rest.

4thly. The said Mason speaks of many thousands of pounds expended upon the place, which with submission cannot be made out, and if it could, what then have the poor planters expended in so many years labour since their first sitting down upon it, when they found it an howling wilderness and *vacuum domicilium*, besides a great expence of blood and estate, to defend it in the late Indian war, nor can they to this day, make both ends meet, by all their labour and frugality, and therefore must needs sink under the exaction of such a proprietor.

5thly. The land which Mr. Mason claims as proprietor, is the land on which such vast expense hath been laid out by his grandfather Capt. John Mason, for the peopling of it, and the land from whence his said grandfather's servants were violently driven out, or expelled by the inhabitants of the Massachusetts, but upon this land there was no such expence laid out by his grandfather, Captain John Mason, for the end aforesaid, nor is this the land from whence any servants of his said grandfather were so expelled, and therefore, we, that are possessed of this land, are not concerned in his claim, he hath mistaken his province, and may endeavour to find it some other where, for here is no such place.

6thly. If Mr. Mason had a patent here, why did he not take possession in the day thereof? If he were in possession, why did he not keep it still? None ever drove him out as he informs; had he been once settled, he might to this day have kept it, as the rest of the inhabitants have done, without the least molestation, but I am humbly of opinion, that if he, the said Mason, or any of his heirs came hither, they only came as many ships did to Newfoundland and to this country, to make a fishing voyage or beaver trade, and that being at an end, departed, and left their room to the next taker.

This is the sum of what I have at present to answer, humbly requesting of your honor, the stating of the case, with your opinion thereupon, to his majesty as the commission directs ; and when his majesty shall, in his wisdom and justice, see meet to order an hearing of the matter in his courts of judicature, upon the place, before a jury of uninterested and indifferent persons, which may be had out of the neighboring province, (and possibly Mr. Mason may think not attainable in this province, wherein all persons are concerned,) as he hath been pleased to do by that part of Mr. Mason's claim, which lies under his majesty's government of Massachusetts, I hope to be able upon these and other grounds so far to make out my title as to be held unblamable, before God and man, for not complying with his demands. Or, if I should see cause to appeal to his majesty and honorable council, that I shall be put beyond all need of paying quit rent to the pretended proprietor.

Thus begging your honor's favor, I subscribe,
Sir, your humble servant,
E. S.

(The two preceding papers are in the hands of the Hon. President Weare.)

No. 33. *Edmund Randolph's Letter to the Lords of Trade and Plantations, giving an account of the Rebellion in New-Hampshire, 1683.*

To the right honorable the lords of his majesty's most honorable privy council, appointed a committee for trade and plantations :

A short narrative of the late transactions and rebellion in the province of New-Hampshire, in N. E., humbly presented by Edward Randolph, collector of his majesty's customs there :

His majesty having thought fit to establish his royal authority more immediately in New-England, was pleased, by his commission under the great seal, to appoint Edward Cranfield, Esq., to be governor of that province, who arrived in New-England upon one of his majesty's frigates, about the beginning of October, 1682.— The countenance, with his indulgence to the people, obtained his easy admission into the government, in which he was very obliging to all, but especially to the late ruling party ; but, withal, made it his business to put the fort, which commandeth the mouth of the harbor, and militia, into safe hands, and put good men into places of civil administration ; and likewise, provided as well as he could, during the short time the frigate lay there, for the future quiet and settlement of that government.   Upon the 14th of November following, a general assembly of the province was called, wherein, after several warm debates, some laws were made and passed by the governor, and adjourned that assembly till the 9th of January following, being at that time unwilling to break with them, in hopes they would better understand, for the future.

Some time in December following, the governor, with Major Waldron, late president of the province, Mr. Moodey, minister, and other chief men amongst them, go to Boston, where he is civilly entertained. But his main design in that journey was, to feel

the temper of that government, and the rather, because he found
they had such an influence upon the people of this province, that
they advised and adhered to them, in the conduct of all their public and private affairs, which in a little time began to discover itself, for no sooner had Governor Cranfield openly discoursed with
me, in Boston, about my prosecuting a seizure made by me, at
Portsmouth, in October last, of a Scotch vessel, belonging to one
Jeffreys, a Scotchman, a church member and inhabitant of that
province, but it discomposed the whole party, and it was contrived
in their return home, that I might have no better success in his
majesty's immediate government, than in my former trials at Boston, to which end Mr. Hammond, candidate for a magistrate the
ensuing year in that colony, and brother-in-law to Mr. Moodey,
comes in the extremity of bad weather, upon the 19th December,
to Portsmouth, (although two or three days before he had declared
he would not go thither till spring.) Governor Cranfield being
returned from Boston, appoints a special court for a trial of the
Scotch vessel, and I went to Portsmouth to attend it ; but the
party, believing the governor to be wholly their own, and one of
the chief of them openly saying, whatever came out of the ketch
should never come into my hands, so continued the matter, that
she was carried by the fort out of the river at Pascataqua in the
day time ; although Major Stileman, one of the committee, was
commander of the fort, had express orders from the governor to
stop her ; whereupon the governor put him out of all office, and
made Captain Barefoote, one of the present council, captain of the
fort, and of the foot company, belonging to the great Island : upon
which, the fort is built. Now the better to color this matter, it
was presently given out, and by many believed, that the master
and sailors aboard, without consent or knowledge of the owner,
had run away with the ketch, as Jeffreys upon his oath voluntarily did avouch, taken before the governor. The party hoping by
this means, to persuade the governor to take no further notice of
it, the rather because the frigate was then gone out of the river.
But I had certain advice that one of Jeffreys' servants was privately sent out of the way, harbored in a very obscure place in
the province of Maine ; upon which, Mr. Martin, by his letter,
desired the justices of the peace there, to send their constables
with a warrant, to bring Jeffreys' servant before the governor to
be examined, what they knew concerning [   ] away the
Scotch ketch, they conferred and deposed that Mr. Jeffreys, the
owner, employed them, and being upon the place, stood by, gave
orders and directions, when and how the ketch should be carried
away, so that the governor, by this means, finding it out to be a
mere continuance, advised me to continue my prosecution on his
majesty's behalf, against the ketch, and all persons concerned in
her escape. The party now find no way to avoid the trial, however, it is so ordered that the jury, on which were four leading
men, church members, are prevailed upon, that against clear proof
of the breach of the acts of trade, they find against his majesty's
intended to admit them upon the statute made in the 23 of Henry

VIII., for preventing perjuries and false verdicts, which so startled them all, that some of the council intercede on their behalf, and prayed liberty to amend their ·verdicts, which being by the court agreed to, they found for his majesty, and the ketch was condemned. January the 9th.—The assembly being adjourned to that day, meet; the governor recommended to them several good bills, that had passed the council, but instead of their concurrence, they either rejected or put them into such a disguise, as rendered them altogether useless, and afterwards would not take notice of any bills, which did not arise from themselves. They likewise peremptorily insisted to have the nomination of judges and the appointing courts of judicature, powers solely invested in the governor by commission from his majesty; and lastly, they had prepared bills repugnant to the laws of England; upon which the governor, finding them to act without any regard to his majesty's service, or benefit of the province, after he had passed some bills, not knowing where these matters would end, dissolved the assembly. In a short time after, one Edward Gove, who served for the town of Hampton, a leading man, and a great stickler in the late proceedings of the assembly, made it his business to stir the people up to rebellion, by giving out that the governor, as vice admiral, acted by his royal highness' commission, who was a papist, and would bring popery in amongst them, that the governor was a pretended governor and his commission was signed in Scotland. He endeavored with a great deal of pains, to make a party, and solicited many of the considerable persons in each town to join with him, to recover their liberties, infringed by his majesty's placing a governor over them, further adding that his sword was drawn, and he would not lay it down till he knew who should hold the government. This he discoursed at Portsmouth, to Mr. Martyn, treasurer, and soon after to Capt. Hull, at Dover, which they discovered to the governor, who immediately despatched away messengers with warrants to the constables of Hampton and Exeter, to apprehend Gove—and fearing he might get a party too strong for the civil power, (as indeed it proved, for Justice Weare and a marshal were repulsed) the governor (although much dissuaded) forthwith ordered the militia of the whole province to be in arms, and understanding by the marshal that Gove could not be apprehended at Hampton, by himself, and a constable, but was gone to his party at Exeter, from whence he suddenly returned with 12 men, belonging to that town, mounted and armed with swords, pistols and guns, and a trumpet sounding, and Gove with his sword drawn, riding in Hampton at the head of them was taking horse, and with a part of the troop intended to take Gove and his company, but the governor was prevented by a messenger from Hampton, who brought word that they were met withal and taken by the militia of that town, and secured with a guard; the trumpeter forcing his way, escaped, after whom a hue and cry was sent to all parts, but as yet he is not taken. This rising was unexpectedly to the party made up on the 21st day of January last. It is generally believed, many considerable persons, at whose houses Gove then either sent or called, to come out and stand up for their liberties, would have joined with him, had he not discovered his desigas, or appeared in arms at that time. For upon the 30th day of January, being appointed by the governor a day of public humiliation, they designed to cut off the governor, Mr. Mason, and some others whom they affected not. The governor sent a strong party of horse to guard the prisoner, then in irons, from Hampton to Portsmouth. They were brought and examined before the governor and council, where Gove behaved himself very insolently; they were all committed to custody, and Capt. Barefoote, having the trained band of Great Island then in arms, was ordered to take care of the prisoners and keep a strict watch upon them, in regard the prison was out of repair. All this while the governor was at great charge and expense in suppressing this rebellion, and keeping up guards, to secure the peace of the province. We therefore, judged it necessary to bring them to a speedy trial, and to that end directs a commission of oyer and terminer to Richard Waldron, Thomas Daniel and William Vaughan, Esq'rs, for their trial, to be had upon the first day of February next, at which time Gove and the other prisoners were brought to the court, then holden at Portsmouth, in the said province, the grand jury found the bill, the next day they were all arraigned and indicted upon the 13th of the king, for levying war against his majesty. Gove pleaded to the indictment, not guilty; then Mr. Martyn, treasurer of the province, and Capt. Hull, both of Portsmouth, with two justices of the peace and a lieutenant of the foot company at Hampton, who was at the taking of them, were all sworn in court; then Gove owned the matter of fact, and to justify his taking up of arms, pleaded against the governor's power, that he was only a pretended governor, by reason his commission, as he said, was sealed in Scotland, likewise that the governor had by his proclamation, appointed the 30th January to be annually observed and kept a day of humiliation, and obliged the ministers to preach that day; that the governor had at his house discoursed to Gove and shewed him out of the 10 chapter of St. Mark, the necessity of children's baptism; this he urged to be a great imposing upon the ministry. The other prisoners pleaded not guilty; but had little to say in defence for themselves, further than they were drawn in by Gove. The jury, after long consideration, found Gove guilty of high treason upon the indictment, and all the rest in arms; upon which the court proceeded to give judgment, and passed the sentence of condemnation upon Gove, but in regard the other prisoners were specially found, the governor ordered the court to respite their judgment till his majesty's pleasure should be known therein; most of them being young men and altogether unacquainted with the laws of England. Herewith I humbly present your lordships a particular account of their trial, signed by Richard Waldron, Esq. judge of that court and passed under the seal of the province.

(The foregoing, copied from the Massachusetts colony files, was communicated to the editor by Mr. Joshua Coffin, S. H. S. Mass.)

No. 34. *Copy of a letter from Edward Gove, of Hampton, to the Court of Sessions, January, 1683.*

[This letter may be found in a Note, pages 99 and 100, of this volume.]

No. 35. *Copy of Cranfield's order for the administration of the sacraments, according to the mode of the church of England.*

At a council, held at Great Island, December 10, 1683.

By the governor and council.

New-Hampshire,—

It is hereby required and commanded, that all and singular, the respective ministers within this province, for the time being, do, from and after the first day of January next, ensuing, admit all persons that are of suitable years, and not vicious and scandalous in their lives, unto the blessed sacrament of the Lord's supper, and their children unto baptism. And if any persons shall desire to receive the sacrament of the Lord's supper, or their children to be baptized according to the liturgy of the church of England, that it be done accordingly, in pursuance of the laws of the realm of England, and his majesty's command to the Massachusetts government. And if any minister shall refuse so to do, being thereunto duly required, he shall incur the penalty of the statutes, in that case made and provided, and the inhabitants are freed from paying any duties to the said minister.

The aforesaid order was published,

R. CHAMBERLAIN, Clerk Council.

(This paper is in the council minutes, second book.)

No. 36. *Copy of the information against Rev. Joshua Moodey, 1683.*

New-Hampshire, in New-England.

To Walter Barefoote, Esq., judge of the court of pleas of the crown, &c., now sitting at Great Island ; and to Nathaniel Fryer and Henry Green, Esquires, assistants.

The information of Joseph Rayn, his majesty's attorney general for the said province of New-Hampshire, against Joshua Moodey, of Portsmouth, in the said province, clerk, in his said majesty's behalf.

The said Joseph Rayn informeth, that the abovesaid Joshua Moodey, being the present minister of the town of Portsmouth, aforesaid, within the dominions of our sovereign lord, Charles the second, king of England, is by the duty of his place, and the laws and statutes of the realm of England, (viz., the statutes made in the fifth and sixth of king Edward the sixth, and the statute of the first year of the reign of the late queen Elizabeth, which is confirmed by the statute made in the thirteenth and fourteenth year of the reign of our sovereign lord, king Charles the second,) required and commanded to administer the sacrament of the Lord's supper, in such manner and form as is set forth in the book of common prayer and administration of the sacraments, and other rites and ceremonies of the church of England, and shall use no other manner or form than is mentioned and set forth in the said book. Nevertheless, the said Joshua Moodey, in contempt of the said laws and statutes, hath wilfully and obstinately refused to administer the sacrament of the Lord's supper, according to the manner and form set forth in the said book of common prayer, unto the honorable Edward Cranfield, Esq., governor of his majesty's said province of New-Hampshire, Robert Mason, Esq., proprietor, and John Hinks, Esq., of the said province; and doth obstinately and wilfully use some other form than is by the said statutes ordained, contrary to the form thereof : Therefore, the said Joseph Rayn, in behalf of our sovereign lord, the king, doth pray, That the said Joshua Moodey, being thereof convicted according to law, may suffer such penalties, as by the said statute are made and provided in that case.

No. 37. *Copy of a second information against the same.*

New-Hampshire, in New-England.

To the honorable Walter Barefoote, Esq., judge of the court of pleas of the crown, and other civil pleas, held at Great Island, and now sitting, this 6th February, 1683-4, &c.

The information of Joseph Rayn, his majesty's attorney general for the said province, in his majesty's behalf, against Joshua Moodey, of Portsmouth, clerk.

Whereas, the said Joshua Moodey hath, in open court of the quarter sessions of the peace, held at Great Island, aforesaid, upon record, confessed and owned before the justices, that he hath administered the sacraments contrary to the rites and ceremonies of the church of England, and the form prescribed and enjoined by the statute made in the first year of the late queen Elizabeth, and so stands convicted of the said offence before the justices at the said sessions ; Joseph Rayn, his majesty's attorney general for the said province, who prosecutes for our sovereign lord, the king, doth, (according to the ancient law of the statute made in the forty-second year of the reign of king Edward the 3d, now in force,) in his majesty's behalf, exhibit his information to this honorable court against the said Joshua Moodey, for that he having for many years had the *appearance* and *reputation* of a minister of God's word in the said province, being within the king's dominions, and having wilfully and obstinately refused to administer the sacraments according to the rites of the church of England, hath administered the sacraments of baptism and the Lord's supper in other manner and form than is appointed and commanded by the statute of the first of queen Elizabeth and other statutes, contrary to the form thereof, and in contempt of his majesty's laws : and doth pray the court's judgment, and that the said Joshua Moodey may suffer the penalties by the said statute in this case made and provided.

No. 38. *Warrant and Mittimus against the Same.*

New-Hampshire in New-England.

To James Sherlock, gent., prov. marshal and sheriff of the said province, or his deputy.

In his majesty's name, you are hereby required forthwith, to take and apprehend the body and person of Joshua Moodey, of Portsmouth, in the said province, clerk, and carry him to the prison of Great Island, in the said province ; and the prison-keeper, Richard Abbot, is hereby required to receive him, the said Joshua Moodey, and keep him in safe custody, in the said prison, he having been *convicted of administering the sacraments contrary to the laws and statutes of England, and refusing to administer the sacraments according to the rites and ceremonies of the church of England, and the form enjoined in the said statutes.* There to remain for the space of six months next ensuing, without bail or mainprize. Fail not.

Dat. the 6th of Feb. 1683-4.

WALT. BAREFOOT,	(Seal.)
PETER COFFIN,	(Seal.)
HEN. GREEN,	(Seal.)
HEN. ROBY,	(Seal.)

Vera copia,

Teste, Richard Chamberlain, Clro. P.

(The three preceding papers, are in the Recorder's office.)

No. 39. *Copy of Cranfield's order, for raising money without an assembly.*

New-Hampshire.

At a council held at Great-Island, Feb. 14, 1683-4.

By the Governor and Council.

Whereas we have lately had intelligence by a letter from Capt. Hook to Capt. Barefoot one of the council of this his majesty's province, that he had advice from the captain of the Fort at Casco of a sudden rising and onset intended by the Indians upon the English at the eastward : And whereas the assembly have been lately tendered a bill for raising a revenue for the fortifying and defending ourselves against his majesty's enemies, did absolutely refuse and reject the same without giving any reason for so doing, or preparing any other for defraying the charge of the public service. We his majesty's governor and council finding the public treasury so empty and bare that there is not so much money as to pay a single messenger ; and those persons that are the support of the province have not estates to support themselves in the war (if any should happen) without due payment for their service, in consideration of the premises, by virtue of his majesty's royal commission bearing date the ninth of May, 1682, and also of his majesty's royal instructions to the governor bearing date the 29th of April, 1682, have, for the raising a revenue for fortifying and defraying the necessary charges of the government, that there may be a magazine of ammunition and provision, and of money to pay indigent soldiers, as also for such emergencies as a war will necessarily produce, thought fit to continue, and do hereby continue all such taxes and impositions as have been formerly laid upon the inhabitants (excepting only the rate of the penny in the pound raised in time of usurpation without a general assembly) commanding and requiring all and singular the constables and collectors forthwith to perform their duty in levying and collecting the same, and paying it into the treasurer.

No. 40. *Copy of a letter from the Council to Governor Dongan.*

Province of New-Hampshire, March 21, 1683-4.

Sir,

By several advices we have received of a sudden rising intended by the Indians in these eastern parts to fall upon the English, we judged it absolutely necessary without delay to provide for the safety and preservation of his majesty's subjects inhabiting this province, and to give relief (if need be) to our neighboring colonies. We have therefore upon consideration of the best means for the securing of these provinces concluded it very necessary to entertain a number of southern Indians for soldiers, who are best acquainted with the manner of these Indians' skulking fight ; and this being *a work of piety and charity* for preventing the effusion of christian blood : And knowing that your honor has an influence upon the southern Indians our honorable governor was willing to take the trouble upon himself of a journey to New-York to treat with your honor for sending of such a number of Mahiquas, or other Indians, as may be convenient to assist in this service, and to make such capitulations and agreement as to his honor shall seem reasonable. We doubt not your honor's readiness in any thing that may tend to his majesty's service and the safety of his subjects, having often heard a noble character of your honor from our governor, whom we have intreated to present our letter with our most humble service. We have committed all matters to his honor's prudence and management and what his honor shall judge fit to be done we shall see performed. So praying for your honor's health and prosperity, we subscribe ourselves, (being his majesty's council of New-Hampshire.)

May it please your honor, your most humble servants,

To the Hon. Col. Tho. Dongan, governor of his royal highness his colony of New-York, and the territories thereto belonging, humbly present.	ROBT. MASON, WALTER BAREFOOT, R. CHAMBERLAIN, ROBT. ELLIOT. JOHN HINKS.

(The two preceding papers are in the Council's Minutes, second book.)

No. 41. *Address and Petition of the Inhabitants of Exeter, Hampton, Portsmouth and Dover, against Cranfield.*

To the King's Most Excellent Majesty.

The humble address and petition of sundry of your majesty's loyal subjects the freeholders and inhabitants of your majesty's province of New-Hampshire in New-England,

Most humbly sheweth,   [From the town of Exeter.

That your petitioners' predecessors having under the encouragement of your majesty's royal ancestors by their letters patents to the great council of Plymouth, removed themselves and some of us into this remote and howling wilderness in pursuance of the glorious ends proposed, viz. The glory of God, the enlarging his majesty's dominions, and spreading the gospel among the heathen : And in order thereunto either found the lands we now possess *vacuum domicilium*, or purchased them of the heathen the native proprietors of the same, or at least by their allowance, approbation or consent, have sat down in the peaceable possession of the same for the space of above fifty years ; hoping that as we had attended the ends, so we should have shared in the privileges of those royal letters patents above mentioned, and thereupon did the more patiently bear and cheerfully grapple with those innumerable evils and difficulties that must necessarily accompany the settlers of new plantations, especially in such climates as these besides the calamities of the late Indian war to the loss of many of our lives, and the great impoverishment of the survivors. We were also further encouraged from your majesty's princely care in taking us by your late commission under your majesty's immediate government, and appointing some among ourselves to govern us according to those methods there prescribed, being particularly bound to discountenance vice and promote virtue and all good living, and to keep us in a due obedience to your majesty's authority and continuance of our just liberties and properties, together with liberty of conscience in matters of worship, and all in order to our living in all godliness and honesty, fearing God and honouring the king, which we profess to be our desire to do.

But contrariwise partly by the unreasonable demands of our pretended proprietor, Robert Mason, Esq., and partly from sundry other reasons, that are either effects or concomitants thereof, we are in a far worse condition than any other your majesty's plantations, and reduced to such confusions and extremities, that necessitate our humble application to your majesty, upon whose clemency and justice only, under God, we depend for our relief.

Your poor, distressed and oppressed petitioners, do therefore, most humbly supplicate your most gracious majesty, that you will vouchsafe to give leave unto one of ourselves, Mr. Nathaniel Weare, whom we have sent for that end, to spread before your sacred majesty, and your most honorable privy council, our deplorable estate, the beholding of which we doubt not, will move compassion towards us, and your majesty's propensity to justice, will incline to the using such means as to your wisdom shall seem best, that the oppressed may be relieved, wronged ones righted, and we, your majesty's almost undone subjects, now prostrate at your feet, may upon the tasting of your equity and goodness, be raised, and further engaged, in all humility and thankfulness, as in duty bound evermore heartily to pray, &c.

[The following names having been derived from copies, not originals, there occurred a number of mistakes in the former editions, which I have endeavored to correct.]

Andrew Wiggin,
Thomas Wiggin, senior,
Thomas Wiggin, junior,
Robert Smart, senior,
John Young,
John Foulsham,
Edward Smith,
Peter Foulsham,
Theophilus Durdly,[1]
Richard Morgan,
Samuel Leavitt,
John Cotton, junior,
John Gilman, senior,
Edward Gilman,
Moses Leavitt,
Jonathan Robinson,
Thomas Rawlins,

David Robinson,
Kinsley Hall,
Bily Dudley,
James Sinkler,
Christian Dolhoff,
Philip Charte,
Jeremiah Low,
Ralph Hall,
Samuel Hall,
John Sinkler,
John Wadleigh,
Samuel Foulsham,[2]
Eleazar Elkins,
Ephraim Foulsham,
Humphrey Wilson,
Nathaniel Foulsham,
Jonathan Thing.

The like petition from the town of Hampton, in said province, signed by,

Nathaniel Bachiler,[3]
John Marston,
James Philbrick,
Jacob Browne,
Thomas Browne,
Henry Lamper,
Jonathan Wedgwood,
Henry Moulton,
John Moulton,
Joseph Smith,
David Wedgwood,
James Cheuse,
James Perkins,
Morris Hobbs, senior,
Joseph Moulton,
Benjamin Moulton,
Thomas Leavitt,
Thomas Dearborne,
John Leavitt,
Henry Dearborne,
Aratus Leavitt,
Christopher Hussey,

John Tucke,
John Smith,
Thomas Page,
Philip Towle,
Josiah Sanbourne,
William Sanbourne, senior,
Ruth Johnson, widow,
Richard Sanbourne,
Thomas Walker,
Isaac Godfrey,
Humphrey Perkins,
David Lamprey,
Benjamin Lauyre,[4]
William Fuller,
John Sanbourne,
Hesron Leavitt,
Samuel Sherborne,
Francis Page,
Peter Weare,
Benjamin Browne,
Thomas Philbrick,
Timothy Blake,

[(1) Probably Theophilus Dudley, son of Rev. Samuel Dudley.
(2) This name is now written *Folsom*.
(3) Son of Rev. Stephen Bachiler, and died 2 January, 1710, aged 80.
(4) Perhaps Benjamin Lavers.]

Jacob Perkins,
Jonathan Philbrick,
Ebenezer Perkins,
Caleb Perkins,
Joseph Perkins,
Joseph Dow,
John Clifford, senior,
Samuel Philbrick,
Joseph Shaw,
John Clifford,
Benjamin Shaw,
Samuel Cogg,
Timothy Hilliard,
Anthony Stanyan,
John Stanyan,
Joseph Sanbourne,
Isaac Perkins,
Moses Swett,
Joseph Swett,
Joseph Cass,
Duel Clemens,
Samuel Cass,
John Sanbourne, senior.

The like petition from Portsmouth, in said province, signed by,

George Hunt,
Peter Ball,
John Sherburne, senior,
Samuel Wentworth,
Splan Lovell,
Richard Webber,
Richard Waterhouse,
William Davell,
John Cotton,
Colomart Mashawes,[1]
John Barsham,
John Shipway,
John Johnson,
John Sherburne, junior,
Thomas Pickering,
Thomas Wacombe,
Obadiah Mors,
Nicholas Morrell,
Samuel Keais,
John Dennett,
John Tooke,
Edward Melcher,
George Lavers,
Jacob Lavers,
John Brackett,
Matthius Haines,
Samuel Haines,
Samuel Haines, junior,
William Fifield, senior,
Walter Neal,
John Light,
William Pitman,
James Jones,
William Cotton,
James Levitt,
Jethro Furber,
Edward Ball,
Thomas Cotton,
Daniel Duggen,
Francis Jones,
John Pattridge,
Robert Purinton,
Nehemiah Partridge,[2]
Jotham Lewis,
Anthony Brackett,
Leonard Weeks,
Nathaniel Drake,
John Hunking,
Richard Jose,
Jane Jose,
John Fletcher,
Richard Martyn,
Ph. Suret,
Richard Waldron,
Ben. Hull,[3]
John Cutt,
William Vaughan,
George Jaffrey,
John Pickering,
John Bruster.

[(1) Probably Matthews.
(2) Yartridge in the former editions.
(3) This name appears to be *Reuben* in contemporary records.]

The like petition from the town of Dover, signed by,

Job Clements,
Thomas Roberts,
Edward Allen,
William Furber, senior,
Henry Senter,
Richard Rowes,
Anthony Nutter,
John Dam,[1]
William Furber, junior,
John Dam, junior,
John Nutter,
Thomas Row,
Edward Row,
John Meadow,[2]
Philip Chesley,
Joseph Stevenson,
Thomas Chesley,
Joseph Kinneder,[3]
Stephen Jones,
Edward Small,
Nathaniel [Lomax?][4]
James Huckins,
Gatharias Jerlld,
Ezekiel Wentworth,
Paul Wentworth,
Gerard Gyner,
Jenkins Jones,
Joseph Canne,
Richard Waldron,

John Winget,
John Gerrish,
William Wentworth,
John Heard,
John Roberts,
John Hall, junior,
Robert Burnham,
Samuel Burnham,
Jeremiah Burnham,
Samuel Hill,
Ralph Wormley,
William Horn,
Peter Mason,
John Woodman, senior,
John Woodman, junior,
Jonathan Woodman,
John Davis, senior,
John Davis, junior,
Joseph Fields,
John Bickford,
Thomas Bickford,
Thomas Edgerly,
John Hill,
Charles Adams,
Samuel Adams,
William Parkinson,
Joseph Hill,
Nathaniel Hill,
John Roberts.

(From a copy in the hands of the Honorable President Weare, and now (1830) in the hands of J. B. Moore, Esq.)

No. 42.　*The deposition of Peter Coffin relating to Cranfield's conduct towards William Vaughan.*

The deposition of Peter Coffin, Esq., one of his majesty's justices of the peace for New-Hampshire, being sworn, saith,

That sometime in the beginning of February, A. D. 1683-4, I the deponent, was present at the house of Mr. John Hincks, in company with the Hon. Edward Cranfield, Esq. governor of this province, where I heard the said governor send for Mr. William Vaughan, and when the said Vaughan came, the governor inquired of him what affidavits those were he had that day desired to be taken. The said Vaughan answered, those that concerned his cause against Mr. Mason. The governor asked him who they

[(1) Now spelled Dame.
(2) Probably John Meader, who was of Dover.
(3) Perhaps Joseph Kennedy.
(4) A Nathaniel Lomax or Lummus, from Ipswich, was of Dover about this time.]

were, he answered, if he might have summons he would bring them before his honor to be sworn; and then the governor brake out into a passion, and told him, the said Vaughan, that he was a mutinous fellow, and asked him what he went lately to Boston for; the said Vaughan answered he went about his business. Then the governor said, he went to carry a mutinous petition, to be sent to England by Weare, and asked him what vessel Weare went in; Mr. Vaughan answered, that he left Weare in Boston. Then the governor said, that by the next ships after Weare was got to England, and had presented his petition, he should have an account of the persons' names that subscribed it, returned to him, and that it would be the best haul he ever had, for it would be worth £100 a man. The governor further said, that the said Vaughan was a mutinous fellow, and required of him bonds to the good behaviour; Mr. Vaughan answered, he knew none of the king's laws he had broken, but if he could be informed of his crime, he was ready to give bonds. And that in the whole discourse, Mr. Vaughan demeaned himself with a great deal of moderation and submission.— Notwithstanding which, the governor commanded a mittimus to be writ, and signed the same with his own hand, whereupon the said Vaughan was forthwith committed to prison.

PETER COFFIN.

Peter Coffin, Esq., the above named deponent, appearing in the town of Kittery, in the province of Maine, this 27th of January, 1684–5, made oath to the above written, before me,

CHARLES FROST, Just. of Peace.

No. 43. *The warrant and mittimus whereby William Vaughan, Esq. was committed to prison.*

New-Hampshire.

To James Sherlock, gent. sheriff and provost marshal of the said province, or his deputy.

In his majesty's name you are hereby required to take and apprehend the body of William Vaughan, of Portsmouth, Esq. and carry him to the prison of Great Island; and Richard Abbot, the prison keeper thereof, is hereby required to receive the said Vaughan into said prison, and there keep him in safe custody, till he shall give good security to our sovereign lord the king, his heirs and successors, for his, the said Vaughan's, good behaviour towards the same, our sovereign lord the king, *he having refused to find security for his said good behaviour* the sixth day of February, 1683. Given under my hand and seal the said sixth day of February, 1683–4.

EDWARD CRANFIELD, (L. S.)

(The two preceding papers are in the Recorder's office.)

No. 44. *A letter from William Vaughan, Esq., containing a journal of transactions during his imprisonment, &c. to Nathaniel Weare, Esq., agent in London.*

Portsmouth, 4th Feb. 1683-4.

Mr. Nathaniel Weare,

Sir,—These serve to give covert to the enclosed, which were unhappily mislaid, and so brought to Portsmouth, instead of being carried by you to London, though on the other hand you carried many papers for London, which ought to have been at Portsmouth. There were several papers in the bundle which were very impertinent unto your business, and the transporting of them very prejudicial to some here ; your especial care about them is expected, yet may be safely returned with you, if not transmitted by you before your return. We are now a doing about getting evidences sworn, which you shall have a further account by the first, though retarded much by having no copies of them as we expected.— Since your departure, much ado has been made; many executions extended, viz. upon Messrs. Cutts, Daniel, myself, Mr. Fletcher, Moodey, Hunking, Earl, Pickering, Booth, &c. I went to prison, but was redeemed with money; several doors were broken open by Matthews, the marshal's deputy, chests also and trunks, and carried out of the houses till redeemed with money. John Partridge and William Cotton are in prison, and have been sundry days. No pay (as fish, sheep, horses, &c.) would be taken for their executions, so their bodies were levied upon, and there they lie. Our minister, for refusing to administer the sacrament to the governor, is bound over to the quarter sessions, to sit to-morrow, the issue we know not, but six months imprisonment threatened. Your wife and family well. Great bluster at Hampton about the petition ; some weaklings were wheedled into a confession and they discovered the persons that carried the petition, who were by justices G. and R. bound over to the quarter sessions ; but last Saturday night (on what ground know not) Mr. Green burnt their bonds, and only told them they must appear when called for.— Charles Hilton is lately dead ; as other news arrives shall hand it to you by all occasions, and do you the like by us.

5th. Quarter sessions are come, and there Capt. Barefoote, Messrs. Fryer, Coffin, Greene, Roby, Edgerly, were justices, Raines was attorney. It was brought in as a plea of the crown. Mr. Moodey pleaded his not being ordained, having no maintenance according to statute, and therefore not obliged to that work which the statute required. Besides, these statutes were not made for these places, the known end of their removal hither being that they might enjoy liberty in these foreign plantations, which they could not have by virtue of the statutes at home, and were allowed to have here, especially our commission granting liberty of conscience. These things were pleaded, but to no purpose. After a short pleading, and that not without many interruptions and smiles by the pragmatic, busy, impertinent attorney, he was committed to the marshal, (viz. Long Matthews) and held in custody that night, though permitted to lodge at Capt. Stileman's. The jutices debated a little ; four of them entered their dissent, viz. Messrs. Fryer, Green, Roby, Edgerly, but Capt. Barefoote and Coffin were for his condemnation. Judgment of the case, every man's was entered by the secretary over night, but being deferred till next morning, information was given to somebody, who came in and threatened and hectored after such a rate, that Green and Roby also consented, as you see by the enclosed, and he was committed to prison. Petition was by him made to the court, and afterwards to the governor, that he might step up at night to his family and settle matters there, and that he might not go into the dismal place the common prison. The court could not, the governor would not, of first, though in fine gave leave to the marshal to drop him at Capt. Stileman's, where he is confined to his chamber, though not without leave to go down stairs, or into the backside, and this was done 6th instant. At night, I having moved for the taking of evidences, which was in words owned, went to the secretary for summonses, intending to begin with Lieut. Hall and Thomas Wiggin, he refused to give summonses, but first (I suppose) must inform somebody, I was sent for by the marshal, huffed and hectored strangely, threatened, &c. in fine, must give bonds to the good behaviour. I refused; thereupon he made and signed my mittimus to the prison, though by the way, I know not how, was also dropped at and confined to Mr. Moodey's chamber, where we have been these two nights, very cheerful together.

Poor Wadleigh, who was left to the governor's mercy, is come out upon security for forty pounds money, and your Gove for a like sum, only William Partridge is to do it in work, building and fencing, &c. The actions go on, and are turned off hand apace, *twelve at a clap*, after the old manner. Roby, though a justice, is still of the jury. A new trick is on foot. Several of us that were executed upon, and paid our money the first suit, are sued again for illegal withholding possession, though the marshal (who was by execution required to give possession, never came to demand it;) the issue of which we know not, matters being yet depending.

9th. The prisoners Vaughan and Mr. Moodey were fetched out of prison to plead their cases at the court. Messrs. Cutt, Daniel, John Partridge and myself and Mr. Moodey were sued, and all cast, but the last, who had something particularly to say, and so he cast Mr. Mason, though we thought we all said enough to cast him,—viz. that he had an execution for the land sued for, and when he levied his execution might have taken the land also, with many other things, (enough of, we thought,) to have turned the case against him, before any indifferent judges and jurors, but thus we are treated.

But above all, our minister lies in prison, and a famine of the word of God coming upon us. No public worship, no preaching of the word, what ignorance profanes, and misery must needs ensue ! By the premises, you see what need there is you should be vigorous and speedy as you may, about your business, to do what may be to the preventing of utter ruin.

My imprisonment is a present stop to the getting what evidences is needful, and it is like we shall not make any further attempt here, but with what convenient expedition, will be done what is needful and necessary. Mr. Martin was sued at the court in two actions, one by Mr. Mason, for fines and forfeitures, collected and received by him as treasurer, from seventy-nine to eighty-two, and another action, by the governor, for fines, &c., from April, eighty-two. He is cast in both actions, to the value of about seventy pounds, although he pleaded, that what he received was disposed by order of the authority which made him treasurer, and had as good commission from his majesty, as that was in being ; neither did it legally appear, that either Mr. Mason or the governor have any right to fines and forfeitures, the king appointing all public money to be disposed or improved for the support of the government : however it is but ask and have ; their demands in any case have the force of an execution.

10th. The sabbath is come, but no preaching at the Bank, nor any allowed to come to us, we had none but the family with us, the poor people wanting for lack of bread. Motions have been made, that Mr. Moodey may go up and preach on the Lord's day, though he come down to prison at night, or that neighbor ministers might be permitted to come and preach, or that the people might come down to the prison and hear, as many as could, but nothing will do; an unparalleled example amongst christians to have a minister put out and no other way found to supply his place by one means or other. Mr. Fryer was severely threatened for refusing to subscribe Mr. Moodey's commitment, but hath obtained fairly a dismission from all public offices. Justice Edgerly also cashiered, and bound over to the Quarter Sessions.* It is said that Justice Green is much afflicted for what he has done, but Roby not. Peter Coffin can scarce show his head in any company.†

14th. News came from the fort at Casco, that there was great danger of the Indians rising, which hath occasioned a meeting of the council and some discourse, but hear no more since, and hope it may vanish.

15th. Good Mrs. Martin was buried, being not able to live above one sabbath after the shutting up the doors of the sanctuary. Somebody has said that the imprisoning of the minister is none of his work, he did but constitute the court, they did it themselves, though also hath said he would have done it himself if they had not.

* [Tho. Edgerly was, by the governor's order of the sessions, discharged from being justice of the peace, and of being in any other public employment. Records of Court of Q. S.]

† Mr. Moodey, in the church records, remarks thus on his judges. ' Not long after, Green repented, and made his acknowledgment to the pastor, who frankly forgave him. Robie was excommunicated out of Hampton church, for a common drunkard, and died excommunicate, and was by his friends thrown into a hole near his house for fear of an arrest of his carcase. Barefoote fell into a languishing distemper, whereof he died. Coffin was taken by the Indians, (at Cochecho, 1689) his house and mill burnt, himself not being slain but dismissed ; the Lord give him repentence, though no signs of it have yet appeared.'

17th. Another sad Sabbath.

18th. Came Messrs. Mason, Barefoot and secretary, with Thurton who swore against me a false oath, of which I have enclosed a copy. Thurton said he was sent for on purpose to give in his testimony against me ;—they went away, and soon after came the enclosed mittimus directed to Mr. Raines, who is sheriff and marshal in Mr. Sherlock's room, that have been out of favor of late, though now it is said in favor, but not in place again. Mr. Estwicke is also put out of all office. Note, that when I went to him for taking oaths, he said all oaths should be taken before the governor and council, but now could send to justices to do it. We had for some nights our key taken away from the chamber door about 8 or 9 at night, but have since left off that trade. Sewall of Exeter is dead.* Several overtures were made this week to John Partridge and William Cotten by Raines to come out of prison he giving them 3 months time to provide money or any other current pay, though they tendered fish, plank, &c. before they were put in, they refused to accept.

24th. This sabbath our wives, children and servants came down and spent the day with us in our chamber, and we yet hear nothing said against it.

25th. The marshal goes and levies upon John the Greek's† sheep and cattle for the execution, for which he had lain about three weeks in prison, and then came and ordered him to go about his business, 15 sheep, sundry lambs, and two heifers seized for six pounds odd money. This day also Mr. Jaffery having had sundry warnings the week before to clear his house because Mr. Mason would come and take possession of it, went nevertheless to the Bank upon business ; meanwhile came Mr. Mason with the marshal and turned all his servants out of doors, set another lock on the door, and at night when his servants came home wet ; they would not suffer them to come in, but there lodged Mathews and Thurton all night. Mr. Mason said, while about this work, that he was sorry Weare had no more of this news to carry home with him.

The governor having sent to Mr. Cotton,‡ that when he had prepared his soul, he would come and demand the sacrament of him, as he had done at Portsmouth, already. Mr. Cotton, the latter end of the week before last, went to Boston, and has been out two Lord's days, already ; all is well with yours there, so far as I can learn, I cannot go to see, else, might have given them a visit.

One word more about my business. I am under imprisonment, about Thurton's business, being seized by the marshal, and committed, when in prison before, for not giving bond for the good behaviour, though nothing charged upon me, any more than before, which you well know. I know nothing, but they intend to keep me here endlessly. It is said, I must pay one hundred pounds, for

* [Probably Edward Sewall, who died in 1684.]

† [This person is called in the Records of the Court of Quarter Sessions, John Greek, alias Amazeen.]

‡ [Rev. Seaborn Cotton, of Hampton.]

striking one of the king's officers, and must have my name returned into the exchequer, and must lie in prison, till the money
be paid, and I am discharged from the exchequer. The design
you may easily see, is to ruin me, and how vain my pleas will be,
you may easily guess. Though I have many things to say, viz.
that Thurton was either no officer, or at least, not known to be so,
however not sworn, nor did I strike him in the high-way, as he
swears, nor is there any proof, but his own single testimony, which
how far it avails in such a case, would be considered ; it is also
worthy of inquiry, whether ever that law was intended for us,
here being no customs to be gathered, no exchequer to be applied
to, and therefore, how these methods can be observed, is not in-
telligible. You may easily imagine how things will be if I am
forced to comply with their humors. Pray consult, consider, and
see if something may not be done to put a stop to such arbitrary
proceedings, a trial on the place, by indifferent, unconcerned
judges and jurors, if, at least, there can any such be found, who
will not be forced into what some will have done, but I shall not
need to instruct you. There you have better, counsel, then I can
give you, and of your fidelity to inquire and remit by the first,
what is needful on this account I doubt not.

I have given you but a taste, we that see it, know more than
can possibly be understood by those, that only hear, in a word
such is the height of their heat and rage, that there is no living for us
long in this condition. But we hope God will be seen in the
Mount.

I should have inserted what fell out after the dissolving of the
rebelious assembly, there was discourse of constables, and instead
of the freemen choosing as formerly, they took a short and cheaper
course, and at the Quarter Session, constables where chosen, and
to begin with Mr. Speaker,* he has the Honor to be constable for
Portsmouth, Capt. Gerrish, Lt. Anthony Nutter and John Woodman, for Dover, John Smith† the cooper, for Hampton, John Foul-
som, at Exeter. Whether Mr. Speaker shall sew or fine, is not
yet determined. And now I am speaking of the General Assembly, must hint what was formerly forgotten, viz. that they convened on the Monday, and the choice of the speaker (their old
one) in words highly approved, and he complimented alamode.
Then a bill was sent them down, (of which if I can get it, being
now in prison, shall inclose a copy) which they talked a little of,
and then brake up for the night and went up to the Bank to lodge,
(the tide serving very well to go and come) the report of which
highly disgusted, and the next morning the answer to the bill vehemently urged, which was in fine a negative. Hereupon, in a
great rage, telling them they had been up to consult with Moodey,
an utter enemy to church and common wealth, with much of like
nature, he dissolved them, which was done on the Tuesday, after

* [Richard Waldron, who, it appears from the Records of the Court of
Quarter Sessions, was appointed constable for Portsmouth, 5 February, 1683
–4, but refused to serve.]

† [John Smith, of Hampton. Records of C. Q. Sessions.]

which he came up to the Bank and gave order for a sacrament on the next Lord's day, as you have heard, and since the assembly men pricked for constables.

By the premises, you will see how the governor is making good his word. *He came for money, and money he will get*, and if he get it, you know who must lose it, and how miserable must our condition quickly be, if there be no remedy quickly provided. He contrives and cuts out work, and finds evil instruments to make it up, and these some among ourselves. Thus we are cloven by our own limbs.

28th. Since Mr. Jaffrey was dispossessed, Raines offered him for five shillings per annum quit-rent to Mr. Mason, he should have his house again, provided he would own him proprietor, but he refusing, it is said he shall never have it again. The talk is, that his house must be court-house and prison both, and standing so near the governor, it is judged suitable for both those ends, that he may have the shorter journey to court, and the prisoners may be always under his eye.

29th. John the Greek having lain some weeks in prison upon execution, his goods having been levied upon, (as above) was by Raines locked out of the prison, and bidden to be gone, but he would not, keeps his quarters still with the other two. This day his goods were sold by the marshal, and bought by Thurton.

Mr. Cotton* is come home from Boston. Great offence taken here at a sermon he preached in Boston, on Acts xii. v. though pleasing to the hearers.

March 2d. This day Mr. Jaffrey's goods were all turned out of doors by the sheriff, &c. his man received and disposed of them. Against Jaffrey there are two oaths taken, single oaths, but being for the king, will pass, and orders are given for warrants to apprehend him, he appears not.

March 5. It is said that they are going this day to Major Waldron's, to serve him as they have done Mr. Jaffrey, and it is given out that the rest will be treated in like manner; the court was adjourned yesterday to the next month, probably that they might levy the executions that are in bank before they cut out any more work. Justice Green seems something troubled for sending the minister to prison, and saith he will never do such a thing again, but Peter Coffin saith it is a nine days' wonder, and will soon be forgotten, but others think otherwise. If they go on thus, we are utterly ruined, must go away or starve, if at least we be not so confined that we cannot go away neither. I question whether any age can parallel such actions.

In my last I sent you a letter to Sir Josiah Child, my master, of which also you have another copy herewith. My design is, that you carry the letter yourself, wait on him while he reads it, and if he will please to hear you, (as I hope he may) that you amplify matters, inform him what further intelligence you have, and attend his direction, if God move his heart to do ought for us. This day,

---

* [Rev. Seaborn Cotton, of Hampton. See page 107.]

the governor sent us word by the marshal that we must remove to Mr. Jaffrey's house to-morrow, which house is made the prison.— We hope the news of the rising of the Indians will fall to nothing.

Ditto 5th. Thus far was sent you by way of Barbadoes. It follows. The governor did say to a Salem man, that Moodey might go out of the prison, if he would go out of the province, but we hear no more since.

James Robinson under great wrath and in much danger only for speaking something to Thurton (of his being a pitiful fellow, &c.) while said Thurton was active in turning out Mr. Jaffrey's goods.

6th. Matthews and Thurton hunted for Mr. Jaffrey, searched in Mrs. Cutt's house, went into every room above and below stairs, searched under her bed where she lay sick in it, but found him not. They carried it very rudely and basely in their work. Matthews said he would catch him, or have his heart's blood, but he was not there. Mr. Jaffrey's goods were carried to the other side by night.

It is said that our imprisonment has much [*alarmed*] the whole country, and made them more fond of their liberties. This night, Matthews was beaten at Mercer's,* (some fuddling about it, it is like) but it is made a mighty thing on, said to be a deep plot, deeper than Gove's, managed by strong heads, and abundance of that nature, and because the persons concerned were under the influence of Vaughan and Moodey, they should suffer for it, for not teaching them better. Though we know no more of it than you, nor is there ought in it worth notice, but thus we are treated. The governor went up to the Bank and made great inquiries about it. Capt. Pickering and others that were in the fray, are bound over.

7th. They had six pounds, five shillings, of Obadiah Morse, by way of execution. Raines was discarded, being put out of being sheriff, &c. though he had his commission under the seal but the other day. Matthews is made provost marshal (at least) in his room, and Thurton, marshal's deputy. Good birds for such offices. Lord have mercy upon us. They had also eighteen shillings from Samuel Case,† the rest is deferred, and he has put away his goods and intends to remove or go to prison, and so we must all.

11th. The Indian news occasioned an order to the trustees to get ammunition, they came down and pleaded their time was up ; it was said, you shall keep in during my pleasure. They said they had no money of the towns in their hands, nor could any be raised without a general assembly. Then lay out your own money, or else wo to you ; and this they are fain to comply with.

He said and swore that if Mason would not acknowledge a judgment next court, of six hundred pounds, he would take all his business from him, and sue in his own name. He swore he would turn out that rogue Eliet, who is as bad as any other.

Mr. Waldron being sent for by warrant to come before the jus-

* [Francis Mercer, who was an alehouse keeper.]
† [Probably Cass.]

tices to take the constable's oath, appeared before Mr. Mason and Capt. Barefoote, but excusing it, and giving good reason, was dismissed upon paying five pounds; but poor Capt. Barefoote was most fearfully rated at for his labor, many oaths sworn that Waldron should either take the oath or either take up with a goal.— The next day, (though the justices, whose business it is, had fairly dismissed him) he was convented again, the oath tendered, he threatened with a prison immediately, but told them he knew the law better than so, then they took his own bond to answer it at quarter sessions, and so far of that matter as yet. Another constable is chosen, viz. Capt. Pickering, though he has as yet waived the oath, having lately served in that place, and pleading his being bound to good behaviour for that last fray. He talks much of frigates to scare the poor people.

14th. Council sat, and could not agree about raising money, which highly provoked somebody. They said the general assembly only could raise money.

The governor told Mr. Jaffrey's negro he might go from his master ; he would clear him under hand and seal ; so the fellow no more attends his master's concerns.

15th. This day the secretary was in a great rage turned out of all his offices, except secretary to the council, (an empty name, little profit) and the books sent for out of his hands. He is much concerned and dejected.

I am credibly informed, and you may believe it, that the governor did in the open council yesterday, say and swear dreadfully, that he would put the province into the greatest confusion and distraction he could possibly, and then go away and leave them so, and then the devil take them all. He also then said, that Mr. Mason said he would drive them into a second rebellion, but himself would do it before; and I wonder he has not; such actings are the ready way, but God hath kept us hitherto, and I hope he will do so still. He also said and swore that any person that should have any manner of converse with us, or any of our mind, he would count them his utter enemies and carry toward them as such.

17th. The governor having formerly prohibited the prisoners from making shingles, went himself this day to the prison, and prohibited John Partridge from making shoes ; bade the marshal throw them into the sea.

This day Raines being not willing to give up a warrant that he had executed, during the short time of being sheriff, was sent for by the governor, and not appearing, the governor came to his chamber, and did beat him dreadfully, and bade the marshal carry the rogue to jail. He remains out of favor still. The governor also went over to Capt. Hooke's, and got him to give warrants to the constables on the other side, to search all houses for Mr. Jaffrey, and bring him over, but they found him not, nor is he yet found, though proclamation was made at Wells court, for his seizure, though not yet done.

March 18. This morning came Matthews to our chamber, and

said the governor sent him to carry me to the prison, where I am, where I still lie; being put in only for Thurton's action, and kept in, though I offered security to respond it. I think they have let fall the other about the good behaviour, seeing they can make nothing of it, and before my coming in, John the Greek's bed, &c. was turned out of prison, and he forced away, who would not depart before.

21st. Mr. Martyn came to discourse about the money he was cast for, which they have not yet levied upon him, but intend to lay it upon all the old council equally, that each may bear his share. At same time, the governor told Mr. Martyn that he would send his execution. Said Mr. Martyn, you know it is not my due to pay the money. No matter, (said he) *I want money, and will have it.* But *I have none,* said he; then I will take your house.— He added also, to Mr. Martyn, that he was a church member, and he would watch him and all such, and be sure to pay them off if he could catch them.

22d. The sorest storm and the highest tide that ever was known. Many thousands of pounds damage in Boston, and much here.— The bridge to the Great Island broken off in the middle, to the great joy of many.

24th. The governor went to Boston in Fox's sloop, intending thence to New-York, pretending to discourse Colonel Dungan, and bring down two hundred Mohawks to kill the eastward Indians. What is at the bottom, or will be the issue, God knows. He had a cold treat at Boston, staid not a night in town. Since his going, we have had little news worthy of your notice, but all things have been very quiet hitherto.

I have not enlarged upon these particulars to my master Child, but if he will take any notice of the thing and be concerned about it, he will then give you opportunity of discoursing him, and you may inform what is further needful.

31st. This month passed out and the other came in, without any noise, unless the great joy that was at the Bank, by Mr. Moodey's going up thither, and my going once or twice after, with our keepers, by Mr. Mason's permission, who presides in the governor's absence, but we soon returned to the place from whence we came.

April 8. Nathaniel Fox, who married Mrs. Stileman's daughter, sent Matthews to arrest Capt. Stileman for his wife's portion, (though it was often tendered him in such pay as the court ordered it, but he would have it in money.) Capt. Stileman gave his own house and all that was in it, for security to answer the action, but Matthews bringing Thurton with him at his instigation, who was terribly insolent, they *arrested the woman, Mrs. Stileman, and carried her to prison with much violence and coarse usage, though her husband had given security.* She was carried in the evening. Capt. Stileman wrote to Mr. Mason; he protested against it, and wrote to the marshal, it would not do. He went again, and Mr. Mason wrote again, but to no purpose; they kept her there till the next morning; a thing not to be paralleled in the English nation !—

Complaint hath been made, but no remedy. Abbot being up at the Bank with me, Thurton took the key of the prison, and when Abbot came, would not permit him to go in, but turned him away. Brave doings ! No tongue can tell the horrible imperiousness and domineering carriage of that wretch. The next morning, Mr. Mason (much ado) got Mrs. Stileman out, and the jailor into his place again.

Mr. Mason gave leave for any minister to come and preach at the Bank, so that we got Mr. Phillips* for two Lord's days, viz. 13 and 20th, having been nine Lord's days without a sermon.

April 14th. Came H. Greene to Mr. Moodey's chamber, and made a confession of his fault, and begged his pardon for putting him in prison, and said he would get him out quarter sessions, &c. Good words, but ——. Capt. Barefoote went to the prison, and told John Partridge that if he would give an order to allow so much as his charges came to, out of what the provinces owed him about Gove, for the soldiers, &c. he should come out of prison, and they would pay him the remainder, the whole being about thirty pounds, but he was not forward lest he should in so doing quit them of false imprisoning him; but if they would do it themselves, stop so they might. Nothing is done in it.

15th. Matthews and Thurton were sent to Hampton to levy executions and serve attachments, and warn jurymen for the court in May.

They arrested seven, among which Captain Sherburne one, warned the old jurymen, executed upon William Sanborn, took four oxen which were redeemed by money, drove away seven cows from Nathaniel Bachiler, went to your house, met your son Peter going with his four oxen into the woods, commanded him to turn the oxen home, he would not; they cursed, swore, drew upon him, threatened to run him through, beat him, but he did not strike again. They came to your house, were shut out, your wife fearfully scared for fear of her son who was out with them. At length she let them in, laid three pounds on the table, which they took, and then levied on several young cattle, but released and left them. Your son came hither to advise, but complaining is bootless, such a dismal case are we in. They took away two beds from old Perkins, but his son offered his person, and they took it, and quitted the other ; what more they did there we as yet hear not.

Capt. Gerrish, John Woodman, Lieut. Nutter and Nathaniel Bachiler are sworn constables.

17th. I went to Mr. Mason at Capt. Barefoote's house and had several witnesses with me, and desired him to take depositions that I might send them home, about my case and the rest of the cases, but he refused. The governor had put me in prison when I asked him, and now in his absence, the deputy governor denies to grant them. I hope this will be matter of just complaint, that we should be hindered from applying to his majesty for relief under

* [Rev. Samuel Phillips, of Rowley.]

our oppressions. You will have evidence of his denial sent home, sworn before some of the Bay magistrates. We can do no more unless the Bay should assist us, which they are loath to do, and we are loath to put them upon, as matters are circumstanced with them ; but we think it should be taken very heniously by all that love justice and willing to administer it, that his majesty's subjects should be thus treated. Surely they are afraid or ashamed of their actions, (and they may be both) else they would not be so shy of having them known.

This is what offers here ; what more needful, cousin Waldron will advise from Boston.

With due respects remain,

Your assured friend and servant.

For Mr. Nathaniel Weare, in London.

A discourse with the governor about my imprisonment, May, 1684.

[Subjoined to the foregoing letter.]

At a sessions held the 6th May, 1684, I was denied counsel, and to have witnesses sworn. Mr. Waldron, Captain Stileman and Captain Frost were presented.

10th. The governor was with me in prison. Mr. Chamberlain, Mr. Hinkes and Mr. Sherlock with him.

The governor proffered me, (that whereas, I was fined by the justices in Thurton's case, that I might think they had not done me right,) that if I would prosecute it (giving security so to do,) in the king's bench, at Westminster, the exchequer, or before king and council, I should ; though by his commission he could not do it. My answer was, unless I could have security given me, that in case I should recover, I might have my charge and damage made me good ; it would be of no benefit to me. He said there was no reason for that, because it was for the king ; though it was his, because Mr. Mason had resigned up to the king all fines and forfeitures, and the king had given it to him. But he said, if I would deposit a valuable sum he would do the like, and would give bond, and have it tried as abovesaid. My answer was, I thought the forty pounds was enough, and that I expected execution would come out at the time, and should endeavor by the time, to provide enough for it, but withal, told the governor it was at his liberty to remit it, if he pleased, by virtue of his commission.

Also, for my being in prison for not giving bond for my good behaviour, when the sessions came I was not brought to my trial for that, but remanded to prison again.

At ditto, time the governor told me he had put me in prison on that account, and he would abide by it, till I would give two hundred pounds bond. My answer was, I had rather lay in prison, than give bond to tempt such a fellow as Thurton, (or such others) that had sworn against me already, and falsely, and judged it might be no scruple to him to do the like again. And withal, told him, that if his honor pleased to let me out of prison, I would engage myself, by bond, to live out of the province, though that would be very detrimental to my concerns, and by that, I hoped he would have no thoughts of my misbehaving myself, that would be detrimental to the king's government here, or himself. Not that I scrupled giving bond for my good behaviour, though not accused for any thing, but for laying a temptation to some base minded person or persons to forswear themselves, as one had done before, in another case relating to me.

May 12. Was informed, that whereas, Thurton had a commission to be prison keeper, (and withal, had vapored, and said the prison was too good for Vaughan, and the room that he had fitted up, did intend to keep it himself, and that Vaughan should take his quarters where he would assign it, and that the prisoners should not be waited on as Abbot had done, for he would keep them locked up, only come morning and evening,) lost his pocket book, wherein was his commission and sundry papers of concernment.

(The original of this letter and journal is in the hands of the Honorable President Weare.)

No. 45. *Copy of a letter from the governor and council to the lords of trade.*

Province of New-Hampshire, May 23, 1684.

May it please your lordships,—

Since Robert Wadleigh is returned from England, having lately had an appeal dismissed by the council-board, by taking advantage of Mr. Randolph's absence, who was attorney for the parties, he hath put the people of this province into such a ferment and disorder, that it is not possible to put his majesty's commands in execution, or any ways govern them. And, though notwithstanding, in obedience to your lordships' commands, we have called an assembly, (a copy of the proclamation for that purpose being herein inclosed,) we cannot think it prudent or safe to let them sit ; they being of the same ill humor, or worse, as when Gove went into arms, his design being hatched at the time the assembly sat. And it looks more like a design, they having those four constables into the assembly, that the king's peace may not be preserved, (the whole number of the assembly being eleven :) This Wadleigh being formerly an assembly man, and hath three sons condemned in Gove's rebellion, (and himself now chosen again ;) the oldest of them I have pardoned, one of them is dead, and the other I keep in prison till I receive your lordships' further order. All the other offenders being pardoned. Major Waldron's son is constantly of the assembly and speaker, (this being the third that hath been called.) I wish his majesty's clemency do not cause some great mischief to be done here. They have never given TWO PENCE* to the support of the government, and that very rate that was made in the time of presidents Cutt and Waldron, we have according to his majesty's royal commission continued ; but do not think it safe to publish it, unless we had strength to countenance

*The first assembly voted two hundred pounds to the governor, but it is not certain that he accepted it though he consented to the act.

our proceedings. This we conceived it our duty to inform your lordships, and are,

May it please your lordships,

Your most humble and most obedient servants,

The appellants claim by grant from	EDW. CRANFIELD,
Mr. Mason; and as for Wadleigh,	ROBT. MASON,
he hath been these sixteen days	WALT. BAREFOOT,
in the country, and though I have	R. CHAMBERLAIN,
heard much of him, I have not	JOHN HINKS,
yet seen him.	JAMES SHERLOCK.

To the right honorable, the lords of the committee }
of trade and plantation, at Whitehall,   }

(From the Council Records.)

No. 46.   *Copy of a letter from Cranfield to Sir Leoline Jenkins,*
of the same date.

May it please your honor,—

We humbly beg, after your honor hath perused this letter to the lords of the council, you would be pleased to lay it before their lordships, and desire their lordships to come to some speedy resolution ; for it is no longer in my power to promote the honor and interest of his majesty here, without a small frigate to second his majesty's broad seal and other his royal commands. As to the pirates, your honor may be assured, that myself and the council will punish them according to their demerits, if they shall at any time happen to come within this jurisdiction ; and carefully obey all other commands which shall be sent unto,

May it please your honor,

Your honor's most humble and most obedient servant,

EDW. CRANFIELD.

I most humbly beseech your honor by the first opportunity, to send the king's letter to give me liberty to go off to Jamaica or Barbadoes for my health ; finding so great a weakness in my legs, which indisposition hath been contracted by the severity of the cold.

To the Right Honorable Sir Leoline Jenkins, one of his }
majesty's principal secretaries of state at Whitehall.   }

(The two preceding papers are in the council minutes, second book.)

No. 47.   *Copy of Nath'l Weare's first complaint against Cranfield.*

To the king's most excellent majesty, and the lords of his most honorable privy council,—

The humble representation of Nathaniel Weare, inhabitant and planter in your majesty's province of New-Hampshire, in New-England, in America, on behalf of himself and other your majesty's loyal subjects, inhabitants and planters there, whose names are subscribed to the four annexed petitions, as follows :—

1. That the honorable Edward Cranfield, Esq., your majesty's governor of the said province, upon his first entrance on that government, in order to the enlargement of his power as governor there, beyond the just bounds and limits your majesty was by your royal commission pleased to set him, and to engross the whole power of erecting courts, with all necessary fees, powers and authorities thereto, into his own hands, exclusive of the general assembly there. The said Mr. Cranfield, at the first general assembly there, when the words of his commission ran, 'And we 'do hereby give and grant unto you full power and authority to 'erect, or constitute and establish, such and so many courts of ju- 'dicature and public justice within the said province and planta- 'tion, within your government, as you *and they* shall think fit and 'necessary for the hearing and determining of all causes, as well 'criminal as civil, according to law and equity, and for awarding 'execution thereupon, with all reasonable and necessary powers, 'authorities, fees and privileges belonging unto them,' caused his commission to be entered in the council books there, and delivered a copy thereof to the general assembly without the words [*and they*,] affirming those words to have been put in by mistake of the clerk, in engrossing the commission; whereby the said Mr. Cranfield has enhanced the fees upon trials there, to his own advantage, as will appear in one of the articles following.

2. Although your majesty has been graciously pleased by your said commission to interpose between the inhabitants of the said colony and Mr. Robert Mason, *pretended* proprietor thereof, and to direct—

'That on non-agreement between those inhabitants and Mr. Mason, the said Mr. Cranfield should interpose, who if he could not end the differences between, was by the said commission directed to transmit to England such cases impartially stated, with his opinion and reasons on the same, that your majesty with advice of your privy council, might hear and determine the same.' That nevertheless, the said Mr. Cranfield, instead of keeping himself indifferent between the contending parties, Mr. Mason and the said inhabitants, hath by purchase or mortgage from Mr. Mason, made himself owner of the province : And the better to come by what he hath so purchased, he hath under color of the authority of your majesty's commission, made courts, whereof both judges and jurors have agreed with Mason for their own lands, and some of them have taken grants from Mason of other men's lands. That nevertheless this jury is continued from month to month, and kept for this service.

That Mr. Mason has cast forty persons on suit by that jury, the court rejecting all pleas, and though the verdict be given for Mr. Mason according to your majesty's royal commission, (which directs as before) and the judgment entered accordingly, yet, upon the execution the inhabitants are turned out of their lands and houses, as it hath fared with Wm. Vaughan and others, and deprived of all subsistance.

3. That the charge of every action is raised from 20s. to 6l.,

which is exacted in money, and though goods tendered, (as usual) the persons are imprisoned for want of money in kind, and Mr. Cranfield himself, takes ———— of the 6*l.*

4. That the said Mr. Cranfield, under color of trying actions, has, by setting the fees so extraordinary, forced several to quit their claims, for want of money to carry on the suit.

5. That the said governor taking upon himself the power of priceing money not entrusted with him by his commission, hath, against the agreement of the general assembly, by advice of his council, ordered pieces of eight, however wanting in their weight, to pass for 6 shillings.

6. That the said governor, without good and lawful cause, hath taken upon him to commit several men to prison, particularly Wm. Vaughan, until bonds given for their appearances and good behaviour, when nothing further objected to them.

7. That the said governor and his council, took upon them to make laws and put them in execution, without the general assembly.

8. That to prove the articles above, against Mr. Cranfield, the complainants have successlessly endeavored to procure warrants or summons from the secretary, to summon their witnesses to be sworn, (which cannot otherwise be so) the seeking of such summons has occasioned being bound to the good behaviour, so as the complaining of a wrong done one, does, under Mr. Cranfield's management, but draw a new punishment on the afflicted, but no manner of redress.

All which, the said Nath. Weare, humbly lays at your majesty's feet, imploring your majesty's present hearing what your petitioner is able to make out of the premises, and ordering some commission to examine the truth of the residue of the said allegations (since your majesty's governor on the place will not admit of such evidence.) That on the return thereof, your majesty's subjects in that province, may find such relief as to your princely wisdom shall seem meet.

And that, in the mean time, Mr. Cranfield, be admonished not to exceed the bounds of his commission.

And your petitioner shall ever pray, &c.

No. 48. *Reference of the same, to the Lords of Trade.*

At the court at Hampton court, this 11th day of July, 1684.

By the king's most excellent majesty, and the lords of his majesty's most honorable privy council.

Upon reading this day at the board, the petition and complaint of Nathanial Weare, inhabitant and planter in his majesty's province of New-Hampshire, in New-England, in America, in behalf of himself and others, his majesty's loyal subjects and inhabitants and planters there, whose names are subscribed to the four petitions thereto annexed against Edward Cranfield, Esq., his majesty's governor thereof;

His majesty was pleased to order, that the said petition and complaint be, and they are hereby referred to the right honorable, the lords committees of this board for trade and foreign plantations, who are to consider thereof, and to report to his majesty at this board their opinion thereupon, and then his majesty will declare his further pleasure.

PHILIP LLOYD.

A true copy.

(The two preceding papers, are in hands of the Hon. President Weare.)

No. 49. *Letter from the Lords of trade to Edward Cranfield*

After our hearty commendations to you. His majesty having received the petitions and complaints of divers of his subjects, inhabitants and planters of New-Hampshire, against you for certain irregular proceedings alleged by them to be had by you, in the execution of your commission and administration of justice ; and it being ordered in council, that the said petitions and complaints be examined and considered by us, that we may report to his majesty our opinions, to the end his majesty's further pleasure, may be signified thereupon. We have, therefore, herewith sent unto you copies of the said petitions and representations, that you may return your particular answer thereunto with all speed, and that we may the better distinguish the truth of what is alleged or complained of, and of such defence as you shall be able to make. We do think fit, that all persons whatsoever, have free liberty to depose upon oath what they know, and to take copies of all records, in these or any other cases relating to yourself, or the said province, and that the said depositions be taken in writing by any member of the council or justice of the peace in that colony, whom you are duly to authorize thereunto, and as we cannot believe that you will put any restriction or discouragement whatsoever, upon the taking and transmitting of all necessary proofs and records, attested by the proper officers, for the clearing of truth in the matters complained of, so we think it requisite, that copies of all affidavits be interchangeably delivered, to each party concerned as soon as they shall be taken, and so not doubting of your compliance herein, we bid you heartily farewell.

From the council chamber in Whitehall, this 23d day of July, 1684.

Your very loving friends,

Radnor.	Guilford, C. S.	Halifax, C. P. S.
Craven.	Rochester.	Ernle. Godolphin.
		L. Jenkins.

To our very loving friend, Edward Cranfield, Esq., Lieutenant Governor and commander in chief of his majesty's province of New-Hampshire, in New-England.

A true copy,

WILLIAM BLATHWAYT.

(This paper is in the council minutes 2d book.)

No. 50. *A Brief, containing the substance of the affidavits, objec-*
tions and replies at the hearing before the Lords Committee of the
Council for Trade and Plantations, 10th of March, 1684-5.

[Not inserted in the former editions.]

To the first article of the complaint, Anthony Nutter and John
Woodman, depose—

That Mr. Cranfield declared in the assembly, that the words
[and they] were inserted in his commission by mistake, and
dd. a copy without those words. That Mr. Cranfield accordingly made Capt. Barefoote a judge of the pleas and chief justice
of the province, without the council's advice, and appointed a
court once in every month. That the fees for trying all actions
were first set at 20s. A former bill of costs in the like case but
£1 1s. Another but £1 10s. But now there is added to that
20s. by the said judge, £5 1s. 2d. in Mr. Mason's case.

Note. The costs are signed by the judge and not by the governor.

Note. The witnesses in Mason's cases were always some of
the jury.

1st Objection. That the assembly were of opinion, that the governor alone had the power of erecting courts of judicature.

Answer. That in November, 1682, the assembly then dispu-
ted this matter, and the order produced has no date. Besides,
Tipping signs the assembly's acts, and this is only signed by
Chamberlain.

2d Objection. Mason swears that the governor gave copies of
his commission, with the words [and they] inserted. Mr. Elliot
swears the same. And that the council set the fees, which the
governor afterward allowed.

Answer. The council were at the governor's pleasure.

3d Objection. Walter Barefoote, the judge, swears that the
late president and council took 20s. for every action, before it
should be called, and there is now no more taken. And the
plaintiff's or defendant's costs or charge, were, as now, taxed by
the court, and are very reasonable. That Waldron, when judge,
made Randolph pay £8 2s. 6d. costs, in a trial for the king, besides damages.

Answer. 1. That the fact is otherwise, as will appear, costs
being now altered, £3 to Mr. Mason, in every action, and 12 of
them in a day tried. 2. That Randolph's costs were for a special
court for that one trial.

To the second.

Note. That at first, Mr. Cranfield gave public notice that all
persons might come in, and agree with Mr. Mason. But, John
Winget, Thomas Rogers, and Elias Stileman, deponents, came
in, and the governor would not intermeddle.

Reuben Hull, deposes,—That Mr. Cranfield owned he had
bought the province of Mason.

William Vaughan and Richard Waldron,—That he shewed his
deeds from Mason, of purchase of that province, to the deponents.

Nathaniel Foulsham proves possession given Mason of Capt. Gilman's house and lands.

Benjamin Moulton and William Fifield—The like of Sanburn's house and lands, and the imprisoning of Sanburn.

No more turned out of possession, but executions granted against several.

To the third.

The raising of the costs from 20s. to £6, is proved in the first.

Nathaniel Weare.—To prove that costs were, before, always taken in goods, and not in ready money, and that where goods to be had, the persons never taken.

John Pickering and William Cotton.—That for Cotton's costs to Mason, plank or other goods would not be taken, but for want of money Cotton was imprisoned.

Christopher Noble.—The same fully.

H. Axwell, John Partridge, William Cotton and Richard Nicholas.—That Partridge's costs, goods tendered as before, but refused, and Partridge imprisoned ; that he was forbid to work in prison, and forced to live upon his friends' charity.

John Geare and Walter Windsor.—The same to Thomas Pickering.

John Smith.—The same to Christopher Hussey.

Mr. Weare knows him to be 86 years old.

To the fourth.

Jacob Perkins and Timothy Hilliard.—That seeing how others were dealt with, by Mr. Mason, by imprisonment for want of money to pay court charges, they were forced to yield to Mr. Mason's demands.

To the fifth.

14 Nov. 1682. The general assembly ordered pieces of 8, rials and dollars, to pass at 6s. 8d. per ounce, troy weight.

4 Oct. 1683. Mr. Cranfield and his council reciting an act of January then last, but must intend that above, of November, order those pieces should go at 6s. apiece, without respect to the weight, so that some dollars not worth 3s. by weight, pass at 6s.

William Sanburn, swears, he lost 16s. in receiving £5, Spanish money, by reason of the order above.

Jacob Browne.—That he lost a 6th part of £5, Spanish money, by reason as before.

Objection. Mason swears, that he first proposed to the governor and council, putting a value on Spanish money, as it is at London his majesty's mint. That the council agreed thereto, and the governor approved it.

Walter Barefoote and Robert Elliot swear the same.

Answer. 1. It is pretty bold swearing he first proposed it.— 2. His proposing it, does not make it lawful for the governor and council to do it without the assembly.

To the sixth.

The mittimus for sending Mr. Vaughan to prison, until £500 bail to the peace. Oct. 22, 1683. No crime alleged, nor particular breach of the peace.

Upon this commitment, the jailor took Mr. Elliot and Mr. Daniel's bond for his appearance.

The same day Mr. Vaughan was discharged from being of the council.

The next day, the governor, by a new warrant, taking notice of the bond taken by the jailor, and that the taking such was an escape in the jailor, orders his commitment anew, until he give £500 security for the peace and good behaviour.

25 Oct. 1683. Mr. Vaughan and Mr. Daniel gave the governor a recognizance of £500, conditioned for Vaughan's being of good behaviour and keeping the peace, and should appear at the next quarter sessions, to answer what should be objected against him.

6 Nov. 1683. At the next quarter sessions, Mr. Vaughan appeared, but there being no prosecution he and his bail were discharged.

Objection. 24 Oct. 1684. Thurton swears, that in September, 1683, he desired Mr. Cranfield to bind Mr. Vaughan to his good behaviour, for beating him, so as he durst not execute his office.

Answer. That this was not thought of at the time of his commitment, for if it had, Mr. Cranfield must have bound him to good behaviour expressly to said Thurton, which he did not.

February, 1683. One Joseph Dow, and other jurymen, passing by the governor's house, were invited in, and friendly received. But on asking the question, whether they might not, when they were sworn (as before they had done) hold up their hands, instead of kissing the book, the governor fell into a rage, and asked them how they came there. To whom Dow replied, " at your honor's invitation." That Mr. Cranfield complaining of this matter to the next court, as a riot, Dow was forced to give £100 bond, for his appearance next sessions. When Dow appeared, nothing being alleged against him, he was discharged and his arms restored. But at a another session after, Dow was called again, on the same bond, and the penalty was estreated against him, and he forced to fly out of the province, with his wife and nine children, leaving his house and grounds, with the corn in the ground, to the governor. This, Mr. Vaughan and Mr. Weare can also prove.

February 6, 1683-4. The governor again committed Mr. Vaughan, for want of security for his good behaviour. Upon which Mr. Vaughan lay in prison *nine months.*

Peter Coffin swears, February, 1683, That Vaughan demeaned himself civilly to the governor, and offered to give security to the peace, if the governor could give one instance wherein he had broken the law. But the governor, in great heat, charged him with having gone to Boston, with a mutinous petition to his majesty, and said he would make a good haul of it, and get £100 of every man that had signed that petition, and then ordered his commitment, as above.

August 5, 1684. Mr. Vaughan petitioned the president Barefoote, and the rest of the justices, at the then quarter sessions, that he might be brought, by *habeas corpus*, to answer to what should be objected, and so be either acquitted or condemned.

August 5, 1684. Mr. Cranfield writes to that court, and instances many crimes, in general, against Mr. Vaughan, as promoting tumultuous petitions, &c., and then requires their binding him over to the next sessions ; and then concludes, not doubting of their care, that he wholly left the determination of it to them, urging, that, if he denied the matter, he had evidence to prove it. The same day, the court continued him in custody accordingly.

September 16, 1684. Mr. Barefoote and the other justices, when the governor was present, committed Vaughan to Hampton prison, until he gave good security for his good behaviour, and for his appearance next sessions, to answer misdemeanors to be objected against him, on his majesty's behalf.

October 18, 1684. After two quarter sessions past, and nothing objected against Mr. Vaughan, when his majesty's letter came over on Mr. Weare's complaint, Mr. Vaughan was released by the governor's warrant, but to return to prison in two months.

September 12. 35 Car. 2. Mr. Joshua Moodey being to take a journey out of the province, was forced to give a recognizance of £200 to return in three weeks, if alive and well.

To the seventh.

December 22, 1683. The governor and council order sale of goods, taken on execution, to be sold by outcry, in 14 days.

That they impose taxes on the inhabitants, to £500, without the general assembly.

That the justices empowered the marshals, by warrant, to levy the same, on the constables' refusing.

That the justices fined the constables for not collecting the rates —and that the marshals levied these taxes.

October 22, 1683. The governor and comp. order, no vessels or sloops should come from any other colonies, unless licensed by him, which is, in effect, setting up a license office, whereby the governor got as follows—

7 November, 1684. Daniel Gent, master of a sloop of Boston, swears, that he paid 2d per M., for 100,000 feet boards, landed at Broad Island, in governor Cranfield's time, and never any thing before.

8 November, 1684. John Usher proves the same, paid for the like, though Mr. Cranfield had, by letter, promised they should go free.

6 November, 1684. William Ardel proves the same, for the like.

To the eighth.

William Vaughan and John Pickering.—Prove that, in February, 1683, the secretary denied to swear their witnesses, or to attend the governor therein, or grant any summons for witnesses, to prove that the governor's secretary would not grant summons, to bring in witnesses, to be sworn, to make out Mr. Weare's complaint, nor swear any that came in without summons, unless his

secretary might have the modelling of their evidence as he pleased ; though his majesty had commanded affidavits should be taken
indifferently.

6 November, 1684. Thomas Wiggin and Thomas Graffort.—
Prove the denial of swearing twenty-eight persons, in the matters
in question.

And Mr. Vaughan was committed the same day, as appears by
commitment before, for desiring the same.

11 December, 1684. John Foulsham and Nathaniel Bachiler.—
Swear that, in July last, the governor said he would fine all the
petitioners £100 each, and that it should be the best toll that ever
came to his mill.

11 December, 1684. John Partridge and Nehemiah Partridge.—
Swear that the secretary denied them copies of several records,
the governor, in March, 1682–3, having ordered the contrary.

Objection. James Sherlock, swears that, the 16th October,
1684, Mr. Cranfield offered Major Waldron to call a council and
swear his evidences, before Weare went to England.

Walter Barefoote, the same, and that the governor offered him
what copies of records he desired.

Answer. This is true, in fact, the offer was made, but when
it was desired, Vaughan was committed.

(Found among Weare's MSS.)

No. 51. *A brief of Cranfield's commission, and of the evidence, in
support of the complaint, and against it.*

[Not inserted in the former editions.]

New-Hampshire, in New-England.

1. IX no. Maii, XXXIIIto. Car. 2di. The king by letters
patent, under the great seal of England, constitutes Edward Cranfield, Esquire, lieutenant-governor and commander in chief of all
that part of New-Hampshire province, in New-England, extending from three miles northward of all or any part of Merrimack
river, unto the province of Maine.

To execute all things belonging to his commission, as per instructions therewith, or such further powers and instructions as,
under his majesty's sign manual, shall be sent, and according to the
reasonable laws in being there, and such other as shall be made
and agreed on by him, with the advice and consent of the council
and assembly there, as hereafter.

2. Robert Mason, Richard Waldron, Thomas Daniel, William
Vaughan, Richard Martyn, John Gilman, Elias Stileman, Job
Clements, Walter Barefoote, and Richard Chamberlain, Esquires,
to be of his majesty's council there, and to assist in the government.

Cranfield to take an oath for due execution of his office and
trust, to be administered by any five of the said council ; and he
to give the oaths of allegiance and supremacy, and the test in the
act for the prevention of dangers from popish recusants, and the
oath for due execution of their places and trusts.

3. Power of suspending members in just cause, five to be a quorum.

To certify vacancies by death, departure or suspension, that new may be appointed under his majesty's sign manual.

Power to Cranfield, out of the principal free householders, to fill up the council, when less than seven on the place, and not more, till they confirmed, or others made under the sign manual.

Suspended or displaced members, not to be of the general assembly.

4. Power to call assemblies of freeholders, with consent of the council, till further pleasure signified, which assemblies are to take the oaths of allegiance and supremacy, or be incapacitated.

And the governor and assembly to make laws agreeable, as near as may be, to those of England, to be allowed or disallowed by his majesty, under his sign manual.

5. Governor to have a negative voice in making laws, with power to dissolve and prorogue general assemblies at pleasure—to use the public seal.

Power to give the oath of allegiance by himself, or others, to whom he pleases.

Power to himself to erect what courts he thinks necessary for law and equity in matters both civil and criminal. To make judges, justices of the peace, sheriffs, and other necessary officers, and to administer necessary oaths to them.

Power to pardon criminals, (except in treason and wilful murder,) and to reprieve therein also, until his majesty's pleasure be known ; and to remit fines, &c.

6. Appeals to the king and his council, in all actions real and personal, of above £ 50 value, and not under, the appellant giving good bail, to answer costs and charges, which shall be awarded by his majesty here, and execution not to be suspended by the appeal.

In cases of life or limb (wilful murder excepted) the party convict to be either sent to England or his case ; and execution respited until orders therein returned by the king or his council.

Power to levy men and transfer them from one place to another in America.

7. To execute the office of captain general, and martial law in time of war. The governor, with consent of the council, to erect forts, platforms, castles, cities, boroughs, towns, and fortifications, necessary, and the same to fortify or dismantle. Invasion to be repelled by force of arms.

To discourage vice and encourage virtue.

Liberty of conscience to all protestants, and those of the church of England to be principally encouraged.

8. The present taxes to be continued until the general assembly fix others. Public money to be issued by the governor's warrant, with consent of the council, and to be used for support of the government, and not otherwise.

The governor to be vice-admiral of all the seas and coasts belonging to his government, and to receive instructions therein from the D. of Y. lord high admiral there.

Power to appoint fairs, marts, and markets, with advice of the council.

The like for ports, harbors, havens, &c. for shipping, &c. and custom houses and officers for the same, and those to alter and diplace, following the rules of the acts of trade and navigation.

9. All officers and inhabitants to be aiding to the governor in execution of the said powers.

Power to appoint and displace a deputy governor ; who is to be of the council.

The council to govern on the death of the governor, and in his absence when no deputy appointed.

10. Recites that the land in New-Hampshire was held and improved by several, under title from the Massachusetts, since evicted.

And Mr. Robert Mason's claim thereto; for prevention of whose being unreasonable in his demands, his majesty had obliged him under hand and seal, to demand nothing for the time past, until the 24th June, 1679, nor molest any for the time to come, but make them titles forever, paying 6d. per £. for the true yearly value of all houses built, and of all lands, whether gardens, orchards, herbal or pasture, improved by them, which shall be bounded to them, provided Mason have the residue to make the best of.

11. On non-agreement between the inhabitants and Mason, the governor to interpose, who, if he cannot end the differences between them, is to transmit to England such cases, impartially stated, with his opinion and reasons on the same, that his majesty, his heirs and successors, with advice of the privy council, may hear and.determine the same.

The governor to hold his office and said powers, during his majesty's pleasure. The commission of 18 September, 1679, to be void.

William Vaughan will depose, that at a court on Great-Island, 6 Nov. 1683, Walter Barefoote, deputy-governor, Nathaniel Fryer and H. Greene, judges, Robert Mason, plaintiff, W. Vaughan, R. Waldron, N. Weare, and Eleanor Cutt, widow, defendants, concerning title of lands, judgment was given for the plaintiff, from which defendants appealed, and their appeals were admitted. And the 16th following, Mr. Mason promised to attend at Mr. Vaughan's house, to take the security, where the appellants and security attended, but no Mr. Mason nor secretary. But appellants and security went and found out the secretary, to whom they tendered security, who said he had no orders to take it, and refused taking it, whereby the seizin and appeal lost.

That in order for the trials for Mr. Mason's land ; 1. There is a standing jury kept from month to month. 2. That by report, those jurymen have agreed with Mason for their lands. 3. That several pleas have been refused, and the defendants told p. judges, they would not make record for them by entering their pleas. 4. That the courts refused reading the stat. 27 Eliz. c. 6, sect. 2. Coke's Inst. lib. 2, cap. 12, p. 156, and other statutes.

17th Feb. 1682. The governor, Mr. Cranfield, by note affixt on the church doors, gave notice, that if the inhabitants of that province came not in within a month, to take leases from Mr. Mason, pursuant to his majesty's commission, he would certify the refusal to his majesty, that Mr. Mason might be discharged from his obligation to grant such.

Signed,   ED. CRANFIELD.

4th Jan. 1683. Joshua Moodey will depose, that Gov. Cranfield, about December, 1682, shewed the deponent writings, under the hand and seal of Robert Mason, conveying his right to New-Hampshire Province to Mr. Cranfield.

4th Jan. 1683. William Vaughan and Richard Waldron, jr. will depose the same.

4th Jan. 1683. Reuben Hull will depose, that in December last, Mr. Cranfield said Mason had given him deeds for his province, which he had shewn to Mr. Vaughan and Mr. Waldron, and intended suing Mason at the next court for the same.

William Fifield, jr., Richard Sanbourn, and Nathaniel Sanbourn, will depose, that in October, 1682, being at J. Sanbourn, senior's, house, when Robert Mason, Sherlock, the marshal, and James Leach, came to give Mason possession : when Sanbourn not opening the door, Leach, per marshal's order, broke it open and gave Mason possession, and Sherlock took Sanbourn prisoner. When Mason openly told the people, " this is what you shall all come to."

Thomas Wiggin swears, 13 April, 1683, that in March last, he and Robert Mason and Robert Hall, being at Deputy-Governor Barefoote's house, Mason said he would seize Major Waldron's, Joshua Moodey's, John Partridge's and Capt. Tippen's lands, who should not have one foot in the province, and that he would live in Andrew Wiggin's farm, being a good one. That the people had been in one rebellion, and he would force them into a second, and then hang them. That shortly there would be a frigate there with soldiers, whom he would quarter in the province, at the people's cost, and that then they would rebel. That let Wadleigh go for England if he would, New-England had now no friend in the council or committee, but formerly they had the lord privy seal. That he and his two sons would fight any six there, for the province, at sharps.   Sworn before

WM. VAUGHAN, Just. Peace.

18 April, 1683. Lieut. Robert Hall, justice of peace there, swears the same, before Justice Vaughan.

14 April, 1683. Shadrach Walton swears, that about three weeks before, he heard Mason say, that he looked for a frigate with soldiers, and would quarter ten at each house, till they eat up all the people's cattle and sheep, and beggar them, and that then he should see what they would do ; and upon inquiry of the reason why, said it was because they would not comply with him according to his majesty's order. Said he would speedily seize Major Waldron's, Mr. Moodey's and J. Partridge's estates, and bade deponent tell Lieut. Nutter his estate was going after the rest.   Sworn before   W. VAUGHAN.

Against us.

27 Sept. 1683. R. Mason, R. Chamberlain, and Joseph Rayne swear, that 25 Sept. 1683, in a trial between Mason and R. Waldron, the defendant excepted against the whole jury, and openly told the people they were all concerned, that his would be a leading case, and that they must all be Mason's tenants, and that they being all parties, could not be of the jury. That Barefoote being the judge there, would have committed him for the words as mutinous. That the said Waldron, in March, 1630, said they were not the more bound to believe the king's letter, because the king had writ it.

Thomas Philbrick speaks of some discourse between him and Henry Greene, Esq. about Henry Roby and Nathaniel Boulter, two standing jurymen's having had land from Mason, which was worth £100, above the 2d. per acre to be paid. Note.—H. Greene is one of the judges.

Henry Dow can testify, that the 11th October, 1683, Henry Roby had land measured out to him of 100 acres upland and marsh, appointed him by Mason. And Nathaniel Boulter, senior, and his sons, had 20 acres, which he said was too little, in that Mason had promised him 30. And Robert Smith had a piece of marsh land, he claiming the same from Mason. That these grounds were part of the unfenced pasture, where the milch cows of Hampton inhabitants used to feed, the loss whereof is of great prejudice to the town.

Ephraim Marston says the same.

17 July, 1683. R. Waldron, John Windiat and Thomas Roberts, certify, that upon the governor's summons of the 17th Feb. 1682, above, within the time set, attended the governor, to know his pleasure therein, who bade them agree with Mason ; on discourse with whom, in another room, the governor overhearing, came in, and told Col. Waldron that they should not hector so in his house, and bade them begone; that they propounded to Mason to refer the matter to the governor, or otherwise, that the governor should state the case to his majesty, according to the commission ; which Mason refused, saying that unless they owned his title, he would have nothing to do with them.

Richard Waldron, senior, fined £5, for mutinous words spoke at a trial, between him and Mason. And fined £10, for words spoken to the dishonor and contempt of his majesty, from which sentences he desired leave to appeal.

Cert. p. RICH'D CHAMBERLAIN, Prothon.

11 Sept. 1683. Warrant to James Sherlock, marshal, or deputy, to attach the goods, or for want thereof, the body of R. Waldron, and take bond, with sureties of £4000, for his appearance, in trespass for lands held and woods felled to £4000 value ad. s. R. Mason. Sept. 19, 1683. The warrant served on part of the defendant's goods, in the name of the whole. 6th Nov. 1683.— Judgment for the plaintiff, 10s. damages, and £5 8s. costs. The defendant appeals, which allowed, on £200 security before the 16th, to pay the cost of the appeal, and to prosecute it in six months. 23 Nov. 1683. Warrant for costs.

10 Dec. 1683. The governor and council commanded the ministers there, to admit all persons, not scandalous, to the sacrament, and their children to baptism. That if any desire the sacramant or baptism, according to the liturgy of England, that it be done, pursuant to the laws of England and his majesty's command to the Massachusetts. Ministers refusing, being duly required, to incur the penalty of the state, and the inhabitants freed from paying tithes or other duties to such minister. And the governor ordered Joshua Moodey, minister of Portsmouth, personally to read that order at his meeting-house, the next Lord's day.

4 Dec. 1683. The governor and council ordered all the ministers in New-Hampshire, to attend the Monday following, to give their reasons why they did not administer the sacraments according to his majesty's letters sent the Massachusetts, and the statute in that case.

15 Jan. 1683-4. James Sherlock gives Moodey notice, in writing, that Cranfield, Barefoote, Chamberlain and Hincks, would receive the sacrament, according to the liturgy of the church of England, the next Sunday.

April, 33tio. car. 2di. 1681. By indenture between Robert Mason and Richard Rich, Mason, in consideration of 20s. bargains, sells, enfeoffs, &c. to Rich and his heirs, an house and orchard at Dover, a field of 8 acres, 2 acres on the common, another field of 3 acres and a half, and 6 acres. Land at Hilton's point of 20 acres, 3 acres marsh land, 10 acres upland, leaving highways, with liberty of feeding cattle and cutting necessary woods, *excepting mines and minerals*, and pine trees of 24 inches and more diameter.— Habend. to Rich and his heirs as parcel of *Dover manor*, reddend 25s. per annum, with a clause of distress. Covenant for the grantees building two houses, in two years, at Hilton's point and to pay 2s. per annum rent, for each, to Mason and his heirs. Covenant for quiet enjoyment under the said rents, and against incumbrances. Covenant for the grantees payment of said rents, and preservation of the boundaries. The grantee, &c. at every ten years to deliver engrost terrars of the premises.

ROB'T MASON.

24 May, 1681. Robert Mason, by writing, made Nicholas Shapleigh his attorney, with power to make deeds to the inhabitants for the lands they now possess, and what other they had occasion for, which he obliged himself and heirs to ratify. Gave notice he would return from England the next spring, and by his majesty's grace ease them of the heavy taxes then imposed.

ROB'T MASON.

7 Jan. 1683-4. Richard Waldron, William Furber, senior, and Henry Langstaff,* offer to depose, that the 20 acres on Hil-

* [In Rev. Mr. Pike's MS. Journal, I find the following note on this person, who was at Pascataqua as early as 1631. " July 18, 1705. Mr. Henry Langstar, of Bloody-point, deceased, after ten days sickness, occasioned by a fall into his Leanto, four stairs high, whereby being greviously bruised, it brought an inflammation upon him. He was above 100 years old, hale, strong, hearty man, and might have lived many years longer, if, &c."]

ton's point, granted by deed above, of the 29 April, 1681, with some other lands therein, were fenced in for pasture 50 years ago, and so held by the people of Dover ever since.

(Found among Weare's MSS.)

No. 52. *Report of the Lords of Trade against Cranfield, and the King's order.*

At the court at Whitehall, the 8th of April, 1685.

By the king's most excellent majesty, and the lords of his majesty's most honorable privy council.

Upon reading a report from the right honorable the lords of the committee of trade and plantations, in the words following :

May it please your majesty,—

Having received an order in council, dated the 11th day of July last, upon the petition and complaint of Nathaniel Weare, inhabitant of your majesty's province of New-Hampshire, in New-England, in the behalf of himself and others, your majesty's subjects and planters there, against Edward Cranfield, Esq., your majesty's governor of that province, whereby we were directed to report our opinions upon the said complaint. We did accordingly transmit a copy thereof to the said Edward Cranfield, and upon receiving his answer, and hearing what the complainants could allege and make out against him,—We find that the said Edward Cranfield has not pursued his instructions, in reference to the propriety of soil which Robert Mason, Esq., claims in that province, inasmuch as the said Edward Cranfield, by his instructions, is directed, that in case the inhabitants of New-Hampshire should refuse to agree with the said Mason, he should interpose and endeavor to reconcile all differences, which, if he could not bring to effect, he was then to send into England such cases, fairly and impartially stated, together with his opinion, for your majesty's determination ; whereas, instead thereof, he has caused courts to be held in New-Hampshire, and permitted titles of land to be decided there, and unreasonable costs to be allowed, without first representing the particular cases to your majesty. As to the complaint of his having raised the value of coins, against the laws of the assembly there, we are most humbly of opinion, that although it be your majesty's undoubted prerogative to set and determine the price and value of coins, within your dominions, yet your majesty's governor ought not to have made any alterations therein, without having received your majesty's special directions ; all which we humbly propose may be signified to him, by your majesty's order, and that the differences depending between the said Robert Mason and planters, in that part of New-Hampshire, may be at length decided. We further offer, that William Vaughan, one of the complainants attending this board, may have opportunity allowed him of appealing to your majesty, within a fortnight, from all verdicts and judgments given in New-Hampshire, in his private case, upon hearing whereof, and by the relation it has with others, your majesty will be best able to judge of the right and title of the said Robert Mason, to that part of the province of New-Hampshire aforesaid, and upon bringing the said appeal, that all proceedings at law, relating to the said title, may forthwith cease, until your majesty's further pleasure be known.

All which is nevertheless most humbly submitted.

Rochester,	Arlington,
Halifax, P.	Oxford,
Clarendon, C. P. S.	Chesterfield.
Beaufort,	

Council chamber, 27 March, 1685.

His majesty in council was graciously pleased to approve of the said report, and to order that his majesty's pleasure therein be signified to Mr. Cranfield accordingly. It was also ordered, that Mr. William Vaughan be allowed to appeal to his majesty, within a fortnight, from all verdicts and judgments given in his private case, in New-Hampshire, according to the said report.

A true copy, WM. BRIDGEMAN.

No. 53. *The King's Order for hearing Vanghan's Appeal.*

[Not inserted in the former editions.]

At the court at Whitehall, the 29th of April, 1685. Present—the king's most excellent majesty in council.

Upon the petition of William Vaughan and Nathaniel Weare, of New-Hampshire, in New-England, setting forth among other things, that in obedience to a late order of council, the petitioner, William Vaughan, hath appealed against several verdicts and judgments, one fine and one decree, given, entered up, imposed and ordered against him, in New-Hampshire, as in the petition is at large set forth, it is this day ordered, that copies of the said petition and appeal be sent to the right honorable the lords of the committee for trade and plantations, who are to examine the allegations thereof, and to report to this board how they find the same, together with their lordship's opinion thereupon.

PHIL. MUSGRAVE.

(The two preceding papers, are in the hands of the Hon. President Weare.)

No. 54. *Letter from the Lords of Trade to Cranfield.*

After our hearty commendations unto you, we have, in obedience to his majesty's commands, received and examined your answer to the complaint of Nathaniel Weare, inhabitant of his said province of New-Hampshire, in behalf of himself, and others of his majesty's subjects and planters there, and having likewise heard what the said Weare could bring in evidence of the said complaints, and thereupon reported our opinions to his majesty, we are commanded hereby to signify unto you, that you have not pursued your instructions in reference to the propriety of the soil which Robert Mason, Esquire, claims in the province of New-Hampshire, inasmuch as you were directed, that, in case the inhabitants of New-Hampshire should refuse to agree with the said Mason, you should interpose, and endeavor to reconcile all differences, which, if you could not bring to effect, you were then to send to his majesty such cases, fairly and impartially stated, together with your opinion for his majesty's determination ; instead whereof, you have caused courts to be held in New-Hampshire, and permitted titles of land to be decided there, and unreasonable costs to be allowed, without first representing the particular cases to his majesty. And yet, although it be his majesty's undoubted prerogative, to set and determine the price and value of coin, within his majesty's dominions, you have not done well in directing any alterations therein, without his majesty's special order. In both which, you have been wanting in your duty to his majesty. But, that the chief occasion of dispute in that province may be removed, we are farther directed to acquaint you, that, as to the differences depending between the said Robert Mason and the planters, his majesty hath been graciously pleased, by his order in council, dated the 8th of this instant, April, to permit William Vaughan, one of the complainants, attending this board, to appeal to his majesty within a fortnight from the date of the said order, from all the verdicts and judgments given in New-Hampshire, in his private case, upon hearing whereof, and by the relation it has with others, his majesty will be best able to judge of the right and title of the said Robert Mason, to that part of the province of New-Hampshire. And his majesty doth likewise think fit, that, upon bringing the said appeal, by the said William Vaughan, all proceedings at law, relating to the said title, do forthwith cease, until his majesty's pleasure be known. Whereof you are to take notice, and to govern yourself accordingly. And so we bid you very heartily farewell. From the council chamber, at Whitehall, the 29th day of April, 1685,

Your loving friends,

(Signed)

W. Cant.	Bridgwater,
Guilford, C. S.	Chesterfield,
Rochester,	Sunderland,
Halifax, P.	Craven,
Clarendon, C. P. S.	Alesbury,
Beaufort,	Middleton,
Lindshy,	Godolphin,
Arlington,	J. Ernle,
Hunington,	Geo. Jaffrey.

Directed to our loving friend, Edw. Cranfield, Esq., lieutenant-governor and commander in chief of his majesty's province of New-Hampshire, in New-England.

No. 55. *Letter from the same to the same, respecting Vaughan's Appeal.*

After our hearty commendation : His majesty hath received the petition and appeal of William Vaughan, inhabitant of New-Hampshire, from several verdicts and judgments given against him in that province, which being referred to us by his majesty's order in council of the 29th of April last, that we should examine the allegations thereof, and make report of the same, with our opinion thereupon, we have accordingly appointed to hear all parties concerned in the several cases therein contained, on the first Tuesday, after midsummer day, which shall be in the year 1686. To which end, we herewith send you a copy of the said petition and appeal, which you are to communicate unto Robert Mason, Esq., and to all others whom it may concern, who are to take notice thereof, and to give their attendance at that time either by themselves or by their agents sufficiently empowered by them, to answer the said appeal, and to submit to such judgment hereupon as his majesty in council shall be thought fit. And you are likewise to permit all persons to have free access to, and take copies of all records within that province relating to the matters in dispute, and to depose upon oath what they know concerning the same, which depositions are to be taken in writing by any of the members of the council or justices of the peace in that province, without any hindrance or discouragement whatsoever, in order to be transmitted unto us, for the clearing of truth in that appeal. And so we bid you heartily farewell. From the council chamber in Whitehall, the 22d day of May 1685. Your loving friends,

Guilford, C. S. Rochester,
Halifax, Pr. Clarendon, C. P. S.
Ormond, Sunderland.

Lieut. Governor of New-Hampshire, or
Commander in Chief for the time being.

(The two preceding papers are in the possession of John Penhallow, Esq.)

No. 56. *Copy of the Petition of the Inhabitants against Mason.*

To the king's most excellent majesty.

The humble petition and address of your majesty's dutiful and loyal subjects, inhabiting in the province of New-Hampshire, in New-England. [1685.]

Most humbly sheweth,—

That your majesty's loyal subjects of this province, had for more than fifty years been peaceably possessed of the lands lately challenged by Mr. Mason, and having found the same an utter desert and forest land, with excessive cost and hard labor, reduced the same to a tolerable support of ourselves and families, and lately maintained the same, with a vast expense of our estates and lives, against the incursions of a barbarous enemy, who had otherwise reduced the same to utter confusion.

That upon his late majesty's declaration and order for the settlement and government of this province, we accounted ourselves
happy for that therein we were by his said majesty's princely
grace and favor, saved from the unreasonable demands which Mr.
Mason might have made upon us, by the limitations in the
commission for government, wherein it was provided that the said
president or governor, for the time being, should use all methods
by his good advice, to settle and quiet the people, in the matter of
Mr. Mason's title, or otherwise impartially to state the case, and
report the same to his majesty, that a final determination might
thereupon have been made, by his majesty in council, which if it
had been duly attended, had, we doubt not, long since, by your
majesty's justice and favor, put us into a happy estate of quiet and
repose.

That, notwithstanding his said majesty's command and limitation, the said Mr. Mason hath been allowed to pursue many of
the inhabitants, in several suits and actions, wherein the government have taken to themselves power of an absolute judgment,
without any regard had to the said commands and limitations, and
with that excess and rigor as to assign the said Mr. Mason sometimes ten pounds, other times twenty pounds costs, when damages
have been sometimes not above two shillings, very seldom ten,
according to the orders and limitations abovesaid.

That the said Mr. Mason, beyond and beside the said quit rents,
and directly against his majesty's order in the said commission,
wherein the tenure of improved lands is assured to the ter-tenants,
upon payment of the said quit rent, or otherwise, as his majesty
in council should determine, hath disposed or given away the fee,
to several persons, of several lands, which were, long before his
challenge, fenced and improved by others, to the great damage and
injury of his majesty's good subjects, beside many other irregularities in the management of the government, to the great oppression
and destruction of trade within your majesty's province, and the
utter impoverishing thereof.

That for the last two years and upward, during the whole management of Mr. Mason's suits at law, against your majesty's subjects, there hath been generally one jury returned to serve all the
said issues, with little alterations, and almost constantly one foreman, (who for that end we are apt to fear) was early complied
with by Mr. Mason for all the lands in his own possession formerly, with addition of several other lands to his own profit.

That notwithstanding your majesty's late gracious order, and inhibiting of any further procedure in the case of Mr. Mason's title,
until the cause were brought before your majesty in council, Mr.
Walter Barefoote, who was left deputy governor, hath since the
arrival of your majesty's commands, permitted executions to be
extended, and persons thereupon imprisoned, in causes concerning the said Mason's title, with excessive and unreasonable costs
and damages.

And lastly, whereas your majesty hath, upon complaint made
against the irregular proceedings done and suffered, been gracious-

ly pleased to permit Mr. William Vaughan, one of the principal inhabitants and merchants in this province, to take his appeal to your majesty in council for relief, against several oppressive judgments, one whereof refers to the title of his lands within this province, holden in the same form with the rest of his majesty's good subjects here, we do, with all humble gratitude, acknowledge your majesty's justice and favor herein, and for that the pursuance and issue of the said appeal, will therefore necessarily affect the whole province and be introductory to the determination of all Mr. Mason's challenge, we have judged it our duty in most humble manner, to prostrate ourselves at your majesty's feet, and have therefore betrusted and fully impowered Mr. Nathaniel Weare, one of the inhabitants of this your majesty's province, our agent, to lay before your majesty and most honorable privy council, the common case and condition of your majesty's poor and distressed subjects in this province, who is fully instructed humbly to represent the same, and the arbitrary and severe oppressions we have labored under, from which we are well assured of relief by your majesty's most just and gracious determination, and to make an humble and entire submission of ourselves, unto your majesty's pleasure, most humbly beseeching, that we may henceforward have our perfect and immediate dependence upon your majesty and the crown of England, as well in the tenure of our lands as in the affairs of government, which gracious influence of your majesty is only able to revive and restore this province to its former flourishing estate and growth, whereby we may at length be made serviceable to your most sacred majesty and the crown, which we are devoted to serve, resolving therein to be exemplary to all other your majesty's subjects in the territory of New-England, and for which we shall every pray, &c.

(This paper is in the hands of the Hon. President Weare.)

No. 57. *Copy of the Decision of King James II. against William Vaughan.*

At the court at Whitehall, the 19th of November, 1686.

(L. S.)   Present—The king's most excellent majesty.

Lord Chancellor,	Earl of Plymouth,
Lord Treasurer,	Earl of Morray,
Lord President,	Earl of Middleton,
Duke of Ormond,	Earl of Melford,
Duke of Albemarle,	Earl of Tyrconnel,
Duke of Beaufort,	Viscount Stauronberg,
Lord Chamberlain,	Viscount Preston,
Earl of Oxford,	Lord Bishop of Durham,
Earl of Huntington,	Lord Arundel of Wardour,
Earl of Peterborough,	Lord Dartmouth,
Earl of Craven,	Lord Dover,
Earl of Powis,	Mr.Chancellor of the excheq'r,
Earl of Nottingham,	Mr. Chancellor of the Dutchy.

Upon reading this day at the board, a report from the honorable the lords of the committee of council for trade and foreign plantations, bearing date the 6th day of November instant, setting forth, that in obedience to his majesty's orders in council, of the 25th of April, 1685, and the 3d of July last, they have examined the appeal of William Vaughan, from a verdict and judgment given against him, on the 6th day of November, 1683, in his majesty's courts in New-Hampshire, in New-England, at the suit of Robert Mason, Esq., as proprietor of that province, for certain lands and tenements in Portsmouth, in the said province, and that they having heard the said Robert Mason, and Nathaniel Weare, attorney for the appellant, and his counsel learned in the law, are humbly of opinion that his majesty be pleased to ratify and affirm the verdict and judgment aforesaid.

His majesty in council was pleased to approve of their lorships' said opinion and report, and to order the said verdict and judgment given against the said William Vaughan, on the sixth day of November, 1683, in his majesty's courts in New-Hampshire, in New-England, at the suit of Robert Mason, Esq. as proprietor of that province, for certain lands and tenements, in Portsmouth, in said province, be ratified and affirmed, and they are hereby ratified and affirmed accordingly.   WM. BRIDGEMAN.

Vera copia, per RICHARD PARTRIDGE, Clerk.

Copy as on file in the case, Allen vs. Waldron,
                         Exam. per GEO. JAFFREY, Cl.

No. 58. *Four letters or petitions from John Hogkins, commonly called Hawkins, one of the sachems of the Penacook Indians.*

                                        May 15th, 1685.
Honor governor my friend,—You my friend I desire your worship and your power, because I hope you can do som great matters this one. I am poor and naked and I have no men at my place because I afraid allwayes Mohogs he will kill me every day and night. If your worship when please pray help me you no let Mohogs kill me at my place at Malamake river called Panukkog and Nattukkog, I will submit your worship and your power.— And now I want pouder and such alminishon, shatt and guns, because I have forth at my hom and I plant theare.

       This all Indian hand, but pray you do consider your
                humble servant,   JOHN HOGKINS.

Simon Detogkom,	Peter ◯ Robin,
Joseph ☓ Traske,	Mr. Jorge ☓ Rodunnonukgus,
King ⅏ Hary,	Mr. Hope ⋈ Hoth,
Sam ⅏ Linis,	John x Toneh,
Wapeguanat ⅏ Saguachuwashat,	John *a* Canowa,
Old Robin ⅏,	John x Owamosimmin,
Mamanosgues ◯ Andra,	Natonill † Indian.

Another from the same.

May 15, 1685.

Honor Mr. Governor,—Now this day I com your house, I want se you, and I bring my hand at before you I want shake hand to you if your worship when please then you receive my hand then shake your hand and my hand. You my friend because I remember at old time when live my grant father and grant mother then Englishmen com this country, then my grant father and Englishmen they make a good govenant, they friend allwayes, my grant father leving at place called Malamake rever, other name chef Natukkog and Panukkog, that one rever great many names, and I bring you this few skins at this first time I will give you my friend. This all Indian hand.

[The rest as before.]   JOHN ⋈ HAWKINS, Sagamor.

Another from the same.

Please your worship,—I will intreat you matther you my friend, now   this if my Indian he do you long pray you no put your law because som my Indians fooll, som men much love drunk then he no know what he do, may be he do mischif when he drunk if so pray you must let me know what he done because I will ponis him what he have done, you, you my friend if you desire my business, then sent me I will help you if I can.

Mr. JOHN HOGKINS.

Another from the same.

Mr. Mason,—Pray I want speake you a few words if your worship when please, because I com parfas [on purpose] I will speake this governor but he go away so he say at last night, and so far I understand this governor his power that your power now, so he speake his own mouth. Pray if you take what I want pray com to me because I want go hom at this day.

Your humble servant,

May 16, 1685.   JOHN HOGKINS, Indian sogmon.

(From the originals in the Recorder's office.)

No. 59.   *Letter from Capt. Francis Hooke, advising of danger from the Indians.*

Capt. Barefoot, Sir,

This is to informe you that just now there cam to me a post, wherein I am fully informed that there is just ground to feare that the heathen have a souden desyne against us ; they havinge lately about Sacoe affronted our English inhabitants there by threatening of them, as alsoe by killinge theyre doggs ; but more pertickularly in that on Friday, Saturday, and Lord's day last they have gathered all theyre corne, and are removed both pack and packidge. A word to the wise is enough. The old proverb is, forewarned, forearmed. Myself and rest in commission with us are fourthwith settinge ourselves in a posture, and tomorrow our counsell meet for to consider what is needful to be done. Not els, beinge in great hast, butt remayn, Sir, your obliged servant,

Kittery, 13 Aug. 1685.   FRANCIS HOOKE.

No. 60. *Report of persons sent to inquire into the above matter.*
[No date or signature.]

To the Honorable Walter Barefoote, Esq. and the council of Great-Island.

Gentlemen,—According to your command and order to me, bearing date the 2d instant, I have to the utmost of my power observed every particular. Upon our arrival there, on Friday night, they were all very courteous to us, and in the morning my orders were read, which was very kindly received by them, and the reasons why they deserted the places where they usually abode among the English was ;—

1. That four Indians came from fort Albany to the fort at Penacook, and informed them that all the Mohawks did declare they would kill all Indians from Uncas at mount Hope to the eastward as far as Pegypscot.

2. The reason of Natombamat, sagamore of Saco, departed his place was, because the same news was brought there, as himself declared, upon reading my orders at Penacook.

3. Natombamat, sagamore of Saco, is gone to carry the Indians down to the same place, where they were before departed from us, on Sunday morning, and desired Capt. Hooke to meet him at Saco five days after.

4. Both sagamores of Penacook, viz. Wonalanset and Mesandowit, the latter of which is come down, did then declare they had no intention of war, neither indeed are they in any posture for war, being about 24 men, besides squaws and papooses.

5. Asking the reason why they did not come among the English as formerly, they answered they thought if the Mohawks came and fought them, and they should fly for succor to the English, that then the Mohawks would kill all the English for harboring them.

No. 61. *Articles of Peace with the Indians inhabiting New-Hampshire and Maine.*

Articles of peace agreed upon the eighth day of September, in the year of our Lord, 1685, between the subjects of his majesty, king James the second, inhabiting the provinces of New-Hampshire and Maine, and the Indians inhabiting the said provinces.

It is agreed there shall be for the future, a lasting peace, friendship and kindness, between the English and the Indians, and that no injury shall be offered by the one to the other.

That if any Englishman doth any injury to an Indian, upon complaint made to any justice of peace, the Englishman shall be punished, and the Indian shall have present satisfaction made him. And if any Indian doth an injury to the English, or threaten to do any injury, the sagamore to whom that Indian doth belong, shall punish him in presence of one of the king's justices of the peace.

That if any other Indian shall design any mischief or harm to the English, the Indians inhabiting the aforesaid provinces shall give present notice thereof to the English, and shall assist the English.

That so long as the aforesaid Indians shall continue in friendship with the English, they shall be protected against the Mohawks, or any others, and may freely and peaceably set down by the English near any their plantations.

Robert Mason,	Walter Barefoote,
Robert Elliot,	Henry Green,
John Davis,	Francis Hooke.

The mark of ⌠ Mesandowit.
The mark ⋈ of Wahowah, alias Hopehood.
The mark ౮ of Tecamorisick, alias Josias.
The mark ௦ of John Nomony, alias Upsawah.
The mark W of Umbesnowah, alias Robin.

We whose names are hereunto written, do freely consent and engage to comply and perform the within written articles, as our neighbors have done, and do further engage as followeth :

Lastly, That the Indians shall not at any time hereafter remove from any of the English plantations, with their wives and children, before they have given fair and timely notice thereof, unto the English, from whence they do so remove; and in case the said Indians shall remove with their wives and children, without such fair and timely notice given to the English, that then it shall be taken pro confesso that the Indians do intend and design war with the English, and do thereby declare that the peace is broken ; and it shall and may be lawful to and for the English, or any on their behalfs, to apprehend the said Indians, with their wives and children, and to use acts of hostility against them, until the sagamores shall make full satisfaction for all charge and damage that may arise thereby.
                                        John Davis,
                                        Francis Hooke.

The mark   of Netambomet, sagam. of Saco.
The mark X of Wahowah, alias Hopehood.
The mark) of Ned Higgon.
The mark ౧ of Newcome.
Kancamagus, alias John Hawkins, sagamore, signed this
    instrument, 19 7ber, 1685, his G mark.
Bagesson, alias Joseph Traske, O his mark.
And agreed to all within written.
                        Testis, JOSEPH RAYN.

No. 62. *Petition of William Houchins for aid to obtain a cure of the King's Evil.*
            Portsmouth, the 7th of Sept. 1687.
To the much honred cort now sitting in said Portsmouth, for the
            prouince of Newhampshir,
The humbel petishon of William Houchins, on of his magesty
    subgicts belonging to said prouinc, humbly seweth for aduic,
    ade and releff in his deplorabell estat and condition.
That whereas it has plesed God to lay his hand uppon him, and

that hee is in such a condition not being abell to help him selff, as to the geting a liuing or proquering help or remedy for my distemper, being low in the world, and hauing useed ail the menes and aduic posabell for nere fiue years past; hauing bin informed by som that it is a distemper caled the *king's euell*,* so can not be qureed but by his magesty. Hauing littell or nothing in this world, if my liff should go for it am not abell to trancsport my selff for England to his magesty for releff; thareffor humbly and hartly beg the help, ade and asistanc of this honred cort, that thay would so far commiserat my deplorabell condition as order som way ether by breff or any other way that youer honors shall think most meet to moue the harts of all cristen people with compation to besto somthing uppon mee, to trancsport mee for England, whar, God willing, I intend forth with to goo iff posabell, but without help not posabell. This humbly leuing my selff in the sad condition I am in, trusting in God and youer honors for help and aduice, subscrib youer por deplorabell saruant,

WILLEAM HOUCHINS.

No. 63.   *A letter from Secretary Addington to Major Waldron, apprizing him of his danger from the Indians.*

Boston, 27 June, 1689.

Honorable Sir,—The governor and council having this day received a letter from Major Hinchman, of Chelmsford, that some Indians are come into them, who report that there is a gathering of some Indians in or about Penacook, with design of mischief to the English. Among the said Indians, one Hawkins is said to be a principal designer, and that they have a particular design against yourself and Mr. Peter Coffin, which the council thought it necessary presently to despatch advice thereof to give you notice, that you take care of your own safeguard, they intending to endeavor to betray you on a pretension of trade.

Please forthwith to signify the import hereof to Mr. Coffin and others, as you shall think necessary, and advise of what informations you may at any time receive of the Indians' motions.

By order in council,   ISA. ADDINGTON, Sec'y.

For Major Richard Waldron and Mr. Peter Coffin, or either of them, at Cocheco; these with all possible speed.

* This petition is inserted merely as a curiosity. It was a received opinion in that day that the distemper called the king's evil could be cured only by the royal touch. The following advertisement taken from an old London Gazette, is of the same nature.

"These are to give notice, that the weather growing warme, his majesty will not touch any more for the evil till towards Michaelmass. And his majesty's chirurgeons desire, to prevent his majesty being defrauded, that greater care be taken for the future in registring certificates given to such as come to be touched." London Gazette, May 29, 1682.

END OF THE FIRST VOLUME.